MySQL®/PHP Database Applications, Second Edition

MySQL®/PHP Database Applications, Second Edition

Brad Bulger, Jay Greenspan,
and David Wall

Wiley Publishing, Inc.

MySQL®/PHP Database Applications, Second Edition

Published by
Wiley Publishing, Inc.
10475 Crosspoint Boulevard
Indianapolis, IN 46256
www.wiley.com

ISBN: 0-7645-4963-4

Manufactured in the United States of America

10 9 8 7 6 5 4 3 2 1

2O/RW/RQ/QT

Published by Wiley Publishing, Inc., Indianapolis, Indiana
Published simultaneously in Canada

For general information on our other products and services or to obtain technical support, please contact our Customer Care Department within the U.S. at (800) 762-2974, outside the U.S. at (317) 572-3993 or fax (317) 572-4002.

Wiley also publishes its books in a variety of electronic formats. Some content that appears in print may not be available in electronic books.

Library of Congress Cataloging-in-Publication Data: 2002114859

About the Authors

Brad Bulger can remember when computers were as big as refrigerators and old-timers would come into the machine room and call them "mini." After working for several companies that no longer exist, he is now a member of The Madfish Group (`http://www.madfishgroup.com`), where he builds Web sites for money. He would still like to know when the future is going to get here but has a sneaking suspicion he already knows.

Jay Greenspan is a New York–based writer, editor, and technical consultant. He has contributed to sites run by Apple Computer and *Wired Digital,* and is author of *MySQL Weekend Crash Course*. He runs Trans-City Productions, Inc. (`http://www.trans-city.com`), a firm that provides editorial services to high-tech companies.

David Wall is a freelance technical consultant, lecturer, and writer. He specializes in Linux/Apache/MySQL/PHP (LAMP) servers and in Voice over IP technologies from IBM and Cisco Systems. His consultancy, David Wall Enterprises (`http://www.davidwall.com`), has offices in Washington, D.C., and Sydney.

Credits

ACQUISITIONS EDITORS
Debra Williams Cauley
Jim Minatel

PROJECT EDITORS
Kevin Kent
Neil Romanosky

TECHNICAL EDITORS
Zak Greant
Bill Patterson
Liz Warner

COPY EDITOR
S. B. Kleinman

EDITORIAL MANAGER
Mary Beth Wakefield

VICE PRESIDENT & EXECUTIVE GROUP PUBLISHER
Richard Swadley

VICE PRESIDENT AND EXECUTIVE PUBLISHER
Bob Ipsen

VICE PRESIDENT AND PUBLISHER
Joseph B. Wikert

EXECUTIVE EDITORIAL DIRECTOR
Mary Bednarek

PROJECT COORDINATOR
Maridee Ennis

GRAPHICS AND PRODUCTION SPECIALISTS
Beth Brooks
Jennifer Click
LeAndra Hosier
Michael Kruzil

PERMISSIONS EDITOR
Carmen Krikorian

MEDIA DEVELOPMENT SPECIALIST
Angela Denny

PROOFREADING AND INDEXING
TECHBOOKS Production Services

To Lizma, who's still here; Jon Postel, who isn't;
and a free Internet, which might not be much longer

For Catou

Preface

Welcome. If you are thumbing through these pages, you're probably considering writing Web-based applications with PHP and MySQL. If you decide to go with these tools, you'll be in excellent company. Thousands of developers – from total newbies to programmers with years of experience – are turning to PHP and MySQL for their Web-based projects, and for good reason.

Both PHP and MySQL are easy to use, fast, free, and powerful. If you want to get a dynamic Web site up quickly, there are no better choices. The PHP scripting language was built for the Web. All the tasks common to Web development can be performed in PHP with an absolute minimum of effort. Similarly, MySQL excels at tasks common to dynamic Web sites. Whether you're creating a content-management system or an e-commerce application, MySQL is a great choice for your data storage.

Is This Book for You?

Quite a few books deal with PHP, and a few cover MySQL. We've read some of these and found a few to be quite helpful. If you're looking for a book that deals with the gory details of either of these packages, you should probably look elsewhere.

The focus of this book is applications development. We are concerned with what it takes to get data-driven Web sites up and running in an organized and efficient way. The book does not go into arcane detail of every aspect of either of these tools. For example, in this book you will not find a discussion of PHP's LDAP functions or MySQL's C application program interface (API). Instead, we focus on the pieces of both packages that affect one another. We hope that by the time you're done with this book you'll know what it takes to get an application up and running using PHP and MySQL.

How This Book Is Organized

We have organized the book into five parts.

Part I: Working with MySQL

Before you code any PHP scripts you need to know how to design a database, create tables in your database, and get the information you want from the database. Part I of this book shows you just about everything you need to know to work with MySQL.

Part II: Working with PHP

As an applications developer, you will spend the bulk of your time writing scripts that access the database and present HTML to a user's browser. Part II starts by showing you the basics of the PHP scripting language, covering how PHP works with variables, conditions, and control structures. Part II also covers many of PHP's functions and discusses techniques for writing clean, manageable code.

Part III: Simple Applications

In this part we present two of the nine applications in this book: a guestbook and a survey. Here you see the lessons from Parts I and II put into practice as we build working applications.

Part IV: Not So Simple Applications

Here the applications become more complex, as we present applications commonly used on the Web. You see how you can design a content management system, a discussion board, a shopping cart, and other useful applications. Along the way we show you some tips and techniques that should be helpful as you write your applications.

Part V: Appendixes

The appendixes cover several topics of interest to the MySQL/PHP developer. In them you can find installation and configuration instructions, quick reference guides to PHP and MySQL functions, a regular expressions overview, and guides to MySQL administration. In addition, you can find a few helpful resources, some snippets of code, and instructions on using the CD-ROM.

Acknowledgments

I owe so many people so many bags of chocolate peanuts for helping me that I should start a chocolate-peanut farm. Making this book happen, trying to cover products under very active development, has been like trying to paint an oil portrait of a manic chameleon in a camouflage factory. I must single out Debra Williams Cauley, Acquisitions Editor, and Kevin Kent, Development Editor, for their help and their patience – they have been the essence of diplomacy; Jay Greenspan, for getting me into this; and Liz Warner, for all disclosed and undisclosed forms of assistance, but especially for helping me stay sane(ish). Thanks so much to MySQL AB for the generous use of the MySQL Function Reference in Appendix J, and to Zak Greant, Erik Granstrom, Bill Patterson, and David Sides, CEO of Dolphin, for all their assistance. To everyone who helped, thank you – you have our gratitude. – Brad Bulger

Thanks to my friends, family, and colleagues for their support and freely shared expertise during the creation of this book. – David Wall

Contents at a Glance

Part V Appendixes

Contents

Part II Working with PHP

Part IV Not So Simple Applications

Introduction

Soon we will head off on a fabulous journey, a journey on which we will explore the ins and outs of MySQL and PHP database applications in great detail. It's going to be a fun trip; we just know it.

Okay, maybe we're being a bit optimistic. If you're anything like us, points of this particular journey will be a lot more tedious than they are exciting. Let's face facts: Application development isn't always the most exciting thing in the world. And as with any other venture that involves programming, some very frustrating times are sure to be ahead, whether because of a syntax error you can't find or a piece of code that won't do what you think it ought to do. But despite all that, here you are, and we think there is a very good reason for that.

Web applications are the present and the future. No matter your background, whether you have a history with Visual Basic or COBOL, or maybe just some HTML and JavaScript, your résumé is only going to improve with some Web application development experience. We don't think there's a better combination of tools to have under your belt than PHP and MySQL. The numbers bear us out. PHP and MySQL are becoming increasingly popular, and the demand for people who can use these tools will only increase.

A bit later in this introduction we go into a more detailed explanation of why you should use PHP and MySQL. However, before we can get to that, we want take a bit of time to go over the architecture of Web applications. Once we've done this, we can explain in detail why PHP and MySQL should be the centerpieces of your application-development environment. Once we've sold you on these tools, we present a very quick and grossly under-coded application. As you look over this application, you can see the basic syntax and principles behind PHP and MySQL.

As we proceed with the book, we assume that you have read and understand everything presented in this introduction.

Basic Architecture

At the most basic level, the Web works off a client/server architecture. Simply stated, that means that both a central server and a client application are responsible for some amount of processing. This setup differs from that of a program such as Microsoft Word, which operates just fine without any help from a server. Those of you who used older VAX machines might remember the days of dumb terminals, which had no processing power whatsoever. Depending on where you work today, perhaps in a university or a bank, you might still use applications that are in no way dependent on the client. In other words, applications in which all the work is done on the central computer.

The client

In this book, you'll learn how to use MySQL and PHP to create applications that make use of a single client: the Web browser. This is not the only possibility for Internet-based applications. For very sophisticated applications that require more client-side processing or that need to maintain state (we talk about maintaining state later in the introduction) a Java applet may be necessary. But unless you're coding something like a real-time chat program, client-side Java is completely unnecessary.

So the only client you need to be concerned with is the Web browser. The applications need to generate HTML to be rendered in the browser. As you probably already know, the primary language of browsers is the Hypertext Markup Language, or HTML. HTML provides a set of tags that describe how a Web page should look. If you are new to the concept of HTML, get on the Web and read one of the many tutorials out there. It shouldn't take long to learn the basics. Some of the best include:

- National Center for Supercomputer Applications (`http://archive.ncsa.uiuc.edu/General/Internet/WWW/HTMLPrimer.html`)
- Davesite (`http://www.davesite.com/webstation/html/`)
- Webmonkey (`http://hotwired.lycos.com/webmonkey/teachingtool/`)

Of course, most browsers accept more than HTML. All kinds of plug-ins, including RealPlayer, Flash, and Shockwave, are available, and most browsers also have some level of support for JavaScript. Some can even work with XML. But, like most Web developers, we are taking a lowest-common-denominator approach in this book. We're going to create applications that can be read in any browser. We don't use JavaScript, XML, or anything else that could prevent some users from rendering the pages we serve. HTML it is.

The server

Almost all of the work of Web applications takes place on the server. A specific application, called a Web server, is responsible for communicating with the browser. A relational-database server stores whatever information the application requires. Finally, you need a language to broker requests between the Web server and the database server; it is also used to perform programmatic tasks on the information that comes to and from the Web server. Figure I-1 represents this system.

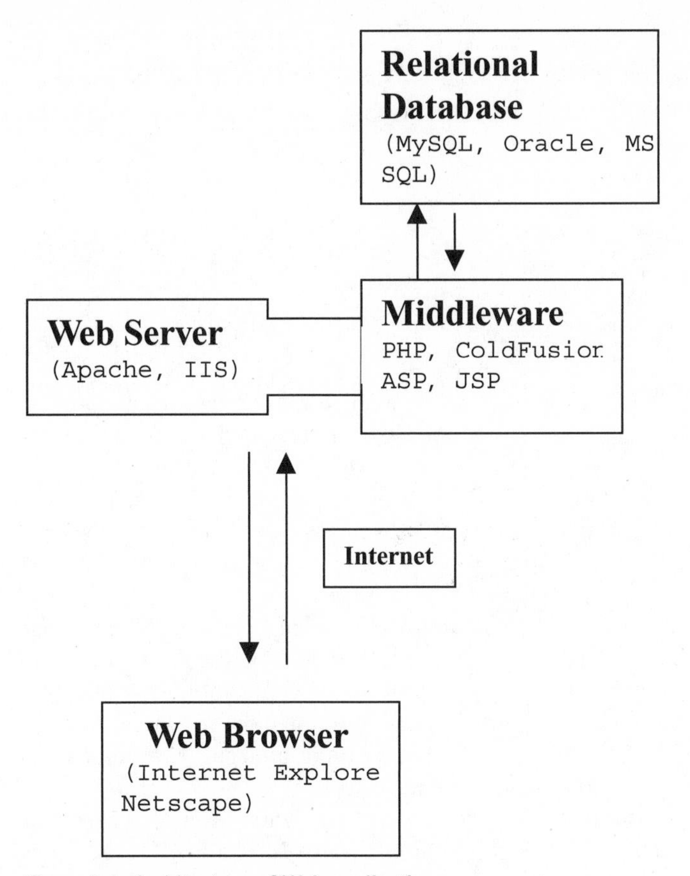

Figure I-1: Architecture of Web applications

But, of course, none of this is possible without an operating system. The Web server, programming language, and database server you use must work well with your operating system.

THE OPERATING SYSTEM

Many operating systems are out there. Windows 98/2000/CE/XP and Macintosh OS are probably the most popular. But that's hardly the end of it. Circumstances might have forced you to work with some obscure OS for the past few years. You might even be under the impression that your OS is the best thing going. That's fine. But if you're planning on spending a lot of time on the Web and on running applications, you're best off getting to know either Windows NT/2000 or some version of Unix. These two account for well over 90 percent of all the servers on the Web. It is probably easier for you to learn a little NT/2000/XP or Unix than it is to convince everybody else that the AS/400 is the way to go.

Apple's Mac OS X is based on a FreeBSD/Unix foundation and gives you everything you expect from a Unix OS.

Which should you use? Well, this question is a complex one, and the answer for many will be based partially on philosophical approach. In case you're unaware of it, let's take a moment to talk about the broad topics in this philosophical debate.

If you don't know what we are talking about, here are the basics. PHP and MySQL belong to a class of software known as *open source*. This means that the source code for the heart of the applications is available to anyone who wants to see it. These applications make use of an open-source development model, which enables anyone who is interested to participate in the development of the project. In the case of PHP, coders all over the world participate in the development of the language and see no immediate pay for their substantial work. Most of the people who participate are passionate about good software and code for the enjoyment of seeing people like you and me develop with their tools.

This method of development has been around for some time, but it has gained prominence as Linux has become increasingly popular. More often than not, open-source software is free of charge. You can download the application, install it, and use it without getting permission from anyone or paying a dime to anyone.

Suffice it to say that Microsoft, Oracle, and other traditional software companies do not make use of this method of development.

If you are not an open-source adherent, there are excellent reasons for choosing NT/2000/XP. Usually, the thing that steers people towards NT/2000/XP is inertia. If you or your company has been developing with Microsoft products for years, it is probably going to be easier to stay within that environment than to make a change. If you have a team of people who know Visual Basic, you are probably going to want to stick with NT/2000/XP. But even if this is the case, there's nothing to prevent you from developing with PHP and MySQL. Both products run on Windows 95/98 and Windows NT/2000/XP/CE.

But in the real world, almost all PHP/MySQL applications are running off some version of Unix, whether Linux, BSD, Irix, Solaris, HP-UX, or one of the other flavors.

The major advantage of Unix is its inherent stability. Boxes loaded with Linux have been known to run for months or years without crashing. Linux and BSD also have the advantage of being free of charge and able to run on standard PC hardware. If you have any old 486, you can load it up with Linux, MySQL, PHP, and Apache and have yourself a well-outfitted Web server. You probably wouldn't want to put it on the Web, where a moderate amount of traffic might overwhelm it, but it can serve nicely as a development server, a place where you can test your applications.

THE WEB SERVER

The Web server has what seems to be a fairly straightforward job. It sits there, running on top of your operating system, listening for requests that somebody on the

Web might make, responding to those requests, and serving out the appropriate Web pages. In reality, it is a bit more complicated than that, and because of the 24/7 nature of the Web, the stability of the Web server is a major issue.

There are many Web servers out there, but two dominate the market. These are Apache and Microsoft's Internet Information Server (IIS).

INTERNET INFORMATION SERVER IIS is deeply tied to the Windows environment and is a key component of Microsoft's Active Server Pages (ASP). If you've chosen to go the Microsoft way, you'll almost certainly end up using IIS.

There is a certain amount of integration between the programming language and the Web server. At this point, PHP 4 and 5 integrate well with IIS.

APACHE The Apache Web server is the most popular Web server there is. It, like Linux, PHP, and MySQL, is an open-source project. Not surprisingly, Apache works best in Unix environments, but also runs just fine under Windows.

Apache makes use of third-party modules. Because it is open source, anyone with the skill can write code that extends the functionality of Apache. PHP most often runs as an Apache extension, known as an Apache module.

Apache is a great Web server. It is extremely quick and amazingly stable. The most frequently stated complaint about Apache is that, like many pieces of Unix software, the graphical tools for manipulating the application are limited. You alter Apache by specifying options on the command line or by altering text files. When you come to Apache for the first time, all this can be a bit opaque.

Though Apache works best on Unix systems, versions also run on Windows operating systems. Nobody, not even the Apache developers, recommends that Apache be run on a busy server under Windows. If you have decided to use the Windows platform for serving Web pages, you're better off using IIS.

But there are conditions under which you'll be glad Apache does run under Windows. You can run Apache, PHP, and MySQL on a Windows 98 machine and then transfer those applications to Linux with practically no changes to the scripts. This approach is the easiest way to go if you need to develop locally on Windows but to serve off a Unix/Apache server.

MIDDLEWARE

PHP belongs to a class of languages known as *middleware*. These languages work closely with the Web server to interpret the requests made from the World Wide Web, process these requests, interact with other programs on the server to fulfill the requests, and then indicate to the Web server exactly what to serve to the client's browser.

The middleware is where you'll be doing the vast majority of your work. With a little luck you can have your Web server up and running without a whole lot of effort. And once it is up and running, you won't need to fool with it a whole lot.

But as you are developing your applications, you spend a lot of time writing code that makes your applications work. In addition to PHP, several languages perform similar functions. Some of the more popular choices are ASP, Perl, and ColdFusion.

RELATIONAL DATABASES

Relational database management systems (RDBMSes) provide a great way to store and access complex information. They have been around for quite a while. In fact, they predate the Web, Linux, and Windows, so it should be no surprise that there are many RDBMSes to choose from. All the major databases make use of the Structured Query Language (SQL).

Some of the more popular commercial RDBMSes are Oracle, Sybase, Informix, Microsoft's SQL Server, and IBM's DB2. In addition to MySQL, there are now two major open-source relational databases. Postgres has been the major alternative to MySQL in the open-source arena for some time. For a while, Borland released its Interbase product under an open-source license and allowed free download and use. The results of that release are a software project called Firebird.

Why These Products?

Given the number of choices out there, you might be asking yourself why you should choose PHP and/or MySQL. We answer this question in the following sections.

Why PHP?

Programming languages are a lot like shoes. Some look good to some people yet look really ugly to others. To carry the analogy a little further, some shoes just fit well on some feet.

What we mean is this: When it comes to Web programming, all languages do pretty much the same things. They all interact with relational databases, they all work with file systems, and they all interact with Web servers. The question of which language is best is rarely a matter of a language's ability or inability to perform certain actions. It's usually more a matter of how quickly and easily you can do what you need to do.

IT'S FAST AND EASY

What about speed? There are really only three things that we know for sure when it comes to comparing the speeds of Web-programming languages.

- Applications written in C will be the fastest.
- Programming in C is rather difficult and takes much longer than programming in any of the other languages mentioned so far.
- Comparisons among languages are extremely difficult.

From everything we know, we feel safe in saying that PHP is as fast as anything out there.

More often than not, choosing a language comes back to the same issues involved in buying shoes. You want to go with what's most comfortable. If you're like us, you find that PHP represents the perfect combination of power, structure, and ease of use. Again, this is largely a matter of opinion, but we do believe that the syntax of PHP is superior to those of ASP and JSP. And we believe it puts more power at your fingertips more quickly than ColdFusion and is not as difficult to learn as Perl.

In the end, we believe PHP offers you the best opportunity to develop powerful Web applications quickly. That generalization made, we do believe there are other excellent reasons for choosing PHP.

IT'S CROSS-PLATFORM

In the rundown of Web architecture, we mentioned that PHP runs on Windows 2000/NT/CE/XP and Unix and with both IIS and Apache. But the cross-platform abilities of PHP go far beyond these platforms. If you happen to be using Netscape, Roxen, or just about anything else, it is likely PHP works with it.

Yes, ASP can be run on Linux, ColdFusion can work on Solaris and Linux, and JSP is adaptable across many platforms. At this point, PHP works as well on as wide a variety of systems as any other available product.

IT ACCESSES EVERYTHING

What do you need to access in the course of creating your Web applications? LDAP? IMAP mail server? Oracle? Informix? DB2? Or maybe you need an XML parser or WDDX functions.

Whatever you need to use, it is more than likely that PHP has a built-in set of functions that make getting whatever you need very easy. But what if it doesn't have something built in that you'd like? That brings us to our next point.

IT'S CONSTANTLY BEING IMPROVED

If you are new to open-source development, you might be surprised by the high quality of the software. There are thousands of very technical, very talented programmers out there who love to spend their time creating great, and mostly free, software. In an active project such as PHP, a variety of developers look to improve the product almost daily.

It is truly remarkable. If you happen to find a bug, you can submit a report to a mailing list that the core developers read. Depending on its severity, it is likely that the bug will be addressed within a couple of hours to a couple of days.

When PHP was put together, it was done so in a modular fashion. This makes adding greater functionality reasonably easy. If there are sets of functions you'd like added to PHP, there's a good chance that someone can do it with minimal effort.

YOUR PEERS CAN SUPPORT YOU

Most languages have active mailing lists and development sites. PHP is no exception. If you run into trouble – if there's a bug in your code that you just can't figure out or if you can't seem to fathom some function or another – someone among the hundreds subscribed to PHP mailing lists will be happy to check and fix your code.

The open-source nature of PHP creates a real feeling of community. When you get into trouble, your PHP-hacking brethren will feel your pain and ease it.

IT'S FREE

If you have a computer, Linux, Apache, and PHP are all completely free.

Why MySQL?

This one is perhaps a little tougher to answer. Although MySQL has much to recommend it, it also has a variety of competitors, many of whom may be better suited for a particular task.

In Part I of this book we discuss MySQL in some detail. In these chapters we mention features available in other relational databases that MySQL does not support. (If you know your way around databases and are curious, these include stored procedures, triggers, and subqueries.)

Given these limitations, MySQL is definitely not the best choice in certain environments. If you are planning on starting, for example, a bank or a savings and loan, MySQL probably isn't for you.

But for the majority of people using the majority of applications, MySQL is a great choice. It is particularly well suited for Web applications.

IT'S COST-EFFECTIVE

Think you need an Oracle installation? Get ready to shell out tens of thousands of dollars at a minimum. There's no doubt that Oracle, Sybase, and Informix create terrific databases, but the cost involved is prohibitive for many.

MySQL is free for development and can be used in a live production environment for a minimal cost (see `https://order.mysql.com/index.php?infopage=1` for more details on licensing MySQL).

IT'S QUICK AND POWERFUL

MySQL might not have every bell and whistle available for a relational database, but for most users it has plenty. If you are serving out Web content or creating a moderately sized commerce site, MySQL has all the power you need.

For small to-medium-sized databases, MySQL is extremely fast. The developers of MySQL take great pride in the speed of their product. For applications like the ones presented in Parts III and IV of this book, it is unlikely you'll find a database that's any faster.

IT'S IMPROVING ALL THE TIME

MySQL is improving at a staggering rate. The developers release updates frequently and are adding impressive (and we do mean impressive) features all the time. It's even possible that at the time you're reading this book MySQL will support subqueries and stored procedures.

Your First Application

Enough of the prelude. Now we turn to writing an application so you can see how all these parts come together in a real live application. By the time you have finished reading this introduction, you should have a pretty good idea of how it all comes together.

Tool check

You need a few key elements to get going. We run through them here so you know what you need.

SOFTWARE

This is a Web-based application, so you're clearly going to need a Web server. You will probably be using Apache, whether you are using Windows or Unix. You need to install Apache so that it can access the PHP language.

In addition, you need to have MySQL installed. And PHP has to be able to recognize MySQL. Apache, MySQL, and PHP are provided on the accompanying CD, and installation instructions are provided in Appendix C. You might want to install these packages before proceeding, or you can just read along to get an idea of what we're doing and install the packages later when you want to work with the more practical examples in this book.

TEXT EDITOR/INTEGRATED DEVELOPMENT ENVIRONMENT

To code PHP and your Web pages, you need, at a minimum, a text editor. You can use Notepad or something similarly basic, but if you're starting without an allegiance to any particular editor, we suggest you get something with good syntax highlighting. On Windows, Macromedia HomeSite (`www.macromedia.com`) is a tool that works well with PHP, and we've heard excellent things about Editplus (`www.editplus.com`).

If you have been working on Unix for some time, it is likely that you already know and love some text editor or another, whether it be Emacs, vi, or Kedit. If not, any of these are fine, though the first two do take some getting used to. If you're working on Unix, but don't have the patience to learn vi, try Pico. It's very easy to use.

In the last couple of years, a few companies have released integrated development environments (IDEs) for use with PHP. Zend Technologies (`www.zend.com`), whose employees have been deeply involved with PHP for years, sells a suite of products that can make your PHP coding life much easier. Based on code that was originally open source, NuSphere Corporation (`www.nusphere.com`) has also created a very competent IDE for Windows and Linux.

Application overview

We start this book with an example of a simple Web application that stores user information, a place where users can enter their names, email addresses, URLs, and maybe even comments – in essence, a *guestbook*.

The guestbook is a simplified example, something you would never want to run on a live Web server. We re-create this application in a more robust form in Chapter 8.

Creating the database

Now that you know exactly what you need, the first step is to create a database that stores this information. To do this, you use the language common to most every database server: SQL. You read a lot more about this later, so don't worry if you don't understand everything right away. Just read through the rest of the Introduction and then read Chapter 1.

Start up the MySQL command-line client. If you're working on Unix, typing **mysql** at the shell should do the trick (or you might have to go to the directory that contains the MySQL executable – typically /mysql/bin or /usr/local/mysql/bin).

If you are on Windows, you need to go to the DOS prompt, find the path to mysql.exe, and execute it. Then, at the prompt, create a new database. When you're done, you should have something that looks very much like this:

```
[jay@mybox jay]$ mysql
Welcome to the MySQL monitor.  Commands end with ; or \g.
Your MySQL connection id is 716 to server version: 4.0.1-log

Type 'help' for help.

mysql> create database guestbook;
Query OK, 1 row affected (0.00 sec)

mysql>
```

Now, within the database named guestbook you need a table that stores the user information. This table is also created in the MySQL monitor. The command to create the table isn't very complex. You basically need to let MySQL know what kind of information to expect, whether numbers or strings, and whether or not any of the information can be omitted (or `NULL`). Details appear in Chapter 2, but for now just note that the basic command is `create table`; you get something that looks about like the following:

```
mysql> use guestbook;
Database changed
mysql> create table guestbook
    -> (
    ->          name         varchar(40) null,
    ->          location         varchar(40) null,
    ->          email            varchar(40) null,
    ->          url              varchar(40) null,
    ->          comments         text null
    -> )
    -> ;
Query OK, 0 rows affected (0.00 sec)

mysql>
```

Then you have to give your application permission to use the table:

```
mysql> grant delete, insert, select, update on guestbook
    ->          to nobody@localhost identified by 'ydobon';
Query OK, 0 rows affected (0.00 sec)
```

Then you issue a quick statement that forces the server to re-read the permissions tables, effectively putting the new ones into effect:

```
mysql> FLUSH PRIVILEGES;
```

So now you have a database named guestbook and a table, also named guestbook, within the database. Now it's time to write an application in PHP that will enable you to insert, edit, and view information kept in this guestbook.

Your PHP script

Now's the time to move to the text editor. In the course of configuring your Web server, you need to let it know which files should be handed off to PHP so the engine can interpret the page. Most often these files have a .php extension, though it is possible to have PHP interpret anything, including .html files. These scripts live inside the folder designated to hold Web pages. For Apache, this is usually /htdocs.

BASIC SYNTAX

One neat thing about PHP is that it lets you move between straight HTML and commands that are part of the PHP programming language. It works like this: The sections of your script between the opening tag (`<?php`) and the closing tag (`?>`) are interpreted by the PHP engine, and portions not within these tags are treated as plain HTML. Check out the following PHP page.

```
<?php
echo "Hi, ";
?>
mom.
```

When run through the Web server, this code creates a Web page that prints, simply, `Hi, mom.` PHP's `echo` command manages the first part of the line. But, of course, PHP can do quite a bit more than that. Like any other programming language, it can work with variables and make decisions.

```
<?php
echo "Hi, mom. ";

$var = date("H");
if ($var <= 11)
{
    echo "good morning";
}
elseif ($var > 11 and $var < 18)
{
    echo "good afternoon";
}
else
{
    echo "good evening";
}
?>
```

In the preceding code, after printing out the greeting, there is some real programming. We have used PHP's built-in date function to grab the hour of the day in 24-hour format. That value is immediately assigned to a variable named `$var`. Then a decision is made, and the appropriate text is printed, depending on the time of day. Notice the syntax here. Each PHP command ends with a semicolon (:). In the `if` statement, curly braces (`{}`) hold the commands to be executed depending on the condition. And the condition itself is held within parentheses (`()`).

The `date()` function and `echo`, which are used in the previous example, are just two of the hundreds of functions built into PHP, many of which you learn to use in the course of this book. If you are going to access the database, you're going to need a few more.

CONNECTING TO THE DATABASE

While you're installing PHP you should let it know that you plan on using MySQL with it. If you don't do this, what we discuss now won't work. Even if PHP is aware that you're using MySQL, in your specific scripts you must identify the exact database you need access to. In this case, that is the guestbook database you just created.

```
mysql_connect("localhost","nobody","ydobon")
    or die("<h3>could not connect to MySQL</h3>\n");
mysql_select_db("guestbook")
    or die("<h3>could not select database 'guestbook'</h3>\n");
```

The first line in the preceding code tells MySQL that the Web server (the entity running the script) is on the local machine, has a username of *nobody*, and has a password of *ybodon*. Then, if the connection is successful, the specific database is selected with the `mysql_select_db()` command. With these lines safely tucked away in your scripts, you should be able to manipulate the database with your commands.

Because you're going to need these lines in every page in this application, it makes sense to save some typing, put them in a file of their own, and include them in every page. If you've done any programming at all, you know that this involves dumping the entire contents of that file into the file being accessed. These lines are kept in a file called dbconnect.php. At the top of every other file in this application will be the following line:

```
include('dbconnect.php');
```

INSERTING INFORMATION INTO THE DATABASE

Because you have yet to put any users in the database, we start by reviewing the script that enables you to do that. But first, we need to tell you a little bit more about PHP variables. A bit earlier in this introduction in the section "Basic Syntax," we showed that you can create variables within a PHP script, but because this is a client/server environment, you're going to need to get variable data from the client (the Web browser) to PHP. You usually do this with HTML forms.

There's a basic rundown of HTML forms in Appendix B. Check that if you need to. For now we just want to point out that every form element has a name and that when a form is submitted, the names of those form elements become available as variables in the PHP script the form was submitted to.

In older versions of PHP, these variables would automatically be created as global variables: If you submitted a form with a field named `firstname`, the script receiving the form would have a variable named `$firstname` defined when it began. This can lead to some serious security problems, however. So now, the values are available as elements in the system-defined "superglobal" arrays, such as `$_GET` (for fields passed in as part of the URL) and `$_POST` (for fields submitted from forms). The simplest of these to use is `$_REQUEST`, which combines `GET`, `POST`, and cookie values. If you're not understanding all of this right now, don't worry about it; these concepts are covered in greater detail later in the book, particularly in Chapter 9.

As soon as the following form is submitted, the variables `$_REQUEST['surname']` and `$_REQUEST['submit']` become available in the PHP script myscript.php. The value of `$_REQUEST['surname']` is whatever the user enters into the text field. The value of `$_REQUEST['submit']` is the text string `submit`.

```
<form action="myscript.php">
    <input type="text" name="surname">
    <input type="submit" name="submit" value="submit">
</form>
```

Before we show the script itself, now is a good time to note that Web programming is slightly different from other types of programming in one important respect: It is stateless. To display a page, a Web server must first receive a request from a browser. The language they speak is called HTTP, the Hypertext Transfer Protocol. The request includes several things – the page the browser wishes to see, the form data, the type of browser being used, and the IP address the browser is using. Based on this information, the Web server decides what to serve.

Once it has served this page, the server maintains no connection to the browser. It has absolutely no memory of what it served to whom. Each HTTP request is dealt with individually with no regard to what came before it. For this reason, in Web programming you need to come up with some way of maintaining state. That is, if you are progressing through an application, you need some way of letting the server know what happened. Essentially, you need ways of passing variables from page to page. This comes up in our applications. The applications have three ways in which to do this: by passing hidden form elements, by using cookies, or by using sessions.

Now back to the script.

```
<form action="myscript.php">
    <input type="text" name="surname">
    <input type="submit" name="submit" value="submit">
</form>
```

You can decide what you display on a page based on the variable information that comes from HTML forms. For example, you can find out whether the preceding form has been submitted by checking if the variable name `$_REQUEST['submit']` has a value of `submit`. This very technique comes into play when it we create the page for inserting information into the database.

There is one page in our application, called sign.php, that has an HTML form. The action of the form (the program to run as a result of the submission) in this page is create_entry.php. Here's the page in all its glory:

```
<h2>Sign my Guest Book!!!</h2>

<form method="post" action="create_entry.php">

<b>Name:</b>
<input type="text" size="40" name="name">
<br>
```

```
<b>Location:</b>
<input type="text" size="40" name="location">
<br>
<b>Email:</b>
<input type="text" size="40" name="email">
<br>
<b>Home Page URL:</b>
<input type="text" size="40" name="url">
<br>
<b>Comments:</b>
<textarea name="comments" cols="40" rows="4"
wrap="virtualv></textarea>
<br>

<input type="submit" name="submit" value="Sign!">
<input type="reset" name="reset" value="Start Over">

</form>
```

When the user fills out this form and submits it, the information is sent to create_entry.php. The first thing to do on this page is to check if the form has been submitted. If it has, take the values entered into the form and use them to create a query to send to MySQL. Don't worry about the specifics of the query just yet. Just know that it inserts a row into the database table you created earlier.

```
<?php
include("dbconnect.php");

if ($_REQUEST["submit"] == "Sign!")
{
        $query = "insert into guestbook
(name,location,email,url,comments) values ('"
                .$_REQUEST["name"]
                ."', '"
                .$_REQUEST["location"]
                ."', '"
                .$_REQUEST["email"]

                ."', '"
                .$_REQUEST["url"]
                ."', '"
                .$_REQUEST["comments"]
                ."') "
        ;
```

```
        mysql_query($query);
?>
<h2>Thanks!!</h2>
<h2><a href="view.php">View My Guest Book!!!</a></h2>
<?php
}
else
{
        include("sign.php");
}
?>
```

If the form, which is in sign.php, hasn't been submitted, it is included and, therefore, shows the same form. You might notice that this page is submitted to itself. The first time the create_entry.php page is called, the form in sign.php is displayed. The next time, though, the data are inserted into the database.

Figures I-2 and I-3 show the pages that this script creates.

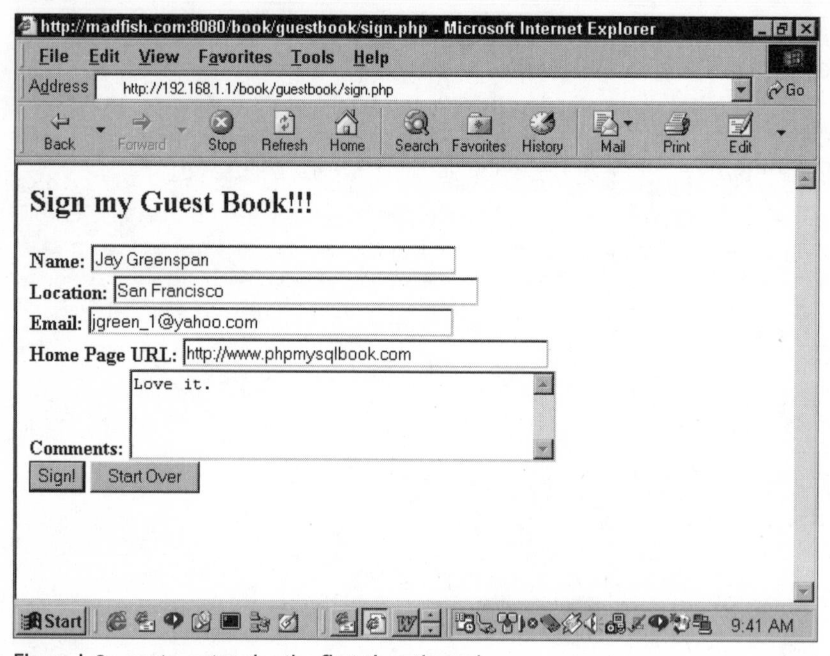

Figure I-2: create_entry.php the first time through

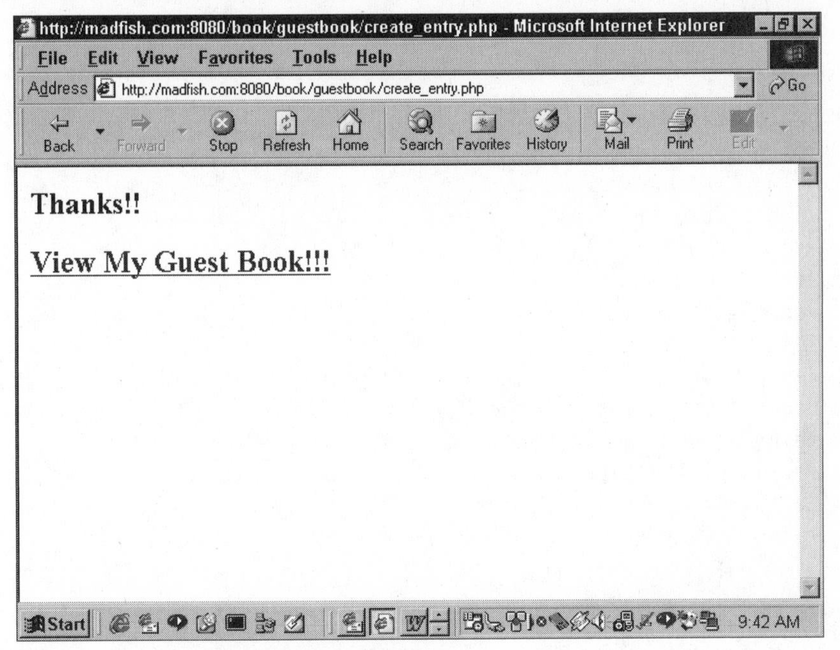

Figure I-3: create_entry.php after submission

VIEWING INFORMATION IN THE DATABASE

This shouldn't be too tough. You already know that the file needs to include dbconnect.php. Other than that, we've already mentioned that databases store information in tables. Each row of the table contains information on a specific person who signed the guestbook, so to view all the information the page needs to retrieve and print out every row of data. Here's the script that can do it (you should notice that it's pretty sparse):

```
<?php include("dbconnect.php"); ?>

<h2>View My Guest Book!!</h2>

<?php

$result = mysql_query("select * from guestbook")
        or die(mysql_error());
while ($row = mysql_fetch_array($result))
{
```

```
        echo "<b>Name:</b>";
        echo $row["name"];
        echo "<br>\n";
        echo "<b>Location:</b>";
        echo $row["location"];
        echo "<br>\n";
        echo "<b>Email:</b>";
        echo $row["email"];
        echo "<br>\n";
        echo "<b>URL:</b>";
        echo $row["url"];
        echo "<br>\n";
        echo "<b>Comments:</b>";
        echo $row["comments"];
        echo "<br>\n";
        echo "<br>\n";
        echo "<br>\n";
}
mysql_free_result($result);
?>

<h2><a href="sign.php">Sign My Guest Book!!</a></h2>
```

The query in the preceding code asks MySQL for every row in the database. Then the script enters a loop. Each row in the database is loaded into the variable `$row`, one row at a time. Rows continue to be accessed until none is left. At that time, the script drops out of the `while` loop.

As it works through the loop, each column in that row is displayed. For example, the following code prints out the email column for the row being accessed:

```
echo $row["email"]
```

When run, the simple script at the beginning of this section prints out every row in the database. Figure I-4 shows what the page will look like.

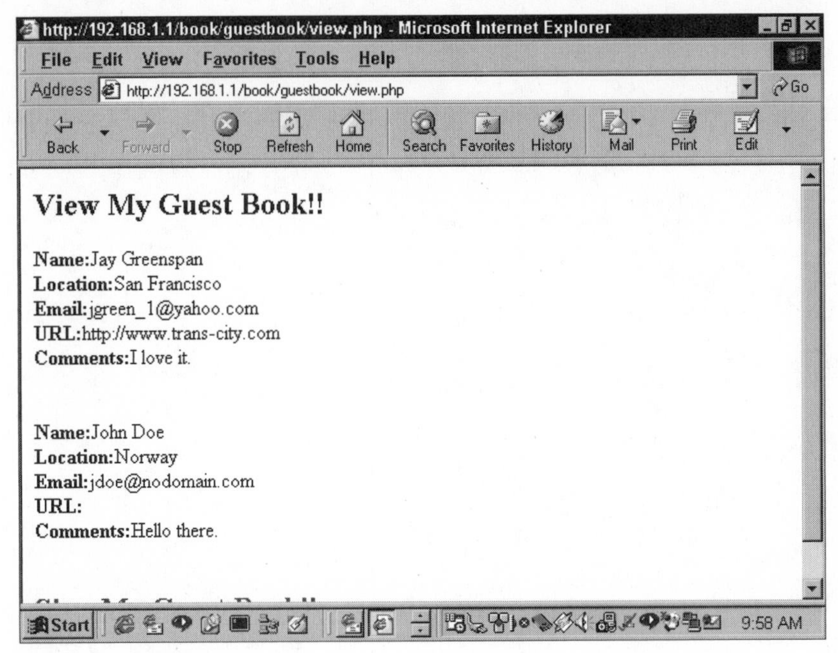

Figure I-4: view.php

And that about does it for our first application.

WHY YOU SHOULD NOT USE THIS APPLICATION

Again, we strongly recommend against putting the application discussed in this introduction anywhere that the general public can get to it. If you want a guestbook, use the application made exclusively for this book, which you find in Chapter 8. We call this application Guestbook 2003. But we cover a lot of ground and present a lot of information before we get there.

We hope you enjoy the read!

Part I

Working with MySQL

Chapter 1

Database Design with MySQL

IN THIS CHAPTER

- Identifying the problems that led to the creation of the relational database
- Learning the normalization process
- Examining advanced database concepts

THE BULK OF THIS CHAPTER is for those of you who have made it to the early twenty-first century without working with relational databases. If you're a seasoned database pro, having worked with Oracle, Sybase, or even something like Microsoft Access or Paradox, you may want to skip this little lesson on database theory. However, we do suggest that you look at the final section of this chapter, where we discuss some of MySQL's weirder points. MySQL's implementation of SQL is incomplete, so it might not support something you want to use.

Why Use a Relational Database?

If you're still here and are ready to read with rapt attention about database theory and the wonders of normalization, you probably don't know much about the history of the relational database. You may not even care. For that reason, I'll keep this very brief. Dr. E. F. Codd was a research scientist at IBM in the 1960s. A mathematician by training, he was unhappy with the available models of data storage, finding them all prone to error and redundancy. He worked on these problems and then, in 1970, published a paper with the rousing title "A Relational Model of Data for Large Shared Data Banks." In all honesty, nothing has been the same since.

A programmer named Larry Ellison read the paper and started work on software that could put Dr. Codd's theories into practice. If you've been a resident of this planet during the past 20 years, you may know that Ellison's product and company took the name Oracle and that he is now one of the richest individuals in the world. His earliest product was designed for huge mainframe systems. Responding to market demands over the years, Oracle, and many other companies that have sprung up since, have designed systems with a variety of features geared toward a variety of operating systems. Now relational databases are so common that you can get one that runs on a Palm Pilot.

To understand why Dr. Codd's theories have revolutionized the data-storage world, it's best to have an idea of what the troubles are with other means of data storage. Take the example of a simple address book – nothing too complex, just something that stores names, addresses, phone numbers, emails, and the like. If you have no persistent, running program to put this information into, the file system of whatever OS you're running becomes the natural choice for storage.

For a simple address book, a delimited text file can be created to store the information. If the first row serves as a header and commas are used as delimiters, the text file might look something like this:

```
Name, Addr1, Addr2, City, State, Zip, Phone, Email
Jay Greenspan, 211 Some St, Apt 2, San Francisco, CA, 94107,
4155551212, jay@not.real
Brad Bulger, 411 Some St, Apt 6, San Francisco, CA, 94109,
4155552222, brad@not.real
John Doe, 444 Madison Ave, , New York, NY, 11234, 2125556666,
nobody@mysqlphpapps.com
```

This isn't much to look at, but it is at least machine-readable. Using whatever language you wish, you can write a script that opens this file and then parses the information. You will probably want it in some sort of two-dimensional or associative array so that you'll have some flexibility in addressing each portion of each line of the file. Any way you look at it, there's going to be a fair amount of code to write. If you want this information to be sortable and queryable by a variety of criteria, you're going to have to write scripts that will, for instance, sort the list alphabetically by name or find all people within a certain area code. What a pain.

You might face another major problem if your data needs to be used across a network by a variety of people. Presumably more than one person is going to need to write information to this file. What happens if two people try to make changes at once? For starters, it's quite possible that one person will overwrite another's changes. To prevent this from happening, the programmer has to specify file locking if the file is in use. While this might work, it's kind of a pain in the neck for the person who gets locked out. Obviously, the larger the system gets the more unmanageable this all becomes.

What you need is something more robust than the file system – a program or daemon that stays in memory seems to be a good choice. Furthermore, you'll need a data-storage system that reduces the amount of parsing and scripting that the programmer needs to be concerned with. No need for anything too arcane here. A plain, simple table like Table 1-1 should work just fine.

Now this is pretty convenient. It's easy to look at and if a running program accesses this table it should happen pretty quickly. What else might this program do? First, it should be able to address one row at a time without affecting the others. That way, if two or more people want to insert information into this table they won't be tripping over each other. It would be even spiffier if the program provided a simple and elegant way to extract information from a table such as this. There should be a quick way to find all of the people from California that doesn't involve parsing and sorting the file. Furthermore, this wondrous program should be able to accept statements that describe what you want in a language very similar to English. That way you can just say: "Give me all rows where the contents of the `state` column equal `CA`."

Yes, this program is great, but it isn't enough. Major problems still need to be dealt with. These problems, which we'll discuss in the following pages, are the same ones that made Dr. Codd write his famous paper, and the same ones that made Larry Ellison a billionaire.

Blasted Anomalies

Dr. Codd's goal was to have a model of information that was dependable. All of the data-storage methods available to him had inherent problems. He referred to these problems as *anomalies*. There are three types of anomalies: update, delete, and insert.

The update anomaly

Now that you can assume that a table structure can quickly and easily handle multiple requests, you need to see what happens when the information gets more complex. Adding some more information to the previous table introduces some serious problems (Table 1-2).

Table 1-2 is meant to store information for an entire office, not just a single person. Since this company deals with other large companies, there will be times when more than one contact will be at a single office location. For example, in Table 1-2 two contacts are present at 1121 43rd St. At first this may appear to be okay; you can still get at all the information available relatively easily. The problem comes when the BigCo Company decides to up and move to another address. In that case, you'd have to update the address for BigCo in two different rows. This may not sound like such an onerous task, but consider the trouble if this table has 3,000 rows instead of 3 – or 300,000 for that matter. Someone, or some program, has to make sure the data are changed in every appropriate place.

Another concern is the potential for error. It's very possible that one of these rows could be altered while the other one remained the same. Or, if changes are keyed in one row at a time, it's likely that somebody will introduce a typo. Then you'd be left wondering if the correct address is 1121 or 1211.

The better way to handle this data is to take the company name and address and put that information in its own table. This process of separating a table out into multiple new tables is usually called *decomposition*. The two resulting tables will resemble Table 1-3 and Table 1-4.

Now the information pertinent to BigCo is in its own table, Companies. If you look at the next table (Table 1-4), Contacts, you'll see that we've inserted another

TABLE 1-1 SIMPLE TABLE FOR DATA STORAGE

name	addr1	addr2	city	state	zip	phone	email
Jay Greenspan	211 Some St.	Apt. 2	San Francisco	CA	94107	4155558888	jay@not.real
Brad Bulger	411 Some St.	Apt. 6	San Francisco	CA	94109	4155552222	brad@not.real
John Doe	444 Madison Ave.		New York	NY	11234	2125556666	nobody@ mysqlphpapps.com

TABLE 1-2 PROBLEMATIC TABLE STORAGE

id	company_name	company_address	contact_name	contact_title	phone	email
1	BigCo Company	1121 43rd St.	Jay Greenspan	Vice President	4155551212	jay@not.real
2	BigCo Company	1121 43rd St.	Brad Bulger	President	4155552222	brad@not.real
3	LittleCo Company	4444 44th St.	John Doe	Lackey	2125556666	nobody@hotmail.com

TABLE 1-3 COMPANIES

company_id	company_name	company_address
1	BigCo Company	1121 43rd St.
2	LittleCo Company	4444 44th St.

TABLE 1-4 CONTACTS

contact_id	company_id	contact_name	contact_title	phone	email
1	1	Jay Greenspan	Vice President	4155551212	jay@not.real
2	1	Brad Bulger	President	4155552222	brad@not.real
3	2	John Doe	Lackey	2125556666	nobody@mysqlphpapps.com

column, company_id. This column references the company_id column of the Companies table. In Brad's row, you see that the company_id (the second column) equals 1. You can then go to the Companies table, look at the information for company_id 1, and see all the relevant address information. What's happened here is that you've created a relationship between these two tables – hence the name *relational database.*

You still have all the information you had in the previous setup, you've just segmented it. In this setup you can change the address for both Jay and Brad by altering only a single row. That's the kind of convenience you want to be after.

Perhaps this leaves you wondering how you get this information un-segmented. Relational databases give you the ability to merge, or join, tables. Consider the following statement, which is intended to give all the available information for Brad: "Give me all the columns from the contacts table where contact_id is equal to 1, and while you're at it throw in all the columns from the Companies table where the company_id field equals the value shown in Brad's company_id column."

In other words, in this statement, you are asking to join these two tables where the company_id fields are the same. The result of this request, or query, looks something like Table 1-5.

In the course of a couple of pages, you've learned how to solve a data-integrity problem by segmenting information and creating additional tables. But we have yet to give this problem a name.

When we learned the vocabulary associated with relational databases from a very thick and expensive book, this sort of problem was called an *update anomaly.* There may or may not be people using this term in the real world; if there are, we haven't met them (people in the real world call it "breach of contract" when addressing their consultants). However, we think this term is pretty apt. In Tables 1-1 and 1-2, if you were to update one row in the table, other rows containing the same information would not be affected.

The delete anomaly

Now take a look at Table 1-6, focusing on row 3.

Consider what happens if Mr. Doe is deleted from the database. This may seem like a simple change but suppose someone accessing the database wants a list of all the companies contacted over the previous year. In the current setup, when you remove row 3, you take out not only the information about John Doe, you remove information about the company as well. This problem is called a *delete anomaly.*

If the company information is moved to its own table, as you saw in the previous section, this delete anomaly won't be a problem. You can remove Mr. Doe and then decide independently if you want to remove the company he's associated with.

The insert anomaly

Our final area of concern is problems that will be introduced during an insert. Looking again at the Table 1-6, you can see that the purpose of this table is to store information on contacts, not companies. This becomes a drag if you want to add a

TABLE 1-5 QUERY RESULTS

company_id	company_name	company_address	contact_id	contact_name	contact_title	phone	email
1	BigCo Company	1121 43rd St.	2	Brad Bulger	President	4155552222	brad@not.real

TABLE 1-6 TABLE WITH DELETE ANOMALY

company_id	company_name	company_address	contact_name	contact_title	phone	email
1	BigCo Company	1121 43rd St	Jay Greenspan	Vice President	4155551212	jay@not.real
2	BigCo Company	1121 43rd St	Brad Bulger	President	4155552222	brad@not.real
3	LittleCo Company	4444 44th St	John Doe	Lackey	2125556666	nobody@mysqlphpapps.com

company but not an individual. For the most part, you'll have to wait to have a specific contact to add to the database before you can add company information. This is a ridiculous restriction. The solution is to store contact information in one table and company information in another. By storing company information in its own table, you can add a new company there even if you (as yet) have no contacts to go with it. Ditto for contacts with no matching companies.

Normalization

Now that we've shown you some of the problems you might encounter, you need to learn the ways to find and eliminate these anomalies. This process is known as *normalization.* Understanding normalization is vital to working with relational databases. But to anyone who has database experience normalization is not the be-all and end-all of data design. Experience and instinct also play a part in the creation of a good database. The examples in this book will usually be normalized. However, in some cases, a denormalized structure is preferable, for performance reasons, code simplification, or so on.

One other quick caveat. The normalization process consists of several *normal forms.* Normal forms are standards of database regulation that promote efficiency, predictability of results, and unambiguousness.

In this chapter we cover first, second, and third normal forms. In addition to these, the normalization process can involve four other (progressively more rigorous) normal forms. (For the curious, these are called Boyce-Codd normal form, fourth normal form, fifth normal form, and Domain/Key normal form.) We know about these because we read about them in a book. In the real world, where real people actually develop database applications, these normal forms aren't discussed. If you get your data into third normal form that's about good enough – mainly because data in the third normal form meets the requirements of the first and second normal forms, by definition. Yes, a possibility exists that anomalies will exist in third normal form, but if you get this far you should be OK.

First normal form

Getting data into first normal form is fairly easy. Data need to be in a table structure and to meet the following criteria:

- Each column must have a unique name and define a single attribute of the table as a whole.
- Each row in the table must have a set of values that uniquely identifies the row (this is known as the *primary key* of the table).
- No two rows can be identical.

- Each cell must contain an *atomic* value, meaning that each cell contains only one value. No arrays or any other manner of representing more than one value can exist in any cell.
- No repeating groups of data are allowed.

The final item here is the only one that may require some explanation. Take a look at Table 1-7.

As you've already seen with these data, row 1 and row 2 contain two columns that contain identical information. This is a repeating group of data. Only when you remove these columns and place them in their own table will these data be in first normal form. The separation of tables that we did in Tables 1-3 and 1-4 will move this data into first normal form.

Before we move on to chat about second and third normal form, you're going to need a couple of quick definitions. The first is of the term *primary key.* The primary key is a column or set of columns by which each row can be uniquely identified.

Primary keys, while very important, are difficult to understand both in theory and in practice. The theory is straightforward: Each row in the column designated as the primary key must have a unique value. In practice, the easiest way to get a series of unique numbers is to use a series of sequential numbers, in which the value of the primary key column in each row increments the previous row's primary key value by one. Because this is such a popular solution to the primary key problem, all database servers of any consequence create the incremental values for you as records are created. MySQL has such a mechanism; you use it by designating your primary key column as type `auto_increment`.

Depending on your data, all kinds of values will work for a primary key. Social Security numbers work great, as do email addresses and URLs. The data just need to be unique. In some cases, two or more columns may comprise your primary key. For instance, to continue with the address-book example, if contact information needs to be stored for a company with many locations, it is probably best to store the switchboard number and mailing address information in a table that has the `company_id` and `company_location` as its primary key.

Next, we need to define the word *dependency,* which means pretty much what you think it means. A dependent column is one that is inexorably tied to the primary key. It can't exist in the table if the primary key is removed.

With that under your belt, you are ready to tackle second normal form.

Second normal form

This part of the process only comes into play when you end up with one of those multi-column primary keys that we just discussed. Assume that in the course of dividing up your address tables you end up with Table 1-8. Here, the `company_name` and `company_location` columns comprise the multi-column primary key.

TABLE 1-7 TABLE WITH REPEATING GROUPS OF DATA

company_id	company_ name	company_ address	contact_ name	contact_ title	phone	email
1	BigCo Company	1121 43rd St.	Jay Greenspan	Vice President	4155551212	jay@not.real
2	BigCo Company	1121 43rd St.	Brad Bulger	President	4155552222	brad@not.real
3	LittleCo Company	4444 44th St.	John Doe	Lackey	2125556666	nobody@hotmail.com

TABLE 1-8 TABLE NOT IN SECOND NORMAL FORM

company_name	company_location	company_ceo	company_address
BigCo Company	San Francisco	Bill Hurt	1121 43rd St.
LittleCo Company	Los Angeles	Bob Ouch	4444 44th St.

You should be able to see pretty quickly that an insertion anomaly would work its way in here if you were to add another location for BigCo Company. You'd have the CEO name, Bill Hurt, repeated in an additional row, and that's no good.

You can get this table into second normal form by removing rows that are only partially dependent on the primary key. Here, the CEO is dependent only on the `company_name` column. It is not dependent on the `company_location` column. To get into second normal form, you move rows that are only partially dependent on a multi-field primary key into their own table (see Tables 1-9 and 1-10). Second normal form does not apply to tables that have a single-column primary key.

TABLE 1-9 TABLE IN SECOND NORMAL FORM

company_id	company_name	company_ceo
1	BigCo Company	Bill Hurt
2	LittleCo Company	Bob Ouch

TABLE 1-10 TABLE IN SECOND NORMAL FORM

company_id	company_location	company_address
1	San Francisco	1121 43rd St.
2	Los Angeles	4444 44th St.

Third normal form

Finishing up the normalization process, third normal form is concerned with *transitive dependencies*. A transitive dependency describes a situation in which a column exists that is not directly reliant on the primary key. Instead, the field is reliant on some other field, which in turn is dependent on the primary key. A quick way to get into third normal form is to look at all the fields in a table and ask if they all describe the primary key. If they don't, you're not there.

If your address book needs to store more information on your contacts, you might find yourself with a table like Table 1-11.

TABLE 1-11 TABLE NOT IN THIRD NORMAL FORM

contact_id	contact_name	contact_phone	assistant_name	assistant_phone
1	Bill Jones	4155555555	John Bills	2025554444
2	Carol Shaw	2015556666	Shawn Carlo	6505556666

You might think we're doing OK here. But look at the `assistant_phone` column and ask if that really describes the primary key (and the focus of this table), which is your contact. It's possible, even likely, that one assistant will serve many people, in which case it's possible that an assistant name and phone will end up listed in the table more than once. That would be a repeating group of data, which you already know you don't want. Tables 1-12 and 1-13 are in third normal form.

TABLE 1-12 TABLE IN THIRD NORMAL FORM

assistant_id	assistant_name	assistant_phone
1	John Bills	2025554444
2	Shawn Carlo	6505556666

TABLE 1-13 TABLE IN THIRD NORMAL FORM

contact_id	contact_name	contact_phone	assistant_id
1	Bill Jones	4155555555	1
2	Carol Shaw	2015556666	2

Types of Relationships

In the applications you'll see later in this book we create a bunch of tables that don't have anomalies. We include columns that maintain relationships among these tables. You'll encounter three specific types of relationships in database land.

The one-to-many relationship

This is by far the most common type of relationship that occurs between two tables. When one value in a column references multiple fields in another table, a one-to-many relationship is in effect (Figure 1-1).

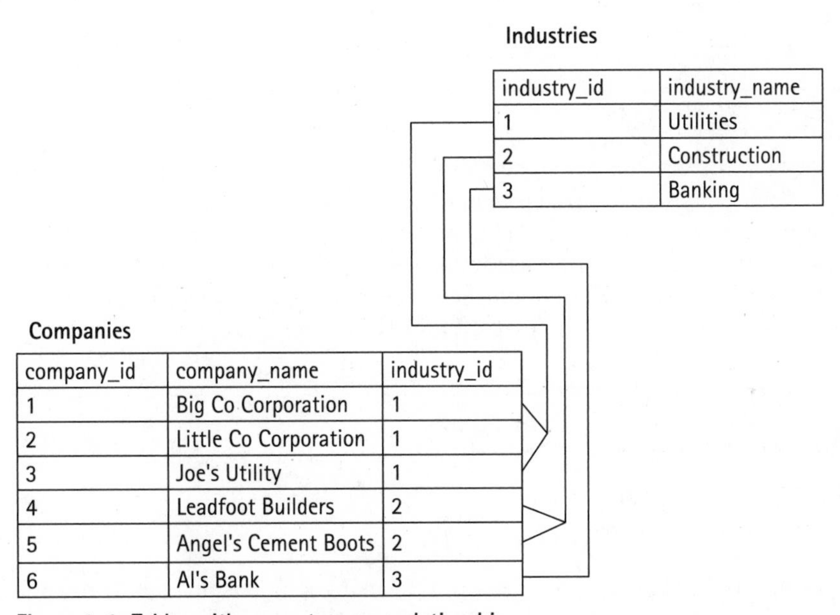

Industries

industry_id	industry_name
1	Utilities
2	Construction
3	Banking

Companies

company_id	company_name	industry_id
1	Big Co Corporation	1
2	Little Co Corporation	1
3	Joe's Utility	1
4	Leadfoot Builders	2
5	Angel's Cement Boots	2
6	Al's Bank	3

Figure 1-1: Tables with a one-to-many relationship

Figure 1-1 shows a classic one-to-many relationship. Here, each company is associated with a certain industry. As you can see, one industry listed in the industry table can be associated with one or more rows in the company table. This in no way restricts what you can do with the companies. You are absolutely free to use this table as the basis for other one-to-many relationships. Figure 1-2 shows that the Companies table can be on the "one" side of a one-to-many relationship with a table that lists city locations for all the different companies.

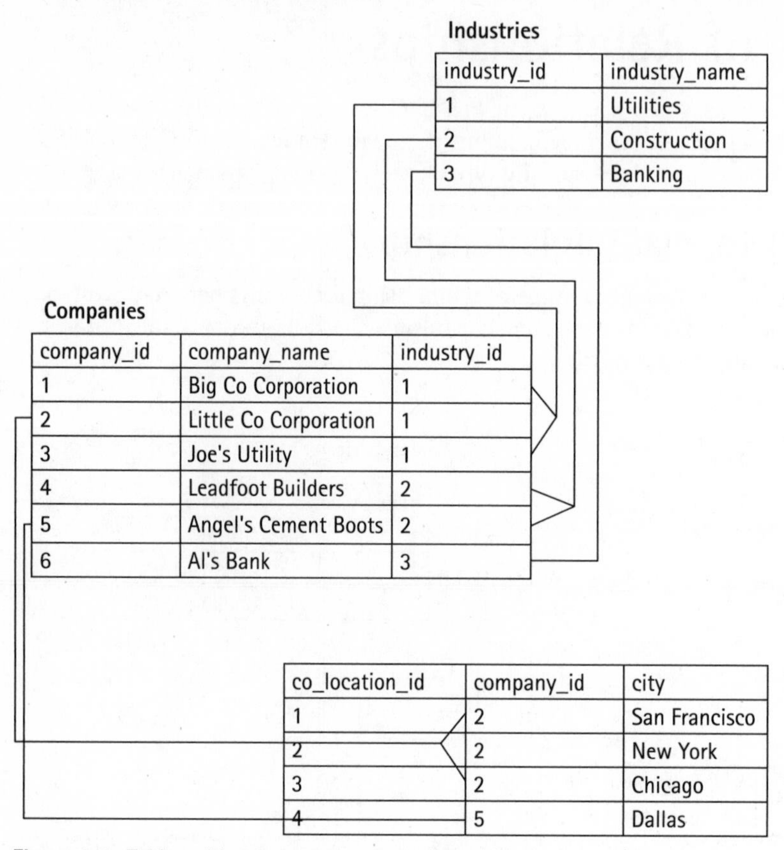

Industries

industry_id	industry_name
1	Utilities
2	Construction
3	Banking

Companies

company_id	company_name	industry_id
1	Big Co Corporation	1
2	Little Co Corporation	1
3	Joe's Utility	1
4	Leadfoot Builders	2
5	Angel's Cement Boots	2
6	Al's Bank	3

co_location_id	company_id	city
1	2	San Francisco
2	2	New York
3	2	Chicago
4	5	Dallas

Figure 1-2: Tables with two one-to-many relationships

The one-to-one relationship

A one-to-one relationship is essentially a one-to-many relationship where only one row in a table is related to only one row in another table. During the normalization process, we mentioned a situation in which one table holds information about corporate executives and another holds information about their assistants. This could very well be a one-to-one relationship if each executive has one assistant and each assistant works for only one executive. Figure 1-3 gives a visual representation of this relationship.

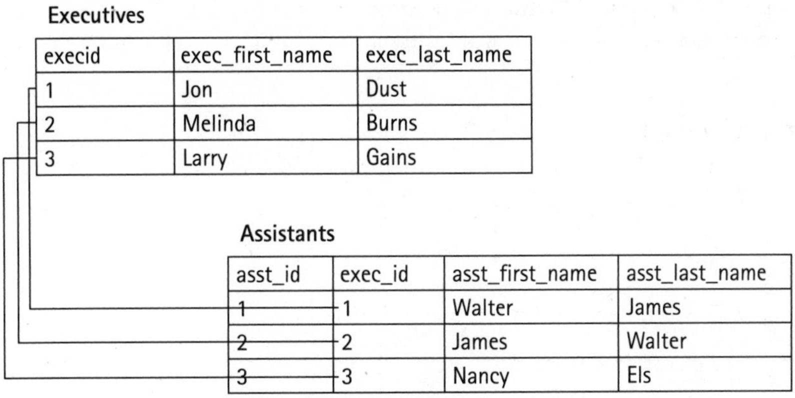

Executives

execid	exec_first_name	exec_last_name
1	Jon	Dust
2	Melinda	Burns
3	Larry	Gains

Assistants

asst_id	exec_id	asst_first_name	asst_last_name
1	1	Walter	James
2	2	James	Walter
3	3	Nancy	Els

Figure 1-3: Tables with a one-to-one relationship

The many-to-many relationship

Many-to-many relationships work a bit differently from the other two kinds of relationships. For instance, suppose that the company keeping the data has a variety of newsletters that it sends to its contacts, and suppose that it needs to add this information to the database. There's a weekly, a monthly, a bi-monthly, and an annual newsletter, and to keep from annoying clients, the newsletters must only be sent to those who request them.

To start, you could add a table that stores the newsletter types (Table 1-14).

TABLE 1-14 NEWSLETTERS TABLE

newsletter_id	newsletter_name
1	Weekly
2	Monthly
3	Bi-monthly
4	Annual

Table 1-14 can't be directly related to another table that stores contact information. So it's not sufficient to define which clients have requested which types of newsletters. The only way to make that work is to add a column to the Contacts table that stores the newsletters that each contact receives. Right away, you should notice a problem with Table 1-15. In Table 1-15 the Newsletters column contains more than one value. The value looks a lot like an array. As mentioned earlier, this should never occur within a database – you want only atomic values in each column.

TABLE 1-15 REVISED CONTACTS TABLE

contact_id	contact_first_name	contact_last_name	Newsletters
1	Jon	Doe	1,3,4
2	Al	Banks	2,3,4

In situations like this you'll need to create another table, of a type often known as a *mapping table* because it maps the relationship of one table to another. Figure 1-4 shows how the relationship between these values can be made to work.

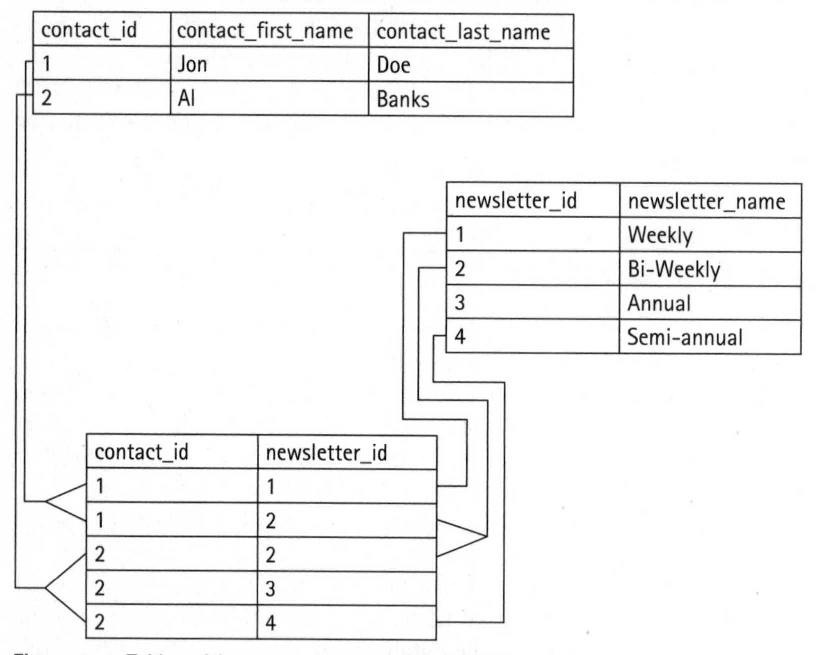

Figure 1-4: Tables with a many-to-many relationship

With this structure, any number of contacts can have any number of newsletters and any number of newsletters can be sent to any number of contacts.

Newcomers to databases often overlook many-to-many relationships and instead choose designs that require excessive columns within a table or arrays within a column. Make sure to consider a many-to-many relationship if your structure seems unmanageable.

Advanced Database Concepts

For a long time MySQL was a polarizing piece of software in the applications-development community. It had (and still has) aspects that many developers loved: it's free (at least, when used in applications that conform to the GNU Public License), it doesn't take up a whole lot of resources, it's very quick, and it's easy to learn compared to packages like Oracle and Sybase. However, it didn't originally offer features common in other databases, such as subselects or joins in updates, and these shortcomings kept many from adopting MySQL for their applications. But since the publication of the first edition of this book a lot of work has been done on MySQL, and it now offers at least partial support for the features discussed in the following sections.

Referential integrity

Every example used so far in this chapter has made use of *foreign keys*. A foreign key is a column that references the primary key of another table in order to maintain a relationship. In Table 1-4, the Contacts table contains a `company_id` column, which references the primary key of the Companies table (Table 1-3). This column is a foreign key to the Companies table.

In Chapter 2 we demonstrate how to create tables in MySQL. It's easy enough to create tables with all the columns necessary for primary keys and foreign keys. However, in MySQL foreign keys are not universally available.

In packages like Oracle, Sybase, or PostgreSQL, tables can be created that explicitly define foreign keys. For instance, with Oracle the database system could be made aware that the `company_id` column in the Contacts table has a relationship to the company_id column in the Companies table. This capability is potentially a very good thing and is known as a *foreign-key constraint*. If the database system is aware of a relationship, it can check to make sure the value being inserted into the foreign-key field exists in the referenced table. If it does not, the database system will reject the insert. The capability of the database server to reject records because they don't satisfy the requirements of linked tables is known as *referential integrity*.

With MySQL, at the time of this writing, foreign-key constraints are only available when you're using the InnoDB table type. You'll see how to work with foreign-key constraints in InnoDB in Chapter 2.

To demonstrate the importance of foreign-key constraints we'll show you how you'd achieve the same effect using MySQL table types other than InnoDB. Before inserting or updating records in your table, you have to take some extra steps.

To be ultra-safe, you would need to go through the following steps in order to insert a row in the Contacts table (Table 1-4), for example:

1. Get all the values for `company_id` in the Companies table.
2. Check to make sure the value for `company_id` to be inserted into the Contacts table exists in the data you retrieved in Step 1.
3. If it does, insert values.

The developers of MySQL had long argued that referential integrity was not necessary and that including it would slow down MySQL. Further, they argued that it is the responsibility of the application interacting with the database to ensure that the inserted data is correct. There is a logic to this way of thinking. In Parts III and IV of this book we present several applications that would work just fine without enforcing referential integrity or the method of checking shown above. In general, in these applications, all the possible values are pulled from a database anyway and there's very little opportunity for errors to creep into the system.

But there's no doubt that having the option of enforcing referential integrity is a good thing.

Transactions

In relational databases, things change in groups. As shown in a variety of applications in this book, many changes require that rows be updated in several tables concurrently. An e-commerce site may contain code that works in the following manner:

1. Insert a customer into the Customers table.
2. Check the inventory table to see that a sufficient quantity of the item exists to place the order.
3. Add invoice information into the Invoice table.
4. Reduce the quantity available for the item in the inventory table by the quantity ordered.

When you're working with a series of steps like this, serious problems can occur. If the operating system crashes or power goes out between steps three and four, the database will contain bad data. It's also important to remember that MySQL and other relational databases are multi-threaded, which means that they can process directives from multiple clients simultaneously. Imagine what would happen with the previous listing if two orders were placed almost simultaneously for an item that was nearly out of stock. Two threads (in the case of an e-commerce site, two customers working through their browsers) could find themselves requesting the final item at the same time. If precautions are not taken, it's possible that one person might receive confirmation that the order is available when in fact it is not.

To prevent such occurrences, most sophisticated database systems make use of *transactions*. A transaction is a bundle of commands treated as an indivisible unit. If any one of these commands fails to go through, the whole group of commands fails, and the database returns to the state it was in before the first command was attempted. This is known as a commit/rollback approach. Either all the requests are committed to the database, or the database is rolled back to the state it was in prior to the transactions. This works both to prevent threads from stepping on each other and to protect data in the event of a crash.

With the example given above, if in Step 2 the application were to discover that no items are left, a `ROLLBACK` command will be given and no items will be removed from the inventory. In the case of a crash, the in-progress transactions will be automatically rolled back.

A transaction-capable database must support the four properties that go by the acronym ACID, which are defined as follows:

- **Atomicity** – The operations that make up each transaction are treated collectively as a single, or atomic, unit. Either all changes are committed or none are.
- **Consistency** – The available data will never be in an inconsistent state; either other threads will see the data in the state it was in prior to the transaction, or other threads will see the data in the state it winds up in after the transaction is completed.
- **Isolation** – Each transaction is isolated from all others. The effects of Transaction A are not visible to Transaction B until Transaction A is completed. If a transaction is in progress, the interim state of the data will not be visible to other transactions.
- **Durability** – When a transaction is complete, the changes are permanent. Even if a database crashes, the information from a committed transaction will be available and complete.

In older versions of MySQL transactions were not supported. This was a major problem for many developers, who could not fathom the idea of designing proper applications without this feature. Now MySQL features several table types (including InnoDB and BerkeleyDB) that support transactions. You read more about these tables in Chapter 2.

Stored procedures

The big fancy database systems allow for procedural code (real computer code, similar to PHP or Perl) to be placed within the database. Using stored procedures provides a couple of key advantages. First, it can reduce the amount of code needed in middleware applications. If MySQL accepted stored procedures (which it unfortunately does not — yet), a single PHP command could be sent to the database to query data, do some string manipulation, and then return a value ready to be displayed in your page.

The other major advantage comes when you are working in an environment in which more than one front-end is accessing the same database. Consider a situation in which there happens to be one front-end written for the Web and another, accessible on Windows machines, written in Visual C++. It would be a pain to write all the queries and transactions in two different places. You'd be much better off writing stored procedures and accessing those from your various applications. Stored procedures are planned for MySQL version 5.0.

Summary

At this point you should have a pretty good idea of how relational databases work. The theory covered here is really important, as quality data design is one of the cornerstones of quality applications. If you fail in the normalization process, you could create difficulties that will haunt you for months or years.

In the applications in Parts III and IV of this book, you see how we approach and normalize several sets of data.

Now that you know how tables in a relational database work, move on to Chapter 2, where you see how to make these tables in MySQL.

Chapter 2

The Structured Query Language for Creating and Altering Tables

IN THIS CHAPTER

- Creating tables and databases in MySQL
- Choosing the proper column type and column attributes for tables
- Choosing the proper tables for your applications
- Altering existing tables
- Using phpMyAdmin
- Using MySQLCC
- Using MacSQL

IN CHAPTER 1 you learned that tables are the basis of all the good things that come from working with relational databases. You can do a fair amount with these tables, as you'll see throughout this book. So it should come as no surprise that creating and maintaining them requires some knowledge.

If you're coming to MySQL from a background in Microsoft's SQL Server or a desktop package like Access, you may be used to creating tables with a slick WYSIWYG (what you see is what you get) interface. There's no doubt that working with a graphical interface can be a lot more pleasant than figuring out the syntax of a language – any language. In fact, you can use any of several GUI tools to create and manipulate tables, and we'll discuss some of these later in the chapter. However, even if you plan on installing and using a GUI tool, you should take some time to learn how to create and maintain tables using the Data Definition Language (DDL), which is part of SQL. Specifically, it will be a great help to you to understand the `create` and `alter` commands. Before too long you will have to use these commands within your scripts. There also may be an occasion when you don't have access to the graphical interface, and you'll need this knowledge to fall back on.

Essential Definitions

Before we get to creating tables and databases in MySQL, you'll need to understand a couple of items. The concepts we're about to present are very important – make sure you understand how to deal with these before you move forward in your database design.

Null values

One of the first decisions you will have to make for every column in your table is whether or not to allow *null values*. If you remember back to your basic math, you may recall the null set – a group that contains nothing. In relational databases, null has the same meaning: A null field contains nothing.

The concept of nothing is different from the concept of zero. A field that is null is distinctly different from a field containing a text string with no characters (a *zero-length* string) or a numerical value of 0. The difference is that empty strings and zeros are values.

This SQL statement . . .

```
select * from mytable where myfield = 0;
```

returns rows in which the myfield column contains the numerical value 0. In contrast, the statement . . .

```
select * from mytable where myfield = '';
```

returns an entirely different set of rows: those with nothing at all in their myfield columns.

Value comparisons do not work with null. Since null is the absence of value, any comparison with any value (including another null) is meaningless. In Chapter 3 you can see that using null values requires that the application developer be very careful when writing table joins. To give you a quick preview, consider what would happen if we wanted to join Table 2-1 and Table 2-2:

In your SQL select statements (covered in Chapter 3), you can determine if a field contains a null value in a couple of ways. First, you can use MySQL's isnull() function. For example, to find rows in a table where the middle_name column contains null values, you could run the following query:

```
select * from names where isnull(middle_name);
```

Or, to exclude null values from the query result:

```
select * from names where !isnull(middle_name);
```

The exclamation point means "not."

You can also use the `is null` and `is not null` statements. For example:

```
select * from users were addr2 is null;
select * from users where addr2 is not null;
```

TABLE 2-1 CONTACTS

first_name	last_name	fantasy_spouse_id
Jay	Greenspan	1
Brad	Bulger	NULL

TABLE 2-2 desired_spouse

fantasy_spouse_id	First_name	last_name
1	Nicole	Kidman

If you wanted to find the authors of a great book on MySQL and PHP and their dream spouses, you would have to join these tables on the `fantasy_spouse_id` field. (Don't worry if you don't understand the exact syntax, it will be covered in the next chapter.)

```
SELECT * FROM contacts, desired_spouse
   WHERE contacts.fantasy_spouse_id =
desired_spouse.fantasy_spouse_id;
```

This statement works fine for Jay, but there's going to be a problem for Brad because he's a happy bachelor and his `fantasy_spouse_id` field is null. He will not show up in the result set even though the goal of the query is to get all the people in the contacts table and the associated fantasy spouses, if the retrieved contacts have them.

Again, this is just a preview, an example of why null is so important. In Chapter 3 you can see how the outer join solves problems like this.

Indexes

Arguably the single greatest advantage of a relational database is the speed with which it can query and sort tremendous amounts of information. To achieve this great speed, MySQL and all other database servers make use of optimized data-retrieval mechanisms called *indexes*.

An index allows a database server to create a representation of a column that it can search with amazing speed. Indexes are especially helpful in finding a single row or group of rows from a large table. They can also speed up joins and aggregate functions, like `min()` and `max()`, which we cover in Chapter 3.

Given these advantages, why not just create an index for every column for every table? There are some very good reasons. First, indexes can actually slow some things down. It takes time for your database server to maintain indexes. You wouldn't want to create overhead for your server that is not going to be a benefit to you down the road. Also, on some occasions the indexes themselves are slower. If you need to iterate through every row in a table, you're actually better off not using an index. Also, unnecessary indexes will use a lot of disk space and memory.

A table's primary key is often the subject of searches (for obvious reasons). Thus the column or columns that you declare as your primary key in a table definition will automatically be indexed.

We'll talk more about creating indexes later in this chapter.

The create database Statement

Before you can get to creating your tables, you'll need to create a database to hold them. This should take all of a second. The basic `create database` statement is fairly simple and can be run from any interface that has access to MySQL.

The general syntax is as follows:

```
create database database_name
```

In case you're wondering, after running this command, MySQL creates a folder in which it stores all the files needed for your database. On our Linux machines the database folders are stored in /usr/local/mysql/lib.

When naming databases, or for that matter columns or indexes, avoid using names that will cause confusion down the road. On operating systems in which file names are case-sensitive, such as most Unix systems, database names will also be case-sensitive. Come up with conventions that you plan on sticking to, such as using all-lowercase names for tables and columns. Spaces are not allowed.

Though MySQL can work around potentially bad choices, you should avoid using words that MySQL uses in the course of its business. For instance, naming a table "Select" is a really bad idea. Chapter 6 of the MySQL reference manual lists over 150 reserved words. If you stay away from words used by SQL or MySQL functions, you should be okay.

From the MySQL command-line client, you can simply type in the following command:

```
mysql> create database my_database;
```

The MySQL command-line client is in the bin/ directory of your MySQL installation and has the file name mysql (in Unix) or mysql.exe (in DOS/Windows).

From PHP, you can use the `mysql_query()` function. The following piece of code would create two databases. (Keep in mind that you need to log into MySQL as a user with the proper rights for the code to work.)

```
$conn = mysql_connect("localhost","username", "password")
  or die ("Could not connect to localhost");


mysql_query(" CREATE DATABASE IF NOT EXISTS my_database ") or
    die ("Could not create database");
```

The use database Statement

Before you can begin making tables in MySQL you must select a database that has been created. Though you can do this in individual `SELECT` statements, it's easier to define a default working database with the `use` command. If you are accessing MySQL through the MySQL command-line client, you will have to enter this statement:

```
use database_name
```

If you're accessing a database through PHP, use the `mysql_select_db()` function:

```
$conn = mysql_connect("localhost","username", "password")
  or die ("Could not connect to localhost");

mysql_select_db("test", $conn) or
    die ("Could not select database");
```

The create table Statement

Once you have created and selected a database, you are ready to create a table. The basic `create table` statement is fairly simple and takes this basic form:

```
create table table_name
(
    column_name_1 column_type column_attributes,
    column_name_2 column_type column_attributes,
    primary key (column_name),
    index index_name(column_name)
)type=table_type
```

Column types, column attributes, and details on indexes are covered in the following sections. Before we get to those, we should mention two simple column attributes:

- `null | not null`
- `default`

The first gives you the opportunity to allow or forbid null values. If you don't specify `null` or `not null` it is assumed that null values are allowed. The second, if declared, sets a value if none is declared when you insert a row into the table. (If a column is defined as "`not null`" and no default value is specified, MySQL assigns a default value for the column based on its data type. See the "CREATE TABLE Syntax" section of the online MySQL Language Reference Manual for details.)

Here's an example `create` statement that demonstrates these two attributes, and a few others.

```
create table topics (
        topic_id        integer not null auto_increment,
        parent_id       integer default 0 not null,
        root_id         integer default 0,
        name            varchar(255),
        description     text null,
        create_dt       timestamp,
        modify_dt       timestamp,
        author          varchar(255) null,
        author_host     varchar(255) null,
primary key(topic_id),
index my_index(parent_id)
)type=myisam;
```

This statement creates a table named topics with nine columns and two indexes, one for the primary key and one for the parent_id column. In the preceding statement four column types are used: integer, varchar, text, and timestamp. These and many other column types are discussed in further detail in the following example. Before you set out to create tables you should have a good understanding of all the column types available as well as of ways to create indexes.

To create tables from the command-line client, key in the entire command. From PHP, use the mysql_query() function as follows:

```
$conn = mysql_connect("localhost","username","password") or
    die ("Could not connect to localhost");

mysql_select_db("test", $conn) or
    die("could not select database");
$query = "create table my_table (
    col_1 int not null primary key,
    col_2 text
)";
mysql_query($query) or
    die(mysql_error());
```

Column Types

MySQL provides you with a range of column types. While several are similar, subtle yet important differences exist among them. Give this section a read and choose carefully when deciding on column types for your tables.

String column types

Eight MySQL column types are suitable for storing text strings:

- char
- varchar
- tinytext/tinyblob
- text/blob
- mediumtext/mediumblob
- longtext/longblob
- enum
- set

char

Usage: `char(length)`

The `char` column type has a maximum length of 255 characters. This is a fixed-length type, meaning that the field will be right-padded with spaces when a value is inserted that has fewer characters than the maximum length of the column. So if a column has been defined as `char(10)` and you want to store the value `happy`, MySQL will actually store `happy` and then five spaces. The spaces are removed from the result when the value is retrieved from the table. Values longer than the column width are truncated.

varchar

Usage: `varchar(length)`

This type is nearly identical to `char` and is used in many of the same places. It also has a maximum length of 255 characters. The difference is that `varchar` is a variable-length column type, meaning that values will not be padded with spaces. Instead MySQL will add one character to each `varchar` field to store the length of the field.

MySQL removes spaces from the end of strings in `varchar` fields, but this behavior might change in future releases of the language.

If you define a column as `varchar` with a column length of less than four, MySQL will automatically change the column to the `char` type. Similarly, if you try to mix `char`s and `varchar`s with a column length of more than four, they all become `varchar`s.

Using char or varchar

For the most part, there is little practical difference between `char` and `varchar`. Which one you decide to use will depend on which will require more space, the trailing spaces in a `char` column or the size byte in `varchar`. If your field stores something like last names, you'll probably want to allow 25 characters, just to be safe. If you were to use the `char` column type and someone had the last name Smith, your column would contain 20 trailing spaces. There's no need for that; you're much better off using `varchar` and allowing MySQL to track the size of the column. However, when you want to store passwords of five to seven characters, it would be a waste to use `varchar` to track the size of the column. Every time a `varchar` field is updated, MySQL has to check the length of the field and change the character that stores the field length. You'd be better off using `char(7)`.

tinytext/tinyblob

Usage: `tinytext/tinyblob`

These are the first of the four *binary* (or *blob*) column types. You can use these columns to store both large strings and binary objects. Notice that we have paired a text and a blob column here and in the following three listings. The only difference between the paired items is the way in which MySQL will sort and compare the values stored in the columns. For blob-column types (`blob`, `tinyblob` `mediumblob`, `largeblob`), MySQL will perform case-sensitive comparisons. For text-column types (`tinytext`, `text`, `mediumtext`, `largetext`), MySQL will perform case-insensitive comparisons.

For example, if you were to make a table with the following `create` statement:

```
create table blob_test
(
    blob_column text
);
```

and then insert a row with the following data into the table:

```
insert into blob_test (blob_column) values ('THIS IS A STRING FOR MY BLOB');
```

MySQL would run case-insensitive comparisons. Therefore, the following `select` statement would return the inserted row:

```
mysql> select * from blob_test where blob_column like 'this%';
+--------------------------------+
| blob_column                    |
+--------------------------------+
| THIS IS A STRING FOR MY BLOB |
+--------------------------------+
```

If, however, the column were declared as a `blob`:

```
create table blob_test2
(
    blob_column blob
);
```

and the same data were inserted, the previous `select` statement would not match the row.

All of the statements used in this example will be explained in the remainder of Chapter 2 and in Chapter 3.

All of these types (`tinytext/tinyblob`, `text/blob`, `mediumtext/mediumblob`, and `largetext/largeblob`) are variable column types, similar to `varchar`. They differ only in the size of the string they can contain. The `tinytext/tinyblob` type has a maximum length of 255, so in fact it serves the same purpose as `varchar(255)`. An index can be created for an entire `tinytext` column, but remember that `tinytext` and `tinyblob` fields preserve trailing whitespace characters.

text/blob

Usage: `text/blob`

The `text/blob` type has a maximum length of 65,535 characters.

mediumtext/mediumblob

Usage: `mediumtext/mediumblob`

The `mediumtext/mediumblob` type has a maximum length of 16,777,215 characters.

longtext

Usage: `longtext/longblob`

The `longtext` type has a maximum length of 4,294,967,295 characters. However, this column currently is not very useful, as MySQL allows strings of only 16 million bytes.

enum

Usage: `enum ('value1', 'value2', 'value3' ?) [default 'value']`

With `enum`, you can limit the potential values of a column to those you specify. It allows for 65,535 values, though it's difficult to imagine a situation in which you'd want to use this column with more than a few potential values. This type is of use when, for example, you want to allow only values of `yes` or `no`. The `create` statement that makes use of `enum` will look like this:

```
create table my_table (
   id int auto_increment primary key,
   answer enum ('yes', 'no') default 'no'
);
```

set

Usage: `set ('value1', 'value2', 'value3' ?) [default 'value']`

This column type defines a superset of values. It allows for zero or more values from the list you specify to be included in a field. You will not see this column type used in this book: We do not like to see multiple values in a single field, as it violates very basic rules of database design. (Reread Chapter 1 if you don't know what we mean by this.) You can see an example of where `set` makes sense in the MySQL grant tables, which are discussed in Appendix E.

Bear in mind that `set` columns can yield big savings in storage space and improvements in performance as databases get bigger. Suppose you have 20,000,000,000 rows and you need to store the state of eight binary switches for each row. To normalize this out would require a `bigint` and a `tinyint` for each switch. Even without indexes you are looking at about 185GB for the table. Using a `set` column, you would require only 37.25GB for this problem. However, this isn't something you'll see in this book.

Numeric column types

MySQL provides you with seven column types suitable for storing numeric values. Note that the following are synonyms: `int` and `integer`; `double`, `double precision`, and `real`; and `decimal` and `numeric`.

- `int/integer`
- `tinyint`
- `mediumint`
- `bigint`
- `float`
- `double/double precision/real`
- `decimal/numeric`

Be aware that `real` is synonymous with `float` when running in ANSI mode.

For all numeric types the maximum display size is 255. For most numeric types you will have the option to *zerofill* a column — to left-pad it with zeros. For example, if you have an `int` column that has a display size of `10` and you insert a value of `25` into this column, MySQL will store and display `0000000025`. The numeric column types may also be defined as `signed` or `unsigned`. `signed` is the default definition.

int/integer

Usage: `int(display size) [unsigned] [zerofill]`

If you use the `unsigned` flag, this column type can store integers from 0 to 4,294,967,295. If you use the `signed` flag, the range is from -2,147,483,648 to 2,147,483,647. `int` will often be used with `auto_increment` to define the primary key of a table:

```
create table my_table (
   table_id int unsigned auto_increment primary key,
   next_column text
);
```

Note that we've used an `unsigned` column because an `auto_increment` column has no need for negative values.

tinyint

Usage: `tinyint(display size) [unsigned] [zerofill]`

If `unsigned`, `tinyint` stores integers between 0 and 255. If `signed`, the range is from -128 to 127.

mediumint

Usage: `mediumint(display size) [unsigned] [zerofill]`

If you use the `unsigned` flag, `mediumint` stores integers between -8,388,608 and 8,388,607. If you use the `signed` flag, the range is from 0 to 1677215.

bigint

Usage: `bigint(display size) [unsigned] [zerofill]`

If you use the `signed` flag, `bigint` stores integers between -9,223,372,036,854, 775,808 and 9,223,372,036,854,775,807. If you use the `unsigned` flag, the range is from 0 to 18,446,744,073,709,551,615.

float

Float has two distinct usages.

- Usage: float(precision) [zerofill]

  In this usage, `float` stores a floating-point number and cannot be unsigned. The `precision` attribute can be ≤ 24 for a single-precision floating-point number, and between 25 and 53 for a double-precision floating-point number.

- Usage: float[(*M*,*D*)] [zerofill]

  This is a small (single-precision) floating-point number and cannot be unsigned. Allowable values are -3.402823466E+38 to -1.175494351E-38, zero, and 1.175494351E-38 to 3.402823466E+38. `M` is the display width and `D` is the number of decimals. If the `float` attribute is used without an argument or with an argument of ≤ 24, the column will store a single-precision floating-point number.

double/double precision/real

Usage: `double[(M,D)] [zerofill]`

This column stores a double-precision floating-point number and cannot be unsigned. Allowable values are -1.7976931348623157E+308 to -2.2250738585072014E-308, zero, and 2.2250738585072014E-308 to 1.7976931348623157E+308. `M` is the display width and `D` is the number of decimals.

decimal

Usage: `decimal[(M[,D])] [zerofill]`

Numbers in a decimal column are stored as characters. Each number is stored as a string, with one character for each digit of the value. `M` is the display width, and `D` is the number of decimals. If `M` is left out, it's set to 10. If `D` is 0, values will have no decimal point. The maximum range of `decimal` values is the same as for `double`. Remember, though, that `decimal`, like all real types, can cause rounding errors.

Date and time types

MySQL provides you with five column types suitable for storing dates and times:

- `date`
- `datetime`
- `timestamp`
- `time`
- `year`

MySQL date and time types are flexible, accepting either strings or numbers as part of `insert` statements. Additionally, MySQL is pretty good at interpreting dates that you give it. For instance, if you create this table:

```
create table date_test(
   id int unsigned auto_increment primary key,
   the_date date
);
```

the following `insert` statements are all interpreted correctly by MySQL:

```
insert into date_test (a_date) values ('00-06-01');
insert into date_test (a_date) values ('2000-06-01');
insert into date_test (a_date) values ('20000601');
insert into test6 (a_date) values (000601);
```

MySQL prefers to receive dates as strings, so `000601` is a better choice than a similar integer. Using strings for date values may save you from encountering some errors down the road.

Extracting information from date and time columns can be a challenge. MySQL provides many functions that help manipulate these columns.

date

Usage: `date`

The `date` column type stores values in the format `YYYY-MM-DD`. It will allow values between 1000-01-01 and 9999-12-31.

datetime

Usage: `datetime [null | not null] [default]`

The `datetime` type stores values in the format `YYYY-MM-DD HH:MM:SS`. It will allow values between 1000-01-01 00:00:00 and 9999-12-31 23:59:59.

timestamp

Usage: `timestamp(size)`

This is a handy column type that will automatically record the time of the most recent change to a row, whether from an `insert` or an `update`. Size can be defined as any number between 2 and 14. Table 2-3 shows the values stored with each column size. The default value is `14`. Bear in mind that if there are multiple 'Timestamp' fields, only the first will be automatically changed. A timestamp field can later be forced to update by explicitly assigning it to NULL.

TABLE 2-3 timestamp FORMATS

Size	Format
2	YY
4	YYMM
6	YYMMDD
8	YYYYMMDD
10	YYMMDDHHMM
12	YYMMDDHHMMSS
14	YYYYMMDDHHMMSS

time

Usage: `time`

This type stores time in the format `HH:MM:SS` and has a value range from -838:59:59 to 838:59:59. The reason for the large values is that the `time` column type can be used to store the results of mathematical equations involving times.

year

Usage: `year[(2|4)]`

In these post-Y2K days it's hard to imagine that you'd want to store your years in two-digit format, but you can. In two-digit format, allowable dates are those between 1970 and 2069, inclusive. The digits 70–99 are prefaced by 19, and 01–69 are by 20.

Four-digit–year format allows values from 1901 to 2155.

Creating Indexes

MySQL can create an index on any column. There can be a maximum of 16 indexed columns for any standard table. (MyISAM tables support 32 indexes by default and can be made to support 64.) The basic syntax is as follows:

```
index [index_name] (indexed_column)
```

Although the index name is optional, you should always name your indexes. It becomes very important should you want to delete or change your index using the SQL `alter` statement. If you don't specify a name, MySQL will base the index name on the first column in your index.

Another way to create an index is to declare a column as a primary key. Note that any `auto_increment` column must be defined as part of a unique index and is normally (but not necessarily) the primary key of the table. In the following code, the `id_col` column is indexed:

```
create table my_table (
    id_col int unsigned auto_increment primary key,
    another_col text
);
```

The primary key can also be declared like other indexes, after the column definitions, as in the following code:

```
create table my_table (
    id_col int unsigned not null auto_increment,
    another_col text,
    primary key(id_col)
);
```

Indexes can span more than one row. If a query uses two rows in concert during a search, you can create an index that covers the two with this statement:

```
create table mytable(
    id_col int unsigned not null,
    another_col char(200) not null,
    index dual_col_index(id_col, another_col)
);
```

The preceding index will be used for searches that start on `id_col` and can include `another_col`. Indexes of this kind work from left to right. So this index will be used for searches that are exclusively on `id_col`. However, it will not be used for searches on `another_col`.

You can also create indexes on only part of a column. For `char`, `varchar`, and `blob` columns, you can create indexes for the initial portion of a column. Here the syntax is as follows:

```
index index_name (column_name(column_length))
```

For example:

```
create table my_table(
    char_column char (255) not null,
    text_column text not null,
    index index_on_char (char_column(20)),
    index index_on_text (text_column(200))
);
```

An index can also assure that unique values exist in every row in a table by using the `unique` constraint, as follows.

```
create table my_table(
    char_column char (255) not null,
    text_column text not null,
    unique index index_on_char (char_column)
);
```

Table Types

MySQL offers several table types: MyISAM, BDB, InnoDB, and Heap. The default table type is MyISAM. The syntax for declaring a table type is as follows:

```
create table table_name (
    column_name column_type column_attributes
)type=table_type
```

In Chapter 1 we discussed transactions and the importance of that concept to relational databases and the applications built around relational databases. For a long time MySQL didn't support transactions, and this absence was seen by many as a fatal flaw. A lot of developers wouldn't go near MySQL because of it.

But that is no longer the case: MySQL does support full ACID transactions (see Chapter 1 for the definition of ACID). But in order to make use of transactions you need to use table types that support this feature. The following discussion of the table types available in MySQL is extremely important. Make sure to read it carefully and keep up on changes to MySQL table types by checking the MySQL online manual semi-regularly. If you have further questions about MySQL table types you should consult the online manual for the latest information.

MyISAM

On most installations MyISAM is the default MySQL table type. A couple of generations back it was the only table type available in MySQL. MyISAM tables are extremely fast and stable; however, they do not support transactions. They only offer table-level locking of data.

MyISAM tables are optimized for speed in retrieving data with `select` statements. Because of the optimization and lack of transaction support, MyISAM tables are best for tables that are going to run `select` operations far more frequently than they run `update` or `delete` operations.

For example, if you are creating a shopping cart (as we do in Chapter 14) you likely have a table or two dedicated to the product catalog and other tables dedicated to recording user information and orders. The tables that hold catalog information (the items available in your store) probably won't change all that frequently – at most a couple of times a day. And if your store is doing well, these data will be queried frequently, as users browse the items you have available. MyISAM tables are perfect for tables that serve this purpose. The tables that store shopping-cart data and record sales information are going to be subject of `insert` and `update` queries far more frequently than they will be subject of `select` queries. For these sorts of tables you're much better off using one of the transactional table types: InnoDB, Gemini, or BerkeleyDB.

On almost all systems, MyISAM will be the default table type. You'll be able to run any valid `create` statement, and MySQL will create a MyISAM table, even if you don't include a type attribute in your `create` statement. If you want to be extra careful, however, you can include `type=myisam` in your statement, like so:

```
create table mytable(
   col1 int,
   col2 text
) type=myisam;
```

InnoDB Tables

InnoDB tables provide full ACID transaction support (see Chapter 1 for the definition of ACID) and row-level locking. Though other transactional table types are available in MySQL, InnoDB is probably the transactional table that most readers of this book will decide to use. MySQL AB (the company that maintains MySQL) packages InnoDB tables with its standard distribution and is working closely with Innobase (`www.innobase.com`) to see that these tables work well with MySQL.

If you're hosting your application at an ISP, you'll want to make sure that the host supports InnoDB tables before you write your applications for those tables. You can check to see that these tables are available by running the following query: `show variables like 'have%'`.

```
mysql> show variables like 'have%';
+---------------+-------+
| Variable_name | Value |
+---------------+-------+
| have_bdb      | NO    |
| have_innodb   | YES   |
| have_isam     | YES   |
| have_raid     | NO    |
| have_symlink  | YES   |
| have_openssl  | NO    |
+---------------+-------+
6 rows in set (0.30 sec)
```

As you can see from the preceding output, the value for `have_innodb` is `YES`. If the value on your or your ISP's system is `NO`, InnoDB tables are not available.

To create InnoDB tables add `type=innodb` to your `create` statement, as follows:

```
create table mytable(
   col1 int,
   col2 text
) type=innodb;
```

In the applications presented in this book, we have chosen to implement transactions using InnoDB tables. Even if you come to this book with a strong background in relational databases, you will need to read Chapter 12, where we discuss InnoDB's transactional model in detail.

BerkeleyDB

BerkeleyDB tables come from Sleepycat software. This table type provides transaction support but offers only page-level locking. While these tables are reasonably good, there's very little reason to use Berkeley tables when InnoDB tables are available. And at this point InnoDB tables are available to just about everyone. Sleepycat's Web site is `www.sleepycat.com`.

Heap

Heap tables are actually memory-resident hash tables. They are not stored in any physical location and therefore will disappear in case of a crash or power outage. But because of their nature, they are blazingly fast. You should use these tables only for temporary tables – but remember that all users can access heap tables.

The alter table Statement

If you're not happy with the form of your table, you can modify it with the `alter table` statement. Specifically, this statement enables you to rename tables, columns, and indexes; add or drop columns and indexes; and change the definitions of columns and indexes. It also enables you to change tables from one type to another (from MyISAM to InnoDB, for example). This statement always starts with `alter table` *table_name*. The rest of the command depends on the action needed, as described in the following sections.

Changing a table name

The syntax for changing a table name is as follows:

```
alter table table_name rename new_table_name
```

To rename a table named `users` to `users_old`, you would use the following command:

```
alter table users rename users_old;
```

If you have MySQL version 3.23.27 or higher you can make use of the `rename` statement. The basic syntax of this statement is as follows:

```
rename table_name TO new_table_name
```

Adding columns

When adding a column, include all column definitions expected in the `create` statement (column name, type, null|not null, default value, and so on). The basic syntax is as follows:

```
alter table table_name add column column_name column_attributes
```

For example, to add a column to a table named `users` that stores a cell-phone number, you could run the following command:

```
alter table users add column cell_phone varchar(14) not null;
```

In MySQL you can also specify the location of a column – that is, where in the listing of columns it should appear (first, last, or before or after a specific column). Use the word `first` at the end of your `alter` statement to place your inserted column as the first column in the table; use the phrase `after` *`column-name`* to place the column after a column that already exists, as shown in the following examples. So if you wanted to put the `cell_phone` column first in your `users` table, you would use the following command:

```
alter table users add column cell_phone varchar(14) not null first;
```

If you wanted to place the `cell_phone` column between the `home_phone` and `work_phone` columns, you would use the following:

```
alter table users add column cell_phone varchar(14) not null after
home_phone;
```

Don't spend a lot of time worrying about the order of your columns within a table. One of the tenets of database design holds that column order is arbitrary. Any time the order of columns retrieved form the database is important, you need to specify the column order in your query.

Dropping columns

To drop a column, you need only the following command:

```
alter table table_name drop column column_name
```

So to drop the cell_phone column, use this:

```
alter table users drop column cell_phone;
```

Adding indexes

You can add indexes using the index, unique, and primary key commands in the same way you would use them in the create statement:

```
alter table my_table add index index_name (column_name1, column_name2, ?)
alter table my_table add unique index_name(column_name)
alter table my_table add primary key(my_column)
```

For example, if you wanted to add an index on the email column of the users table the following would do the trick:

```
alter table users add index index_on_email (email);
```

Dropping indexes

Making your indexes go away is easy enough with the drop command:

```
alter table table_name drop index index_name
```

To drop the index on the email column, use:

```
alter table users drop index index_on_email;
```

Changing column definitions

It is possible to change a column's name or attributes with either the change or modify command. To change a column's name you must also redefine the column's attributes. The following will work:

```
alter table my_table change my_col2 my_col3 int not null;
```

But this will not:

```
alter table my_table change my_col2 my_col3;
```

If you wish to change only the column's attributes, you can use the change command and make the new column name the same as the old column name. For example, to change the lname column from a varchar(25) column to a char(25) column, you can use the following:

```
alter table users change lname lname char(25);
```

Or you may prefer the modify command:

```
alter table users modify lname char(25);
```

When altering a table, try to get all of your changes into a single alter statement and separate the different portions with commas. It's better practice than, for example, deleting an index in one statement and creating a new one in another statement. For example, the following statement would run a single alter command on a table named users that modifies the column type of lname and adds an index on the email column:

```
mysql> alter table users
    -> modify lname char(25),
    -> add index index_on_email(email);
```

Using the show Command

A series of commands in MySQL enables you examine the databases on your system and lets you know what is available in your MySQL installation. Keep these commands in mind, because they come in handy at times.

show databases

When you start your MySQL command line, you are connected to the MySQL server but are initially given no indication as to what is available to the server.

```
shell> mysql -u root;
Welcome to the MySQL monitor.  Commands end with ; or \g.
Your MySQL connection id is 73 to server version: 3.23.39

Type 'help;' or '\h' for help. Type '\c' to clear the buffer.

mysql>
```

That prompt is nice but not especially helpful. Your initial interest is probably in seeing what databases are available. You can get a list of databases by issuing the `show databases` command:

```
mysql> show databases;
+----------+
| Database |
+----------+
| mysql    |
| store    |
| test     |
+----------+
3 rows in set (0.14 sec)
```

The MySQL installation includes the other two databases (`mysql` and `test`) automatically. The `mysql` database is covered in great detail in Appendix D.

If you want to work with any of these databases in the command-line client, issue the `use` command:

```
mysql> use store;
Database changed
```

show tables

After you are connected to a specific database, you can view the tables that make up the database by running the `show tables` command:

```
mysql> show tables;
+-----------------+
| Tables_in_store |
+-----------------+
| addresses       |
| formats         |
| items_for_sale  |
| order_items     |
| orders          |
| places          |
| products        |
| users           |
+-----------------+
8 rows in set (0.01 sec)
```

show columns

You can get specific information about the columns within a table. The syntax of the command is `show columns from table_name`. Note that there are two synonyms to `show columns`: `show fields` (`show fields from table_name`) and `describe` (`describe table_name`).

```
mysql> show columns from users;
+------------+-------------+------+-----+---------+----------------+
| Field      | Type        | Null | Key | Default | Extra          |
+------------+-------------+------+-----+---------+----------------+
| user_id    | int(11)     |      | PRI | NULL    | auto_increment |
| fname      | varchar(25) |      |     |         |                |
| lname      | varchar(40) |      |     |         |                |
| email      | varchar(60) | YES  |     | NULL    |                |
| home_phone | varchar(14) | YES  |     | NULL    |                |
| work_phone | varchar(14) | YES  |     | NULL    |                |
| fax        | varchar(14) | YES  |     | NULL    |                |
+------------+-------------+------+-----+---------+----------------+
7 rows in set (0.12 sec)
```

The preceding query lists most of what you need to know about this table. The first column, `Field`, shows the column name; `Type` (logically enough) shows the column type; `Null` indicates whether or not null values are permitted in the column; `Key` shows if an index was created for the column, and if so what kind; `Default` shows the default value (if one was indicated in the `create` statement); and `Extra` gives some added information (in the preceding table, you can see that `user_id` is an `auto_increment` column).

show index

There will come times when you will need to examine the indexes on your tables. You can get a lot of information from the `show index` command. The following command lists all indexes on the `addresses` table:

```
mysql> SHOW INDEX from addresses \G
*************************** 1. row ***************************
       Table: addresses
  Non_unique: 0
    Key_name: PRIMARY
Seq_in_index: 1
 Column_name: address_id
   Collation: A
 Cardinality: 7
    Sub_part: NULL
```

```
      Packed: NULL
     Comment:
1 row in set (0.13 sec)
```

Notice that in the preceding command we used `\G` to terminate the command. This lets the MySQL command-line client know that the data are listed in the preceding format, rather than in the tabular format you've seen so far. This kind of layout, showing the column name, a colon, and then the value, is convenient when a query result contains more rows than can comfortably fit in a table.

show table status

If you want to get more detailed information on each table, you can run the `show table status` command. This command will show you the number of rows in each table, the time the table was created, and quite a few other interesting tidbits. You can get the information on all tables in a database at once by simply running `show table status`, or you can get the information on a specific table by using a command like the following (wildcards % and `''` are legal):

```
mysql> show table status like 'addresses' \G
*************************** 1. row ***************************
           Name: addresses
           Type: MyISAM
     Row_format: Dynamic
           Rows: 7
 Avg_row_length: 58
    Data_length: 412
Max_data_length: 4294967295
   Index_length: 2048
      Data_free: 0
 Auto_increment: 8
    Create_time: 2001-10-25 15:32:08
    Update_time: 2001-10-27 08:51:44
     Check_time: 2001-11-27 09:45:46
 Create_options:
        Comment:
1 row in set (0.01 sec)
```

show create table

Before running an `alter` command, you may want to know exactly what statement was used to create the table in the first place. You can get this information using the `show create table` command:

```
mysql> SHOW CREATE TABLE addresses \G
```

```
*************************** 1. row ***************************
       Table: addresses
Create Table: CREATE TABLE `addresses` (
  `address_id` int(11) NOT NULL auto_increment,
  `user_id` int(11) default NULL,
  `place` varchar(25) NOT NULL default '',
  `addr_1` varchar(255) NOT NULL default '',
  `addr_2` varchar(255) default NULL,
  `city` varchar(50) NOT NULL default '',
  `state` char(2) NOT NULL default '',
  `ZIP` varchar(5) NOT NULL default '',
  `country` varchar(5) default NULL,
  PRIMARY KEY  (`address_id`)
) TYPE=MyISAM
1 row in set (0.00 sec)
```

GUI Tools for Manipulating MySQL Tables and Data

So far in this book we've shown you how to work with MySQL tables and data using standard SQL statements. However, the process of creating tables and viewing table data can a bit of a drag when you're using the command-line client. Happily, a variety of programs are available that will help you create and alter tables and view table data.

Using phpMyAdmin

phpMyAdmin is probably the most widely used MySQL-administration tool. It's written in PHP and can therefore run on any platform on which PHP can run. (And given the subject of this book, we feel safe in assuming that you're running a PHP-capable platform.) Be aware, though, that you have to carefully follow the installation instructions to prevent security problems.

The first step in working with phpMyAdmin is to grab a copy of the source files. A version is on the book accompanying this CD, but we recommend getting the latest possible source files. You can get the most recent release from `http://www.phpmyadmin.net/`. If you're working off of a Unix or Mac OS X machine, you'll want to get the copy of the source that has a .tar.gz extension; for example, `phpMyAdmin-2.5.1-rc3-php.tar.gz`. For Windows, get a copy of the source with the .zip extension (for example, `phpMyAdmin-2.5.1-rc3-php.zip`).

You'll want to copy the folder to your Web server's root directory. On Apache installations, this directory is usually called /htdocs. You can then uncompress the file using the following command:

```
shell> tar xvzf phpMyAdmin-2.5.1-rc3-php.tar.gz
```

phpMyAdmin will then be available through your Web server via a URL like the following: `http://localhost/phpMyAdmin-2.5.1-rc3/`

On Windows, you'll use a zip utility like WinZip or pkzip to unzip the files.

Before you can access the application, you'll need to make changes to the config.inc.php file. In most cases, all you'll need to do is put the appropriate username and password on the following lines:

```
$cfg['Servers'][$i]['user']             = 'root';       // MySQL user
$cfg['Servers'][$i]['password']         = 'mypass';     // MySQL
password
```

If you're finding an error that states you don't have iconv support compiled in, simply change the following entry in the config.inc.php file to `FALSE`.

```
$cfg['AllowAnywhereRecoding'] = TRUE
```

Once you are done with the configuration you should be able to go to the /index.php page and start using phpMyAdmin.

Using phpMyAdmin is fairly straightforward, and we won't explain it here. Just spend some time clicking around and you'll get a good idea of how it works. Figures 2-1 and 2-2 show what you can expect from a couple of phpMyAdmin's screens.

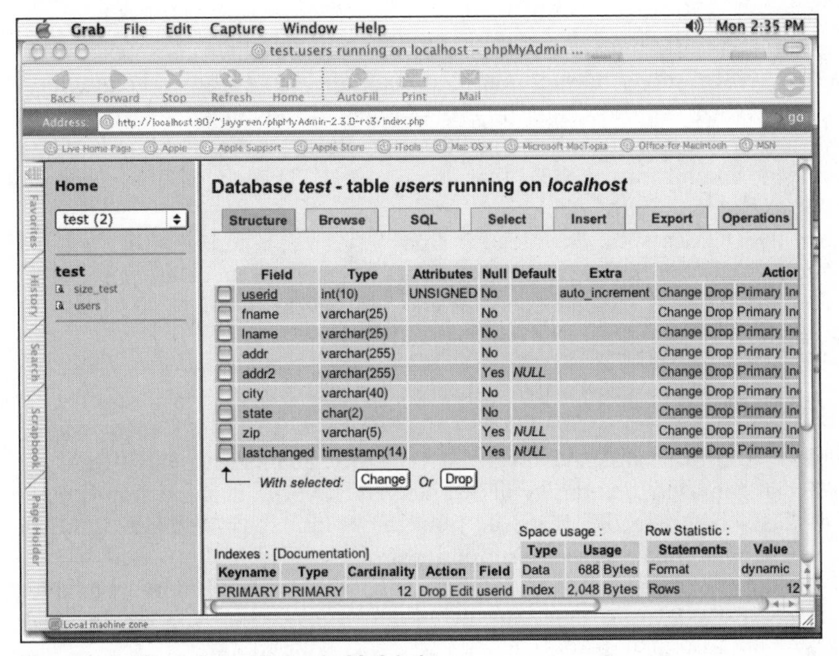

Figure 2-1: View of a table in phpMyAdmin

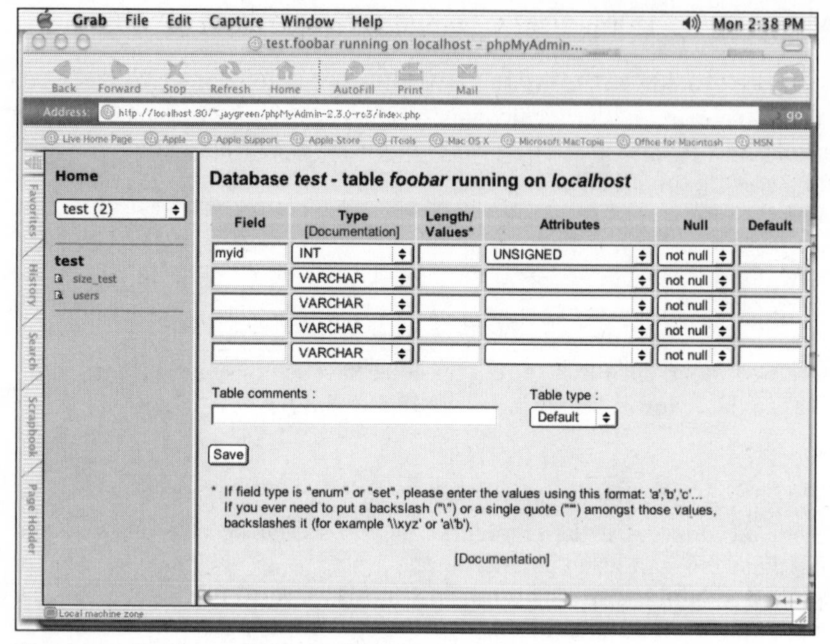

Figure 2-2: Creating a table in phpMyAdmin

MySQL Control Center

This program is an offering from MySQL AB, the company that does most of the work on the MySQL server daemon and that maintains `mysql.com`. The graphical client, called MySQL Control Center (MySQLCC), has the advantage of working on a wide variety of systems, including FreeBSD, OpenBSD, Solaris, and Linux. If you want a graphic administrative client that doesn't use HTTP, as phpMyAdmin does, this will be one of your better choices.

To give MySQLCC a spin, download it from `www.mysql.com/downloads/` and follow the installation instructions. Figure 2-3 shows what you can expect MySQLCC to look like. It includes tools for creating tables, viewing table contents, and running queries (manually and automatically).

Using MacSQL

The people at Runtime Labs have created a very nice, sophisticated GUI front for Mac OS X that connects to a variety of SQL Servers, MySQL included. You can get a copy of this software, called MacSQL, from the `rtlabs.com` Web site. Runtime provides a free demo that you can take for a test run.

After you download and install MacSQL, you can start the application by double-clicking the MacSQL icon. At that point MacSQL will detect that you have MySQL installed and will offer you a screen like the one shown in Figure 2-4.

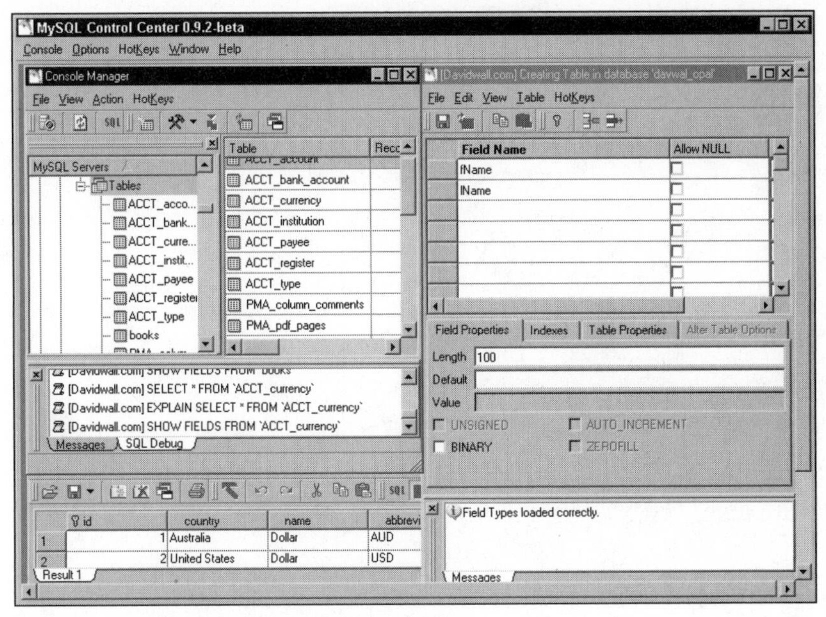

Figure 2-3: The MySQL Control Center interface

New Connection
Database Type: Connect via:
MySQL Parameters
Host: Port:
localhost
Userid: Password:
root ••••••
Database:
Cancel Connect

Figure 2-4: The Connections screen for MacSQL

To make a connection to MySQL on the local machine, make sure that the Port item is blank and that the username, host (localhost), and password are appropriate. At this point you'll be presented with a screen, like the one shown in Figure 2-5, that offers several options.

If you're using OS X, we recommend that you download the free demo and work through each of the options on this screen. You'll find that most anything you want to do with MySQL you can accomplish with this software. At that point you may decide that it's worth the $99 for a version of MacSQL Lite.

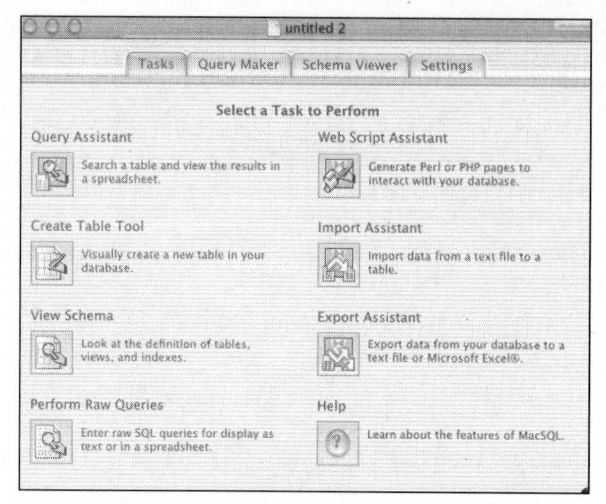

Figure 2-5: Options for MacSQL

Summary

This chapter discussed what you need to know in order to create and maintain databases and database tables when working with MySQL. It is possible that you will never need to commit the details of the `create` statement to memory, as graphical tools like phpMyAdmin can help you create and alter tables. Still, it is important to understand the column types and the purposes of indexes, as a quick and efficient database will always use the correct data type and will only include indexes when necessary.

This chapter also introduced you to some of the GUI tools that can be used to administer a MySQL installation. In the end, most find that using some type of GUI tool is easier than manually inputting SQL commands for creating and altering databases and tables. With these highly useful tools, you'll likely come to the same conclusion.

Chapter 3

The Structured Query Language for Inserting, Editing, and Selecting Data

IN THIS CHAPTER

- Using the `insert` statement
- Using the `update` statement
- Using the `replace` statement
- Using the `delete` statement
- Using the basic `select` statement
- Joining tables

NOW THAT YOU KNOW how to make tables, you need to learn how to put data into them and get data out of them. You need to familiarize yourself with only a few simple SQL statements in order to get data into tables, and you need only another couple to edit data once it's in your tables. Following that, you need to learn the `select` statement, which retrieves your data in about as many ways as you can imagine, either from a single table, or by joining two or more tables together.

The insert Statement

You will use the `insert` statement to place rows of data into your tables. The basic form of the SQL `insert` statement is as follows:

```
Insert into tablename ( column1 [, column2 [, column3 [, ...] ] ] )
values ( value1 [, value2 [, value3 [, ...] ] ] )
```

If a column in your table allows null values, you can leave that column out of the insert statement.

Text strings must be surrounded by single quote marks ('), or double-quote marks (' ') if you're not running in ANSI mode. For example:

```
insert into table_name (text_col, int_col) values ('hello world', 1)
```

This can cause a problem because undoubtedly someone is going to want to insert a contraction into a table and that would confuse your database because it would interpret the first single quote it sees (after the start of the string) as the end of the string, and it then wouldn't know what to do with the remainder of the string. Therefore you'll need a way of *escaping*, or working around, the single quote character, by preceding it with a backslash (\). The same applies to the backslash character itself:

```
insert into mytable ( mycolumn ) values ('This is\'nt going to
fail.');
insert into mytable ( mycolumn ) values ('this \\ stores a
backslash');
```

It's worth noting that % and _ need to be escaped only in contexts where wildcard matching is allowed. You can also escape single quotes by using two consecutive single quote marks (' '), and double quotes within a double-quoted string by using two consecutive double quotes (" ").

The following characters are identified in MySQL by their typical escape sequences:

- \n (newline)
- \t (tab)
- \r (carriage return)
- \b (back space)

For the most part, you won't have to worry about escaping all of these characters while doing your PHP programming. As you'll see, functions and settings built into PHP handle this automatically. The addslashes() function and the magic quotes settings in the php.ini (covered in the MySQL documentation at http://www.mysql.com) are particularly helpful.

In MySQL you can also use the insert statement to add more than one row of data at a time. All you need to do is include additional sets of values. For example:

```
insert into table_name (text_col, int_col)
values
    ('hello world', 1),
    ('hello mars', 2)
;
```

This approach has a few significant benefits, including that the database has less parsing to do and that less data has to be sent to the database server over a network. It's a matter of reducing overhead.

The update Statement

The SQL update statement is slightly different from the others you have seen so far in that it makes use of a where clause. A where clause enables you to pick out particular rows from your table – the rows *where* these conditions are true. Most often, the conditions have to do with matching the values of fields in the row to the particular values you're looking for. The general syntax is as follows:

```
update table_name set col_1=value1, col_2=value_2 where col=value
```

Once again, if you're inserting a string you'll need to surround it with single quotes and escape special characters properly. Keep in mind that the comparisons in the where portion of the update statement can use any comparison operator (for example, 'col = value', 'col > value', and so on).

Often the where clause will be used to identify a single row by its primary key. In Table 3-1, id is the primary key. (The where clause is discussed in more detail later in the chapter.)

TABLE 3-1 THE FOLKS TABLE

id	Fname	lname	Salary
1	Don	Ho	25,000
2	Don	Corleone	800,000
3	Don	Juan	32,000
4	Don	Johnson	44,500

The following statement would affect only Don Corleone:

```
update folks set fname='Vito' where id=2;
```

As you can see, it would be risky to run an `update` statement based on the `fname` column, as you could accidentally update every column in this table.

```
update folks set fname='Vito' where fname='Don';
```

You can also use `update` to give your underpaid employees a raise:

```
update folks set salary=50000 where salary<50,000;
```

As of MySQL 4.0, you can also update a table based on data in other tables. This is an extremely helpful feature, since it enables you to make changes using only SQL statements that previously would have required a program or script (or some very dodgy workarounds).

To demonstrate, we add another table (Table 3-2) to the example set, recording the income brought in by the people in `folks`:

TABLE 3-2 THE INCOME TABLE

id	Income
1	500,000
2	1,500,000
3	250
4	1,250,000

We can use a multi-table update to give the top performers a raise:

```
update folks, income
       set folks.salary = folks.salary * 1.1
       where folks.id = income.id and income.income >= 1000000
;
```

As you might guess from the syntax, you can update multiple tables with a single `update` statement. You might have good reasons to do that, but be careful – the results might not be what you expect. The reason is that the order in which you update columns in the query makes a difference. To illustrate, we add a salary column to the income table, not something you'd want to do if this were a real database, by the way:

```
alter table income add salary numeric(10,2);
```

Then we update the records in income to fill in the salary with the values from the folks table:

```
update income, folks set
  income.salary = folks.salary
  where income.id = folks.id
;
```

Now the income table looks like Table 3-3:

TABLE 3-3 THE INCOME TABLE

id	Income	Salary
1	500,000	50,000
2	1,500,000	880,000
3	250	50,000
4	1,250,000	55,000

Next, we redo the previous query, giving a raise to people who have brought in an income of at least $1,000,000. This time, we update the salary field in both tables at the same time:

```
update folks, income set
   folks.salary = folks.salary * 1.1
   , income.salary = income.salary * 1.1
   where folks.id = income.id and income.income >= 1000000
;
```

If we run a select on the two tables now, the results (Table 3-4) look reasonable:

```
select f.id, f.fname, f.lname, i.income, f.salary as folks_salary,
i.salary as income_salary from folks f, income i where f.id = i.id;
```

TABLE 3-4 RESULTS OF THE UPDATE

id	fname	lname	Income	folks_salary	income_salary
1	Don	Ho	500,000	50,000	50,000
2	Vito	Corleone	1,500,000	968,000	968,000
3	Don	Juan	250	50,000	50,000
4	Don	Johnson	1,250,000	60,500	60,500

However, if we change the query to use the value from the `salary` column in the `folks` table to update both tables, as in the following code, the results are a bit odd (Table 3-5).

```
update folks, income set
    folks.salary = folks.salary * 1.1
    , income.salary = folks.salary * 1.1
    where folks.id = income.id and income.income >= 1000000
;
```

TABLE 3-5 RESULTS OF THE UPDATE

id	fname	lname	Income	folks_salary	income_salary
1	Don	Ho	500,000	50,000	50,000
2	Vito	Corleone	1,500,000	968,000	1,064,800
3	Don	Juan	250	50,000	50,000
4	Don	Johnson	1,250,000	60,500	66,550

What's happening is that in the first part of the `set` clause, `folks.salary = folks.salary * 1.1`, the `salary` field is being set to its current value times 1.1; but in the second part of the `set` clause, `income.salary = folks.salary * 1.1`, the *new* value of `folks.salary` is being used. Thus, `income.salary` ends up being set to the original value of `folks.salary` times 1.21 (1.1 twice).

Plus, for even more fun, if we switch the order in which the tables to be updated are listed, as in the following code, we see "reasonable" results again (Table 3-6).

```
update income, folks set
    income.salary = folks.salary * 1.1
    , folks.salary = folks.salary * 1.1
    where folks.id = income.id and income.income >= 1000000
;
```

Table 3-6 RESULTS OF THE UPDATE

id	fname	lname	income	folks_salary	income_salary
1	Don	Ho	500,000	50,000	50,000
2	Vito	Corleone	1,500,000	968,000	968,000
3	Don	Juan	250	50,000	50,000
4	Don	Johnson	1,250,000	60,500	60,500

The tables are updated in the order in which they are listed, and the query runs as if it were actually two updates in order:

```
update income, folks set
    income.salary = folks.salary * 1.1
    where folks.id = income.id and income.income >= 1000000
;
update income, folks set
        folks.salary = folks.salary * 1.1
        where folks.id = income.id and income.income >= 1000000
;
```

When you look at it as two queries, the results make sense. We recommend that you stick to updating a single table at a time for the sake of clarity if nothing else, unless you have a good reason to do otherwise.

Note that this syntax is not standard ANSI SQL syntax. This matters primarily for the portablility of your application; it's a good reason to isolate the code that actually performs `updates`.

The delete Statement

The `delete` statement removes a row or multiple rows from a table. The syntax is as follows:

```
delete from table_where where-clause
```

To remove Don Ho from Table 3-1, you'd run the following statement:

```
delete from folks where id=1;
```

You can delete records from one or more tables at a time, based on the data in those tables as well as others (this capability is as of MySQL 4.0):

```
delete from table1 [, table2 [, ...]] using table1 [, table2 [,
...]] [, additional_table_1 [, additional_table2 [,...]]] where
where-clause
```

This is just one of a few supported formats for a multi-table `delete` statement. We're using it because it is most similar to the single-table `delete`, which means we're a smidge less likely to get the syntax wrong.

The tables listed in the `from` clause are the ones from which records are deleted. Those same tables appear again in the `using` clause, along with any other tables you wish to query to determine what records you want to delete.

To illustrate, we can remove the underachievers from the `folks` table. Tables 3-7 and 3-8 provide the data used in the example again.

TABLE 3-7 THE FOLKS TABLE

id	Fname	Lname	Salary
1	Don	Ho	25,000
2	Don	Corleone	800,000
3	Don	Juan	32,000
4	Don	Johnson	44,500

TABLE 3-8 THE INCOME TABLE

id	Income
1	500,000
2	1,500,000

id	Income
3	250
4	1,250,000

Now we can use the delete statement to remove records from the folks table for people whose income is too low, as demonstrated in the following code. Table 3-9 displays the results.

```
delete from folks using folks, income
  where folks.id = income.id and income.income < 100000
;
```

TABLE 3-9 THE FOLKS TABLE

id	Fname	lname	Salary
1	Don	Ho	25,000
2	Don	Corleone	800,000
4	Don	Johnson	44,500

The replace Statement

You won't find MySQL's replace statement in other database systems, and it is not part of the SQL standard. However, it is convenient in places. The replace statement works with a row for which you know what the primary key should be. When you run the replace statement, MySQL searches for a row with the primary key indicated in the statement. If a row with the indicated primary key exists, that row is updated. If not, a new row is inserted. The basic syntax is as follows:

```
Replace into table_name (col_1, col_2, ?) values (val_1, val_2, ?)
```

For an example of a situation in which replace would be helpful, imagine you have a table with two columns, email and full_name, with email as the primary key. If you want to write a script that gives a user the opportunity to insert and edit this information, you would have some sort of form with which the user could enter the data. Then, when the user submits the form, the script would have to go through some decision logic. Without replace, the logic would be something like this:

```
examine form data
delete record from database with the submitted primary key value
   (this will run with no results if no such record exists)
run insert statement
```

But because MySQL has the replace statement, you can lose all of this logic and just run replace. For example:

```
replace into users (email, full_name) values ('jon@doe.com', 'Jon
Doe')
```

Note that you don't need to use a where clause to identify the row that you are replacing; MySQL handles this, based on the value of the primary key. (If you use the replace statement on a table with no defined primary key, MySQL inserts a new record into the table.)

However, you can use a where clause to identify the source of the new data, and that can come in very handy. Suppose you want to change the values of a field in one table to reflect the result of an aggregate query against another table. You can't do this with an update statement because group by clauses are not allowed there. But replace accepts a select statement as its source (just like insert). If the table you are updating has a unique key (see why they're so handy?), you're in gravy.

To illustrate, we add a third table to the set of example tables. Table 3-10 records donations brought in by each of the fellows:

TABLE 3-10 THE DONATIONS TABLE

Id	amount	date
1	5000	3/1/2003
1	5000	3/2/2003
1	5000	3/3/2003
2	25000	3/1/2003
2	3000	3/2/2003
2	4000	3/2/2003
2	10000	3/3/2003
3	1000	3/1/2003

Id	amount	date
3	3.15	3/2/2003
3	25	3/3/2003
4	10000	3/1/2003
4	20000	3/2/2003

We want to be able to update the `income` field of the `income` table to the sum of the donations acquired by each person. As before, we can do this by deleting the current records in the `income` table and then creating new ones. Or, we can just use `replace`, as in the following code:

```
replace income (id, income)
        select id, sum(amount) from donations group by id
;
```

Table 3-11 shows the results.

TABLE 3-11 THE INCOME TABLE

Id	income	salary
1	15000	NULL
2	42000	NULL
3	1028.15	NULL
4	30000	NULL

Notice that we've lost the data from our `salary` column. The trouble is that we are not allowed to include the table we are replacing into the `select` statement. To change some fields and keep others, we have to create a temporary table storing the current values in `income` and join it to `donations` in the `replace` statement. How much better that is than a `delete` and an `insert` is a matter of taste. Remember, `replace` follows the same syntax as `insert`. There is no `where` in `replace`.

The Basic select Statement

When it comes time to take the information from your database and lay it out on your Web pages, you'll need to limit the information returned from your tables and join tables together to get the proper information. So you'll start with your database, the superset of information, and return a smaller set. In the `select` statement you'll choose columns from one or more tables to assemble a result set. This result will have columns and rows and thus can be effectively thought of as a table (or a two-dimensional array, if your mind works that way). This table doesn't actually exist in the database, but it helps to think about it this way.

The basic `select` statement requires you to indicate the table or tables you are selecting from and the column names you require. If you wish to select all the columns from a given table, you can substitute an asterisk (*) for the field names. For example:

```
select column_1, column_2, column_3 from table_name
```

or

```
select * from table_name
```

Keep in mind that with a `select` statement you are not actually altering the tables involved in the query. You are simply retrieving information. From PHP, you will send the query to MySQL from the `mysql_query()` function.

There are all sorts of ways you can choose to lay out the information, but at times you're going to want a simple HTML table with the column names put in a header row. The simple PHP code in Listing 3-1 will lay out any SQL query in an ultra-simple HTML table. It includes a simple form that will enable you to enter a query. If you don't understand this code just yet, don't worry about it; all the PHP functions will be covered in Chapter 6. Alter the `mysql_connect()` and `mysql_select_db()` functions if you wish to change the database used. I wouldn't advise putting this script on a server that is publicly available, as it would open up a huge security hole.

Listing 3-1: A PHP Script That Converts a SQL Query to an HTML Table

```
<?php
mysql_connect("localhost", "username", "password") or
    die("Could not connect to database.");

mysql_select_db("test") or
    die("Cannot select database");
```

```
if( !empty($_GET["query"]) ){
    $query = stripslashes($_GET["query"]);
} else {
    $query = "SELECT * FROM users";
}

$result = mysql_query($query) or
    die( mysql_error() );

$number_cols = mysql_num_fields($result);

echo "<b>Query: $query</b>",
     '<table border="1">',
     '<tr align="center">';

for ($i=0; $i < $number_cols; ++$i) {
   echo '<th>' . mysql_field_name($result, $i) . "</th>\n";
}
echo "</tr>\n";

while( $row = mysql_fetch_row($result) ){
   echo "<tr>\n";
   foreach( $row as $field ){
      echo '<td>' . (is_null($field) ? 'NULL' : $field) . "</td>\n";
   }
   echo "</tr>\n";
}

echo '</table>';
?>

<form action="<?php echo $_SERVER['PHP_SELF']; ?>" method="GET">
  <input type="text" name="query" size="50" value="<?php echo
$query; ?>"><br>
  <input type="submit">
</form>
```

For the remainder of this chapter you will see how to build on the complexity of the `select` statement. To show you things in action, we created a table in MySQL against which we can run these queries. The `create` statement in Listing 3-2 makes a table named `users` that holds basic personal information.

Listing 3-2: A create Statement for the users Table

```
CREATE TABLE users (
    userid int(10) unsigned NOT NULL auto_increment,
    fname varchar(25) NOT NULL,
    lname varchar(25) NOT NULL,
    addr varchar(255) NOT NULL,
    addr2 varchar(255),
    city varchar(40) NOT NULL,
    state char(2) NOT NULL,
    zip varchar(5),
    lastchanged timestamp(14),
    PRIMARY KEY (userid)
);
```

To get things started, we loaded up the database with a few rows of information. The `insert` statements that load this data are shown in Listing 3-3.

Listing 3-3: insert Statements for the users Table

```
INSERT INTO users (userid, fname, lname, addr, addr2, city, state,
zip, lastchanged)       VALUES (1,'Jason','Greenspan','555 5th
St','apt 204','San Francisco','CA','94118',20020626134625);
INSERT INTO users (userid, fname, lname, addr, addr2, city, state,
zip, lastchanged) VALUES (2,'Brad','Bulger','666 6th St','apt
17','San Francisco','CA','94116',20020626134704);
INSERT INTO users (userid, fname, lname, addr, addr2, city, state,
zip, lastchanged) VALUES (3,'John','Doe','279 66th St',NULL,'New
York','NY','11100',20020627120644);
INSERT INTO users (userid, fname, lname, addr, addr2, city, state,
zip, lastchanged) VALUES (4,'Jane','Doe','987 67th
St',NULL,'Windsor','MA','14102',20020627120644);
INSERT INTO users (userid, fname, lname, addr, addr2, city, state,
zip, lastchanged) VALUES (5,'Jean','Banks','4 Elm
St','','Eugene','OR','98712',20020627120644);
INSERT INTO users (userid, fname, lname, addr, addr2, city, state,
zip, lastchanged) VALUES (6,'Donny','Alphonse','25 14th
St',NULL,'New York','NY','11104',20020627120644);
INSERT INTO users (userid, fname, lname, addr, addr2, city, state,
zip, lastchanged) VALUES (7,'Meghan','Garcis','44 Maple
Dr',NULL,'Nashville','TN','37114',20020627120644);
INSERT INTO users (userid, fname, lname, addr, addr2, city, state,
zip, lastchanged) VALUES (8,'Kenny','Clark','General
Delivery',NULL,'Washeegan','VT','10048',20020627120644);
INSERT INTO users (userid, fname, lname, addr, addr2, city, state,
zip, lastchanged) VALUES (9,'Danny','Briggs','8 Palm Way','ste
222','Miami','FL',NULL,20020627120644);
```

```
INSERT INTO users (userid, fname, lname, addr, addr2, city, state,
zip, lastchanged) VALUES (10,'Luke','Gnome','8 Palm Way',NULL,'San
Francisco','CA','94118',20020627120644);
INSERT INTO users (userid, fname, lname, addr, addr2, city, state,
zip, lastchanged) VALUES (11,'Alan','Paine','27 Casa Way',NULL,'Los
Angeles','CA','94204',20020627120644);
INSERT INTO users (userid, fname, lname, addr, addr2, city, state,
zip, lastchanged) VALUES (12,'Jay','Grimes','718 Field
St',NULL,'Pierre','ND','44221',20020627120644);
```

When run through the PHP code above, the query `select * from users` will return the results shown in Figure 3-1.

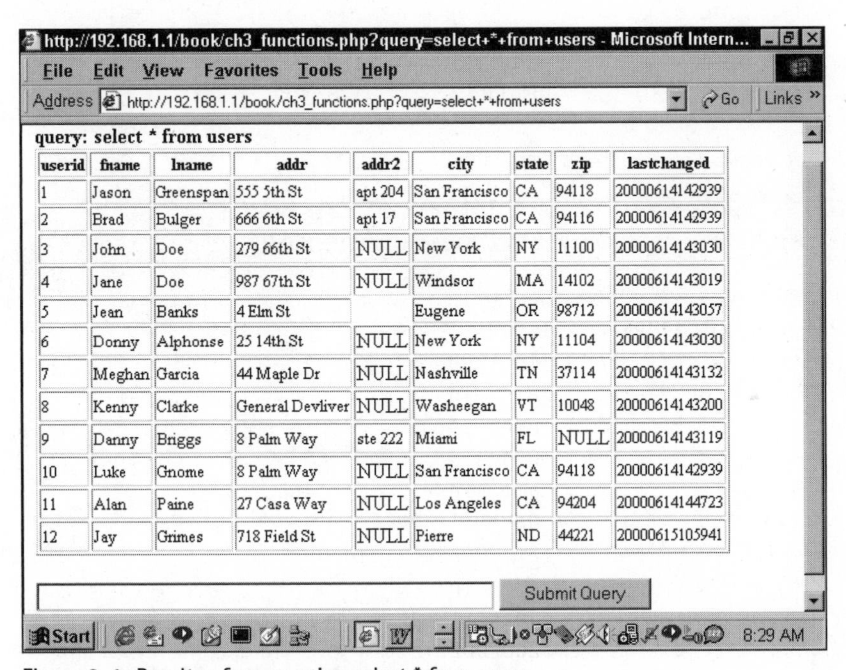

query: select * from users

userid	fname	lname	addr	addr2	city	state	zip	lastchanged
1	Jason	Greenspan	555 5th St	apt 204	San Francisco	CA	94118	20000614142939
2	Brad	Bulger	666 6th St	apt 17	San Francisco	CA	94116	20000614142939
3	John	Doe	279 66th St	NULL	New York	NY	11100	20000614143030
4	Jane	Doe	987 67th St	NULL	Windsor	MA	14102	20000614143019
5	Jean	Banks	4 Elm St		Eugene	OR	98712	20000614143057
6	Donny	Alphonse	25 14th St	NULL	New York	NY	11104	20000614143030
7	Meghan	Garcia	44 Maple Dr	NULL	Nashville	TN	37114	20000614143132
8	Kenny	Clarke	General Devliver	NULL	Washeegan	VT	10048	20000614143200
9	Danny	Briggs	8 Palm Way	ste 222	Miami	FL	NULL	20000614143119
10	Luke	Gnome	8 Palm Way	NULL	San Francisco	CA	94118	20000614142939
11	Alan	Paine	27 Casa Way	NULL	Los Angeles	CA	94204	20000614144723
12	Jay	Grimes	718 Field St	NULL	Pierre	ND	44221	20000615105941

Figure 3-1: Results of query using select * from users

The where clause

The `where` clause limits the rows that are returned from your query. To get a single row from a table you would a run the query against the primary key. For instance, to get all the information on Brad you would use this query:

```
select * from users where userid = 2;
```

Figure 3-2 shows the results of this query.

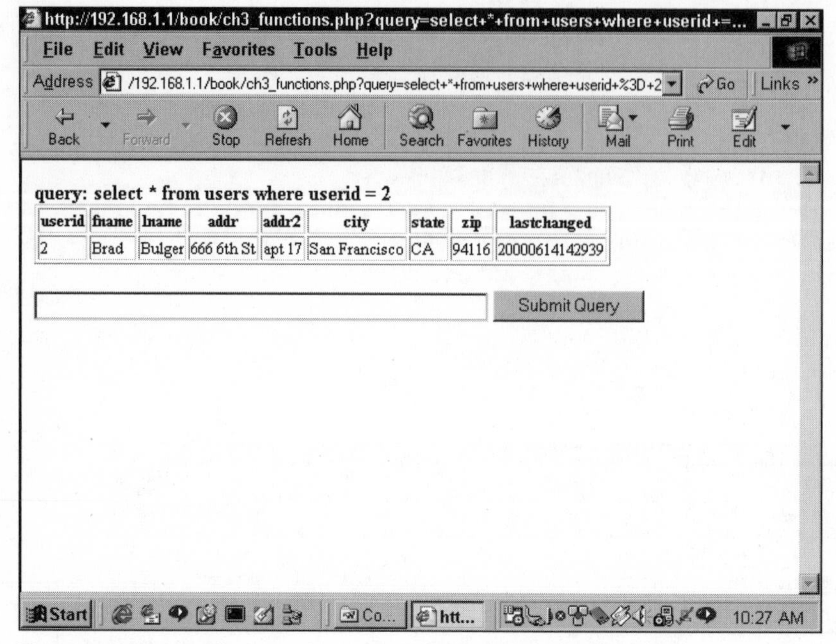

userid	fname	lname	addr	addr2	city	state	zip	lastchanged
2	Brad	Bulger	666 6th St	apt 17	San Francisco	CA	94116	20000614142939

Figure 3-2: Results of query using select * from users where userid=2;

If you're doing a comparison to a column that stores a string (`char`, `varchar`, and so on), you will need to surround the string used for comparison in the `where` clause with single quotes.

```
select * from users where city = 'San Francisco';
```

MySQL has several comparison operators that can be used in the `where` clause. Table 3-12 lists these operators.

Don't be confused by the fact that the "equal to" operator is = in MySQL and == in PHP. Be careful.

You can combine several comparisons with `and` or `or`:

```
select * from users
where userid = 6 or
     city = 'San Francisco'
;
select * from users
```

```
where state = 'CA' and
      city = 'San Francisco'
;
```

TABLE 3-12 MYSQL COMPARISON OPERATORS

Operator	Definition
=	Equal to
<> or !=	Not equal to
<	Less than
<=	Less than or equal to
>	Greater than
>=	Greater than or equal to
like	Compares a string (discussed in detail later in this chapter)
<=>	NULL-safe comparison

It's important to note that fields with null values cannot be compared with any of the operators used in Table 3-12. For instance, in the table shown in Figure 3-1, you might think that the following statement would return every row in the table:

```
select * from users where zip <> '11111' or state = '11111';
```

But in fact, row 9 will not be returned by the query. Null values will test neither `true` nor `false` to any of these operators. Instead, to deal with null values, you will need to make use of the `is null` or `is not null` predicates.

To get the previous query to work as we had intended you'd need to augment your original query, as follows:

```
select * from users
where zip <> '11111' or
      zip = '11111' or
      zip is null
;
```

Or if you want to find all the rows where `zip` contains any value (except null) you can use the following:

```
select * from users where zip is not null;
```

USING distinct

At times, your query will contain duplicate data. For instance, if your goal is to see all the cities in California, your first instinct might be to run a query like `select city, state from users where state='CA'`. But look at the result returned in Figure 3-3.

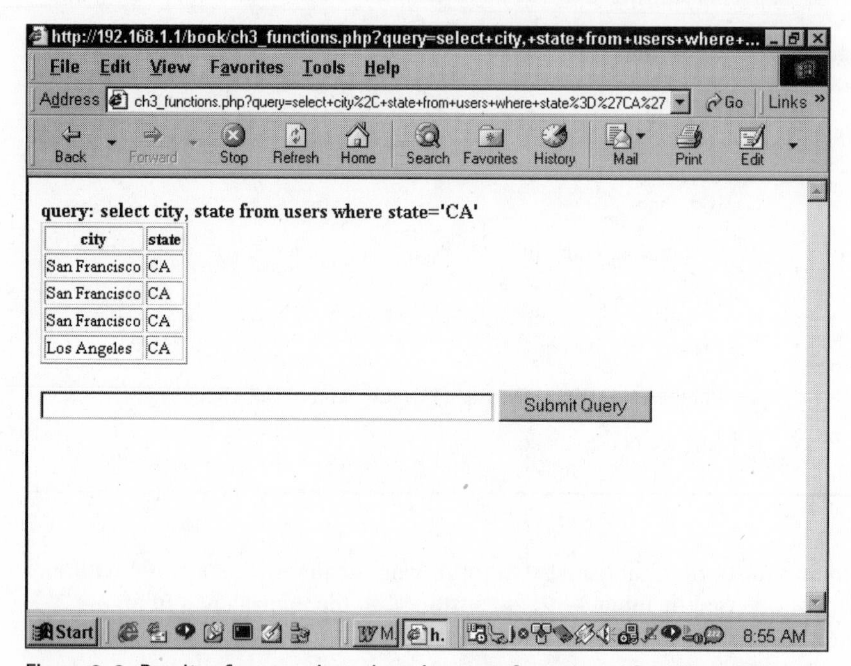

Figure 3-3: Results of query using select city, state from users where state='CA'

Notice that the first three rows are identical. You could use PHP to sort through the identical results and return only unique city names in California, but that would be a fair amount of scripting. You can get what you want directly from the database by using `select distinct`. When you use `distinct`, the MySQL engine will remove rows with identical results. So here the better query is `select distinct city, state from users where state='CA'`, which returns the data in Figure 3-4, which is exactly what you want.

USING between

You can also choose values within a range by using the `between` predicate. The `between` predicate works for numeric values as well as dates. In the following query, `lastchanged` is a `timestamp` column. If you want to find the people who signed up on June 26, 2002, you could use this query:

```
select * from users where lastchanged between 20020626000000 and
20020626235959;
```

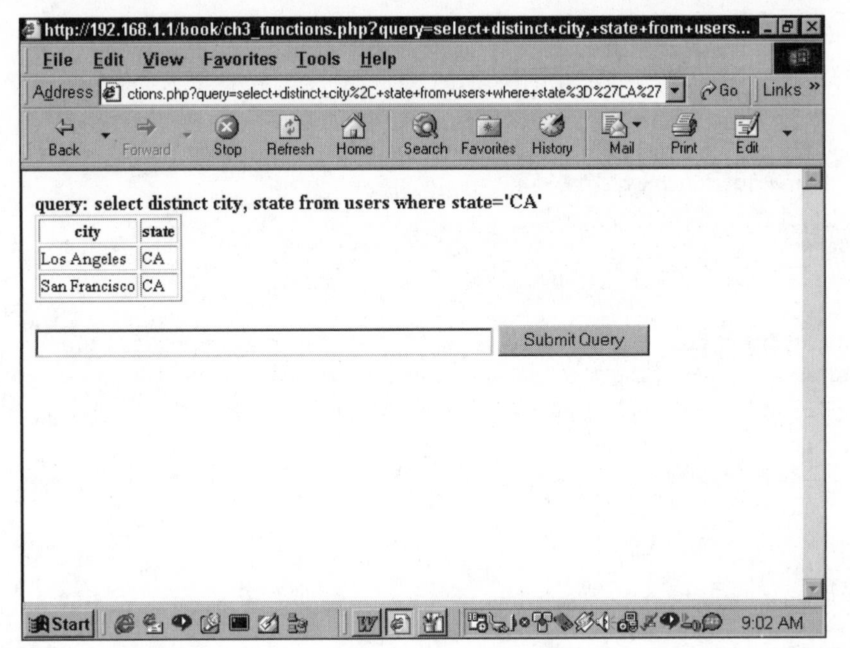

Figure 3-4: Results of query using select distinct city, state from users where state='CA'

This is a shorthand way of saying:

```
select * from users where lastchanged >= 20020626999999 and
lastchanged <= 20020626335959;
```

Remember that the default timestamp column type stores dates in the form `YYYYMMDDHHMMSS`, so to get all entries for a single day you need to start your range at midnight (00:00:00) and end it at 11:59:59 p.m. (23:59:59).

You can also use `between` on text strings. If you wish to list all the last names that start with the letters *A* through *G*, the following query would work. Note that it will not include names that start with *A*.

```
select * from users where lname between 'a' and 'g';
```

USING in/not in

The `in` predicate is helpful if a single column that can be returned has several possible values. If you want to query the users table to get all the states in New England, you could write the query like this:

```
select * from users
 where state = 'RI' or
       state = 'NH' or
       state = 'VT' or
```

```
        state = 'MA' or
        state = 'ME'
;
```

Using in, you can specify a set of possible values and simplify this statement. The following query achieves the same result:

```
select * from users
   where state in ('RI', 'NH', 'VT', 'MA', 'ME');
```

If you want the same effect in reverse you can use the not in predicate. To get a listing of all people in the table *not* living in New England, simply throw in the word not:

```
select * from users where
       state not in ('RI', 'NH', 'VT', 'MA', 'ME');
```

USING like

Of course there will be occasions when you are searching for a string, but aren't exactly sure what the string looks like. In cases like these you will need to use wildcard characters. In order to use wildcards, you need the like predicate.

Two wildcard characters are available: the underscore (_) and the percent sign (%). The underscore stands for a single character; the percent sign represents any number of characters, including none.

So, for example, if you were looking for someone with the first name of Daniel or Danny or Dan, you would use the percent sign:

```
select * from users where fname like 'Dan%';
```

Note that because the percent sign will match on zero characters, the preceding query matches the name Dan.

However, if for some odd reason you need to find all of the people in your database with four-letter first names beginning with the letter *J*, you'd construct your query like this (note that three underscores follow the *J*):

```
select * from users where fname like 'J___';
```

The three underscores will match any characters and return names like Jean, John, and Jack. Jay and Johnny will not be returned.

In MySQL the like comparison is not case-sensitive. This makes it quite different from most SQL implementations.

order by

There is one thing you should always keep in mind when working with relational databases: The storage of rows in any table is completely arbitrary. In general, you'll have no idea of the order in which your database has decided to put the rows you've inserted. When it matters, you can specify the order of rows returned in your query by tacking `order by` on the end of it.

The `order by` command can sort by any column type: alphabetical, chronological, or numeric. In addition, you can sort in either ascending or descending order by placing `asc` or `desc`, respectively, after `order by`. If neither is included, `asc` is used by default.

To alphabetize a list of the entries in the table, you probably want to make sure that the entries were sorted by both the `fname` and `lname` columns:

```
select * from users order by lname, fname;
```

You can sort by as many columns as you wish, and you can mix the `asc` and `desc` as necessary. The following query isn't particularly useful, but it is possible:

```
select * from users order by lname asc, fname desc;
```

limit

The `limit` predicate will restrict the number of rows returned from your query. It enables you to specify both the starting row and the number of rows you want returned. To get the first five rows from the table, run the following query:

```
select * from users limit 0,5;
```

To find the first five rows alphabetically, you can use `limit` with `order by`:

```
select * from users order by lname, fname limit 0,5;
```

You'll probably notice that the numbering is like arrays – the first row is row 0. To get the second five rows of the table, you'd run the following:

```
select * from users limit 5,5;
```

The `limit` predicate is particularly useful in situations where you want to restrict the display on any one page. You'll see the use of `limit` throughout this book. Even Chapter 8, which describes the first application in this book, uses `limit`. It's worth noting that `LIMIT n` is the same as `LIMIT 0, n` and that negative values are illegal after `LIMIT`.

group by and aggregate functions

Remember back to when we were talking about using `select` with `distinct` and how that removes rows you don't need? That may have seemed pretty cool, but it's nothing compared to what you can get out of the `group by` predicate and its associated aggregate functions.

Consider this task: You wish to know the number of entries from each state in the database (for example, six from California, seven from New York, two from Vermont). If you did a `select distinct state from users order by state` query, you would get a listing of each state in the database, but there would be no way to get the numbers. As MySQL goes through the table to process the query it simply skips over rows that would return identical values.

However, with `group by`, MySQL creates a temporary table where it keeps all the information on the rows and columns fitting your criteria. This allows the engine to perform some very important tasks on the temporary table. Probably the easiest way to show what `group by` can do is by showing one of the aggregate functions. We'll start with `count()`.

MySQL may not actually create a temporary table for each `group by`; however, the actual inner workings of a `group by` are pretty complex, and this is a good way to think about what MySQL is doing.

count()

Once again, the goal of your query is to find out the number of people from each state in your users table. To do that you will use `group by` with `count()`.

Remember that when the `group by` clause is used you can imagine MySQL creating a temporary table where it assembles like rows. The `count()` function then (you guessed it) counts the number of rows in each of the groups. Check out the following query and the result returned in Figure 3-5:

```
select state, count(*) from users group by state;
```

Here the asterisk (*) indicates that all rows within the group should be counted. The `count(*)` function is also handy for getting the total number of rows in a table.

```
select count(*) from users;
```

Within a `group by`, you can also indicate a specific field that is to be counted. `count` will look for the number of non-null values. Take, for example, the table in Figure 3-6.

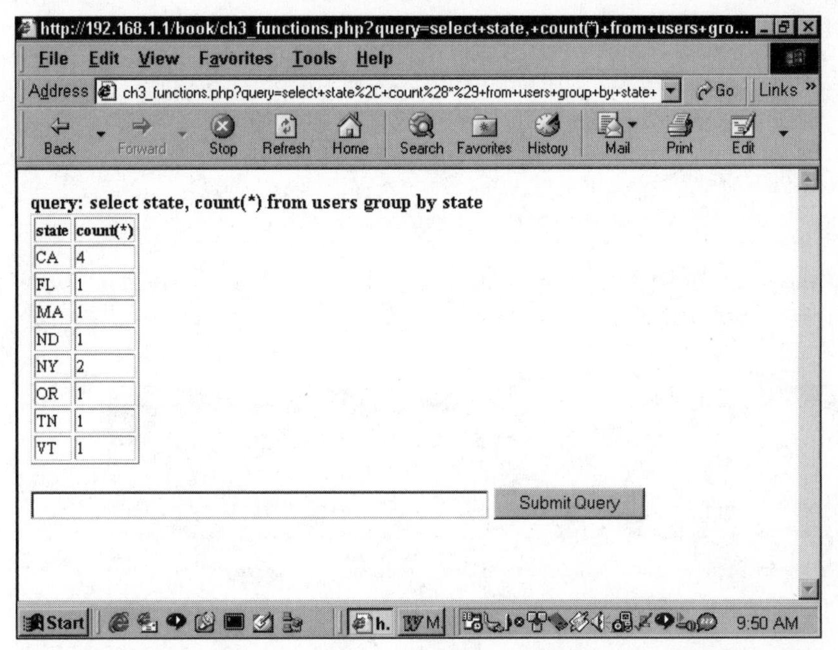

Figure 3-5: Results of a query using select state, count(*) from users group by state

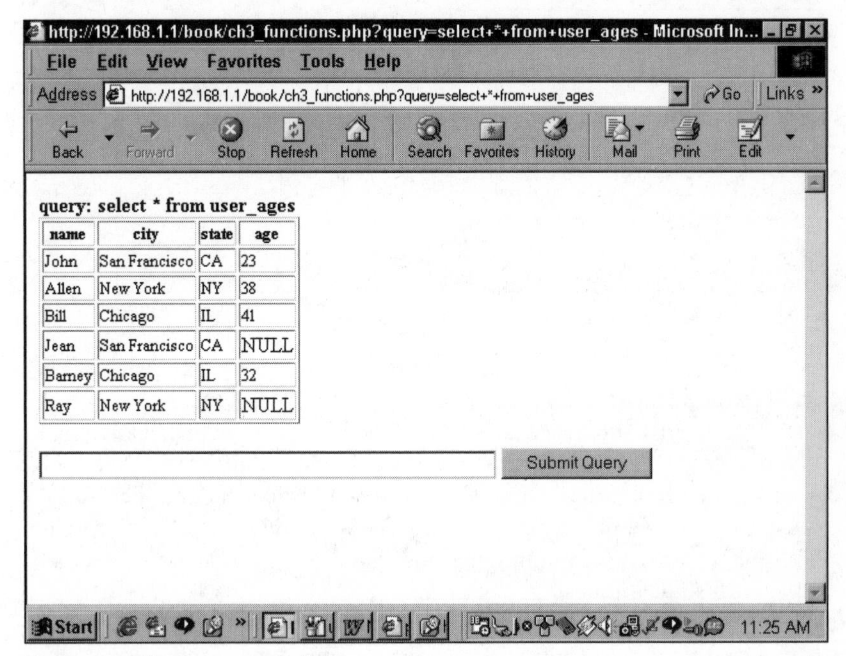

Figure 3-6: The users_ages table

If you're the type that's really into statistics, you can use this table to figure out what percentage from each city feels comfortable indicating its age. First, you need a count of all the entries from each specific city and state; following that you need a count of all the non-null values in the age field.

```
select city, state, count(*), count(age) from user_ages
group by state, city;
```

From the result in Figure 3-7, you can see that Chicagoans are far more forthcoming than those from the coasts.

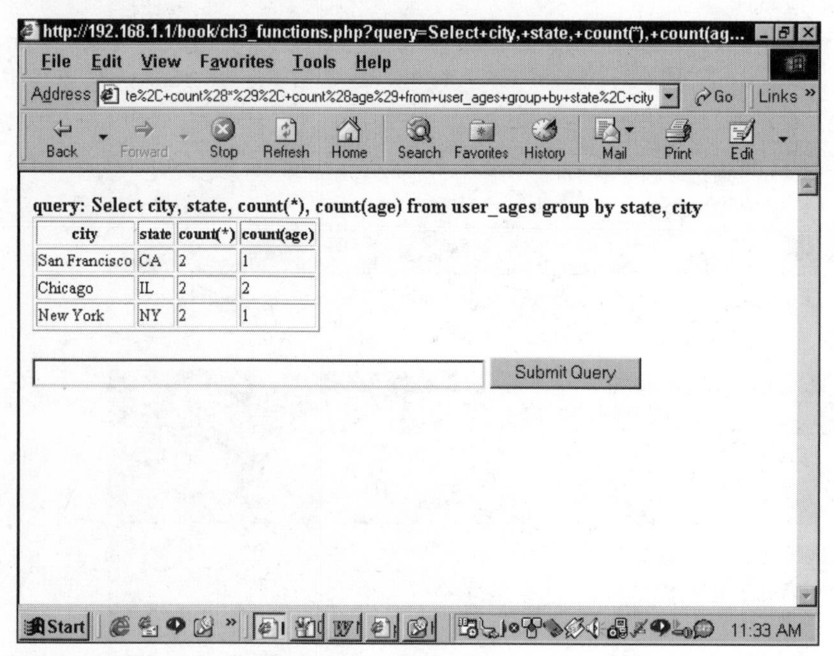

Figure 3-7: Results of query using count() function

There will be times, particularly when you're working with functions, when the column name returned by the query isn't what you'd like it to be. For example, in Figure 3-7 you may wish for a table header a bit more descriptive than `count(*)`.

You can follow any function or column name with the word `as` and then specify a name you prefer. `as` simply designates an *alias* – an identifier that represents something else. If you need a column name that is more than one word, surround the text string with single quotes.

While on the topic of aliases, we'll also mention that a variety of functions and operators are available in MySQL (see Appendix J). They range from simple math functions to more complex operations. The following is some math we've thrown in to clarify the purpose of the query. Notice the use of `as` for the alias and the way it affects the display of the query (shown in Figure 3-8).

```
select city, state, count(*) as 'Total Rows',
       count(age) as 'The Willing',
       (count(age)/count(*)*100) as 'Percent Responding'
from user_ages
group by state, city;
```

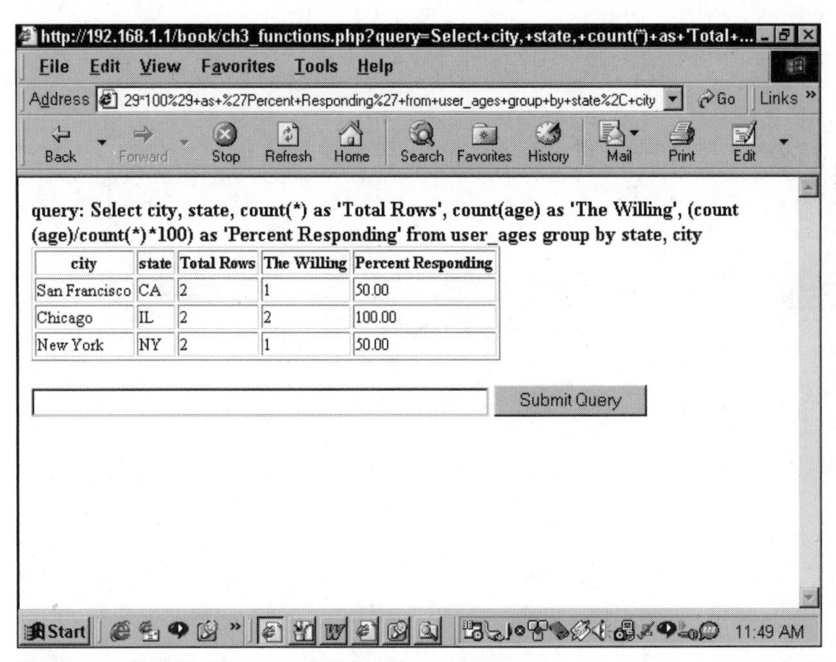

Figure 3-8: Results of query using functions and aliases

You can also use aliases on tables. This will be particularly helpful when you're dealing with multiple tables. You can read about this in further detail in the section "The multi-table join."

sum()

The `sum()` function returns the sum of a given column and is almost always used with a `group by` clause. For instance, if you are running an application for a non-profit, you might want to know the total contributions from each state. The table you're working with might look like the one in Figure 3-9.

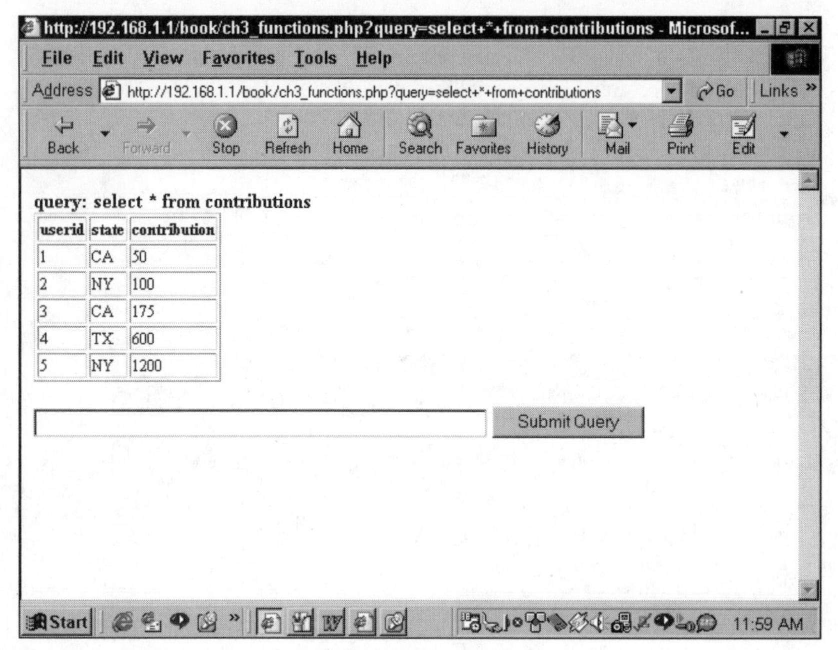

Figure 3-9: Table where using sum() would be helpful

To get the total from each state you'd run the following query:

```
select state, sum(contribution) from contributions group by state;
```

min()

The `min()` function pulls out the lowest value in each grouping. To find the lowest contribution from any state just make a small change to the previous query:

```
select state, min(contribution) from contributions group by state;
```

max()

As you probably guessed, `max()` will return the highest value in a group:

```
select state, max(contribution) from contributions group by state;
```

avg()

`avg ()` returns the average of the group:

```
select state, sum(contribution) from contributions group by state;
```

You can throw all these together to create a pretty useful query, as Figure 3-10 and the following query show:

```
select state, sum(contribution) as 'Total',
       avg(contribution) as 'Average',
       min(contribution) as 'Minimum',
       max(contribution) as 'Maximum'
from contributions
group by state;
```

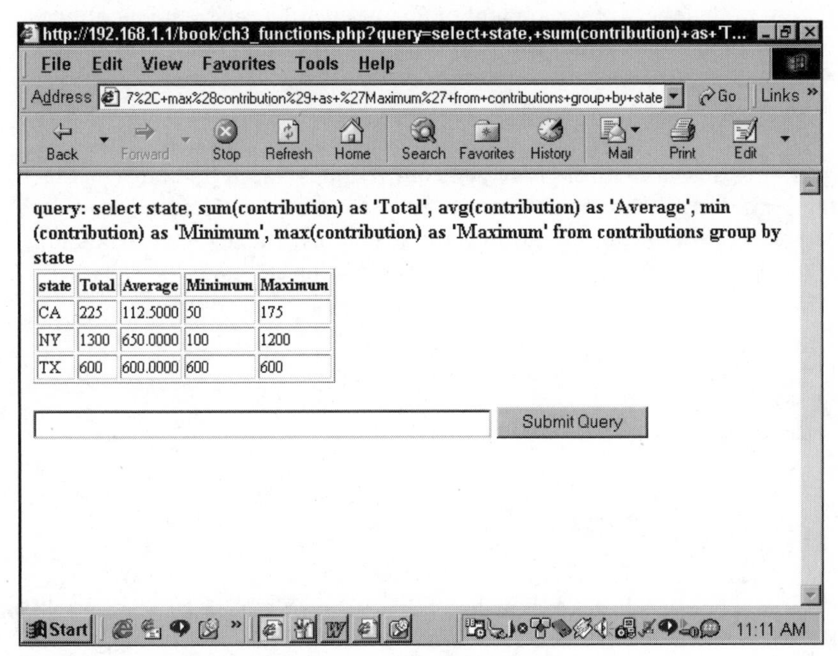

state	Total	Average	Minimum	Maximum
CA	225	112.5000	50	175
NY	1300	650.0000	100	1200
TX	600	600.0000	600	600

Figure 3-10: Using multiple aggregate functions together

group by OPTIONS

Most relational databases require that fields listed in the `select` clause be used in the `group by` predicate. But MySQL gives you a second option: You can group a subset of the columns listed. For instance, if you want to find out the number of people in one city and get a look at a sample ZIP code from that city, you could run the following:

```
select city, zip, count(*) from users group by city;
```

The query would return a listing of cities, the number of entries for each city, and one sample ZIP code. These results are quite different from those from the following query:

```
select city, zip, count(*) from users group by city, zip;
```

This returns a separate row for each city/ZIP combination and provides a count for each unique combination.

having

The having predicate restricts the rows displayed by a group by. This predicate is not the same as the where clause. The where clause actually restricts the rows that are used in the group by, whereas the having clause only prevents their display.

If you need to find the average amount of donations from each state for all those who contributed more than $100, you could run the following:

```
select avg(donations), state from contributions where donations> 100;
```

However, if you want to display average contributions for all the states in which the average was over $100, you have to use the having clause. Because the having clause does not restrict rows that go into the group by, the aggregate functions, like avg()in this case, use all the rows in their calculations.

```
select avg(contribution) as avg_contrib, state
from contributions
group by state
having avg(contribution)>100;
```

Joining Tables

If you read Chapter 1, you know that relational databases work so well because they segment information. Different tables hold information on different topics, and fields are inserted into the tables to maintain relationships. After you finish the normalization process, it's likely that none of your tables will be usable without the others. That is why you'll need to join tables in your SQL select statements.

The two-table join (equi-join)

For the sake of continuity, we're going to reprise a couple of tables first seen in Chapter 1. Take a look at the familiar tables in Figure 3-11.

If you're looking to do a mailing to all the people in the contacts table, you are going to need to join the contacts table to the companies table, because the street address is in the companies table (and that's exactly where it should be). The company_id column in the contacts table creates the relationship between these tables. And if you join these tables on occasions in which the company_id field in the contacts table is equal to the company_id field in the contacts table, all the information will be at your fingertips.

companies

company_id	company_name	address
1	Big Co Company	1121 43rd St
2	Little Co Company	4444 44th St

contacts

contact_id	company_id	Name	Title	Phone	Email
1	1	Jay Greenspan	Vice President	4155551212	1121 43rd St
2	1	Brad Bulber	President	4155552222	4444 44th St
3	2	John Doe	Lacky	2125556666	4444 44th St

Figure 3-11: Tables in need of a join

Making this join is easy enough in SQL. All the tables to be joined must be listed in the `from` portion of the `select` statement. And the fields on which the join takes place must be listed in the `where` portion:

```
select *
from companies, contacts
where companies.company_id = contacts.company_id;
```

At those times when a reference to a field name is ambiguous, you need to specify which table the column comes from by using the syntax `table_name.column_name`. You can do this in the `where` clause in Figure 3-12. If you fail to indicate the table from which you're pulling the column in the SQL statements, MySQL will return an error.

This type of join, in which tables are merged based on quality in a common field, is extremely common. It is known as an *equi-join* or *inner join*. The name "inner join" will make more sense when you learn about the *outer join* later in this chapter.

Once you begin performing joins, aliases become convenient. By specifying an alias in the `from` clause you can save yourself some typing. In the following code, `t1` is an alias for `companies` and `t2` is an alias for `contacts`.

```
select *
from companies t1, contacts t2
where t1.company_ID = t2.company_ID;
```

The multi-table join

An equi-join can be applied to more than one table. Many of your SQL statements will join three, four, or more tables. All you'll need to do is add additional columns after `select`, additional tables in the `from` clause, and the additional join parameters in the `where` clause. Take a look at the tables that need multiple joins in Figure 3-13.

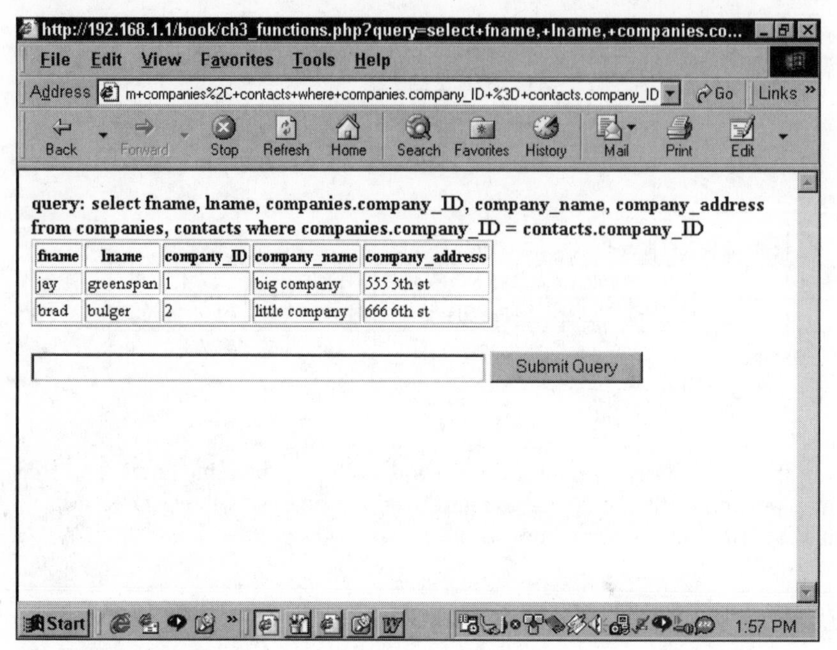

Figure 3-12: A basic join

If you want to find the addresses for all the companies with offices in California and that have expertise in consulting, you have to join all four of these tables. The following query gets the job done. Here the `where` clause contains quite a few tests: The first two lines of the `where` clause limit the rows that will be returned to those companies that match your criteria. The remainder of the `where` clause takes care of the joins.

```
select *
from companies, locations, expertise, companies_expertise
where state = 'CA' and
    companies_expertise.expertise_ID = 3 and
    companies.company_ID = companies_expertise.company_ID and
    companies.company_ID = locations.company_ID and
    companies_expertise.expertise_ID = expertise.expertise_ID
;
```

The outer join

The challenges presented by null values have shown themselves repeatedly in this book. In Chapter 2, we presented Tables 2-1 and 2-2, which we're re-presenting here as Tables 3-13 and 3-14.

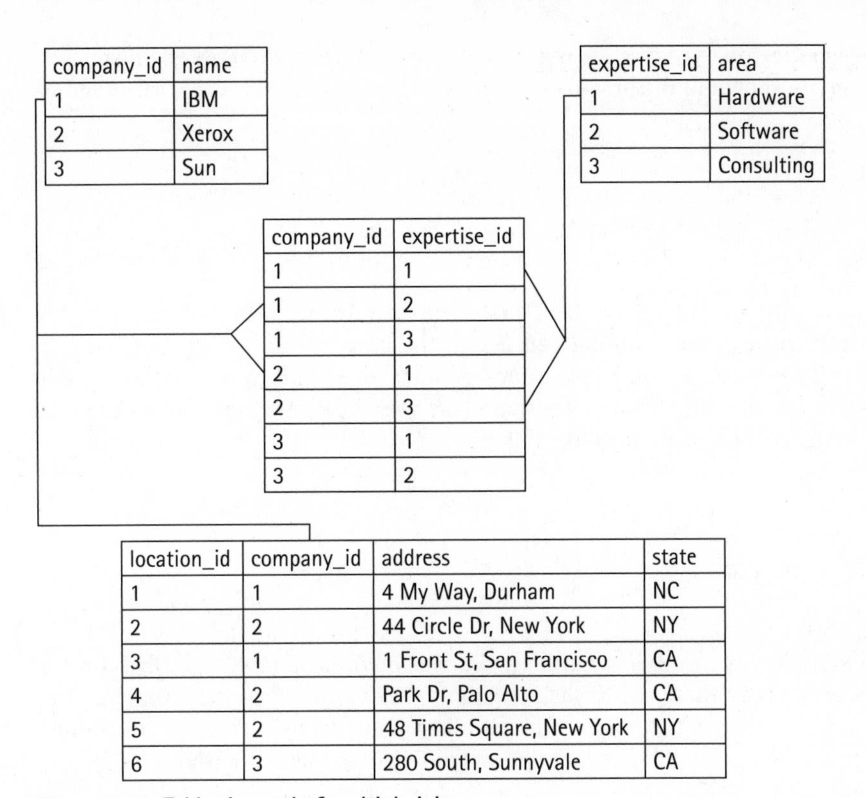

company_id	name
1	IBM
2	Xerox
3	Sun

expertise_id	area
1	Hardware
2	Software
3	Consulting

company_id	expertise_id
1	1
1	2
1	3
2	1
2	3
3	1
3	2

location_id	company_id	address	state
1	1	4 My Way, Durham	NC
2	2	44 Circle Dr, New York	NY
3	1	1 Front St, San Francisco	CA
4	2	Park Dr, Palo Alto	CA
5	2	48 Times Square, New York	NY
6	3	280 South, Sunnyvale	CA

Figure 3-13: Tables in need of multiple joins

TABLE 3-13 THE CONTACTS TABLE

first_name	last_name	fantasy_spouse_id
Jay	Greenspan	1
Brad	Bulger	NULL

TABLE 3-14 desired_spouse

fantasy_spouse_id	first_name	last_name
1	Nicole	Kidman

Now imagine that you need to get a list of the contacts and their desired spouses. The equi-join shown in the previous section will not work in this case. Take the following query:

```
select *
from contacts, desired_spouse
where contacts.fantasy_spouse_id = desired_spouse.fantasy_spouse_id;
```

Only the first row of the contacts table will be returned. The null value in the second row ensures that nothing can match the criterion in the `where` clause. In cases like this, wherein you need to preserve one table and join the second table when there are matching values, you can make use of the outer join (also known as the *left outer join*), which looks like this:

```
select *
from contacts
left join desired_spouse
on contacts.fantasy_spouse_id = desired_spouse.fantasy_spouse_id;
```

This statement says, "I want to keep the entire contacts table, and tack on the spouses table when these two fields are equal." The word *left* in the term *left outer join* refers to the fact that when you visualize your database tables, you should visualize the first table, the one that appears in the `from` clause, on the left side, and the joined table on the right.

Depending on the database package you're using, the syntax of the outer join may vary. Some databases support left, right, and full (both left and right) outer joins. MySQL only has the left outer join, but in practice that's usually all you need. You can either use the syntax in the previous query or use `left outer join on`.

Outer joins will come up frequently out of necessity. Additionally, it is often good practice to use outer joins even when you feel an inner join will do the trick. It's just a matter of being safe: You'd rather not have important rows of data come up missing because you forgot to account for null values. Throughout the book you will see occasions when we have used outer joins because we just wanted to be extra careful.

There may come times when you will need to do more than one outer join. Say, for instance (and for no particularly good reason), you wanted to store information regarding spouses' siblings. You'd add another table listing the siblings, and add a column to the desired_spouse table, which maintains the relationship. So if you were to design a query that maintained everyone in the contacts table and everyone returned from the spouses table, you'd have to throw in two outer joins:

```
select *
from contacts
left join desired_spouse on contacts.spouse_id =
desired_spouse.fantasy_spouse_id
left join on siblings desired_spouse.sibling_id =
siblings.sibling_id;
```

The self join

As bizarre as it may sound, the time will come when you'll need to join a table to a copy of itself. You'll usually run into the need to do this when looking for duplicates in a table. If you had a sneaking suspicion that there was a bigamist in Table 3-15, how would you search out the two people with the same spouse?

TABLE 3-15 THE CONTACTS TABLE

contact_id	first_name	last_name	spouse_id
1	Jason	Fullman	1
2	Brad	Bulger	
3	John	James	2
4	Elliot	Simms	2

You would need to discover if the value in this spouse_id field was repeated (in this case, the number 2 appears more than once). You could do a group by, but then there would be no way of getting the names of the people involved. Using group by along with the count() function, you could find the occasions on which one person appears more than once, but it would take a second query to find out who those people were. With a self join you can do it all in one step. But it needs to be a carefully considered step.

You might think that the following query would do the trick. Notice that we again use an alias, so that we have two table names we can address:

```
select t1.first_name, t1.last_name, t2.first_name, t2.last_name
from contacts t1, contacts t2
where t1.spouse_id = t2.spouse_id;
```

But this is going to return more rows than we need. Specifically, each name will match itself, providing duplicates of each returned entry. Given this query, when the row for Jason is compared to itself, it will test true and be returned in the result. You can eliminate redundancy here by ensuring that the contact_id field from the first table is not equal to the contact_id field in the second table:

```
select t1.first_name, t1.last_name
from contacts t1, contacts t2
where t1.spouse_id = t2.spouse_id
and t1.contact_id != t2.contact_id;
```

This is good but not perfect. Take the example of Elliot and John. A row will be returned when Elliot is in t1 and John is in t2; another will be returned when John is in t1 and Elliot is in t2. The easiest way to address that problem here is to make use of the numeric primary key. You know one ID will be greater than the other, and by using that information you can get rid of all duplicates.

```
select t1.first_name, t1.last_name
from contacts t1, contacts t2
where t1.spouse_id = t2.spouse_id
and t1.countact_id < t2.contact_id;
```

Unions

Unions allow queries with the same number of columns to be returned in one result set. For instance, if you have two tables storing user names, you can have all of the names in one query returned with a statement like this:

```
select first_name, last_name
from table_1
union
select first_name, last_name
from table_2;
```

Correlated subqueries

Subqueries are a new feature in MySQL version 4.1. Their addition is welcome, particularly for developers with Oracle or PostgreSQL familiarity, who have been able to use them all along.

For those new to the concept, subqueries enable you to define an entire query in the where clause. For example, if you have a table that stores students and their test scores, you can easily find all the students with better-than-average test scores:

```
select first_name, last_name, score
from test_scores
where score > (select avg(score) from test_scores);
```

You can achieve the same effect by running two queries, storing the results of the first query in program variables or a temporary table, and then using those results in the second query. In most cases you can work around the absence of subqueries by running additional queries. You lose some elegance, but the effect is identical.

Summary

You can get through the better part of your life without committing some portions of SQL to memory. If you are using graphical tools you may not need to learn the specifics of the `create` or `alter` commands. The same cannot be said of the `insert`, `update`, `delete`, and `select` statements.

Everything covered in this chapter is really important to your life as an applications developer. The `insert`, `update`, and `delete` statements are what enable you to have a database in the first place. They're what you need to add records, change records, and remove records. The `select` statement enables you to efficiently retrieve and sort information from your databases, and if you understand the intricacies of the `select` statement you'll be able to write applications more efficiently and elegantly. And if you're able to combine all of those statements with effective table-joining techniques, you're well on your way to managing data in MySQL efficiently.

Part II

Working with PHP

Chapter 4

Getting Started with PHP – Variables

IN THIS CHAPTER

- Assigning variables within PHP scripts
- Handling data passed from HTML forms
- Working with PHP's built-in variables, including Apache variables
- Testing for and assigning variable types

PHP MAKES WORKING with variables extremely easy. PHP is smart about understanding variable types and keeps the syntax to an absolute minimum. Those coming to PHP from a C, Java, or Perl background may find PHP comparatively easy to deal with, but the ease of syntax can present its own problems.

All variables in PHP start with a dollar sign ($). It doesn't matter what kind of variables they are, whether strings, integers, floating-point numbers, or even arrays. They all look identical in the code. The PHP engine keeps track of the type of information you are storing.

In general, variables will come from three places: They are either assigned within a script, passed from an HTML page (often from form input), or are part of your PHP environment. We'll talk about each of these in the following sections.

Assigning Simple Variables Within a Script

PHP does not require explicit variable declaration. All you have to do is assign a value to a variable and it exists. And as we already mentioned, all variable types look identical. The following code shows how to assign values of string, integer, and floating-point (double) types to variables:

```
$a = "this is a string"; //this is a string
$b = 4; //this is an integer
$c = 4.837; //this is a floating-point number
$d = "2"; //this is another string
```

Notice that the = is the assignment operator. For comparison, you must use two consecutive equals signs (= =). For example, `if($x==1)`.

If you try to use a variable without having assigned a value to it, your code still runs – treating the unheard-of variable as having a value of `NULL` – but PHP issues a notice (an `E_NOTICE` level error message) warning you that the variable is undefined. Since it's best practice to make sure your variables have been initialized with some value, even if it's just `NULL`, this is a good reason to make sure your error reporting levels are set to display or log all PHP errors, at least during development.

For more information about error reporting, see the Error Handling and Logging Functions section of the PHP Manual (`http://www.php.net/errorfunc`).

Typing is flexible, and PHP is pretty smart about handling changes in types. For example, given the code you just saw, the following would evaluate as you'd probably hope:

```
$e = $b + $d;
echo $e;
```

PHP would recognize that you want to treat the string in `$d` as an integer. The variable `$e` will be an integer type and will equal 6. In fact, PHP will also evaluate the following as an integer:

```
$a = 2;
$b = "2 little piggies";
$c = $a + $b;
```

Here, `$c` will equal 4. If an integer or floating-point number is at the beginning of a string, PHP can evaluate it as such. Similarly, PHP handles automatic conversion sensibly as well, as seen in the following code:

```
$f = 2; //$f is an integer
$g = 1.444; // $g is a double (floating-point) type
$f = $f + $g;  //$f is now a double type
```

PHP will also do type conversions when comparing two variables. This is a good thing, because the most common values for a script, entries submitted from an HTML form, always come in as strings. Here's an example:

```
$a = '1.3';
if ($a == 1.3)
{
```

```
    echo "'$a' is 1.3\n";
}
else
{
    echo "'$a' is not 1.3\n";
}
```

The result:

```
'1.3' is 1.3
```

If you need to make a strict comparison, where the types as well as the values must match, you can use a triple equal sign (===) operator (or its inverse, !==). This most commonly arises when you need to distinguish between 0, NULL, FALSE, and an empty string, since in a normal comparison these will all be treated as equal. The following code demonstrates:

```
$a = 0;
if ($a === 0)
{
    echo "'$a' is 0\n";
}
else
{
    echo "'$a' is not 0\n";
}
if ($a === FALSE)
{
    echo "'$a' is FALSE\n";
}
else
{
    echo "'$a' is not FALSE\n";
}
```

The result:

```
'0' is 0
'0' is not FALSE
```

This kind of flexibility is nice, but it can lead to some difficulty. There will be times when you're not sure what variable types you are working with. We'll show you how to deal with these circumstances in the section "Testing Variables" later in this chapter.

Delimiting strings

In the preceding code, all the strings were surrounded by double quotes. You can also delimit strings in PHP in two other ways. If you surround your strings with double quotes, variables within the string will be expanded. For instance,

```
$my_name = "Jay";
$phrase = "Hello, my name is $my_name";
echo $phrase;
```

will print "Hello, my name is Jay". But if you want to include any of the following characters within your string, they must be escaped with backslashes:

- Double quotes (")
- Backslash (\)
- Dollar sign ($)

For example, to print an opening `form` tag using double quotes you would have to do the following:

```
echo "<form action=\"mypage.php\" method=\"get\">";
```

You can also surround strings with single quotes ('). If a string is within single quotes, variables will not be expanded. So this code –

```
$my_name = "Jay";
echo 'Hello, my name is $my_name';
```

– will print "Hello, my name is $my_name". The only characters that need to be escaped within single quotes are single quotes and backslashes.

The flip side of this is that variable references will not be expanded inside single quotes. If we repeat the first example in this section with single quotes:

```
$my_name = 'Jay';
$phrase = 'Hello, my name is $my_name';
echo $phrase;
```

PHP prints out "Hello, my name is $my_name".

Since PHP knows that it does not have to parse a single-quoted string for variable references, it's marginally faster to use single-quotes to delimit constant values in your code. In recent releases, however, the performance difference between the two styles has shrunk to insignificance. So it's a matter of your personal preference, and of which style is most convenient for what you're trying to do.

Finally, you can also make use of *heredoc syntax* to delimit strings. The heredoc syntax can be thought of as a hybrid of the single- and double-quote styles that can be convenient in many circumstances. Heredoc text is delimited at the start of the string with three less-than signs (<<<) and an identifier. An identifier must contain only numbers, letters, and underscores and begin with either a letter or an underscore; in the book we use the identifiers `EOQ` and `EOT`. The text is terminated with the same identifier followed by a semicolon (`;`), on the left margin of the code. This is important to remember – heredoc terminators must not be indented, and the terminator and semicolon must be the only characters on the line, with no spaces before or after the semicolon. In the following code, `$my_string` is a string properly delimited using heredoc syntax.

```
$my_string = <<<EOQ
My string is in here.
EOQ;
```

If you use heredoc syntax, variables are expanded and double quotes do not need to be escaped. We make frequent use of the heredoc syntax when working with form elements, as is the case here:

```
$element = <<<EOQ
<textarea name="$name" cols="$cols" rows="$rows"
wrap="$wrap">$value</textarea>
EOQ;
```

In a case like this we don't need to litter the string with backslashes, and we still get the convenience of having variables expanded within the string.

Note that when using heredoc syntax your file format should match the operating system it runs on. PHP is expecting a newline character as defined by the operating system to be the last character before the beginning of the heredoc terminator, and for the terminator and a semicolon to be the only characters on their line. It will produce an error if it is not. Unix-based operating systems (which includes Mac OS X) use a newline character (`\n`) to terminate lines, while classic Mac (OS 9 and earlier) files use a carriage return (`\r`), and DOS and Windows files use both (`\n\r`). Editing your files on one operating system and running them on a different one can cause difficult-to-diagnose errors. Most text editors enable you to save as a Unix file type, and if you are running your scripts on a Unix server, choosing that option saves you a lot of trouble.

If you want to reference an element in an associative array, an object property, or make any other kind of variable reference that could be interpreted ambiguously, you should enclose the variable in curly braces, like so:

```
$array = array ("fname"=>"jay", "lname"=>"greenspan");
$fields = <<<EOQ
```

```
The value in array of 'fname' is {$array['fname']}
EOQ;
foreach ($array as $key => $value)
{
    $fields .= <<<EOQ
['']<input type="text" name="{$key}_value"
value="$value">
EOQ;
}
```

Assigning arrays within a script

Arrays are variables that contain multiple values. For example, a simple array might store the months of the year. To assign this array, you could use the following:

```
$months = array("January", "February", "March", "May", "June",
"July", "August", "September", "October", "November", "December");
```

This array has 12 elements, and you can address them by their order in the array, starting with `0`. So the command `echo $months[0]` would print "January" and `echo $months[11]` would print "December". To print out all the values within an array, you could get the length of the array and then set up a loop, as follows:

```
$months = array("January", "February", "March", "May", "June",
"July", "August", "September", "October", "November", "December");
for ($i=0, $mcount=count($months); $i<$mcount; $i++)
{
  echo $months[$i] . "<br>\n" ;
}
```

The `for` loop is explained in Chapter 5.

You can also assign values to arrays with a simple assignment operator. The following would work:

```
$dogs = array();
$dogs[0] = "shepherd";
$dogs[1] = "poodle";
```

If you don't specify an index value, the value will be tacked onto the end of the array. The following line would assign `"retriever"` to `$dogs[2]`.

```
$dogs[] = "retriever";
```

A variety of functions work with arrays. Many of these are covered in Chapter 6.

Like many programming languages, PHP makes use of associative arrays. If you are new to the concept, elements in associative arrays have *keys* that reference individual elements. (In fact, all array values have keys. The difference with an associative array is that the keys are meaningful and can be strings as well as integers, whereas in a simple list array, they represent only the position of the value in the array.) Keys are particularly important when you're dealing with databases. When you fetch rows from your database query you will usually refer to the elements by their keys.

You can assign an associative array by using keys. Here, `first_name`, `last_name`, and `email` are the keys:

```
$person = array (
   "first_name" => "Jay",
   "last_name" => "Greenspan",
   "email" => "jgreen_1@yahoo.com"
);
```

If you wanted to add to this array, you could assign another value. Notice that the next line would add an integer to the array, so this array would then contain four values - three strings and one integer:

```
$person['age'] = 32;
```

Typically, if you wanted to access both the keys and the values in an associative array, you would use the `list()=each()` construct or the `foreach()` loop. Here are some examples:

```
while (list($key, $value) = each($person))
{
   echo "<b>key:</b> $key, <b>value</b> = $value <br>\n";
}
```

Chapter 5 describes the `list()=each()` construct in more detail. Basically, `each()` pulls the key and value of a single array element; `list()` takes those values and assigns them to `$key` and `$value`, respectively. This process continues until each element in the array has been accessed. If you want to go through the array a second time, you will need to reset the array pointer with `reset($person)`.

If you wanted to get only the value without the key, or if you were using a nonassociative array and wanted to use the `list()=each()` structure, you would have to do this:

```
while (list( , $value) = each($person))
{
   echo "value = $value <br>\n";
}
```

Or, if you wanted to get at just the keys, you could do this:

```
while (list($key) = each($person))
{
   echo "key = $key <br>\n";
}
```

You can also cycle through arrays using the `foreach()` loop. The following will print out the keys and values for each element of the `$person` array:

```
foreach($person as $key=>$value)
{
   echo "key = $key; value = $value <br>\n";
}
```

And the following will print out just the values of array elements:

```
foreach($person as $value)
{
   echo "value = $value <br>\n";
}
```

With `foreach()` there's no need to reset the array pointer after looping through the array. It is also appreciably faster than the `list()=each()` syntax.

Think about PHP arrays this way: All arrays are associative. A couple of pages back you saw that you can assign a basic array without specifying associative keys. For example, `$myarray= array ("pug", "poodle")`. When this is done, PHP assigns `$myarray` consecutive numeric keys starting at `0`.

They behave just like associative keys. You step through them using `list()=each()` or `foreach()`. They make use of the same array functions, many of which are explained in Chapter 6.

Assigning two-dimensional arrays in a script

PHP also supports multidimensional arrays. The most commonly used multidimensional array is the two-dimensional array. Two-dimensional arrays look a lot like tables. They store information that is based on two keys. For instance, if you wanted to store information on more than one person, a two-dimensional array would work well. You would assign an array named `$people`, which would contain individual arrays addressing each person:

```
$people = array (
            "jay" => array (
                "last_name" => "greenspan",
                "age" => 32
             ),
             "john" => array (
                  "last_name" => "doe",
                  "age" => 52
             )
);
```

Here the `$people` array contains information on two people, Jay and John. To access information on any single value, you would need to use both keys. To print out John's age, the following two commands would work:

```
echo $people['john']['age']; //prints 52
```

You could access all of the elements in a two-dimensional array by looping through both of the array's dimensions:

```
foreach ($people as $person => $person_array)
{
    echo "<b>What I know about $person</b><br>\n";
    foreach ($person_array as $person_attribute => $value)
    {
        echo "$person_attribute = $value<br>\n";
    }
}
```

Accessing Variables Passed from the Browser

The whole point of using PHP, or any other middleware package for that matter, is to deliver customized information based on user preferences and needs. Often, the information will come via HTML forms. But information can come from other places, including HTML anchors, cookies, and sessions.

HTML forms variables

One of the most common ways in which variable information is delivered is through HTML forms.

Appendix B presents detailed information on creating HTML forms. Refer to that appendix before you read this section if you are unfamiliar with this topic.

For each of your form elements you have to assign name and value attributes (name and value are settings defined in HTML code). When the form is submitted, the name/value pairs are passed to PHP. They can be passed to PHP by either the GET or POST methods, depending on what you chose in the METHOD attribute of your <FORM> tag (the default is GET).

In older versions of PHP (prior to PHP 4.2), once a form was submitted, the form elements automatically become global variables in PHP. (Global variables and variable scope are discussed in Chapter 7). Consider the following simple HTML form:

```
<form action="mypage.php" method="POST">
   <input type=text name=email>
   <input type=text name=first_name>
   <input type=submit name=submit value=add>
</form>
```

Once the user hit the Submit button, variables named $email, $first_name, and $submit were made available in the called PHP page. Listing 4-1 is a brief example of how scripts were usually written for PHP versions 4.1 and lower. (Assume the name of the page is mypage.php.)

Listing 4-1: Common Variable Use in Older Versions of PHP

```
<?php
if (isset($submit) && $submit=="yes")
{
    echo "thank you for submitting your form.";
```

```
}
else
{

?>
<form action="mypage.php" method="POST">
   <input type="text" name="email">
   <input type="text" name="first_name">
   <input type="submit" name="submit" value="yes">
</form>

<?php
}
?>
```

On his or her first visit to this page the user would be presented with a form. Once the form was submitted and the page had recalled itself with the new variable information, only the "thank you" message would appear. There was, however, a major problem with the global variables that came from forms. Even the code in Listing 4-1, which is about as simple as scripting gets, demonstrates this problem.

The user-entered variables should come to the PHP script by way of the `POST` method – not by way of `GET`. However, if a user wanted to see the "thank you" message without entering anything into the form elements, he or she could simply tack some information onto the URL typed into the browser. For example:

```
http://localhost/mypage.php?submit=yes
```

In older versions of PHP, when the PHP engine encountered the `submit` variable in the querystring, it would automatically register the variable as a global and thus the test at the beginning of this script – `if (isset($submit) && $submit=="yes")` – would be true.

Many programmers wrote applications that took advantage of the global variables and unintentionally made their scripts vulnerable to attacks. We won't get into the details of the exploits here; it's enough to mention that, even if you have the opportunity, you should not be using global variables that come from form elements. Instead you should use a series of arrays that contain variables sent via HTTP.

In PHP 4.2 and higher you can opt to have `GET`, `POST`, session, and cookie variables available as globals by altering the `register_globals` item in the php.ini file. Current versions of PHP default to a setting of `off`, meaning that HTTP variables will not be available as globals. In most circumstances you should keep this setting the way it is. However, if you are running older scripts that you don't have time to change, you may have to alter this setting.

In PHP versions 4.2 or later, you should be getting your form data via the superglobal (so called because they are globally available without ever having to be declared as global) array variables `$_POST` and `$_GET`, depending on the method used in your form. You can also use the `$_REQUEST` variable, which is a combination of `GET`, `POST`, and cookie values.

To add a bit more security to the previous listing, you could rewrite Listing 4-1 to look like Listing 4-2:

Listing 4-2: Simple Script That Does Not Use Globals

```
if (isset($_POST['submit']) && $_POST['submit']=="yes")
{
    echo "thank you for submitting your form.";
}
else
{
?>
<form action="test1.php" method="POST">
  <input type="text" name="email">
  <input type="text" name="first_name">
  <input type="submit" name="submit" value="yes">
</form>

<?php
}
```

You can access any individual element as you would an element in any associative array (`$_POST ['email']`). Or you can loop through all the contents of an array as follows:

```
foreach ($_POST as $key => $value)
{
   echo "variable = $key value = $value <br>";
}
```

Passing arrays

Sometimes passing scalar variables won't be enough, and you'll need to pass arrays from your HTML page to your PHP script. This will come up when the user can choose one or more form elements on a page. Take, for example, multiple select boxes, which enable users to pass one or more items from a number of items. The form element is made with the HTML in the following code example. The `multiple` attribute indicates that the user can choose more than one element, as shown in Figure 4-1. To choose more than one element on the PC, hold down the Ctrl key while selecting additional values. On the Mac, use the Apple key. Gnome users can select and unselect individual elements with a click.

```
<form action="mypage.php" method="POST">
   <select name="j_names[]" size="4" multiple>
       <option value="2">John
       <option value="3">Jay
       <option value="4">Jackie
       <option value="5">Jordan
       <option value="6">Julia
   </select>
   <input type="submit" value="submit">
</form>
```

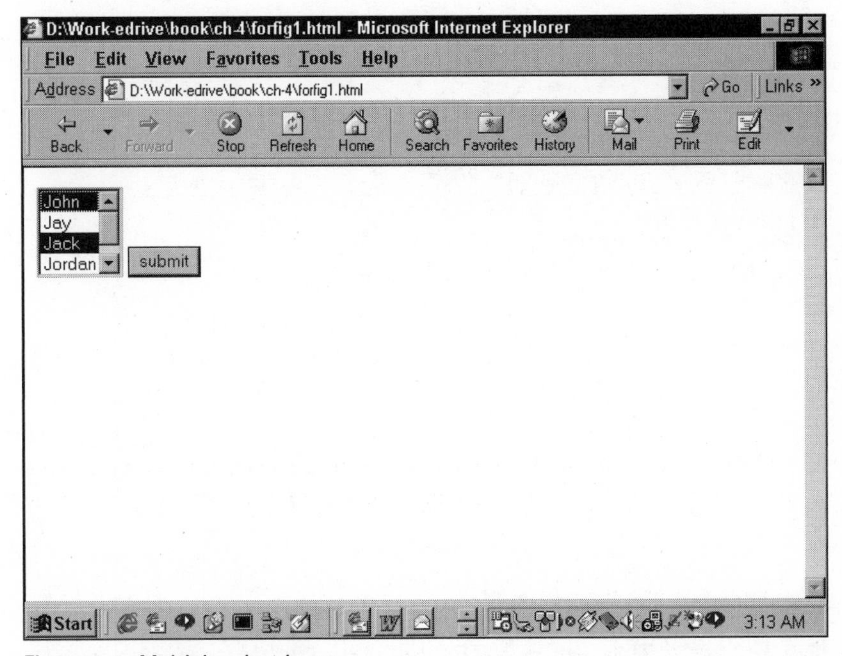

Figure 4-1: Multiple select boxes

Notice that in the `select name` attribute we've added opening and closing brackets (`[]`). This tells PHP to expect an array. If we didn't include the brackets, two values might end up fighting for the same variable name, and that's no good at all.

Once it has been submitted you can address this array like any other two-dimensional array:

```
if (is_array($_POST['j_names']))
{
   echo "<b>the select values are:<br> <br>";

   foreach ($_POST['j_names'] as $value)   {
```

```
        echo $value . "<br>\n";
    }
}
```

Passing arrays can also be useful when you want to present a series of checkboxes that the user may or may not check before pressing the Submit button. Chapter 8 contains a code example for a page that enables the program's administrator to use checkboxes to select which entries should be deleted. Figure 4-2 shows a sample of this type of page. If you were to assign a different name to each checkbox, you would have to check each one individually. With arrays, you can write a three-line loop to check them all.

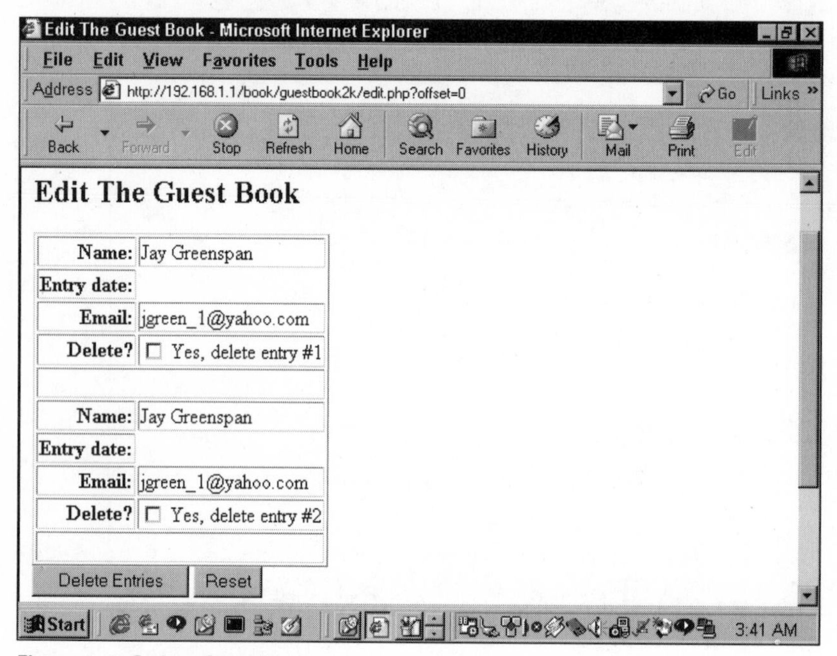

Figure 4-2: Series of checkboxes

Arrays passed from forms can also have associative keys, which can be multidimensional. The name of the form element should take the form `name="array_name[element_name]"`. Or, for a multidimensional array, `name="array_name[element_name][subelement_name]"`.

Cookies

Cookies are small pieces of information that are stored by a user's Web browser. Some are kept in memory and discarded after a short time, and others are written to the user's hard drive for long-term use. Once a Web browser has accepted a cookie from a server, it resends the same cookie to its owner(s) on each HTTP request until the cookie expires or is deleted. Cookies provide the only way to keep track of users over the course of several visits. Remember that the Web is a stateless environment. Your Web server really has no idea who is requesting a page. Cookies help you keep track of users as they move around your site.

When they exist, cookies become part of the HTTP request sent to the Web server. But first you'll need to set a cookie. The PHP developers have made this, like everything else in PHP, exceedingly simple. Use the `setcookie()` function. This function takes the following arguments:

```
setcookie(name [, value [, time_to_expire [, path [, domain [,
security setting]]]]]);
```

We will discuss this function in more detail in Chapter 6, but for now, suffice it to say that the following statement –

```
setcookie("mycookie",
"my_id",time()+(60*60*24*30),"/",".mydomain.com", 0)
```

– would set a cookie with the following parameters:

- Stores a variable named `my_cookie`
- The value of `mycookie` is `"my_id"`.
- The cookie will expire 30 days from the time it is set (current time plus the number of seconds in 30 days).
- The cookie will be available to every page in the domain. (You could restrict it to a specific path within a domain by including a path.)
- The cookie will be available to every site with a `mydomain.com` address.
- There are no special security settings.

Once the cookie is set, you can retrieve cookie values through the `$_COOKIE` superglobal array variable. The value of the cookie set with the previous `setcookie()` function is available as `$_COOKIE['mycookie']`.

You can also set cookies that are accessible as arrays:

```
setcookie("mycookie[first]",
"dddd",time()+2592000,"/","192.168.1.1", 0);
setcookie("mycookie[second]",
"my_second_id",time()+2592000,"/","192.168.1.1", 0);
```

These two variables would be accessible as associative arrays within the `$_COOKIE` array.

The preceding code works fine on Internet Explorer 5 on the PC. However, it might not work on other browsers. In any case, you are probably better off avoiding situations that require arrays within cookies.

Sessions

PHP, like ASP and ColdFusion, natively supports sessions, only it does a much better job. What's a session? Basically, it's another means of maintaining state between pages. Your script declares that a session should start by accessing the $_SESSION superglobal variable (you can also use the older-style session_start() function). At that point PHP registers a unique session ID, and usually that ID is sent to the user via a cookie. PHP then creates a corresponding file on the server that can then keep track of any number of variables. The file has the same name as the session ID.

Once the session is created, you can register any number of variables. The values of these variables are kept in the file on the server. As long as the session cookie lives, these variables will be available to any page within the same domain that wishes to access them. This setup is much more convenient than sending variables from page to page through hidden form elements or bloated cookies.

Of course, it is possible that some users will not allow cookies. For this reason, PHP enables you to track the session ID through the querystring. You can do this manually by appending the session ID to the querystring, or by changing the session.use_cookies value in your php.ini file to equal 1.

The constant SID is predefined as "*session-name=session-ID*". To add it to the querystring manually, use <?php echo SID; ?>. This automatically prints out a string like this:

```
PHPSESSID=07d696c4fd787cd6c78b734fb4855520
```

Adding this value to a link will cause PHPSESSID to be passed via the querystring. Use something like this:

```
<a href="mypage.php?<?php echo SID; ?>">click to page</a>
```

The following script will register a session variable named my_var, and will assign it a value of "hello world".

```
<?
$_SESSION['my_var'] = "hello world";
?>
```

On subsequent pages, you are able to access this by simply referring to $_SESSION['my_var'].

It can take a little work with `if` statements to make your session variables properly accessible. Look at the short script in Listing 4-3 for an example.

Listing 4-3: Code Using Sessions

```
<?php

//check to see if $_SESSION['your name'] contains anything
if (!empty($_SESSION['your_name']))
{
    //this portion will run the first time to
    //this page.
    echo "I already know your name," ,  $_SESSION['your_name'];
}
else
{
   if (empty($_POST['submit']))
   {        echo "<form name=myform method=post action=$PHP_SELF>
        <input type=text name=first_name> first name<br>
        <input type=text name=last_name> last name<br>
        <input type=submit name=submit value=submit>
        </form>";


    }
    else
    {
       //if the form has been submitted, this portion will
       //run and make an assignment to $_SESSION['your_name'].
       $_SESSION['your_name'] = "$first_name $last_name";
       echo "Thank you, {$_SESSION['your_name']}";
    }
}
?>
```

After running this code, hit Refresh on your browser. You will see that the script remembers who you are.

If your script sends anything to the browser prior to setting a cookie — even so much as a blank line at the end of an included file — you will get error messages. So if you are setting cookies manually, or using cookies to store your session ID, you should make sure that either that part of your code is at the very top of your script file or use the output-buffering functions to keep your script from sending anything to the browser until you're ready.

Using Built-In Variables

A variety of variables are set by your server and PHP environment. You can find a complete list of these variables by running phpinfo(). If you haven't done it yet, go to your keyboard, run the following script:

```
<?php
phpinfo();
?>
```

This script delivers a page listing these variables.

It's a good idea to delete this page when you're done with it. No need to give crackers any more information than absolutely necessary.

You can use this variety of variables in a variety of ways. We'll take a look at some of these variables now, and show you where and when you might use them. Some variables come from the PHP engine, while others originate from your Web server.

PHP variables

Many of the most useful values supplied by PHP are available as keys of the $_SERVER superglobal.

$_SERVER['PHP_SELF']

The relative path of the script being run. This is very helpful when a form is both presented and processed in the same PHP page.

```
<?
if(isset($_POST['submit']))
{
  //do some form processing here
  echo "thanks for the submission";
} else {
?>
<form name="myform" method="POST" action="<?php echo  $PHP_SELF; ?>>
        <input type="text" name="first_name"> first name<br>
        <input type="text" name="last_name"> last name<br>
        <input type="submit name="submit" value="submit">
 </form>
```

```
<?
}
?>
```

Keep in mind that PHP_SELF always refers to the name of the script being executed in the URL. So in an include file, PHP_SELF will not refer to the file that has been included; it will refer to the script being run.

It's worth noting that PHP_SELF behaves strangely when PHP is run on Windows or as a CGI module. Make sure to look at phpinfo() to see the value of $PHP_SELF on your system.

$_SERVER['HTTP_HOST']

Returns the domain of the host serving the page.

$_SERVER['REMOTE_ADDR']

Returns the IP address of the host serving the domain.

$_SERVER['DOCUMENT_ROOT']

Returns the path of the document being accessed, relative to the root directory of the filesystem.

$_SERVER['REQUEST_URI']

Very similar to PHP_SELF, except that querystring information is maintained in this variable. So if you were visiting http://www.mydomain.com/info/products/index.php?id=6, $_SERVER['REQUEST_URI'] would equal /info/products/index.php?id=6.

See your phpinfo() page for a full list of PHP variables.

Apache variables

Apache keeps track of dozens of variables. We can't include a complete list of them here, as the variables you use will vary depending on your current setup. Here are some of the ones you might use frequently in your scripts.

As you look at this list and phpinfo(), keep in mind that if you are not getting what you want out of your Web server variables, you will need to make changes to your server configuration, not PHP. PHP just passes the information along and cannot alter these variables. There is also a fair amount of overlap between PHP and Apache variables. These are also available as keys of the $_SERVER array variable.

$_SERVER['DOCUMENT_ROOT']

Returns the full path to the root of your Web server. (For most Apache users this directory will be something like /path/to/htdocs.) We use this variable throughout the book to make our applications portable. Take this `include` statement as an example:

```
include("{$_SERVER['DOCUMENT_ROOT']}/book/functions/charset.php");
```

By using the `$_SERVER['DOCUMENT_ROOT']` variable instead of an absolute path, we can move the book directory and all its sub-folders to any other Apache server without worrying that the `include` statements will break. Keep in mind that if you are using a Web server other than Apache, `$_SERVER['DOCUMENT_ROOT']` may not be available.

If you set the `include_path` directive in your php.ini file, you will not need to worry about specifying any path in your `include` statement — PHP will look through all the directories you specify and try to find the file you indicate.

$_SERVER['HTTP_REFERER']

Contains the URL of the page the user viewed prior to the one he or she is currently viewing. Keep in mind when using `$_SERVER['HTTP_REFERER']` that not every page request has a referrer. If the user types the URL into a browser, or gets to your page via bookmarks, no referrer will be sent. This variable can be used to present customized information. If you had a relationship with another site and wished to serve up a special, customized header for only those referred from that domain, you might use a script like this:

```
//check if my user was referred from my_partners_domain.com
if(ereg ("http.*my_partners_domain.com.*" ,
$_SERVER['HTTP_REFERER']))
{
   include'fancy_header.php';
}else{
   include 'normal_header.php';
}
```

Keep in mind that `$_SERVER['HTTP_REFERER']` is notoriously unreliable. Different browsers serve up different `values` in certain situations. It is also easily spoofed. So you wouldn't want to use a script like the preceding to serve any secure information.

$_SERVER['HTTP_USER_AGENT']

Anyone who has built a Web page knows how important browser detection is. Some browsers will choke on fancy JavaScript, and others require very simple text. The `user_agent` string is your key to serving the right content to the right people. A typical `user_agent` string looks something like this:

```
Mozilla/4.0 (compatible; MSIE 5.01; Windows 98)
```

You can then parse this string to get what you are looking for.

You may be interested in PHP's `get_browser()` function. Theoretically, this function will determine the capabilities of your user's browser so you can find out if your script can safely serve out, for example, frames or JavaScript. The PHP manual has instructions for installation and use of `get_browser()`, but we do not recommend using it. Why? Using `get_browser()` you will be told that both Internet Explorer 5 for the PC and Netscape Navigator 4.01 for the Mac support CSS (Cascading Style Sheets) and JavaScript. But as anyone with client-side experience knows, writing DHTML that works on both of these browsers is a major task (and a major pain). The information you get from `get_browser()` can lead to a false sense of security. You're better off accessing `$_SERVER['HTTP_USER_AGENT']` and making decisions based on the specific browser and platform.

$_SERVER['REMOTE_ADDR']

The IP address of the user that sent the HTTP request. `$_SERVER['REMOTE_ADDR']` is easily spoofed and doesn't necessarily provide information unique to a user. You might want to use it for tracking, but it should not be used to enforce security. On some servers – notably the default Apache installation shipped with Mac OS X – this is available as `$_SERVER['HTTP_PC_REMOTE_ADDR']` instead.

$_SERVER['REMOTE_HOST']

The host machine sending the request. This has a value only if your server is configured to do reverse DNS lookups, something that is commonly turned off for performance reasons. When I dial it up through my ISP (`att.net`), `$_SERVER['REMOTE_HOST']` looks like this: `119.san-francisco-18-19rs.ca.dial-access.att.net`.

$_SERVER['SCRIPT_FILENAME']

Contains the filesystem's complete path to the file.

Other Web server variables

As mentioned earlier, `phpinfo()` is your friend. We developed applications for this book on Unix systems running Apache Web servers. But, as PHP runs on a variety of operating systems and Web servers and MySQL runs on Windows as well as Unix, you should be aware of the different variables associated with whatever Web server and operating system you're running.

You'll see that the files imported into in our applications via include statements make use of the DOCUMENT_ROOT Apache variable. If you were to attempt to move the application files to a server other than Apache on Windows, you would get an error in the include statements. The better choice when using Microsoft's Personal Web Server is the $APPL_PHYSICAL_PATH variable.

Testing Variables

At the start of this chapter, we showed that assigning data to a variable determines the variable type. The appearance of the variable gives no indication as to what the variable contains. If you see $var sitting in a script you'll have no idea if it contains a string, an integer, a floating-point number, or an array. In fact, many times in your scripts you won't be sure if the variable contains a value, or even if it exists at all. For all these reasons, you need to perform tests. The following sections describe the types of tests you can perform.

isset()

This function tests whether a variable has any value, including an empty string. It returns a value of either TRUE or FALSE. If the variable has not been initialized or has been set to NULL, isset() will return FALSE. In code snippets throughout this chapter we showed the use of isset() to test whether the script was encountering a submitted form.

If you wish to destroy a variable, use the unset() function.

empty()

The empty() function overlaps somewhat with the isset() function. It returns TRUE if a variable is not set, is an array with no elements, or has a value of "" (an empty string), 0, NULL, or FALSE. It is useful for, among other things, processing form data. If you want to determine if the user has put something in a text field, for example, you might try something like this:

```
if ($_POST["first_name"] == "")
{
  echo "Please enter your first name. It is a required field";
  exit;
}
```

However, PHP complains that first_name is an undefined index value. That's because if you leave a text field on a form blank, nothing is submitted by the form for that field. So no entry with the field's name exists in $_POST. But the empty() function enables you to check for things that aren't there:

```
if (empty($_POST['first_name']))
{
  echo "Please enter your first name. It is a required field";
  exit;
}
```

is_null()

Starting in version 4.2, PHP supports the `NULL` variable type. Most often you will be using `NULL` when examining data returned from a database.

is_int()

This function tests whether a variable is an integer. It has two synonyms: `is_integer()` and `is_long()`. You may need this function to troubleshoot a script when you're not sure whether a variable is an integer or a string containing numerals.

```
$a = "222";
$b = 22;
```

Given these two variable assignments, `is_int($a)` would test `FALSE` and `is_int($b)` would test `TRUE`.

is_double()

This function tests whether a variable is a floating-point (or double) number. It has two synonyms: `is_float()` and `is_real()`.

is_string()

This function tests whether a variable is a text string.

is_array()

This function tests whether a variable is an array. It is used frequently in the course of this book. A good example can be found in Chapter 6, in the discussion of the `implode()` function.

is_bool()

This function tests whether a variable is Boolean (contains either `TRUE` or `FALSE`). Note that the following examples are not Boolean:

```
$a = "TRUE";
$b = "FALSE";
```

In Chapter 6 you will see a variety of functions that return FALSE on failure. In these, FALSE is a Boolean value.

is_object()

Returns TRUE if the variable is an object. See Chapter 7 for a discussion of objects and object-oriented programming if you don't know what an object is.

is_resource()

Returns TRUE if the variable is a resource. An example of a resource variable is the connection value returned by mysql_connect().

is_scalar()

Returns TRUE if the variable is of any type other than array, object, or resource.

gettype()

This function will tell you the type of variable you have. It will return the expected values (string, double, integer, array, boolean, or resource), and it can also return types related to object-oriented programming (object). You can find more information on PHP object-oriented programming in Chapter 7.

Note that gettype() returns a string. So in the following example, the conditional would test as true and print "Yes":

```
$str = "I am a string";
$type = gettype($str);
if ($type == "string")
{
    echo "Yes";
}
```

Changing Variable Types

You can change the type of any variable in three ways.

Type casting

You can change the variable type by placing the name of the variable type you require in parentheses before the variable name:

```
$a = 1;
$b = (string) $a;
```

```
echo gettype($a), "<br>\n";
echo gettype($b), "<br>\n";
```

This code would print

```
integer
string
```

Using this method you can cast a variable as an array, a double, an integer, or, as in the preceding code, a string. Casting to type `object` is less reliable.

Using settype()

This function takes two arguments. The first is a variable name. The second specifies the variable type. The advantage of using this function over casting is that `settype()` will return a value of `FALSE` if the conversion fails, while there is no way to detect a failed casting. This function can take the same types as listed in type casting.

```
$a = 1;
settype($a, "string");
```

intval(), doubleval(), and stringval()

Finally, if you don't have enough ways to evaluate variable types, use one of these functions. They do not actually change the type of the variable, but return a value of the specified type. So in the following examples, you can be sure `$a` will be treated like an integer:

```
$a = "43";
$b = (intval($a) * 2);
```

Variable Variables

PHP includes variable variables, which, in the wrong hands, could be used to write the most incomprehensible code imaginable. Variable variables enable you to take the contents of a variable and use them as variable names. Two consecutive dollar signs let PHP know to take the value of the variable and use it as a variable name. The following creates a variable name `$foo` with a value of "bar":

```
$a = 'foo';
$$a = 'bar';
```

In the context of a database application, variable variables might be used to create a series of variables against which you compare other variables. In the following example, `$firstrow` is an associative array:

```
$firstrow = array ("firstname"=>"jay", "lastname"=>"greenspan");
foreach ($firstrow as $field => $value)
{
    $field = "first_{$field}";
    $$field = $value;
}
echo $first_firstname, " ", $first_lastname;
```

When your script runs through the `foreach` loop, the following variables would be created and printed:

```
$first_firstname = "jay"
$first_lastname = "greenspan"
```

Summary

If you read this chapter attentively (or even if you didn't) you should have a pretty good idea of how to work with PHP variables.

PHP does a better job than any scripting language of making variables easy to access and process. If you want to get a feel for how PHP variables are used, take a look at Chapter 8, which contains the first application in the book. There, many of the functions and concepts presented here are put to work. By flipping back and forth between this chapter and those scripts, you will see how variables are used and how scripts come together.

One very important point: This chapter did not discuss variable scope, which is an important topic. See Chapter 7 where we discuss functions, for an explanation of this topic.

Chapter 5

Control Structures

IN THIS CHAPTER

- Understanding the syntax of `if` statements
- Determining true and false values with PHP
- Learning PHP loops
- Choosing loops to use in your scripts

CONTROL STRUCTURES ARE the building blocks of programming languages. PHP has all the control structures needed to make a language work. If you're familiar with C or Perl, none of the features we discuss in this chapter should come as much of a surprise. However, if you're approaching PHP from a background in VBScript or Visual Basic, the syntax will probably be different from what you're used to. (If you aren't familiar with functions, you might want to peek ahead to the beginning of the next chapter for a quick overview – but come right back!) If you find the syntax to be a little heavy at first, stick with it. You might find that the extra brackets and parentheses actually help you write readable code.

The if Statement

The `if` statement is pretty much the cornerstone of all programming languages. In PHP, an `if` statement typically takes this basic form:

```
if (condition or set of conditions)
{
    actions to perform if condition is true.
}
```

After the word `if` is a set of parentheses. Within those parentheses is the single condition or set of conditions to be tested. If the condition is evaluated as being true, the code within the curly braces will execute. The following will test true and print "I'm True!" to a Web page.

```
<?php

$foo = 100;
$bar = 10;

if ($foo > $bar)
{
    echo "I'm True!";
}

?>
```

This is clear enough. But before we mention the complexities of the `if` statement, you should know how PHP determines whether a condition is true or false.

Determining true or false in PHP

The next section shows the operators commonly used in `if` statements. These are fairly easy to understand. In the preceding code example, 100 is greater than 10, so `($foo > $bar)` will test true. No problem. But there's a bit more to these tests in PHP.

The words *TRUE* and *FALSE* also carry the expected meanings.

```
if (TRUE)
{
    echo "Yup!"; //this will be printed
}
if (FALSE)
{
    echo "Nothing doing.";  //this will not be printed
}
```

But you're not limited to simple mathematical operators or the words *TRUE* and *FALSE* when you're testing for a true or false condition. As you can see in Chapter 4, you often test for the existence of a variable using `isset()` or `empty()`. These functions, like many others in PHP, return a value of `FALSE` if the condition is false, and a value of `TRUE` if the condition is true. If used as a simple value, `FALSE` converts to `0` and `TRUE` to `1`. For example, the following prints out "1":

```
$myvar = "I am setting a variable";
echo isset($myvar), "\n";
```

But though `FALSE` and `0` are equivalent (just as `0` and an empty string are equivalent) and `TRUE` and `1` are equivalent, they are not the same. You can see this using the built-in PHP function var_dump(), which shows you the internal representation of a value. If we use it with the previous example:

```
$myvar = "I am setting a variable";
var_dump(isset($myvar));
```

the output is now "bool(true)".

When you need to test if two values are not just equivalent, but identical, you use the === operator (or !== to test if the values are not identical). The following shows you what we mean:

```
$myvar = "I'm setting a variable again";
if (isset($myvar) == 1)
    echo "isset(\$myvar) is equivalent to 1\n";
if (isset($myvar) === 1)
    echo "isset(\$myvar) is exactly the same as 1\n";
if (isset($myvar) == TRUE)
    echo "isset(\$myvar) is equivalent to TRUE\n";
if (isset($myvar) === TRUE)
    echo "isset(\$myvar) is exactly the same as TRUE\n";
```

The output of this code is:

```
isset($myvar) is equivalent to 1
isset($myvar) is equivalent to TRUE
isset($myvar) is exactly the same as TRUE
```

It's not just 1 that is true – any non-zero, non-empty value tests as true (an array with no elements is empty, so it tests as false). This gives you some flexibility in your tests.

When working with Web pages, you'll usually be doing some sort of text manipulation. Often you'll need to test whether the text string you're working with has a certain structure. For example, you might want to test whether a string contains certain characters. You can use one of the regular expression functions for this, but you can also use the strstr() function. The strstr() function takes two arguments, both of them strings. It searches the first argument for the first occurrence of the string specified in the second argument. It returns the string in the second argument plus all of the characters following that string. However, if the string isn't found, the function will return a value of FALSE. In the following example strstr() returns "text string":

```
$str = "my little text string";
strstr($str, "text");
```

Since the result of this function is not empty and not 0 it can be used in a test. The following code would test `TRUE` and print out "Yeah!"

```
$str = "my little text string";
if (strstr($str, "text"))
{
    echo "Yeah!";
}
```

But in the string is not found in the following example, so the function will return a value of `FALSE` and nothing will print:

```
$str = "my little text string";
$new_str = strstr($str, "nothing");
if ($new_str)
{
    echo "nothing to print"; //this will not be printed
}
```

However, you need to be careful with these kinds of simple tests. For instance, using `strstr()` just to test if one string contains another is something of a waste of resources – it's handing you back a whole substring value that you don't need. So say you decide to use the `strpos()` function instead. This built-in function returns the position of one string within another, or `FALSE` if the string is not found. The problem is that the code we've used in the previous two examples can produce some odd results:

```
$str = "my little text string";
if (strpos($str, "text"))
{
    echo "Found 'text'\n";
}
else
{
    echo "Did not find 'text'\n";
}
if (strpos($str, "my"))
{
    echo "Found 'my'\n";
}
else
{
    echo "Did not find 'my'\n";
}
```

This produces the following output:

```
Found 'text'
Did not find 'my'
```

But we can see that `'my'` clearly is inside `'my little text string'`. What gives?

The problem is that in PHP, string positions start with `0`. The string `'my'` is at the beginning of `'my little text string'`, and so its position is `0`, which is what `strpos()` returns. Just testing for zero or non-zero values isn't good enough. We need to check explicitly for a return value of `FALSE`:

```
if (strpos($str, "my") !== FALSE)
{
    echo "Found 'my'\n";
}
else
{
    echo "Did not find 'my'\n";
}
```

This produces the correct result:

```
Found 'my'
```

You have to be careful to match your tests to the values you might be testing. Usually, that's just a matter of – surprise! – checking the documentation.

This is a good place to note that the functions you create in the course of your programming will often need to return a value indicating success or failure. You can make your functions do this by returning `TRUE` or `FALSE`.

Take a look at this example that looks for `http://` at the beginning of a string (a common task and one that illustrates the technique):

```
//tests whether a variable starts with "http://"
function url_test ($url)
{
    if (strtolower(substr($url,0,7)) == "http://")
    {
        return TRUE;    }
    else
    {
        return FALSE;    }
}
```

```
$myurl = "http://www.theonion.com";
if (url_test ($myurl))
{
    echo "Thanks for entering a valid URL.";
}
```

Comparison operators

Table 5-1 lists the relatively few comparison operators in PHP.

TABLE 5-1 PHP'S COMPARISON OPERATORS

Symbol	Operator	Description
== (2 equals signs)	Equal to	Determines if two quantities are equivalent.
=== (3 equals signs)	Identical to	Determines if two values have equivalent values and are of the same variable type.
!=	Not equal	Determines if two values are not equivalent.
!==	Not identical to	Determines if two values are not equivalent, or not of the same variable type.
>	Greater than	Determines if the value to the left of the symbol is greater than the one to the right.
<	Less than	Determines if the value to the left of the symbol is less than the one to the right.
>=	Greater than or equal to	Determines if the value to the left of the symbol is greater than or equal to the one on the right.
<=	Less than or equal to	Determines if the value to the left of the symbol is less than or equal to the one on the right.

Logical operators

In addition to comparison operators, you will be using logical operators in your scripts. Table 5-2 lists PHP's logical operators.

TABLE 5-2 PHP'S LOGICAL OPERATORS

Symbol	Example	Description
`and`	`if ($a ==0 and $b==1)`	Checks both conditions.
`&&`	`if ($a ==0 && $b==1)`	Same as the previous symbol, but has a higher precedence (see Note below).
`or`	`if ($a ==0 or $b ==1)`	Determines if one or the other operand meets the condition.
`||`	`if ($a ==0 || $b ==1)`	Same as the previous symbol, but has a higher precedence (see Note below).
`xor`	`if ($a ==0 xor $b==1)`	This is known as *exclusive or.* It determines if one of the two operands is true but not both. If both of these conditions are true, the overall test will be false.
`!`	`if (!empty($a))`	Determines if something is not the case. In this example the condition will be true if `$a` is not empty.

The difference between `&&` and `and`, and between `||` and `or`, is the order of precedence. PHP must determine which operators to compare first. It does this according to the list found at `http://php.net/operators`. Don't forget, though, that parentheses override the order of precedence. The contents of inner parentheses get evaluated before those of outer parentheses.

Complex if statements

Using the operators in Table 5-1 and 5-2, you can create `if` statements that are a bit more complex than the basic one at the beginning of this chapter.

Here are a few quick examples:

```
if ($var == 1 && $var2 <= 5 && !empty($var3))
{
    //do some stuff
}
```

Since this is a book dealing with MySQL databases, we'll show some examples of `if` statements you can use when playing with database queries.

To test if a `select` query returned any rows, you can use either of the following:

```
$query = "select * from my_table";
$result = mysql_query($query)or
    die(mysql_error());
if (mysql_num_rows($result) > 0)
{
    //do something here.
}


//this would also work
$query = "select * from test.foo";
$result=mysql_query($query);
if (!($row = mysql_fetch_assoc($result)))
{
    echo "there were no rows to fetch, so the query must have
returned no rows.";
}
```

The following tests if an update query actually changed anything. A similar construct would work for `delete` statements.

```
$query = "update mytable set col1='my text' where id = 1";
mysql_query($query) or
    die(mysql_error());
if (mysql_affected_rows() == 0)
{
    echo "query did nothing";
}
```

As is noted in Chapter 3, be careful to remember that the "equal to" operator is = in MySQL, but == in PHP. A common typo is to write `if ($a = $b) ...` in PHP. This assigns the value of `$b` to `$a`, and always tests as true, so it can be easy to miss.

if ... else statements

If you're clear on the previous sections, nothing here will surprise you. The `else` portion of an `if ... else` statement enables you to specify code that will be executed if the condition specified is false. The following code prints `"it is not equal"`:

```
$a = 2;
if ($a == 1)
{
    echo "it's equal";
}
else
{
    echo "it is not equal";
}
```

if ... elseif statements

You will often have to check a variable against more than one set of conditions. For instance, you might have a single page that will insert, edit, and delete records in a database. It is fairly typical to indicate which portion of the script you wish to run by assigning different values to a submit button in an HTML form. When the form is submitted, the value of the submit button can be checked against several `elseif` statements, as follows:

```
if ($_POST['submit'] == "edit")
{
    // code for editing database
}
elseif ($_POST['submit'] == "update")
{
    //code for updating records
}
elseif ($_POST['submit'] == "delete")
{
    //code for deleting records
}
else
{
    echo "I have no idea what I should be doing.";
}
```

elseif is technically not the same as else if. If you put that space between the words you will not get an error, but you could conceivably get different behavior. In practice, the two variations are equivalent.

switch ... case

The switch structure is an alternative to multiple if ... elses. It won't work for everything, but in some situations switch will help you remove some ugly syntax.

Choose a variable against which you wish to run a comparison. Continuing the example given in the discussion of if ... else, you may wish to execute different parts of a script based on the value passed by a submit button:

```
switch ($_POST['submit'])
{
    case "insert":
        // code to insert to database
        break;
    case "update":
        //code to update database
        break;
    case "display":
        //code to display
        break;
    default:
        echo "Unexpected value {$_POST['submit']} for 'submit'\n";
}
```

Here the code tests against the value in $_POST['submit']. If the variable is equal to "insert", that portion of code is run.

Note the use of break in the preceding code. If break is not included, the code will continue to run. For example, if $_POST['submit'] was equal to "update", the following would run the code for both the update and display portions:

```
switch ($_POST['submit'])
{
    case "insert":
        // code to insert to database
        break;
    case "update":
        //code to update database
    case "display":
```

```
        //code to display
        break;
}
```

Loops

No matter what programming language you've used in the past, you know that loops are an essential part of programming. PHP has a rich set of loops that should satisfy your every programming need.

while ...

This is probably the most common loop, so we'll discuss it first. You give the `while` loop a condition to validate. As long as that condition is true, the code within the curly braces will be executed.

```
while (condition)
{
    //code to execute here;
}
```

As a very basic example, the following code prints all the numbers between 0 and 10:

```
$a = 0;
while ($a<=10)
{
    echo "$a <br> \n";
    $a++;
}
```

For something a bit more practical, you will use a `while` loop to iterate through every row returned by a database query. Since `mysql_fetch_assoc()` will return false if there's no row to be fetched, it works quite nicely with a `while` loop.

```
$query = "select fname, lname from people";
$result = mysql_query($query) or
    die(mysql_error());
while ($row = mysql_fetch_assoc($result))
{
    echo $row["fname"] , " " , $row["lname"] , "<br> \n";
}
```

USING while WITH list() = each()

Another place while ... often comes into play is with arrays, when you are using the list() = each() structure. This structure assigns elements in an array to named variables. It will iterate through the array, and when no more elements are left to pull from, it will test false and the while loop will stop. When pulling from an array, list() is expecting an associative array and will take two variables: the first for the key and the second for the value, as illustrated in the following code:

```
$knicks = array (center => "Ewing", point => "Childs",
shooting_guard => "Houston",
forward => "Sprewell", strong_forward => "Johnson"
        );
echo "<h2>The Knicks 1999 Starting Five Were</h2>";
while (list($key,$value) = each ($knicks))
{
    echo "$key: $value <br>\n";
}
```

After you run the preceding code the array pointer will be at the end of the array. If you wish to loop through it again, you will have to move the pointer to the beginning of the array with reset. In the preceding example, reset($knicks) would work.

Note that if you don't have an associative array and you wish to grab array values, you will need to account for it in your list(). Do this by including a comma within the list parentheses, as follows:

```
$names = array("John", "Jacob", "Jason", "Josh");
while (list ( , $value) = each ($names))
{
    echo "$value <br> \n";
}
```

If no comma preceded $value in the preceding code, the ordinal placement of each element would be assigned to $value and the code would print "0, 1, 2, 3".

If you want to get only the keys out of an associative array, your list statement should contain something like list($key,).

Though we're stressing list's use with the each() statement, it can generally be thought of as an "array destructor." – that is, it pulls elements out of an array. Similarly, each() is an "array iterator," meaning that it walks through all the elements in an array. It doesn't need to be used with list(), though that is by far the most common usage.

USING MULTIPLE while LOOPS

Continuing with the subject of `while` loops and MySQL queries, you probably need a quick piece of code that prints out the results of any query. For this, you can use a nested set of `while` loops. The outer loop fetches each individual record from the database, and the inner one prints out the contents of each individual record:

```
while($row = mysql_fetch_assoc($result))
{
    while (list($key, $value) = each ($row))
    {
        echo "<b>$key:</b> $value <br>\n";
    }
}
```

do ... while

The `do ... while` loop is nearly identical to the `while` loop. The only difference is that the condition is tested after the code in question has been run once, as follows:

```
do
{
    //code to be used here.
} while (condition);
```

The preceding structure may be useful to you. It may even be vital to scripts you need to write. But in the course of writing the large applications for this book, we didn't need to use it once.

for

The `for` loop takes three expressions.

- The first is evaluated once before the second expression is tested.
- The second argument is a condition that is evaluated each time through the loop; if the condition in the second argument tests false, the loop ends (or never begins if it tests false right away).
- The third expression is executed after the body of the loop is run.

As an example, the following code iterates through every value in an array and prints the value for each element:

```
$myarray = array ('jay', 'brad', 'john', 'kristin');
for ($i = 0; $i < count($myarray); $i++)
{
```

```
    echo $myarray[$i] . "<br>\n";
}
```

The first time through, `$i` is assigned the value of 0, so the first element in the array will be printed. The next time and each subsequent time through, `$i` will be incremented by one. The loop will end as soon as `$i` is equal to the length of the array (which is 4). Remember that the elements in the array start at 0, so the last element in the above array is `$myarray[3]`.

You can also leave any of the three expressions in the `for` loop empty. If you leave the second expression empty, the `if` condition will evaluate to true, and you will need to make sure that your loop will eventually hit a `break` statement (we discuss `break` in the section "break" later in this chapter).

Running the following code would be very bad: It would run indefinitely, using up your memory and CPU. You'd have to kill the Web server to get this script to stop. It could bring your entire machine down.

```
for ($i = 0;; $i++)
{
    echo "$I <br>\n";
}
```

foreach

The `foreach` structure is used exclusively with arrays. You can use it in place of `list() = each()` on most occasions. This structure will work from the beginning to the end of an array, assigning each element to a scalar variable (a variable that has only one value, such as an integer or a Boolean value, as opposed to a multi-element array or complex object) that you indicate with the word `as`. The following prints all the values in the array `$names_array`:

```
$names_array = array("jay", "brad", "ernie", "bert");
foreach ($names_array as $first_name)
{
    echo $first_name;
}
```

If you are working with an associative array, you will likely need to access both the key and the value of every array element. The following syntax will enable you to do this:

```
$jay_info = array ("fname" => "jay", "lname" => "greenspan", "hobby"
=>"juggling");
```

```
foreach ($jay_info as $key => $value)
{
    echo "<b>$key:</b> $value <br>\n";
}
```

Unlike `list() = each()`, `foreach()` does not require you to reset the array afterwards. It works with a temporary copy of the array. Since it is also generally faster than `list() = each()`, it's preferable.

continue and break

Within loops you may need to either break out of the loop entirely or skip to the next item to be addressed in the loop. For these situations, you can use `continue` and `break`, respectively. Both `continue` and `break` can accept a numeric argument. The argument specifies how many levels of loop to break out of. This capability is rarely used.

continue

Consider a situation in which you're reading from the file system and would like your script to address each file in a specific directory, but have no need to address any subdirectories. When PHP reads names from the directory, you don't know if the item is a file or directory, so you need to run a test using the `is_dir()` function. You want to skip over listings that are directories. The script looks something like this:

```
$directory=opendir('/home/jay/');
echo "Files are:<br>\n";
while ($file = readdir($directory))
{
    if (is_dir($file)){continue;}

    echo "$file <br>\n";
    //process files here;
}
closedir($directory);
```

Note that `continue` isn't necessary here. You can also code this script as in the following example, and some feel this a better way of going about it:

```
$directory=opendir('/home/jay/');
echo "Files are:<br>\n";
while ($file = readdir($directory))
{
   if (!is_dir($file)){
```

```
            echo "$file <br>\n";
        }
    }
    closedir($directory);
```

break

`break` will release the script from a control structure without stopping the execution of a script. It is almost always best to avoid using `break`. `if` statements can usually accomplish the same thing and make for cleaner code.

A situation in which you might want to use `break` would be in response to an error inside your loop. In the following example, we loop through the rows returned by a MySQL query, calling one function to do some initial processing and then calling a second function to do something with the first function's results. If either of those two functions fail, we want to stop the process right there and not continue with the rest of the rows.

```
while ($row = mysql_fetch_assoc($result))
{
    $setup_result = setup($row);
    if ($setup_result === FALSE)
    {
        print "Error in calling 'setup()'\n";
        break;
    }
    $process_result = process($setup_result);
    if ($process_result === FALSE)
    {
        print "Error in calling 'process()'\n";
        break;
    }
}
```

Summary

In this chapter you saw the building blocks of the PHP language. You saw how to make use of loops and `if` blocks. If you read Chapter 4, where variables were discussed, you now know all the basics you need for programming with PHP.

Coding is all about working with variables, loops, and `if` blocks. The various combinations of these will take care of everything you will need to accomplish in your applications. However, one major portion remains to be learned: functions. Chapter 6 shows how PHP's built-in functions operate on your scripts.

Chapter 6

PHP's Built-in Functions

IN THIS CHAPTER

- Using PHP's built-in functions
- Function syntax
- Working with functions

PHP HAS AN AMAZING NUMBER of built-in functions and extensions (An 'extension' is a related collection of functions that are not part of the core PHP code). Many are available to you only if PHP is compiled with certain options. If, for example, you need to do some Extensible Markup Language (XML) parsing, PHP has two extensions that can help you. (One uses an event-based approach, the other a document approach.) If you need Lightweight Directory Access Protocol (LDAP), Internet Mail Access Protocol (IMAP), or Portable Document Format (PDF) functions, an extension is there for you. Additionally, PHP has an application program interface (API) for just about every relational database on the planet. But there's no need to cover most of these functions in this book.

Another thing to keep in mind is that the function set is changing almost daily. PHP is internally structured in a way that makes it extremely easy for programmers to add additional functions. In fact, if you know your way around C, you can probably add a new function to PHP in a few hours. So you can expect regular additions to the core function set.

Your best friend, as always, is the online PHP manual: `http://www.php.net/manual`. It's the only source of which you can be sure that the list of functions will be more or less up to date. If you want to go directly to the explanation of a function, all you need to do is point your browser to `http://www.php.net/function_name`.

We want to point out one more thing before we get started here. The final two portions of this book contain a number of applications. In the course of creating these applications, we made use of a little over 150 of PHP's built-in functions. So while thousands of built-in functions exist, you will probably make regular use of only a relatively small number.

A pretty neat resource is the function table at `http://www.zugeschaut-und-mitgebaut.de/php/`.

Function Basics

Functions all take the same basic form:

```
return_type function_name (argument1, argument2, argument3)
```

First, `return_type` is the type of output that the function returns when called: integer, Boolean, array, string, and so forth. These are called *return values*. Next is the function's name; note that the name of the function is not case-sensitive.

Finally, following the function name is a set of parentheses. Inside the parentheses are any arguments required by the function, separated by commas. While having any arguments at all is optional, the parentheses themselves are not. We will discuss arguments first, followed by return values, because that's the order in which the function deals with them.

Arguments

An argument is simply a value (or a reference to a value) that the function is expecting. A function might expect zero, one, two, three, or more arguments, and any of the arguments can be of any variable type – it may be a string, an integer, an array, or something else. To give you a better idea of what arguments are, here's an example: a function that does string handling.

The `str_replace()` function is extremely helpful. Suppose you have the following string:

```
$str = "My name is Jay.";
```

Say that in the `$str` variable you need to search for `Jay` and replace it with `John`. The function that does the replacement takes three arguments: the string to be searched through, the string to be searched for, and the replacement string. It so happens that in PHP, the arguments come in this order:

```
str_replace(string to search for, replacement string, string to be
searched through);
```

Or, to put it in practice:

```
$str = "My name is Jay.";
$new_str = str_replace("Jay", "John", $str);
```

Keep in mind that certain functions will have optional arguments and that a few will take no arguments at all. Take the `substr()` function, for example. This function takes a large string and extracts a smaller string from it by using index numbers that are provided as arguments. The letters in the original (larger) string are numbered (starting with 0 at the leftmost end), and the arguments refer to these numbers. To get everything from the second character in a string on, you would use the following code:

```
$str = substr ($str_var,1);
```

However, the `substr()` function also has an optional third argument, which you can use to limit the size of the string that it returns. A positive value counts forward from the position given in the second argument. A negative value counts backwards from the end of the string. So to get everything from the second character to the next-to-last character in a string, you would use the following code:

```
$new_str = substr ($str_var,1,-1);
```

We'll point out optional arguments as we move through the functions. The details of working with `substr()` will be covered later in the chapter.

On a few occasions a function will take no arguments at all. A good example is `time()`, which returns the current Unix timestamp. When this is the case, in the description of the function in the documentation, the keyword `void` will be used to explicitly tell you that the function takes no arguments:

```
int time ( void)
```

Return values

When using a function, you should always be aware of what the function will return – specifically, what variable type. In the previous case, `str_replace()` returns a string. What you do with this string is your business. You could assign it to a variable or print it out, or do whatever else seems appropriate. The following code echoes its output string:

```
//assign to variable
$new_str = str_replace("Jay", "John", $str);
//print directly
echo str_replace("Jay", "John", $str);
```

Note that functions can return arrays, integers, doubles (floating-point numbers), objects, floats (long floating-point values), or (sometimes) Boolean values. In Chapter 5 you saw a good example of a function that returns a Boolean value (that is, `TRUE` or `FALSE`). If you want to determine whether a variable is an array you can use the `is_array()` function, as in the following.

```
if (is_array($var))
{
    //process array
}
```

Some functions will return a value if there is a value to be returned, and will return FALSE if there is no value to be returned. A good example of this is the mysql_fetch_array() function. This function will grab rows from a result set returned by a query, as long as there are results to grab. When no more rows are to be had it returns FALSE. As you saw in Chapter 5, this is very helpful for looping through all rows returned by a query.

```
$result = mysql_query("select * from my_table") or
    die ( mysql_error() );
while($row = mysql_fetch_array($result))
{
 //process row
}
```

Finally, a function will occasionally return no value at all. This is rare, as most functions at least return TRUE on success and FALSE on failure. If a function does not return any value, the keyword 'void' again is used in the documentation to tell you so:

```
void function_name(arg1, arg2, ...)
```

Function Documentation

As we say repeatedly throughout this book, the PHP online manual is your friend. The documentation team is amazing, and we really believe that the quality of the online manual is one of the reasons for the success of the language. As we cannot realistically cover every PHP function in this book, you will need to consult the online manual or one of the excellent PHP encyclopedias that exist (try *PHP Functions: Essential Reference* by Zak Greant and others). For that reason, we want to take a minute to go over the way in which it presents the functions.

A typical manual reference will look something like this:

```
int mysql_affected_rows ([int link_identifier])
```

This function returns the number of rows affected by an update, insert, or delete query. Looking at this, you can see that the first portion (int) indicates the variable type that will be returned. This can be any of the variable types or void (meaning that the function will return nothing). Then comes a list of arguments in parentheses. The type of argument is listed as well as what it represents. Note that optional arguments are placed in brackets. In the preceding code sample, therefore, the function requires no arguments but has one optional argument: the connection identifier grabbed from `mysql_connect()`.

In the preceding example, if you pass an argument, it had better be an integer. If you were to use an array, for example, you would get an error.

Important PHP Functions

In this section we will attempt to break down PHP functions into logical groupings. Along the way we will cover the functions used in the applications presented in this book.

String handling functions

In creating Web-based applications, string handling and manipulation are among the most critical tasks of the language you work with. Text cleanup and validation are extremely important, and good Web middleware will make working with text relatively easy. PHP excels in this department: It contains built-in functions that cover most anything you'd want to do to text.

In fact, far more string handling functions exist than we could cover here. At the time this book was written, 88 string handling functions were listed on `http://www.php.net/manual/en/ref.strings.php`. In this book we can cover only a portion of these. We will cover all the string handling functions we used in the course of creating the applications in Parts III and IV, and we will cover some other notable functions that we didn't have the opportunity to use.

STRING FUNCTIONS USED IN THIS BOOK

We thought it would be nice to start with a function that clearly demonstrates why PHP is so cool.

STRIP_TAGS() This function removes HTML and PHP tags.

```
string strip_tags (string str [, string allowable_tags])
```

One of the most important things you will need to do with every Web-based application you write is make sure that the users of your Web pages haven't passed you malicious text. As we discuss in Chapter 8, if you're not careful, you might find your pages filled with HTML tags (`<img>`, `<div>`, and the like) or JavaScript code that you don't want. You could also find yourself in real trouble if some cracker decides to litter your form fields with something like `<script> alert("you stink");</script>`.

The `strip_tags()` function will remove all HTML and PHP tags, except for those explicitly allowed in the second argument. If you want to allow `<b>` and `<i>` tags, you can use this:

```
strip_tags($str, "<b><i>")
```

ADDSLASHES() This function is intended to work with your database `insert` and `update` queries.

```
string addslashes (string str)
```

If you take a look at a typical `insert` query you can see a potential problem:

```
insert into table_name(char_field, numeric_field)
values ('$str', $num);
```

What if the value in `$str` contains a contraction such as "ain't"? You could get an error because the apostrophe is going to confuse MySQL. You need to escape all occurrences of single quotes ('), double quotes ("), and `NULL`s in the string. For example:

```
$str1 = "let's see";
$str2 = "you know";
$str1 = addslashes($str1);
$result = mysql_query("insert into show_stuff
    (stuff_desc, stuff_stuff) values('$str1', '$str2')");
echo mysql_affected_rows();
```

So, given this potential problem, do you need to put all of your form-input information through `addslashes()`? Not necessarily. It depends on the `magic_quotes_gpc` setting in your php.ini file. If it is set to `on`, data that comes from HTTP `GET`, HTTP `POST`, or cookies is automatically escaped, so you don't need to worry about putting the information through `addslashes()`.

Make sure to check your `magic_quotes` settings in your php.ini file. Note that if set to `yes`, `magic_quotes_runtime` will automatically add slashes to data returned from queries and files. See Appendix Cfor more discussion on `magic_quotes` settings.

STRIPSLASHES() This function reverses the operation of `addslashes()`. It returns an unescaped string from which all backslashes have been removed.

```
string stripslashes (string str)
```

If you are writing code for distribution, where you won't be able to know how your user's PHP installation is configured, you might want to use `stripslashes()` and `addslashes()` in combination:

```
$var1 = $_GET['var1'];
$stripped_var = stripslashes($var1);
$slashed_var = addslashes($stripped_var);
$result = mysql_query("insert into mytable (mycol) values
('$slashed_var')");
```

This code runs regardless of the setting of `magic_quotes_gpc`.

The following sections contain some more PHP string functions that are used in this book.

HTMLENTITIES() AND HTMLSPECIALCHARS()

```
string htmlentities (string string [, int quote_style [, string charset]])
```

```
string htmlspecialchars (string string [, int quote_style [, string charset]])
```

These two functions translate characters into their HTML escape codes. `htmlspecialchars()` translates only the characters that might be interpreted as markup on an output page (namely &, <, >, ', and "), whereas `htmlentities()` translates every character that has an HTML equivalent.

CRYPT()

```
string crypt (string str [, string salt])
```

Given a string, this function returns a one-way hash of the string, using either the optionally provided salt or a randomly generated one. Providing your own salt allows reproducibility in testing and also allows you to specify the hashing algorithm that's used.

TRIM()

```
string trim (string str [, string charlist])
```

This function returns a string with all white space trimmed from the beginning and end. With the second argument, you can specify an additional list of characters to be trimmed off.

STR_REPEAT()

```
string str_repeat (string input, int multiplier)
```

This function returns a string consisting of the input string concatenated to itself the specified number of times.

STR_REPLACE()

```
mixed str_replace (mixed search, mixed replace, mixed subject)
```

Given three arguments as input, this function returns a string consisting of a modified version of the third argument with every instance of the first argument replaced by the second argument. This is a lightweight alternative to the regular expression functions and should be used when the power of regular expressions is not required.

STRCHR() AND STRSTR()

```
string strchr (string subject, string search)
```

```
string strstr (string subject, string search)
```

```
string stristr (string subject, string search)
```

These functions behave identically, except that `strchr()` and `strstr()` are case-sensitive and `stristr()` is case-insensitive. They search for the second argument in the first, and return the part of *`subject`* following the first instance of *`search`*.

STRLEN()

```
int strlen (string str)
```

Given a string, this function returns a character count.

STRPOS()

```
int strpos (string haystack, string needle [, int offset])
```

This function returns the position of the first occurrence of the string *needle* in the string *haystack*, starting at the position in *haystack* specified by *offset*, or at 0 (the beginning of the string) if *offset* is not specified. If *needle* is not found, the function returns `FALSE`.

STRRPOS()

```
int strrpos (string haystack, char needle)
```

This function behaves similarly to `strpos()`, but it returns the position of the *last* occurrence of the search character. Note that with this function the string to be found can only be a single character.

STRREV()

```
string strrev (string string)
```

This function reverses a string.

SUBSTR()

```
string substr (string string, int start [, int length])
```

This function returns a substring of the input string, delineated by the `start` and `length` arguments. If `length` is absent, the substring will go to the end of the string.

STRTOLOWER(), STRTOUPPER(), UCFIRST(), AND UCWORDS()

```
string strtolower (string str)
```

```
string strtoupper (string str)
```

```
string ucfirst (string str)
```

```
string ucwords (string str)
```

These functions change the capitalization of alphabetic strings. `strtolower()` and `strtoupper()` change the case of the entire string to lower or upper case, respectively; `ucfirst()` capitalizes only the first character of the input string; and `ucwords()` capitalizes the first character of each white space-delineated word in the string – to lower or upper case, respectively.

HELPFUL STRING FUNCTIONS NOT USED IN THIS BOOK

Just because we didn't use them doesn't mean you won't. And again, it's entirely possible that something we didn't cover will suit your needs perfectly. Please look over the PHP manual for a complete list.

NL2BR() This function adds an HTML break (`<br>`) after each newline (`\n`) in a string.

```
string nl2br (string string)
```

Note that the newline characters will remain after going through this function. For example, this code

```
$str = "jay
john
bob
stan";

echo nl2br($str);
```

will print the following (note that this is the HTML source of the resulting page):

```
jay
<br>
john
<br>
bob
<br>
stan
```

MD5() `md5()` is a one-way algorithm that encrypts information.

```
string md5 (string str)
```

This function is often used for passwords. If you were to put a password in a text file, it is possible that someone who had (legitimate) access to your system could view the passwords. However, if you pass it through `md5()`, the correct password is unknowable. For example, `md5("jay")` is `baba327d241746ee0829e7e88117d4d5`. If this is what is entered in the text file, those who have rights to view the database will not know what the clear text password is.

A safe password will be a lot more complex than `jay`. A cracker can (and will) run an entire dictionary through `md5()` to see if something allows entry to the system.

Regular expression functions

Regular expressions offer a method for complex pattern matching. If you're new to the concept of regular expressions, consider this: Given the string handling functions you have seen so far, how can you insert a newline and a break (`\n<br>`) after every 45 characters? Or, how can you find out if a string contains at least one uppercase letter? You may be able to pull it off, but it won't be pretty.

The following code will solve the problems posed by the previous two questions.

```
//insert \n<br> after each 45 characters
$new_str = ereg_replace("(.{45})", "\\1\n<br>", $str);

//check if string contains uppercase letter
if (ereg("[A-Z]", $str))
{
    echo "yes it does.";
}
```

Statements like these may seem a bit opaque at first, but after working with them for a while, you will grow to love the convenience they offer.

See Appendix G for a rundown on how regular expressions work.

Note that regular expressions are a good deal slower than string handling functions. So if you have, for example, a simple `replace` that doesn't require regular expressions, use `str_replace()` and not `ereg_replace()`.

REGULAR EXPRESSION FUNCTIONS USED IN THIS BOOK

The following regular-expression functions are used in the applications in this book.

EREG() `ereg()` tests whether a string contains a match for a regular expression.

```
int ereg (string pattern, string string [, array regs])
```

You can use this function in two ways. First, you can place a regular expression in the first argument and search for its existence in the second argument. The function will return `TRUE` or `FALSE`, depending on the outcome of the search. For example:

```
if ( ereg("^http://.*", $str) )
{
   echo "This is a URL";
}
```

Alternatively, the optional third argument is an array that is created from the regular expression. The portions of the regular expression that will become elements in the array are indicated by parentheses in the regular expression.

```
ereg("(....)-(..)-(..)", $publish_date, $date_array);
```

This example, which was taken from the content-management application in Chapter 11, creates an array named `$date_array`, wherein the first element will be the complete string matched by the regular expression. The next three elements in the array will be the portions indicated by the parentheses. So `$date_array[1]` will contain four characters, and `$date_array[2]` and `date_array[3]` will contain two characters each.

So, after running this code

```
$publish_date = "2000-10-02";
ereg("(....)-(..)-(..)", $publish_date, $date_array);
```

`$date_array` will contain the following:

```
[0] => 2000-10-02
[1] => 2000
[2] => 10
[3] => 02
```

Note that `ereg()` performs a case-sensitive match.

EREGI() This function is a case-insensitive version of `ereg()`.

```
int eregi (string pattern, string string [, array regs])
```

EREG_REPLACE() You can use this function for string replacement based on complex string patterns.

```
string ereg_replace (string pattern, string replacement, string
string)
```

For example, if you want to delete the querystring from a URL, you can use this:

```
$url= "http://www.mysqlphpapps.com/index.php?var=hello";
$parsed_url = ereg_replace("\?.*\$", "",$url);
echo $parsed_url;
```

The preceding code prints `http://www.mysqlphpapps.com/index.php`. This regular expression matches a question mark and all characters that occur after it until the end of the line. The question mark must be escaped with a backslash because it has a specific meaning to the regular expression (regular expressions are covered at `http://www.php.net/manual/en/ref.pcre.php`). Following the question mark the regular expression matches any number of characters until the dollar sign, which is the endline character. It needs to be escaped with a backslash because otherwise PHP will think it represents a variable.

Often you will need a bit more functionality than this. What if you want to preserve the string you are searching for in the replacement string? Or what if your search contains distinct portions offset by sets of parentheses? Here's a simple example. We want to replace the current querystring by placing an additional `name=value` pair between the two `name=value` pairs currently in the string. That is, we want to put `newvar=here` after `var=hello` and before `var2=yup`, as follows:

```
$url= "http://www.mysqlphpapps.com/index.php?var=hello&var2=yup";
$parsed_url = ereg_replace("(\?.*&)", "\\1newvar=here&",$url);
echo $parsed_url;
```

This creates the following string:

```
http://www.mysqlphpapps.com/index.php?var=hello&newvar=here&var2=yup
```

Here the single set of parentheses indicates portion 1. Then, by using the notation `\\1`, we can include that portion in the newly created string. If more than one portion is indicated by additional parentheses, you can echo the others back into the result by noting which portion you need.

```
$url= "this is a test ";
$parsed_url = ereg_replace("(this.*a).*(test)", "\\1 regular
expression \\2",$url);
echo $parsed_url;
```

The result of these commands is the phrase `this is a regular expression test`.

The regular expression matches everything between `this` and `test`. You can use parentheses to indicate a substring that starts with `this` and ends with the letter `a`. The next `.*` portion matches any number of characters. Finally, `test` is another substring. These substrings are echoed back in the second argument, with `\\1` echoing the first substring and `\\2` echoing the second substring.

The regular expression match is case-sensitive.

EREGI_REPLACE() This function is the same as `ereg_replace()`, except that the match is case-insensitive.

REGULAR EXPRESSION FUNCTION NOT USED IN THIS BOOK – sql_regcase()

This regular expression function, while not used in the examples in this book, is still useful to know.

`sql_regcase()` alters strings so that you can use them in case-insensitive regular expressions.

```
string sql_regcase (string string)
```

This might be of use if you are doing a regular-expression search in a database server that doesn't support case-insensitive regular expressions. It will save you from having to type in every character in a string as both an uppercase and a lowercase letter. For example:

```
echo sql_regcase("this string");
```

produces:

```
[Tt][Hh][Ii][Ss] [Ss][Tt][Rr][Ii][Nn][Gg]
```

PERL-COMPATIBLE REGULAR EXPRESSIONS (PCRE)

For years, the Perl programmers of the world have had regular expressions unlike any others. If you have some experience with Perl, it's likely that you've come to love the additional power these regular expressions give you. If you don't come from a Perl background, you might enjoy learning a bit about the features.

PCREs are, however, a fairly large topic, one that Appendix G explains only briefly. However, if you're looking to get a good jump on learning about Perl's regular expressions and how they can work for you, the information at `http://www.perldoc.com/perl5.8.0/pod/perlre.html` is a good read. You'll also find a decent description of Perl regular expressions in the PHP manual, at `http://www.php.net/manual/en/ref.pcre.php`.

The major reason for using PCRE functions is that they give you a choice between "greedy" and "non-greedy" matching. For a quick example, take the following string:

```
$str = "I want to match to here. But end up matching to here"
```

Using `ereg()` or `ereg_replace()` you have no way to match from `I` to the first occurrence of `here`. The following will not work as you might expect:

```
$str = "I want to match to here. But end up matching to here";
$new_str = ereg_replace("I.*here", "Where", $str);
echo $new_str;
```

This will print `Where` and nothing else. The entire string will be replaced. Using `ereg_replace()` you cannot indicate that you want to match to the first occurrence of `here`. However, using `preg_replace()`, you can do the following:

```
$str = "I want to match to here. But end up matching to here";
$new_str = preg_replace("/I.*?here/", "Where", $str);
echo $new_str;
```

In this instance, `.*?` means "match all characters until the first occurrence."

PCRE FUNCTIONS USED IN THIS BOOK

The following PCRE functions are used in the applications created in this book.

PREG_MATCH() This function is similar to the ereg() function in that you can assign the optional third argument an array of matched subpatterns, if any are found in the regular expression. preg_match returns the number of pattern matches found, or FALSE if no match is found.

```
int preg_match (string pattern, string subject [, array matches])
```

PREG_REPLACE() This function makes replacements based on Perl regular expressions.

```
mixed preg_replace (mixed pattern, mixed replacement, mixed subject
[, int limit])
```

preg_replace() is similar to ereg_replace(), though the pattern here must be a Perl regular expression. It can also make use of *digit* to echo the matched substring into the result. The optional fourth argument limits the number of replaces that preg_replace makes.

Consider the following example:

```
preg_replace("/(<br>| |[\s])*$/i","",$body);
```

Note that \s denotes all whitespace characters. This example will remove all occurrences of breaks (<br>), non-breaking spaces ($nbsp;), or white space (spaces, tabs, new lines) at the end of the string in $body. This replacement is not case-sensitive (the i flag determines that) to ensure that both <BR> and <br> are matched.

The parentheses indicate that you are specifying a pattern made up of several parts. The | character means *or* here; you want to match
 or   *or* any whitespace characters. The asterisk after the closing parenthesis indicates that you want to match any number of repeated occurrences of this pattern (for example, in

, the pattern occurs three times, and this expression would match all of them). The final dollar sign character represents the end of the string. By using it, you are saying that you want to match only occurrences of this pattern that are at the string's end, and not globally remove every whitespace character from $body, which would likely be a bad thing.

PREG_GREP()

```
array preg_grep (string pattern, array input)
```

Given a regular expression string and an array, this function returns an array containing only those elements of the input array that match the regular-expression pattern.

PREG_MATCH_ALL()

```
int preg_match_all (string pattern, string subject, array matches [,
int flags])
```

This function searches a string for matches to a regular-expression pattern. It places the matches it finds in the `matches` array.

Variable functions

PHP has a number of functions that deal directly with variables and constants. Some of these functions deal with the types of variables: These are covered in the next section.

is_array(), is_numeric(), and is_string()

```
bool is_array (mixed var)
```

```
bool is_numeric (mixed var)
```

```
bool is_string (mixed var)
```

These three Boolean functions test whether the given variable is of a particular type.

isset()

```
bool isset (mixed var [, mixed var [, ...]])
```

This useful function returns `TRUE` if every argument is an existing variable containing a non-null value, and `FALSE` otherwise.

unset()

```
void unset (mixed var [, mixed var [, ...]])
```

This function unsets the specified variable(s).

empty()

```
boolean empty (mixed var)
```

If a variable is undefined, an empty array, or equivalent to 0 (`0.00`, `FALSE`, an empty string, and so on); `empty()` returns `TRUE`. This code summarizes the behavior of the function:

```
$a = 0   ; print empty($a) ? "TRUE" : "FALSE"; //TRUE
$b = "0" ; print empty($b) ? "TRUE" : "FALSE"; //TRUE
$c = ""  ; print empty($c) ? "TRUE" : "FALSE"; //TRUE
$d = 1   ; print empty($d) ? "TRUE" : "FALSE"; //FALSE
print empty($e) ? "TRUE" : "FALSE"; //TRUE
$f= TRUE ; print empty($f) ? "TRUE" : "FALSE"; //FALSE
$g= FALSE; print empty($g) ? "TRUE" : "FALSE"; //TRUE
$h=array();print empty($h) ? "TRUE" : "FALSE"; //TRUE
```

floor()

```
float floor (float value)
```

Given a floating-point variable, `floor()` rounds down any fractional amount and returns the highest integer value less than or equal to the value of the variable.

constant()

```
mixed constant (string constantname)
```

This function simply returns the value of a defined constant.

define()

```
bool define (string name, mixed value [, bool case_insensitive])
```

This function defines a constant with a specified name and value. If the third argument is set to `TRUE` the constant will be defined as case-insensitive.

get_defined_constants()

```
array get_defined_constants (void)
```

This function returns an array containing the names and values of all the currently defined constants.

Type-conversion functions

This is a category of our own making. In the manual, these functions will fall under other headings. However, we feel that the specialized nature of these functions demands a unique category.

Chapter 4 discusses PHP variables in detail, including PHP's flexible variable typing. If you recall, if you need to evaluate a string as if it were an integer, you can make use of the `intval()` function. (See Chapter 4 for similar variable-conversion functions.)

But at times the variable conversion will be a bit more extreme, turning strings into arrays and arrays into strings. Why, you ask, might you want to do this? Consider a string like the following:

```
24,16,9,54,21,88,17
```

So you have this string of integers, maybe retrieved from a text file. How would you go about sorting it in ascending order? If you have to deal with it as a string the code is going to get very nasty. However, if you can make use of PHP's myriad of array functions, life gets quite a bit easier. You can simply use the `sort()` function. Take a look:

```
$str = "24,16,9,54,21,88,17";
//turn $str into an array
$array = explode(",", $str);
//sort the array in ascending order
sort($array, SORT_NUMERIC);
//turn the array back into a string and print
$new_str = implode(",", $array);
echo $new_str;
```

This will print the following:

```
9,16,17,21,24,54,88
```

More on the `sort()` function a bit later in the chapter.

TYPE CONVERSION FUNCTIONS USED IN THIS BOOK

The following type conversion functions are used in the examples in this book.

EXPLODE() This function transforms a string into an array.

```
array explode (string separator, string string [, int limit])
```

The first argument is the character or characters that separate the different elements. In the preceding example the string is separated by a comma. The second argument is the string you wish to break into an array.

The third argument limits the number of elements in the resulting array. If you use the following code

```
$str = "24,16,9,54,21,88,17";
//turn $str into an array
$my_array = explode(",", $str, 3);
```

`$my_array` will have three elements: `$my_array[0] => 24 $my_array[1] => 16 $my_array[2] => 9,54,21,88,17`. You can see that the last element contains what's left of the original string. If you want to sort only the first three elements in a string and discard the rest you might do this:

```
$str = "24,16,9,54,21,88,17";
//turn $str into an array
$array = explode(",", $str, 4);
unset($array[3]);
sort($array, SORT_NUMERIC);
echo implode(",", $array);
```

If the string separator does not exist, the entire string will be placed in array element zero. If the string does not exist, an empty string will be placed in the first element.

IMPLODE() As you might expect, `implode()` is the opposite of `explode()`: It turns an array into a string.

```
string implode (string glue, array pieces)
```

The first argument is the string that will separate the string elements. The second is the array to be separated.

A good example of where you might use `implode()` is a page that runs a SQL `delete` command. Suppose you have presented a series of checkboxes to indicate the rows you wish to delete from the database. You are probably going to want to pass the elements you wish to delete within an array. In the script that does the deletes, you can then run something like this:

```
//say $delete_items from an HTML page and
//contains (1,3,7)
if( is_array($delete_items) )
{
    $str = implode("," , $delete_items);
    $query = "delete from table where item_id in ($str)";
    mysql_query($query);
}
```

SPLIT() The `split()` function does the same thing as `explode()`, but it enables you to specify a regular expression as the separation string.

```
array split (string pattern, string string [, int limit])
```

The `split()` function can come into play if you want to separate a string based on more than one element. Say you have a string you need as an array, the elements of which can be separated by either a newline (\n) or a tab (\t). The following will do the trick:

```
//note there is a tab between 524 and 879
//and a tab between 879 and 321
$items = "524	879	321
444
221";
$array = split("[\n\t]", "$items");
```

`split()` is more flexible than `explode()`, but it's also slower.

PREG_SPLIT()

```
array preg_split (string pattern, string subject [, int limit [, int flags]])
```

This function works like `split()`, only it uses a Perl regular expression as the pattern.

Note that if the flag is `PREG_SPLIT_NO_EMPTY`, empty items will not be placed in the array.

Again, if `explode()` can do the same task, make sure to use it instead of `preg_split()` because `preg_split()` is slower.

To divide a sentence into its component words (splitting by white space), you can do the following:

```
$sentence = "Soup is good food."
$words = preg_split("\s", $sentence);
```

The content of `$words` will be as follows:

```
[0] => Soup
[1] => is
```

```
[2] => good
[3] => food.
```

`gettype()` and `settype()` can be used to directly change the type of variables.

GETTYPE()

```
string gettype (mixed var)
```

This function returns the type of a variable as a string: Boolean, string, array, integer, and so forth.

SETTYPE()

```
bool settype (mixed var, string type)
```

Given a variable as argument, this function sets the variable to the specified type: Boolean, integer, float, string, array, object, or null.

INTVAL() AND FLOATVAL()

```
int intval (mixed var [, int base])
```

```
float floatval (mixed var)
```

These two functions take any scalar variable and return an integer or a floating-point variable, respectively.

COMPACT() `compact()` and `extract()` are used to convert array elements into variables and vice versa, respectively.

```
array compact (mixed varname [, mixed ...])
```

Given a list of variable names (passed either as individual arguments or as an array), `compact()` outputs an array whose keys are the variable names and whose values are the respective values of those variables. Only variables whose values are set will be included in the output array.

EXTRACT()

```
int extract (array assoc_array [, int extract_type_constant [, string prefix]])
```

To pull key/value pairs from an array and make them into standalone variables, use `extract()`. The element key will become the name of the variable, and the element value will become the value of the variable. Therefore, this code

```
$array = array("name" => "Jay",
               "brand" => "Cohiba");
extract($array, "name");
echo $name;
```

will output this:

```
Jay
```

The *extract_type_constant* argument controls how namespace collisions are handled. The constant takes any of eight predefined values (see the PHP manual page on this at http://php.net/extract) such as EXTR_OVERWRITE and EXTR_SKIP. These dictate what the parser should do when it encounters collisions.

NUMBER_FORMAT()

string number_format (float *number* [, int *decimals* [, string *dec_point* , string *thousands_sep*]])

Given a floating-point number, this function returns a string formatted for human consumption, containing the number with thousands separators and a decimal separator. By default these are a comma and a dot, respectively, but other symbols can be specified.

JOIN()

string join (string *glue*, array *pieces*)

Given an array and a string, join() returns a string comprised of the elements of the array concatenated in order, with the *glue* string between each two elements.

join() is identical to the implode() function.

RANGE()

array range (mixed *from*, mixed *to* [, int *increment*])

This function creates an array and automatically populates it with elements ranging from from to to. If a step increment is specified in the third argument, that will be the increment between elements; otherwise the increment will be one.

TYPE CONVERSION FUNCTIONS NOT USED IN THIS BOOK

In addition to the functions in the previous section, you can make use of `spliti()`, which uses a case-insensitive pattern match. Other than the case-insensitivity with respect to alphabetic characters, `spliti()` works just like `split()`. Consider these:

```
$audienceResponse1 = "oooooAAAooooh";
$audienceResponse2 = "oooooaaaooooh";
list ($part1, $part2)  = split('[AAA]', $audienceResponse1);
list ($part3, $part4)  = spliti('[aaa]', $audienceResponse2);
```

As a result of that, `$part1` and `$part3` contain `ooooo`, while `$part2` and `$part4` contain `ooooh`.

Array functions

We are big fans of the array functions available in PHP. Just about anything you'd like to do to an array you can do with a built-in function. The developers of PHP have done a good job of making sure you don't have to loop though arrays very frequently, if ever.

The PHP manual lists exactly 60 array functions as of this writing. It's likely that by the time you read this chapter, there will be several more. So make sure you scan the manual to see the full range of available array functions.

See Chapter 5 for a discussion of how to create, add to, and walk through an array.

ARRAY FUNCTIONS USED IN THIS BOOK

Here's a rundown of the array functions we use in this book.

ARRAY_FLIP() This function, which is useful with associative arrays, exchanges keys and values. That is, the keys become the values and the values become the keys.

```
array array_flip (array trans)
```

We use this function once in the course of the book, in the following code:

```
$trans = array_flip(get_html_translation_table(HTML_ENTITIES));
$title = strtr($title, $trans);
```

Before the array_flip() function, the array holds many elements. Here are a couple of examples:

```
[(c)] => &copy
[(r)] => &reg
```

Once the array is flipped, these entries will look like this:

```
[$copy] => (c)
[&reg] => (r)
```

Then strtr() replaces each value with its key. So in the end this code will make sure that any character that needs to be represented by an HTML entity will be.

Note that if an array has two keys with identical values before being flipped, only one can survive in the flipped array. You can't have two array elements with same key. If conflict arises, the element in the position with the highest index value will be maintained.

ARRAY_MERGE() As you can probably guess, this function merges, or concatenates, two or more arrays.

```
array array_merge (array array1, array array2 [, array ...])
```

If two or more of the arrays contain the same associative keys, the elements with the highest index values will be preserved.

ARRAY_SPLICE() This function takes the array indicated in the first argument and removes all elements following the offset specified in the second argument. It can then insert additional elements.

```
array array_splice (array input, int offset [, int length [, array
replacement]])
```

If the offset is a positive number, the elements will be counted from the left; if the offset is a negative number, all items to the left of the indicated number will be deleted. The optional third argument can indicate how many elements after the offset you wish to delete. For example, this code

```
$knicks_array = array ("Childs", "Sprewell", "Ewing",
"Johnson","Houston");
array_splice($knicks_array, 2,1);
```

will remove elements starting at offset 2 and remove only one element. So Ewing will be deleted from this array. array_splice() also gives you the ability to replace the deleted portion with another array. So, to account for trades, you can do this:

```
$knicks_array = array("Childs", "Sprewell", "Ewing",
"Johnson","Houston");
$new_knicks = array("Longley","Rice");

array_splice($knicks_array, 2,1,$new_knicks);
```

Following this code, `$knicks_array` will contain six elements: `Childs`, `Sprewell`, `Longley`, `Rice`, `Johnson`, `Houston`.

Note that the value returned by this function is an array of the deleted items. In the code that follows, `$traded_knicks` will be an array with one element, `Ewing`:

```
$knicks_array = array("Childs", "Sprewell", "Ewing",
"Johnson","Houston");
$traded_knicks = array_splice($knicks_array, 2,1);
```

COUNT() This function returns the number of elements in an array, and is frequently used with loops.

```
int count (mixed var)
```

For example:

```
$array = array(1,2,3,4,5);
$len = count($array);
for ($i=0; $i < $len; $i++)
{
   echo $array[$i] . "<br>\n";
}
```

Note that `sizeof()` is a synonym for `count()`.

ARRAY_FILTER()

```
array array_filter (array input, callback function)
```

This function returns a new array consisting of only those elements of the input array that pass through a filtering function.

Here is a simple code snippet illustrating how the function can be used:

```
function test_score($var) {
       global $score;
       return ($var > $score);
}
$winners = array_filter($players, "test_score");
```

To illustrate the behavior of that function, imagine that `$players` initially contained this list:

```
45, 35, 21, 8, 17, 12, 10
```

Further imagine that the global variable `$score` held `10`. At the end of the code snippet just illustrated, `$winners` would contain this:

```
45, 35, 21, 17, 12
```

ARRAY_KEY_EXISTS()

```
bool array_key_exists (mixed key, array search)
```

This function takes a key name and an array as arguments, and returns a Boolean value indicating whether the key exists in the array.

ARRAY_KEYS()

```
array array_keys (array input [, mixed value])
```

With only one argument, this function returns all the keys of an array. If it is given a value as a second argument, it returns all keys with that value.

ARRAY_MAP()

```
array array_map (mixed function, array array1 [, array array2...])
```

This function takes an array and a function as arguments, and passes each element of the array to the function. It returns an array consisting of the return values generated by the called function for each element, in the original order. So, given

```
function halve($var) {
     return $var / 2 ;
}
$half = array_map("halve", array(16, 8772, 566, 100));
```

now `$half` contains:

```
Array
(
    [0] => 8
    [1] => 4386
    [2] => 283
    [3] => 50
)
```

Note that the called function must not modify the array itself.

ARRAY_DIFF() If given two arrays, this function will return all the elements that are in the first array but not in the second array.

```
array array_diff (array array1, array array2 [, array ...])
```

For example:

```
$knicks = array("sprewell", "houston", "ewing", "childs");
$all_stars = array("mourning", "houston", "carter", "davis",
"miller");
$non_knick_allstars = array_diff($all_stars, $knicks);
```

Note that in the returned array, the elements maintain the keys they had in the array from which they were taken. So, after this code is run, `$non_knick_allstars` will contain the following:

```
[0] => mourning, [2] => carter, [3] => davis, [4] => miller
```

Additional arrays can be added to the function. For example:

```
$knicks = array("sprewell", "houston", "ewing", "childs");
$all_stars = array("mourning", "houston", "carter", "davis",
"miller");
$non_knick_allstars = array_diff($all_stars, $knicks,
array("carter"));
```

Given this, `carter` will also be removed from the returned array.

ARRAY_INTERSECT() This function returns the array elements that two (or more) arrays have in common.

```
array array_intersect (array array1, array array2 [, array ...])
```

IN_ARRAY() This very convenient function will search all the values of an array and return `TRUE` if the value in the first argument is found in the array in the second argument.

```
bool in_array (mixed needle, array haystack)
```

ARRAY_KEY_EXISTS()

```
bool array_key_exists ( mixed key, array search )
```

This function returns TRUE if the key value key exists in the array search. The difference between this function and isset($array['key']) is that if $array['key'] has a value of NULL, isset($array['key']) returns FALSE, while array_key_exists() returns TRUE.

ARRAY_POP() The array_pop() function returns the last element in an array, and removes that element from the original array.

```
mixed array_pop (array array)
```

For example:

```
$array = array(1,2,3,4,5);
$int = array_pop($array);
```

After this runs, $array will contain (1,2,3,4) and $int will contain 5.

ARRAY_PUSH() This function adds elements to the end of the array indicated in the first argument.

```
array_push (array array, mixed var [, mixed ...])
```

The additional arguments will be values you wish to tack onto the array:

```
$array = array (1,2,3);
array_push($array,4,5,6);
```

The resulting array will contain 1,2,3,4,5,6.

ARRAY_SHIFT()

```
mixed array_shift (array array)
```

This function works identically to array_pop(), except that it takes the first element instead of the last.

ARRAY_UNSHIFT()

```
array_unshift(array array, mixed var [, mixed ...])
```

This function works identically to array_push(), except that it adds new elements to the beginning instead of the end of the array.

ARRAY_VALUES()

```
array array_values(array input)
```

Given an input array, array_values() returns all the values from the array. Note that it does not return key names; instead, it outputs numbered values. The following is an example output:

```
Array
(
    [0] => Jay
    [1] => 5.4
    [2] => blue
)
```

ARRAY_WALK()

```
array array_walk (array array, callback function, [mixed data])
```

This function takes an array and a function as arguments and passes each element of the array through the function. It returns an array containing all transformed elements, in the original order.

So if you have defined a function altupper, which modifies the case of strings in an annoying way, then, given

```
$alternating_uppercase = array_walk(array('blue', 'red', 'pink',
'yellow'), "altupper");
```

$alternating_uppercase will contain the following:

```
[0] => bLuE
[1] => rEd
[2] => pInK
[3] => yElLoW
```

Note that the called function must not modify the array itself.

EACH()

```
array each (array array)
```

This function returns the key/value pair at the current location of the array cursor (the logical pointer that indicates which element of the array is being examined) and advances the cursor one element.

RESET()

```
mixed reset (array array)
```

This function resets the cursor of an array to the beginning, and returns the value of the array's first element.

ARRAY FUNCTIONS NOT USED IN THIS BOOK

Again, PHP contains many great array functions. Here are some of the highlights (from our point of view, anyway).

ARRAY_COUNT_VALUES() This nifty function will return an associative array, the keys of which will be all of the unique values within the array.

```
array array_count_values (array input)
```

The values of the resulting array will be an integer representing the number of times the value appears within the array:

```
$array = array("yes","no","no","yes","why");
$result = array_count_values($array);
```

After this `$result` will contain:

```
[yes] =>, 2, [no] => 2, [why] => 1
```

ARRAY_RAND() This function will pick one or more random elements from an array.

```
mixed array_rand (array input [, int num_req])
```

Note that `array_rand()` does not pick the value; rather, it picks the key of the chosen elements. For example:

```
srand ((double) microtime() * 1000000);
$names = array("jay", "brad", "john", "Jeff");
$rand_keys = array_rand ($names, 2);
```

In this example, `$rand_keys` will contain an array with two numbers. To get the values from the `$names` array, you will first need to get to the key value extracted by `array_rand()`, and so you will need to use something like this:

```
echo $names[$rand_keys[0]];
```

Seed the random number generator only once per script. You might even want to think about using a shared variable so that you can seed the generator only once, period, to deal with a problem that's beginning to appear more frequently as processors get faster. If processor speed continues to increase and transaction volume increases, there is a ceiling to reach at which point the random numbers stop being random because your `microtime()` value is the same in two consecutive calls.

SHUFFLE() This function randomizes the elements in an array.

```
void shuffle (array array)
```

You will need to seed the random number generator before using it. For instance:

```
srand ((double) microtime() * 1000000)
shuffle ($array);
```

SORT() If no second argument is given, this function will sort an array in ascending or alphabetical order.

```
void sort (array array [, int sort_flags])
```

The flags can be of two kinds:

- `SORT_NUMERIC` – Compare items numerically
- `SORT_STRING` – Compare items as strings

If the array you wish to sort contains only numbers, PHP will sort it numerically; if the array contains only strings, it will be sorted alphabetically. If the array contains both strings and numbers, it defaults to sorting by a string.

PHP offers many other ways to sort arrays. Please look at the manual entries for `arsort()`, `ksort()`, `rsort()`, and `usort()`.

Object/class functions

PHP has a number of functions concerned with classes (which are templates from which objects are created) and objects themselves. The examples in this book use a few functions that retrieve information about the defined objects, classes, and methods. Here they are.

is_a()

Use this function to determine whether a given object is an instance of a given class or an instance of a class descended from the given class. Specify the object in the first argument and the class name in the second; the function will return `TRUE` if the one is an instance of the other.

```
bool is_a (object object, string class_name)
```

is_object()

This function, much like the other `is_` functions, returns `TRUE` if the argument is an object, and `FALSE` otherwise.

```
bool is_object (mixed var)
```

get_class()

Given an object, this function returns the name of the class of which the object is an instance.

```
string get_class (object obj)
```

get_object_vars()

Given an object, this function returns an associative array containing the object's current properties.

```
array get_object_vars (object obj)
```

method_exists()

Given an object and a method name, this function returns `TRUE` if the method (function) is defined for the object.

```
bool method_exists (object object, string method_name)
```

Print functions

Several functions enable you to print information to the screen. Only two pop up in this book, but you should be aware of all the functions listed in this section.

PRINT FUNCTIONS USED IN THIS BOOK

In this case the word "functions" may be something of a misnomer. For instance, `print()` is probably better described as a language construct. (The useful difference is that you are not required to use parentheses around the arguments.) In any case, you will use all of these very much as you will use functions; thus, they are included here.

PRINT() As you would expect, this prints what you specify.

```
void print ( string str )
```

ECHO() This also isn't a function, but a language construct. We use it constantly throughout this book, so at this point you probably know what it does.

```
void echo ( string str1 [, string strN ...] )
```

Keep in mind that you can mix variables and literal strings within double quotes:

```
$var = "this string";
echo "Please print $var";
```

This will print `Please print this string.`

However, within single quotes the string will be treated literally:

```
$var = "this string";
echo 'Please print $var';
```

The preceding code will print `Please print $var`. The concept of mixing variable names and string literals is discussed in greater detail in Chapter 4.

`print` versus `echo`. Which should you use? This is very much a matter of personal preference: Use whichever you think looks better in your script. There's only one major difference between the two, and this may influence your decision. `echo` can take multiple arguments. That is, with `echo`, different portions can be separated by commas. This will work:

```
echo "this is part 1", "this is part 2";
```

But this will not:

```
print "this is part 1", "this is part 2";
```

PRINT FUNCTIONS NOT USED IN THIS BOOK

They didn't come up here, but these are really important to know about.

SPRINTF()

```
string sprintf (string format [, mixed args])
```

This function can be used to output a string formatted according to a specified C-style pattern. The parameters of the pattern are covered in detail in the online PHP documentation (http://www.php.net/sprintf).

PRINT_R() This function is great for putting to productive use the time you'd otherwise spend pulling your hair out. It prints the entire contents of any variable – most notably arrays and objects – to the screen.

```
void print_r (mixed expression)
```

It is invaluable for debugging. We use it frequently when we're not getting the results we expect from arrays or objects.

Do not do `print_r($GLOBALS)`. You will create a very large output.

VAR_DUMP() This function behaves like `print_r`, but gives you a bit more information.

```
void var_dump (mixed expression)
```

In addition to printing out the contents of a variable, it includes the data type – including the data type for each element in an array or object. The same caution given for `print_r()` applies to `var_dump()`.

Date/time functions

Dealing with PHP and MySQL as a team, you will have to get to know two sets of date/time functions – and they are quite different. See Appendix J for detailed coverage of MySQL's time and date functions.

DATE/TIME FUNCTIONS USED IN THIS BOOK

The following are some date/time functions used in the applications in this book.

DATE() You can use this function and the indicators outlined next to return the date and time.

```
string date (string format [, int timestamp])
```

If you include a second argument, that time/date value will be formatted as you prescribe. Otherwise, the current time and date will be used.

The time and date the functions return are based on the time on the server. You will need to make use of JavaScript to get an idea of the time on the client's computer.

Often the second argument will be a product of the `mktime()` function, which we discuss next.

You can format the date using any of the indicators in Table 6-1.

TABLE 6-1 INDICATORS FOR THE date() FUNCTION

Indicator	Meaning
a	am or pm
A	AM or PM
B	Swatch Internet time
d	Day of the month, two digits with leading zeros; 01 to 31
D	Day of the week, textual, three letters; for example, Fri
F	Month, textual, long; for example, January
g	Hour, 12-hour format without leading zeros; 1 to 12
G	Hour, 24-hour format without leading zeros; 0 to 23
h	Hour, 12-hour format; 01 to 12
H	Hour, 24-hour format; 00 to 23
i	Minutes; 00 to 59
I [capital *i*]	1 if Daylight Savings Time, 0 otherwise
j	Day of the month without leading zeros; 1 to 31

Continued

Table 6-1 INDICATORS FOR THE date() FUNCTION *(Continued)*

Indicator	Meaning
l (lowercase *l*)	Day of the week, textual, long; for example, Friday
L	Boolean for whether it is a leap year; 0 or 1
m	Month; 01 to 12
M	Month, textual, three letters; for example, Jan
n	Month without leading zeros; 1 to 12
s	Seconds; 00 to 59
S	English ordinal suffix, textual, two characters; for example, th, nd
t	Number of days in the given month; 28 to 31
T	Time-zone setting of this machine; for example, MDT
U	Seconds since the epoch (midnight, January 1, 1970)
w	Day of the week, numeric; 0 (Sunday) to 6 (Saturday)
Y	Year, four digits; for example, 1999
y	Year, two digits; for example, 99
z	Day of the year; 0 to 365
Z	Time-zone offset in seconds; -43200 to 43200

For example, if you want to print the date in the format, `June 5, 2003 4:22 pm`, this would do the trick:

```
echo date("F d, Y g:i a");
```

MKTIME() This function is most useful for calculating valid dates.

```
int mktime (int hour, int minute, int second, int month, int day,
int year [, int is_dst])
```

For example, say you have a form that collects a date – maybe the current month, day, and year. You want to calculate and set a due date exactly 30 days from the date submitted.

```
$year = 2003;
$month = 5;
$day = 24;
echo date("l F d, Y", mktime(0,0,0,$month,$day+30, $year) );
```

This will output 30 days from May 24, 2000, and will print out `Friday June 23, 2000`.

Keep in mind that this function enables you to add or subtract dates without worrying that PHP will return a fictitious result. In the previous example, you could subtract six from the month value of `5`, and PHP would return a meaningful date. You can add or subtract any number of years, months, or days without worrying that PHP will return a bad result. For instance, the following is a perfectly acceptable way to get date information about the last day of 1999:

```
$year = 2000;
$month = 1;
$day = 1;
echo date("l F d, Y", mktime(0,0,0,$month,$day-1, $year) );
```

This code will let you know that December 31, 1999 was a Friday.

Notice that the preceding code first calculates the timestamp of the date indicated by `mktime()` and then prints that out using the date function.

If you exclude arguments from the right, those parameters will be retrieved from the current timestamp. So, to print what the date and time will be in five hours, this will do the trick:

```
echo date("l F d, Y g:i a", mktime( date('H')+5) );
```

Note the nesting of functions here. Starting at the innermost function, `date('H')` returns the current hour, in 24-hour format. Then five is added to that, and the timestamp is calculated for five hours in the future. The timestamp is then formatted using the string indicated.

TIME() This function returns the current time measured in the number of seconds since the Unix Epoch. The Unix Epoch is the beginning of time in Unix terms – the time with timestamp 0. It's arbitrarily defined as January 1 1970 00:00:00 GMT.

```
int time(void);
```

MICROTIME() This function returns the string *`msec sec`* where *`sec`* is the current time measured in the number of seconds since the Unix Epoch (0:00:00 January 1, 1970 GMT), and *`msec`* is the microseconds part.

```
string microtime(void);
```

This function is only available on operating systems that support the `gettimeofday()` system call.

The returned string will look something like `0.12082400 969034581`. You can be reasonably sure that this function will never return the same number twice. It is often used to seed the random number generator.

DATE/TIME FUNCTIONS NOT USED IN THIS BOOK

A few other time/date functions may prove useful to you. They include several for printing the current date and time. If you need to know about something specific that isn't discussed here, take a look at the manual: `http://www.php.net/manual/ref.datetime.html`.

File-system functions

PHP has a whole range of functions that enable you to manipulate files and directories on the host computer. In the course of creating applications for this book, we encountered only one instance in which files needed to be written to or taken from the file system: in the Catalog and Shopping Cart applications, when we needed to provide the user with the ability to store images that have been uploaded. But if you work with PHP frequently there's little doubt that you will need to become familiar with these functions. By way of introduction, we will say that the directory and file-system functions in PHP are simply terrific. The PHP developers have really done a great job of making working with files, either on the local system or elsewhere on the Internet, a piece of cake. Just to give a quick example, it took about two minutes to write the following script, which will grab a stock quote from a site we will not specify for legal reasons.

```
$farray = file("http://domain.com/stockquote?symbols=ORCL", "r");
foreach ($farray as $value)
{
        if( ereg("last:.*$", $value) )
        {
                $value = strip_tags($value);
                break;
        }

}
```

This brief script slurps up an entire page and assigns each line to an element in the `$farray`. We then loop through the array looking for the string `last`. On the site we played with, the word "last" indicates the most recent quote. All we had to do was strip the HTML tags, and we had all the information we needed. If we had wanted to, we could have done some more string processing to format the information in a way we liked.

FILE SYSTEM FUNCTIONS USED IN THIS BOOK

If you would like to see these in use, check out Chapters 12 and 14.

FOPEN() This function opens a file pointer to the indicated file or URL in the first argument. (The pointer is very much like the result identifier returned by `mysql_connect()`.)

```
int fopen (string filename, string mode [, int use_include_path])
```

The mode determines what you can do with the file. Table 6-2 shows the available modes.

TABLE 6-2 MODES FOR THE fopen() FUNCTION

Mode	Meaning
r	Open for reading only; place the file pointer at the beginning of the file.
r+	Open for reading and writing; place the file pointer at the beginning of the file.
w	Open for writing only; place the file pointer at the beginning of the file and truncate the file to zero length. If the file does not exist, attempt to create it.
w+	Open for reading and writing; place the file pointer at the beginning of the file and truncate the file to zero length. If the file does not exist, attempt to create it.
a	Open for writing only; place the file pointer at the end of the file. If the file does not exist, attempt to create it.
a+	Open for reading and writing; place the file pointer at the end of the file. If the file does not exist, attempt to create it.

Note that this function returns a resource identifier. If you wish to read from or write to a file you will need to do something like this:

```
//open a file and read contents into a variable
$filename="test99.txt";
$fp = fopen($filename, "r+") or
    die("could not open $filename");
$contents = fread ($fp, filesize($filename));
//replace all occurrences of Jayson
$new_contents = str_replace("Jayson", "Jay", $contents);
//write out new file contents.
```

```
rewind($fp);
fwrite($fp, $new_contents);
//ftruncate assures there won't be extra
//characters if the resulting file is shorter
//than the original.
ftruncate($fp,ftell($fp));
fclose($fp);
```

FCLOSE() This function closes the pointer to a file.

```
int fclose (int fp)
```

It is good form to use it when you are done with a file. If you don't, PHP will do it for you, just like `mysql_close()`.

FWRITE()

```
int fwrite (int fp, string string [, int length])
```

`fwrite()` writes the value of the string argument to the file indicated by the file pointer. The function returns a value of `-1` if an error is encountered; otherwise it returns the number of bytes it wrote successfully.

FREAD()

```
string fread (int fp, int length)
```

`fread()` reads from the file pointer given in the first argument the number of bytes given in the second argument, or until the end of the file, whichever comes first.

FEOF() This function tests whether a file pointer has reached the end of a file.

```
bool feof (int fp)
```

See the `fgets()` function for an example of `feof()`.

FGETS() This function returns a single line from the file indicated by the file pointer (usually taken from `fopen()`). If you are working with a large file, it's easier on the system to load files into memory one line at a time, rather than in one big chunk as is done with `fread()`.

```
string fgets (int fp, int length)
```

This function will read a line up until a newline character. Optionally, you can specify the maximum number of bytes to read within a line in the second argument. The number 2048 is traditionally used in the second argument because on many old file systems that was the maximum line length. These days, you're safe using something larger. You shouldn't use this function with binary files.

```
$fp = fopen("/path/to/file","r");
while ($fp && !feof($fp))
{
        print fgets($fp,2048);
}
fclose($fp);
```

FILE() This function reads a file line by line, each line becoming an element in an array.

```
array file (string filename [, int use_include_path])
```

UMASK() This function sets the umask value (see your Solaris man page – `man umask` – if you don't know what this is).

```
int umask (int mask)
```

`umask()` sets PHP's umask to `mask & 0777` and returns the old umask.

FILE_EXISTS()

```
bool file_exists (string filename)
```

If the local file specified in the argument exists, this function returns `TRUE`.

```
file_get_contents()
```

```
string file_get_contents (string filename [, int use_include_path])
```

The contents of the file specified in this function's argument are returned in a string. If the optional second argument is set to `1`, the function looks for the file in the include path specified in the configuration.

COPY() This function makes a copy of the file in argument one and copies it to the location in argument two.

```
bool copy (string source, string dest)
```

If the copy works, the function returns TRUE. If not, it returns FALSE. This function is used in Chapter 12.

TEMPNAM() This function creates a unique file name in the directory indicated in the first argument.

```
string tempnam (string dir, string prefix)
```

The string prefix in argument two will be placed before each file name. This can help you keep track of what files belong to what scripts.

DIRNAME() This function will return the directory name of the supplied string.

```
string dirname (string path)
```

For example,

```
echo dirname("/www/htdocs/testfile.txt");
```

will return

```
/www/htdocs
```

MKDIR()

```
int mkdir (string pathname, int mode)
```

This function creates in the local file system a directory with the name pathname and the permissions given by the octal integer *mode*. Permissions in this form are governed by standard Unix rules, nicely explained by Linux vendor Slackware here: http://www.slackware.com/book/index.php?source=x2163.html.

IS_DIR()

```
bool is_dir (string pathname)
```

If the argument is an existing directory, this function returns TRUE.

IS_UPLOADED_FILE()

```
bool is_uploaded_file (string filename)
```

If the specified file was uploaded via HTTP by the user, this function returns TRUE. It is useful for determining that the files a script is operating on are not native system files.

MOVE_UPLOADED_FILE()

```
bool move_uploaded_file (string filename, string destination)
```

This function incorporates the functionality of `is_uploaded_file()`. It first checks whether the argument file name was uploaded via `HTTP POST`, and, if so, moves it to the destination location. If it is not an uploaded file, the function returns `FALSE`.

BASENAME()

```
string basename (string path [, string suffix])
```

Given a file path, this function will cut off all elements of the path except the base file name. If a suffix is given as an optional argument, that suffix will also be cut off of the file name. For example:

```
$path = "/www/htdocs/testfile.txt";
echo basename($path, ".txt");
```

will output

```
testfile
```

REALPATH()

```
string realpath (string path)
```

Given a pathname containing symbolic links or `../` shortcuts, `realpath()` will return an absolute pathname with none of these components.

FILE SYSTEM FUNCTIONS NOT USED IN THIS BOOK

File system functions are an important topic, and one you should spend some time learning about. Most of the more popular file system commands are available through PHP, and many commands are available for opening, reading, writing, and displaying files. But, as this book deals with a relational database for data storage, we will not cover them here.

Script Control functions

This is a group of functions and language constructs that can be used to control the execution of PHP scripts.

call_user_func()

```
mixed call_user_func (callback function [, mixed parameter [, mixed ...]])
```

This function takes a user-defined function as its argument and calls the function, passing it any parameters given.

call_user_func_array()

```
mixed call_user_func_array (callback function [, array parameters])
```

This function is fundamentally the same as `call_user_func()`, with the difference that, instead of passing a single parameter or list of parameters, it passes an array to the called function.

die()

```
void die ([string status])
```

This function outputs the argument string and then terminates the script. It is used very commonly to abort a function when an error is encountered.

Note that this function is equivalent to `exit()`.

eval()

```
mixed eval (string code)
```

This function is used to execute code stored in a variable. The function evaluates and executes the code string contained in the argument, and returns the return value of the code.

Using `eval()` with poorly escaped or terminated code will result in parse errors that can be tricky to debug.

func_get_arg(), func_get_args(), and func_num_args()

```
mixed func_get_arg (int arg_num)
```

```
array func_get_args (void)
```

```
int func_num_args (void)
```

When called within a function, these three functions give information about the function's arguments:

- `func_get_args()` returns an array consisting of the function's argument list.
- `func_get_arg()` returns argument number `arg_num` in the function's argument list.
- `func_num_args()` returns the number of arguments passed to the function.

Each of these functions generates a warning if it is not called from within a user-defined function.

function_exists()

```
bool function_exists (string functionname)
```

If the function specified in the argument exists, this function returns `TRUE`. This function can be useful for testing the runtime environment, although some functions that exist may not be usable in the current configuration.

include(), include_once(), require(), and require_once()

These are special language constructs used to control the execution of scripts. Each takes a PHP file name as an argument, and includes and evaluates the file in the course of execution. `require()` and `include()` behave identically, with the difference that `require()` will generate a fatal error if the file to be included is missing, whereas `include()` merely generates a warning.

`include_once()` and `require_once()`, as their names imply, will only include the specified file if it has not already been included.

The format is simple:

```
include(remote_file);
include_once(remote_file);
require(remote_file);
require_once(remote_file);
```

Random number generator functions

Every now and then you will need to pick something at random. It may be an individual element, or it may be something that has to do with randomizing an array with `shuffle()` or getting a random element from an array with `array_rand()`. In any case you will need to make use of PHP's random number generator functions.

Note that the random number generator needs to be seeded before use. That is, it has to be given a number that is reasonably unique to begin with. For this, as you will see, the `microtime()` function will be of great use.

Keep in mind that really two sets of random number generators exist. There are the standard `rand()`, which doesn't take a seed, and `srand()`, which does and which you need in order to seed the generator for `shuffle()` and `array_rand()`. However, if you just want to get a random number and not use it with any other functions, use the `mt` functions described below – they're faster and more random.

Now we examine some important random number generator functions used in the applications in this book.

mt_srand()

This function seeds your random number generator.

```
void mt_srand (int seed)
```

Use the following line and you can be sure your numbers will be plenty random:

```
mt_srand ((double) microtime() * 1000000);
```

Seed the random number generator only once per script.

mt_rand()

This function returns a random number. You can specify a minimum value and/or a maximum value.

```
int mt_rand ([int min [, int max]])
```

So to get a random number between 1 and 100, do the following:

```
mt_srand((double)microtime() * 1000000);
$number = mt_rand(1,100);
echo $number;
```

rand()

```
int rand ([int min, int max])
```

`rand()` generates a (pseudo)random number between *min* and *max*.

`mt_rand()` returns better, faster results than `rand()`.

Session functions

These are explained in detail in Chapter 14. Sessions are means by which state is maintained between pages. Remember that HTTP, the language of the Web, does not allow servers to remember much of anything between requests for pages from a specific user. Sessions allow the server to keep track of activities by a single user.

MySQL functions

These functions are explained in detail in Appendix J.

A total of 48 MySQL functions are available in the library. Only about a third of these are used in the applications in this book. You may find uses for some of the other MySQL functions in your applications, but you probably won't use all of them.

HTTP header functions

Three vital HTTP header functions exist, both of which you will need to get to know.

header()

If you are going to be communicating with the browser or with other HTTP servers, this is the function to use.

```
int header (string string)
```

Essentially, you can send any header that would be expected under RFC 2616 (`ftp://ftp.isi.edu/in-notes/rfc2616.txt`), which defines HTTP. The RFC itself is a handful (and perhaps the sleepiest reading you'll do all year). Here is a common header you are likely to send:

```
header("Location: http://www.php.net");
```

This is nothing more than a redirect: It sends the browser to a page you specify. If you have been working with straight HTML and JavaScript or the `<META type=refresh>` tag to do your redirects, you should switch to this type of header whenever possible. It will work for all browsers and the redirection will be totally transparent to the user.

IMPORTANT — no, make that VERY IMPORTANT — you cannot send a header after anything — ANYTHING — has been sent to the browser. If you send a header after even a hard return, you will get an error. If you send a hard return before your opening `<?php` tag, you will get an error. If there is a hard return in an included file that precedes your `header()` function, you will

get an error. This should not be a problem you encounter frequently; your pages should be designed so that most of the logic is handled prior to the display. However, if you have a situation you just can't work around, take a look at the output buffering functions.

setcookie()

This is basically a specialized header function, because a cookie is set by nothing more than a specific HTTP header.

```
int setcookie (string name [, string value [, int expire [, string
path [, string domain [, int secure]]]]])
```

The first argument will be the name of the cookie. The second will be the value. The `expire` value should be set with the `time` function. The following is a pretty typical use of `setcookie()`:

```
setcookie("id",$id_val,time()+(24*60*60),"/",".domain.com",0);
```

This will set a cookie that will expire in 24 hours (24 × 60 × 60). The cookie will be available to every directory within `domain.com`. If you want to restrict it to a specific directory, you can change the / to a directory name.

You can find more on cookies in Chapter 4 in the discussion on variables.

In some versions of Internet Explorer, you must either give both time and path values or neither.

header_sent()

This function can keep you from sending headers after some text has been sent to the browser.

```
bool header_sent(void)
```

If you are relying heavily on this function, you are probably not coding your pages properly.

Image functions

PHP provides very powerful functions for generating and manipulating images.

IMAGE FUNCTIONS USED IN THIS BOOK

Here is a rundown of the image functions used in this book.

GETIMAGESIZE()

```
array getimagesize (string filename [, array imageinfo])
```

Given an image file as argument, this function returns an array containing the width of the image in pixels, the height of the image in pixels, a numeric flag containing the type of the image, and a text string containing the dimensions that can be used directly in an HTML IMG tag. Valid numeric flags include `1` for GIF, `2` for JPEG, and `6` for BMP.

So, given a JPEG of 468 × 60 pixels, `getimagesize()` would return the following:

```
Array
(
[0] => 468
[1] => 60
[2] => 2
[3] => height="60" width="468"
)
```

IMAGECOPYRESIZED()

```
int imagecopyresized (resource dest_im, resource src_im, int destX,
int destY, int srcX, int srcY, int destW, int destH, int srcW, int
srcH)
```

This function is used to copy part of one image (referred to above as a `resource`), delineated by rectangular X and Y coordinates and offset, to another image. The arguments it takes are as follows:

- The destination image identifier
- The source image identifier

- The starting X coordinate on the destination image
- The starting Y coordinate on the destination image
- The starting X coordinate on the source image
- The starting Y coordinate on the source image
- The width in pixels of the destination image
- The height in pixels of the destination image
- The offset width to take from the source image
- The offset height to take from the source image

IMAGECREATE()

```
resource imagecreate (int x_size, int y_size)
```

This function creates a new image with the given dimensions, and returns its identifier.

IMAGECREATEFROMSTRING()

```
resource imagecreatefromstring (string image)
```

This function creates a new image from the image stream given in the argument string, and returns its identifier.

IMAGEPNG()

```
int imagepng (resource image [, string filename])
```

Given an image identifier, `imagepng()` outputs an image stream, in PNG format, to either the user's browser or, if it is given a file name as a second argument, to the specified file.

IMAGESX(), IMAGESY()

```
int imagesx (resource image)
```

```
int imagesy (resource image)
```

These two functions return the dimensions of the referenced image: `imagesx()` returns the width, and `imagesy()` returns the height.

IMAGETYPES()

```
int imagetypes (void)
```

This function checks the configuration of the GD library that PHP is using to see which image types are supported. It returns a bitmask containing a value that corresponds to the AND sum of the constants that represent each image type. You can test for PNG support, therefore, with code like the following:

```
if (imagetypes() & IMG_PNG)
    echo "PNG support is enabled.";
}
```

EXIF_IMAGETYPE()

```
int exif_imagetype (string filename)
```

exif_imagetype() examines an image file and determines the type of image it is, returning a numeric code, or FALSE if it is not a recognizable image type. PHP must be compiled with – enable-exif.

Refer to the online PHP manual (http://www.php.net/manual/en/ref.image.php) for a list of image types and their codes.

EXIF_THUMBNAIL()

```
string exif_thumbnail (string filename [, int width [, int height [, int imagetype]]])
```

If an image contains an embedded thumbnail, this function will retrieve the thumbnail as a data stream. For example:

```
<?php
$thumb= exif_thumbnail($imagefile, 40, 50);
echo $thumb;
?>
```

If the preceding code is stored as a file called thumbnail.php, a subsequent HTML call to this file as an image will display the thumbnail:

```
<img src="thumbnail.php" height="50" width="40">
```

Mail function

If you have Sendmail or another suitable email program installed on your system, this function will take all the fuss out of sending email from your PHP pages.

Sendmail is the program most commonly used with PHP's `mail` function, but qmail with Sendmail wrappers will work, and Pegasus (`http://pegasus.usa.com/`) can apparently work on Windows (though we haven't tested it).

The `mail()` function sends an email from your PHP script.

```
bool mail (string to, string subject, string message [, string
additional_parameters] )
```

Your basic email will look like this:

```
mail("name@domain.com","Subject Text", "The complete message goes here");
```

And if you want to get a little fancier and include a From and a Cc:, use the following:

```
mail("jay@trans-city.com","Test Message", "Here I am",
"From: Jay G\r\nCc: webmonkey@trans-city.com\r\nReply-to:
myname@mydomain.com");
```

Additional parameters have been added in the fourth argument, and the different parameters are separated by line feeds and newlines (`\r\n`).

If you want to set up a large email system, don't use PHP. Better tools are out there. This function is intended for sending an occasional email from within PHP scripts.

If you'd like to send attachments in your PHP email, check out this excellent article at `phpbuilder.com`: `http://phpbuilder.com/columns/kartic20000807.php3`.

URL functions

If you've ever looked at a query string, you may have noticed that the text you entered into your form fields has been changed. For examples, spaces are turned into plus signs (+) and each ampersand (&) becomes `%26`. Many other characters are encoded. (All non-alphanumeric characters other than the hyphen (`-`), underscore (`_`), and dot (`.`) are replaced by a percent sign (`%`) and two characters).

On occasion you will need to encode or decode text. For that you will use the functions below.

urlencode()

This function encodes a string so that it's URL-ready. Most often you will use this function if you want to send variable information to another page.

```
string urlencode(string str)
```

For example:

```
$myvar="this string with weird &* stuff";
$encoded = urlencode($myvar);
header("Location: http://www.mydomain.com?var=$encoded");
```

Notice that this code snippet has only encoded the values of a querystring element. If you were to `urlencode` the entire URL, you would not be happy with the results. The result of this code

```
urlencode("http://www.mydomain.com");
```

is `http%3A%2F%2Fwww.mydomain.com`.

urldecode()

This function undoes the encoding process. It's usually unnecessary because the variable created from your `GET` or `POST` data is decoded in your variables.

```
string urldecode(string str)
```

rawurlencode()

This function returns a string in which all non-alphanumeric characters except the hyphen, underscore, and dot have been replaced with a percent (`%`) sign followed by two characters.

```
string rawurlencode(string str)
```

This is the encoding described in RFC 1738 for protecting literal characters from being interpreted as special URL delimiters, and for protecting URLs from being mangled by transmission media with character conversions (like some email systems). For historical reasons, spaces are encoded as plus (+) signs.

rawurldecode()

This function unencodes according to the same provisions as `rawurlencode()`.

```
string rawurldecode(string str)
```

base64_encode()

This function encodes a specified string in such a way as to eliminate all possible control characters, meaning the string can be sent over any transmission medium without the need to worry that the string could be interpreted as a command.

```
string base64_encode(string str)
```

base64_decode()

This function undoes what `base64_encode()` does. That is, it converts the encoded string back into its original form.

```
string base64_decode(string str)
```

Error functions

PHP gives you a high level of control over how errors are handled and reported to the user. Here is an overview of some of the important error-handling functions that are offered.

error_reporting()

This function sets the level of error reporting.

```
int error_reporting ([int level])
```

Possible levels of reporting are:

- 0 – No reporting
- 1 – Errors
- 2 – Warnings
- 4 – Parse errors
- 8 – Notices

You are encouraged to use the predefined named constants instead of raw numbers: `E_ERROR`, `E_WARNING`, `E_PARSE`, `E_NOTICE`, `E_ALL`, and so on. See the online PHP documentation (`http://www.php.net/manual/en/function.error-reporting.php`) for more details about levels of error reporting.

If you want a particular expression to cast no errors, you can prefix it with the `@` operator.

error_log()

```
int error_log (string message [, int message_type [, string
destination [, string extra_headers]]])
```

If you want to log a custom error message, this is the function to use. It can send a message to the server's logger (as specified in the `error_log` directive), to an email address, or to a file.

set_error_handler()

```
string set_error_handler (callback error_handler)
```

In scripts in which errors must be handled by a custom function, `set_error_handler()` enables you to specify that function. All error messages (as controlled by `error_reporting()`) are sent to the specified function.

trigger_error() and user_error()

```
void trigger_error (string error_msg [, int error_type])
void user_error (string error_msg [, int error_type])
```

These two functions are synonymous. Both send a user-level error message.

Output buffering

Output buffering is the process of writing the results of your script to a temporary buffer. Instead of being sent out over the Web the results will gather in a buffer, where you can manipulate them if you wish.

Probably the most common use of output buffering is to ensure that you don't get errors caused by sending headers after text has been sent to the browser. To prevent this from happening you can start a buffer, write some of an HTML page to the buffer, and then, given a specific condition, write a header (maybe a cookie), and then output the rest of the page. When you flush the buffer, the contents will be written to the browser without error.

If you are frequently using buffering to prevent headers from causing errors, rethink your page logic. Decisions first, output second.

People have also been playing with using output buffering to gzip page contents. In browsers that are capable of unzipping, the page can be downloaded a lot faster this way. However, given browser craziness, we don't recommend this.

BUFFERING FUNCTIONS USED IN THIS BOOK

Object buffering allows you to cache instances of object in a region of memory, making them easily accessible across multiple sessions. Quite a few object-buffering functions exist. We used very few of them.

OB_START() This function starts the buffer.

```
void ob_start(void)
```

FLUSH() This function clears the buffer.

```
void flush(void)
```

OB_END_CLEAN(), OB_END_FLUSH()

```
void ob_end_clean (void)
```

```
void ob_end_flush (void)
```

These two functions both turn off output buffering, but `ob_end_flush()` sends the contents of the buffer to output first, whereas `ob_end_clean()` deletes the contents of the buffer without sending them.

BUFFERING FUNCTIONS NOT USED IN THIS BOOK

Check the online manual for some more sophisticated buffering functions.

Information functions

These functions will give you information about the environment in which you are working.

phpinfo()

```
int phpinfo ([int option])
```

This is your guide to all that is available in your PHP environment. Use it. Use it. Use it. And then take it off your system. There's no point in letting crackers get a look at the specifics of your system.

The *option* argument specifies what you want information about, such as installed modules. Have a look at the manual page (`http://php.net/phpinfo`) for a list of legal option values.

phpversion()

```
string phpversion (void)
```

This function returns only the version of PHP you are using.

php_sapi_name()

```
string php_sapi_name (void)
```

This function returns a string indicating the type of Server Application Programming Interface (SAPI) interface that exists in the current configuration. For example, if the CGI version of PHP is running, the string will be `cgi`.

extension_loaded()

```
bool extension_loaded (string extensionname)
```

This function returns `TRUE` if the input PHP extension is loaded, and `FALSE` if it is not.

ini_get()

```
string ini_get (string varname)
```

This function returns the value of a PHP configuration option.

ini_set()

```
string ini_set (string varname, string newvalue)
```

This function assigns a new value to a PHP configuration option. Refer to the PHP online documentation for information on which options can be controlled by this function.

Summary

As you've seen, PHP has more functions than you will be able to commit to memory anytime soon. It can seem intimidating, but the quantity and quality of these functions are what make PHP such a great language. Most anything you need to do can be done quickly and painlessly.

At first you may need to study and play with the functions in order to get them to work. But in time it will get a lot easier. You'll be making use of more and more functions, and keeping your scripts more compact and easier to read.

Chapter 7

Writing Organized and Readable Code

IN THIS CHAPTER

- Keeping your code tidy
- Understanding the power and convenience of functions
- Using object-oriented code
- Learning the importance of comments

THIS CHAPTER PRESENTS a run-through of the preferred ways to present and organize code. Along the way you will see how to construct functions and classes in PHP. By the end of this chapter you should have a good idea of how write efficient, readable applications in PHP, and you should be ready to dive into the applications in Parts III and IV of this book.

Indenting

If you have done coding in any language, this point should be pretty obvious. But it is an important point and, therefore, deserves some mention. In the type of coding needed for Web applications, following a few indenting rules can help make your life a little easier.

How far should you indent? Some feel that each level of code should be indented by three spaces. Others, like us, think a single tab is the way to go. If you use spaces, it is possible that your code will look terrible in a different text editor (maybe the one used by your co-worker). We believe tabs are a better choice anyway, but some people have the opposite opinion with the same motivation. So really, what's important is consistency.

Code blocks

The most obvious use of indenting comes in differentiating blocks of code. For instance, it is fairly typical to have an `if` block within a `while` loop:

```
$i = 0;
while ($i < 100)
{
    $i++;
    if ($i  < 50 )
    {
        echo "Within the first 49.";
    }
    else
    {
        echo "Between 50 and 99.";
    }
}
```

As you can see in this PHP code, each block is delimited by curly braces (`{}`); this goes for both `while` loops and `if` blocks. When a block is entered with an opening curly brace, the next line should be indented. Each line following at the same level of execution should be indented at the same level. Additional nested blocks should be indented another level.

Looking at the preceding brief snippet of code, it is easy enough to see that it contains three distinct blocks. This might not seem like such a big deal with a small bit of code like this, but as scripts get longer, and levels of nesting get deeper, you will see how important it can become. We're not going to belabor this point because it should be pretty clear. But, for a quick example, we present the previous code without indents. Note that it works just fine – PHP doesn't care if you don't write your code neatly. But imagine coming back to this a month after you wrote it and having to troubleshoot or add code. Life is a lot easier if you can easily find the block that needs work.

```
$i=0;
while ($i < 100)
{
$i++;
if ($i  < 50 )
{
echo "Within the first 49.";
}
else
{
```

```
echo "Between 50 and 99.";
}
}
```

If you like, you can even run everything together, like this:

```
$i=0; while ($i < 100) {$i++; if ($i  < 50 ) { echo "Within the
first 49."; } else { echo "Between 50 and 99."; } }
```

The interpreter truly does not care. Indeed, you'll sometimes see code generated by other programs that looks that way. Such organization is obviously a nightmare to analyze and maintain.

You can also omit some of the braces, like so:

```
$i = 0;
while ($i < 100)
{
    $i++;
    if ($i  < 50 )
        echo "Within the first 49.";
    else
        echo "Between 50 and 99.";
}
```

This is an easy way make your code a little more compact, and in some ways easier to read, if – and let's stress that *if* – you're writing simple `if-else` statements like this one. Remember, though, indenting alone does not a code block make. This code:

```
$i = 0;
while ($i < 100)
{
    $i++;
    if ($i  < 50 )
        echo "Within the first 49.";
    else
        echo "Between 50 and 99.";
        echo " (which is getting up there)";
}
```

will not treat those last two `echo` statements the same, even though it looks like it might. In fact, the preceding code is equivalent to the following:

```
$i = 0;
while ($i < 100)
```

```
{
    $i++;
    if ($i  < 50 )
    {
        echo "Within the first 49.";
    }
    else
    {
        echo "Between 50 and 99.";
    }
    echo " (which is getting up there)";
}
```

When in doubt, use braces.

Are you getting a parse error you can't identify? Make sure you have an identical number of opening and closing curly braces and parentheses. If you have, for example, five closing curly braces in a page and only three opening ones, you haven't opened at least two of your code blocks. Most code editors — which are really just text editors with a few extra features for programming — enable you to park your cursor on a single brace and either use a hotkey combination to find its match or highlight the block of code it marks. If the matching brace or marked region isn't what you expect, you know how to advance further down the road to bug-free code.

Function calls

Indenting code should not stop at code blocks. Often you need to use nested function calls or complex variables that take up several lines. You will be much happier in your coding life if you use indents in these situations. Take a look at the following, which is borrowed from the Catalog application:

```
$file_ext = strtolower(
    substr(
        $file
        , strrpos($file,".")
    )
);
```

The purpose of this code is pretty simple: It takes the name of a file and assigns its extension (the characters following the final dot (.)) to `$file_ext`. It takes three separate built-in PHP functions to get this done. PHP executes the innermost level first. There, strrpos() finds the numeric position of the final dot. For example, for the string myfile.jpg it would return 6. Then the substr() function returns only the characters following the dot. Finally, that string is set in lowercase characters.

This code can be written on one line, but as you can see, it becomes rather difficult to read:

```
$file_ext = strtolower(substr($file, strrpos($file,".")));
```

Or maybe you find this easier to read. A lot of things we talk about in this chapter are matters of personal preference. The important thing is that you spend a lot of time considering how to make your code as readable as possible. On the other hand, if you plan to share your code with others (especially via public repositories like SourceForge), you should adhere to style conventions. There doesn't appear to be an official (or generally recognized) document that describes PHP-coding style conventions. The PEAR folks have a style guide you might want to peruse, at http://pear.php.net/manual/en/standards.php.

In the first example of this code, it's much easier to see what each of the closing parentheses relates to, and you can more quickly get an idea of what the code accomplishes and how.

You might be tempted to write the preceding code using temporary assignments to variables. That would look something like this:

```
$file_ext = strrpos($file, ".");
$ext_letters = substr($file, $file_ext);
$lower_ext_letters = strtolower($ext_letters);
```

But this code is slower at execution time (not to mention at coding time), though a code optimizer could reduce the problem. Variable assignments do take time, and in a short piece of code where they aren't necessary, stay away from temporary-variable assignment. That said, you should avoid sacrificing readability. In some places temporary variables can help make code much easier to read. And there are circumstances when using a temporary variable speeds up your code — by avoiding repetition of a function call whose results aren't going to change, for example:

```
$len = count($array);
for ($i = 0; $i < $len; $i++)
{
```

```
    ...
}
```

In neither case is the speed difference phenomenal. So, as usual, it ends up being a question of what makes the most sense for you.

SQL statements

In Web-database applications, SQL statements are interspersed throughout PHP code. Usually PHP variables are included within SQL statements to get specific results based on variable data. Indenting SQL statements helps keep the code readable and maintainable. In the following example we show you a few examples of SQL statements of various types. You can see many examples of these in the applications in Parts III and IV of this book.

```
//2 table select
$query = "select n.fname, n.lname
        , c.co_name, c. co_address, c.co_zip
    from names n, companies c
    where n.name_id = $name_id
        and n.co_id = $c.co_id
";

//update query in heredoc style
$query = <<<EOQ
update products
set product = '$product'
    , description = '$cleandsc'
    , price = $nullprice
    , image_src = $nullimage_src
where product_id = $product_id
EOQ;

//insert query
$query = "insert into products (category_id, product)
    values ($category_id, '$product')
";
```

We've heard stories of database engines refusing to process queries that, like the ones preceding, have newlines in them. This issue is not a problem with MySQL and won't be a problem with most database engines. However, there are other perfectly acceptable ways to write queries that do not put newlines in the queries, yet show indenting to the reader. Here are a couple of examples using the concatenation operators:

```
$query = "select col_1, col2 ";
$query .= " from table_1, table_2 ";
$query .= " where col_1 = $var";
```

or

```
$query = "select col_1, col_2 "
              . " from table_1, table_2 "
              . " where col_1 = $var"
;
```

Choose whichever you like best.

Includes

Every language has a facility for including external files. PHP has four commands that enable you to do this. Before we get to those, we briefly discuss why includes are so critical for writing organized and readable code. And we start with a very common example.

In most Web sites, header information varies little from page to page. There are opening tags (<HTML>, <HEAD>, and so on) and perhaps some navigation information. The following is a typical HTML-page header:

```
<HTML>
<HEAD>
   <TITLE>My Page Name</TITLE>
</HEAD>
<body bgcolor="#FFFFF" link="#8E0402" vlink="#20297C">
```

It is an absolute waste to type this text into every file within a Web site. Moreover, it can be a real pain. Suppose you want to change the `bgcolor` attribute of the `<body>` tag throughout the site. If this information were hard-coded in every file, you would have no choice but to either go into each file individually and make the change or write a script to do it for you.

You are far better off keeping all of this information in a single file (maybe called header.php) and then using a command that spits the contents of that file into the file being accessed. For this, you can use one of the PHP functions discussed in the next section. For this example we use `include()`.

You might want to give your include files a distinct extension — .inc is a typical choice. One advantage of this approach is that the files can't be run directly from a browser, since the Web server is (usually) not configured to recognize .inc as a PHP file. You can also store your include files outside of your Web server's document path for even more security (since some servers respond to unknown extensions by printing out the file — oops, there's your source code.)

Suppose you have two files, header.php and index.php. (Notice that we have made an important change in header.php: The `<TITLE>` tags now contain a PHP variable.)

```
<HTML>
<HEAD>
   <TITLE> <?php echo $page_title; ?> </TITLE>
</HEAD>
<body bgcolor="#FFFFF" link="#8E0402" vlink="#20297C">
```

You may have seen code like the above written like this:

```
<TITLE> <?= $page_title ?> </TITLE>
```

These "short tags" involve less typing, it's true, but whether or not they work is dependent on how PHP is configured. They're likely to be disabled by default, now or in future releases, so you should avoid using them.

Now for the index.php file:

```
<?php

$page_title = "Welcome to My Site";
include('header.php');

echo "Here are the contents of my PHP pages. Anything could be
here.";

?>
```

Notice that the variable `$page_title` is visible to the file pulled in by the `include` statement. When index.php is served, the resulting HTML page will be as follows:

```
<HTML>
<HEAD>
   <TITLE> Welcome to My Site </TITLE>
</HEAD>
<body bgcolor="#FFFFF" link="#8E0402" vlink="#20297C">
```

Keep any code, whether HMTL or PHP, that is needed in a variety of pages within include files. Header and footer information, database-connection code, and pages that contain functions or classes are all good candidates for includes.

At the start of an included file PHP reverts to HTML mode. If code within the file needs to be parsed as PHP, you must first indicate that with the `<?php` marker.

PHP contain a variety of commands that do slightly different things with included files. We look at these commands in the following sections.

include() and require()

These commands are very similar and can usually be used interchangeably. However, you should know what distinguishes the two, because at times using the wrong one can cause problems.

The primary difference is indicated by the names. The `require()` command fails with a fatal error if it can't find the file it is trying to import; the file is "required" to continue. The `include()` command, on the other hand, issues a non-fatal error (which you can block with the @ operator) only if it can't find the file, and PHP continues processing your script.

include_once() and require_once()

In addition to `include()` and `require()`, PHP provides `include_once()` and `require_once()`. These are provided to keep you, the developer, from stepping on your own toes. As you might expect, they keep you from including the same file twice, which, were it possible, could cause some problems when it comes to calling user-defined functions.

For example, suppose you have a file that contains a function, but that the function relies on another function from an outside file. Your file would contain lines like these:

```
require 'helpful_file.php';
function short_function()
{
```

```
    [...]
    the_function_from_helpful_file();
}
```

Suppose you give the name short_function.php to the file containing the preceding lines. Later, if you try to include both short_function.php and helpful_file.php in a third file, you'll have a problem. The second time that helpful_file.php gets included, it will try to redeclare functions that have already been declared once. PHP will not let you do this and will spit out an error. So in cases like this use `include_once()` or `require_once()`. Note that if files are included more than once you might also have a problem dealing with variables that inadvertently overwrite each other.

User-Defined Functions

Chapter 6 shows many of the functions built into the PHP processing engine. If you are a humble person and look at Appendix F or visit the online PHP manual, you should be duly impressed by the quantity and power of PHP's built-in functions. But it isn't enough – and no matter how much work the able developers put into the language, it never will be enough. That is because every developer on the planet has unique needs. You need to accomplish specific tasks, and you need to do it in ways that fit your own styles and predilections.

User-defined functions enable you to create blocks of code that achieve specific tasks. The great thing about user-defined functions is that the code becomes reusable. Any piece of code that you find yourself writing over and over should be committed to a function. This saves you time in the long run.

In the applications presented in this book nearly all of the code is within functions. The files that you see in your browser typically result from a number of function calls. This approach helps to keep things readable.

Function basics

You can start by writing a simple function that writes out the start of an HTML table.

```
function start_table()
{
    echo "<table border=1>\n";
}
```

To call this function within your PHP page, you access it just like a built-in PHP function:

```
start_table();
```

That's easy enough. But what if you want the border to vary in given situations? You can make the border a variable, and then in the function call specify the value for `border`:

```
function start_table($border)
{
    echo "<table border=$border>\n";
}

start_table(1);
```

Now suppose that most of the time you want the border to be `1`, but that you want to be able to change the border within the function call. The following does the trick:

```
function start_table($border=1)
{
    echo "<table border=$border>\n";
}
```

Here `$border` has been given a default value of `1`. But you can overwrite that value by specifying a different value when calling the function. For example, if you call the function with the following command, the table has a border of `2`:

```
start_table(2);
```

Once again, `1` is the default value, so if this function is called with the following code the table border is `1`:

```
start_table();
```

If you know your HTML, you know that the `table` tag can have multiple attributes: `cellspacing` and `cellpadding` are two others. You can add those to the function, along with default values:

```
function start_table($border=1, $cellspacing=2, $cellpadding=2)
{
echo "<table border=$border cellspacing=$cellspacing
 cellpadding=$cellpadding>\n";
}
```

Then, in the call to this function you can alter any of these:

```
start_table(4,5,5);
```

The table created with this command has a `border` of 4, `cellspacing` of 2, and `cellpadding` of 5.

The values that the function accepts are known as *arguments.* So the `start_table` function shown here takes three arguments. The more pedantic members of the audience might point out that the values sent to the function are arguments, while the values received by and used within the function are parameters. Practically speaking, they're the same thing, and you see the words used interchangeably all the time.

When constructing functions, be aware that if you wish to change one of the default values in your function call, you must specify all the arguments that precede it (that is, that occur to the left of it). For instance, the first command in the following code produces an error. However, the second one works and creates a table tag with a `border` of 4, `cellspacing` of 3, and `cellpadding` of 2.

```
//this will cause an error
start_table( ,5,5);
//this will work
start_table(4,3);
```

Also, if you don't specify a default value for an argument in your function definition, then you must supply a value for it when you call it. If you had written the `start_table()` function like this:

```
function start_table($border=1, $cellspacing=2, $cellpadding)
```

Then this call . . .

```
start_table(4,3);
```

would fail. You need to supply a value for `$cellpadding`, like this:

```
start_table(4,3,2);
```

Functions can accept more than simple variables; you can pass any of the scalar types (string, integer, double), any array (numeric, associative, or multidimensional), resources (like a MySQL connection handle), or objects. You might want to make use of a function that turns a PHP array (in other words, a list of stuff) into an HTML unordered list (a visible list of stuff).

```
function create_ul($array)
{
    echo "<ul>\n";
    foreach ($array as $value)
    {
        echo "<li>$value</li>\n";
    }
    echo "</ul>\n";
}
```

Returning values

Of course, your functions do more than print HTML. Functions can perform database calls or mathematical computations or do some string handling. They can do just about anything, and often you want to make the rest of the script aware of the results of your function. You can do this by using the keyword `return`. When a function hits the word `return` it leaves the function, and it returns whatever value you specify – a variable, a Boolean value (`TRUE` or `FALSE`), or nothing at all, if that's what you prefer. (Note: a plain '`return;`' statement is equivalent to '`return NULL;`'.)

```
function basic_math($val_1, $val_2)
{
    $added = $val_1 + $val_2;
    return $added;
}
```

You can then call this function and print the results:

```
$added_value = basic_math(5,4);
echo $added_value;
```

If fact, the following works equally well:

```
echo basic_math(5,4);
```

Functions can return any variable type (strings, object, arrays, and the like), or, in the case of database calls, they can return result identifiers. Additionally, functions can return `FALSE`. If you read Chapter 5, you might remember that in PHP any non-zero, non-false value is evaluated in an `if` statement as `TRUE`. So you might want to improve the previous function by making sure the values passed can be added.

```
function basic_math($val_1, $val_2)
{
    if (!is_int($val_1) || !is_int($val_2))
    {
        return FALSE;
    }
    $added = $val_1 + $val_2;
    return $added;
}
```

If either of the arguments in the call to this function is not an integer, the function returns `FALSE` and stops. A call to this improved function might look like this:

```
if (($added_value = basic_math(7, 5)) === FALSE)
{
    echo "What exactly are you doing?";
}
else
{
    echo $added_value;
}
```

If the function returns a value (any value), that value is added. If not, a special message is printed. Notice how this mimics the behavior of many of the PHP built-in functions. Its purpose is to perform a task, and if it fails to do so, it returns `FALSE`.

Take a quick look at the following function. It's a good example of how functions can really save you time, headaches, and keystrokes. The `mysql_query` function is fine; it sends a query from PHP to MySQL and, if it succeeds, returns a result identifier. If it fails, however, it does not automatically return any error information. Unless you do a bit of digging, you won't know what the problem was with the query. So for every query in your applications (and there will be plenty), you tack on an `or die` phrase:

```
mysql_query("select * from table_name") or die
  ("Query failed:" . mysql_error());
```

But life gets quite a bit easier if you create a function like the following and then send all of your queries through that function:

```
function safe_query ($query = "")
{
    if (empty($query)) { return FALSE; }
    $result = mysql_query($query)
        or die("ack! query failed: "
            ."<li>errorno=".mysql_errno()
```

```
            ."<li>error=".mysql_error()
            ."<li>query=".$query
        );
    return $result;
}
```

So your applications might include a file with this function on every page, and then you can use `safe_query()` in place of `mysql_query()`.

Using a variable number of arguments

One nice feature of PHP is that you can pass an indefinite number of arguments to a function and then assign the list of arguments to an array. Consider the following code:

```
function print_input_fields()
{
    $fields = func_get_args();
    foreach ($fields as $field)
    {
        if (isset($GLOBALS[$field]))
        {
            $value = $GLOBALS[$field];
        }
        else
        {
             $value = '';
        }
        print " <tr>\n";
        print "  <td valign=top
align=right><b>".ucfirst($field).":</b></td>\n";
        print "  <td valign=top align=left><input type=text
name=$field size=40 value=\"$value\"></td>\n";
        print " </tr>\n\n";
    }
}
start_table();
print_input_fields("name","location","email","url");
end_table();
```

The `$GLOBALS` array is discussed later in this chapter in the "Variable scope" section.

This function prints out form fields within a table. First, `func_get_args()` creates an associative array, with the name of the argument as the key. Then each form field is printed out. This strategy is pretty convenient because you can call a function in a number of situations and vary the output by including as many arguments as needed.

If you're wondering how this might work if your function contains some required parameters prior to the set of arguments that might vary, good for you. That's an excellent question.

Two other PHP functions work in such situations: `func_num_args()`, which returns the number of arguments sent to a function, and `func_get_arg()`, which returns a specific argument based on its numeric index, starting at `0`. So, for example, you might have a function that prints an HTML form with a variable number of input fields, like the following:

```
function print_form($action="", $method="POST")
{
    if (empty($action)){return FALSE;}
    echo "<form action=$action method=$method>";
    $numargs = func_num_args();
    for ($i = 2; $i < $numargs; $i++)
    {
        echo "<input type=text name=" . func_get_arg($i). ">";
    }
    echo "</form>";
}

print_form("myurl.php", "", "myfield1", "myfiels2");
```

Be aware that `empty()` might behave differently than you expect. It returns true if the evaluated variable is not defined, or if it contains `""`, `0`, `"0"`, `NULL`, `FALSE`, or an array with no elements.

Variable scope

To work with functions you need to understand how PHP handles variable scope. Scope is an important topic in any programming language, and PHP is no different.

In PHP, variables assigned outside of functions are known as *global variables*. These can be variables that you create, they can come from HTML form elements through either `GET` or `POST`, or they can be any of the variables inherited from the Apache environment. All globals are accessible from an array known as `$GLOBALS`. You can add to and delete from this array.

We've said it before, and we'll say it again: Use `phpinfo()` to get information about variables in your environment or your configuration.

In PHP a global variable is not automatically available within a function. If you want to use a global within a function you must indicate within the function that the variable you are accessing is a global.

Here is an example of using a global within a function:

```
function add_numbers($val_2)
{
    global $number;
    echo $number + $val_2;

}
$number = 10;
add_numbers(5);
```

This code prints `15`. Here `$number` is a global because it is assigned outside of a function. Using the keyword `global` tells PHP that you want to fetch the specified number from the `$GLOBALS` array. The preceding code can also be written like this:

```
function add_numbers($val_2)
{
    echo $GLOBALS["number"] + $val_2;;
}
$number = 10;
add_numbers(5);
```

In the applications in this book we use the technique shown in the first example because it seems a little cleaner, and because directly manipulating the `$GLOBALS` array is not really encouraged. It's nice to see where your variable is coming from at the top of the function.

Within your functions, you might want to make variables available as globals. That way they are available in the body of your script and in other functions. You can create a global variable the same way you access a previously defined one, with the `global` keyword. Here's a quick example:

```
function assign_to_global($val_1, $val_2)
{
    global $sum;
```

```
    $sum = $val_1 + $val_2;
}

assign_to_global(5,6);
echo $sum;
```

This script prints 11. For something a bit more complicated, we borrow the following function from the applications section of the book:

```
function set_result_variables ($result)
{
    if (!$result) { return; }
    $row = mysql_fetch_array($result,MYSQL_ASSOC);
    while (list($key,$value) = each($row))
    {
        global $$key;
        $$key = $value;
    }
}
```

This function expects a result identifier gathered by `mysql_query()` in an earlier function. Assume that the query run prior to this function call returns a single row. That row is then assigned to an associative array named `$row`. Then each column taken from the query (which is now the key in the associative array) and its value are available as a global. This availability can be useful if the values retrieved from the query are needed in many other functions. However, beware of having columns with the same names as PHP variables – particularly global variables. You should try to not let that happen, lest conflicts occur.

Global variables are used sparingly within functions throughout the applications in this book. This is because it is easier to keep track of your variables if you are passing them through arguments and retrieving them through return values. If you start using globals extensively you might find that your variables are returning unexpected values in different places – and finding the functions that are causing the error can be a major pain.

Here's another reason to avoid globals when possible: You will be using the same variable names over and over and over again. We don't know how many times in these applications the variable names `$query`, `$result`, `$row`, or `$i` are used, but trust us when we say that they are used frequently. All kinds of hassle are introduced if you have to keep track of each time you use a variable name.

At times you have little choice but to use global variables, but before you do, make sure that you can't accomplish what you're trying to do using variables of local scope.

Object-Oriented Programming

A few years back there was a large move toward object-oriented programming. Some people thought that the procedural approach – that is, coding strictly with functions – just wasn't enough. Therefore, the folks working on languages like C++ and Java popularized an approach that enables a developer to think about code in a different way.

The idea behind object-oriented programming is to think of portions of your application as objects. What is an object? Well, it's an amorphous thing, a kind of black box – a superstructure of variables and functions. But if you are new to the concept, this description may not be so clear.

To make things clearer conceptually, we provide a few examples. In our examples, our objects are things that can be displayed as part of a Web page. For each of the different kinds of elements of a page, you might want to know different things. If you're displaying an image, for example, you might want to know how wide it is. For an HTML table, you might want to know if it has a color. By treating the elements as objects, you can effectively ask them how wide they are or what color they are without having to dig inside them to find out yourself. You can also tell the elements to do things, like draw themselves on the page.

Now all you need is the correct nomenclature. Descriptions of the object (such as width and color) are called *properties*, and descriptions of the actions an object can take (such as draw) are known as *methods*. Some methods are a bit of both, and you can think of them as descriptions of the questions you can ask the object – a `width()` method might tell you how wide the object is and whether it has one property named `width` or a dozen different properties that it has to add together first. And as it happens, in the actual code of a class, you use the word `function` just as you would in a regular user-defined function, so you might hear both terms used interchangeably. Here's an example of what a PHP class looks like:

```
class TextBox
{
    var $_text;

    function TextBox($text)
    {
        $this->_text = $text;
    }
    function style()
    {
        return "font-family:'Helvetica Neue',Helvetica,sans-serif;";
    }
    function text()
    {
```

```
        return <<<EOT
<font style="{$this->style()}">{$this->_text}</font>
EOT;
    }
}
```

Before you get to using objects, however, we want to explain a couple of the advantages of this object-oriented approach. Suppose some programmer has created an object and tells you about its methods and properties. You don't really need to know *how* any of it works; you just need to know that it does. You can make use of the methods and properties of the object in your scripts with little effort.

Of course, the same could be said of a well-designed procedural approach. A well-documented collection of functions can work equally well. Time was when objects in PHP weren't much more than collections of function libraries and arrays that used little arrows instead of square brackets. That has changed dramatically with PHP 5, and the language is now much closer to other object-oriented languages like Java. However you look at it, you should be able to write good procedural code before you move on to objects.

By using objects, not only can you make use of methods and properties in the heart of your scripts, but also you can extend the functionality of a class in a number of different ways, with one of the most basic being the use of a concept called *inheritance*. Going back to the previous example, for example, an image and a table both might have a height and a width. We can create a class called a `Rectangle` that knows about heights and widths and then have our `Image` class and `Table` class inherit `Rectangle`, automatically being able to make use of all its properties and methods. (In object terminology, we call `Rectangle` the *parent* class, and `Image` and `Table` are both *children*.)

There's a lot more to object-oriented programming (or OOP for short – not to be confused with OOPS, which is the kind of programming we're trying to avoid) than just inheritance, though. We can't do full justice to the topic here, but we'll try to cover some of the basics.

Classes, Continued

In object-oriented programming, you work with classes and objects. A *class* is a definition describing properties and methods, while an *object* is a variable that has those properties and can use those methods. You could think of the blueprints for the chair you're sitting in now as a kind of `Chair` class. That would make your actual chair an object, or *instance*, of the `Chair` class. If your chair came from a factory, there might be thousands of `Chair` instances out there in the world, but still only one `Chair` class.

You can use a few different kinds of classes. Let's start out our small example with one of the most minimal kinds of classes, an *interface*.

INTERFACES

```
interface Color
{
    public function color();
}
interface Drawable
{
    public function draw($return=false);
}
interface Rectangle
{
    public function height();
    public function width();
}
```

Not much code there. But then that's the point – an interface isn't about how you will do something, so much as what you will be able to do. An interface is like a promise: Any class that builds on the Color interface, for example, swears that it will have a method named `color` with no arguments that you will be able to call. In this case, we're not promising anything about what that method will do (or what it will return to you, for that matter). But if you're dealing with an object that has Color in its background, you know that you'll be able to call `$object->color()` and get some kind of response.

So what does that get you besides a new buzzword? Well, without claiming to describe all of the benefits, here are a couple of basic ones.

In PHP, normal classes are *inherited*, while interfaces are *implemented*, like so:

```
class AlertBox extends TextBox implements Color, Rectangle
```

Here, `extends` means that the AlertBox class is inheriting the properties and methods of the TextBox class. You can inherit only from a single class in PHP, but you can implement as many interfaces as you like. The benefit comes from the fact that you can tell if a particular object implements the interface in which you're interested, using the `instanceof` operator. Say that you've got a section of code that doesn't care about anything but rectangles. Circles, triangles, lines of text – let somebody else deal with those; we just want rectangles. You can make that work like this:

```
if ($object instanceof Rectangle)
{
    $width = $object->width();
    $height = $object->height();
}
```

To write the same code without the concept of an interface, you'd have to do something like this:

```
$methods = get_class_methods($object);
if (in_array('width', $methods) and in_array('height', $methods))
{
    $width = $object->width();
    $height = $object->height();
}
```

Even then, you don't know if that object's `width()` method is going to require an argument that you can't supply. Plus, clearly, this is going to be a lot slower to run. The Rectangle interface tells you very simply that this is a proper Rectangle that knows how to respond to a decent `width()` call, regardless of what other kinds of foolishness it might get up to somewhere else.

Another benefit of using interfaces can come when you have multiple people working on different parts of the same project. By laying out a set of interfaces as the first step, each person can write code that will call on the other classes being built by other people, whether or not those other classes have actually been written yet, and without worrying about how they're going to work when they are written.

We can take that approach one step further, to specific properties and methods, by moving on to inheritance and *abstract* classes.

ABSTRACT CLASSES

An *abstract* class is sort of a blueprint's blueprint. It looks just like a regular class, because that's what it is, except for one difference: You can't make an object out of it. To add another $5 word to our pile, we can say that an abstract class cannot be *instantiated* – meaning that you can't create an instance of one, at least not directly.

Instead, abstract classes are there solely to be inherited. One way you can use them is as a place to put utility code – code that all of your classes will use, but that doesn't really have a purpose outside of the specific context of one of those classes. Maybe your abstract class has a method that does some complex mathematical calculations or one that picks one string at random from an array of strings.

PHP considers a class to be abstract if you explicitly declare the class that way – `abstract class MyClass { ... }` – or if one of the class's methods is declared to be abstract – `abstract function some_function();`. Another, indirect way of making a class abstract is by declaring that it implements an interface without supplying one or more of the methods that the interface defines. The effect is to shift the burden of supplying those required methods onto the class's children.

Here's another step in our example that shows what we mean: an abstract class that implements one of the interfaces we declared previously – except not really:

```
abstract class TextBox implements Drawable
{
```

```
    private $_text;

    public function __construct($text)
    {
        $this->_text = $text;
    }
    private function style()
    {
        return "font-family:'Helvetica Neue',Helvetica,sans-serif;";
    }
    final protected function text()
    {
        return <<<EOT
<font style="{$this->style()}">{$this->_text}</font>
EOT;
    }
}
```

This is a class that defines the way text will be displayed by later, non-abstract classes. A couple of new keywords pop up here that need some explanation.

`Public`, `protected`, and `private` define who has access to a property or a method. In this class, you can see that the `$_text` property is `private`. That means that only the methods of the `TextBox` class can read or change the contents of that property, not even classes that inherit from `TextBox`. The same applies to the `style()` method.

The `__construct()` method, on the other hand, is `public`. That means anyone can call it. This is a special method that gets called automatically when you create an object, using the keyword `new`, like so:

```
$object = new MyClass;
```

In prior versions of PHP, the *constructor* method had to have the same name as the class. In our first example of what a class looks like, for instance, the `TextBox()` is the constructor method. Now we can use the generic name `__construct()` instead. This not only makes maintenance easier, but also solves some issues with inheritance in earlier versions.

In between `private` and `public` is `protected`. A `protected` property or method can be used directly by the class in which it's declared and any child of that class, but not by the general public (that is, code outside of the classes). So, in our example here, a class that extends `TextBox` can't call the `style()` method, but it can call `text()`.

What it can't do is declare its own version of `text()`, though. That's because of the other keyword we use in its declaration, `final`. `Final` means what it sounds like it means: the end of the road for this method name. For protected or public methods that aren't declared to be `final`, you can do things like this:

```
class ParentClass
{
    public function sayHello()
    {
       print $this->Hello();
    }
    protected function Hello()
    {
       return "Hello!\n";
    }
}
class ChildClass extends ParentClass
{
    protected function Hello()
    {
       return "Howdy!\n";
    }
}
$p = new ParentClass;
$p->sayHello();  // prints out "Hello!\n"
$c = new ChildClass;
$c->sayHello();  // prints out "Howdy!\n"
```

However, if we declare the `Hello()` method of the `ParentClass` class to be `final`, instead of printing out Howdy!, you get:

```
PHP Fatal error:  Cannot override final method parentclass::hello()
in /my/pathname/test.php on line 13
```

So in our example, `TextBox` is reserving to itself the definition of `text()`. This means that we have some degree of confidence that we can change, say, the style definitions used to format text and have it be reflected in all the classes that are descended from `TextBox`.

The other thing to note about `TextBox` (which is a busy little class for something that isn't even real) is this:

```
abstract class TextBox implements Drawable
```

But doesn't the `Drawable` interface require a `draw()` method? No `draw()` method in `TextBox`? Typo?

Nope. Instead, by declaring that it implements `Drawable` without doing anything about it, `TextBox` is forcing any class that inherits it to supply its own `draw()`

method, doing whatever is appropriate for that particular class, like the TitleBox does in the next section:

INHERITANCE

```
class TitleBox extends TextBox
{
    public function draw($return=false)
    {
        $output = "<h3>{$this->text()}</h3>";
        if ($return)
            return $output;
        else
            print $output;
    }
}
```

Okay, so we've actually talked about inheritance before this. But now you can see it in action. TitleBox is a regular old class that you can use to create regular old objects. And as you can see in Figure 7-1, it doesn't have to do very much – just define the draw() method required by the Drawable interface, which TitleBox gets from its parent class, TextBox. If we put all of the pieces together, and add one last step – the creation of an object that we can use – we can even make words appear on a Web page (see Figure 7-1):

```
$title = new TitleBox("Greetings!");
$title->draw();
```

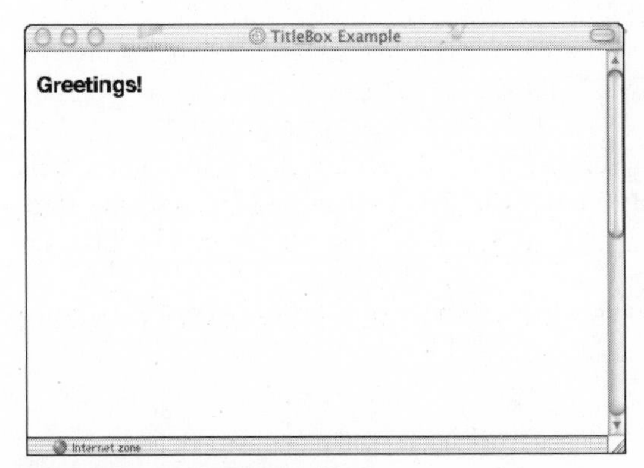

Figure 7-1: A TitleBox example

And here's a slightly fancier example, again building on the code we've seen up until now, only this time in color!

```
class AlertBox extends TextBox implements Color, Rectangle
{
    protected $_color;

    public function __construct($text='oops',$color = 'yellow')
    {
        // notice that we could be setting height and width
        // in the constructor, but instead
        // this class has them hard-coded
        // (i.e. all alert boxes are the same size)

        $this->_color = $color;
        parent::__construct($text);
    }

    public function height()
    {
        return 100;
    }

    public function width()
    {
        return 200;
    }

    public function color()
    {
        return $this->_color;
    }

    public function draw($return=false)
    {
        $output = <<<EOT
<table height="{$this->height()}" width="{$this->width()}"
border="1">
 <tr>
  <td bgcolor="{$this->color()}" align="center">{$this->text()}</td>
 </tr>
</table>
EOT;
        if ($return)
            return $output;
        else
            print $output;
    }
```

```
}
$alert = new AlertBox("Warning! Object Alert!");
$alert->draw();
```

Notice the `height()` and `width()` methods. These are good examples of methods that answer questions, rather than perform actions. An AlertBox doesn't even have a width or height property; instead, the methods return hard-coded values. But code that uses an AlertBox object doesn't have to care at all about any of that. It knows that it can call `$object->height()` to find out how tall it is and `$object->width()` to find out how wide, and that's all it needs.

Figure 7-2 shows you what it looks like in action.

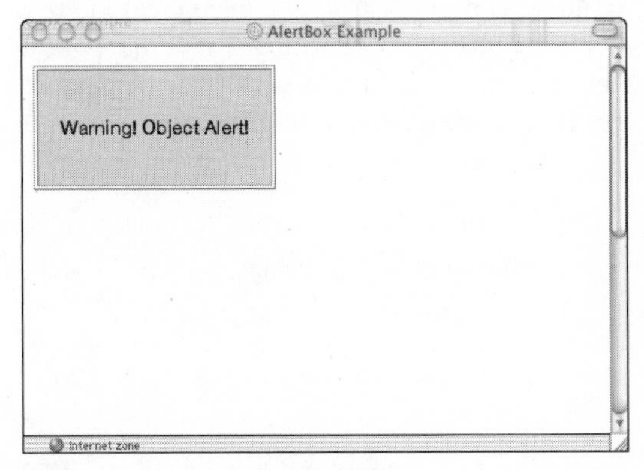

Figure 7-2: An AlertBox example

Where this all gets good is in the combination of features, of course. On the CD, there's a more complete example using the code we've seen in this chapter, in the /oop directory. One part of what you'll find in there is a `Page` class that draws an entire HTML page built up out of smaller components that are themselves instances of the kinds of classes we've been looking at. You just line them up when you create your Page object and tell the Page to draw:

```
$page = new Page($title,$logo,$alert,$ad,$biglogo);
$page->draw();
```

The `Page` class takes care of making sure that everything you hand it can be drawn:

```
class Page implements Drawable
{
    protected $_things = array();

    public function __construct()
```

```
    {
        $args = func_get_args();
        foreach ($args as $i => $arg)
        {
            if ($arg instanceof Drawable)
                $this->_things[] = $arg;
            else
                error_log("Rejecting Page item #{$i} - not drawable:
".var_export($arg,TRUE));
        }
    }
```

Then it calls its own `draw()` method to display them. You can even create a new subclass of `Page`, something like `SubPage` or `BoxSet` that arranges its objects in a particular way, and then hand an instance of that subclass to your Page object like any other Drawable object. You can see the possibilities that might have.

Object cloning

In prior versions of PHP, making a copy of an object was nothing special:

```
$a = new MyClass();
$b = $a;
```

Voila, $b was a copy of $a. But returning a reference to a particular object was more of a chore:

```
function &returnObject()
{
    $a =& new MyClass();
    return $a;
}
$b =& $a;
```

Now, it's the other way around. All object variables are references. If you create a new instance of `MyClass` in `$a` and assign `$a` to `$b`, you still have only one `MyClass` object out there. You've just got two different variables referencing it. Normally, that's what you want – it makes it a lot easier to pass objects in and out of methods and function calls, for one thing. But sometimes you need the old behavior – you want to end up with two different instances of `MyClass`, one in `$a` and the other in `$b`. For that, you have the `__clone()` method.

```
$a = new MyClass();
$b = $a->__clone();
```

Every class can just leave cloning to the built-in `__clone()` method, available with every object at no extra cost. Or you can write your own `__clone()` method to do things like create new separate database connections, erase temporary storage variables, reset counters, and so on.

Destructors

PHP now lets you declare not only generic constructor methods, using the name `__construct()`, but also *destructor* methods as well, named `__destruct()`. A destructor function gets called when you destroy an object – at the end of a script, for instance. Or say you create an object inside of a procedural function. When a function ends, all of its local variables go out of scope, so in a general sense the memory assigned to them is released and the variables are destroyed. If you've written a `__destruct()` function for your object, it would be called at that point.

You can use destructor functions to do any clean-up work that's necessary: roll back any open transactions, close database connections or logging files, and so on.

Exceptions

PHP 5 includes an exception scheme similar to that of the Java programming language. In other words, it supports `try/catch` blocks, which were not supported in earlier versions of the language.

You can, for example, define an exception class for later invocation, as in the following example:

```
class DemoException
{
    function __construct($exception)
    {
        $this->exception = $exception;
    }

    function Display()
    {
        print "DemoException: $this->exception\n";
    }
}

class DemoExceptionTosser extends DemoException
{
    function __construct($exception)
    {
        $this->exception = $exception;
    }
```

```
    function Display()
    {
        print "DemoExceptionTosser: $this->exception\n";
    }
}

try
{
    throw new DemoExceptionTosser('Hello');
}
catch (DemoException $exception)
{
    $exception->Display();
}
```

This code works by attempting to execute what's in the `try` block. When that code uses the `throw` keyword to indirectly construct a `DemoException` object, the exception is caught by the code in the `catch` block and subsequently printed out by the `Display()` function.

Object-Oriented Code versus Procedural Code

Here's the million-dollar question: In your applications, should you use object-oriented code or procedural code? This question can inspire heated debate. But really such heated debate is unnecessary because there is a correct answer: It depends upon the situation. If a given application can be designed to take advantage of object orientation (in other words, if the problem at hand can be modeled as a series of elements that interact), object orientation may be the way to go. And since it's possible to think of the entire world as a bunch of objects interacting with each other, that's a pretty strong possibility.

Object-oriented code comes with advantages and disadvantages. Weigh them and decide for yourself if you should use classes or just functions.

The following are the advantages of object-oriented programming:

- In the long run (that is, across several projects), you can save time using the object-oriented approach.
- You can make easily reusable pieces of code.
- You can make use of extensive class libraries available for free on the Web.

The following are the disadvantages of object-oriented programming:

- It's slower than the procedural approach in the short term.
- The syntax can be confusing at first.
- Web programming does not make use of many of the advantages of object-oriented code.
- If you're using very large class libraries, you might experience a performance reduction.

Comments

In any programming language, comments are essential – not only to you as you're writing the code, but to those who come to the code after you. What may be crystal-clear to you may be absolutely unreadable to others. Or, if you've had to do something particularly complex, you might find that you don't even understand what you were thinking if you come back to the code a couple of months after you wrote it.

In PHP you can indicate comments with two slashes (//), with a hash (#), or by bracketing commented code with /* and */. This last method is particularly helpful for multi-line comments.

Comment all of your functions, what they do, what they are expecting, and what they return. Make sure to note any variables that might be tough to track.

As you look through the functions directory of the CD, you will see that every function has an initial comment that mimics the style used in the PHP manual. For example:

```
int fetch_record (string table_name [, mixed key [, mixed value]])
```

Then you provide some description as to what these arguments mean and the significance of the return value. When writing the body of the function, you should comment on anything that is not going to be intuitive to someone coming to the script at a later date. If you have a series of functions that perform some complex string handling or use lengthy regular expressions, make sure to note exactly what those functions are intended to accomplish. For example, consider this line of code:

```
$file_ext = strtolower(substr($file, strrpos($file,".")));
```

It isn't especially difficult to figure out, but you can sure help the next person coming to this line with a simple comment:

```
//get characters following the final dot
//and make lowercase
$file_ext = strtolower(substr($file, strrpos($file,".")));
```

The other important thing to comment is the overall logic of pages, especially long pages. Often a script behaves differently under different circumstances. Variables passed from forms, errors, and other factors affect what portions of the script run. At the top of the page, you can indicate what factors affect the page's logic and then, as you reach different `if` blocks, explain where the conditions are coming from and what they mean.

For a brief example, take the confirm_delete.php page from Chapter 8, which makes advantageous use of comments

```
/*
 /*
********************************************************
*** This script from MySQL/PHP Database Applications ***
***         by Jay Greenspan and Brad Bulger         ***
***                                                  ***
***   You are free to reuse the material in this     ***
***   script in any manner you see fit. There is     ***
***   no need to ask for permission or provide       ***
***   credit.                                        ***
********************************************************
*/

/*
Application: Guestbook2k
Described in: Chapter 8
Name: confirm_delete.php
Purpose: Confirm, then perform, deletion of entries from the guestbook.

This script will be accessed in two circumstances:

- The 'Delete Entries' button on the edit.php page was pressed.
  This should be the first time that the script is called. The ids
  of the records to be deleted should be passed in via the entry_id[]
  array.

- The 'Confirm Delete' button on this page was pressed. This confirms
  the deletions and will run the delete queries against the database.

The $offset variable is preserved to allow navigation to other entriesin the
guestbook after or instead of confirming the deletion.

This script must be run by an authenticated user - i.e., only guestbook
administrators.

*/
```

```
// turn on PHP output buffering - only HTTP headers will be sent
// to the browser while this is on. it will prevent an accidental
// blank line or some such from breaking HTTP authentication.

ob_start();

require_once('header.php');
guestbook_authenticate();

// turn off output buffering and send the accumulated output
// to the browser

ob_end_flush();

guestbook_start_page('Confirm Changes');


$submit = (string)array_key_value($_POST,'submit');

// if $entry_id hasn't been passed in - because the user
// hit the 'Delete' button without checking off any
// entries, say - initialize it to an empty array.

$entry_id = (array)array_key_value($_POST,'entry_id',array());

if ($submit == 'Delete Entries' && !empty($entry_id))
{
    // presumably coming from edit.php. print out id values to be
    // deleted and the 'Confirm Delete' submit button

    // because the <form> tag contains no action attribute, it
    // will submit back to this script

    print "<form method=post>\n<ul>\n";

    foreach ((array)$entry_id as $value)
    {
        print <<<EOQ
<li>Delete entry #$value?
<input type=hidden name="entry_id[]" value="$value">
EOQ;
    }

    print <<<EOQ
</ul>
```

```
<br>
<input type=submit name=submit value="Confirm Delete">
<input type=hidden name=offset value="$offset">
</form>
EOQ;

}
else
{
    // just in case this script is called directly or in some other
    // unanticipated manner
    print "<h4>No action to confirm</h4>\n";
}

// display navigational links and end the page
nav($offset, 'edit.php');
guestbook_end_page();
```

We end this section on a word of caution: don't over-comment. Commenting every single line, or making the obvious even more obvious, is annoying. For example, the following comments are completely unnecessary and only make a script difficult to read:

```
//make string lowercase
$str = strtolower($str);
//increase $i by 1
$i++
```

Commenting calls for good judgment. You don't want to comment too much; you don't want to comment too little. Our best advice is to take a look at how other programmers comment their code and to pick a style that you like. We use one method for the applications in this book; others have different styles.

The PEAR directory of your PHP installation is a great place to look for tips on good coding style. PEAR stands for PHP Extension and Application Repository. It is a growing set of scripts that contains a series of best practices for programming with PHP. The folks working on PEAR are real pros who write terrific code. We recommend looking through the scripts in that directory to glean some tips on writing quality code.

Summary

In this chapter, we have presented some ways to write clean and organized code. When you look at your scripts, you should ask yourself a few questions.

- **Are there blocks of code that are common to every page?** Maybe those blocks can be moved into an include.
- **Are there chunks of code that I'm writing over and over again?** Perhaps writing a function or class might save time.
- **Is the next person who comes to this script going to be able to figure out what I've been doing?** If not, make sure that you add enough comments to make things clear.

You need to decide if an object-oriented approach is good for you and the application you're writing. Our advice: make sure you are comfortable writing clean procedural code before you jump into object-oriented programming.

Part III

Simple Applications

Chapter 8

Guestbook 2003, the (Semi-)Bulletproof Guestbook

IN THIS CHAPTER

- Learning the power of Guestbook 2003
- Organizing your code in a reasonable way
- Writing good, reusable functions

IN THIS CHAPTER WE DEVELOP the first of our applications – a guestbook. Guestbooks aren't complex and they aren't very exciting. However, this application does give us the chance to introduce some concepts, such as validation, and put many of the practices discussed earlier in this book to work.

In the introduction of this book we provided some code that could be used for the most basic guestbook possible. However, using that code for your guestbook is not a good idea: It's got all kinds of holes that will allow malicious people out there to mess with your pages. The ultra-basic guestbook has another problem: Given the way the code is just dumped into one page, there's not a line that's reusable. One of the main goals of developing any application is to create chunks of reusable code.

Determining the Scope and Goals of the Application

The easiest way to get yourself into trouble when coming at an application is not to know exactly what you are trying to achieve. A vital part of the developer's job is to figure out exactly what is needed in the application. Usually doing this will involve extensive discussion with the people for whom the application is being developed. During these discussions, it is important to think a step ahead and ask questions that may not have been asked before. What if the scope increases in a certain way? What if additional but related information needs to be tracked?

Considering these and similar scenarios will affect the way you design your database and your scripts, and that is why it is best to know the exact scope and goals of your application. Depending on whom you're working with, you may want to get some sketches of pages that need to be developed.

The scope of this application is small and the goals are minimal. The guestbook stores names, addresses, and the like. (To tell the truth, the purpose of this chapter is not so much to show you how to write a guestbook as it to show you how to write good, reusable, organized code for your applications.) In any case, you should know what Guestbook 2003 looks like before you proceed.

In this chapter we're not going to take the notion of creating good functions as far as it can go. In Chapter 9 we present a more extensive set of functions that we'll use throughout the rest of the book.

Necessary pages

This guestbook has three basic pages: one for signing, one for viewing, and one for administering.

Figure 8-1 shows the page that gives the user the opportunity to sign the guestbook. It's pretty simple, a form with four text fields and one text area field. Additionally, there are a submit button and a reset button.

Figure 8-1: Page for signing the guestbook

Next, there must be a way to see who has signed the guestbook. For the sake of having readable Web pages, we created a standard style, shown in Figure 8-2, in which only two entries are printed on each page. At the bottom of the page are navigational elements that indicate whether previous or additional entries exist. These should be conditional and should disappear appropriately when you are at the beginning or end of the guestbook.

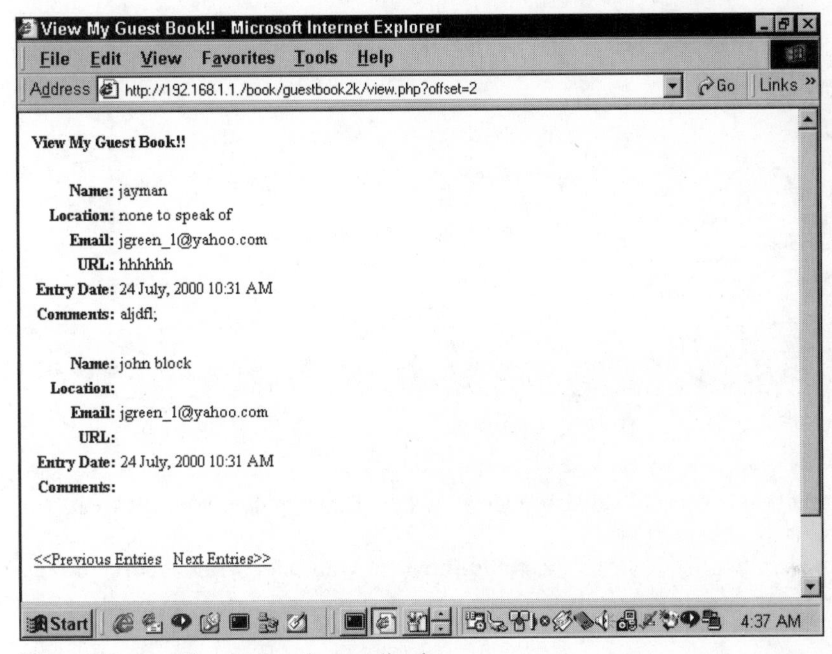

Figure 8-2: Page for viewing the guestbook

Finally, we need a page that enables us to delete entries we don't want. The page in Figure 8-3 seems to do the trick. Access to this page needs to be limited to authorized users: We don't want any old schmo going in and cleaning out our guestbook.

What do we need to prevent?

The major problem that we need to tackle in the guestbook application is one that is common to any application with form input: It is possible for vandals to input nasty code into your forms that will screw up the pages for everyone else who comes along. If you used the guestbook application in the introduction you could be in serious trouble. Consider what would happen if someone inserted the following code into a text field:

```
<script>alert("boo");</script>
```

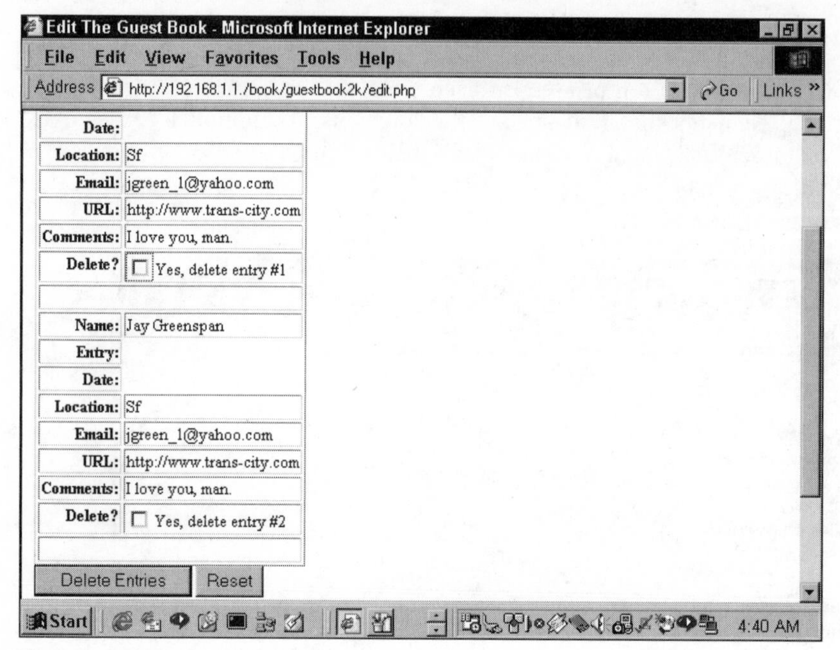

Figure 8-3: Page for administering the guestbook

The next time the page loaded, the viewer would be greeted with a little treat seen in Figure 8-4.

If some jerk felt like it, he or she could screw up your page with all sorts of tags, as follows:

```
<img src=http://www.britney-spears.fsnet.co.uk/britney4.jpg>
```

Additionally, this application requires some validation. When the user enters information, the application is going to see that it makes sense. The application will check for the following:

- Email addresses should contain an at symbol (@), one or more characters before the @, and a dot somewhere after the @. Email validation can get more complex (and will in later chapters).
- URLs should look like URLs, complete with an `http://` prefix and at least one dot.
- Some text must be entered in the name field. There's little point to a guestbook entry without a name.
- No email address should appear more than once in the database.

Once the application has checked all of this, the user will need to be made aware of any errors. Figures 8-5 and 8-6 show how we will indicate these errors.

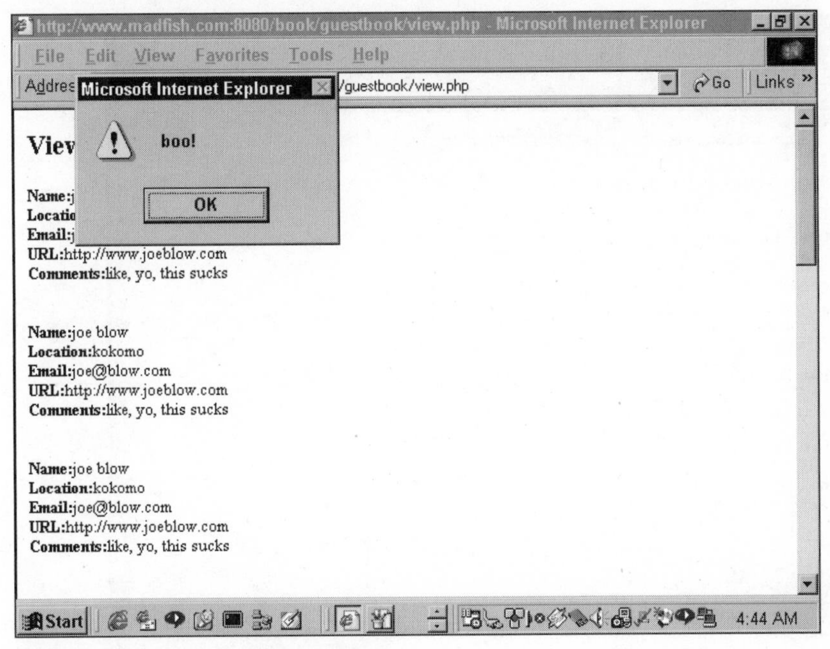

Figure 8-4: Results of a problem entry

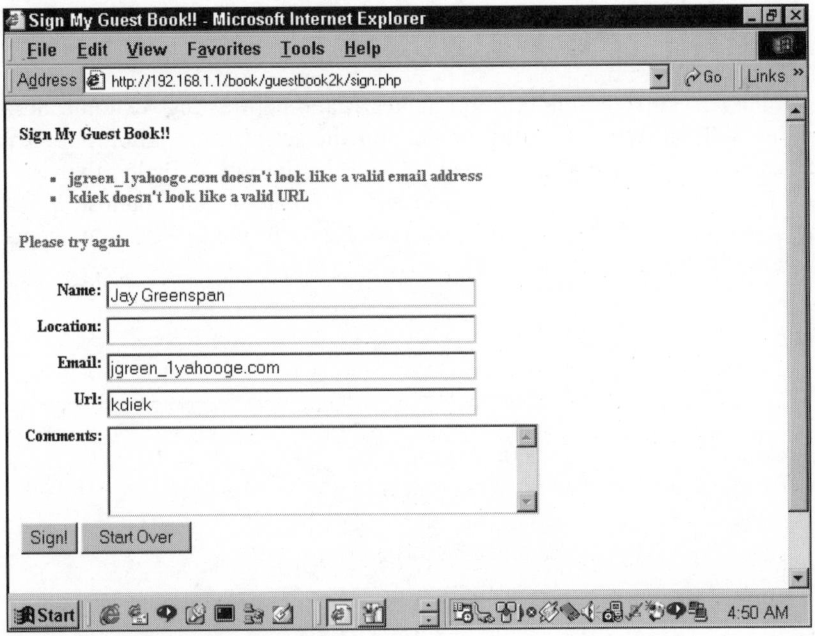

Sign My Guest Book!! - Microsoft Internet Explorer

File Edit View Favorites Tools Help

Address http://192.168.1.1/book/guestbook2k/sign.php Go Links

Sign My Guest Book!!

- jgreen_1yahooge.com doesn't look like a valid email address
- kdiek doesn't look like a valid URL

Please try again

Name: Jay Greenspan

Location:

Email: jgreen_1yahooge.com

Url: kdiek

Comments:

Sign! Start Over

Start 4:50 AM

Figure 8-5: Reporting bad information

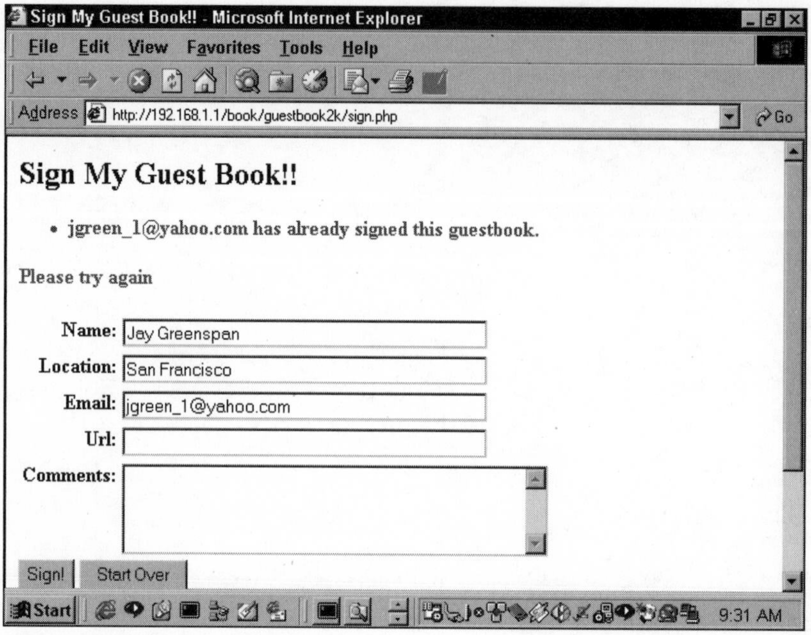

Figure 8-6: Reporting a duplicate entry

Designing the Database

We covered the normalization process in Chapter 1, and before long we'll put these normalization skills to work. For this application the set of information is pretty simple. So simple, in fact, that a single table will do the job. Actually, that isn't quite true. For administrative purposes, you should create a table against which user names and passwords can be authenticated. Here are the `create` statements that will make the tables:

```
drop table if exists guestbook;
create table guestbook
(
        entry_id        integer not null auto_increment
        , name          varchar(40) null
        , location      varchar(40) null
        , email         varchar(40) not null
        , url           varchar(40) null
        , comments      text null
        , created       timestamp
        , remote_addr   varchar(20) null
, primary key (entry_id)
```

```
, unique (email)
);

drop table if exists guestbook_admin;
create table guestbook_admin
(
        username        varchar(50) not null
        , password      varchar(255) not null
, primary key (username)
);
```

When you are adding a user to the guestbook_admin table, it would be best to encrypt the password. The easiest way to do this is by using a built-in MySQL password encryption function like `sha1()`, as follows:

```
insert into guestbook_admin (username, password)
    values ('jay', sha1('rules'));
```

After you've run this command, the actual value stored in the `password` column is `caa155adf81fddd29ab4b21a147927fb0295eb53`. When you need to find out whether a user knows the password, you can use the `sha1` function again:

```
select * from guestbook_admin where
username = 'jay' and
password = sha1('rules');
```

From the latest MySQL documentation: "Note: The `PASSWORD()` function is used by the authentication system in MySQL Server, you should NOT use it in your own applications. For that purpose, use `MD5()` or `SHA1()` instead. Also see RFC-2195 for more information about handling passwords and authentication securely in your application."

Code Overview

In this, the first of your applications, you need to look at the architecture you will use in constructing your applications. The applications on the CD have been constructed so that they are as reusable and portable as possible.

To start with, the CD contains a folder named book, which should be copied to the document root directory of your Web server. On Apache this folder is usually named htdocs by default. The book folder contains all the applications documented in this book.

Within the book folder is a series of folders, one folder for each of the applications presented here, one labeled classes, and one labeled functions. For the purpose of this application we will concern ourselves with the basic.php file in the functions folder; this file defines some functions that you will use in a variety of applications. We'll discuss the functions in basic.php that are used in Guestbook 2003 in the section entitled "Code Breakdown."

The code that is relevant only to Guestbook 2003 is kept in the guestbook2k folder. Here, startup code that needs to be run at the beginning of each page is run by the header.php file. The header.php file contains, in turn, two other files: globals.php and functions.php. This is a structure that we'll be using through all the examples in the book. The globals.php file is where you create global variables and define constants for use in the application. The functions that will need to be addressed across a number of pages are kept in the functions.php file. We will also explain these functions in detail in the "Code Breakdown" section.

The pages that are called from the browser are named intuitively: view.php, sign.php, and edit.php. The other page of the application is confirm_delete.php, which is called only by edit.php and not by the user directly.

You may find the view.php, sign.php, and edit.php files surprisingly short. They only contain a couple of dozen lines of code each. This is because just about everything is written in reusable functions.

So once again the important thing is to understand the functions kept in /book/functions/basic.php and /book/guestbook2k/functions.php, as well as the startup code run in /book/guestbook2k/header.php.

Code Breakdown

As mentioned in the previous section, the vast majority of the work of this application is done in functions, and these functions are kept in files that will be included in the pages called from the browser.

From functions/basic.php

The following are the main functions from basic.php that we'll be using in this application. We'll cover other functions later on, and they're all briefly documented in Appendix F. The functions are grouped by their general purpose, and that's the order in which we'll go through them.

GENERAL UTILITY FUNCTIONS (OR, "IF ONLY PHP HAD A FUNCTION TO . . .")

Here are some utility functions that we find helpful:

ARRAY_KEY_VALUE() With the advent of the new "superglobal" PHP variables like `$_POST`, you'll be getting most of the values you use in your code from associative arrays (`$_GET`, `$_POST`, and so on). The trouble is that if a particular key hasn't been defined in the array, trying to access it causes an error – well, strictly speaking, a warning, but it's a good idea to eliminate those, too. You could type something like

```
$country = isset($my_array['country']) ? $my_array['country'] : '';
```

over and over again, but that isn't great because if `$my_array['country']` is set to `NULL`, `isset()` will return `FALSE`, and that may not be the behavior you want – after all, the key is present in the array. A better choice would be `array_key_exists()`, which returns `TRUE` if the key exists, no matter what its contents. But typing lines like the following repeatedly is no fun at all:

```
$country = array_key_exists('country', $my_array) ?
$my_array['country'] : '';
```

The following function will help:

```
function array_key_value($arr='', $name='', $default='')
{
    // cast in case $arr is an object
    $arr = (array)$arr;
    if (!is_array($name))
    {
        if (array_key_exists($name,$arr))
            $default = $arr[$name];
        return $default;
    }
    $results = array();
    foreach ($name as $n)
    {
        if (array_key_exists($n,$arr))
        {
            $results[] = $arr[$n];
        }
        else
        {
            $results[] = $default;
        }
    }
    return $results;
}
```

You can see this function used on almost every page of the application. For example, the sign.php page contains several lines that look like this:

```
$email = array_key_value($_POST,'email');
```

When `array_key_value()` is called from the preceding example, the first `if` block will be ignored. In the second `if` block, the `array_key_exists()` function checks if a key by name of `email` exists in the `$_POST` array. If it does, the value of `$_POST['email']` will be assigned to `$email` when the function returns a value. If the `email` key does not exist, `$email` will contain an empty string.

IS_ASSOC() Sometimes you need to know not just if a variable is an array, which the PHP function `is_array()` can tell you, but if it's an associative array – in other words, do all the elements have named keys? The `is_assoc()` function exists for this situation.

```
function is_assoc($a)
{
    if (is_array($a) || is_object($a))
    {
        $nkeys = array_filter(array_keys($a),'is_numeric');
        if (empty($nkeys))
        {
            return TRUE;
        }
    }
    return FALSE;
}
```

DEFENSIVE AND TEXT-HANDLING FUNCTIONS

A shocking amount of programming work has to do with the manipulation of strings. It seems there's always text to be chopped up, stuck together, searched for, or formatted. This section deals with some of the text-processing functions available in PHP.

CHARSET() This function sends out an HTTP header that explicitly sets the character-set-encoding value for the page to `ISO-8859-1`:

```
function charset($charset='',$mimetype='')
{
    if (empty($charset))
    {
        $charset = 'ISO-8859-1';
    }
    if (empty($mimetype))
    {
        $mimetype = 'text/html';
    }
    header("Content-Type: $mimetype; charset=$charset");
}
```

If the character set is left undefined, it can be much more difficult to detect and prevent hacks into your scripts (by looking for < and > characters, for example). If you have access to the php.ini file for your site, you can uncomment the 'default_charset' value there to the same effect. You can find more information about this topic at the following sites:

```
http://www.cert.org/tech_tips/malicious_code_mitigation.html
http://www.apache.org/info/css-security/encoding_examples.html
```

CLEANUP_TEXT() This function goes a long way toward making sure we don't insert malicious text into our database.

```
function cleanup_text ($value='', $preserve='', $allowed_tags='')
{
    if (empty($preserve))
    {
        $value = strip_tags($value, $allowed_tags);
    }
    $value = htmlspecialchars($value);
    return $value;
}
```

This function accomplishes two things. First, it removes all HTML tags. The `strip_tags()` function takes care of that. We can indicate tags we want to keep with the third argument (`$allowed_tags`). For instance, if we want to allow bold and italic tags, the second argument to `strip_tags()` can be a string like this: <b><i>. If we want to leave tags as they are, we can indicate this with a non-empty value in the second argument, `$preserve`.

Then `htmlentities()` changes characters like ampersands (&) and double quotes to their equivalent HTML entities (`&` and `"`, respectively). After being run through this little function, your text is ready to be inserted in the database.

REVERSE_CLEANUP_TEXT() So we've run all the text from your users through `cleanup_text()` before storing it in our database, for safety's sake. Now, though, we need to get that text back out of the database and display it on a Web page. If we did allow some HTML tags to be included, we'll need to reverse the effects of `cleanup_text()`, or instead of seeing this –

My mom won't let me watch *The Exorcist* tonight!

– you'll see this:

```
My mom won't let me watch <i>The Exorcist</i> tonight!
```

```
function reverse_cleanup_text ($value)
{
    static $reverse_entities = NULL;
    if ($reverse_entities === NULL)
    {
        $reverse_entities = array_flip(
            get_html_translation_table(HTML_ENTITIES)
        );
    }
    return strtr($value,$reverse_entities);

}
```

The HTML translation table HTML_ENTITIES is a list of all the special characters that have HTML-entity equivalents. Then we use array_flip() to turn it around, so that strtr() can go through the string and replace each HTML entity it finds with the special single character it represents_ < to <' & to &, and so on. (We save the modified translation table in a static variable, so subsequent calls to this function won't have to recreate it.)

MAKE_PAGE_TITLE() For most pages, we use the same text in the <title> that appears in an HTML heading <h1>. But some characters are inappropriate for the <title> tag. For instance, if we set $page_title to "José's Review of <i>The Exorcist</i>", within a rendered <h1> tag we'd see the correct value, Josà's Review of *The Exorcist*. But the title of the browser window will show Josà's Review of <i>The Exorcist</i>. To avoid this, we can use this little function:

```
function make_page_title ($title='')
{
    return reverse_cleanup_text(cleanup_text($title));
}
```

FROM /GUESTBOOK2K/HEADER.PHP

Once again, this file will be included in every page in this application. It includes the functions.php and globals.php files, where we'll keep all the functions and global variables specific to this application. In addition, the first few lines of this application will see to a few details. For instance, it sets the PHP include_path configuration variable to cover the /book/functions directory. (If you can edit the php.ini file for your installation, you can set include_path in there and remove this code.)

```
// make sure that the current directory and book/functions
// are in the include path
```

```
// make sure that the book/functions directory is in the include path

//realpath turns a relative path to an absolute one, and
//DIRECTORY_SEPARATOR is pre-defined PHP constant that on Unix will
//return a slash(/) and on Windows a backslash(\)
$funcdir = realpath('..'.DIRECTORY_SEPARATOR.'functions');
$include_path = ini_get('include_path');
if (strpos($include_path, $funcdir) === FALSE)
{
    // the only time there's a semicolon in the include path is on Windows.
    // (far as i know, at least...)
    $ps = strchr($include_path, ';') ? ';' : ':';
    ini_set('include_path',$include_path.$ps.$funcdir);
}

require_once('basic.php');

// set the character encoding
charset();

// display all errors and warnings, but not notices
error_reporting(E_ALL ^ (E_NOTICE | E_USER_NOTICE));

require_once('globals.php');
require_once('functions.php');

mysql_dbconnect();
```

A few words about including files. You'll notice that we use two different functions to do this, `require_once()` and `include_once()`. They work exactly the same way, except that – as the name implies – `require_once()` won't take no for an answer. If it can't find the file it's trying to include, the script will fail right there. The `include_once()` function will just issue a warning and move on.

We also generally prefer the `include_once()` and `require_once()` functions over `include()` and `require()`. Again, as the names imply, the difference is that the `_once` functions will only include a file if it hasn't already been included at some point. This enables us to put calls to a file like header.php in all of our files, even if some of them might end up including others.

FROM /GUESTBOOK2K/GLOBALS.PHP

In the following code, we have included something interesting: a constant, here named `DEFAULT_LIMIT`. A constant is like a variable in that it contains a value (in this instance `2`). However, that value cannot be changed by a simple assignment; in fact, once a constant has been defined with the `define()` function, it can't be changed at all. Constants do not run into the same scope problems that are encountered with variables, so you can use them within functions without having to pass them in as arguments or worry about declaring globals. After you run the `define()` function, the constant `DEFAULT_LIMIT` will be available everywhere in the application.

We'll use `DEFAULT_LIMIT` to decide the number of entries that will be viewable on each page. You are welcome to change the value if you would like to see a larger number.

```
// constants
define('DEFAULT_LIMIT', 2);

// global variables

// we'll look for offset in the $_REQUEST superglobal because it
// could be coming in from either the URL or a form. $_REQUEST is
// a combination of GET, POST, and cookie-based values.

$offset = array_key_value($_REQUEST,'offset',0);
```

If you are putting together a query using a constant, you will have to end your quoted string in order to make use of the constant value. For example,

```
$query = "select * from db_name limit DEFAULT_LIMIT"
```

will confuse MySQL, because PHP has not replaced the name of the constant with its value. However, this will work:

```
$query = "select * from db_name limit " .
DEFAULT_LIMIT
```

PHP has many built-in constants you can use within your scripts, like the `DIRECTORY_SEPARATOR` constant seen in the header.php file. A list of constants is included in the PHP manual at `http://www.php.net/manual/language.constants.php`.

FROM /GUESTBOOK2K/FUNCTIONS.PHP

On top of the standard PHP functions are those that were created for the Guestbook 2003 application. The following sections take a look at the guestbook library.

MYSQL_DBCONNECT() This is a slightly prettier version of the original `dbconnect()` function included in the first edition of this book.

```
function mysql_dbconnect()
{
    $link = @mysql_connect('localhost','nobody','ydobon');
    if ($link === FALSE)
    {
        $private_error = 'mysql_dbconnect: could not open connection
to mysql:'
            .'<li>errno:'.mysql_errno()
            .'<li>error:'.mysql_error()
        ;
        error_log($private_error, 0);
        die('Error: could not connect to database server. Please
contact the system administrator.');
        exit;
    }
    if (!@mysql_select_db('guestbook2k'))
    {
        $private_error = 'mysql_dbconnect: could not select
guestbook database:'
            .'<li>errno:'.mysql_errno()
            .'<li>error:'.mysql_error()
        ;
        error_log($private_error, 0);
        die('Error: could not connect to guestbook database. Please
contact the system administrator.');
        exit;

    }
    return $link;
}
```

The @ in front of the calls to `mysql_connect()` and `mysql_select_db()` tells PHP not to print out any errors or warnings that happen inside those functions. That enables us to write out the detailed errors to the error log while sending a simpler error to the user.

SAFE_MYSQL_QUERY() This function will save you from pulling your hair out when you're trying to get your queries right.

```
function safe_mysql_query ($query='')
{
    if (empty($query))
    {
        return FALSE;
    }
```

```
    $result = @mysql_query($query);

    if ($result === FALSE)
    {
        // if there was an error executing the query, write out the
        // details to the error log

        $private_error = 'ack! query failed: '
            .'<li>errorno='.mysql_errno()
            .'<li>error='.mysql_error()
            .'<li>query='.$query
        ;
        error_log($private_error, 0);

        // send a generic error message to the user

        die('There was an error executing a query. Please contact
the system administrator.');

        exit;
    }

    return $result;
}
```

Throughout the application, we will run our queries through this function. This way, if the query fails for some reason, we can get a pretty good idea of what happened. This is another example of safe coding. After troubleshooting your code, we won't run into these problems often, but if a change is made somewhere (perhaps without our knowledge) we'll get a pretty good idea of what's going on.

GUESTBOOK_AUTHENTICATE() This function will require the user to enter a name and password and will then validate those against the `guestbook_admin` table in the database. If the username and password don't match any valid entries, or if the user (by hitting Cancel, say) doesn't submit them, an error message will be displayed.

```
function guestbook_authenticate($realm = 'Guest Book Administration'
 , $errmsg = 'You must enter a valid name and password to access
this function'
)
{
// check if we can use HTTP authentication - as of now, that
// means checking if we are running as an Apache module
```

```
    $http_auth_OK = (php_sapi_name() == 'apache');

// $_SERVER['PHP_AUTH_USER'] and $_SERVER['PHP_AUTH_PW'] are values
// supplied by PHP, corresponding to the user name and password
// the user has entered in the pop-up window created by an HTTP
// authentication header. If no authentication header has ever been
// sent, these variables will be empty. If we are not using HTTP
// authentication, the login form will create entries in the
// $_POST superglobal with the same names.

    foreach (array('PHP_AUTH_USER','PHP_AUTH_PW') as $v)
    {
        if (!isset($_SESSION[$v]))
        {
            if ($http_auth_OK)
            {
                $_SESSION[$v] = array_key_value($_SERVER,$v,'');
            }
            else
            {
                $_SESSION[$v] = array_key_value($_POST,$v,'');
            }
        }
    }

    $found_user = 0;
    if (!empty($_SESSION['PHP_AUTH_USER']))
    {
        // ignore case, even if MySQL has been set to
        // pay attention to it
        $query = <<<EOQ
select 1 from guestbook_admin
where password = sha1(lower('{$_SESSION['PHP_AUTH_PW']}'))
and lower(username) = lower('{$_SESSION['PHP_AUTH_USER']}')
EOQ;
        $result = safe_mysql_query($query);
        if ($result)
        {
            list($found_user) = mysql_fetch_row($result);
        }
        else
        {
// if the query didn't work at all (which should have been caught by
// safe_mysql_query() in theory), we're not going to be able to
```

```
// confirm the password, so fail.
            $private_error = "problem running authentication query
($query): "
                .mysql_error()
            ;
            error_log($private_error,0);
            die('Database error: could not check password. Please
contact the system administrator.');
            exit;
        }

// if the query ran but didn't find a match for the user name
// and password, $found_user will not be set to anything.
// if this is so, have the user try again.

        if ($found_user == 0)
        {
            $errmsg .= <<<EOQ
<li>Could not find entry for username ({$_SESSION['PHP_AUTH_USER']})
-
please try again.
EOQ;
        }
    }
    if ($found_user == 0)
    {
        if ($http_auth_OK)
        {
// Send a WWW-Authenticate header, to perform HTTP authentication.
            Header("WWW-Authenticate: Basic realm=\"$realm\"");
            Header("HTTP/1.0 401 Unauthorized");

// The user should only see this after hitting the 'Cancel' button
// in the pop-up form.
            print $errmsg;

            exit;
        }
        else
        {
// Print out an HTML form to obtain a name and password
// for authentication.

            if (!empty($errmsg)) { $errmsg = "<p>$errmsg</p>"; }
```

```
            print <<<EOQ
<h2>$realm</h2>
$errmsg
<form method=post>
Username: <input type=text name="PHP_AUTH_USER"
value="{$_SESSION['PHP_AUTH_USER']}">
<br>
Password: <input type=password name="PHP_AUTH_PW"
value="{$_SESSION['PHP_AUTH_PW']}">
<br>
<input type=submit>
</form>
EOQ;
            exit;
        }
        // should never get here
        $private_error = 'authenticate: error: continued after
requesting password';
        error_log($private_error);
        die('System error: please contact the system
administrator.');
        exit;
    }
    else
    {
        print <<<EOQ
<p><b>Editing as {$_SESSION['PHP_AUTH_USER']}</b></p>
EOQ;
    }
}
```

If PHP is installed as an Apache module, `guestbook_authenticate()` will send out a 401 HTTP response code. This header forces the browser to open the username and password box shown in Figure 8-7.

The values entered into these text fields are set by PHP to the variables `$_SERVER['PHP_AUTH_USER']` and `$_SERVER['PHP_AUTH_PW']`. If PHP isn't running as an Apache module, an ordinary HTML form is displayed, with text fields using the same names. The text fields will be returned as values in `$_POST`.

When the user submits either form the same page is run, and `guestbook_authenticate()` is called again. Now that it has a possible username and password it can query MySQL to check if the values are stored in the database. If they are not, the password form is displayed again.

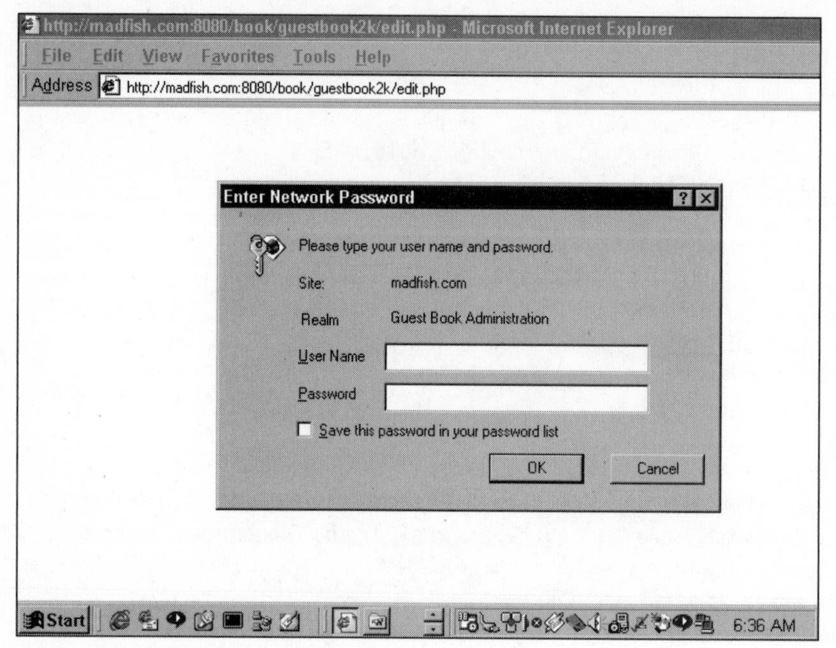

Figure 8-7: Results of a 401 Unauthorized header

PRINT_ENTRY() This prints the results of a query within a table.

```
function print_entry($row,$preserve='')
{
    if (!is_assoc($row))
    {
        return FALSE;
    }

    // walk through any arguments passed in after the first two
    $numargs = func_num_args();
    for ($i = 2; $i < $numargs; $i++)
    {
        $field = func_get_arg($i);

        // This will transform a label string to a valid database
        // field name - e.g., 'Last Name' becomes 'last_name'
        $dbfield = str_replace(' ', '_', strtolower($field));

        $dbvalue = cleanup_text($row[$dbfield],$preserve);
        $name = ucwords($field);
        print <<<EOQ
```

```
 <tr>
  <td valign="top" align="right"><b>$name:</b></td>
  <td valign="top" align="left">$dbvalue</td>
 </tr>
EOQ;
    }
}
```

The easiest way to see how this function works is to take a look at the line of code that calls a function. The following snippet was taken from the view.php file:

```
print_entry($row,$preserve,'name','location','email','URL','entry
date','comments');
```

Notice that the function itself has only two default arguments (`$row` and `$preserve`), while the call to the function has nine arguments. The first argument, `$row`, is a row from a database call. It is expecting that a row was taken from a query by means of `mysql_fetch_array()` so that the contents of the row are an associative array, the keys of which are equal to the column names of the database table. The second argument, `$preserve`, is needed for the `cleanup_text()` function, which we discussed previously in the chapter. The rest of the arguments are equivalent to associative keys in `$row`.

The arguments sent to any user-defined function make up an array. The number of elements in the array can be retrieved with `func_num_args()`. If we were to use the call to `print_entry()` in this example, `func_num_args()` would return 9.

The value of each argument can then be accessed with `func_get_arg()`. This allows for a structure like the one used here, where a loop accesses and then processes each argument sent to the function. The first time through the `for` loop, `$field` is assigned the third element in the array, `name`. You can use the value in `$field` to access an element in the associative array `$row` (`$row['name']`).

After you make sure the argument contains no capital letters or spaces, the value is sent to the `cleanup_text` function and printed.

It's nice to structure a function this way because it allows an arbitrary number of arguments to be sent to the function. We can include one or many fields to print.

PRINT_INPUT_FIELDS() This function works much like `print_entry()`. `func_get_args()` makes `$fields` an array, each element of which is an argument sent to the function. The `foreach()` structure moves through all elements in the array and prints a text field for each. The name of the field will be in one table cell, and the input box will be in an adjoining cell.

```
function print_input_fields()
{
    $fields = func_get_args();
```

```
    foreach ($fields as $field)
    {
        $value = array_key_value($_POST,$field,'');
        $label = ucwords(str_replace('_',' ',$field));
        print <<<EOQ
 <tr>
  <td valign="top" align="right">
   <b>$label:</b>
  </td>
  <td valign=top align=left>
   <input type="text" name="$field" size="40" value="$value">
  </td>
 </tr>
EOQ;
    }
}
```

Notice that we check the `$_POST` global array for the default value of the text field. The check is here in the event that the user enters bad information and the information needs to be re-presented with the values he or she entered. Why would information need to be printed a second time? That should make perfect sense after you read about the next function, `create_entry()`.

CREATE_ENTRY() We are not going to simply dump user information into the database. First it needs to be verified.

```
function create_entry(
  $name='', $location='',$email='',$url='',$comments=''
)
{
    // remove all HTML tags, and escape any other special characters
    $name = cleanup_text($name);
    $location = cleanup_text($location);
    $email = cleanup_text($email);
    $url = cleanup_text($url);
    $comments = cleanup_text($comments);

    // start out with an empty error message.
    // as validation tests fail, add errors to it.
    $errmsg = '';
    if (empty($name))
    {
        $errmsg .= "<li>you have to put in a name, at least!\n";
    }
```

```
    // do a very simple check on the format of the email address
    // supplied by the user. an email address is required.
    if (!empty($email) && !preg_match(
            '/^[\w_-.+]+@[\w_-]+(\.[\w_-])+$/', $email
    ))

    {
        $errmsg .= "<li>$email doesn't look like a valid email
address\n";
    }
    else
    {
        // if the format is OK, check to see if this user has
already
        // signed the guestbook. multiple entries are not allowed.
        $query = "select * from guestbook where email = '$email'";
        $result = safe_mysql_query($query);
        if (!$result)
        {
            $errmsg .= "<li>couldn't check the guestbook for
$email.\n";
        }
        elseif (mysql_num_rows($result) > 0)
        {
                $errmsg .= "<li>The email address '$email' has
already signed this guestbook.\n";
        }
        else
        {
            die('<li>no previous entry found:'
                    .'<li>query='.$query
                    .'<li>rows='.mysql_num_rows($result)
            );
        }
    }

    // perform a very simple check on the format of the url supplied
    // by the user (if any)

    if (!empty($url) && !eregi('^http://[A-Za-z0-9\%\?\_\:\~\/\.-
]+$',$url))
    {
        $errmsg .= "<li>$url doesn't look like a valid URL\n";
    }
```

```
    if (empty($errmsg))
    {
        $query = <<<EOQ
insert into guestbook (name,location,email,url,comments,remote_addr)
values ('%s','%s','%s','%s','%s','%s')
EOQ;
        $query = sprintf($query
            , mysql_real_escape_string($name)
            , mysql_real_escape_string($location)
            , mysql_real_escape_string($email)
            , mysql_real_escape_string($url)
            , mysql_real_escape_string($comments)
            , mysql_real_escape_string($_SERVER['REMOTE_ADDR'])
        );
        safe_mysql_query($query);

        print "<h2>Thanks, $name!!</h2>\n";
    }
    else
    {
        print <<<EOQ
<p>
<font color=red>
<b>
<ul>
$errmsg
</ul>
Please try again
</font>
</p>
EOQ;
    }
    return $errmsg;
}
```

This function is going to make sure that the information entered is moderately useful. If there is a problem with the information, a text string describing the problem will be assigned to the variable `$errmsg`. If, after the function is executed, `$errmsg` is empty, the values will be inserted into the database. Otherwise the error message(s) will be printed, and the values the user entered will be assigned to globals so that they can be printed as the default values in the text fields the next time through.

This function checks for the following in the following order:

- That the name field contains something
- That the email address is potentially a proper address (contains text, an @, and a period (.)) Note that this is not very strong validation of email. It takes a very long and complicated script to thoroughly validate an email, as you will see in later chapters.
- If the email looks OK, that this email address hasn't been entered in the database already
- That the URL is potentially valid

Check Appendix G for more detail on regular expressions.

SELECT_ENTRIES() This function's sole purpose is to put together your database call.

```
function select_entries ($offset=0, $limit=DEFAULT_LIMIT)
{
    // cast to make sure that these are integer values
    $limit = (int)$limit;
    $offset = (int)$offset;

    $query = <<<EOQ
select *, date_format(created,'%e %M, %Y %h:%i %p') as entry_date
from guestbook
order by created desc
limit $offset, $limit
EOQ;
    $result = safe_mysql_query($query);

    return $result;
}
```

You already know that `DEFAULT_LIMIT` sets the number of records displayed per page. As the second argument in the `limit` clause, the `$offset` variable indicates which records will be returned from the query. If you are having problems understanding `$offset`, take a look at the explanation of the `limit` clause in Chapter 3. A value for `$offset` will be passed through the navigational elements. (We'll examine this technique in detail when we discuss the next function.)

To retrieve the date value in a readable way, this query makes use of MySQL's date functions. MySQL stores the date and time as a 14-digit number (`YYYY:MM:DD:HH:SS`), but it's nicer to return the date information in a way that's easier for humans to read. The MySQL `date_format` function retrieves the information in the way we want to use it. This function and many other MySQL functions are discussed in Appendix J.

NAV() This function's sole purpose is to create navigational elements.

```
function nav ($offset=0, $this_script='', $limit=DEFAULT_LIMIT)
{
    $offset = (int)$offset;
    $limit = (int)$limit;

    // don't run things from outside this directory
    if ( empty($this_script) or
        dirname(realpath(__FILE__)) !=
dirname(realpath($this_script))
    )
    {
        $this_script = $_SERVER['PHP_SELF'];
    }

    // get the total number of entries in the guest book -
    // we need this to know if we can go forward from where we are

    $result = safe_mysql_query('select count(*) from guestbook');
    $total_rows = mysql_result($result,0,0);

    print "<p>\n";
    if ($offset > 0)
    {
        // if we're not on the first record,
        // we can always go backwards
        $poffset = $offset - $limit < 0 ? 0 : $offset - $limit;
        print <<<EOQ
<a href="${this_script}?offset=${poffset}">&lt;&lt;Previous
Entries</a>
 
EOQ;
    }
    if ($offset+$limit < $total_rows)
    {
        // offset + limit gives us the maximum record number
        // that we could have displayed on this page. if it's
```

```
        // less than the total number of entries, that means
        // there are more entries to see, and we can go forward
        $noffset = $offset + $limit;
        print <<<EOQ
<a href="${this_script}?offset=${noffset}">Next Entries&gt;&gt;</a>
EOQ;
    }
    print "</p>\n";
}
```

When appropriate, this function will print out links that will enable the user to view the next set of entries, the previous entries, or both. The scope is determined by the `$offset` and `$limit` arguments.

The first time through `$offset` will have no value, and therefore no previous entries link will exist (because `$offset` will not be greater than 0). But if more rows remain to be displayed, a link will be created that creates a value for `$offset` to be accessed if that link is followed.

Say it's the first time we're executing this function, so `$offset` has no value, and the database contains 10 rows. When it reaches the last `if` block the script will see that there are more rows to be displayed (`$offset + $limit` equals two, which is less than 10), and so the following link will be printed:

```
<a href="/book/guestbook2k/view.php?offset=2">Next
Entries&gt;&gt;</a>
```

Interesting code flow

Once you understand how the functions presented thus far work, you should have no problem figuring out how Guestbook 2003 works. For the most part, very, very little work is done in the pages called by the browser. These pages are pretty much an assemblage of function calls.

We will break down one file in detail so you can get the feel of how this structure works. Most of the rest you should be able to figure out by flipping between the files and the explanations of the functions. In the following sections we will walk through the view.php file.

VIEWING ENTRIES

The first thing you need to do in every page is include the header.php file, which enables access to all the functions we outlined previously. After that, you should include standard header information by calling the `guestbook_start_page()` function, passing in the title of the page. Here is the logical flow of the code:

```
<?php

require_once('header.php');
```

```
guestbook_start_page('View My Guest Book!!');

?>



<table border="0">

<?php

// $preserve is passed into the cleanup_text() function (declared in
// /book/functions/basic.php). setting it to an empty value will
// cause any HTML tags in an entry to be stripped out before
// being displayed.

$preserve = '';

// select_entries() (declared in header.php) should return a mysql
// result set identifier

$result = select_entries($offset);

while ($row = mysql_fetch_array($result))
{

print_entry($row,$preserve,'name','location','email','URL','entry
date','comments');
    print "<tr><td colspan=2> </td></tr>\n";
}

// release memory associated with this mysql result set
mysql_free_result($result);

?>

</table>

<?php

nav($offset);

end_page();

?>
```

This is it. You use the global `$offset` variable to run the query with the `select_entries()` function, and then print the results by calling the `print_entry()` function within a `while` loop. Navigational elements are determined by the `nav()` function.

DELETING ENTRIES

The most complex portion of this application involves the ability to delete entries from the guestbook. This stands to reason because you don't want your guestbook being fooled with by anonymous users. So the first thing you need to do before deleting an entry is authenticate users. When discussing the `guestbook_authenticate()` function, we showed how an HTTP 401 header will bring up the browser's username-and-password dialog box. The values entered need to be checked against the guestbook_admin database table. The `guestbook_authenticate()` function takes care of this for you, which is why it's called at the top of the edit.php file.

```
<?php

ob_start();

require_once('header.php');
guestbook_authenticate();

ob_end_flush();

guestbook_start_page('Edit The Guest Book');

?>
```

We use the PHP output buffering functions, `ob_start()` and `ob_end_flush()`, to make sure that no output gets sent to the browser before the HTTP 401 header. Otherwise, a blank line or space outside the `<?php ... ?>` tags in the header.php would prevent `guestbook_authenticate()` from running. If you know you won't be using PHP as an Apache module, then you know PHP won't be trying to send these headers, and you can remove this code. It shouldn't make any visible difference if you leave it in, however.

Once a valid username and password have been entered, the remainder of the edit.php file will be sent. But this time, in addition to all the other information, a checkbox will be included so the user can decide which entries should be deleted. The value of the checkbox will be the primary key of the guestbook table.

```
while ($row = mysql_fetch_array($result))
{
    // call the normal function to display a guestbook entry
    print_entry($row,$preserve,'name','entry date','location','email'
        ,'URL','comments'
```

```
    );

    // now add an extra row to allow the user to mark this entry
    // for deletion
    print <<<EOQ
 <tr>
  <td valign="top" align="right"><b>Delete?</b></td>
  <td valign="top" align="left">
   <input type=checkbox name="entry_id[]"
value="{$row['entry_id']}">
   Yes, delete entry #{$row['entry_id']}
  </td>
 </tr>
 <tr><td colspan=2> </td></tr>
EOQ;
}
```

This form is then submitted to the `confirm_delete.php` file. Notice how we're passing an array here. The name of the form element is `entry_id[]`, which means that when this form is passed to PHP `entry_id` will become an array. The number of values in the array depends on the number of boxes checked. HTTP will not send the unchecked boxes at all.

The first time through the `confirm_delete.php` file, we will print out the entries. This will make the person deleting these entries make sure he or she isn't doing something stupid.

```
    foreach ((array)$entry_id as $value)
    {
        print <<<EOQ
<li>Delete entry #$value?
<input type="hidden" name="entry_id[]" value="$value">
EOQ;
    }
```

If any of these entries are to be deleted, this page will submit to itself, with a different value (confirm delete) sent by means of the submit button. This will make the following code run:

```
    foreach ($entry_id as $value)
    {
        print "<li>Deleting entry #$value\n";
        safe_mysql_query("delete from guestbook where entry_id =
$value");
    }
```

We loop through the `$entry_id` array, deleting records for each member.

Scripts

A few more scripts and functions are available to you, but these don't warrant much discussion. Complete copies of all the files are included on the CD. We suggest you look at them and the comments to get a feel for how they fit into the application.

Summary

The skills you learned here may not get you the big bucks as a programmer, but if you understand everything that is being done here, you should be in pretty good shape as you move forward in your PHP programming life.

In particular, you should see the priority that is put on creating reusable code. Nearly everything in this example is in functions. This makes it much more likely than it would otherwise be that the code we write will be usable in some future application. Additionally, in this chapter you got to see some basic validation. Validation is an important concept and one you will need to take very seriously when your application accepts user input.

Chapter 9

Survey

IN THIS CHAPTER

- Learning functions for creating HTML tags
- Understanding data that use a relational structure
- Putting MySQL's date functions to work
- Working with PHP's error-handling functions

IF GUESTBOOKS are the most common type of application on the Web, surveys are probably second in popularity. Many sites have some sort of widget that enables you to choose you favorite color or sports hero, or whatever, to see what percentage of voters take what stance.

This application will be a bit more complex than the guestbook application you saw in Chapter 8. The programming will get a bit trickier, and the administration of the application will require more work. Unlike the guestbook, this application will require some knowledge of database theory. Related tables, complete with the primary and foreign keys, appear in Part I of this book. This means that your SQL queries will include joins.

Determining the Scope and Goals of the Application

The problem with the Web is that it can be mighty impersonal. You surf around, look at pages, search for information, and have advertisements try to sell you things. But you don't see much evidence of other human beings. A survey on a site gives surfers a clue that other people have been by and that it's possible to leave a mark that others will see later.

A survey application can be ultra-simple. If you want only to gather responses to a single question and return basic statistical information on the responses (how many votes for choice A, B, and so on), you don't need a whole lot of code (or a chapter explaining it). A single table to store answers would do the trick. The question can even be hard-coded into the HTML for the Web site. But that would not make for very interesting learning experience, would it?

It gets more interesting if there can be any number of questions. Instead of just one, this application will allow for two, five, ten, or more – whatever you want. This survey will also record demographic information (such as age and country of origin) and enable sorting on the basis of this information. We also decided to add the ability to pick a winner from those who filled out the personal information. This might encourage people to give real rather than fictitious answers.

There is one more wrinkle to discuss here. It's really not possible to create a survey application that records perfect data. Even if you go to extreme lengths, there will always be an opportunity for the shrewd and persistent to submit multiple answers as long as you allow anonymous access to your survey. But in all likelihood your survey will not have to pass muster with the Federal Elections Commission. A small step to weed out those ruining your survey should do the trick, and you will see one way to accomplish this step later on in the chapter.

Necessary pages

Entering and viewing survey information will require three pages. The first is where the questions will be presented and where the user will enter name, address, and geographic and demographic information. The second page will show the basic survey results. The third will give a detailed breakdown. Figures 9-1, 9-2, and 9-3 show these respective pages.

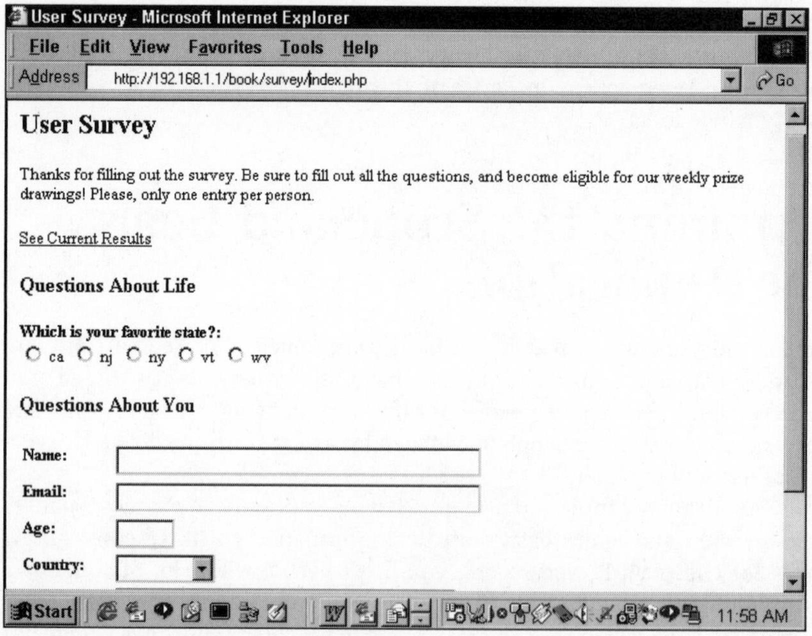

Figure 9-1: Page for filling out survey

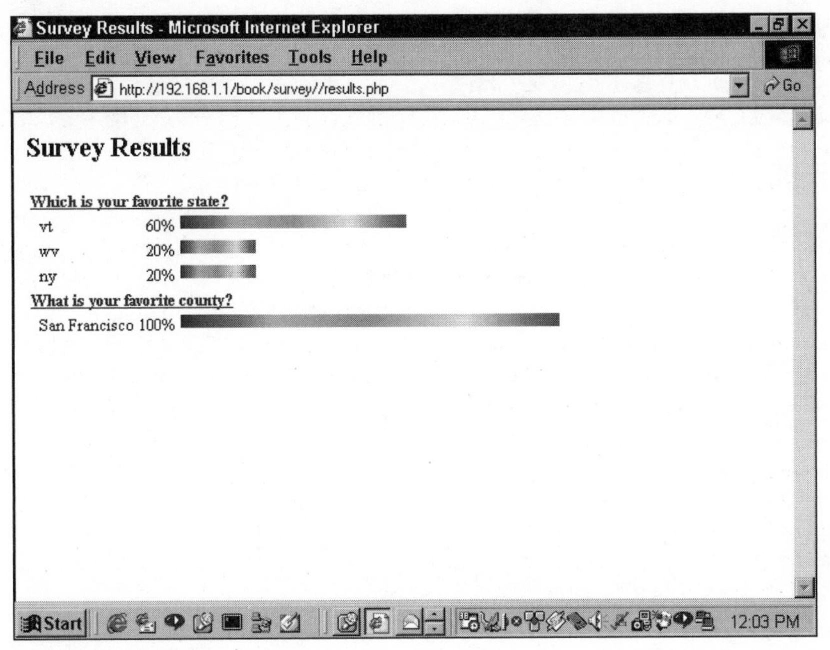

Figure 9-2: Basic survey results

Complex Survey Results - Microsoft Internet Explorer

File Edit View Favorites Tools Help

Address http://192.168.1.1/book/survey//complex_results?question_id=2

Which is your favorite state? (5 total votes)

By age:

Answer	didn't say	under 16	17 to 32	33 to 48	49 to 64	65 and up
vt	33.3%			33.3%	33.3%	
wv					100%	
ny				100%		

By country:

Answer	Canada	Other	USA	USA
vt		33.3%		66.6%
wv			100%	
ny	100%			

By state:

State	vt	wv	ny
CA	66.6%	33.3%	
didn't say	100%		

Start 12:05 PM

Figure 9-3: Detailed survey results

This application, like all others, requires some administrative tools. For starters, you will need to be able to add, delete, and edit questions. Additionally, another page selects a winner at random from the database. Figures 9-4 and 9-5 show the administrative page and the select winner page, respectively.

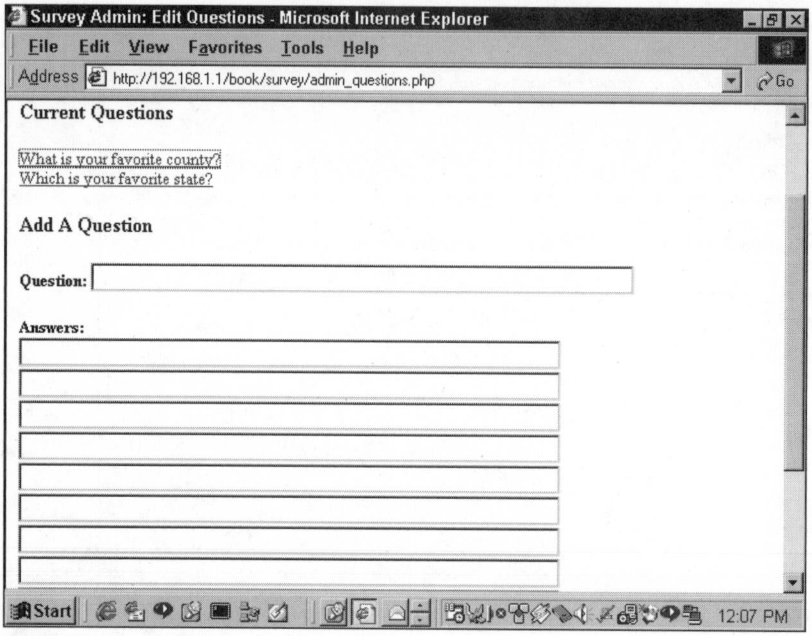

Survey Admin: Edit Questions - Microsoft Internet Explorer

File Edit View Favorites Tools Help

Address http://192.168.1.1/book/survey/admin_questions.php

Current Questions

What is your favorite county?
Which is your favorite state?

Add A Question

Question:

Answers:

Start 12:07 PM

Figure 9-4: Survey-administration page

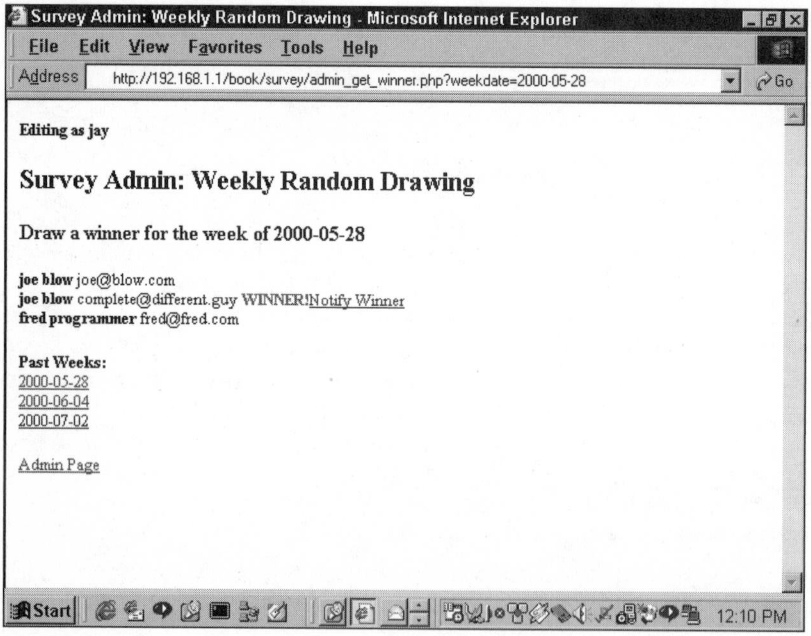

Survey Admin: Weekly Random Drawing - Microsoft Internet Explorer

File Edit View Favorites Tools Help

Address http://192.168.1.1/book/survey/admin_get_winner.php?weekdate=2000-05-28

Editing as jay

Survey Admin: Weekly Random Drawing

Draw a winner for the week of 2000-05-28

joe blow joe@blow.com
joe blow complete@different.guy WINNER!Notify Winner
fred programmer fred@fred.com

Past Weeks:
2000-05-28
2000-06-04
2000-07-02

Admin Page

Start 12:10 PM

Figure 9-5: Select winner page

Winners will be notified via email and sent a URL to claim their prize. The page they get when they open the URL will look like the one in Figure 9-6. Once there, winners will need to confirm who they are, just so you have an extra level of security.

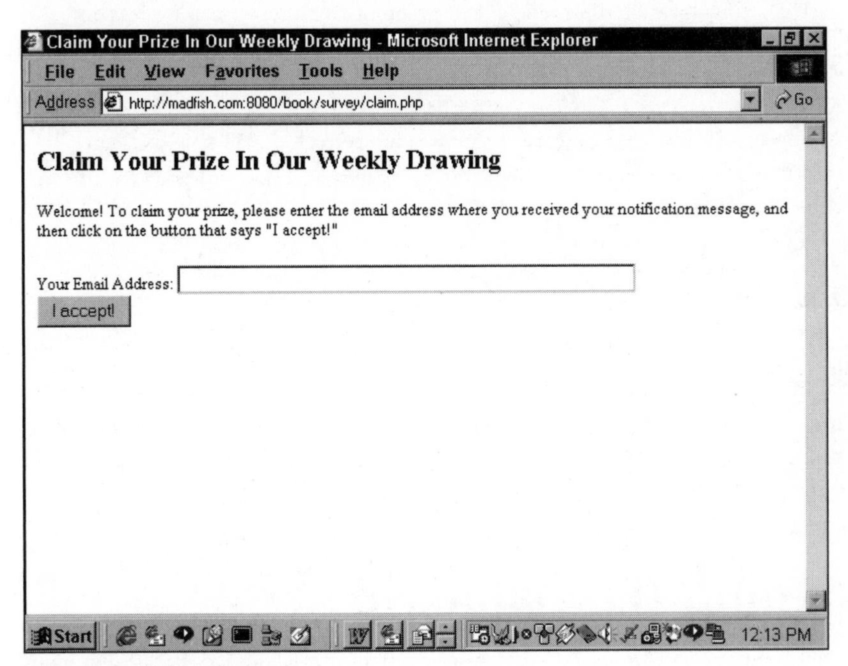

Figure 9-6: Claim prize page

Preventive measures

In the previous chapter we discussed methods for removing junk information that people may attempt to send through the form elements. We will continue to use these functions here. This application will also do some email address validation.

This application will provide you with a simple means of blocking some people from entering information at your site. It's nothing terribly sophisticated; a savvy Internet user would be able to work around it in a minute. Using the form shown in Figure 9-6 you will be able to enter a domain of origin that will be blocked from the site. All users who enter data will have their `$_SERVER['REMOTE_HOST']` and `$_SERVER['REMOTE_ADDR']` values checked against a table in the database (they can turn the presentation of these values off, though). If their host is found, the application will refuse access to the user. Again, this isn't perfect. If you really have sensitive information and need an effective way to block users, you should work with some sort of login scheme. This is just an example of what you could do with a database and HTTP header information.

Email Addresses: To Validate or Not to Validate?

Verifying that an email is in the proper format takes a lot of work. To check a single address thoroughly takes multiple regular expressions. Given that regular expressions are fairly slow, you may be wondering if it is even worth running a script like that, especially if you are running a site with very heavy traffic. You will need to decide that for yourself, based on the amount of traffic you get and the strength of your server hardware. Do you need to make sure emails are perfect, or will a simpler, less robust form of validation be good enough? Even if you make sure the address is in the proper format, that doesn't tell you if the address is attached to an actual mailbox. If you do need to validate your email addresses as much as possible, check around on the Web. Online code archives contain software that will check an address's validity and do rudimentary network lookups to validate domain names and the like.

You'll also need to take some steps to make sure that the wrong people won't be claiming prizes. You'll need to make sure that the people coming to claim prizes are who they say they are.

Designing the Database

This survey application allows for any number of multiple-choice questions. Each question can have any number of answers. To create this relationship you'll need two tables, one named questions and one named answers, that have a one-to-many relationship. (Each question (1) can have any (*n*) number of answers.)

User information is best represented by multiple tables as well, since each user will answer multiple questions. A table named users will store name and address information, while a table named responses will tie together a user and an answer. (User A chose Answer Z to Question 2, for example.) The weekly contest winners will be represented as a link to the appropriate user record in a table named `winners`, where users' names are listed along with the week in which they won. Two other tables, states and age_ranges, are used to help us group responses together in different ways.

Finally, two administrative tables have no relationships to the other tables in the database. The admin table holds usernames and passwords for administrators, and blocked_domains records domains that have been blocked.

Because we have multiple tables that are linked together, in this database we can begin to take advantage of the features of the InnoDB table type. One of those is the ability to create foreign key constraints. (MySQL has always enabled you to declare these, but they have no meaning for other table formats.) A foreign-key table constraint spells out the relationship between the table being defined and another table in the database, such as the relationship in this example between the answers and questions tables. A nice benefit of the foreign key table is the `ON DELETE` part of the constraint definition. If you set this to `ON DELETE CASCADE`, deleting a record in the master table will automatically cause all dependent records in the child table to be deleted as well. Therefore, if you delete a question, all of its answers go away too. Which means that much less code to write (always a good thing).

Figure 9-7 shows a visual representation of the structure of the database. The `create` statements for making these tables are shown in Listing 9-1. Note that these table definitions were copied from the `mysqldump` utility. If you're not aware of `mysqldump`, or the other `mysql` utilities, make sure to read Appendix D.

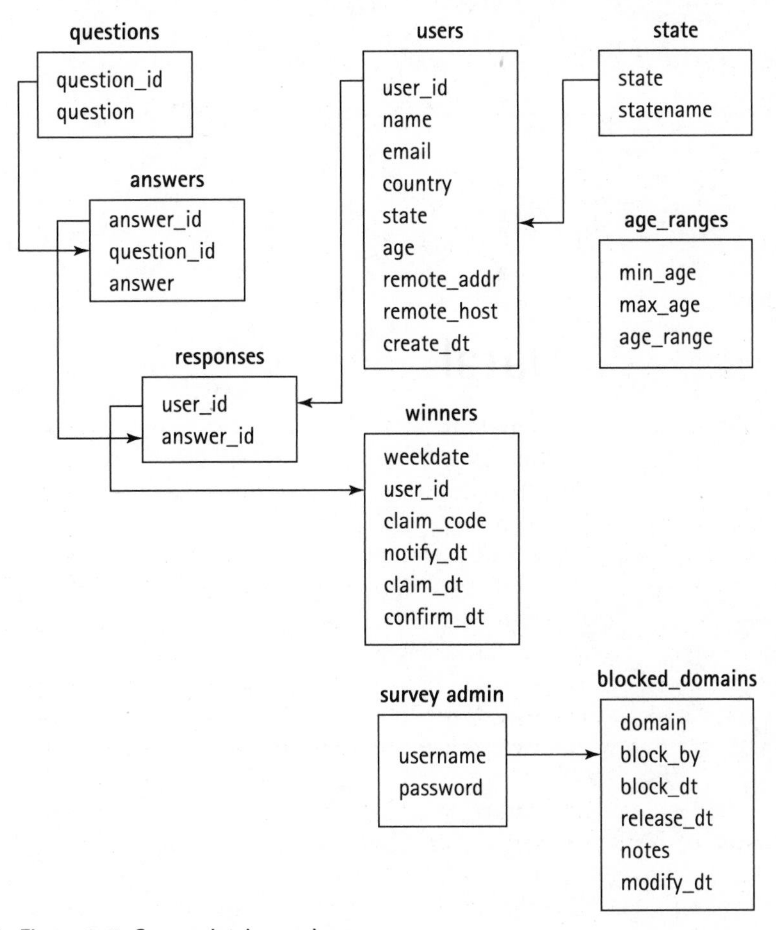

Figure 9-7: Survey database schema

Listing 9-1: Create statements for survey

```
--
-- Table structure for table 'admin'
--

CREATE TABLE admin (
  username varchar(50) NOT NULL default '',
  password varchar(255) NOT NULL default '',
  PRIMARY KEY  (username)
) TYPE=InnoDB;

--
-- Table structure for table 'age_ranges'
--

CREATE TABLE age_ranges (
  min_age int(11) NOT NULL default '0',
  max_age int(11) NOT NULL default '0',
  age_range varchar(10) default NULL,
  PRIMARY KEY  (min_age,max_age)
) TYPE=InnoDB;

--
-- Table structure for table 'answers'
--

CREATE TABLE answers (
  answer_id int(11) NOT NULL auto_increment,
  question_id int(11) NOT NULL default '0',
  answer text NOT NULL,
  PRIMARY KEY  (answer_id),
  KEY question_id (question_id,answer_id),
  FOREIGN KEY (`question_id`) REFERENCES `survey.questions`
(`question_id`) ON DELETE CASCADE
) TYPE=InnoDB;

--
-- Table structure for table 'blocked_domains'
--

CREATE TABLE blocked_domains (
  domain varchar(64) NOT NULL default '',
  block_by varchar(50) default NULL,
  block_dt datetime NOT NULL default '0000-00-00 00:00:00',
```

```
  release_dt datetime default NULL,
  notes text,
  modify_dt timestamp(14) NOT NULL,
  PRIMARY KEY  (domain),
  KEY block_by (block_by),
  FOREIGN KEY (`block_by`) REFERENCES `survey.admin` (`username`) ON
DELETE SET NULL
) TYPE=InnoDB;

--
-- Table structure for table 'questions'
--

CREATE TABLE questions (
  question_id int(11) NOT NULL auto_increment,
  question text NOT NULL,
  PRIMARY KEY  (question_id)
) TYPE=InnoDB;

--
-- Table structure for table 'responses'
--

CREATE TABLE responses (
  user_id int(11) NOT NULL default '0',
  answer_id int(11) NOT NULL default '0',
  PRIMARY KEY  (user_id,answer_id),
  KEY answer_id (answer_id),
  FOREIGN KEY (`user_id`) REFERENCES `survey.users` (`user_id`) ON
DELETE CASCADE,
  FOREIGN KEY (`answer_id`) REFERENCES `survey.answers`
(`answer_id`) ON DELETE CASCADE
) TYPE=InnoDB;

--
-- Table structure for table 'states'
--

CREATE TABLE states (
  state char(2) NOT NULL default '',
  statename varchar(30) NOT NULL default '',
  PRIMARY KEY  (state)
) TYPE=InnoDB;
```

Continued

Listing 9-1 *(Continued)*

```
--
-- Table structure for table 'users'
--

CREATE TABLE users (
  user_id int(11) NOT NULL auto_increment,
  name varchar(50) default NULL,
  email varchar(50) default NULL,
  country varchar(20) default NULL,
  state char(2) default NULL,
  age int(11) default NULL,
  remote_addr varchar(15) default NULL,
  remote_host varchar(80) default NULL,
  create_dt timestamp(14) NOT NULL,
  PRIMARY KEY  (user_id)
) TYPE=InnoDB;

--
-- Table structure for table 'winners'
--

CREATE TABLE winners (
  weekdate datetime NOT NULL default '0000-00-00 00:00:00',
  user_id int(11) NOT NULL default '0',
  claim_code char(8) NOT NULL default '',
  notify_dt datetime default NULL,
  claim_dt datetime default NULL,
  confirm_dt datetime default NULL,
  PRIMARY KEY  (weekdate),
  UNIQUE KEY claim_code (claim_code),
  KEY user_id (user_id),
  FOREIGN KEY (`user_id`) REFERENCES `survey.users` (`user_id`) ON
DELETE CASCADE
) TYPE=InnoDB;
```

Code Overview

If you have already read the section of the same name in Chapter 8, the structure we use here should be familiar to you. Items in the /functions folder are included and ready for reuse. We've also taken the MySQL functions we used for the guestbook, modified them a bit to make them more generally useful, and renamed them `my_connect()` and `my_query()`. These can be found in the /functions/basic directory.

It's obvious that this survey application requires several more pages than the guestbook: More needs to be done. Though you can include several actions in a single page, and sort through the ones you need by passing variables and using `if` statements, it can make code difficult to keep track of. Better to have several intuitively named files that perform specific tasks. That said, some pages in this application make use of variables in order to decide how they should look and behave.

If you've done any Web work at all you know how tedious it can be to deal with HTML tables and forms. On the one hand, putting literal HTML tags into your pages will always be a faster procedure than any code-based method of generating them. On the other hand, propagating changes through all those literal tags can be more than tedious – it's also a great source of bugs). For that reason, in this and most of the other applications in this book, we will try to ease the pain involved in dealing with tables and forms. In the following sections you will see several functions that will make life, in the long run at least, a lot easier. The functions in the coming sections will make a lot more sense if you see what they accomplish first. Here's some code that will work just fine if used with the following functions:

```
print start_table();
print table_row(
    table_cell('Cell text')
);
print end_table();
```

or even just this:

```
print table('Cell text');
```

This will create a table with one cell. You could build on the complexity of the unicellular table by adding additional `table_cell()` calls within the `table_row()` function call. You can do this because of PHP's ability to deal with a variable number of arguments. We designed the `table_row()` function to loop through all of the arguments (some of which are calls to the `table_cell()` function). You may be wondering how these functions deal with table attributes, like `width`, `align`, and others. How could you alter those for particular tables_or for all your tables at once?

If you don't like the functions we've created for tables, forms, and other HTML elements, don't use them. It is perfectly acceptable (and perhaps even more common) to type out HTML elements rather than create them through functions. Like many things in programming, it comes down to a matter of preference. For the question of whether to hard-code HTML or programmatically generate it, there's no right answer. It is true, though, that dynamically generating HTML on a high-traffic site can put a big load on the server. In that situation, you probably will want to put literal HTML in your pages — at least in your live pages — or look into a caching system of some kind.

Here we come to another question of style. You can write your functions to expect certain attributes as arguments, in a particular order, like this:

```
function table_cell ($value='', $align='left', $valign='top', $width='')
```

That's straightforward, and calling the function is pretty simple too:

```
print table_cell('This will be in the upper left corner');
print table_cell('This will end up in the lower right corner',
'right', 'bottom');
```

But the drawback is that you have to remember what attribute goes where. And reading code like this six months later, after you've forgotten you wrote it, or when you didn't write it all, can be a problem. For an example like the `table_cell()` function above, it's not so bad – "right" and "bottom" are clear enough. But a line like

```
print image_tag('/images/b129.gif', 10, 20, 5, 1, 0);
```

is not so clear. As an alternative, you can specify your arguments as named values in an array:

```
print image_tag(array('src'=>'/images/b129.gif', 'width'=>10,
'height'=>20
     , 'vspace'=>5, 'hspace'=>1, 'border'=>0
));
```

That makes the function call easier to read, but the tradeoff is that the function itself is a bit less so:

```
function image_tag ($attributes=NULL)
```

Now the work of figuring out what values are being passed to the function takes place inside the function itself. Still, that keeps it in one place. The function calls are a little more tedious to write, and the functions a little trickier. The benefit is code that's easier to read, easier to maintain, and less ambiguous in the writing; this means fewer bugs. (Unless you're prone to forget parentheses, like some of us.)

The functions we'll use with these examples make something of a lazy compromise between these two approaches. When there's a single most common use of a tag, involving one or two attributes, the function assumes that's what you mean if you hand it an unnamed simple value, like this:

```
print table_cell('This is the stuff that goes between the opening
and closing td tags.');
```

If you want to specify other attributes, then everything has to be in an array:

```
print table_cell(array('value'=>'This is the content of the cell'
     , 'align'=>'right', 'valign'=>'bottom'
));
```

A more complex function call might look like this:

```
print table_row(array(
     'bgcolor' => $bgcolor
     , 'cells'=>array(
          table_cell(array(
               'value'=>'<b>New entry</b>'
               , 'align'=>'right'
          ))
          , text_field(array(
               'name'=>'entered_by'
               , 'value'=>''
               , 'size=>10
          ))
          , submit_field('Insert Record')
     )
));
```

Here the arguments to `table_row()` specify the row's background color (`'bgcolor"=> $bgcolor`) and an array of values to be set up as table cells. Some of those are nothing more than the contents of the cell, and so we can just list them, even when the contents themselves are the results of other function calls to create form fields. But we want the first cell to be aligned to the right, so we make an explicit call to the `table_cell()` function ourselves to build it.

Keep in mind that the methods for achieving nested function calls will be explained later in the "Code Breakdown" section. Throughout the process of creating this application we make more extensive use of MySQL functions than you saw in Chapter 8.

Code Breakdown

As with the guestbook application, the code here is divided for convenience. We've added some final touches to the structure that we'll use for the rest of the book. It's worth taking a minute or two to go over it. Here's a picture:

```
/usr/local/apache/dsn/
     * db_dsnlist.php
     * dsn.ini

/usr/local/apache/htdocs/book/
     * autoload.php
     * book.ini
     * book.php
     * classes.php
     * functions.php
     * index.html
     * phpinfo.php
     * sitemap.php
     * source.php
     * survey/
          + admin/
               o block_domain.php
               o end_page.php
               o get_winner.php
               o header.php
               o index.php
               o login.php
               o questions.php
               o winners.php
          + age_results.php
          + claim.php
          + complex_results.php
          + country_results.php
          + db/
               o admin.sql
               o age_ranges.sql
               o answers.sql
               o blocked_domains.sql
               o grants.sql
               o load_questions.sql
               o questions.sql
               o responses.sql
               o setup.bat
```

```
        o setup.in
        o states.sql
        o users.sql
        o winners.sql
    + functions/
        o check_domain.php
        o fetch_question.php
        o fetch_user.php
        o get_answers.php
        o weekstart.php
    + functions.php
    + header.php
    + index.php
    + results.php
    + state_results.php
    + thanks.php
    + verify_answers.inc.php
```

From the top, we have a file named /book/book.php. This adds the /book/functions directory, where we keep the general-purpose functions used across all the examples to the default PHP `include` path. It also adds the /book directory itself by modifying the PHP configuration variable `include_path`. This in turn enables us to write `include` statements that refer to /book/*thing*/*stuff*.php, even if the book directory is not in the root document directory of your server.

The example application that we are looking at in this chapter, the Survey application, lives in the /book/survey directory. In here are the files for the pages of the application. The administrative pages are in a subdirectory named admin/, which helps keep the file names somewhat regular – the header file is named header.php, the page included at the end of every page is end_page.php, and so on. The header.php file makes reference (via an `include` statement) to a second file, functions.php, which defines the functions specific to this application. If we were using any constants or global variables in this application, those would be defined in a file named globals.php.

Two other subdirectories exist under survey/, standard to all the following examples. The functions/ subdirectory is where the actual code defining our local functions lives. Each function is in its own file in here. That's to make it easier to find later, mostly, but it also makes managing changes to the code a little bit simpler. The functions.php file is just a set of `require_once()` calls that pull in the individual function files. (The functions under /book/functions are set up the same way.)

The db subdirectory is where we keep the SQL files that define the survey database. There is a file in here named setup.bat, which runs `mysql` (the command-line client) as the root user, prompting you for a password, and executes the commands in the setup.in file. setup.in creates the database, includes the table definitions, loads some rather silly sample data, and grants read and write access on the database to the `nobody` account. (If your Web server runs under a different username you should edit this file to reflect the different credentials.) Static lookup tables, like the states table, load the relevant data into their definition files.

We covered some of the functions defined by the /book/functions/basic.php file in Chapter 8, so we won't go over those again here. But we did add a few little bonuses this time around.

HTML functions

As your applications get more complex, you're going to need to continually use some HTML ingredients – forms, tables, paragraph tags, anchors, and the like. For this reason we've added a series of functions that make it easier to create those repetitive HTML elements – and we've done it so as to demonstrate a variety of ways to handle arguments to a function.

ARGUMENT-HANDLING FUNCTIONS

To introduce the techniques used by the HTML functions that we'll cover here, we'll pick a small one – the `image_tag()` function – and show you what it's doing.

This `image_tag()` function returns an HTML `<img>` tag.

```
function image_tag()
{
    static $_defaults = array(
        'src' => ''
        , 'alt' => ''
        , 'border' => 0
        , 'allowed' =>
array('Common','alt','height','width','longdesc'

,'src','usemap','ismap','name','align','border','hspace','vspace'
        )
    );
    static $_simple = array('src');
    $p = func_get_args();
    $p = parse_arguments($p, $_simple, $_defaults);
    if (empty($p['alt']))
        $p['alt'] = $p['src'];
    $attlist = get_attlist($p);
    $output = "<img $attlist />";

    return $output;
}
```

The first thing this function does is declare a couple of static variables (the underscores in their names – `$_defaults` and `$_simple` – are just a convention we've used for these particular variable names, to make them distinct from other variable names; they have nothing to do with the variables being static or not).

Static variables aren't reinitialized every time the function is called. Instead, they retain their values from one call to the next, including any changes. So if we have a function like

```
function count_sales($newsales=0)
{
     static $total_sales = 0;
     $total_sales += $newsales;
     print "Total sales to date: $total_sales\n";
}
```

we can use it to keep a running total, like so:

```
count_sales(10.00);
     OUTPUT ---> Total sales to date: 10.00
count_sales(5.00);
     OUTPUT ---> Total sales to date: 15.00
```

Besides serving as a place to store data, statics are also useful when you have something like a big array that gets used every time you call the function, but that never changes. (Or doesn't change much.) Especially when your function is one that gets called over and over again, it can pay to not have to create those variables from scratch each time. One thing to be aware of: Statics are handled just like references, and that affects how they behave. For instance, you can't store another reference in a static variable. For more information, see the PHP manual section at `http://www.php.net/manual/sv/language.variables.scope.php`.

In `image_tag()` the two static arrays we define are storing two kinds of data:

- `$_defaults` is an associative array that describes attributes of the HTML tag and their default values. Sometimes attributes are listed in here because we really do have default values for them – for example, the default value for the `'border'` attribute of an `<IMG>` tag should be zero. Most of the time, they're here to establish the name of the attribute for later use. In fact, many of the "attributes" listed in the `$_defaults` array in other HTML tag functions aren't strictly attributes of the tag at all. The `'value'` attribute of a `<textarea>` tag, for instance, turns into the string between the opening `<textarea>` and closing `</textarea>` tags.
- `$_simple` sets out how we want to interpret arguments to this function when they don't come neatly labeled in an array. As we mentioned earlier, most of the time we'll be using an array to pass arguments into these functions, so that when we look at the function calls we'll know what we meant to do:

```
image_tag(array('src'=>'/images/chimp.jpg', 'height'=>50,
'width'=>50));
```

But we'd also like to be lazy:

```
image_tag('/images/spacer.gif');
```

`$_simple` is what lets us get away with simplified coding style – it's a list of attribute names to be assigned to unlabeled values. Here, setting it to `array('src')` specifies that if we get just a plain string as an argument, it's meant to be the value of the `src` attribute of the `<img>` tag.

Look at the functions being called here.

First up is the `parse_arguments()` function. We call it with three parameters: an array containing the arguments that were passed into `image_tag()` and the two static arrays. You might notice that even though the arguments are declared as references to the passed-in variables we can still initialize them to default values. This is a very useful feature of the new PHP engine release. Being able to define a default value means that the caller can ignore arguments that don't apply.

In the function itself, we use casting operators to make sure that these are arrays, and set up some variables that we'll use to hold values as we go through the arguments (note that in PHP 5, you can assign default values to by-reference arguments; this makes calling the functions much easier):

```
function
parse_arguments($args=array(),&$simple=array(),&$defaults=array())

{
    $args = (array)$args;
    $simple = (array)$simple;
    $defaults = (array)$defaults;
    $key = NULL;
    $result = $defaults;
    $result['_defaults'] = $defaults;
    $result['_simple'] = $simple;
```

We start out the `$result` variable, which is what the function will eventually return, as a copy of `$defaults`. This ensures that everything defined in the `$_defaults` array will come back as an attribute for the tag. Then we put those arrays themselves into `$result` so that they can be modified or replaced by arguments passed in to the original function. This will let us change the default and simple values in the code of a page, setting up a default image size or border width, for example_ without having to rewrite the function itself.

Next we'll walk through the list of arguments. Associative arrays are merged into `$result`, empty arguments are ignored, and other arguments are assigned to the named parameters from the `$_simple` array:

```
    $i = 0;
    $sc = count($simple);
    foreach ($args as $arg)
```

```
    {

        if ($arg === NULL || (is_array($arg) && count($arg) == 0))
        {
            // do nothing
        }
        elseif (is_object($arg))
        {
            $result = array_merge($result, get_object_vars($arg));
        }
        elseif (is_assoc($arg))
        {
            $result = array_merge($result, $arg);
        }
        else
        {
            if ($i < $sc)
            {
                $key = $simple[$i++];
                if (!empty($arg) || !isset($result[$key]))
                {
                    $result[$key] = $arg;
                }
            }
            else
            {
                if ($key === NULL)
                {
                    user_error("Argument '$arg' was passed with no
available target - aborting...\n", E_USER_ERROR);
                }
                if (isset($result[$key]))
                {
                    if (!is_array($result[$key]))
                    {
                        $result[$key] = array($result[$key]);
                    }
                    $result[$key][] = $arg;
                }
                else
                {
                    $result[$key] = $arg;
                }
            }
        }
    }
```

Two things are worth pointing out here. If a simple argument is encountered after we've run out of parameter names from `$_simple`, it's added into an array by means of the last simple name. This is how a function like `paragraph()` works. It has just one simple argument name, `'values'`, so a list of simple arguments passed in to the function ends up as elements in the `$values` array:

```
paragraph('One line','Another line',$variable,'Yet another line');
```

becomes

```
'values' => array('One line', 'Another line', $variable, 'Yet
another line');
```

If there are no names passed in, however, we won't have anywhere to put any arguments that aren't associative arrays. In this case we use PHP's `user_error()` function to raise an error. This prints out our error message and stops the script, just like a normal PHP error. (The `user_error()` function is one you'll be seeing more of in later examples.)

Finally, to clean up, we take any changes to our list of default and simple arguments and pass them back to the calling function. Because the two arrays are passed in by reference, changes made to them here will update the original variables. And because they're declared as static, those changes will still be there the next time the function is called.

```
    $defaults = array_merge($defaults, $result['_defaults']);
    $simple = $result['_simple'];
    return $result;
}
```

Changes to `$_defaults` are merged into the original list, while a new value for `$_simple` will replace the old one.

After calling `parse_arguments()` in the `image_src()` function, like this,

```
    $p = parse_arguments($p, $_simple, $_defaults);
```

we have an array, `$p`, containing all the attribute values and other parameters from the original call. For example, from this line in the Web page –

```
image_src('/images/monkey.jpg');
```

– we would end up with the following values in `$p`:

```
$p = array('src'=>'/image/monkey.jpg', 'alt'=>'', 'border'=>0);
```

For the <IMG> tag specifically, if the 'alt' attribute is empty, we'll use the name of the image file (from the 'src' attribute) as a default:

```
if (empty($p['alt']))
        $p['alt'] = $p['src'];
```

The next step is to turn the reference to the image file into an HTML tag. So we pass the array to the get_attlist() function. This takes key/value pairs from an associative array and reformats them as a single string of HTML-style attributes. The previous example would come back as the following:

```
    src="/images/monkey.jpg" alt="/images/monkey.jpg" border="0"
```

Therefore, we only need add the name of the tag itself and the opening and closing angle brackets to get this, which image_tag() returns as its result:

```
    <image src="/images/monkey.jpg" alt="/images/monkey.jpg"
border="0">
```

A special constant, STANDALONE, defined in /functions/basic.php, is useful for attributes like 'selected' in an <option> tag. So

```
array('value'=>'CA','selected'=>STANDALONE)
```

becomes

```
value="CA" selected
```

Using this function may seem like a lot of work just to get a simple <img> tag. Well, it is. The payoff is flexibility, the cost is an increase in complexity. In a high-performance environment you would probably end up discarding parts of this code. For instance, you could decree that all function calls will be of the following form:

```
    my_function(array('param1'=>'value1', 'param2'=>'value2', ...)
```

This would enable you to eliminate the call to parse_arguments() and simply merge the passed-in array with $_defaults. Or you could use functions like these in your production/development environment to produce less clever, and thus faster, files that will then get pushed out to your servers.

FUNCTIONS FROM /BOOK/FUNCTIONS/HTML/

These functions make it easier to create common HTML tags. Most of the functions in this file are very similar.

ANCHOR_TAG() This function creates an anchor tag.

```
function anchor_tag()
{
    static $_defaults = array(
        'href'=>''
        , 'text' => ''
        , 'value' => ''
        , 'allowed' => array('Common','accesskey','charset','href'

,'hreflang','rel','rev','tabindex','type','name','target'
        )
    );
    static $_simple = array('href','value');

    $p = func_get_args();
    $p = parse_arguments($p, $_simple, $_defaults);

    if (empty($p['text']))
    {
        $p['text'] = $p['href'];
    }
    if (empty($p['value']))
    {
        $p['value'] = $p['text'];
    }

    $attlist = get_attlist($p);
    $output = "<a $attlist>{$p['value']}</a>";
    return $output;
}
```

You can expect only two things every time with an anchor tag: an `href` attribute and some text to go between the opening and closing `<a>` tags. However, it is possible that a `name` attribute would be more descriptive, and more useful in client-side scripting. But more often than not, the call to this function will look something like this:

```
anchor_tag('myurl.com/index.html', 'this is a great link');
```

PARAGRAPH() This function will either print out opening and closing `<p>` tags and everything between them, or just the opening `<p>` tag, depending on how it's called.

```
function paragraph ()
{
    static $_defaults = array(
        'values' => array()
        , 'allowed' => array('Common','align')
        , 'start' => NULL
    );
    static $_simple = array('values');
    $p = func_get_args();
    $p = parse_arguments($p, $_simple, $_defaults);
    $attlist = get_attlist($p);

    $output = "\n<p $attlist>\n";
    if ($p['start'] !== NULL)
    {
        return $output;
    }
    $output .= implode("\n",(array)$p['values'])
        .end_paragraph($p)
    ;
    return $output;
}
```

The first thing to understand about this function is that by default it will print not only the opening `<p>` tag along with its attributes, but also the closing `</p>` tag and everything that could occur between the two. This could include anchor tags, image tags, or just about anything else. The following function call would work just fine, and in fact is used within the survey application:

```
print paragraph(anchor_tag('block_domain.php','Return to Domain
List'));
```

One argument exists in this function call, and that's another function call with two arguments. In effect, when one function call is nested inside another, PHP executes the internal one first. So first the `anchor_tag()` function is called, creating a string like `'<a href="admin_block.php">'`. Then the outer function is executed, so the call to the paragraph function will actually look something like this:

```
print paragraph('<a href="admin_block.php">Return to Domain
List</a>');
```

Note how flexible this becomes. By looping through the number of arguments you can send any number of additional function calls to the paragraph function. And you can happily mix text and function calls together, because by the time paragraph() sees it, it's all text. So the following is a perfectly fine call to the paragraph function:

```
print paragraph(
     "<b>Blocked by:</b> $block_by <br>"
     , "<b>Date Blocked:</b> $block_dt <br>"
     , "<b>Date Released:</b> $release_dt <br>"
     , "<b>Last Modified:</b> $modify_dt <br>"

);
```

START_PARAGRAPH() You might have noticed that the paragraph() function checked to see if it had been passed an argument named 'start', and if it had, returned only the opening <p> tag. Sometimes you need to use the function that way because what goes inside the paragraph is too complicated to be included in a list of values. In such a case you can just call paragraph() with a 'start'=>TRUE attribute, or you can use the start_paragraph() function, as follows:

```
function start_paragraph ()
{
    $p = func_get_args();
    $p[] = array('start'=>'yes');
    return call_user_func_array('paragraph', $p);
}
```

The start_paragraph() function takes the arguments passed into it and adds a 'start' argument. Then comes the interesting part. The PHP function call_user_func_array () takes a function name and an array of arguments and uses them to make a call to the named function. The elements in the array of arguments are passed in exactly as they would be in a normal function call. So

```
call_user_func_array('myfunc',array(1,2,3);
```

works just like

```
myfunc(1,2,3);
```

The call_user_func_array() strategy lets start_paragraph() work as a kind of front end to the paragraph() function. A call to start_paragraph() like this one:

```
start_paragraph(array('align'=>'center'));
```

is equivalent to

```
paragraph(array('align'=>'center', 'start'=>'yes'));
```

Both calls produce the same HTML output:

```
<p  align="center">
```

END_PARAGRAPH() This function just prints out an end paragraph tag (</p>), as follows:

```
function end_paragraph ()
{
    $output = "\n</p>\n";
    return $output;
}
```

Its main reason for existing, besides making a lovely matched set with `start_paragraph()`, is to let you close any opening tags you might want to hard-code into the opening of a paragraph – a <font> tag, for example.

UL_LIST() With this function you can create a bulleted list. Most frequently, an array will be passed to the function, each element prepended with an <li> tag. The function also deals with occasions in which a string is sent as the only argument.

```
function ul_list ()
{
    static $_defaults = array(
        'values' => array()
        , 'contents' => NULL
        , 'allowed' => array('Common','compact','type')
    );
    static $_simple = array('values');
    $p = func_get_args();
    $p = parse_arguments($p, $_simple, $_defaults);
    $attlist = get_attlist($p);

    $output = "<ul $attlist>\n";

    if (!empty($p['values'])
        && !is_array($p['values'])
        && !is_object($p['values'])
    )
    {
        $output .= $p['values'];
    }
    else
    {
        array_key_remove($p,array('_defaults','_simple','allowed'));
```

```
            foreach ((array)$p['values'] as $p['text'])
            {
                $output .= li_tag($p);
            }
        }
        $output .= $p['contents'];
        $output .= "</ul>\n";
        return $output;
}
```

START_TABLE() Every HTML table begins with more or less the same code, so we have a function to generate it for us.

```
function start_table ()
{
    static $_defaults = array(
        'cellspacing' => 0
        , 'cellpadding' => 1
        , 'allowed' =>
array('Common','border','cellpadding','cellspacing'

,'datapagesize','frame','rules','summary','width','align','bgcolor'
        )
    );
    static $_simple = array('width');
    $p = func_get_args();
    $p = parse_arguments($p, $_simple, $_defaults);
    $attlist = get_attlist($p);
    $output = "\n<table $attlist>\n";
    return $output;
}
```

END_TABLE() The same goes for the end of the table – it's boilerplate, and boilerplate should be generated programmatically. Here's a function that does just that.

```
function end_table ()
{
    $output = "\n</table>\n";
    return $output;
}
```

TABLE() Here, unlike with the similar paragraph functions, `start_table()` is the function that knows how to generate the opening `<table>` tag, and it is the overall `table()` function that calls it. This is because we'd like to be able to pass in the width as an argument when we are only opening a table. However, when we're creating a whole table, any unlabeled arguments are going to be rows in the resulting table. Because the two situations need two different values for `$_simple`, `start_table()` can't be just a front end to `table()`.

```
function table ()
{
    static $_defaults = array(
        'rows' => array()
    );
    static $_simple = array('rows');

    $p = func_get_args();
    $p = parse_arguments($p, $_simple, $_defaults);

    $output = start_table($p);

    foreach ((array)$p['rows'] as $row)
    {
        $output .= table_row($row);
    }

    $output .= end_table($p);

    return $output;
}
```

TABLE_ROW() This function does not only print out the opening `<tr>` tag and its attributes; it also prints the table cells that will be nested within the `<tr>` tags.

```
function table_row ()
{
    static $_defaults = array(
        'cells' => array()
        , 'allowed' =>
array('Common','align','valign','char','charoff'
            ,'bgcolor'
        )
    );
    static $_simple = array('cells');
    $p = func_get_args();
    $p = parse_arguments($p, $_simple, $_defaults);
    $attlist = get_attlist($p);
    $output = "\n <tr $attlist>\n";
```

```
    foreach ((array)$p['cells'] as $cell)
    {
        if (!preg_match('/<t[dh]/i', $cell))
        {
            $output .= table_cell($cell);
        }
        else
        {
            $output .= $cell;
        }
    }
    $output .= "\n </tr>\n";
    return $output;
}
```

The following `table_row()` call has two arguments, one of which is itself another function call. The `table_cell()` function (described later) is executed first, and the results are passed in to `table_row()`.

```
print table_row(
     '<b>A simple cell</b>'
     , table_cell(array('value'=>'A not-so-simple cell',
'align'=>'right'))
);
```

So when `table_row()` goes through the values in its `$cells` argument, it finds one plain string (`'<b>A simple cell</b>'`), which it runs through `table_cell()` itself, and one already-formatted cell (the output of the `table_cell()` call in our initial code), which it just tacks onto its output string as is.

TABLE_CELL() Not too much is new here. It might be worth pointing out the way the `$value` attribute is handled: You check to see if it's an array or an object, because PHP lets you cast an object as an array – you get back an associative array of the properties of the object.

```
function table_cell ()
{
    static $_defaults = array(
        'align' => 'left'
        , 'valign' => 'top'
        , 'value' => ''
        , 'allowed' =>
array('Common','abbr','align','axis','char','charoff'

,'colspan','headers','rowspan','scope','valign','width','height'
```

```
        ,'nowrap','bgcolor'
    )
  );
  static $_simple = array('value');

  $p = func_get_args();
  $p = parse_arguments($p, $_simple, $_defaults);
  $attlist = get_attlist($p);

  if (is_array($p['value']) or is_object($p['value']))
  {
      $p['value'] = implode('',(array)$p['value']);
  }

  $output = "\n  <td $attlist>{$p['value']}</td>\n";
  return $output;
}
```

FUNCTIONS FROM /BOOK/FUNCTIONS/FORMS.PHP

Most of these functions are fairly straightforward and don't require any explanation. We will show a couple just for examples.

text_field() This prints out a text field. All the expected attributes should be passed to the function. (Note: `labelize()` is a function in /book/functions/basic – essentially a slightly trickier version of `ucwords()`.)

```
function text_field ()
{
    static $_defaults = array(
        'type' => 'text'
        , 'size' => 40
        , 'name' => 'textfield'
        , 'label' => NULL
        , 'default' => NULL
        , 'value' => NULL
        , 'source' => NULL
    );
    static $_simple = array('name','label','default');
    $p = func_get_args();
    $p = parse_arguments($p, $_simple, $_defaults);
    array_key_remove($p,array('_defaults','_simple'));
    if ($p['label'] === NULL)
    {
        $p['label'] = labelize($p['name']);
    }
```

```
    $p['value'] =
get_field_value($p['name'],$p['default'],$p['value'],$p['source']);
    return input_field($p);
}
```

Most of the other functions look similar to this one, the only real exceptions being the checkbox and radio button.

checkbox_field() The only thing that may be of interest about this function is how we decide if a checkbox is to be checked by default. We can do this by adding an argument called `$match`. If `$match` equals either the value of the field or the label (unless you tell it not to match the label by setting `label_match` to `FALSE`), the field will be checked when displayed. The `radio_field()` function works the same way.

```
function checkbox_field ()
{
    static $_defaults = array(
        'type' => 'checkbox'
        , 'name' => 'checkboxfield'
        , 'value' => ''
        , 'label' => NULL
        , 'match' => NULL
        , 'default' => NULL
        , 'checked' => NULL
        , 'source' => NULL
        , 'prefix' => '<nobr>'
        , 'suffix' => '</nobr>'
        , 'label_match' => TRUE
    );
    static $_simple = array('name','value','label');

    $p = func_get_args();
    $p = parse_arguments($p, $_simple, $_defaults);
    if ($p['label'] === NULL)
    {
        $p['label'] = labelize($p['value']);
    }

    if (!$p['skip_selection'])
    {
        $p['value'] = get_field_value(              $p['name']
            , $p['default']
            , $p['value']
            , $p['source']
        );
```

```
        $p['checked'] = (
            in_array($p['value'],(array)$p['match'])
            || (
                $p['label_match']
                && in_array($p['label'],(array)$p['match'])
            )
        ) ? STANDALONE : NULL ;
    }
    $output = $p['prefix'].input_field($p).'
'.$p['label'].$p['suffix'];

    return $output;
}
```

FUNCTIONS AND CODE FROM /BOOK/BOOK.PHP

This is a kind of uberheader file, which the following examples include to set up the basic environment and call in the reusable functions from /book/functions.

book_constants() We store information about how your site is configured in a file named 'book.ini', using the same format as PHP's own 'php.ini' file. This lets us use the built-in function `parse_ini_file()` to read it in and set up the location of your /book directory, your /dsn directory, etc. as constants.

```
function book_constants()
{
    static $constants = NULL;
    if ($constants === NULL)
    {
        $ini_file = dirname(__FILE__).'/book.ini';
        if (!file_exists($ini_file))
        {
            generate_ini_file($ini_file);
        }
        $constants = parse_ini_file($ini_file);
        foreach ($constants as $k => $v)
        {
            if (!defined($k))
            {
                define($k, $v);
            }
        }
    }
    return $constants;
}
```

path_separator() This is a simple function to figure out what character separates directory names for your environment:

```
function path_separator()
{
    static $path_separator = NULL;
    if ($path_separator === NULL)
    {
        // if the include path has semicolons in it at all, then
they're
        // there to separate the paths; use a colon otherwise
        if (strchr(ini_get('include_path'),';') === FALSE)
        {
            $path_separator = ':';
        }
        else
        {
            $path_separator = ';';
        }
    }
    return $path_separator;
}
```

add_to_include_path() This function adds a directory to PHP's default include path.

```
function add_to_include_path()
{
    $include_path = ini_get('include_path');


    $ps = path_separator();
    book_constants();

    $paths = explode($ps, $include_path);
    $above_book = realpath(BOOK_ROOT.'/../');
    if (!in_array($above_book, $paths, TRUE))
    {
        $paths[] = $above_book;
    }
    $args = func_get_args();
    foreach ($args as $newpath)
    {
        if ($newpath == '')
```

```
        {
            $newpath = $above_book;
        }
        elseif (strpos($newpath,'/book') === 0)
        {
            $newpath = $above_book.$newpath;
        }
        if (!in_array($newpath, $paths, TRUE))
        {
            $paths[] = $newpath;
        }
    }
    $new_include_path = implode($ps, $paths);
    if (!ini_set('include_path', $new_include_path))
    {
        die("Could not set the 'include_path' configuration variable
to '$new_include_path'");
    }
    return $new_include_path;
}
```

The PHP configuration variable `'include_path'` defines a set of directories that PHP will search through to find files included with the `include()` and `require()` functions. (Several of the built-in file system functions, like `fopen()`, will also use this path if asked politely, a nice feature.) The `add_to_include_path()` function figures out where it is on the actual file system of your server and what character your installation uses to separate directories in `'include_path'` (a semicolon in Windows, a colon elsewhere). This lets us add the /book directory to the include path, even if the example code is not really in the root document directory of your Web server. The only reason the code is in a function, by the way, is to avoid creating global variables, which is considered bad style.

INITIALIZATION CODE Having defined `add_to_include_path`, we promptly call it, and then include the book/functions.php file, which sets up our reusable set of functions:

```
// use the local PEAR libraries
ini_set('include_path', '.');
add_to_include_path('/book', '/book/pear/PEAR', '/book/classes');

require_once('book/autoload.php');

// include the core function set
if (!defined('no_include'))
```

```
{
    require_once('book/functions.php');
}
```

The survey application

We're ready to dive into the code of the survey itself now, starting as always with our header.php file.

CODE FROM /BOOK/SURVEY/HEADER.PHP

This file is included in all the pages of the survey application.

```
<?php
require_once(
 preg_replace('|/survey/.*|','/book.php',realpath(__FILE__))
);

// include the function definitions for this application
// (use a path from book/survey so the include will work if we're
// running a script in the survey/admin directory)
require_once('book/survey/functions.php');

// connect to the database
my_connect('survey','joeuser','resueoj');

// make sure the domain isn't on our blocked list
check_domain();

?>
```

This code has been put inside an `if` statement as a precaution. There is no need to reload the header once it has been loaded. We can make sure that it isn't reloaded by creating a constant named `SURVEY_HEADER`. If by chance this page were loaded a second time, you wouldn't have to worry that included files would be imported more than once.

The first thing we do is include the /book/book.php file. Because the survey header file is included by pages in the /survey/admin subdirectory, as well as the main pages in /survey, we have to specify an absolute location for /book/book.php. We can do this using `__FILE__`. `__FILE__` is a PHP language construct that works like an ordinary constant, and that always contains the full name of the current file.

After /book/book.php has run, all of our main functions are defined. Then we load the local set of function definitions. After connecting to the database, we check to see if we've blocked the user's domain (see the following section).

FUNCTIONS FROM /BOOK/SURVEY/FUNCTIONS

The following are useful functions used in the application.

check_domain() As mentioned earlier, this is a facility to block domains, and we use the `check_domain()` function to enforce the block:

```
function check_domain()
{
    // check to see if the user is coming from a domain that is
listed
    // as currently blocked in the blocked_domains database table,
    // as specified by the $_SERVER values REMOTE_HOST or
REMOTE_ADDR.
    // if it is, print out an error and exit.

    $remote_host =
(string)array_key_value($_SERVER,'REMOTE_HOST','');
    $remote_addr =
(string)array_key_value($_SERVER,'REMOTE_ADDR','');
    $wheres = array();
    if (!empty($remote_host))
    {
        $wheres[] = "'$remote_host' like concat('%',domain)";
    }
    if (!empty($remote_addr))
    {
        $wheres[] = "'$remote_addr' like concat(domain,'%')";
    }
    if (count($wheres) > 0)
    {
        $is_blocked = 0;
        $where = implode(' or ', $wheres);
        $query = "select 1 as is_blocked from blocked_domains
            where release_dt is null and ($where)
        ";
        $result = my_query($query);
        list($is_blocked) = mysql_fetch_row($result);
        mysql_free_result($result);
        if ($is_blocked == 1)
        {
            // Be noncomittal.
            print subtitle('Page unavailable.');
            exit;
        }
    }
}
```

In order to understand this code, look more closely at the query, particularly the like predicates. When we bring up this Web page from my ISP (att.net), $_SERVER['REMOTE_HOST'] is something like this: 119.san-francisco-18-19rs.ca.dial-access.att.net. When you block domains, you'll be blocking the top-level domain – in this case att.net. And this top-level domain is what will reside in the database. So the query will have checked on any number of wildcard characters prior to the top-level domain name.

To achieve the wildcard checking, you will need to concatenate the domain names with the % wildcard character – so that, for instance, the query will work against %att.net. Doing this may seem somewhat different from using your typical like predicate. It's another powerful technique to use with SQL.

Or, since you might not have $_SERVER['REMOTE_HOST'] available on your server, you might have entered a literal IP address instead. In this case, the most general part is the beginning of the string, rather than the end. So when we compare the domain field to $_SERVER['REMOTE_ADDR'], we concatenate the % character onto the end rather than the beginning.

Also note that the start of the select statement contains select 1 rather than select count(*). This leads to a good way of testing if any rows meet the condition of the where clause. If the where clause matches any number of rows the query will return a single column with the value of 1, which in the programming world means TRUE. If no rows are returned you know the where portion of the query had no matches.

This function is just intended to demonstrate some general techniques for checking server variables and comparing them against a database. In the real world it would be about as hacker-proof as a wet tissue.

weekstart() This function generates SQL, MySQL style, to figure out the day of the week for a particular date. You use this in the application to pick a winner for the current week.

```
function weekstart ($when='')
{
    if (empty($when))
    {
        $when = 'now()';
    }
    elseif ($when != 'create_dt')
    {
        $when = "'$when'";
    }
    return "from_days(to_days($when)-dayofweek($when) + 1)";
}
```

The MySQL to_days() function returns an integer of the number of days since January 1, 1000. dayofweek() returns an integer representing the day of the week

(Sunday equals 1, Saturday equals 7). So the portion (to_days($now)-dayofweek($when) + 1) will return an integer representing the Sunday of the week in question. The from_days() function will then turn that number into a date. Here is the result of this query run on Monday August 4, 2002 (the day this chapter was first written):

```
mysql> select from_days(to_days(now())-dayofweek(now()) + 1);
+-------------------------------------------------+
| from_days(to_days(now())-dayofweek(now()) + 1) |
+-------------------------------------------------+
| 2002-08-04                                      |
+-------------------------------------------------+
1 row in set (0.01 sec)
```

Note that the value passed here can be a string representing a date, it can be empty, or it can be a field from the users table – namely the create_dt field.

fetch_question() This function grabs the contents of a row in the questions table and returns them as an associative array.

```
function fetch_question ($question_id=0)
{
    $result = my_query(
        'select * from questions where
question_id='.(int)$question_id
    );
    $output = mysql_fetch_assoc($result);
    mysql_free_result($result);
    return $output;
}
```

This will return from the database all the information regarding a particular question, based on the question_id.

fetch_user() This function grabs the contents of a row in the users table and returns them as an associative array.

```
function fetch_user ($user_id='')
{
    $result = my_query(
        'select * from users where user_id='.(int)$user_id
    );
    $output = mysql_fetch_assoc($result);
    mysql_free_result($result);
    return $output;
}
```

This function returns the result set based on a `user_id`.

get_answers() This function returns an array of answers associated with a question, along with the total number of votes so far for each answer.

```
function get_answers($question_id=0)
{
    $question_id = (int)$question_id;
    $query = "select a.answer, a.answer_id, count(r.user_id) as
votes
        from answers a
            left join responses r on a.answer_id = r.answer_id
        where a.question_id = $question_id
        group by a.answer_id
        having votes > 0
        order by votes desc
    ";
    $answers = array();
    $result = my_query($query);
    while ($row = mysql_fetch_assoc($result))
    {
        $answers[] = $row;
    }
    mysql_free_result($result);
    return $answers;
}
```

Interesting Code Flow

There are a few pages in this application that could stand some explanation. However, you should be able to follow most of them if you understand the functions in the previous section.

admin/questions.php

This is a fairly lengthy page, and for good reason: it is used for adding, editing, and deleting questions in the database. The portion of the page to be run will be determined by the values passed by forms or links. The first time through, there will be no variables passed, so a list of the current questions will be presented along with a form for entering a new question. Each of the links to questions that already exist in the database looks like this:

```
<a href="questions.php?question_id=2" >
```

When a link like this is clicked, and the questions.php script is run again, the very last of the initial `if-else` tests in the setup code at the top of the file run, as shown here:

```
else
{
    // if the ID of a question is passed in, retrieve its
information
    // from the database for editing.
    extract(fetch_question($question_id));

    // set the form title to indicate the action the user can
perform
    $qform_title = 'Edit A Question : #'.$question_id;
}

print subtitle($qform_title);

print start_form('questions.php');


print paragraph(
 '<b>Question:</b>'
 , text_field(array(
     'name'=>'question','value'=>$question,'size'=>60
 ))
 , hidden_field(array(
     'name'=>'question_id', 'value'=>$question_id
 ))
);
```

Notice how you can get all the information associated with `$question_id` with one function call (`fetch_question()`). Since `fetch_question()` is returning an associative array, we can use `extract()` to create variables from the values in the array.

Next, go into this loop:

```
$lines = array('<b>Answers:</b><br>');

// print form elements for answers to the question.
$acount = 0;
if ($question_id > 0)
{
    $query = "select answer_id, answer from answers
```

```
            where question_id = $question_id order by answer_id
        ";
        $result = my_query($query);
        while (list($aid,$atxt) = mysql_fetch_row($result))
        {
            // we increment the count first because we want the
            // first key value to be 1, not 0, to make sure that
            // the key will test as non-empty.
            $acount++;
            $lines[] = text_field(array(
                'name'=>"answer_text[$acount]"
                , 'value'=>$atxt
                , 'size'=>60
            ));
            $lines[] = hidden_field(array(
                'name'=>"answer_id[$acount]"
                , 'value'=>$aid
            ));
            $lines[] = " ($aid)<br>\n";
        }
        mysql_free_result($result);
    }
```

This block gets the answers for the selected question and prints them out inside text fields. Additional information is put inside hidden fields. When printed out the result for one answer will look like this:

```
<input type="text" name="answer_text[1]" value="Answer" size="60" >
<input type="hidden" name="answer_id[1]" value="10">
```

When this form is submitted, `$answer_text` will be an array. `$acount` will see that the key of the array is incremented by one for each additional form field. Note that we need to make use of a hidden form element here, because each answer requires three pieces of information: the answer number (1–10), the answer text, and, if the answer came from the database, the primary key of the row the answer came from. The hidden field will create an array named `$answer_id`. The value in each element of that array will be the primary key of the row storing the answer. The index of that array will be the match for the index of `$answer_text`. In code the technique looks like this:

```
$i = 1;
$answer_text[$i];
$answer_id[$i];
```

You'd know, when receiving and processing the information from this screen, that `$answer_id[$i]` contains the primary key of a row, and `$answer_text[$i]` is the answer text that belongs in that row.

The previous section of code will print out form elements only where an answer exists. But you should offer blank form elements so the administrator can enter new answers:

```
// print out blank fields to bring us up to at least 10 answers
while ($acount < 10)
{
    $acount++;
    $lines[] = text_field(array(
        'name' => "answer_text[$acount]"
        , 'value' => ''
        , 'size' => 60
    ));
    $lines[] = hidden_field(array(
        'name' => "answer_id[$acount]"
        , 'value' => 0
    ));
    $lines[] = "<br>\n";
}
print paragraph($lines);
```

This will complete the form and display it, giving all the blank elements you need. For these blank answers, the form will contain the following:

```
<input type="text" name="answer_text[8]" value="" size="60" >
<input type="hidden" name="answer_id[8]" value="0"><br>
```

In these form elements, the value of the hidden field is set to `0`. That way, when it comes time to process these form elements, the script will have something to evaluate: If `$answer_id[$i]` is equal to `0`, this is a new element.

If the user clicks the Save Changes button to submit this form, the preceding chunk of code will run after handling the update of the database record for the question itself. There will always be 10 elements to be looped through, so a `for` loop works nicely.

```
    $answer_texts =
(array)array_key_value($_POST,'answer_text',array());
    $answer_ids =
(array)array_key_value($_POST,'answer_id',array());

    for ($i = 1; $i <= 10; $i++)
```

```
    {
        $atxt = (string)$answer_texts[$i];
        $aid = (int)$answer_ids[$i];
        if (empty($atxt))
        {
            if (!empty($aid))
            {
```

If no text exists for the answer, and a value exists for the answer ID, the user has blanked out an existing answer. So delete it from the database:

```
                my_query('delete from answers where answer_id =
'.(int)$aid);
            }
        }
        else
        {
            $answer = mysql_real_escape_string(cleanup_text($atxt));
            if (empty($aid))
            {
                // if we have no ID for the answer,
                // it doesn't exist yet. create a new
                // record in the answers table.
                $query = "insert into answers (question_id, answer)
                    values ($question_id,'$answer')
                ";
            }
```

Pay attention to the explicit casting – `(int)` – at the beginning of that passage. It prevents an error when the value is `0`. If the element of `$answer_id` is not empty (which means it can't be equal to `0`), an `insert` statement is run:

```
            else
            {
                // if we do have an ID, the answer is already
                // in the answers table. update it.
                $query = "update answers
                    set question_id = $question_id, answer =
'$answer'
                    where answer_id = $aid
                ";
            }
            my_query($query);
        }
    }
```

Otherwise, if an existing answer was present, an `update` query will do the trick.

admin/get_winner.php

Most of this file is readable by humans. Our goal is to draw a qualified winner at random from the database. First we use the `weekstart()` function (discussed earlier in this chapter in the section "Functions from /book/survey/functions") to get the date on which the current week begins:

```
$weekdate = (string)array_key_value($_REQUEST,'weekdate','');

$result = my_query('select '.weekstart($weekdate));
list($thisweek) = mysql_fetch_row($result);
mysql_free_result($result);

print subtitle('Draw a winner for the week of '.$thisweek);

// get a list of qualifying entries for the given week.
$query = "select name, email, user_id from users
    where week(create_dt) = week('$thisweek')
        and year(create_dt) = year('$thisweek')
        and name is not null and name != ''
        and email is not null and email != '' and email like '%@%.%'
        and age > 0
        and country is not null and country != ''
";
```

We then create a query that will determine who is qualified. As you can see, we've decided that in addition to having signed in during the last week, participants need to have entered a name, an email address, and a legitimate age to qualify.

admin/winners.php

We created a few pages to ensure that the winner selected is notified of the exciting news and that we issue the notification in a way that provides some security. The security isn't much, but to make reasonably sure that the person who claims the prize is the person we intended, we would need to make use of a login system, and users of a silly little survey may not be interested in keeping track of yet another password.

The best we can do here is to try to make sure that if some immoral person sees the claim information one week, that person will not be able to easily spoof our system in future weeks. When we send the winner notification, we will include an eight-character claim code. This prize can only be claimed with the code. To make things as secure as possible, we want to make sure this code is unique and very difficult to guess.

```
    mt_srand ((double) microtime() * 1000000);
    $claim_code = substr(md5(uniqid(rand())),0,8);
```

The preceding code uses the `uniqueid()` and `md5()` functions to create a string that is very random. There's little for a hacker to latch onto in trying to figure out how the string is constructed. `md5()` will create a string that is 32 characters long, but that can be a bit unwieldy. So we're using `substr()` to limit the string to eight characters.

The `user_id`, the claim code, and the week of during which the contest took place are inserted into the winners table:

```
    $query = "replace into winners (weekdate, user_id, claim_code,
notify_dt)
         values ('$weekdate', $user_id, '$claim_code', now())
    ";
```

The winner is sent an email containing a URL that includes a claim code that matches one in the database: `http://mydomain.com/book/survey/claim.php?claim_code=54fa3399`.

If the user is interested, he or she will go to this page.

claim.php

If the winner comes to claim.php, we first need to check that the claim code exists in the database. The query in the following code grabs queries from the database to see if the claim code exists; if it does, the query performs a join and returns the user information associated with the claim code.

```
$user_id = 0;
$winner_email = NULL;
$weekdate = NULL;

$claim_code = (string)array_key_value($_REQUEST,'claim_code','');

if (!empty($claim_code))
{
    $query = "select u.user_id, u.email, w.weekdate from users u,
winners w
         where w.claim_code = '$claim_code' and w.user_id = u.user_id
    ";
    $result = my_query($query);
    list($user_id, $winner_email, $weekdate) =
mysql_fetch_row($result);
    mysql_free_result($result);
```

```
}

if ($user_id == 0)
{
    // we couldn't find a record corresponding to the claim_code
    // submitted (if any). print out an error and exit.
    $msg = <<<EOQ

I'm sorry, that doesn't appear to be a valid claim code.
The URL may not have registered properly.
Make sure to copy the complete link into your browser and try again,
or forward your original prize notification to $admin_email.

EOQ;
    print paragraph($msg);
    exit;
}
```

Once it is established that a claim code is valid, we want to do a bit of double-checking and make sure that the person who submitted this claim code knows the email address to which the notification was sent. The application does this by displaying a form asking the user to enter the correct email. That form is sent and processed by the form page. When the form is submitted, the following code will execute:

```
$user_email = (string)array_key_value($_POST,'user_email','');

if (!empty($user_email))
{
    // the user has submitted an email address to claim
    // the prize.
    if ($user_email != $winner_email)
    {
        // the email address submitted by the user doesn't
        // match the one stored for the winning entry.
        // display an error message.
        $notice = <<<EOQ

I'm sorry, that email address doesn't match our records.
Please try again, or forward your original prize notification
to $admin_email.

EOQ;
    }
```

The comparison `$user_email != $winner_email` will work because the query that ran at the top of the page retrieved the correct winner's email, and we get `$user_email` from the form submitted by the user. If that comparison fails, an error message prints. If it does not fail, the following code updates the winners database, recording the time the prize was claimed, and sends an email to the winner letting him or her know that the claim was successful:

```
    else
    {
        // everything matches. we can update the database
        // to record a valid claim.
        $claimquery = "update winners set claim_dt = now()
            where user_id = $user_id
            and claim_code = '$claim_code'
            and weekdate = '$weekdate'
        ";
        my_query($claimquery);
        if (mysql_affected_rows() > 0)
        {
            // send a notification to the administrator that
            // the prize has been claimed.
            $confirm_url = regular_url('admin/winners.php');
            $msgtext = <<<EOQ

The prize for $weekdate has been claimed by $user_email.

Confirm the prize at

$confirm_url

EOQ;
            $subject = 'Prize Claim';
            $result = mail($admin_email,$subject,$msgtext);

            if ($result)
            {
                // we don't need to re-display the form now.
                // print out congratulations and bail.
                $msg = <<<EOQ
Thanks! Your claim has been accepted.
Your prize should be on its way soon!
EOQ;
                print paragraph($msg);
                exit;
            }
```

```
            else
            {
                $private_error = <<<EOQ
could not send claim notification:
admin_email=($admin_email)
subject=($subject)
msgtext=($msgtext)
EOQ;
                user_error('Warning: Could not notify administrator
of your claim.', E_USER_WARNING);
            }
        }
        else
        {
            // just in case the database is broken or
            // some other horror has occurred...
            $msgtext = <<<EOQ
The prize for $weekdate has been claimed by $user_email, but the
database
update did not work.
EOQ;
            $subject = 'Prize Claim';
            $result = mail($admin_email,$subject,$msgtext);
            if (!$result)
            {
                $private_error = <<<EOQ
could not send claim problem notification:
admin_email=($admin_email)
subject=($subject)
msgtext=($msgtext)
EOQ;
                user_error('Warning: Could not notify administrator
of your claim.', E_USER_WARNING);
            }

            // let the user know that something broke
            // and re-display the form by continuing
            // with the script.
            $notice = <<<EOQ

Your claim is valid, but we were unable to record that fact.
Please try again later, or forward your initial prize notification
to $admin_email and let them know there was a problem.

EOQ;
```

```
            }
        }
    }
```

The final portion of this page simply prints the form in which the user will enter his or her email. There's really no need to show that here.

Summary

The survey application involves quite a bit of code, but it isn't anything that you shouldn't be able to figure out with some close scrutiny of the files and the comments. Take a look at the complex_results.php page and its `includes` (age_results.php, state_results.php, and country_results.php) for a look at how MySQL aggregate functions can come in handy.

This application contains much more complexity than the guestbook. In it is a real database schema complete with related tables. In the course of the application we need to make use of queries that contain MySQL functions. (See Appendix J for more information on MySQL functions.)

Another notable item seen in this chapter is the function set we've created for creating common HTML elements. Whether you want to make use of such functions or not is up to you. You may prefer typing out individual form elements, tables, and the like. But you will be seeing these functions used in the remainder of this book.

Part IV

Not So Simple Applications

Chapter 10

Threaded Discussion

IN THIS CHAPTER

- Adding to your Web site features that promote community
- Using an advanced technique to write functions
- Looking at other criteria to use when designing a database
- Setting up error-handling and debugging functions

IF YOU'VE CREATED a Web site or are looking to create one, it's probably safe to assume that you want people to return frequently to your pages. But as everyone in the Web industry knows, loyalty is fleeting, and people are always looking for something better, more engaging, or closer to their interests.

One way to keep the anonymous masses involved with your site is to offer your visitors a way to contribute to its content. If someone has accessed your site, it's likely that he or she has an opinion on the topic you are presenting. And if our conclusions from 30-plus years of observation are correct, people love to share their opinions.

Using the threaded-discussion application in this chapter, you can create an area on your Web site where your users can share their opinions and interact with you and each other.

Once you have this piece of your site up and running, you are well on your way to creating your own Web community. I make special mention of the word *community* for two reasons.

- First, it is a huge buzzword within the industry. Everyone is looking to create a sense of familiarity and inclusion that tempts users to return.
- Second – and perhaps more importantly – you, the Webmaster, should know what you're getting yourself into. From personal experience, we can tell you that "community" can be a real pain in the butt. On the Web, everyone is pretty much anonymous, and few consequences are associated with antisocial behavior. Thus, in many discussion groups, opinionated windbags have a way of ruining a promising discussion.

Before too long, you will undoubtedly see things that are mean or distasteful, and you must be prepared to deal with it. We're not trying to scare you away from including a discussion list on your site. We're just letting you know that you need to put some effort into administering it. Whether you monitor the list yourself or appoint someone to do it for you, somebody will need to make sure your users behave if you want it to be orderly and functional.

Determining the Scope and Goals of the Application

The purpose of any discussion board is reasonably simple. Any visitor to the site should be able to post a new topic to the board or reply to any of the existing topics. Furthermore, the board must be flexible enough to deal with any number of replies to an existing topic, or replies to replies, or replies to replies to replies, and so on. Put another way, the board must be able to deal with an indefinite level of depth. The script must be able to react appropriately, whether the discussion goes one level deep, five levels deep, or ten levels deep, which requires some new techniques, both in your data design and in your scripts.

What do you need?

You need only two files to generate all the views needed for this application. But these two files can have very different looks, depending on the information that is displayed.

The first file displays topics and their replies. The first time users come to the message board they will not know what threads they wish to read. Therefore, a list of topics will be displayed. Figure 10-1 shows the list of top-level topics.

Once a user chooses a topic the page lists all the posts within that topic. As you can see in Figure 10-2, the top of the page shows the text and subject of the post being read. Below that, immediate replies to that post are indicated with a colored border, and the text of the immediate replies is also printed. Figure 10-2 also shows that the application provides a subject, a name, and a link to posts that are more than one level deep in the thread. You can see that it is rather easy to tell who has replied to what.

This same page provides another view. If a user clicks through to a post that does not start a topic, the page shows all threads beneath that post. At the top of the page the script will print the top-level post (or *root*) and the post immediately prior to the one being viewed (or *parent*). Figure 10-3 shows an example of this view.

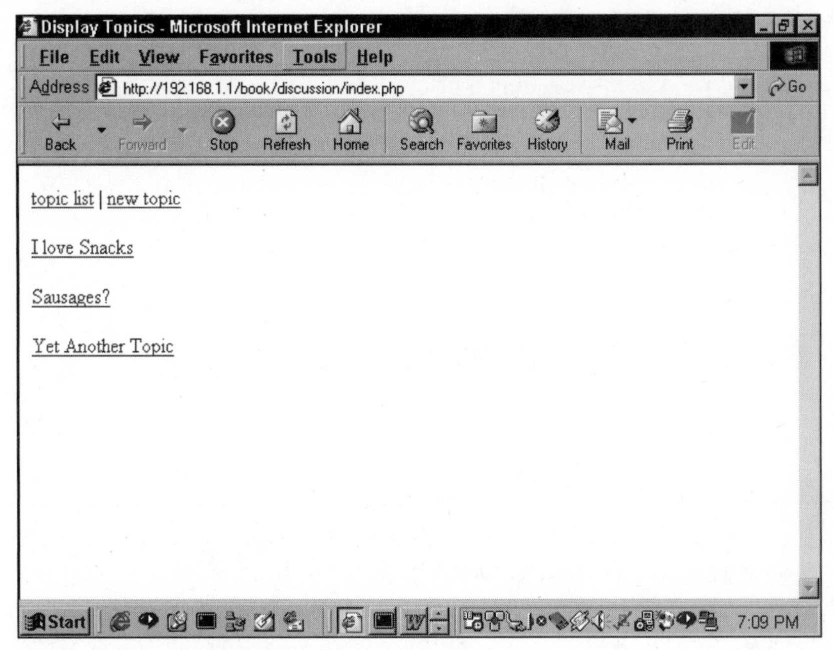

Figure 10-1: List of top-level topics

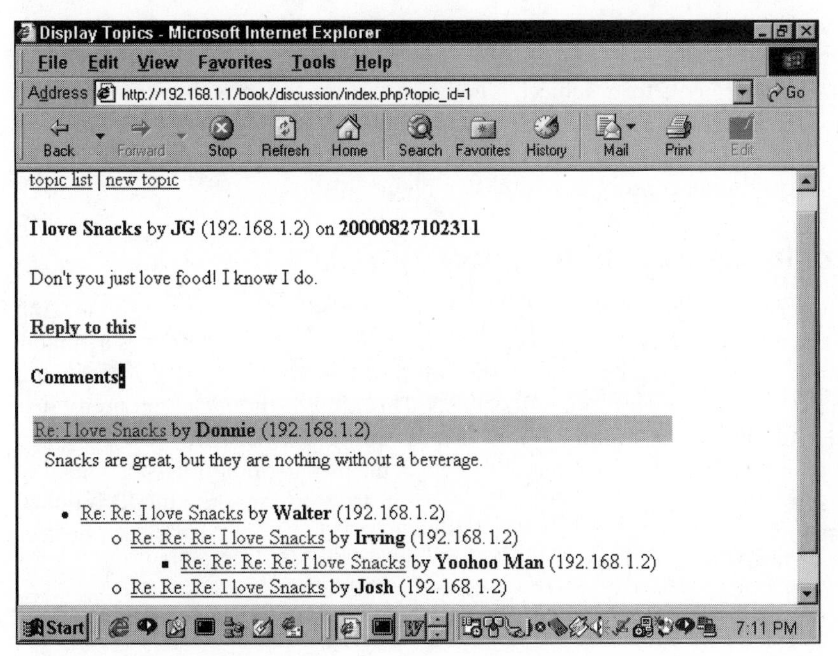

Figure 10-2: Display of a thread

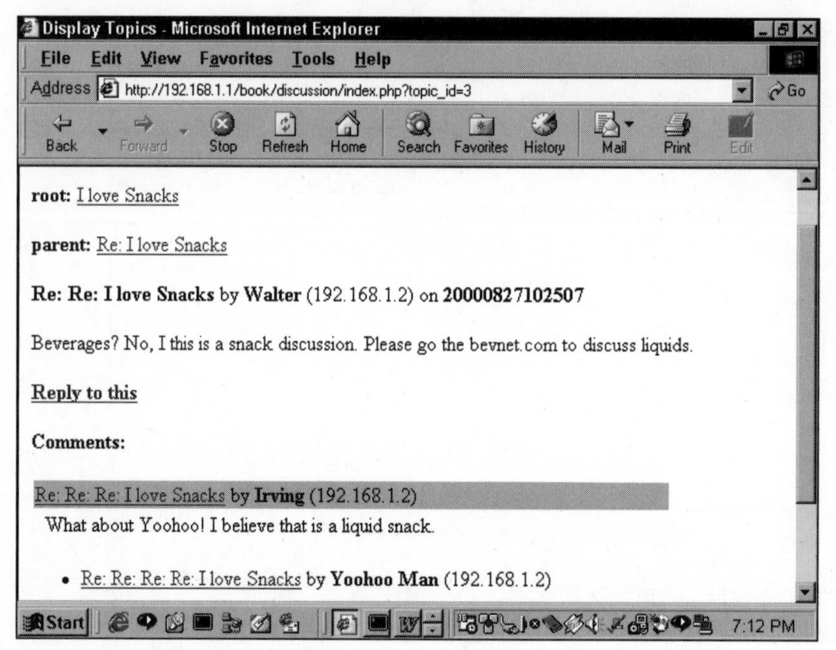

Figure 10-3: View further down a thread

Everything you saw in the previous figures was handled by one page. The second page posts threads to the board. This posting requires only a simple form that contains form elements for a subject, a name, and room for the comment. The form needs to be aware of where in the thread the message belongs. For new top-level topics a form without any context is fine (see Figure 10-4), but for replies within an existing thread some context is helpful (see Figure 10-5).

What do you need to prevent?

As you've seen in previous chapters, you need to spend quite a bit of time making sure things work properly. Unless every post is reviewed before it becomes available on the site, there is no good way of preventing users from posting nonsense and then replying to their own meaningless posts. This kind of thing can get pretty distracting – and again, no foolproof way of preventing it exists. However, you can make it a bit more obvious to other users who is making the nefarious postings. For that reason, this application uses the IP of origin to generate a unique ID number, which can make it more plain who is posting what. This strategy isn't great protection, but it is better than nothing.

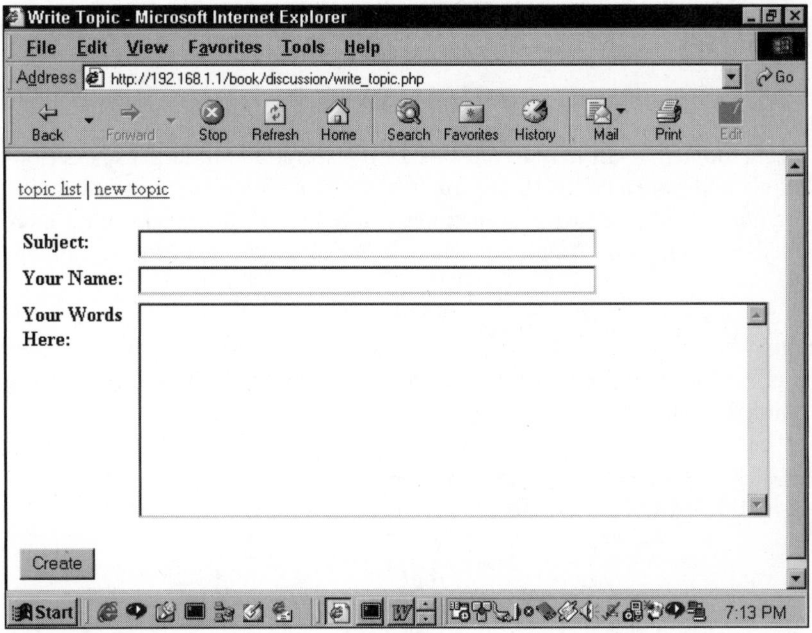

Write Topic - Microsoft Internet Explorer

File Edit View Favorites Tools Help

Address http://192.168.1.1/book/discussion/write_topic.php Go

Back Forward Stop Refresh Home Search Favorites History Mail Print Edit

topic list | new topic

Subject:

Your Name:

Your Words Here:

Create

Start 7:13 PM

Figure 10-4: Form for posting a top-level topic

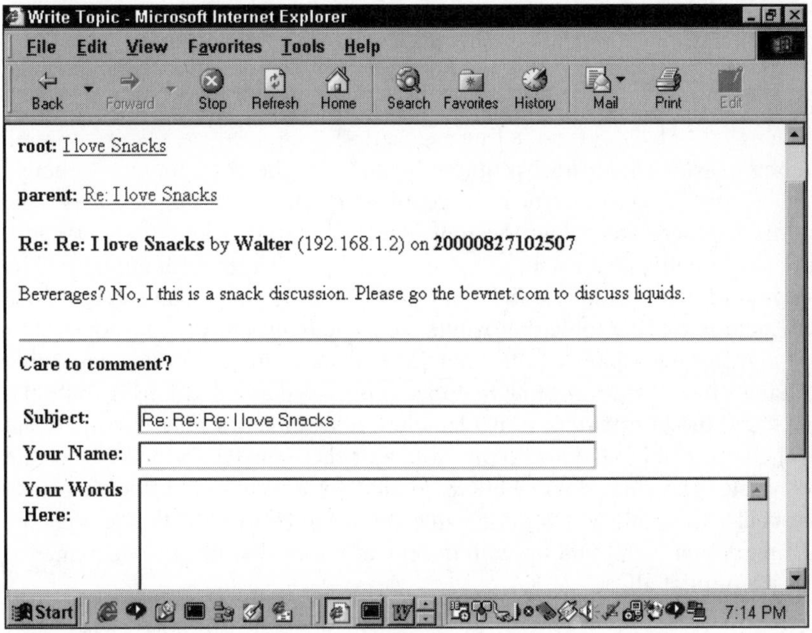

Write Topic - Microsoft Internet Explorer

File Edit View Favorites Tools Help

Back Forward Stop Refresh Home Search Favorites History Mail Print Edit

root: I love Snacks

parent: Re: I love Snacks

Re: Re: I love Snacks by **Walter** (192.168.1.2) on **20000827102507**

Beverages? No, I this is a snack discussion. Please go the bevnet.com to discuss liquids.

Care to comment?

Subject: Re: Re: Re: I love Snacks

Your Name:

Your Words Here:

Start 7:14 PM

Figure 10-5: Form for posting a lower-level topic

The Data

Of all the applications discussed in this book, this one has perhaps the most unexpected data structure.

We'll take a moment right here to tell you a little secret about database development: Though you can usually figure out the structure of a database by going through the normalization process, sometimes you're better off concentrating more on the hoped-for end result. You'll see what we mean as you read the rest of this section.

But before we show you what we created and why it works so well, let us show you an example of what you might have expected – and why it would have been so problematic. You might think that this application would start with a table looking something like Table 10-1.

TABLE 10-1 PROBLEMATIC ROOT_TOPICS

root_ topic_id	root_ topic_date	root_ topic_name	root_ topic_subject	root_ topic_text
1	08/20/2003	Jack	Snacks Rule	I love em.
2	08/20/2003	Edith	More Cheetos	I want my fingers orange.
3	9/1/2003	Archie	M&Ms	Mmmmore.

This table, as you can probably guess, would list the root topics. A simple `SELECT * FROM root_topics` returns a record set of all the root topics. This table doesn't allow for any data below the root level. To take care of this, you might envision a structure in which each `root_topic_id` is associated with another table. Whenever you inserted a row into the `root_topics` table, you'd also run a `CREATE TABLE` statement to make a table that would store the replies to the root topic.

For example, all the replies to the "Snacks Rule" post are stored in a table that looks like Table 10-2. This arrangement works. A one-to-many relationship between the tables exists, and information is available pretty readily. But now consider what happens when somebody wants to reply to one of these posts. You have to create yet another table. And what if you were to go another level or two deeper? It's easy to see that before long this would get completely out of control. With just a couple of active threads you could end up with dozens of tables that need to be managed and joined – no fun at all.

TABLE 10-2 PROBLEMATIC TOPICS

topic_id	topic_date	topic_author	topic_subject	topic_text
1	08/20/2003	Ellen	Re: Snacks Rule	You betcha
2	08/20/2003	Erners	Re: Snacks Rule	Indeed

Now we move away from this ill-considered idea and move toward a more sound plan. Think about what information needs to be stored for each post to the mailing list. Start with the obvious stuff. You need a column that stores the subject of the thread (for example, "Nachos, food of the gods"), one that stores the author's name, and one that records the date the item was posted. So the table starts with these columns – we've thrown in some sample information in Table 10-3 and an `auto_increment` primary key just to keep it clear.

TABLE 10-3 START OF A USEABLE TABLE

topic_id	subject	author	date
1	Nachos rule	Jay	3/12/2003
2	Cheetos are the best	Brad	3/12/2003

But of course this isn't enough. Somehow you need a way to track the ancestry and lineage of any specific topic. (Look again at Figure 10-1 if you are not sure what we mean.) So how are you going to do this? If you are looking to track the ancestry of any particular thread, it probably makes sense to add a field that indicates the topic that started the thread – the root topic.

Take a close look at Table 10-4. Start with the first row. Here the `root_id` is the same as the `topic_id`. Now look at the third row. Here the `root_id` (1) matches the `topic_id` of the first row. So you know that the thread to which row 3 belongs started with `topic_id 1` – "Nachos rule." Similarly, row 6 must be a reply to row 2.

Now look at rows 1, 2, and 5. Notice that in these rows the `topic_id` and the `root_id` are identical. At this point you can probably guess that whenever these two are the same, it indicates a root-level topic. Easy enough, right? The following SQL statement retrieves all the root-level topics:

```
select * from topics where root_id=topic_id.
```

Table 10-4 A MORE COMPLETE TABLE

topic_id	root_id	subject	author	date
1	1	Nachos rule	Jay	3/12/2003
2	2	Cheetos are the best	Ed	3/12/2003
3	1	Re: Nachos rule	Don	3/12/2003
4	1	Re: Nachos rule	Bill	3/13/2003
5	5	What about cookies	Evany	3/14/2003
6	2	Re: Cheetos are the best	Ed	3/13/2003

Now that you've added a `root_id` field to the table, you should know the beginning of a thread. But how can you get all the entries that came between the original topic and the one you're interested in? Initially you might think it would be prudent to add a column that lists the ancestors. You could call the column `ancestors` and in it you'd have a listing of `topic_id`s. It might contain a string like `1, 6, 9, 12`. Taking this approach would be a very, very bad idea. Why, you ask? Well, the most important reason worth mentioning is that you should never put multiple values in a single field – you'll open yourself up to all kinds of hassles.

MySQL does have a column type that takes multiple values. It is called `set`. It is not used anywhere in this book because Dr. Codd would not approve. Do you remember Dr. Codd from Chapter 1? He's the guy who originally developed relational-database theory in the first place. Generally, it's a bad idea to put multiple values in a single field because, except in cases in which the multiple values are always used together (in which case they're not really multiple values), you invariably end up parsing the group to use the values separately. That's extra work you don't need.

So what options are you left with? Create another table to keep track of a topic's lineage? That isn't necessary. The easiest thing to do is add to the previous table a single column that tracks the parent of the current topic, as shown in Table 10-5.

TABLE 10-5 AN EVEN BETTER TABLE

topic_id	root_id	parent_id	subject	author	date
1	1	0	Nachos rule	Jay	3/12/2003
2	2	0	Cheetos are the best	Ed	3/12/2003
3	1	1	Re: Nachos rule	Don	3/12/2003
4	1	3	Re: Nachos rule	Bill	3/13/2003
5	5	0	What about cookies	Evany	3/13/2003
6	2	2	Re: Cheetos are the best	Ed	3/14/2003
7	1	4	Cheetos, are you kidding	Jeff	3/15/2003
8	5	5	Re: What about cookies	Jay	3/15/2003

When you look at the first couple of rows in Table 10-5, you might see little difference between the fields. And that sort of makes sense: If the `topic_id` and the `parent_id` are the same, you already know that it's a root level and that therefore the parent is irrelevant. Move your attention to row `7`. Here you can see that root is row `1`, "Nachos rule." That's easy enough. Now look at the `parent_id`, which is row `4`. If you look at the parent of row `4`, you will find that it's row `3` – and further that the parent of that row is row `1`, which is also the root. So with just this information you can follow a thread to its origin. A very simple script that traces a topic to its origin looks something like this:

```
Select all fields from current topic
If parent_id is not equal to 0 and parent_id does not equal root_id
    Make parent ID current topic
    Go to line 1
```

So that will about do it. Using this data structure, you can get all the information you are going to need. Throw in a couple of timestamps for safekeeping, and you're all set. Listing 10-1 shows the SQL statement that will create the table (using `name` for the subject of the topic, `create_dt` for the date, and `description` for the text):

Listing 10-1: create table Statement for Threaded Discussion

```
create table topics (
    topic_id integer not null auto_increment
    , parent_id integer default 0
```

Continued

Listing 10-1 *(Continued)*

```
    , root_id integer default 0
    , name varchar(255)
    , description text
    , create_dt timestamp(14)
    , modify_dt timestamp(14)
    , author varchar(255)
    , author_addr_id int
, primary key (topic_id)
)
type=InnoDB
;
```

One other table exists in the database, to create the author-ID values we mentioned earlier:

```
create table author_addrs (
    author_addr_id integer default 0 not null auto_increment
    , author_addr varchar(255)
    , entry_dt timestamp
, primary key (author_addr_id)
, unique key (author_addr)
)
type=InnoDB
;
```

As you can see, this code makes use of MySQL's `auto_increment` feature to get a unique value per entry. There is potential here. If you want to add some administrative functions to this application you can add a foreign-key constraint with an `ON DELETE CASCADE` qualifier to the main `topics` table that references `author_addrs`. Then just remove the row from `author_addrs` for the problematic poster and poof, all his or her posts disappear. Bear in mind, though, that the responses to those posts would remain, and the threads the poster started would be orphaned unless they were manually deleted. There are always improvements to be made.

Code Overview

As we mentioned earlier, two main functions are involved in this application:

- Displaying a listing of posts
- Inserting a new post to the database

Thus, it should come as little surprise that at the base level there are only two files: display_topic.php and write_topic.php. In addition to these files, you have a separate file that stores all of your functions (functions.php). If you read the previous section, you probably won't be surprised to find that most of the effort involved in developing this application, and therefore most of the code we are introducing, relates to displaying the ancestors and children of a particular post. Keep in mind that a post can have any number of ancestors and any number of children. So your script has to be flexible enough to deal with a post with one reply or twenty.

The portion that writes a topic to the database should be pretty easy to deal with. In your form you need to have hidden fields that mark the `root_id` and the `parent_id`, and you want to validate the contents of the forms, but other than that it should be pretty easy. The next section of the chapter breaks it down.

Code Breakdown

As usual, most of the fun occurs in the functions. In fact, in this application the only two files actually referenced by URLs are practically empty.

Reusable functions

Again, this application makes use of the functions described in Chapter 8 and Chapter 9. In addition, in this example we introduce some error-handling functions, to give you a finer level of control over what gets displayed to the end user when something goes wrong. When your users can complain about error messages right there in the site itself, this is a topic worth some attention. The code involved is a little more complex than what we've seen so far, so we'll look at it at the end of this chapter, after we've gotten a better idea of what's supposed to happen when things go right.

Functions from /book/discussion/functions

The application itself has just a few functions, one of which uses a technique that requires some explanation. The concept that is new to this application is called *recursion*. It comes up in the `display_kids()` function.

display_kids()

Usually, in this part of the book, a function is displayed and then described. However, this function must be treated a bit differently because recursion can be somewhat difficult conceptually. So before we display the function, we want to take a look at recursion. (If you already know your way around recursive functions, feel free to skim.)

The important thing to keep in mind is that you have no idea how deep any thread will be: There can be one level of replies, or twenty. So to properly lay out all the children of any one thread you need a very, very flexible script. It needs to do something like this:

```
print current topic
while the current topic has unprocessed child topics
    set current topic to next unprocessed child
    go to line 1
end while
if current topic has a parent
   set current topic to that parent and go to line 2
else
   exit
end if
```

This block of code must be repeated indefinitely until no other answers exist. But how do you tell a script to do something until it runs out of answers? The looping mechanisms we've discussed so far won't really work. The `for...`, `while...`, and `do...while` loops that we talked about in Chapter 5 and used in the previous chapters are of no help.

If that isn't clear, take a look at Table 10-6 and the code that follows.

TABLE 10-6 SAMPLE TABLE

topic_id	root_id	parent_id	subject	name	date
1	1	0	Nachos rule	Jay	3/12/2003
2	2	0	Cheetos are the best	Ed	3/12/2003
3	1	1	Re: Nachos rule	Don	3/12/2003
4	1	3	Re: Nachos rule	Bill	3/13/2003
5	5	0	What about cookies	Evany	3/13/2003
6	2	2	Re: Cheetos are the best	Ed	3/14/2003
7	1	4	Cheetos, are you kidding	Jeff	3/15/2003
8	5	5	Re: What about cookies	Jay	3/15/2003

Suppose you want each level to be indented a little farther than the previous one, by means of the HTML `blockquote` tag. Now, assume that you're calling the following function by passing a `topic_id` of `7`.

```
function RecurForMe($topic_id)
{
   $query = "SELECT * from topics  WHERE topic_id =  $topic_id;
   $result = mysql_query($query) or
        die("Query failed");
   $row = mysql_fetch_array($result);
   echo "<blockquote>";
   echo $row["name"], "\n";
   RecurForMe($row["parent_id"]);
}
```

You know by now not to actually run a script like this because there's no error checking, and eventually, when no responses to the query exist, it will cause an error. We wrote this function so you could look at the last line. You see what it does: The function calls itself. If you're not clear about the impact this has, walk through it with us.

The first time through, given the `$topic_id` of `7`, the query returns (surprise, surprise) row number `7`. Then a `blockquote` tag and the name (`Jeff`) is printed out. Then the function calls itself, this time passing the `parent_id` of `4`. The next time through the query returns row `4`, the time after that it returns row `3`, and finally, it returns row `1`. When the function is done, the script output (before the error) looks like this:

```
<blockquote>Jeff
<blockquote>Bill
<blockquote>Don
<blockquote>Jay
```

The `display_kids()` function works in pretty much the same way: It calls itself for as long as necessary. But in the final script you have to take a lot more into consideration. For example, the description field of immediate children is printed out, but farther down the ancestral path you show only subject and name. Before you get caught up in the larger script, look at how to change layout based on ancestry in your simplified script.

```
function RecurForMe($topic_id, $level = 1)
{
   $query = "SELECT * from topics  WHERE topic_id = $topic_id";
   $result = mysql_query($query);
   $row = mysql_fetch_array($result);
   echo "<blockquote>";
   echo $row["name"], "\n";
   if($level == 1) {echo $row["subject"];}
   RecurForMe($row["parent_id"], $level + 1);
}
```

We've added another variable (`$level`) to this function to keep track of the level. The default value is 1, and it is incremented each time through. The first time through the subject is printed, but in subsequent iterations it is not.

Recursion can be an expensive process: It takes up quite a bit of processor time if it goes too far. To prevent a system from being overwhelmed, you might want to limit the depth of any topic.

Armed with this information, you should be able to get through the `display_kids()` function. A lot of info is in there to ensure good layout, but other than that it's all pretty readable. Some comments help you get through.

In the code that follows, note the line

```
$topic_id = (int)$topic_id;
```

This is an example of casting to an `int` value. Casting to an `int` is an easy way of adding safety to your application — you're always sure you'll get an `int` to work with.

```
function display_kids ($topic_id=0, $level=0)
{
    $topic_id = (int)$topic_id;
    $level = (int)$level;

    // make sure that we aren't caught in some terrible loop
    if ($level > 50)
    {
        $private_error = "trying to display topic $topic_id, level
is $level - bailing";
        user_error("Error: Recursion too deep", E_USER_ERROR);
        exit;
    }

    // retrieve topic records from the MySQL database having
    // this topic_id value in their parent_id column (i.e. those
    // for whom this topic is the parent_topic

    $query =
    "select topic_id, name, author
           , date_format(create_dt,'%b %e %Y %r') as create_dt
```

```
            , description
            , author_addr_id
        from topics
        where parent_id = $topic_id
        order by create_dt, topic_id"
    ;

    $result = my_query($query);
    $output = '';
    while ($r = mysql_fetch_assoc($result))
    {
        extract($r, EXTR_PREFIX_ALL, 'r');

        if (empty($r_author))
        {
            $r_author = '[no name]';
        }

        if ($r_topic_id != $topic_id)
        {
            $tag = anchor_tag(
                'index.php?topic_id='.$r_topic_id
                , $r_name
            );
        }
        else
        {
            // this should never happen, but just in case -
            // don't print a link back to this topic
            $tag = $r_name;
        }

        $tag .= " by <b>$r_author</b> (ID#$r_author_addr_id) on
<b>$r_create_dt</b>";

        if ($level)
        {
            // non-zero level - use unordered list format
            $output .= li_tag($tag);
        }
        else
        {
            // zero (first) level - print inside a table
            $output .= table(array(
                'width' => '75%'
```

```
                    , 'rows'=>array(
                        table_row(table_cell(array(
                            'bgcolor'=>'skyblue'
                            , 'colspan'=>2
                            , 'value'=>$tag
                        )))
                        , table_row(
                            table_cell(array(
                                'width'=>'5'
                                , 'value'=>'  '
                            ))
                            , $r_description
                        )
                    )
                ));
            }
            // display any child topics of this child, at the next
            // higher level
            $output .= display_kids($r_topic_id, $level+1);
        }
        mysql_free_result($result);

        if ($output)
        {
            if ($level)
            {
                // if not the first level and at least one child
                // was found,
                // display it as an unordered list
                $output = ul_list(array('contents'=>$output));
            }
            else
            {
                // this is the first child record:
                // - print out a header
                $output = "<b>Comments:</b><br>\n$output";
            }
        }
        return $output;
}
```

display_topic()

This function displays information about a given topic. If no `topic_id` is indicated, a list of the root-level topics is displayed.

```
function display_topic ($topic_id=0, $show_kids=1, $level=0)
{
    $topic_id = (int)$topic_id;
    $show_kids = (int)$show_kids;
    $level = (int)$level;
```

The following portion executes if no `topic_id` is indicated. It displays the root-level topics.

```
    if (!$topic_id)
    {
        // no topic_id given - get all root topics
        $query = 'select topic_id, name from topics where topic_id =
root_id';
        $result = my_query($query);
```

The query in the preceding snippet gets all the root-level topics. The `while...` loop directly following prints each topic as an HTML anchor, something like `<a href="index.php?topic_id=1">Topic name</a>`. When it's finished, it returns from the function.

```
        while (list($r_topic_id,$r_name) = mysql_fetch_row($result))
        {
            // print the name of each topic as
            // a link to this script, passing in
            // the topic_id
            print paragraph(anchor_tag(
                'index.php?topic_id='.$r_topic_id
                , $r_name
            ));
        }
        mysql_free_result($result);
        return;
    }
```

If a `topic_id` is available, the following query gets the parent and root of the indicated `topic_id`. An outer join ensures that the information regarding the current topic is returned by the query, even if the parent or root topic has gone missing.

```
    $query = "select distinct current.parent_id
            , current.root_id
            , current.name
            , current.description
```

```
                , current.author
                , date_format(current.create_dt,'%b %e %Y %r') as
create_dt
                , date_format(current.modify_dt,'%b %e %Y %r') as
modify_dt
                , current.author_addr_id
                , parent.name as parent_name
                , root.name as root_name
            from topics current
                left join topics as parent
                    on current.parent_id = parent.topic_id
                left join topics as root
                    on current.root_id = root.topic_id
            where current.topic_id = $topic_id "
        ;
        $result = my_query($query);
        $r = mysql_fetch_assoc($result);
        mysql_free_result($result);
        if ($r === FALSE)
        {
            print paragraph('<b>Error:</b> No such topic.');
            return;
        }
        extract($r);

        if (empty($author)) { $author = '[no name]'; }

        if ($root_id != $topic_id && $root_id != $parent_id)
        {
            // if the root topic is something other than the current
            // topic or its immediate parent, print out its name
            // as a link to it
            if ($root_name == '') { $root_name = '[no topic name]'; }
            print paragraph(
                '<b>root:</b>'
                , anchor_tag('index.php?topic_id='.$root_id
                    , $root_name
                )
            );
        }
```

If a parent topic exists, the name of the topic is printed, along with a link to it.

```
        if (!empty($parent_name))
        {
```

```
        // if an immediate parent was found, print out its name
        // as a link to it
        print paragraph(
            '<b>parent:</b>'
            , anchor_tag('index.php?topic_id='.$parent_id
                , $parent_name
            )
        );
    }

    // print out the current topic
    print paragraph(
        "<b>$name</b> by <b>$author</b> (ID#$author_addr_id) on
<b>$create_dt</b>"
    );
    print paragraph($description);

    if ($show_kids)
    {
        // print out a link to where the user to reply to
        // the current topic
        print paragraph(
            anchor_tag('write_topic.php?topic_id='.$topic_id
                , '<b>Reply to this</b>'
            )
        );

        // now display any children of the current topic
        print paragraph(display_kids($topic_id, $level));
    }

    // return information retrieved about the current topic
    return array('root_id'=>$root_id, 'parent_id'=>$parent_id,
'name'=>$name);

}
```

create_topic()

This function inserts the data taken from a form into the database. As we mentioned earlier, we are taking the IP address from the `$_SERVER['REMOTE_ADDR']` variable and using it to generate a unique ID number, which is also inserted into the database.

Many of the fields (such as `$root_id`) are coming from hidden form fields. And `root_id` is set to `0` if the user is attempting to create a new top-level topic. In those cases the `parent_id` needs to be set to the same value as the `topic_id`.

```
function create_topic()
{
    static $_defaults = array(
        'name' => '[no name]'
        , 'description' => '[no comments]'
        , 'parent_id' => 0
        , 'root_id' => 0
        , 'author' => '[no author]'
    );
    static $_simple = array();
    $args = func_get_args();
    $p = parse_arguments($args, $_simple, $_defaults);

    // run the topic name, description, and author through the
    // cleanup_text() function (defined in /book/functions/base.php)
    // to remove HTML tags and other special characters.

    $name = cleanup_text($p['name']);
    $description = cleanup_text($p['description']);
    $author = cleanup_text($p['author']);

    // we want to know that the same person is having a conversation
    // with himself, but these days storing real IP addresses is a
    // bit hinky. this serves our purpose just as well.
    $author_addr =
array_key_value($_SERVER,'REMOTE_ADDR','unknown');
    $author_addr = crypt($author_addr,$author_addr);
    $result = my_query("select author_addr_id from author_addrs
        where author_addr = '$author_addr'"
    );
    if (mysql_num_rows($result))
    {
        list($author_addr_id) = mysql_fetch_row($result);
    }
    else
    {
        my_query(
            "insert into author_addrs (author_addr) values
('$author_addr')"
        );
        $author_addr_id = mysql_insert_id();
    }
    mysql_free_result($result);
```

```
    // insert the new record into the topics table
    $query = sprintf(
        "insert into topics
            (name,description, parent_id, root_id, author,
author_addr_id)
            values ('%s','%s',%d,%d,'%s','%s')
        "
        , mysql_real_escape_string($name)
        , mysql_real_escape_string($description)
        , $p['parent_id']
        , $p['root_id']
        , mysql_real_escape_string($author)
        , $author_addr_id
    );

    // begin transaction
    my_query('begin');

    my_query($query);

    $topic_id = mysql_insert_id();
    if ($p['root_id'] == 0)
    {
        // if the root_id is zero, that means that this
        // topic is itself a root topic.  set the root_id
        // column of its database record to that ID value
        // (a root topic is its own root)
        my_query(
            'update topics set root_id = topic_id where root_id = 0'
        );
    }

    // end transaction
    my_query('commit');

    return $topic_id;
}
```

This function simply inserts the data into the database. All the information is coming from an HTML form.

In going through these functions, you might notice that you never check to see if the result of a query is false. You can get away with this because you aren't getting away with it, really; you're just checking in the reusable `my_query()` function.

```
    if ($result === FALSE)
    {
        // if there was an error executing the query, write out the
        // details to the error log
        $private_error = 'ack! query failed: '
            .'<li>errorno='.mysql_errno()
            .'<li>error='.mysql_error()
            .'<li>query='.$query
        ;

        // just in case we were in a transaction
        @mysql_query('rollback');

        // send a generic error message to the user

        user_error('There was an error executing a query. Please
contact the system administrator.', E_USER_ERROR);
    }
```

You use the `$private_error` variable, which your error-handling function checks for, to store the query that failed and the error message. Then the error-causing query can be written out to the server error log, or right to the screen if you're debugging the application. Meanwhile, the user gets a less revealing (and less frightening) error message.

Error-handling and debugging functions

Unlikely as it seems, sometimes you make mistakes in your code. Or the database server won't be running because someone forgot to restart it. Errors happen. When they do, it's useful to have a uniform way of responding to them. PHP enables you to set up a function that gets all the errors in your application (those that come from PHP itself – most of them, at least) and errors you raise in your own code when something doesn't seem right. In this section we cover a set of functions that we use throughout the rest of the book to handle errors. The same functions also prepare your code for debugging in a number of ways, without interfering with its normal use.

PHP has its own error-handling functions. And obviously, doing work that someone else is perfectly willing to do for you is not the simplest path you can take. However, setting up your own error handler is worthwhile for a couple of reasons.

- One, it enables you to exercise a little more control over the user's experience. When something breaks, if you choose, the user sees only a calm report that there seems to be a little problem, while MySQL still writes the scary original error message out to a log file where you can use it to fix whatever's wrong.

- Two, it can make debugging an application a lot easier, especially with some of the functions that now exist in PHP.

For sure, what you see in the following pages is no `Hello_World()` function. A lot is going on in here. And debugging errors when devising your error-handling code is almost more fun than a person should be allowed to have. But once you have it set up, you should find that getting on with the rest of your work is easier because it's there.

error_debugging() and error_logging()

The PHP function `error_reporting()` enables you to modify the level of errors displayed by the default error handler. Here you use one of the oldest tricks in programming – stealing – to set up the same kind of levels for the types of errors (or other things) that you want to write out to the server's error log, or as debugging information:

```
function error_debugging($newlevel=NULL)
{
    static $debug_error_level = 0;
    $output = $debug_error_level;
    if ($newlevel !== NULL)
    {
        $debug_error_level = $newlevel;
    }
    return $output;
}
function error_logging($newlevel=NULL)
{
    static $log_error_level = E_ALL;
    $output = $log_error_level;
    if ($newlevel !== NULL)
    {
        $log_error_level = $newlevel;
    }
    return $output;
}
```

Each function works just like `error_reporting()` – you can change the level by passing in a new value, or just get the current value by calling the function with no arguments. Also, when a new value is set, the previous value is returned.

set_handler()

Now that you have three functions that track how you want to respond to various types of errors – the built-in `error_reporting()` function, and our own `error_debugging()` and `error_logging()` functions – managing all of them could get unwieldy. So you create an interface to them that makes setting up just the conditions you want more straightforward.

```
// create constants to represent normal error reporting,
// error logging, and debugging
define('H_ERROR',1);
define('H_LOG',2);
define('H_DEBUG',4);
define('H_ALL', (H_ERROR | H_LOG | H_DEBUG));

function set_handler($newvalue=NULL, $where=NULL, $direction=NULL)
{
    // store the names of the handling functions

   static $functions = array(
        H_ERROR => 'error_reporting'
        , H_LOG => 'error_logging'
        , H_DEBUG => 'error_debugging'
    );

    // this will hold the last error level that we turned on,
    // so we can easily turn it off (see below)
    static $last_args = array();

    if ($direction === FALSE && $newvalue === NULL && $where ===
NULL)
    {
        // if we just get an argument to turn something off, but
        // not what or where, use the last error level that we
        // turned on
        list($where,$newvalue) = array_pop($last_args);
    }

    if (empty($where))
    {
        // if we don't get a request for a specific kind of
        // handler, pick a default one

        if (error_levels($newvalue))
        {
            // if the error level we're dealing with
            // is one of the standard PHP values, assume that
            // we want to change error handling
```

```
            $where = H_ERROR | H_LOG;
        }
        else
        {
            // if we're dealing with some made-up error level,
            // it's probably for debugging, so use that as
            // the default

            $where = H_DEBUG;
        }
    }


    if ($direction !== FALSE)
    {
        // if we're turning on handling for something, store
        // it for turning off later

        array_push($last_args, array($where,$newvalue));
    }

    $output = 0;
    foreach ($functions as $handler => $handler_function_name)
    {
        if ($where & $handler)
        {
            // if this type of handler is one of the ones we want
            // to change, get its current value

            $handler_level = call_user_func($handler_function_name);

            // either set handling directly to new level,
            // or turn it on or off
            if ($direction === FALSE)
            {
                $handler_level = $handler_level ^ $newvalue;
            }
            elseif ($direction === TRUE)
            {
                $handler_level = $handler_level | $newvalue;
            }
            else
            {
                $handler_level = $newvalue;
```

```
            }

            // add the new level to our result
            $output = $output | $handler_level;

            // call the handler function to set it to the new level
            call_user_func($handler_function_name,$handler_level);
        }
    }

    // return an OR'd sum of the changed handling values
    return $output;

}
```

In this code you set up three constants corresponding to your three ways of responding to an error: H_ERROR for catching errors and displaying them on the screen, set with error_reporting(); H_LOG for writing errors to the server error-log file, set with error_logging(); and H_DEBUG for taking extra steps to debug an error, set with error_debugging(). You use these constants in your code much as you would use the PHP error-level constants (E_ERROR, E_USER_NOTICE, and the like). You also define an H_ALL constant to indicate that you want to affect all of them, just as E_ALL means "all error levels."

The set_handler() function gets called, normally, with three arguments: one to specify whether you want to turn handling of a given error on (TRUE) or off (FALSE); one to specify what error level or other kind of value, such as a debugging constant, you are interested in; and one to specify which of the handlers you want to affect: H_ERROR, H_DEBUG, H_LOG, H_ALL for all of them, or a bitmask combining any two of them, such as (H_ERROR|H_LOG) to affect error reporting and logging.

If you are turning handling on for a given error level, you store the error handler specifications in a static array that functions like a stack. That enables you to call set_handler() without any argument beyond OFF; in that case, you just turn off the last thing that you turned on.

The other interesting thing in this function is the use of the PHP call_user_func() function. For all three handler functions, you make exactly the same kind of calls – once with no arguments at all, to get the current state, and once passing in a new state. Since the steps are the same, you don't need to hard-code them in three separate times. Note that in call_user_func(), the arguments after the function name are passed to the called function just as they are. So this code

```
call_user_func('my_function',3,'hello',$some_variable);
```

is effectively the same as this code:

```
my_function(3,'hello',$some_variable);
```

push_handler() and pop_handler()

These functions use the stack features of set_handler() to make changing error-handling levels even simpler.

```
function push_handler($newvalue=0, $where=NULL)
{
    return set_handler($newvalue,$where,TRUE);
}
function pop_handler($newvalue=NULL, $where=NULL)
{
    return set_handler($newvalue,$where,FALSE);
}
```

The push_handler() and pop_handler() functions don't do much; they're just saving you the trouble of writing the first argument to set_handler(). But in your application code they're much simpler to follow. If you want to turn on logging of user notices – the PHP E_USER_NOTICE error level – you can write this:

```
push_error_handler(E_USER_NOTICE, H_LOG);
```

And to turn it off again:

```
pop_error_handler(E_USER_NOTICE, H_LOG);
```

Or just this:

```
pop_error_handler();
```

It's not quite English, but it's relatively clear.

You're making the same kind of decision here that you made when deciding how to pass arguments to your functions. It would be perfectly valid to skip the set_handler(), push_handler(), and pop_handler() functions and just use the handler functions directly:

```
error_reporting(error_reporting() | E_USER_NOTICE);
error_logging(error_logging() | E_USER_NOTICE);
```

The function calls get a little more obscure, though not terribly so. It's up to you to find the balance. Do you put a pretty complicated chunk of code in one place, or slightly complicated code in lots of places? There's no universal answer to that question.

error_handler()

Speaking of pretty complicated chunks of code in one place, now you are ready to look at your actual error-handling function. You use the PHP function set_error_handler() to tell PHP to call your own function whenever an error occurs in your code. That function is then responsible for doing all the work that PHP's normal error handler does by default. It checks the current error-reporting level to see if it's supposed to react to the particular error, it controls what kind of error message the user sees, and so forth.

Not every PHP error will be sent to the error-handling function. Calls to an undefined function, for example, will not. To quote the manual, "The following error types cannot be handled with a user defined function: E_ERROR, E_PARSE, E_CORE_ERROR, E_CORE_WARNING, E_COMPILE_ERROR, and E_COMPILE_WARNING." For more information, check out the manual page: http://www.php.net/manual/en/function.set-error-handler.php.

```
function error_handler($error_level,$error,$file,$line,$context)
{
    // $context is an array of all the variables defined at the
    // time of the error. so we can check it to see if the
    // variables $public_error, $private_error, or $debug were
    // defined.

    if (array_key_exists('public_error', $context))
    {
        $public_error = $context['public_error'];
    }
    else
    {
        $public_error = $error;
    }
    if (array_key_exists('private_error', $context))
    {
        $private_error = $context['private_error'];
    }
    else
    {
        $private_error = '';
    }

    // the value for $debug that we'll use is a combination of the
    // value of the $debug variable in the scope of the line where
```

```
    // the error occurred (if defined), the setting of the debugging
    // level for the file from debug_file() (if there is one), and
    // the value of the constant DEBUG (if defined).

    if (array_key_exists('debug', $context))
    {
        $debug_scope = $context['debug'];
    }
    else
    {
        $debug_scope = 0;
    }
    $debug_file = debug_file($file);
    if (defined('DEBUG'))
    {
        $debug_constant = constant('DEBUG');
    }
    else
    {
        $debug_constant = 0;
    }

    $debug = $debug_scope | $debug_file | $debug_constant;

    // get the current error handling levels
    $error_reporting = error_reporting();
    $error_logging = error_logging();
    $error_debugging = error_debugging();

    // get the name of the constant that matches the error
    // (if there is one)
    $error_name = error_levels($error_level, "_Error
#$error_level");
    $public_name = substr($error_name,strrpos($error_name,'_')+1);

    // write the error to the server error log if it's of a level
    // that we're interested in

    if ($error_logging & $error_level)
    {
        $logerror = "$error_name file: $file line: $line\n"
            ."    error: $error\n"
        ;
```

```
        if ($public_error && $public_error != $error)
        {
            $logerror .= "    public_error: $public_error\n";
        }

        if ($private_error && $private_error != $error
            && $private_error != $public_error
        )
        {
            $logerror .= "    private_error: $private_error\n";
        }

        error_log($logerror);
    }

    // if $debug is set to something that we're debugging at the
    // moment, add some stuff to the error message and make sure
    // it gets displayed, no matter what the error_reporting level
is

    if ($error_debugging & $debug)
    {
        $debug_error = " <li>error: $error\n";
        if ($public_error && $public_error != $error)
        {
            $debug_error .= " <li>public_error: $public_error\n";
        }
        if ($private_error && $private_error != $error
            && $private_error != $public_error
        )
        {
            $debug_error .= " <li>private_error: $private_error\n";
        }

        $debug_error .= "<li>backtrace:<ul>\n";

        $backtrace = debug_backtrace();

        foreach ($backtrace as $skip)
        {
            $class = 'NoClass';
            $function = 'NoFunction';
            $file = 'NoFile';
            $line = 'NoLine';
            extract($skip, EXTR_IF_EXISTS);
```

```
            $debug_error .= sprintf("\t<li>%s::%s [%s:%s]\n"
                , $class
                , $function
                , $file
                , $line
            );
        }
        $debug_error .= "</ul>\n";

        $public_error .= $debug_error;

        // if E_ALL has been explicitly set in the debug mask
        // dump *everything*...
        if (($error_debugging & E_ALL) == E_ALL)
        {
            // OK, not everything. but you can uncomment this
            // if you want.

            // $context = array_merge(
            //     $context, get_defined_constants()
            // );

            $public_error .= "<li>context:".dumpvar($context)."\n";
        }
    }
    elseif (!($error_reporting & $error_level))
    {
        // if the error is not of a level that we're reporting,
        // blank out the error message
        $public_error = '';
    }

    if (!empty($public_error))
    {
        print <<<EOQ
<blockquote>
<b>$public_name:</b>
$public_error
</blockquote>
EOQ;
    }

    if (error_debugging() & get_constant('fatal'))
    {
        exit;
```

```
    }
    switch ($error_level)
    {
        // the non-fatal errors
        case E_NOTICE:
        case E_USER_NOTICE:
        case E_WARNING:
        case E_USER_WARNING:
            return;

        // everything else is fatal
        default:
            exit;
    }
}
```

The first things we should go over are the arguments. Because PHP is calling the function, it defines what the arguments are. The first one, `$error_level`, is the kind of error, and matches the predefined error-level constants. You can find a list of these online at `http://www.php.net/manual/en/ref.errorfunc.php`.

The second argument, `$error`, is the text of the error message. This might be PHP's own error message; if you've raised an error with `user_error()`, it is the text passed in to that function. The next two arguments, `$file` and `$line`, tell you the name of the file and the line number in that file where the error occurred. The final argument, `$context`, is an associative array of all the variables in scope at the time of the error. (Be careful with this – if the error happens outside of a function, in a global scope, then this contains not only your own global variables but all of the PHP superglobals as well. Because some of these variables incorporate others – `$_REQUEST` containing `$_POST`, `$_GET`, and `$_COOKIE`, for example – trying to dump this array out can lead to recursion problems.)

This last argument, `$context`, is something that you can make good use of. It's where you get the local value of `$debug` from, for one thing. It also enables you to see if you've set up a "private" error message. As an example, in the `my_query()` function, you can use this to capture the MySQL error message:

```
$private_error = 'ack! query failed: '
    .'<li>errorno='.mysql_errno()
    .'<li>error='.mysql_error()
    .'<li>query='.$query
;
```

Then the error handler can write it out to the error log or print it out as debugging output, however you've set it up. Meanwhile, a generic message is set up for the user:

```
user_error('There was an error executing a query. Please contact the
system administrator.', E_USER_ERROR);
```

You can also set up a "public error" message, which gets used instead of the default error message. This strategy is one way to cover situations where a normal PHP error might occur.

Next, you check to see if you have turned on debugging. You can do this just by setting a variable named `$debug` to an appropriate value – this approach is good for debugging inside a function. Or you can set debugging at a file level with the `debug_file()` function (see the next section). You can also just define a constant named `DEBUG` that is visible from anywhere in the application.

You check in with your handler functions to see how you want to react to the error. If logging is turned on, a message is written out to the error log. If debugging is turned on, you create a detailed debugging message for display. If error reporting is set to display this level of error, you prepare a message to be shown to the user.

In setting up the debugging message, you can make use of a very nice new feature in PHP, the `debug_backtrace()` function. This function returns an array of all the functions and files that got you from the initial URL to where you are now, including the relevant line numbers. When you get an error from a function that's five or six levels down, this function is a godsend.

Finally, you display a message to the screen (if there is one), and then either return from the function back to the main program, if it was a warning or notice, or exit, if it was a full error.

debug_file()

You saw this function in the error handler. The `debug_file()` function sets up a debugging level for an entire file:

```
function debug_file()

{
    // store the file names for which we set up debugging levels
    static $debug_files = array();

    // some quick & dirty argument handling. we can do this
    // because we're only interested in two possible arguments,
    // $file and $level

    $args = func_get_args();
    $file = NULL;
    $level = NULL;
    foreach ($args as $arg)
    {
        switch (gettype($arg))
```

```
        {
            case 'array':
            case 'object':
                extract((array)$arg,EXTR_IF_EXISTS);
                break;
            case 'string':
                $file = $arg;
                break;
            case NULL:
                break;
            default:
                $level = (int)$arg;
        }
    }

    if (!$file)
    {
        // if no file name is given, use the current
        //file by default.

        // we want to find the path to the file that called
        //this function,
        // so we can't use __FILE__ - that'll just give
        //us the name of
        // the file where this function is defined.
        //use debug_backtrace()
        // instead.
        $backtrace = debug_backtrace();
        $last = array_shift($backtrace);
        $file = $last['file'];

        if ($level === NULL)
        {
            // if we're using a default file name, then if no level
            // is passed in, set up a default level as well
            $level = get_constant($file);
        }
    }
    else
    {
        $rfile = realpath($file);
        if ($rfile)
        {
            $file = $rfile;
        }
```

```
    }
    }

    if ($level !== NULL)
    {
        // if we're given a level for a file (or have set one
        // as a default case), make a record of it
        $debug_files[$file] = $level;
    }

    // in any case, return the current level for this file,
    // if there is one, or FALSE if there isn't

    if (array_key_exists($file, $debug_files))
    {
        return $debug_files[$file];
    }
    // so now do more tedious file name matching
    $pat = '/'.str_replace('/','.',$file).'/i';
    return current(preg_grep($pat, array_keys($debug_files)));
}
```

Most of the time, if you want to debug a section of your code, you just set `$debug` to a value that you've set up the debug handler to watch. Sometimes, though, you might want to turn on debugging for all the code in a particular file. This can easily be the case with a simple Web page or an included file, where assigning `$debug` a value sets it at a global scope, and possibly triggers a lot of debugging code you don't want to see. That's a problem that `debug_file()` solves. It stores an error level or some other value and associates with a single file. When you get an error, or your code calls `user_error()`, the error-handling routine uses `debug_file()` to see if you've set anything up for the file in which the error occurred.

get_constant()

When you want to define a constant to use in a bitmask, the way you use `E_WARNING` with `error_reporting()`, it doesn't particularly matter what the actual value of the constant is, so long as it doesn't collide with any other constant you're using for the same purpose. That's what `get_constant()` manages for you:

```
function get_constant($constname='')
{
    // start at one above E_USER_NOTICE to avoid conflicts
    // (we can't initialize a static variable to an expression,
```

```
    // so we have to start it off as NULL and then fix that.)

    static $last_constant = NULL;
    if ($last_constant === NULL)
    {
        $last_constant = E_USER_NOTICE << 1;
    }
    static $defined_constants = array();
    static $defined_or = 0;

    $output = 0;
    if (!empty($constname))
    {
        if (!defined($constname))
        {
            define($constname,$last_constant);
            $defined_constants[$constname] = $last_constant;
            $defined_or = $defined_or | $last_constant;
            $last_constant = $last_constant << 1;
        }
        $output = constant($constname);
    }
    else
    {
        // if no constant name is given, hand back the equivalent
        // of E_ALL for the constants defined so far
        $output = $defined_or;
    }
    return $output;
}
```

The other purpose of this function is to enable you to get the value of a constant that you've defined elsewhere – or that you will define, which sounds like some kind of time-travel feature only because that definition isn't really accurate. It works like this: Suppose that in a function named `foo()`, you make a call to `get_constant()`:

```
function foo()
{
    get_constant('MY_CONSTANT');
    print "<h4>my constant is ".MY_CONSTANT."</h4>\n";
}
```

In the normal course of our application, this might be the fifth call made to get_constant(), so MY_CONSTANT would end up being defined as 32768. But suppose you want to watch for MY_CONSTANT somewhere else, such as in a debugging function. You can put the same call to get_constant() in the header file of your application:

```
$global_variable = get_constant('MY_CONSTANT');
```

This is the first call to get_constant() that is executed, so MY_CONSTANT will be defined as 2048. The point is, it doesn't matter. It's the same value that will be returned inside the foo() function when it makes its get_constant() call. As long as MY_CONSTANT represents the same value everywhere in the application, that's what counts.

Summary

If you would like to see how the rest of the code comes together, take a look at the accompanying CD. The other files are well commented and should be relatively easy to follow.

You should come away from this chapter with an understanding of two concepts:

- First, recursion. Recursion is a nifty tool that can be very helpful at times.
- Second, the way we went about organizing the data. We didn't follow a strict normalization procedure, like the one described in Chapter 1. Here we were more concerned with what gets the job done. In the end that's what all application developers are trying to do, right?

Finally, we covered how to set up your own error handler, and some of the uses to which you might put it. As with the HTML functions, you might decide that you want to use a different approach. If so, feel free to ignore our example.

Chapter 11

Content-Management System

IN THIS CHAPTER

- Creating an affordable content-management system
- Maintaining security in your databases
- Anticipating shortcomings in MySQL's privilege scheme

WELCOME TO OUR FAVORITE APPLICATION in this book. Don't get us wrong, we love the guestbook, we love the shopping cart, and we adore the problem tracker. But, as we spent our formative years dealing with Web sites that produced a steady stream of prose, we know the importance of having some sort of content-management system in place.

Content-management systems come in all shapes, sizes, and costs. Depending on your needs (or your company's), you might be inclined to make a five-figure investment in something like Vignette or a six- to seven-figure investment in something like Broadvision. But your choices don't end there. Zope (`http://www.zope.org`), Midgard (`http://www.midgard-project.org/`), and FileNet, formerly eGrail, (`http://www.filenet.com/`) are just three open-source options for content management.

Given all of these options, you might wonder why you should consider using the application presented here – why not just run off one of the aforementioned applications? There is, in fact, an excellent reason. Content management is a field in which a high degree of customization is necessary. Your company's concerns are going to be distinct from any other's, and no matter what system you end up using, you are going to need to do a lot of coding to get your systems working just the way you want. For example, if you decide on Vignette, you'll need to learn a nasty little language called Tcl (pronounced "tickle") or write in Java. If you want to use Zope, you will have to add Python to your repertoire. Midgard is a PHP-based application, and there's no question that there's a lot of good code in there. It's open-source, and presents a nice opportunity to contribute to the development of an increasingly sophisticated piece of software. But you may just want something you can call your own, an application that you know inside out, something built to solve the problems specific to your organization. So take a look at what's available, and see if your challenges, budget, and temperament make one of the ready-made systems a good fit. If not, you can look at the framework and code presented in this chapter and adapt them to your needs, or maybe just recode from scratch.

Determining the Scope and Goals of the Application

For the sake of presenting this content-management application, we've created a fairly basic site (which is in the /book/netsloth directory on the CD-ROM). But given the nature of Web content, whatever site you create is going to require all the design and editorial resources you can muster, and we're not going to worry about that too much here.

Our content-management system is going to need to do several things. Its most obvious purpose is to offer an environment where writers, editors, and administrators can create new stories. Additionally, it must offer a flexible series of stages through which a story moves. For example, if originally implemented with a single editorial stage, the application must be flexible enough to accommodate an additional editorial stage (or several of them) if needed.

Additionally, this application must meet the various demands of a staff. There will be a series of writers, and some byline information will be presented with each story. Further, staff members will be assigned specific functions in the editorial process. Various levels of permission will ensure that not everyone will have the authority to edit or proofread a particular story, or to make that story available to the world at large.

Finally, a sort of super-user authority must exist. A few select people will have the authority to add users and authorities to the editorial staff.

Necessary pages

First off, we need a site, a place where the articles will be displayed. As the site isn't really the focus of this application, we deal with it very briefly. You will obviously need to code a site that fits your needs. Figures 11-1 and 11-2 show the Netsloth site in all its glory.

This application manages content and the creators of the content. We will need a series of editorial stages and a series of users. Users will have access only to the stages that involve them. Figure 11-3 shows a page that lists sample stages and users. Figures 11-4 and 11-5 show pages that administer these rights and stages, respectively.

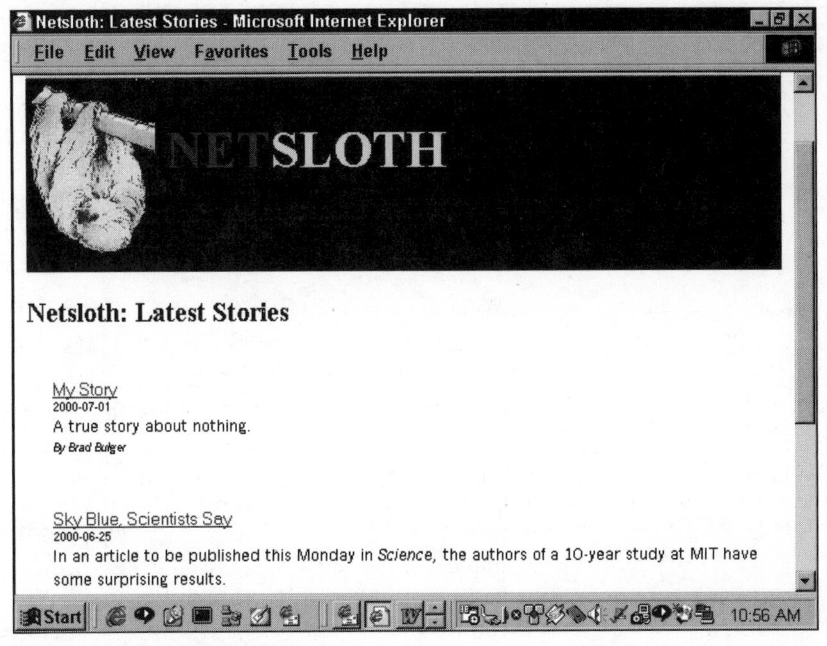

Figure 11-1: Netsloth index page

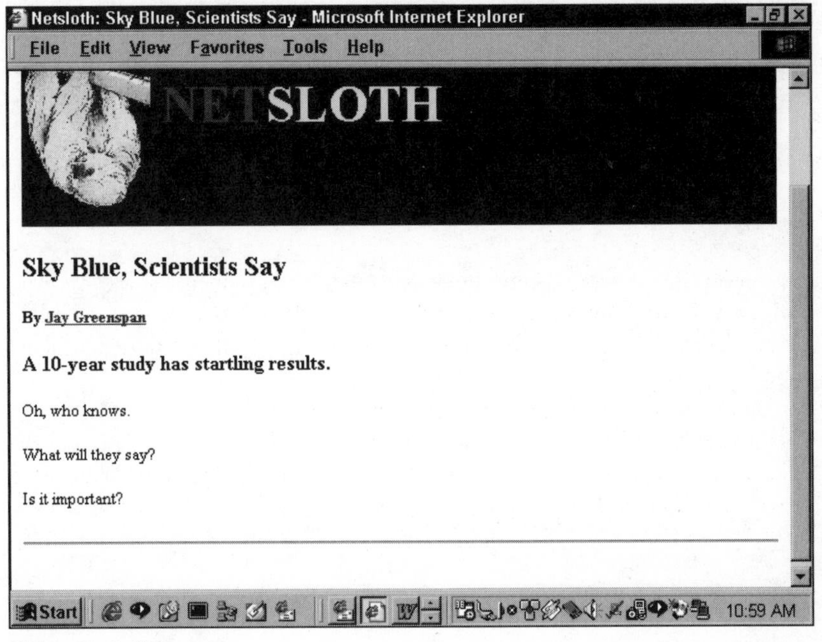

Figure 11-2: Story page

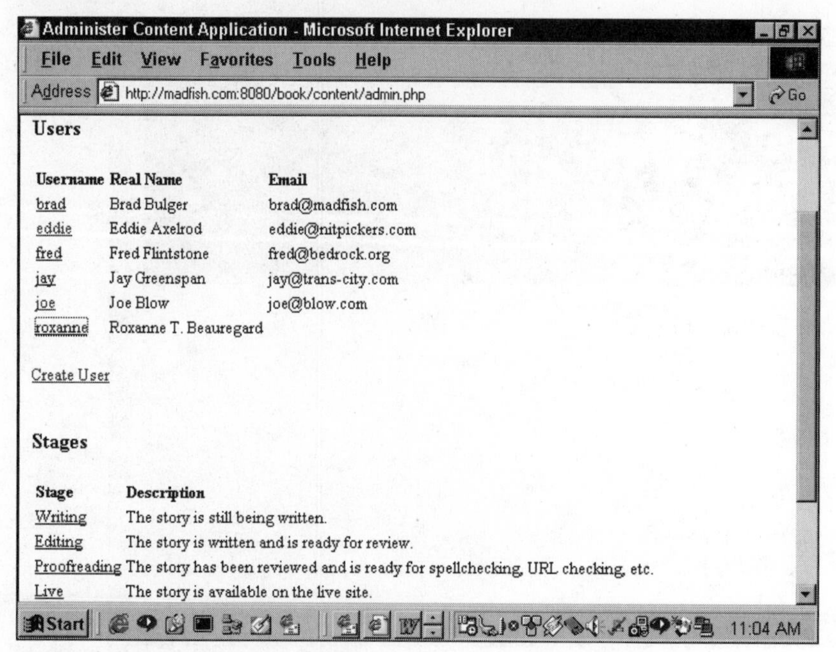

Figure 11-3: Rights and stages page

Administer Content : Users - Microsoft Internet Explorer

File Edit View Favorites Tools Help

Address http://madfish.com:8080/book/content/admin_user.php?user_id=4

Go

Administer Content : Users

User Info

Username: jay

Password:

Real Name: Jay Greenspan

Email: jay@trans-city.com

Stage Access

	Stage	Description
☑	Writing	The story is still being written.
☑	Editing	The story is written and is ready for review.
☐	Proofreading	The story has been reviewed and is ready for spellchecking, URL checking, etc.
☑	Live	The story is available on the live site.

Start

11:05 AM

Figure 11-4: Rights-administration page

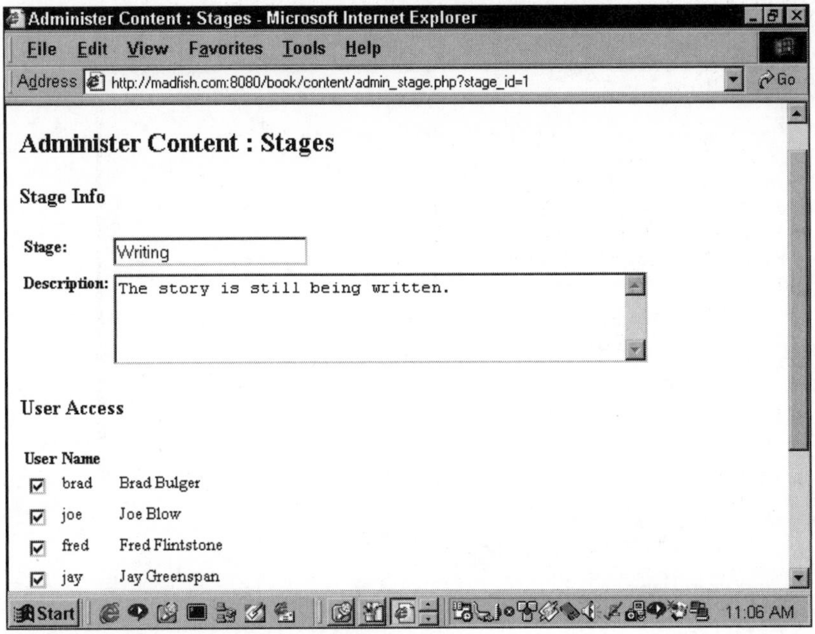

Figure 11-5: Stages administration page

This application also needs a workspace, a page where writers and editors can create stories, and where stories can work their way through the editorial process. The workspace will contain a few fields that identify the author, the date, the body of text, and other necessary information. Additionally, the stage of the editorial process that the story is in is indicated. This page is shown in Figure 11-6.

Another important aspect of an editorial environment is versioning. It's very important to be able to track pieces as they work through the process. We'll want to know who is making changes. Figure 11-7 shows the page that tracks versions, or the story-history page.

This application performs a few more tasks, but they are minor enough to overlook here. Here we have touched on the major functions of the application.

What do we need to prevent?

The major issue in this application is ensuring that users do only what they are permitted to do, and absolutely no more. To do this, the application makes use of MySQL administrative privileges.

All the previous applications have a simple header file that calls a function with which to log in to the database. Each file ends up using the same `my_connect()` call, with the same username and password. But that won't work here because different users need different levels of access.

Netsloth: Edit Story 2 - Microsoft Internet Explorer

File Edit View Favorites Tools Help

Netsloth: Edit Story 2

Headline A Big Test

Publish Date 2000 6 24

Subtitle This is the test you've been waiting for.

Summary Who knew? Testing is important.

Body
<p>
I think this is the first paragraph.
</p>
<p>
Well, no, maybe this one is.
</p>
<p>
No, the other one. Definitely.
</p>

Submit Body File Browse...

Start 11:08 AM

Figure 11-6: Editorial workplace

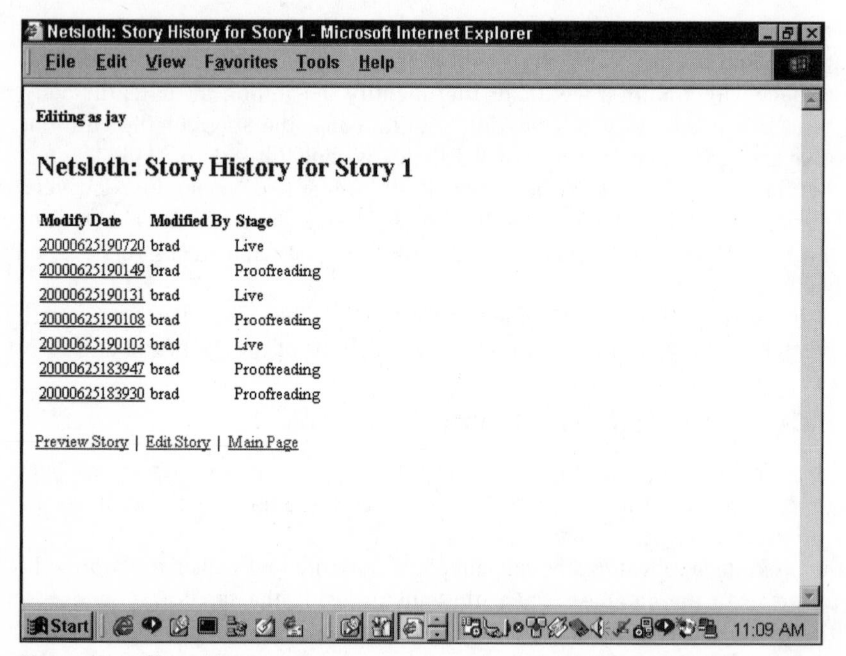

Figure 11-7: Story-history page

Moreover, in this application some users are going to need the ability to grant access to others. Workers will come and go and their responsibilities will change. An administrator will need to be able to change these rights. Since we don't want everybody who logs in to the database to have the same rights, this application will need the facility to have different people log in using different names and passwords.

Privileges in MySQL are granted and revoked with the aptly named `grant` and `revoke` statements. These processes are fairly painless and are described in Appendix E. So before you move forward with this application, it might be worth taking a quick look at that appendix.

In the content-management application you will run into some of the weirder aspects of MySQL. If some of the design of this application seems a little strange, that's because it is. But we'll cross that bridge as we develop our application.

Designing the Database

The schema represented in Figure 11-8 shows how this application divides its data, and Listing 11-1 reveals the MySQL command sequence used to set it up. Keep in mind as you look at it that in database-development land there is usually more than one decent way to go about things. You might find a different way to arrange these types of data that works equally well. In fact, you may even prefer another way. That's fine with us. We encourage independent thought and creativity, as long as it does not result in immoral or ungodly behavior. So normalize your data as you see fit, but in the process please don't violate any natural laws. On the other hand, data normalization makes it easier to grow your databases and adapt them to new purposes. Bear that in mind, too.

Listing 11-1: create Statements for the Content-Management System

```
drop database if exists netsloth;
create database netsloth;
use netsloth;

drop table if exists admin;
create table admin
(
    username    varchar(50) not null
    , password    varchar(255) not null
, primary key (username)
)
type=InnoDB
```

Continued

Listing 11-1 *(Continued)*

```
;

drop table if exists author_seq;
create table author_seq
(
  id int not null auto_increment
, primary key (id)
)
type=InnoDB
;
drop table if exists authors;
create table authors
(
    author_id    integer not null auto_increment
    , author    varchar(50) null
    , email        varchar(255) null
    , bio         text null
    , user_id     int null
, primary key (author_id)
, key (user_id)
, foreign key (user_id) references users (user_id) on delete cascade
)
type=InnoDB
;
-- read-write tables
grant select,update,insert,delete on stories to fake@localhost;
grant select,update,insert,delete on story_seq to fake@localhost;
grant select,update,insert,delete on story_versions to
fake@localhost;
grant select,update,insert,delete on authors to fake@localhost;
grant select,update,insert,delete on author_seq to fake@localhost;
grant select,update,insert,delete on story_author_map to
fake@localhost;

-- read-only tables
grant select on admin to fake@localhost;
grant select on users to fake@localhost;
grant select on stages to fake@localhost;
grant select on user_stage_map to fake@localhost;

-- build local copy
drop table if exists content_tables;
create table content_tables as
    select Table_name, Table_priv
    from mysql.tables_priv
    where Host = 'localhost' and Db = 'netsloth' and User = 'fake'
;
```

```
alter table content_tables add unique (Table_name);

-- delete the slug
delete from mysql.user
    where Host = 'localhost' and User = 'fake'
;
delete from mysql.tables_priv
    where Host = 'localhost' and Db = 'netsloth' and User = 'fake'
;
```

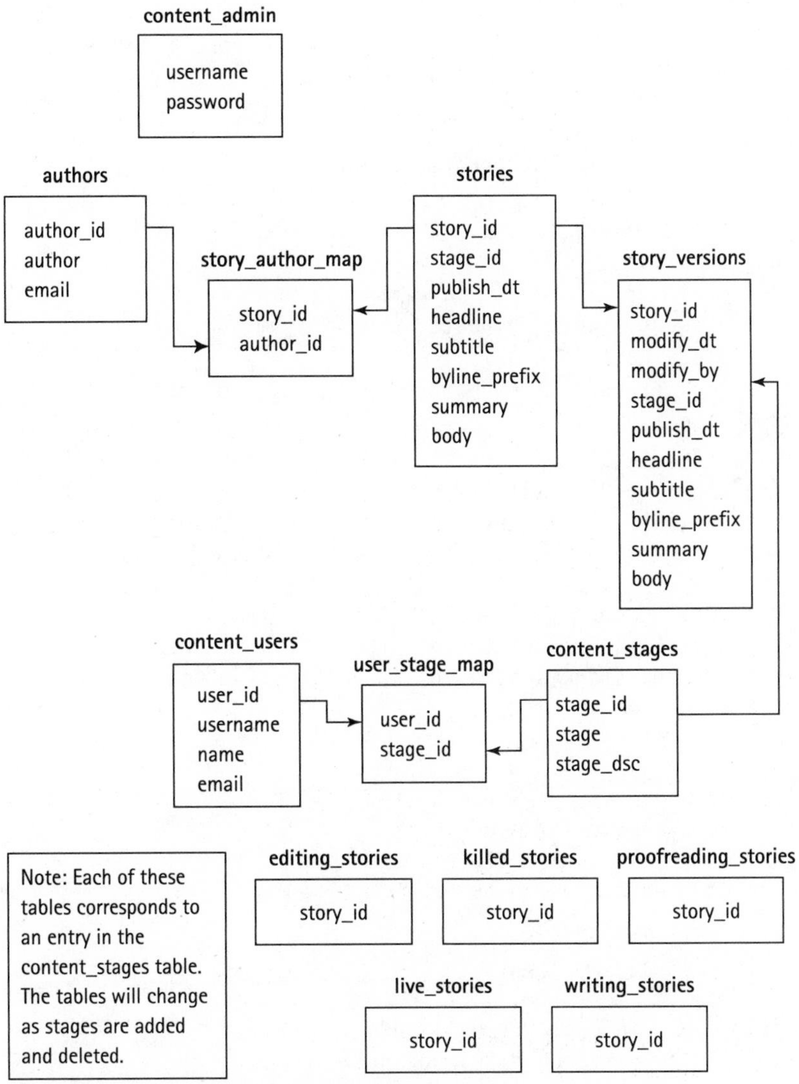

content_admin
username
password

authors
author_id
author
email

story_author_map
story_id
author_id

stories
story_id
stage_id
publish_dt
headline
subtitle
byline_prefix
summary
body

story_versions
story_id
modify_dt
modify_by
stage_id
publish_dt
headline
subtitle
byline_prefix
summary
body

content_users
user_id
username
name
email

user_stage_map
user_id
stage_id

content_stages
stage_id
stage
stage_dsc

Note: Each of these tables corresponds to an entry in the content_stages table. The tables will change as stages are added and deleted.

editing_stories
story_id

killed_stories
story_id

proofreading_stories
story_id

live_stories
story_id

writing_stories
story_id

Figure 11-8: Content management schema

(In these lines, up to 'flush privileges', we are setting up basic permissions for the database, where 'nobody' is the account used by the NetSloth site itself, and 'content_admin' is an example of an account for an administrator of the content management application itself.)

```
delete from mysql.user where user = 'content_admin';
delete from mysql.db where Db = 'netsloth';
delete from mysql.tables_priv where Db = 'netsloth';
grant select on netsloth.*
    to nobody@localhost
    identified by 'ydobon'
;
grant reload on *.*
    to content_admin@localhost identified by 'supersecret'
;
grant delete, insert, select, update, create
    on netsloth.*
    to content_admin@localhost
    with grant option
;
grant delete, insert, select, update, create on mysql.user to
content_admin@localhost ;
grant delete, insert, select, update, create on mysql.db to
content_admin@localhost ;
grant delete, insert, select, update, create on mysql.columns_priv
to content_admin@localhost ;
grant delete, insert, select, update, create on mysql.tables_priv to
content_admin@localhost ;

flush privileges;

drop table if exists stage_seq;
create table stage_seq
(
  id int not null auto_increment
, primary key (id)
)
type=InnoDB
;
drop table if exists stages;
create table stages
(
    stage_id          integer not null auto_increment
    , stage              varchar(20) not null
    , stage_dsc          text null
```

```
    , stage_table    varchar(32) not null
, primary key (stage_id)
)
type=InnoDB
;

drop table if exists stories;
create table stories
(
    story_id    integer not null auto_increment
    , stage_id    integer not null
    , publish_dt    date null
    , headline    varchar(255) null
    , subtitle    varchar(255) null
    , byline_prefix    varchar(20) null
    , summary        text null
    , body        text null
, primary key (story_id)
, index (stage_id)
)
type=InnoDB
;

drop table if exists story_author_map;
create table story_author_map
(
    story_id    integer not null
    , author_id    integer not null
, primary key (story_id)
, index (author_id)
, foreign key (story_id) references stories (story_id) on delete
cascade
, foreign key (author_id) references authors (author_id) on delete
cascade
)
type=InnoDB
;

drop table if exists story_seq;
create table story_seq
(
  id int not null auto_increment
, primary key (id)
)
type=InnoDB
```

```
;

drop table if exists story_versions;
create table story_versions
(
    story_id    integer not null
    , modify_dt    timestamp
    , modify_by    varchar(20) not null
    , stage_id    integer not null
    , publish_dt    date null
    , headline    varchar(255) null
    , subtitle    varchar(255) null
    , byline_prefix    varchar(20) null
    , summary        text null
    , body        text null
, primary key (story_id, modify_dt)
, foreign key (story_id) references stories (story_id) on delete
cascade
)
type=InnoDB
;

drop table if exists user_seq;
create table user_seq
(
  id int not null auto_increment
, primary key (id)
)
type=InnoDB
;
drop table if exists user_stage_map;
create table user_stage_map
(
    user_id        integer not null
        , stage_id    integer not null
, primary key (user_id,stage_id)
, index (stage_id,user_id)
, foreign key (user_id) references users (user_id) on delete cascade
, foreign key (stage_id) references stages (stage_id) on delete
cascade
)
type=InnoDB
;
drop table if exists users;
create table users
```

```
(
    user_id    integer not null auto_increment
    , username    varchar(20) not null
    , password    varchar(16) not null
    , name        varchar(50) not null
    , email        varchar(255) null
, primary key (user_id)
-- , unique (username)
)
type=InnoDB
;
```

Code Overview

At this point, we assume that you are getting comfortable with the way the applications in this book have been constructed. Even with the simple `safe_mysql_query()` function in the guestbook example, you saw the usefulness of having a standard way of working with PHP's native MySQL routines. The built-in routines will let you do what you need to do, no question. But in the course of using them, you may find that you're writing the same kind of code multiple times, a sure signal that some higher-level functions are called for. Also, should you ever want to port your code to a different DBMS for some crazy reason, like because you're being paid to, going through your code and converting those MySQL-specific functions to some other system can be a big pain.

If you've ever done any work with Perl, you may be familiar with the DBI library. It provides a standard interface to multiple database systems. You may have also used Comprehensive Perl Archive Network (CPAN), the big code library where you can find all sorts of previously invented wheels. The same kinds of benefits are available with PHP, thanks to the good people who have built – and are building even now – PEAR.

To quote from the PEAR Manifest (`http://pear.php.net/manual/en/introduction.php`): "PEAR is short for 'PHP Extension and Application Repository' and is pronounced just like the fruit." PEAR has several facets. It's a library of PHP code that solves many common problems encountered by Web developers. It's also a means of packaging and distributing code, to make it simpler to install code from that library, and to encourage people to share their own code. The best place to find out more is at the Web site: `http://pear.php.net`. Here you'll find the code, the main PEAR documentation, mailing lists, and other useful information.

PEAR is very much a moving target, undergoing constant improvement and extension, and it has the rough edges that brings. So by way of introduction, we'll focus on one of the most widely used – and most completely documented – classes, the DB class. It's one of the core PEAR classes that are automatically distributed and installed as part of PHP (at least, as of this writing). Like Perl's DBI class, DB provides a standard interface to multiple database systems. It makes it easy to do the kinds of things you'll want to do to get data out of a database (like building an associative array from the results of a query) and to put data into a database (like handling those pesky quote marks).

As you work through, less and less of the code should require explanation. Thus, our descriptions of the code will deal only with those parts that are really new or tricky.

Here, most of the newer looking code will come from assigning the privileges discussed in the previous section. The application sends queries that you haven't used before.

Code Breakdown

Once again, the code in this application will make heavy use of the functions in the /functions folder. A lot of the code presented here will make calls to those functions. The great thing about functions is that they become part of your library of code that you can re-use for other purposes.

Functions from /dsn

The PEAR DB library takes a connection string that will look somewhat familiar if you've used Perl's DBI class, and that is easy to figure out in any case. It typically looks something like this:

```
phptype://username:password@hostspec/database
```

where *hostspec* might be replaced with the port number and name of the localhost. The routine that accepts connections also accepts an associative array with all the parts spelled out as key/value pairs, so that's what we'll use.

Rather than store usernames and passwords in the code of the example, as we have done up until now, we've moved the connection information for the database to a function in a separate directory, outside the document root of the Apache server. This provides a small amount of extra security – though if you're on a shared server, this information is still vulnerable. But at least moving it out of the Web-server document root means that no one can download the file as a Web page.

In our setup, the /dsn directory is parallel to the /htdocs directory. In there is one file, `db_dsnlist.php`, defining one function, `db_dsnlist()`:

```
function db_dsnlist()
{
    static $_defaults = array(
        'application' => 'default'
    );
    static $_simple = array(
```

```
    'application', 'username', 'password', 'database'
);
$p = func_get_args();
$p = parse_arguments($p, $_simple, $_defaults);

static $dsnlist = array(
    'default' => array(
        'phptype' => 'mysql'
        , 'dbsyntax' => NULL
        , 'username' => 'nobody'
        , 'password' => 'ydobon'
        , 'protocol' => 'tcp'
        , 'hostspec' => 'localhost'
        , 'port' => NULL
        , 'socket' => NULL
        , 'database' => 'test'
    )
    , 'oldcatalog' => array(
        'phptype' => 'mysql'
        , 'dbsyntax' => NULL
        , 'username' => 'nobody'
        , 'password' => 'ydobon'
        , 'protocol' => 'tcp'
        , 'hostspec' => 'localhost'
        , 'port' => NULL
        , 'socket' => NULL
        , 'database' => 'oldcatalog'
    )
    , 'catalog' => array(
        'phptype' => 'mysql'
        , 'dbsyntax' => NULL
        , 'username' => 'nobody'
        , 'password' => 'ydobon'
        , 'protocol' => 'tcp'
        , 'hostspec' => 'localhost'
        , 'port' => NULL
        , 'socket' => NULL
        , 'database' => 'catalog'
    )
    , 'discussion' => array(
        'phptype' => 'mysql'
        , 'dbsyntax' => NULL
        , 'username' => 'nobody'
        , 'password' => 'ydobon'
        , 'protocol' => 'tcp'
```

```
        , 'hostspec' => 'localhost'
        , 'port' => NULL
        , 'socket' => NULL
        , 'database' => 'discussion'
    )
    , 'netsloth' => array(
        'phptype' => 'mysql'
        , 'dbsyntax' => NULL
        , 'username' => 'nobody'
        , 'password' => 'ydobon'
        , 'protocol' => 'tcp'
        , 'hostspec' => 'localhost'
        , 'port' => NULL
        , 'socket' => NULL
        , 'database' => 'netsloth'
    )
    , 'content' => array(
        'phptype' => 'mysql'
        , 'dbsyntax' => NULL
        , 'username' => NULL
        , 'password' => NULL
        , 'protocol' => 'tcp'
        , 'hostspec' => 'localhost'
        , 'port' => NULL
        , 'socket' => NULL
        , 'database' => 'netsloth'
    )
    , 'admin' => array(
        'phptype' => 'mysql'
        , 'dbsyntax' => NULL
        , 'username' => 'admin'
        , 'password' => 'supersecret'
        , 'protocol' => 'tcp'
        , 'hostspec' => 'localhost'
        , 'port' => NULL
        , 'socket' => NULL
        , 'database' => 'netsloth'
    )
    , 'tracking' => array(
        'phptype' => 'mysql'
        , 'dbsyntax' => NULL
        , 'username' => 'nobody'
        , 'password' => 'ydobon'
        , 'protocol' => 'tcp'
        , 'hostspec' => 'localhost'
```

```
            , 'port' => NULL
            , 'socket' => NULL
            , 'database' => 'tracking'
        )
    );
    // remove NULL values to not override entries from dsn
    $p = array_diff($p, array_filter($p,'is_null'));
    if (isset($dsnlist[$p['application']]))
    {
        $dsn = array_merge($dsnlist[$p['application']],$p);
    }
    else
    {
        $dsn = array_merge($dsnlist['default'],$p);
    }
    return $dsn;
}
```

Typically, this function is called with just the application name as a parameter, and will return the entry for that application from the static array of connection parameters. But we can pass in other values as well, which are merged into the returned array.

Functions from /book/functions/database

The functions of the PEAR DB library are powerful enough that in most circumstances you can use them either directly in the code of the Web pages or in functions specific to an example. In a few instances you do the same work in all the examples, though, and these general functions are stored in the /databases directory of the general /functions directory.

db_connect()

The `db_connect()` function is similar to the `mysql_connect()` function we used in previous examples. It creates a persistent connection to the MySQL server, getting connection parameters from the `db_dsnlist()` function described earlier.

```
function db_connect()
{
    static $_connections = array();
    static $_defaults = array(
        'application' => NULL
        , 'database' => NULL
        , 'username' => NULL
        , 'db_error_level' => E_USER_ERROR
        , 'db_error_handler' => 'db_error_handler'
```

```
        , 'options' => array(
            'debug' => 4
            , 'persistent' => TRUE
            , 'autofree' => TRUE
        )
    );
    static $_simple = array('application','username','password');

    $dc = count($_connections);
    $p = func_get_args();
    if (empty($p))
    {
        if ($dc)
        {
            $dbh = array_pop(array_values($_connections));
            if ($dbh === NULL) { user_error('Last connection is
NULL.', E_USER_ERROR); exit; }
            return $dbh;
        }
        user_error('No existing database connection found.',
E_USER_ERROR);
        exit;
    }

    $p = parse_arguments($p, $_simple, $_defaults);

    if (empty($p['application']))
    {
        $p['application'] = $p['database'];
        if (!empty($p['username']))
        {
            $p['application'] .= ':'.$p['username'];
        }
    }

    $dbh = array_key_value($_connections,$p['application'],NULL);
    if ($dbh !== NULL)
    {
        return $dbh;
    }

    $dsn = db_dsnlist($p);
    $dbh = DB::connect($dsn, $p['options']);
    if (DB::isError($dbh))
    {
        $private_error = 'dsn:'.var_export($dsn,TRUE)."\n"
```

```
            .' error:'.var_export($dbh,TRUE)."\n"
        ;
        user_error(
            'Could not connect to database: '.$dbh->getMessage()
            , $p['db_error_level']
        );
        return FALSE;
    }
    if (is_string($p['db_error_handler'])
        && function_exists($p['db_error_handler'])
    )
    {
        // it's a function name - OK
    }
    elseif (is_array($p['db_error_handler'])
        && count($p['db_error_handler']) == 2
        && method_exists($p['db_error_handler'][0],
$p['db_error_handler'][1])
    )
    {
        // it's an object method - OK
    }
    else
    {
        $p['db_error_handler'] = NULL;
    }
    if (!empty($p['db_error_handler']))
    {
        $dbh->setErrorHandling(PEAR_ERROR_CALLBACK,
$p['db_error_handler']);
    }
    else
    {
        $dbh-
>setErrorHandling(PEAR_ERROR_TRIGGER,$p['db_error_level']);
    }
    $_connections[$p['application']] = $dbh;
    if ($dbh === NULL)
    {
        $private_error = var_export($_connection, TRUE);
        user_error('connection is NULL.', $p['db_error_level']);
        exit;
    }
    return $dbh;
}
```

If db_connect() is called with no parameters, it hands back the handle of the last DB object that was created. You'll notice the use of this function throughout this example and the examples that follow; we can call db_connect() from any point in the application – in a Web page, inside a function, and so on – and get access to the database, without having to set up a global variable, and without making multiple connections. The more advanced object-oriented features of PHP 4.3 even let us do away with storing the object handle in a variable, and just use the function in its place. Prior to PHP 4.3 we would have to do something like this:

```
$dbh = db_connect();
$dbh->query('delete * from mysql.users');
```

But the new PHP object handling lets us just write

```
db_connect()->query('delete * from mysql.users');
```

The db_connect() function also sets up how DB errors are handled. They can either be passed on directly to a function or class method, or processed when they trigger a PHP error of a given error level and thus go through whatever error handling we've set up for general PHP errors. For the examples in this book, we normally use the former method, passing DB errors on to a function of our own, db_error_handler().

db_error_handler()

We use a special error-handling function for DB errors rather than only relying on our regular error_handler() function. We do this so that we can roll back any open transaction (if we still have an active database connection) and then trigger a fatal error that will exit the page and stop any other queries from running. This is key to the concept of atomic transactions, which are multi-stage procedures in which, by rule, either all of the steps must occur, or none of them. This prevents such problems as, in the case of a bank, money being credited to one account without being subtracted from another one.

```
function db_error_handler($db_error)
{
    $timestamp = time();
    // this should be unnecessary but can't hurt
    $dbh = db_connect();
    if (is_a($dbh,'DB'))
    {
        $last_query = $dbh->last_query;
        $dbh->query('rollback');
    }
    $skip_past_function = 'mysqlraiseerror';
    $private_error = "DB error ($timestamp): ".$db_error->userinfo;
```

```
    $error_level = E_USER_ERROR;
    user_error(
"Database error - please contact the system
administrator.($timestamp)"
,$error_level
    );
}
```

db_fetch_record()

This function provides a convenient way to get a record or set of records from a table. It makes use of DB's system for token replacement, which is a fancy way of saying "placeholders." As a simple example, you can run a query with DB like this:

```
$result = $dbh->query('select * from mytable where mykey = 1');
```

But you can also pass in two arguments to `DB::query()`, the query string itself, and an array of values to replace into the string:

```
$result = $dbh->query(
    'select * from mytable where mykey = ?'
    , array($mykey)
);
```

The token character ? in the query string tells DB that it should replace it with the content of a value from the array of arguments. If you have two ? characters in your query string, it looks for two values in the array, and so on. The very nice aspect of this – beyond freeing you from having to build a new query string for every new set of values you want to include in your query, which is no small potatoes – is that DB takes care of quoting and escaping characters for you. A statement like this:

```
$mykey = 1;
$myname = "O'Reilly";
$result = $dbh->query(
    'select * from mytable where mykey = ? and myname = ?'
    , array($mykey, $myname)
);
```

results in this query being run by MySQL:

```
select * from mytable where mykey = 1 and myname = 'O\'Reilly'
```

and although this book is about PHP and MySQL, it's worth noting here that DB can be used with a wide variety of databases, handling the proper quotation and escape syntax for each one. If you've ever had to port code from, say, Sybase or PostgreSQL to MySQL, you can appreciate how valuable a feature that is.

You can also make substitutions for literal parts of the query, using the ! token character, like this:

```
$mykey = 1;
$myname = "O'Reilly";
$result = $dbh->query(
    'select * from mytable where mykey = ? and ! = ?'
    , array($mykey, 'myname', $myname)
);
```

DB interprets the ! character to indicate that it should put the corresponding value from the argument list as-is, without quoting it, so that you can change the name of the table of the column you query dynamically. You might be thinking, looking at this example, what is the point of putting the literal string 'myname' in the argument list, when you could have just written it into the query in the first place? It's only to show that you are not limited to using variables in your argument array.

DB even grabs the contents of an entire file for you, using the & token character, like this:

```
$dbh->query(
    'insert into myfiles (filename, filecontents) values (?, &)'
    , array('my file', 'myfile.txt')
);
```

So now that we've seen a little more of what DB can do for us, look at an example of using it, in the db_fetch_record() function:

```
function db_fetch_record()
{
    static $_defaults = array(
        'table' => NULL
        , 'key' => NULL
        , 'value' => NULL
        , 'columns' => '*'
        , 'extra' => NULL
        , 'key_op' => '='
        , 'key_join' => ' and '
        , 'order_by' => NULL
    );
    static $_simple = array('table', 'key', 'value');
    $args = func_get_args();
    extract($_defaults);
    $p = parse_arguments($args, $_simple, $_defaults);
```

```
    extract($p, EXTR_IF_EXISTS);

    $query = 'select ! from !';
    $bind = array($columns,$table);
    $where = NULL;
    if (!empty($key) && !empty($value))
    {
        $where .= implode($key_join, array_fill(0, count($key), "!
$key_op ?"));
        if (is_array($key) && is_array($value))
        {
            foreach ($key as $i => $k)
            {
                $bind[] = $k;
                $bind[] = $value[$i];
            }
        }
        else
        {
            $bind[] = $key;
            $bind[] = $value;
        }
    }
    if ($extra)
    {
        if ($where)
        {
            $where = " ($where) and ";
        }
        $where .= " ($extra) ";
    }
    if ($where)
    {
        $query .= ' where '.$where;
    }
    $order_by = (array)$order_by;
    if (count($order_by) > 0)
    {
        $query .= ' order by '.implode(',',$order_by);
    }
    $result = db_connect()->getAll($query, $bind,
DB_FETCHMODE_ASSOC);
    if (!$result)
    {
```

```
        $private_error = 'could not fetch record: '
            .' query='.$query
            .' bind='.$bind
            .' result='.$result
        ;
        user_error("Could not fetch $table record", E_USER_ERROR);
        exit;
    }
    if (count($result) == 1)
    {
        $result = array_shift($result);
    }
    return $result;
}
```

If the resulting data set has only one row, that row is returned directly. Otherwise, the entire data set is returned. In either case, the constant `DB_FETCHMODE_ASSOC` (defined by the DB library) tells the `DB::getAll()` method to return each row of data as an associative array, with the column names from the query as keys.

db_values_array()

The `db_values_array()` function is similar to `db_fetch_record()` in that it's a shorthand for writing out a whole query. In this case, though, a list of values is always returned and a particular table structure is assumed: that the name of the table is the plural of the name of the label column, and that the name of the key column is the name of the label column plus `_id`. You can pass in corrections to these assumptions as arguments to the function (a common example from our code here: the name of a status lookup table is usually 'status', not 'statuss').

```
function db_values_array ()
{
    static $_defaults = array(
        'label' => NULL
        , 'table' => NULL
        , 'value' => NULL
        , 'sort' => NULL
        , 'where' => NULL
    );
    static $_simple = array('label','table');
    $p = func_get_args();
    extract($_defaults);
    $p = parse_arguments($p, $_simple, $_defaults);
    extract($p, EXTR_IF_EXISTS);

    if (empty($label))
```

```
    {
        $label = str_replace('_id','',$value);
    }
    elseif (empty($value))
    {
        $value = $label.'_id';
    }
    if (empty($table))
    {
        $table = $label.'s';
    }
    if (empty($sort))
    {
        $sort = $label;
    }
    if (empty($where))
    {
        $where = '1=1';
    }

    $output = db_connect()->getAssoc(
        'select !, ! from ! where ! order by !'
        , FALSE
        , array($value,$label,$table,$where,$sort)
    );
    return $output;
}
```

The most common use of db_values_array() is to generate a list of values from a database table for use in a SELECT field or group of option fields (radio buttons or checkboxes).

nullop()

The nullop() function returns either is or is not if the value being checked is equal to NULL, and either = or <> otherwise. We use <> rather than != because the ! character has special meaning to the DB code (see the db_fetch_record() function, described previously in the chapter):

```
function nullop($value=NULL,$op='=')
{
    if ($value === NULL)
    {
        if (strstr($op,'!='))
        {
            $op = 'is not';
```

```
        }
        else
        {
            $op = 'is';
        }
    }
    else
    {
        if (strstr($op, '!='))
        {
            $op = '<>';
        }
    }
    return $op;
}
```

Functions from /content/functions

These functions will be used throughout the application. This section will contain many references to Chapter 9 because in that chapter we first used many of the functions we'll call upon here.

connect_validate_login()

In this example we are using MySQL's own user and password tables to set up accounts that can be used with this application. The success or failure of the attempted connection to a MySQL server tells us if a username is valid or not. We do this by splitting the `authenticate()` function used in previous examples into several pieces, so that we can drop in our own validation code – in this case, `connect_validate_login()`.

```
function connect_validate_login()
{
    // if we haven't started a session yet, the references to
$_SESSION
    // will come up invalid, so start one if we need to.
    check_session();
    if (!isset($_SESSION))
    {
        global $_SESSION;
    }

    static $_defaults = array(
        'application' => 'content'
        , 'username' => NULL
        , 'password' => NULL
```

```
        , 'database' => 'netsloth'
    );
    if ($_defaults['username'] === NULL)
    {
        if (isset($_SESSION['PHP_AUTH_USER']))
        {
            $_defaults['username'] = $_SESSION['PHP_AUTH_USER'];
        }
        if (isset($_SESSION['PHP_AUTH_PW']))
        {
            $_defaults['password'] = $_SESSION['PHP_AUTH_PW'];
        }
    }
    static $_simple = array('username','password');
    $args = func_get_args();
    $p = parse_arguments($args, $_simple, $_defaults);

    $ok = FALSE;

    $p['db_error_level'] = E_USER_NOTICE;
    ob_start();
    $dbh = @db_connect($p);
    ob_end_clean();
    if ($dbh)
    {
        $ok = TRUE;
    }
    else
    {
        $p['error_message'] = "Could not connect\n";
    }
    return $ok;
}
```

fetch_story()

This function enables us to get the record for a story.

```
function fetch_story ($args=NULL)
{
    $story_id=NULL;
    if (isset($_SESSION) && isset($_SESSION['PHP_AUTH_USER']))
    {
        $this_username=$_SESSION['PHP_AUTH_USER'];
    }
```

```
    else
    {
        $this_username = NULL;
    }
    if (is_assoc($args))
    {
        extract($args, EXTR_IF_EXISTS);
    }
    elseif (is_numeric($args))
    {
        $story_id = $args;
    }

    $query = <<<EOQ
select m.user_id as is_ok
    , s.*
    , date_format(s.publish_dt, '%Y') as publish_yr
    , date_format(s.publish_dt, '%m') as publish_mn
    , date_format(s.publish_dt, '%d') as publish_dy
    , t.stage, t.stage_table
from stories s
    left join stages t on s.stage_id = t.stage_id
    left join users u on u.username = ifnull(?, user())
    left join user_stage_map m on s.stage_id = m.stage_id
        and m.user_id = u.user_id
EOQ;

    $bind = array($this_username);
    if ($story_id)
    {
        $query .= ' where s.story_id = ? ';
        $bind[] = $story_id;
    }

    $result = db_connect()->getRow($query, $bind,
DB_FETCHMODE_ASSOC);
    return $result;
}
```

fetch_story_version()

This function works like `fetch_story()`, except that it allows us to specify a value for the `modify_dt` value.

```
<?php
function fetch_story_version ($args=NULL)
```

```
{
    $story_id = NULL;
    $modify_dt = NULL;
    $this_username = $_SESSION['PHP_AUTH_USER'];
    if (is_assoc($args))
    {
        extract($args, EXTR_IF_EXISTS);
    }
    elseif (is_array($args))
    {
        $story_id = array_shift($args);
        $modify_dt = array_shift($args);
        $this_username = array_shift($args);
    }
    elseif ($args !== NULL)
    {
        $story_id = $args;
    }

    $query = <<<EOQ
select m.user_id as is_ok
    , s.*
    , date_format(s.publish_dt, '%Y') as publish_yr
    , date_format(s.publish_dt, '%m') as publish_mn
    , date_format(s.publish_dt, '%d') as publish_dy
    , t.stage, t.stage_table
from story_versions s
    left join stages t on s.stage_id = t.stage_id
    left join users u on u.username = ifnull(?, user())
    left join user_stage_map m on s.stage_id = m.stage_id
        and m.user_id = u.user_id
EOQ;

    $bind = array($this_username);
    $wheres = array();
    if ($story_id)
    {
        $wheres[] = 's.story_id = ?';
        $bind[] = $story_id;
    }
    if ($modify_dt)
    {
        $wheres[] = 's.modify_dt = ?';
        $bind[] = $modify_dt;
```

```
    }
    if (count($wheres) > 0)
    {
        $query .= ' where '.implode(' and ', $wheres);
    }

    $result = db_connect()->getRow($query, $bind,
DB_FETCHMODE_ASSOC);
    return $result;
}
?>
```

function fetch_author()

This function works similarly to the `fetch_story()` function, except that it operates on the authors table to find all the stories by a specified author.

```
function fetch_author ($args=array())
{
    $author_id = NULL;
    $other = NULL;
    if (is_assoc($args))
    {
        extract($args, EXTR_IF_EXISTS);
    }
    else
    {
        $author_id = $args;
    }
    $args = array('table'=>'authors');
    if ($author_id)
    {
        $args['key'] = 'author_id';
        $args['value'] = $author_id;
    }
    if (is_assoc($other))
    {
        $args = array_merge($args, $other);
    }
    return db_fetch_record($args);
}
```

fetch_user()

This function also works similarly to the `fetch_story` function, except it looks for postings by a given user.

```
function fetch_user ()
{
    $params = array('table'=>'users');
    $args = func_get_args();
    foreach ($args as $arg)
    {
        if (is_assoc($arg))
        {
            $params = array_merge($params, $arg);
        }
        elseif (is_numeric($arg))
        {
            $params['key'][] = 'user_id';
            $params['value'][] = $arg;
        }
        elseif (is_string($arg))
        {
            $params['key'][] = 'username';
            $params['value'][] = $arg;
        }
    }
    return db_fetch_record($params);
}
```

stage(), stage_id(), stages()

The `stage()` and `stage_id()` functions are front ends to the main `stages()` function. The first time `stages()` is called, the contents of the stages table from the database are loaded into a static array. This enables us to make subsequent calls to look up a stage name by its ID value, or vice versa, without querying the database.

```
<?php
function stage($stage_id=NULL)
{
    return stages('stage_id',$stage_id);
}
function stage_id($stage=NULL)
{
    return stages('stage',$stage);
}
function stage_table($stage_id=NULL)
{
    return stages('stage_table',$stage_id);
}
function stages($key=NULL,$value=NULL)
{
```

```
        static $stages = NULL;
        if ($stages === NULL)
        {
            $result = db_connect()->query(
                'select * from stages order by stage_id'
            );
            while ($row = $result->fetchRow(DB_FETCHMODE_ASSOC))
            {
                extract($row);
                $stages['stage'][$stage] = $stage_id;
                $stages['stage'][''][] = $stage_id;
                $stages['stage_id'][$stage_id] = $stage;
                $stages['stage_id'][''][] = $stage;
                $stages['stage_table'][$stage_id] = $stage_table;
                $stages[''][] = $row;
            }
            $result->free();
        }
        if (empty($key))
        {
            return $stages[''];
        }
        elseif (array_key_exists($key,$stages))
        {
            if (empty($value))
            {
                return $stages[$key][''];
            }
            elseif (array_key_exists($value,$stages[$key]))
            {
                return $stages[$key][$value];
            }
        }
        return NULL;
    }
    ?>
```

stage_table_name()

We build a separate table for each stage of the workflow through which a story passes. MySQL permissions are assigned, allowing individual users of the application to access these tables. This function converts a stage name into the name of the corresponding stage table.

```
function stage_table_name($stage)
{
```

```
    return preg_replace('/ /', '_',
strtolower(trim($stage)).'_stories');
}
```

write_author()

The `write_author()` function creates or updates a record in the authors table in the database.

```
function write_author($args=array())
{
    $author_id = NULL;
    $author = NULL;
    $email = NULL;
    $bio = NULL;
    if (is_assoc($args))
    {
        extract($args, EXTR_IF_EXISTS);
    }
    else
    {
        $private_error = 'bad arguments to write_author:'
            . var_export($args, TRUE)
        ;
        user_error(
            'Invalid arguments - could not write author'
            , E_USER_WARNING
        );
        return FALSE;
    }

    if (empty($author_id))
    {
        // if we don't have an ID value, no record exists
        // for this author - create one.
        $author_id = db_connect()->nextId('author');
        $stmt = db_connect()->prepare(
            'insert into authors (author,email,bio,author_id) values
(?,?,?,?)'
        );
    }
    else
    {
        // if we have an ID value, a record currently exists
        // for this author - update it.
```

```
        $stmt = db_connect()->prepare(
            'update authors set author=?, email=?, bio=? where
author_id = ?'
        );
    }
    $result = db_connect()->execute($stmt,
array($author,$email,$bio,$author_id));
    if (!$result)
    {
        user_error('Could not update author record',
E_USER_WARNING);
        return FALSE;
    }
    return TRUE;
}
```

write_story()

The `write_story()` function creates or updates a record in the stories table in the database. It also moves a story from one stage to another. Because a user may attempt to modify a story that is in a stage to which the user does not have access, or send a story forward or backward in the workflow to a restricted stage, we may end up getting MySQL permission errors from a query. We don't want the application to simply roll back the transaction and stop when this happens, so we use the DB class `pushErrorHandling()` and `popErrorHandling()` methods (actually, these are methods inherited from the general PEAR Error class) to temporarily change the way database errors are handled.

```
<?php
function start_dbhandler()
{
    db_connect()->pushErrorHandling(PEAR_ERROR_TRIGGER,
E_USER_NOTICE);
}
function end_dbhandler($result=TRUE)
{
    db_connect()->popErrorHandling();
    return $result;
}

function write_story($args=array())
{
    $stage_id = NULL;
    $publish_yr = NULL;
    $publish_mn = NULL;
```

```
$publish_dy = NULL;
$publish_dt = NULL;
$headline = NULL;
$subtitle = NULL;
$byline_prefix = NULL;
$summary = NULL;
$body = NULL;
$story_id = NULL;
$submit = NULL;
$author = NULL;
$author_id = NULL;

if (is_assoc($args))
{
    extract($args, EXTR_IF_EXISTS);
}
else
{
    $private_error = 'write_story: error: bad arguments: '
        . var_export($args, TRUE)
    ;
    user_error('Could not update story', E_USER_WARNING);
    return FALSE;
}

start_dbhandler();

// begin transaction
db_connect()->query('begin');

if (empty($story_id))
{
    // if we have no ID value, this is a new story.
    // get the ID value of a new record from story sequence
    $story_id = db_connect()->nextId('story');
    $result = db_connect()->query(
        'insert into stories (story_id,headline) values (?,?)'
        , array($story_id,'Not Yet Updated')
    );
    if (!$result)
    {
        db_connect()->query('rollback');
        user_error(
            'Could not insert new record into stories table'
```

```
                    , E_USER_ERROR
                );
                return end_dbhandler(FALSE);
            }
        }
        else
        {
            // if we have an ID value, this is an existing story.
            // get the name of its current stage table.
            // (see admin/stage.php for notes about the purpose and
            // use of the stage access tables.)
            $oldstage_table = db_connect()->getOne(
                'select s.stage_table from stages s, stories t
                    where t.story_id = ? and t.stage_id = s.stage_id'
                , array($story_id)
            );
            if (!$oldstage_table)
            {
                db_connect()->query('rollback');
                user_error(
                    'Could not access current stage table for story
'.$story_id
                    , E_USER_WARNING
                );
                return end_dbhandler(FALSE);
            }

            // remove the story from the old stage access table
            $result = db_connect()->query(
                'delete from ! where story_id = ?'
                , array($oldstage_table,$story_id)
            );
            if (!$result or DB::isError($result))
            {
                db_connect()->query('rollback');
                user_error(
                    'Could not delete from current stage table for story
'.$story_id
                    , E_USER_WARNING
                );
                return end_dbhandler(FALSE);
            }
        }

        // get the assigned stage, or the first stage by default
```

```
    $query = 'select stage_id, stage, stage_table from stages
            where stage_id = ?
        union
        select stage_id, stage, stage_table from stages
            having stage_id = min(stage_id)
    ';
    $row = db_connect()->getRow(
        $query
        , array($stage_id)
        , DB_FETCHMODE_ORDERED
    );
    if ($row)
    {
        list($stage_id,$stage,$stage_table) = $row;
    }
    else
    {
        user_error('Unable to get current stage for this story'
            , E_USER_ERROR
        );
    }

    // create or update a record for this story in the stage access
    // table for the new stage.
    $result = db_connect()->query(
        'replace into ! (story_id) values (?)'
        , array($stage_table,$story_id)
    );
    if (!$result)
    {
        if (preg_match('/denied to user/', db_connect()-
>error_message))
        {
            $error = "Access denied to $stage for $username";
        }
        else
        {
            $error = 'Database error - could not update stage';
        }
        user_error($error, E_USER_ERROR);
    }

    if (!empty($publish_yr) && !empty($publish_mn) &&
!empty($publish_dy))
    {
```

```
        // build a publish date from the three related select
        // fields in the form, if all three were set to a value.
        $publish_dt = $publish_yr.'-'.$publish_mn.'-'.$publish_dy;
    }
    elseif ($stage == 'Live')
    {
        // if no publish date was set and the story is being
        // set to the 'Live' stage, use a default publish date
        // of now (i.e., the story will go live immediately).
        $publish_dt = date('Y-m-d');
    }
    else
    {
        // if no publish_dt was set and the story is not Live,
        // set $publish_dt to 'null' for use in the query.
        $publish_dt = NULL;
    }

    // update the story record in the database
    $stmt = db_connect()->autoPrepare(
        'stories'
        , array('stage_id','publish_dt','headline','subtitle'
            ,'byline_prefix','summary','body'
        )
        , DB_AUTOQUERY_UPDATE
        , 'story_id = ?'
    );
    db_connect()->execute(
        $stmt
        , array($stage_id, $publish_dt, $headline, $subtitle
            , $byline_prefix, $summary, $body, $story_id
        )
    );

    // now save a copy of the updated record in the story_versions
    // table. this keeps the history of the story complete up to
    // the present moment.
    $query =
        'insert into story_versions
        (modify_by, story_id, stage_id, publish_dt, headline
            , subtitle, byline_prefix, summary, body)
        select user() as modify_by, story_id, stage_id, publish_dt,
headline
            , subtitle, byline_prefix, summary, body
        from stories where story_id = ?'
```

```
    ;
    db_connect()->query($query,array($story_id));

    if (!empty($author_id))
    {
        // if an author was selected for the story, remove any
        // current link between the story and an author, and
        // add a link for the selected author.
        db_connect()->query(
            'delete from story_author_map where story_id = ?'
            , array($story_id)
        );
        db_connect()->query(
            'insert into story_author_map (story_id, author_id)
values (?,?)'
            , array($story_id, $author_id)
        );
    }

    // end the transaction
    db_connect()->query('commit');

    return end_dbhandler(TRUE);
}
?>
```

Interesting Code Flow

Since most of the more complicated aspects of our application have to do with maintaining users and stages, we will start the breakdown of code with the pages that take care of these stages. Later we will move on to the other features performed by this application.

content/authenticate.php

As we already mentioned, this application differs from the previous ones in that each user will be logging in to the database with his or her own username and password. The script that performs this login will need to be just a touch more flexible than the one we used in the other applications.

This application is going to use the same authentication methods seen in the previous examples, but here the values for `$PHP_AUTH_USER` and `$PHP_AUTH_PW` will also be the values used to log in to the database.

The content/header.php file, which is included in every page in the content-management system, contains the following code:

```
require('authenticate.php');
```

Because we have placed the administrative code in a subdirectory of the main content directory, this one statement will include either the basic authenticate.php file (for normal users) or the content/admin/authenticate.php file (for administrators).

Here are the contents of the basic authenticate.php file.

```
<?php


check_session();
if (!isset($_SESSION))
{
    global $_SESSION;
}

$realm = 'Netsloth Content Management';
$message = 'You must enter a valid name & password to access this
function';

$submit = array_key_value($_REQUEST, 'submit', NULL);
if ($submit == 'logout')
{

    logout();
}

$username = session_auth(array(
    'realm' => $realm
    , 'message' => $message
    , 'validate_function' => 'connect_validate_login'
));
$result = db_connect()->getRow(
    'select u.*, if(a.username is null, 0, 1) as is_admin
        from users u left join admin a on u.username = a.username
        where u.username = ? '
    , array($username)
    , DB_FETCHMODE_ASSOC
);
foreach ($result as $k => $v)
{
```

```
    $_SESSION[$k] = $v;
}
extract($result);
?>
```

The logout() function is one of our standard functions to handle removing a logged-in user. When using HTTP authentication, this can be somewhat tricky. Otherwise, we can just unset the PHP session values $_SESSION[['PHP_AUTH_USER'] and $_SESSION['PHP_AUTH_PW'].

content/admin/user.php

This page, like many you have seen before, has many purposes. The exact portion of the script that will run will depend on the variables sent to the page. It can do the following:

- Enable an administrator to create new users
- Display the information specific to a single user_id, including the stages associated with that user
- Grant additional stages to an existing user
- Revoke the rights to a stage from a user

If the page is accessed without any variable information in the querystring or from POST, the form elements for user information will be blank. This information must be filled in before the form is submitted. When the form is submitted the admin_user.php page will be called again, this time holding the entered form data and with the $submit variable equal to Save Changes.

When submitted, the condition in the if statement at the top of the page will test true:

```
if ($submit == "Save Changes")
```

The page will then call the write_user() function, defined in content/admin/functions/write_user.php, to update or create the user's record in the database. If the user's information must be updated, the form passes a user_id from a hidden form element; otherwise the $user_id variable will be empty. The result of this statement decides whether the script is to perform an update or insert query.

The PEAR DB class provides a simulation of a "sequence" in MySQL. This works like an auto_increment key in a table – in fact, that's exactly what it is – but rather than doing the insert and then discovering what the new key value is, we first get the new key value and then use it in the insert query.

A caution about the `DB::nextId()` method: if the table containing the ID values doesn't exist when this method is called, the method will try to create it. Since it's common for a Web application's user account to not have the privilege to create tables, this is likely to result in a runtime error. You should be sure to have created these tables ahead of time. The table names are *sequencename_seq*, where *sequencename* is the name you pass in to `DB::nextId()`.

```
    if (empty($user_id))
    {
        // if we don't have an ID value, there is no record
        // for this user - create one
        $user_id = db_connect()->nextId('user');
        $query = 'insert into users
            (username, password, name, email, user_id)

            values (?, password(?), ?, ?, ?) '
        ;
    }
    else
    {
        // if we have an ID value, a record for this user
        // currently exists in the users table - update it
        $query = 'update users set username=?
            , password=password(?), name=?            , email=?
where user_id = ? '
        ;
    }
    $stmt = db_connect()->prepare($query);
    $bind = array($username,$password,$name,$email,$user_id);
    if (!db_connect()->execute($stmt,$bind))
    {
        $private_error = db_connect()->last_query;
        user_error('could not update user record', E_USER_WARNING);
        return FALSE;
    }
```

Note that when this section of the script is completed, the `user_id` is known: Either it was passed from the form or it was created by the call to `DB::nextId()`.

Next comes a series of function calls that set up normal permissions on the common tables of the application, such as the stories and authors tables, and the specific permissions on the workflow stage tables that correspond to the stages we chose to give this user access to.

```
if (empty($user_id))
{
    // if we don't have an ID value, there is no record
    // for this user - create one
    $user_id = db_connect()->nextId('user');
    $query = 'insert into users
        (username, password, name, email, user_id)
        values
        (?,password(?),?,?,?) '
    ;
}
else
{
    // if we have an ID value, a record for this user
    // currently exists in the users table - update it
    $query = 'update users set username=?
        , password=password(?), name=?
        , email=? where user_id = ? '
    ;
}
$stmt = db_connect()->prepare($query);
$bind = array($username,$password,$name,$email,$user_id);
if (!db_connect()->execute($stmt,$bind))
{
    $private_error = db_connect()->last_query;
    user_error('could not update user record', E_USER_WARNING);
    return FALSE;
}
```

Returning to the user.php file, the code next prints out the appropriate user information (if existing user information exists) and the stages as a series of checkboxes. The checkboxes are checked if the user has rights for that stage.

The following query is intended to work with the `checkbox_field()` function created earlier. That function takes three arguments (`form name`, `value`, and `match value`). If the `value` and `matchvalue` arguments match, the checkbox will be checked.

```
$query = 'select distinct m.stage_id as matchvalue
        , s.stage_id, s.stage, s.stage_dsc
    from stages s
        left join users u on u.user_id = ?
        left join user_stage_map m on s.stage_id = m.stage_id
            and m.user_id = u.user_id
';
```

This query gathers all the stages and does an outer join on the users table. If the user has been granted access to a stage, that stage name appears in the returned record set, in the `matchvalue` field. If not, a hyphen appears in the field. When the `checkbox_field()` function is run later in the loop, the third argument will either be a hyphen or have the same value as the `stage` field. The results of this query might look like this:

```
+------------+----------+------------+-----------------+
| matchvalue | stage_id | stage      | stage_dsc       |
+------------+----------+------------+-----------------+
|       NULL |        1 | Writing    | the words       |
|       NULL |        2 | Editing    | fixing mistakes |
|          3 |        3 | Publishing | making HTML     |
|          4 |        4 | Live       | On the web      |
|          5 |        5 | Killed     | dead            |
+------------+----------+------------+-----------------+
```

This knowledge should enable you to read the rest of this script. And, of course, further comments are included with the application on the CD-ROM.

content/story.php

At 340 lines or so, this script is long, but it isn't especially complicated. Given the data structure we discussed earlier, it needs to create new stories and update existing stories after they have been through an editorial pass. Along the way the script will need to check if the user has the rights to do the work on the story, and clean up text that users put into the forms.

The file should be made readable by the comments within the page, which are supplied on the accompanying CD-ROM. You must make quite a few decisions in order to get this page to work correctly, and that adds to the length. But decisions to be made within the file are pretty straightforward. Additionally, the page contains quite a few `insert` and `update` statements. If you refer to Figure 11-8 while you're reading through the code, it shouldn't be too tough to get through.

This chapter has spent a fair amount of space discussing how to assign rights to a user using MySQL's grant statements. Hopefully at this point you see how those rights are assigned. The short piece of script that follows tests whether the current user has the rights to work on a story, based on the rights in the grants tables. It first gets the `stage_name`, based on a `stage_id`, and then creates the string of the table name by appending `_table` to the stage name. Then a `select` statement runs that includes the table name we have just created. If that query is not allowed, the query will fail and return `false`. Within the query we are also involving the `user_stage_map` table. That table provides our primary security, and the user must have rights for the current stage in the `user_stage_map` table. If the user does not have rights defined in that table, the query will return no rows. If the query fails or returns nothing, an error will print and the script will exit.

```
    // if we have an ID value, this is an existing story -
    // get information about it from the database

    $result = NULL;
    if (empty($modify_dt))
    {
        // if no timestamp value is passed in, get the
        // current version of the story from the stories
        // table.

        $query = <<<EOQ
select m.user_id as is_ok
    , s.*
    , date_format(s.publish_dt, '%Y') as publish_yr
    , date_format(s.publish_dt, '%m') as publish_mn
    , date_format(s.publish_dt, '%d') as publish_dy
from stories s
    left join user_stage_map m on s.stage_id = m.stage_id
        and m.user_id = ?
where s.story_id = ?
EOQ;
        $bind = array($user_id,$story_id);
    }
    else
    {
        // if a timestamp is passed in, get the version
        // of the story it identifies from the story_versions
        // table.
        $query = <<<EOQ
select m.user_id as is_ok
    , s.*
    , date_format(s.publish_dt, '%Y') as publish_yr
    , date_format(s.publish_dt, '%m') as publish_mn
    , date_format(s.publish_dt, '%d') as publish_dy
from story_versions s
    left join user_stage_map m on s.stage_id = m.stage_id
        and m.user_id = ?
where s.story_id = ? and s.modify_dt = ?
EOQ;
        $bind = array($user_id,$story_id,$modify_dt);
    }

    $result = db_connect()->getRow($query, $bind,
DB_FETCHMODE_ASSOC);
```

```
if (!$result['is_ok'])
{
    // if the query has failed, the user has not been
    // granted MySQL select access to the stage
    // access table, and thus does not have permission
    // to edit this story. print out an error and exit.
    print subtitle(
        'You may not edit stories in the '
        . stage($result['stage_id'])
        . ' stage.'
    );
    print end_page();
    exit;
}
```

Another item of particular interest is the extensive text-processing done in this script. This is an example of the type of processing we might need to do if our users are working with some sort of text-processing tool (such as an HTML editor or word processor). Every tool has its own little quirks that we will need to account for. The only way we are going to find out exactly what type of cleanup we need to do is by examining the code created by the text editor in our workplace.

For instance, we are not going to want to have the beginning and ending tags of a complete HTML page in the body text of an article. So if the user has written the article in a WYSIWYG HTML editor, to make creating links and such easier, we'll want to strip out everything before and after the actual `<BODY>` part of the page, and to get rid of the `<BODY>` and `</BODY>` tags themselves.

```
    $body =
preg_replace('/^.*<body[^>]*>(.*?)<.body.*$/i','$1',$body);
    $body = preg_replace('/[\r\n]{1,2}/',"\n",$body);
```

Of course, PHP's `strip_tags()` function could work for you, if you want to allow a limited tag set and remove all other tags.

Starting at line 157 of the story.php file – at the comment line `fix up paragraph tags` – is a nice block of code that will do a couple of neat things. If it appears the user input the story without using `<p>` tags, the script will add them where it seems appropriate, assuming the user indicated paragraphs with newlines (hard returns). If the user did use `<p>` tags, the script examines the text, making sure that no funky spaces or malformed tags are present. We recommend that you look at the code and comments provided on the CD-ROM to get a good feel for how to do complex text handling.

Summary

In this chapter you saw some of the nifty tricks and techniques that can go into creating a content-management system. Of course an application such as this can be far, far more complex. But this is a good start and presents a reasonable way to organize your code and database tables.

We also made use of MySQL's grant statements when creating this application. As we've said throughout, the grant scheme that we've used here may not be terribly practical. However, it does provide a good example of how you could go about setting up a system where one login name and password isn't enough for the entire application.

Also, make sure to take a look at some of the text-handling code in edit_story.php. Some of the code provides an excellent example of what you can do with PHP's string-handling functions and regular expressions.

Chapter 12

Catalog

IN THIS CHAPTER

- ◆ Working with object-oriented code
- ◆ Looking at database schemas

IN THE COURSE OF THIS CHAPTER we are going to show one way of creating an online catalog. You'll see how to present and administer an application that presents some typical retail items.

We, the authors of this book, feel that you are an intelligent person, as well as someone with great taste in technical literature. We also believe that you picked up this book because you want to learn as much as you can about applications development with PHP and MySQL. That's why we're not wasting any time. Each chapter introduces additional challenges, or at least presents something new and different. This chapter is no exception.

If this chapter were to use the functions presented in the survey application in Chapter 9, we would have little new material to present here. The application would need nothing but a simple database schema, a few queries with some joins, and calls to the HTML functions in the /functions/ folder.

To keep things interesting, we're going to write this example using an object-oriented programming style, and use a few of the OOP techniques we covered in Chapter 7.

Chapter 7 covers the concepts and nomenclature associated with object-oriented programming. In this chapter, we assume that you have read and understood that information.

Determining the Scope and Goals of the Application

The goals we have in mind for this application are pretty modest. Imagine for a moment that you own some sort of retail establishment that has goods you wish to hawk. Further, assume that you have no interest in actually conducting transactions over the Web. Maybe you are just paranoid about this newfangled method of processing credit cards. Or perhaps you are running an elaborate tax-fraud scheme that requires you to deal solely in unmarked twenties.

The code used in this catalog is reused in the creation of shopping-cart application, where we show how to process credit-card transactions. See Chapter 14 for the shopping cart.

Whatever the circumstance, all this site needs to do is show your wares in logical categories and breakdowns. You will hear more about the breakdown of the information when we discuss the database schema.

The chief purpose of this chapter is to show how to create code that makes the best use of the object-oriented approach. The classes must make use of inheritance and encapsulation and should make the task of writing individual scripts a whole lot easier. It's also important to think about modularity. As indicated in the preceding note, the code created here is reused in Chapter 14, so we want to write code in such a way that it becomes easily reusable elsewhere.

Necessary pages

The pages that display the catalog aren't very extravagant. For navigational purposes a simple page displays a list of general product categories. Figure 12-1 shows the category list.

From the list of categories, the viewer of the page clicks through to see a listing of specific types of products available within the general product category. (For example, the category Shirts contains T-shirts, dress shirts, and polo shirts.) Figure 12-2 shows this rather underwhelming page.

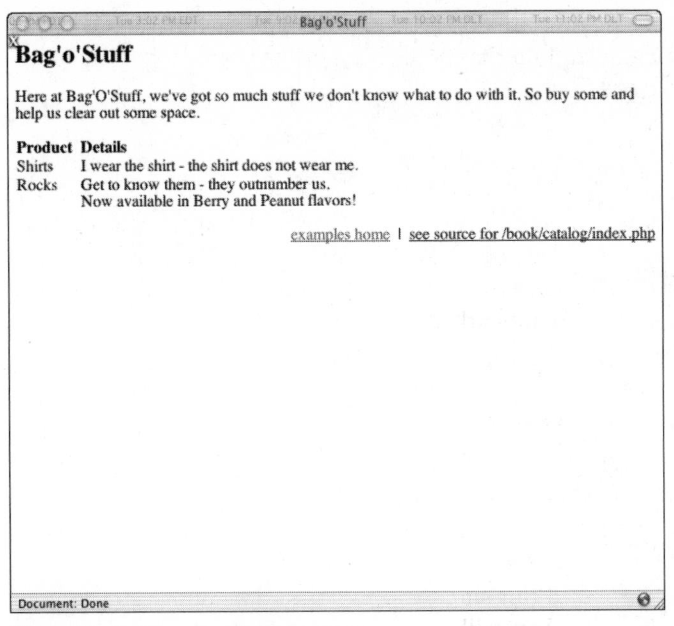

Figure 12-1: General category page

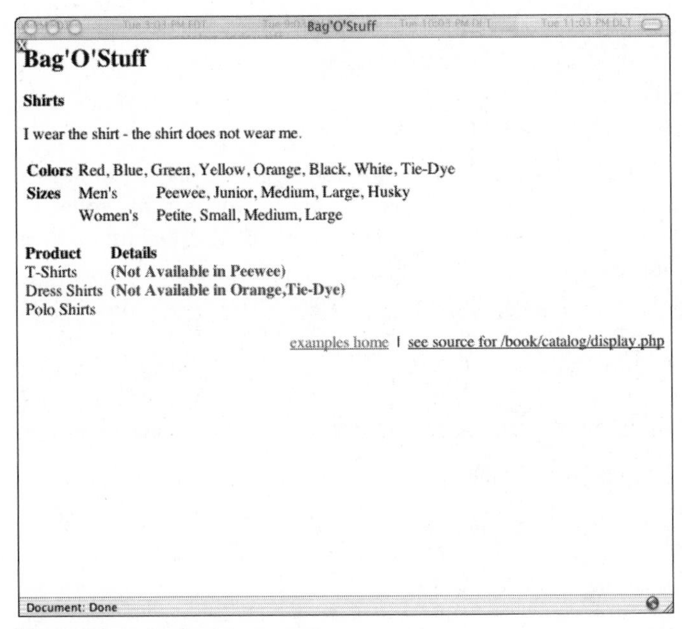

Figure 12-2: Product types page

As a moment's glance at my laundry can tell you, lots of different kinds of T-shirts exist. Descending down into that product type shows a listing of the catalog's selection, as shown in Figure 12-3.

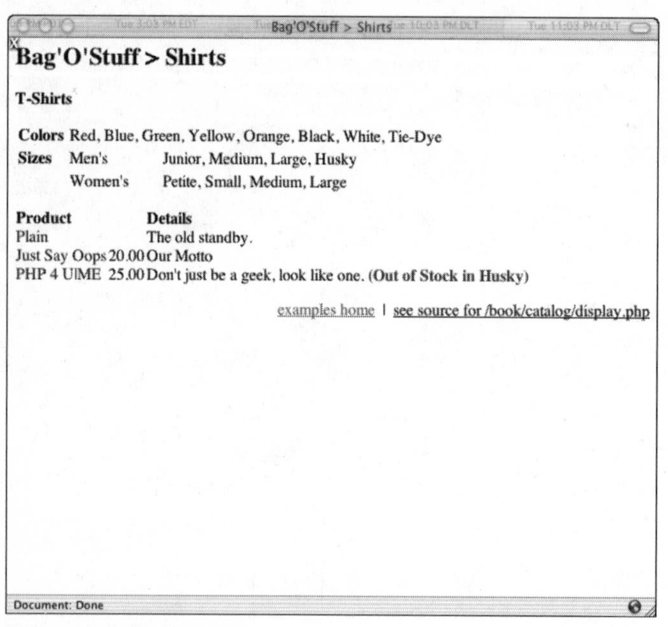

Figure 12-3: Product page

Finally, there is a page that lists an actual item for sale. Notice that a thumbnail of the item is shown, and that under the item is a listing of the various styles in which the item is available. In Figure 12-4 the item is one of the T-shirts, which comes in several sizes and colors.

Like all the applications in this book, this one has a series of administrative pages. Given what you have seen in the previous paragraphs and figures, it should be no surprise that the administrative pages create, delete, and alter information on product groups, individual products, and styles (which can be applied to either product groups or individual products). Some samples of these pages are shown in Figures 12-5, 12-6, and 12-7 respectively.

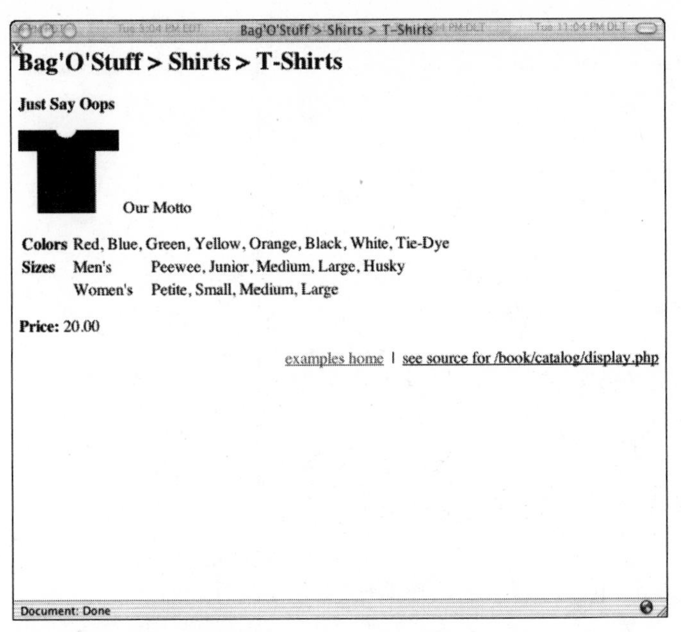

Figure 12-4: Items page

Catalog Admin

Logged in as jay

Catalog Admin

Main Product Lines	Shirts
	Rocks
	Add New Product
General Styles	Colors
	Sizes
	Flavors
	Add New Style

Admin Home | Catalog Home

Document: Done

Figure 12-5: Administration home page

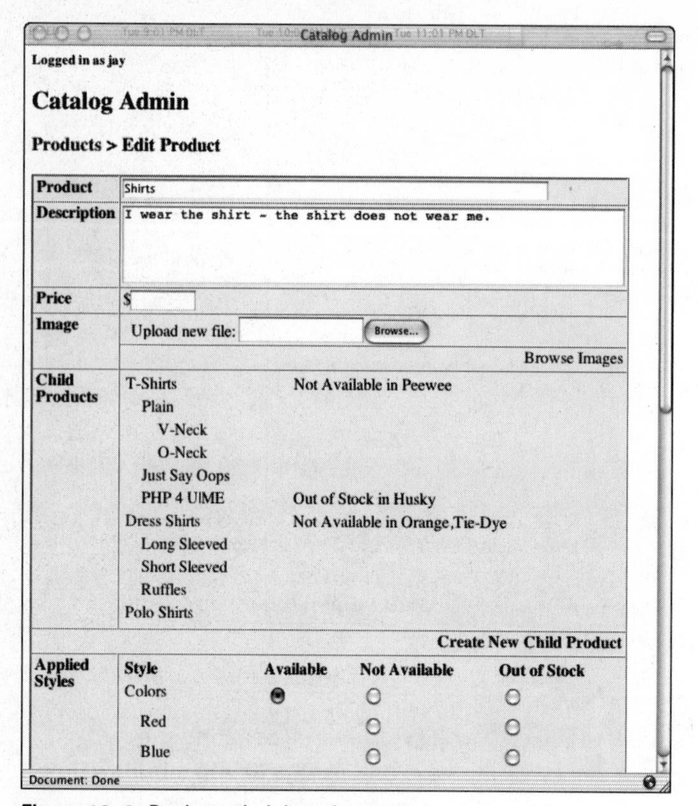

Figure 12-6: Product administration page

What do we need to prevent?

Unlike in the survey and the guestbook, no user interaction exists in this application. To the world at large the catalog is read-only. So you don't need to be quite as concerned with bored people adding unwanted tags and scripts to the pages.

Instead, what you want to be most concerned about preventing is inaccurate and duplicated data. You want to store one fact – that no dress shirts are available in orange, for instance – one time, and have it be applied whenever necessary. If you have to change 50 product entries to remove one style, you're bound to miss some.

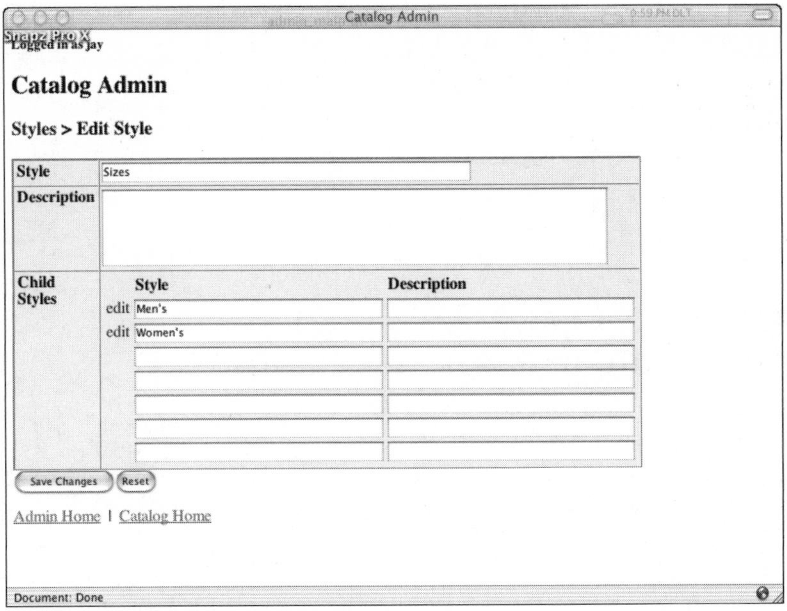

Figure 12-7: Style administration page

The Data

From what we've said about the application so far, you might think that you need at least four main tables in the database: a general product category table, a product types table, an individual products table, and a styles table. But think about how you would naturally describe the data. If someone asked what the store sold, your first answer would be something like "We sell shirts and rocks." What kinds of shirts? T-shirts, dress shirts, and polo shirts. What kinds of T-shirts? You get the idea – in each answer, we're talking about our *products* – just more specifically each time.

The same applies to styles. A product might come in lots of flavors. Some of the flavors are fruit flavors. Some of the fruit flavors are banana, cherry, and orange. If you tried to make a different table for each level, you'd have big problems when you needed to add a new level; the whole application would need to be rewritten.

So the database has just three main tables: a products table, a styles table, and a mapping table to link products and styles together. The following shows the complete schema.

```
+------------------------------------+
| +----------------------------+     |
| |    +----------+            |     |     +--------+
| +--o<| products |-|--+       |     +--o|-| images |
|      |          |    |       |           |        |
+----o<|          |    |       |           +--------+
       |          |    |       |
  +--|-|          |>0--+       |
  |    +----------+            |
  |                            |
  |   +-------------------+    |    +-------------+
  +-o<| product_style_map |    +-o|-| price_types |
      |                   |         |             |
      |                   |>o----o|-|             |
  +-o<|                   |         +-------------+
  |   |                   |       +--------+
  |   |                   |>o---|-| status |
  |   +-------------------+       +--------+
  |
  |    +----------+
  +--|-| styles     |-|--+
       |          |    |
       |          |>0--+
       +----------+
```

Just ignore price_types for now. It's a table we use in the shopping-cart example (which uses this same database) in Chapter 14.

If you remember the discussion-board example in Chapter 10, you have a sense of how the products and styles tables work. Each product can either be a root-level product or belong to another product "above" it in the hierarchy. Shirts are a root-level product, T-shirts belongs to Shirts, Plain belongs to T-shirts, and so on. You use the same structure in the styles table.

It's worth spending a few minutes talking about product_style_map – the table that glues products and styles together. Our T-shirts come in multiple sizes (and different sizes for men's and women's shirts, to boot). They're also available in several different colors. In the most simple approach, product_style_map would contain a row linking every different individual kind of T-shirt to every size and every color in which it's available. But remember what we said about wanting to avoid duplicating data. If you know that you're out of stock in the husky size for all of your T-shirts, or if you add a new color, you don't want to have to change dozens of rows to record that.

Instead, product_style_map has only the minimal number of records needed to represent your actual stock. If there's a standard set of colors for all shirts, you can just map Shirts to Colors. That way when you add a new color it automatically shows up as available for all your shirts. If you don't want the color to apply to plain V-neck T-shirts you can go to that product and mark it "not available" there.

As you'll see, this puts the onus on the application code to interpret the data correctly. You can take an alternate approach to this kind of data that can make coding a bit simpler, but that carries a correspondingly increased risk of inaccurate information showing up on your Web pages. You can add another table to the database – something like derived_product_style_map, for example, that never gets directly updated by the administrators of the site. Instead, the application rebuilds it every time the main tables change. You can think of this kind of table as something like a cache – it stores the results of applying all the varying hierarchies of styles to all of the products, and ends up looking like the very simple mapping table described earlier. The advantage of this approach is probably clear: All the work has been done, and all the Web site has to do is go read the database. The disadvantage is in the process of building it. If anything goes wrong in that process, you end up displaying different information on the site than you see in your administration screens, which is the kind of thing that drives site administrators nuts. Plus, while you're rebuilding it, what do your pages show? There are ways to solve those problems, of course. It's a perfectly legitimate approach to take.

The thing is, every problem we had to solve in our example, which displays pages directly from the source products and styles tables, is one you'd have to solve to create those kinds of derived tables anyway. So if it sounds like a good approach, consider it left as an exercise for you.

The code in Listing 12-1 shows how the Catalog application's database tables are set up. Pay attention to the datatypes – they restrict what we can do later.

Listing 12-1: create Statements for the Catalog Application

```
# -------------------------------------------------------
create table products
(
        product_id              integer not null auto_increment
        , parent_id             integer not null default 0
        , product               varchar(255) not null
        , description           text null
        , price                 decimal(10,2) null
        , price_type_id         smallint null
```

Continued

Listing 12-1 *(Continued)*

```
        , image_id                  integer null
, primary key (product_id)
, key (parent_id)
, key (price_type_id), foreign key (price_type_id) references
price_types (price_type_id) on delete set null
, key (image_id), foreign key (image_id) references images
(image_id) on delete set null
)
type = InnoDB
;

create table styles
(
        style_id                    integer not null auto_increment
        , parent_id                 integer not null default 0
        , style                     varchar(255) not null
        , description               text null
, primary key (style_id)
, index (parent_id)
)
type=InnoDB
;
create table product_style_map
(
        map_id          int not null auto_increment
        , product_id    int not null
        , style_id              int not null
        , status_id             smallint null
        , price                 decimal(10,2) null
        , price_type_id smallint null
        , image_id              int null
, primary key (map_id)
, unique key (product_id, style_id)
, foreign key (product_id) references products (product_id) on
delete cascade
, key (style_id), foreign key (style_id) references styles
(style_id) on delete cascade
, key (status_id), foreign key (status_id) references status
(status_id)
, key (price_type_id), foreign key (price_type_id) references
price_types (price_type_id)
, key (image_id), foreign key (image_id) references images
(image_id)
)
```

```
type=InnoDB
;
create table status
(
        status_id               smallint not null
        , status                varchar(255) not null
        , description   text null
, primary key (status_id)
)
type = InnoDB
;
insert into status (status_id,status,description) values
(0,'Inherited','derived from parent');
insert into status (status_id,status,description) values
(1,'Available','ok to show');
insert into status (status_id,status,description) values (2,'Not
Available','not ok to show');
insert into status (status_id,status,description) values (3,'Out of
Stock','temporarily unavailable - ok to show, with warning');
create table images
(
        image_id                integer not null auto_increment
        , image                 varchar(255) not null
        , width                 integer null
        , height                integer null
        , alt                   text null
, primary key (image_id)
)
type = InnoDB
;
create table admin
(
        username        varchar(50) not null,
        password        varchar(255) not null
)
type=InnoDB
;
insert into admin values ('jay', sha1('rules'));
```

A note on this last line: `sha1()` is an encryption function like `md5()` or `password()`. It stores the password in an encrypted format so that we can still use it for login verification, but anyone looking at the contents of the table would not be able to see the actual password string.

Code Overview

The code in this section is going to look substantially different from that in the chapters you have seen so far.

The object-oriented approach

In the preceding applications we made use of a procedural approach. That is, there is a series of functions, and each function performs a fairly specific procedure. In the actual application, little remains to be done but to call these functions. But in an application such as this, in which the data are largely hierarchical, it's helpful to make use of OO programming's inheritance. It enables you to solve some problems – like how to upload an image file – once, not just for this application, but for subsequent ones as well, by creating a common library of classes much like the sets of functions we've used up until now. In fact, you can even let other people solve your problems for you, by using publicly available class libraries like the ones available from PEAR.

Problems more specific to this application are handled by a single common class, and those specific to each set of data – here, products and styles – are addressed in individual classes. Your code maps more directly to your data.

If you use objects, the contents within the files called by URLs will be even sparser. Almost all the work is performed within the classes. Once you understand what actions the class files perform, there is little else for you to do.

To advocates of OO programming, this is a major advantage. You, the programmer, can get a class file and not really know what happens inside it. All you need to know is what attributes it has and what its methods do. Then you can just include it in your application and painlessly make use of its sophisticated functionality.

We said it in Chapter 7, but it's worth repeating here: You can write procedural code that encompasses most of the benefits discussed here. If you're not careful with OO programming, your code can end up being much more difficult to maintain and use.

Accessing the file system

You have probably noticed by now that in this book almost all of our data are stored within the MySQL database. But even when you're using MySQL you are sometimes better off using the file system for storage. Images (.jpegs, .gifs, .pngs) are a perfect example. Even if your database supports binary data, there's little advantage in putting an image in a database. You need a database for storing and querying normalized data. In your database you are much better off maintaining the path to the image stored in your file system. That way it is easy enough to fill in the `src` attribute in your `<img>` tag.

Uploading files

This is the first application that enables users to upload files; specifically, the administrators of the catalog need to be able to upload images of their products. Uploading files is easy enough in PHP, but before you understand how the upload works you need to know how PHP handles uploaded files.

In your HTML page you have a form like the following:

```
<form action="admin_product.php" method="post"
enctype="multipart/form-data" >
<input type=file name="imagefile">
</form>
```

When you allow file uploads, you open yourself up to denial-of-service (DoS) attacks. If you're not careful, someone could send many multi-megabyte files to your system simultaneously, which could bring your machine to a crashing halt. There are two things you can do about this. The first is to put a hidden form field before your `<INPUT TYPE="file">` tag. The hidden field should look like this:

```
<INPUT TYPE="hidden" name="MAX_FILE_SIZE" value="1000">
```

where `value` indicates the maximum size allowed, in bytes. This is a reasonable first step and can be of help in stopping someone who didn't know you have a size limit. However, this measure will not stop anyone with stronger malicious intent. All that person has to do is look at the source code of your page and make the needed changes.

The other security measure has to do with altering the php.ini file, which contains the `upload_max_filesize` item. If you have access to your php.ini, you can set the value of this item to a number that you think is reasonable. (By default php.ini will allow 2MB uploads.) By making the change in the php.ini file you prevent the attacker from altering it.

When a file is specified and this form is submitted, PHP automatically creates a few variables. They are as follows:

- `$_FILES[`*`yourfieldname`*`][`*`tmp_name`*`]` — The name of the file as stored in the temporary directory on the server
- `$_FILES[`*`yourfieldname`*`][`*`name`*`]` — The name of the file as it was on the user's machine

- `$_FILES[yourfieldname][size]` – The size of the file, in bytes
- `$_FILES[yourfieldname][type]` – The MIME type, in this case image/gif, image/png, or image/jpg (if it was provided by the browser)

The image is stored in the temp directory specified in the php.ini file; if no temp directory is specified in php.ini, the operating system's default temporary directory is used.

The Paths and Directories category of php.ini controls many of the file-upload options.

Code Breakdown

In OO coding, good documentation is your best friend because, as has already been stated, it almost shouldn't matter how the classes you are using accomplish their tasks. You just need to know that they work.

PHPBuilder has an excellent article on software that can help document classes: `http://www.phpbuilder.com/columns/stefano20000824.php3`.

Objects in theory

For example, if we were to tell you about a class named `Product`, we could just tell you the following:

Class Product:

Inherits `CatalogBase`

Properties:

- `product_id`
- `product`
- `description`

Methods:

- `fetch_from_db`: Retrieve all data about this product from the database
- `write_to_db`: Write a new or updated product record to the database
- `delete_from_db`: Remove a product from the database
- `print`: Display a product to the browser

Knowing this information, and really nothing else, you could write a new script that displayed a product. The script that follows assumes that a `product_id` was passed through the querystring or via a `POST`.

```
$p = new Product(array('product_id'=>$product_id));
$p->fetch_from_db();
$p->print();
```

But if we left it at this, your learning experience would be only a fraction of what it should be. Of course, in the next section, we go over the code in depth. For one thing, in this application the display of an object is left to the user of the object – we use regular functions, rather than having a print method in each object.

Classes

We designed the classes in this application so that most of them look and behave similarly. As you look at the classes, you should notice that all but the `Base` class have methods with similar names. Our hope is that once you understand one class, the workings of the others will be pretty clear. For this reason, we're only going to break down two classes in this chapter. Note that the each method in each class is extensively commented on the CD. If you have a specific question as to the working of a snippet of code, you will likely find the answer within the comments.

In the following pages we break down code in the following classes: `Base` and `Product`. For the other classes we describe only how to use the methods and properties. But once you understand the `Product` class, the other classes should be easy enough to figure out.

Please be sure that you have mastered the concepts in Chapter 7 before reading this section.

Breaking the classes into includes also enables you to selectively reuse specific classes when you need them. This becomes important in Chapter 14, when we reuse some of these classes in creating the shopping cart.

PHP 5 also has a new feature that gives objects a bit of an advantage over functions. You can create a function named `__autoload ()` that PHP calls whenever you reference a class that you have not yet declared. This function can then include the file that declares that class. What this means is that you don't have to include a whole raft of class declarations just because you might use them in your script. Neither do you have to do the bug-prone work of spreading the `include` statements throughout your code. We use the `__autoload()` feature in these examples, but files that include the class definitions, like the preceding one, are included in a commented-out version as well – you can use them if you wish.

BASE

There is usually a base class on which your other classes are built (though it's not always named `Base`). In this application `Base` contains a set of utilities that all of the other classes make use of. The class is declared with the following statement:

```
class Base
{
```

Next you declare a couple of constants used by methods of the class. They're not exactly the most original or purposeful constants you'll ever see, but are mostly here as examples:

```
const ON = TRUE;
const OFF = FALSE;
```

Now on to the properties. Most of the classes are built to handle reading, writing, and manipulating data pertaining to a single table in a database. Those common functions are what the `Base` class is built to handle, and its properties show that:

```
var $table = NULL;
var $idfield = NULL;
var $id = NULL;
var $what = NULL;
var $fields = NULL;
var $appname = 'test';

var $error = NULL;
```

The properties are all assigned values of `NULL` in `Base` because it's up to each child class to fill them in with the values specific to the table it will be handling. For example, the `Product` class sets the `$table` property to `products` and the `$idfield` property to `property_id`.

The $appname property is typically set in the base class of an application – in this example, CatalogBase – because it's what you use to determine what database to use when connecting to MySQL.

__construct() In earlier versions of PHP a class's constructor method – the method that is run every time you instantiate a new object of that class – had to be given the same name as the class itself. In PHP 5 constructor methods can all be given the same name, __construct(). Here you are taking any arguments passed into the class in a new Classname() statement and handing them off to the build() method, and then setting up the $idfield and $id properties and connecting to the database:

```
function __construct()
{
    $args = func_get_args();
    call_user_func_array(array($this,'build'), $args);
    if (!empty($this->idfield))
    {
        $f = $this->idfield;
        $this->id =& $this->$f;
    }
    if ($this->table !== null)
        $this->dbh();
}
```

dbh() This method shows the use of static variables in methods. As with regular functions, a static variable retains its value from one call to the next. In the context of a class method, what that means is that two objects of the same class – or of classes that inherit the same class – make use of the same single static value. This makes good sense for something like a database connection, as shown in the following code. If you have four objects in your script, after all, they're all still talking to the same database (probably), and so they need only the one connection.

```
function dbh()
{
    static $dbh = NULL;
    if ($dbh === NULL)
    {
        $dbh = db_connect($this->appname);
        if ($dbh === NULL)          {
            user_error(
                'Received NULL db connection'
                , E_USER_ERROR
            );
```

```
            return FALSE;
        }
        $dbh->setFetchMode(DB_FETCHMODE_ASSOC);
    }
    return $dbh;
}
```

build() This method takes a list or array of arguments and uses them to set values for the properties of the object. We have a couple of points to make here:

- You can use built-in PHP functions to figure out what your objects' property names are at runtime, and use that information to pay attention only to incoming values that match those properties. This enables you do things like

  ```
  $product->build($_POST);
  $style->build($_POST);
  ```

  knowing that each object picks out from `$_POST` only the fields that it needs.

- You can check to see if your class has a method with the same name as the property you've been given a value for. If it does, you can hand that new value off to that method. This capability makes it easier to ensure that only legal values are assigned to an object's properties – that a `$quantity` property is never set to a negative number, for example.

```
function build()
{
    $args = func_get_args();
    if (count($args) == 0)
    {
        return;
    }
    $simple = array_keys(get_object_vars($this));
    $p = parse_arguments($args, $simple);
    $args = array_key_remove($p, $simple);
    foreach ($args as $k => $v)
    {
        if (method_exists($this, $k))
            call_user_func(array($this,$k),$v);
        else
            $this->$k = $v;
    }
}
```

fetch_simple_query() This method lives to be overwritten. The default is about as simple as the code here gets. Anticipating the ability of the database to substitute values into the text of a query, it just returns a query getting everything from a table to be named later. The purpose of the method is to allow child classes to substitute less simple queries in their place. Subsequent methods of the `Base` class can use these queries. Consider a common example: If you have a table that has multiple lookup values, like a `product_type_id` field, you can use a query that joins your main table with the lookup table and returns the appropriate `product_type` for storage in a property of the object:

```
function fetch_simple_query()
{
    return 'select * from !';
}
```

fetch_simple() Using this method is another step along the path to retrieving a record from the database and storing it in the object, but `fetch_simple()` can have other uses as well. The method requires a table name and optionally accepts a field name, a value, and an operator (usually just an equals sign). It runs the query supplied by `fetch_simple_query()` and returns the result. Normally the table name will be the value from the `$table` property of the object, but you can also call this method directly, on any table, querying the value of any single field. That lets you do something like

```
$result = $p->fetch_simple('products','product','S%','like');
```

to get a `DB` result handle for all of the rows in the products table wherein the product name begins with *s*. If nothing else, it saves typing.

Notice that you can use the result of the `dbh()` method as if it were a property. Because it returns an object of the `DB` class (one of `DB`'s subclasses, to be exact), it has its own properties and methods you can use, as shown in this example in which we populate an array with pieces of what will become (thanks to the `dbh()` function) a database query:

```
function fetch_simple($table,$idfield=NULL,$id=NULL,$op='=')
{
    $result = FALSE;
    $bind = array($table);
    $query = $this->fetch_simple_query();
    if ($idfield !== NULL)
    {
        $query .= ' where ! ! ?';
        $bind[] = $idfield;
        $bind[] = nullop($id,$op);
```

```
            $bind[] = $id;
        }
        $result = $this->dbh()->query($query,$bind);
        return $result;
    }
```

fetch_record() This method uses `fetch_simple()` to get a single record from a table in the database and return it:

```
    function fetch_record($table=NULL,$idfield=NULL,$id=NULL)
    {
        if (empty($table))
            $table = $this->table;
        if (empty($idfield))
            $idfield = $this->idfield;
        if (empty($id))
            $id = $this->id;
        $result = $this->fetch_simple($table,$idfield,$id);
        if (!$result)
        {
            return FALSE;
        }
        $row = $result->fetchRow();
        $result->free();
        return $row;
    }
```

fetch_from_db() Finally, we come to the method you'll see most frequently used in the actual child classes that work with a particular table. This method enables you to get the record corresponding to a supplied unique ID value, or the ID value already specified by the `$id` property of your object, and to assign the values from that record to the properties of your object using the building-block methods described in the beginning of the section on object-orientation in this chapter:

```
    function fetch_from_db($id=NULL)
    {
        if ($id !== NULL)
        {
            $this->id = $id;
        }
        $row = $this->fetch_record(
            $this->table
            , $this->idfield
            , $this->id
```

```
        );
        if (!$row)
            return FALSE;
        $this->build($row);
    }
```

fetch_all() This is just a shortcut method for getting all the records from a table that match a particular field value. In practice, using DB's `getAll()` method is about as easy.

```
    function fetch_all($table=NULL,$idfield=NULL,$id=NULL,$op='=')
    {
        if (empty($table)) { $table = $this->table; }
        $result = $this->fetch_simple($table,$idfield,$id,$op);
        if (!$result)
        {
            return FALSE;
        }
        $rows = array();
        while ($row = $result->fetchRow())
        {
            $rows[$row[$this->idfield]] = $row;
        }
        $result->free();
        return $rows;
    }
```

delete_from_db() This method deletes a record from the database:

```
    function delete_from_db($id=NULL)
    {
        if ($id === NULL)
        {
            $id = $this->id;
        }
        $result = $this->dbh()->query(
            'delete from ! where ! = ?'
            , array($this->table, $this->idfield, $id)
        );
        return $result;
    }
```

fieldlist() Now we begin building up to the other main purpose of a class, writing its values to the database. This method hands back a list of fields that, in theory, correspond to the fields of the table the object represents. If the list is not predefined – as it generally is – the method gets a list of fields from the database. (Note that this is a very MySQL-specific query in that it uses the MySQL reserved word `describe`.)

```
function fieldlist()
{
    if (is_array($this->fields) && count($this->fields) > 0)
    {
        return $this->fields;
    }
    if ($this->dbh() && $this->table)
    {           $this->fields = $this->dbh()->getCol(
            "describe {$this->table}"
        );
        return $this->fields;
    }
    return NULL;
}
```

data_fields() You might have a table with 25 fields defined, but use only three of them in a form. When you write the record out to the database you don't want to unwittingly change the other 22 fields. This method returns an associative array of field names and values built from the properties of the object, leaving out properties that are `NULL` or set to empty strings when the corresponding fields in the table are integers:

```
function data_fields()
{
    $fields = array();
    foreach ($this->fieldlist() as $f)
    {
        if (!isset($this->$f))
            continue;
        $v = $this->$f;
        if ($v === NULL)
            continue;
        if ($v === '' && strstr($f, '_id'))
            continue;
        $fields[$f] = $v;
    }
    return $fields;
}
```

create_record() This method inserts into the database a new record corresponding to the value stored in the properties of the object. It uses the PEAR `DB` class' `nextId()` function to get the next ID value for the table (rather than letting MySQL automatically assign it – though in practice PEAR itself is using MySQL's `auto_increment` feature to come up with the new ID value). Generating ID values is dead simple thanks to `DB`'s `autoPrepare()` method, which takes a table name and an array of column names and values and gives you back a fully-baked `insert` query.

```
function create_record()
{
    if ($this->what)
        $this->id = $this->dbh()->nextId($this->what);
    $data_fields = $this->data_fields();
    $stmt = $this->dbh()->autoPrepare(
        $this->table
        , array_keys($data_fields)
        , DB_AUTOQUERY_INSERT
    );
    $result = $this->dbh()->execute(
        $stmt
        , array_values($data_fields)
    );
    return $result;
}
```

update_record() This method updates the record in the database that corresponds to the current object, as indicated by the unique ID value in the `$id` property. Once again, `DB` makes it easy.

```
function update_record()
{
    $data_fields = $this->data_fields();
    $stmt = $this->dbh()->autoPrepare(
        $this->table
        , array_keys($data_fields)
        , DB_AUTOQUERY_UPDATE
        , '! = ? '
    );
    $bind = array_values($data_fields);
    $bind[] = $this->idfield;
    $bind[] = $this->id;
    $result = $this->dbh()->execute($stmt,$bind);
    return $result;
}
```

write_to_db() This method ties it all together, taking the values in the object and saving them to the database as a new record or as an update to an existing one:

```
function write_to_db()
{
    $args = func_get_args();
    call_user_func_array(array($this,'build'), $args);
    $result = FALSE;
    $this->id = $this->{$this->idfield};
    if ($this->id)
    {
        $result = $this->update_record();
    }
    else
    {
        $result = $this->create_record();
    }
    return $result;
}
```

legal_values() You frequently have tables, like status or product_type, that translate a unique ID value to an English word or phrase. This method makes it easy to use an inherited class built on such a table to get the name for a particular ID within a script (or vice versa). Note that it stores all the values from the object's table in a static variable in the method.

You wouldn't want to use this method with a million-record table, where you'd see a big performance problem. Ten is more like it. For large tables, you'll need to run individual queries for each validation.

```
function legal_values($id=NULL, $use_values=NULL)
{
    static $values = NULL;
    if ($use_values !== NULL)
        $values = $use_values;
    if ($values === NULL)
        $values = $this->fetch_all();
    if ($id !== NULL)
    {
        if (isset($values[$id]))
            return $values[$id];
```

```
            elseif (($value = array_search($id, $values)) !== FALSE)
                return $value;
            else
                return FALSE;
        }
        return $values;
    }
```

transaction() This method enables you to set up a multi-statement transaction that can span multiple method calls, even when each of those calls is itself normally a multi-statement transaction. Rather than directly issuing `begin` and `commit` queries to MySQL, the methods call the `transaction()` method (through a series of front methods, which we'll see in the next section), specifying what they want they want to do and how. If they want to begin a transaction, and one is already in progress, nothing happens; otherwise a transaction is begun. Similarly, if they want to commit a transaction that hasn't begun, nothing happens; otherwise the transaction is committed. If called for, a rollback is always performed immediately, of course.

```
    function transaction($what=NULL,$how=NULL)
    {
        static $states = array();
        static $state = NULL;

        if ($what === self::ON)
        {
            if ($state !== self::ON)
            {
                $this->dbh()->query('begin');
                $state = self::ON;
            }
            array_push($states, self::ON);
        }
        elseif ($what === self::OFF)
        {
            if ($how !== 'commit')
                $how = 'rollback';
            if ($how === 'rollback')
                $states = array();
            else
                array_pop($states);
            if ($state !== self::OFF && count($states) == 0)
            {
```

```
                $this->dbh()->query($how);
                $state = self::OFF;
            }
        }
        return $state;
    }
```

begin(), commit(), and rollback() These are the methods actually called by other methods in the child class. To prevent any more queries from being executed, the `rollback()` method issues a fatal error after rolling back the transaction.

```
    function begin()
    {
        self::transaction(self::ON);
    }

    function commit()
    {
        self::transaction(self::OFF,'commit');
    }

    function rollback($error=NULL)
    {
        self::transaction(self::OFF,'rollback');
        if ($error === NULL && isset($this) && isset($this->error))
            $error = $this->error;
        if ($error)
            user_error($error, E_USER_ERROR);
    }
```

PRODUCTS

Before we get started explaining this class, we want to restate that it is very similar to the other classes in this application. If you understand how this class works, the rest of the classes should be relatively easy to figure out.

__construct() This is the constructor of the class. It is very brief.

```
    function __construct()
    {
        parent::__construct();
        $args = func_get_args();
        call_user_func_array(array($this, 'build'), $args);
        $this->id =& $this->product_id;
    }
```

Note that this constructor runs if a Product object is instantiated within a script. But after the object is instantiated, the information associated with the `product_id` is not automatically loaded. The `fetch_from_db()` method, which you saw in the `Base` class, is needed for that.

price() You only want to store prices greater than zero. This method takes care of that. Remember that in the `Base` class's `build()` method, if your object has a method defined with the same name as an incoming property value, that new value is passed to the method rather than just being assigned to the property. So if you have a form with a field named `price`, it is submitted to your script with the `POST` method; when you call `$product->build($_POST)`, you end up calling `$product->price($_POST['price'])`.

```
function price($newprice=NULL)
{
    if ($newprice !== NULL)
        $this->price = $newprice;
    if ($this->price == 0)
        $this->price = NULL;
    return $this->price;
}
```

list_all_children() and list_children() These methods override methods of the `CatalogBase` class, the parent class of `Product` and itself a child class of the main `Base` class we looked at earlier. Here, we are overriding the parent class' methods to call an additional method of our own, `add_notes()` (described in the next section).

```
function list_all_children()
{
    parent::list_all_children();
    if (count($this->child_ids) > 0)
    {
        $this->add_notes(
            $this->all_children
            , array_keys($this->child_ids)
        );
    }
    return $this->all_children;
}

function list_children()
{
    parent::list_children();
```

```
        if (count($this->child_ids) > 0)
        {
            $this->add_notes(
                $this->children
                , array_keys($this->child_ids)
            );
        }
        return $this->children;
    }
```

add_notes() This method checks the database to see if any of the children of this product are mapped to a status other than "Available." If so, it adds a `notes` element to the array entry for those children describing that status (for example, "Not available in orange").

```
    function add_notes(&$kids,$ids)
    {
        if (empty($kids) or empty($ids))
            return;

        $query = 'select m.product_id, t.status, s.style
            from product_style_map m, styles s, status t
            where m.product_id in (!)
                and m.style_id = s.style_id
                and m.status_id in (?,?)
                and m.status_id = t.status_id'
        ;
        $stmt = $this->dbh()->prepare($query);
        $result = $this->dbh()->execute(
            $stmt
            , array(
                implode(',', $ids)
                , Product::NotAvailable
                , Product::OutOfStock
            )
        );
        $notes = array();
        while ($r = $result->fetchRow())
            $notes[$r['product_id']][$r['status']][] = $r['style'];
        $result->free();

        foreach ($kids as $i => $c)
        {
            $cnotes = array();
```

```
            if (isset($notes[$c['product_id']]))
            {
                foreach ($notes[$c['product_id']] as
                $status=>$styles)
                {
                    $cnotes[] = $status.' in '.implode(',',$styles);
                }
            }
            $c['notes'] = implode('; ', $cnotes);
            $kids[$i] = $c;
        }
        return;
    }
```

list_unmapped_styles() This method retrieves all root-level styles that are not mapped to the current product (or one of its parents). It is used in the administration page for the `Product` class to display a list of styles available to be mapped to the product.

```
    function list_unmapped_styles()
    {
        $query = 'select distinct s.style_id, s.parent_id
                , s.style, s.description, m.product_id as map_id
            from styles s
                left join product_style_map m
                on s.style_id = m.style_id and m.product_id in (!)
            where ifnull(s.parent_id,0) = 0
            having map_id is null'
        ;
        $stmt = $this->dbh()->prepare($query);
        $ids = $this->get_parent_ids();
        $ids[] = $this->product_id;
        $result=$this->dbh()-
        >execute($stmt,array(implode(',',$ids)));
        $styles = array();
        while ($row = $result->fetchRow())
        {
            unset($row['map_id']);
            $styles[] = $row;
        }
        $result->free();
        return $styles;
    }
```

list_mapped_styles() This method retrieves all the product-style mappings for the current product and its children, whether those mappings are explicitly stored in the database or are inherited. You use it by running a query against the style table, with a left join to the product_style_map table to get any mappings to the current product or one of its parents. If a style is not explicitly mapped to any of those products, the `product ID` field from the query (aliased to the column name map_product_id) will be null. When you come upon such a row as you walk through the results of the query, you check to see if there was an explicit mapping to the parent of the style. If there was, you copy the status from that mapping. Because you can't create a child record without having created its parent first, parent style ID values are always smaller than those of child IDs. By sorting by parent ID and then child ID, you know that you will run into the parents first – and so the records will be there for the child style to find.

```
function list_mapped_styles()
{
    $this->styles = array();
    $this->mapped_styles = array();
    $ids = $this->get_parent_ids();
    $ids[] = $this->product_id;
    $idlist = implode(',', $ids);
    $bind = array($idlist);

    // we could omit this part and the rest of this
    // function would still run correctly. but if you
    // had a large number of styles, only a few of which
    // applied to any one product line, you'd end up
    // throwing away more rows than you used. so let's
    // narrow the search down a bit by limiting it to
    // only descendants of root styles mapped to this
    // product or one of its parents

    $stylewhere = '';
    if ($this->product_id)
    {
        $style_ids = $this->dbh()->getCol(
            'select m.style_id from product_style_map m, styles
             s
            where m.product_id in (!) and m.style_id =
            s.style_id
            and ifnull(s.parent_id,0) = 0 '
            , 0
            , array($idlist)
        );
        $style_ids = $this->get_child_ids(
```

```
                'style_id'
                , 'styles'
                , $style_ids
            );
            if (count($style_ids) > 0)
            {
                $bind[] = implode(',', $style_ids);
                $stylewhere = 'where s.style_id in (!)';
            }
        }

        $query = <<<EOQ
select distinct s.style_id as id, s.style_id
    , ifnull(s.parent_id,0) as parent_id
    , s.style, s.description
    , m.product_id as map_product_id
    , m.status_id, m.price, m.price_type_id
from styles s
        left join product_style_map m
                on s.style_id = m.style_id
                and m.product_id in (!)
$stylewhere
order by parent_id, style_id, map_product_id
EOQ;
        $result = $this->dbh()->query($query, $bind);
        $values = array();

// what we want to end up with:
// values = array(
//  parent_id => array(style_id=>row,style_id=>row)
//   , parent_id => array(style_id=>row,style_id=>row)
// )
        while ($row = $result->fetchRow())
        {
            if (empty($row['map_product_id']))
            {
                // throw out unmapped root styles
                if ($row['parent_id'] == 0)
                    continue;

                // throw out children of unmapped parents
                if (!isset($this->styles[$row['parent_id']]))

                // inherit values from parent
                $prow = &$this->styles[$row['parent_id']];
```

```
                    $row['map_product_id'] = $prow['map_product_id'];
                    $row['price'] = $prow['price'];
                    $row['price_type_id'] = $prow['price_type_id'];
                    if ($prow['status_id'] == Product::NotAvailable
                    || $prow['status_id'] == Product::OutOfStock
                    || $prow['status_id'] == Product::ParentUnavailable
                    )
                    {
                        $row['status_id'] = Product::ParentUnavailable;
                    }
                    else
                    {
                        $row['status_id'] = Product::Inherited;
                    }
                }
                $values[$row['parent_id']][$row['id']] = $row;
                $this->styles[$row['style_id']] = $row;
            }
            $result->free();

            $this->mapped_styles = $this->sort_list($values);
            return $this->mapped_styles;
        }
```

write_to_db() This method overwrites the write_to_db() method from the Base class. It's derived from the multi-statement transaction methods defined in Base, because writing a product to the database means not just storing information about the product as a record in the products table, but also storing mappings of that product to a style or set of styles.

After setting empty numeric properties to NULL, this method calls the parent write_to_db() method to save the product record itself. It then deletes all existing mappings between the current product and any styles and recreates them based on the values in the $status_id property (which is an array passed in from a form).

```
    function write_to_db()
    {
        static $numeric_fields = array(
            'price','price_type_id','image_id','parent_id'
        );
        $this->dbh()->query('begin');
        foreach ($numeric_fields as $f)
        {
            if (empty($this->$f))
                $this->$f = NULL;
```

```
        }
        parent::write_to_db();
        $this->dbh()->query(
            'delete from product_style_map where product_id = ?'
            , array($this->product_id)
        );
        foreach ((array)$this->status_id as $style_id => $status_id)
        {
            $this->map_style($style_id,$status_id);
        }
        foreach ((array)$this->new_style_id as $nid)
        {
            $this->map_style($nid, Product::Available);
        }
        $this->dbh()->query('commit');
    }
```

MAP_STYLE() You saw this method called from the `write_to_db()` method. It does a simple insert into the product_style_map table, after checking that the status of the mapping is not one derived from a parent of the current product:

```
    function map_style($style_id=0,$status_id=Product::Available)
    {
        if (!$style_id)
        {
            return;
        }
        $this->dbh()->query(
            'insert into product_style_map
                (product_id,style_id,status_id)
                values (?,?,?)'
            , array($this->product_id,$style_id,$status_id)
        );
    }
```

IMG() This method creates an instance of the `CatalogImage` class and stores it in the `$img` property of the current object:

```
    function img()
    {
        if (!isset($this->img))
        {
            $this->img = new CatalogImage(array(
                'image_id'=>$this->image_id
```

```
            ));
        }
        return $this->img;
    }
```

upload() This method is a front end to the `upload()` method of the `CatalogImage` object created by the `img()` method. It passes on any arguments received to the image's `upload()` method, getting back the ID value of the new record created in the images table (if there is one), which it then stores in the `$image_id` property of the current product:

```
    function upload()
    {
        $args = func_get_args();
        $func = array($this->img(), 'upload');
        $image_id = call_user_func_array($func, $args);
        if ($image_id)
        {
            $this->image_id = $image_id;
        }
        return $image_id;
    }
```

thumbnail() This is another front end method to the `CatalogImage` object. It sets the `$alt` property of the image to the name of the current product, so that the `alt` attribute of the `<IMG>` tag, which will ultimately be returned, matches the product being displayed:

```
    function thumbnail($href=NULL)
    {
        $this->img()->check();
        $this->img()->alt = $this->product;
        return $this->img()->thumbnail($href=NULL);
    }
```

__get() and __call() These are special methods, called "overloading" methods. Their names are predefined by PHP. If you access an undefined property of an object, the `__get()` method is called. Similarly, accessing an undefined method causes `__call()` to be run. These methods enable you to use the properties and methods of the `CatalogImage` object directly, as if they were properties and methods of the Product object.

```
    function __get($property)
    {
        return $this->img()->$property;
```

```
}
function __call($method, $args)
{
    $img = $this->img();
    return call_user_func_array(array($img,$method),$args);
}
```

OTHER CLASSES

Now that you have seen one class in its entirety, and have a feel for how the data structures are created, it would be a waste of paper, as well as your time, to lay out all the other classes here. As we've said, they're designed to work similarly. If you understand one, you really understand all of them.

If you'd like more detail on any of the remaining classes, see the comments within the files on the CD.

In this section we're going to tell you what you need to know to make use of the remaining classes. (Note that the `Catalog` class was described earlier.)

Class Name:

`CatalogBase` – Extends `Base`

Default Properties:

- `$parents;`
- `$parent_ids;`
- `$children;`
- `$child_ids;`
- `$depth = 0;`
- `$appname = 'catalog';`

Methods:

- `get_parent` – Retrieves the parent record from the table specified in the `$table` property for the ID specified in the `$id` parameter. If it finds a parent record, it calls itself to get the parent of that record, walking back up the tree of ancestors until it comes to a root-level record (one where the `parent_id` field is zero or `NULL`). The record is then stored in the `$parent_ids` property, indexed by ID value, and returned. The result is a sequential list of parent records in inheritance order.

- `list_parents` – Calls `get_parent()` on the current record and stores the result in the `$parents` property. Also sets the `$depth` property to reflect how far down the current record is (for example, a depth of zero means this is a root-level record, a depth of two means this is the child of a child of a root-level record, and so on).
- `get_parent_ids` – Returns the ID values of the parent records retrieved by `list_parents()`.
- `get_child_ids` – A similar method to `get_parent`, except in the other direction. This method gets the ID values of all the records descended from the current one and returns them as an array.
- `get_child` – Gets descendant records (as opposed to just ID values) of the current record. Optionally stops at a specified maximum depth – for example, setting a maximum depth of zero results in the retrieval of only the first generation of child records.
- `list_children` – Calls `get_child`, limiting the result to the immediate children of the current record.
- `list_all_children` – Calls `get_child` with no maximum depth, retrieving all descendant records of the current record.
- `sort_list` – Turns a nested associative array into a flat list, setting a `depth` element in each record to indicate how far into the original array's nesting it was found.

Class Name:

`CatalogImage` – Extends `Image`

Default Properties:

- `$table = 'images';`
- `$idfield = 'image_id';`
- `$what = 'image';`
- `$fields = array('image_id','image','width','height','alt');`
- `$id = NULL;`

- `$image_id = NULL;`
- `$appname = 'catalog';`
- `$src_dir = '/book/catalog/images';`

Methods:

- `__construct` – Sets the `$file_dir` property (inherited from `Image`) to the full file system path of the /images directory of the Catalog application. It then calls the `__construct` and `build` methods of its parent classes and sets the `$id` property as a reference to the `$image_id` property.
- `upload` – Calls the `upload()` method of the `Image` class, with a default field name of `imagefile`. If the upload succeeds, the `upload()` method writes itself to the images table in the database and returns the ID value of the database record.
- `check` – Fetches information from the database for the current image and then calls the `check()` method of the parent `Image` class.

Class Name:

`Style` – Extends `CatalogBase`

Default Properties:

- `$table = 'styles';`
- `$idfield = 'style_id';`
- `$what = 'style';`
- `$fields = array('style_id','parent_id','style','description');`
- `$id = 0;`
- `$style_id = 0;`
- `$parent_id = 0;`
- `$style = '';`
- `$description = '';`
- `$price = NULL;`
- `$price_type_id = NULL;`

Methods:

- __construct – Calls the __construct and build methods of the parent CatalogBase and Base classes, and then sets the $id property as a reference to the $style_id property.

Sample script

Now that you understand the classes available, we show you how they are put to work in one of the scripts. We give you a look at display.php. This page is looking for a product ID value to be passed in. If none is given, it displays some default values for the main page of the catalog.

```
<?php
require_once('header.php');

// if no product_id value is supplied, display the main page
// of the catalog
$product_id = (int)array_key_value($_REQUEST,'product_id',0);
$p = new Product(array('product_id'=>$product_id));

if (empty($p->product_id))
{
    $p->description = <<<EOT
Here at Bag'O'Stuff, we've got so much stuff
we don't know what to do with it. So buy some
and help us clear out some space.
EOT;
    $p->subproduct_title = "What've We Got?";
    $page_title = "Bag'o'Stuff";
}
```

If you do get a product ID, you retrieve it from the database. You are going to be using breadcrumbs for navigation, so you use the list_products() method to get the list of parent products above the current one and convert the list of parent products into a series of anchor tags.

```
else
{
    $p->fetch_from_db();
    // begin constructing the page title with a link to the main
page
    // of the catalog

    // add a link back to the product level to the page title,
```

```
    // followed by the name of this product, and print out the
    // top of the page

    $titlebits = array(anchor_tag('index.php', "Bag'O'Stuff"));
    foreach ($p->list_parents() as $t)
    {
        $titlebits[] = anchor_tag(
            'display.php?product_id='.$t['product_id']
            , $t['product']
        );
    }
    $page_title = implode(' > ', $titlebits);
}
print start_page($page_title);
```

Then all you do is hand off the Product object to the `print_product()` function and call the usual `end_page()` function, and the page is ready to go:

```
// print out information about this product, and any styles and
// substyles it contains
print_product($p);

// print out the bottom of the page
print end_page();

?>
```

Now we want to take a look at the `print_product()` function and the functions it uses to display the product.

print_product()

This function does only a few things. It prints out a description of the product, including a thumbnail image if one exists. Then it prints out the available styles for the product and any child products, using the other two main display functions of the application.

```
function print_product($p)
{
    $image_tag = $p->thumbnail();
    if (!empty($image_tag))
    {
        // if an image has been uploaded for the product,
        // include the thumbnail version of the image,
        // displayed as a link to the full-size version.
```

```
        $image_tag = anchor_tag($p->img->src, $image_tag);
    }
    print paragraph('<b>'.$p->product.'</b>');
    print paragraph($image_tag, nl2br($p->description));

    print_styles($p);

    print_children($p);
}
```

print_styles()

This function is a lot longer than `print_product()`, but really, not that much more is going on here. Mostly what it's doing is building up an array of the styles that apply to the product, in such a way that you can turn that array into an HTML table on the page. If a style is marked as "Not available," you don't even mention it. If it's only "Out of stock," you want people to know that you'll have it eventually, so you go ahead and display it, with a warning flag. The result looks something like this:

Colors	Red, Blue, Green, Yellow, Orange, Black, White, Tie-Dye	
Sizes	Men's	Peewee, Junior, Medium, Large, Husky (Out of stock)
	Women's	Petite, Small, Medium, Large

```
function print_styles(&$p)
{
    $styles = $p->list_mapped_styles();

    $style_table = array();
    $row = 0;
    $last_depth = 0;
    $max_depth = 0;
    foreach ($styles as $s)
    {
        $style = $s['style'];
        if ($s['status_id'] == Product::NotAvailable)
            continue;
        if ($s['status_id'] == Product::OutOfStock)
            $style .= ' <b style="color:red">(Out of Stock)</b>';
        settype($s['depth'], 'int');
        if ($s['depth'] < $last_depth)        {
            $row++;
            for ($cell = 0; $cell < $s['depth']; $cell++)
                $style_table[$row][$cell] = '';
        }
        $last_depth = $s['depth'];
```

```
        $style_table[$row][$last_depth][] = $style;
        $max_depth = max($last_depth, $max_depth);
    }
    foreach ($style_table as $r => $cells)
    {
        $i = 0;
        foreach ($cells as $k => $v)
        {
            if (is_array($v))
                $v = implode(', ', $v);
            if ($k == 0 && $v != '')
                $v = "<b>$v</b>";
            $style_table[$r][$k] = $v;
            $i = $k;
        }
        if ($i < $max_depth)
        {
            $style_table[$r][$i] = table_cell(array(
                'value'=>$style_table[$r][$i]
                , 'colspan'=>(($max_depth - $i)+1)
            ));
        }
    }
    print paragraph(table(array(
        'rows' => $style_table
        , 'border' => 0
        , 'cellpadding' => 3
    )));
}
```

print_children()

This function is similar to `print_styles()`. It displays the list of immediate child products of the current product, with each product name displayed as a link to display.php for more detailed information about that product:

```
function print_children(&$p)
{
    $child_price_count = 0;
    $child_rows = array();
    $children = $p->list_children();
    if (count($children) > 0)
    {
        $child_url = 'display.php?product_id=';
        foreach ($children as $c)
        {
```

```
            if ((int)$c['price'] > 0 && $c['price'] != $p->price)
                $child_price = $c['price'];
            else
                $child_price = ' ';
            if (!empty($c['description'])
                 && $c['description'] != $p->description
)
            {
                $child_description = nl2br($c['description']);
            }
            else
            {
                $child_description = '';
            }
            if (!empty($c['notes']))
            {
    $child_description .= " <b
style='color:red'>({$c['notes']})</b>";
            }
            $child_rows[] = table_row(
                anchor_tag(
                    $child_url.$c['product_id'], $c['product']
                )
                , $child_price
                , $child_description
            );
        }
    }

    if (!$child_price_count)
    {
        // if no child of this product has its own separate price,
        // print out the product's price now, and set the title of
        // the price column to blank. (this will make that column
        // essentially invisible.)
        if ((int)$p->price > 0)
        {
            print paragraph('<b>Price:</b> '.$p->price);
        }
        $price_label = ' ';
    }
    else
    {
        $price_label = '<b>Price</b>';
    }
```

```
    if (count($child_rows) > 0)
    {
        // print out products belonging to this product
        array_unshift(
            $child_rows
            , table_row('<b>Product</b>'
                , $price_label
                , '<b>Details</b>'
            )
        );
        print paragraph(
            table(array('rows'=>$child_rows,'border'=>0))
        );
    }
}
```

Summary

You might have found this chapter to be quite a handful. In addition to adding code for file uploads, we have used a completely different method for the organization of the code.

The object-oriented approach used in this chapter might not be your cup of tea. And if it's not, you're in good company. Many people who work with PHP feel that object-oriented programming makes little sense in a Web-development environment. But it has its advantages. And the object model in the new version of PHP is greatly enhanced over that of previous versions, too.

As you can see in this application, once the classes are created you don't need to do much to get great functionality within your scripts. Further, in Chapter 14, you can see how we take the code created here and build on it.

Chapter 13

Problem-Tracking System

IN THIS CHAPTER

- Designing a problem-tracking system
- Protecting yourself from redundant data
- Using the `IntegratedTemplate` class from the PEAR class libraries
- Creating a site that has both public and private portions

GOT PROBLEMS? Don't worry, we've all got problems. Relationships falter, bosses make capricious demands, and family – oh, we all know about family. Sadly, in the crazy lives that we all live, PHP and MySQL can do nothing to make your girl/boyfriend love you more or make your dealings with your parents or in-laws any easier. But no scripting language or relational database is better equipped in these areas.

But if you're working for a company that sells or otherwise dispenses goods, it is a virtual guarantee that someone somewhere is going to be unhappy with what he or she has received. When that person complains, you are going to want to have a place in which to record the problems and the steps required for resolution.

The problem-tracking application in this chapter can be used for that purpose. What we have here is fairly generic, and depending on the goods involved with your business, it is likely that you are going to want some fields that apply to your specific products. Anyhow, this application should get you moving in the right direction.

Determining the Scope and Goals of the Application

This problem-tracking system should have aspects that are publicly available and others that only someone with the proper authorization can view. It makes sense to have a form that users can access over the Web in order to report their problems. Alternatively, someone on the support staff should be able to report problems – for example, while taking a phone call from a dissatisfied customer.

Once the problem is entered, it should be tracked by the staff. Each action taken in the attempt to solve the problem should be noted. And the tracking should have a public and a private realm – actions that you want the user to see must be differentiated from those that you do not want the user to see.

Those with problems should be able to keep track of them in two ways. They should be emailed whenever a publicly viewable update is made to their case, and a Web page detailing their problem should be available.

What do you need?

The first thing you need is a form into which people can enter their complaints. What we present in Figure 13-1 is fairly generic; remember that for your own applications you will probably want to add information regarding specific products.

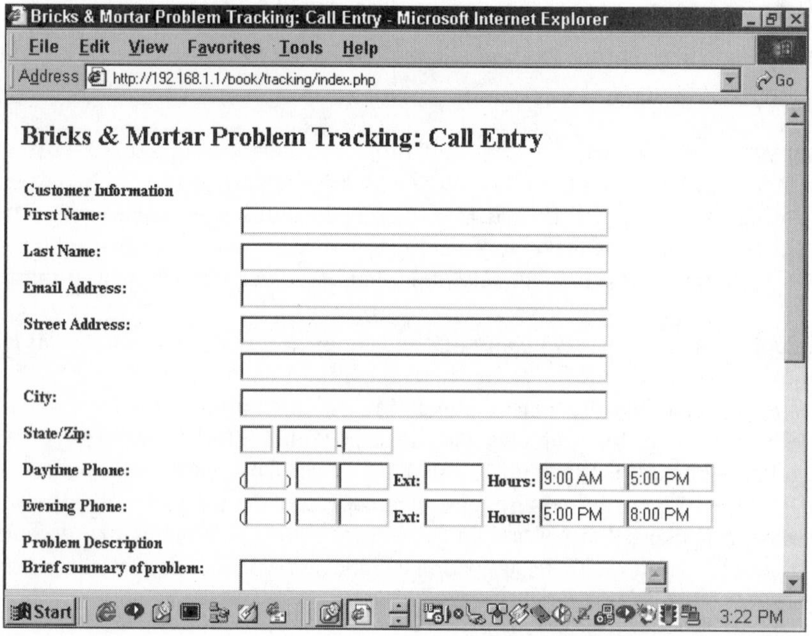

Figure 13-1: Problem entry form

Once a problem is entered, there must be a place for the staff to work on the complaint. It should include all the information about the user, the history of the complaint, and a place to enter new information. This problem-update form would look something like the one in Figure 13-2.

The support-staff members need a home, a place where they can log in and see both unassigned tasks and those that are assigned to them and are still open. The staff page would look something like the one in Figure 13-3.

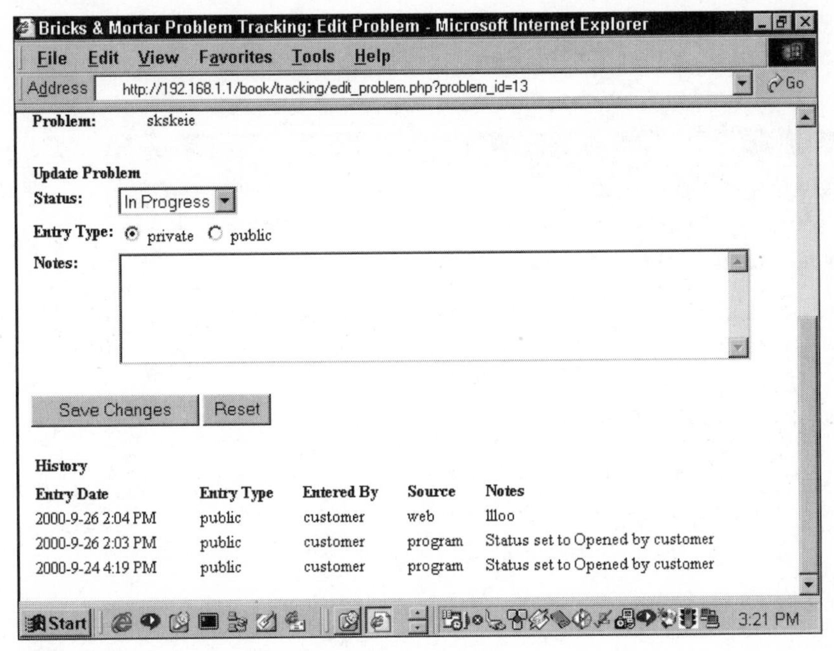

Figure 13-2: Problem update form

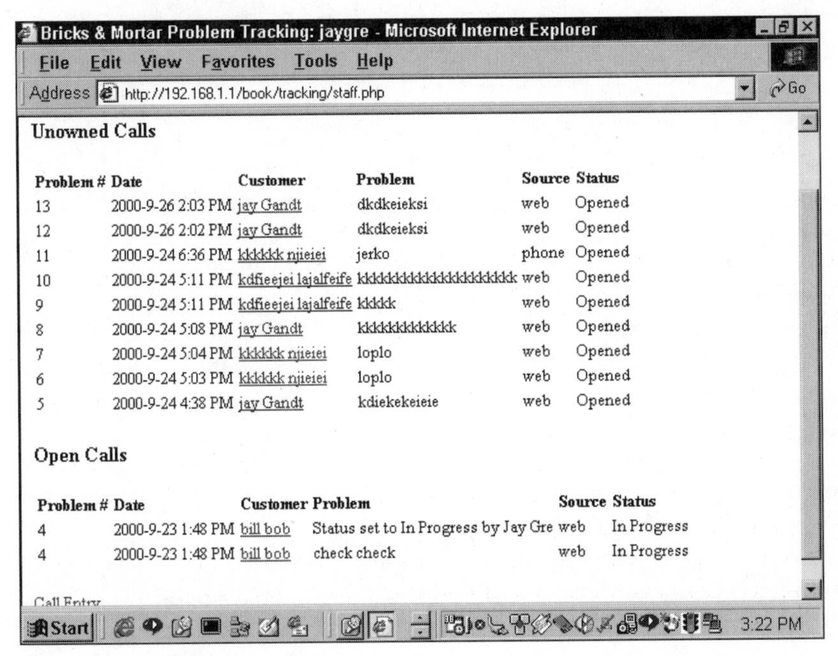

Figure 13-3: Staff page

If you want to see if any of your users are hypochondriacs, you can use the user-history page shown in Figure 13-4, which lists all problems associated with a user.

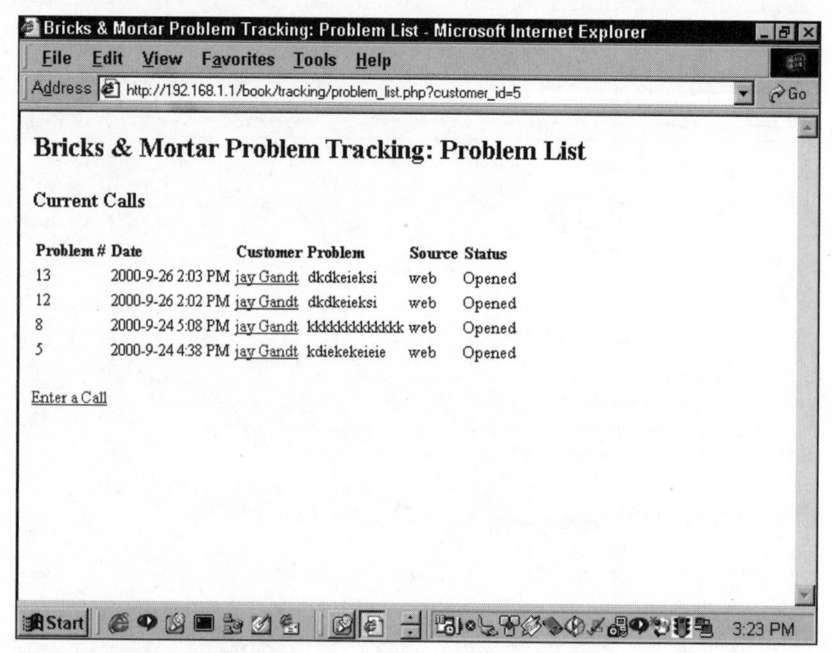

Figure 13-4: User history page

What do you need to prevent?

In setting up this part of the application, you're concerned with gathering information efficiently and in a way that's pleasant for the user. Therefore, your worries are more of an interface-design nature, and thus more in the realm of Web design than application development.

Developers, though, are concerned with making sure that the data collected is valid, and complies with database limitations. You might want to endow your forms with some client-side scripting that checks values for obvious problems before sending them in.

Designing the Database

As you can see from Figure 13-5, the problems table is at the center of the schema.

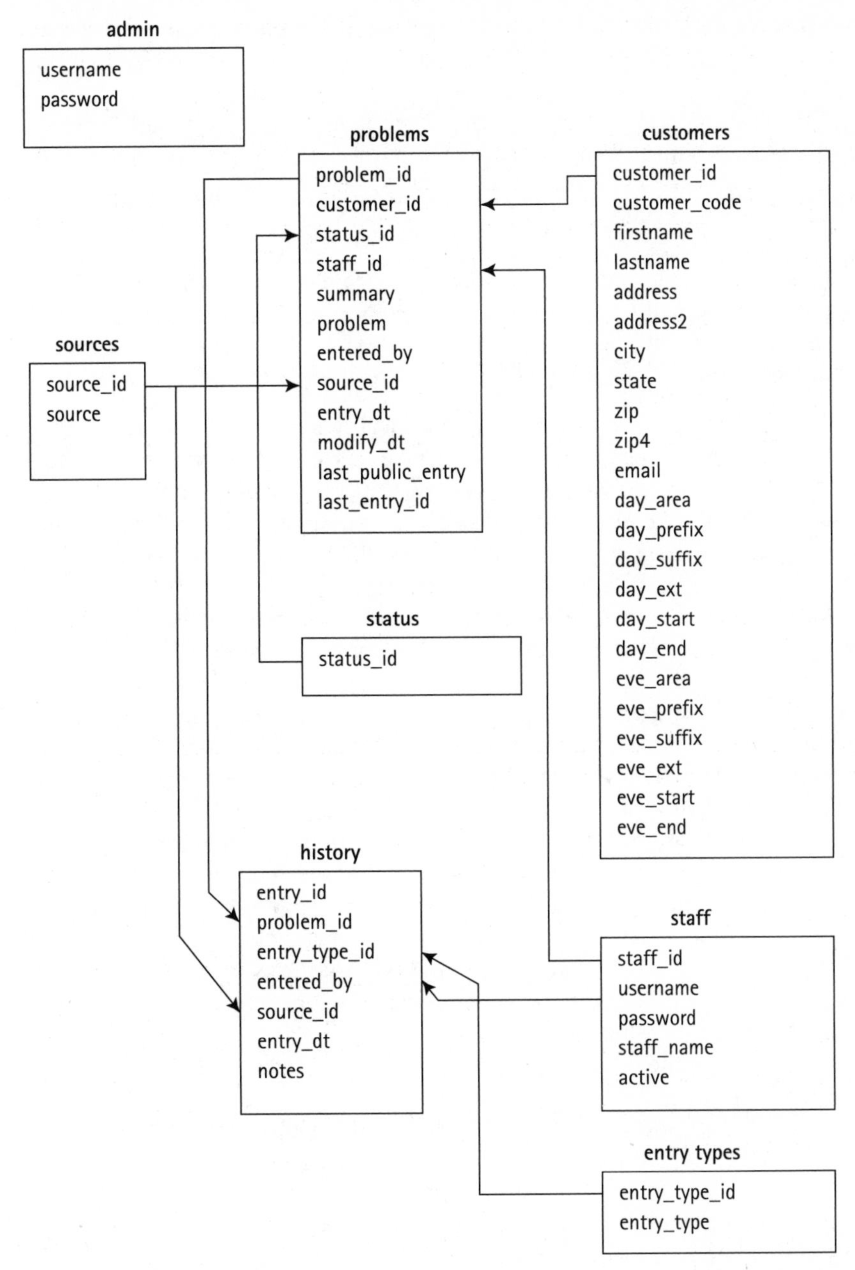

Figure 13-5: Tracking system schema

Here are some design considerations we had to keep in mind as we designed our database:

- Each customer can have one or many problems. The history table records the steps taken to remedy the problem or problems.
- The status table is a lookup table, containing the possible states of a problem, notably *open*, *closed*, *in processing*, and so on.
- The sources table is another lookup table, which records where the problem was originally recorded. If a user enters a complaint over the Web, the sources table will record that; complaints received by the support staff might originate from a phone call, email, or flaming arrow.
- The entry_types table notes whether a specific item in the history table should be public or private. If it is private, it will not be available on the Web page when the user comes to view the progress of the problem, and an email will not be sent to the user when an update takes place. The public updates will be viewable and the user will receive email notification.

Now for a couple of notes on this schema and the `create` statements that follow. Depending on how you plan on running your site, you may wish to add a table or change a column definition or two.

Notice that we have a `problem_code` column in the problems table. However, if you will be emailing users regarding the status of problems, you may want something a little less transparent than the following: `http://yoursite.com/tracking/problems.php?problem_id=7`.

In Chapter 9 we take some precautions when we run into a similar situation. We didn't want people to gain access to restricted parts of our data simply by guessing at variable names in the URL. Here we adopt the same technique we used there in the survey application, creating a random 8-character alphanumeric string from the `md5()` and `uniqueid()` functions. It's true that we run a risk of the same random number coming up twice, and in fact this approach might not be right for a very large application. But it works here.

Listing 13-1 shows the `create` statements for the tables we used in this application. In addition to the `create` statements, this listing includes some of the default data you will need to start the application. Note that if you install this application from the CD-ROM you will have a full set of dummy data you can play with.

Listing 13-1: create Statements Used in the Problem-Tracking System

```
drop table if exists status;
create table status
(
    status_id   tinyint not null auto_increment
    , status        varchar(20) not null
, primary key (status_id)
```

```
)
type=InnoDB
;
insert into status (status) values ('Opened');
insert into status (status) values ('In Progress');
insert into status (status) values ('Closed');
insert into status (status) values ('Re-opened');
drop table if exists status_seq;
create table status_seq
(
  id tinyint not null auto_increment
, primary key (id)
)
type=InnoDB
;
insert into status_seq (id) select max(status_id)+1 from status;
drop table if exists sources;
create table sources
(
    source_id   tinyint not null auto_increment
    , source        varchar(10) not null
, primary key (source_id)
)
type=InnoDB
;
insert into sources (source) values ('web');
insert into sources (source) values ('email');
insert into sources (source) values ('phone');
insert into sources (source) values ('in-store');
insert into sources (source) values ('staff');
insert into sources (source) values ('program');
drop table if exists source_seq;
create table source_seq
(
  id int not null auto_increment
, primary key (id)
)
type=InnoDB
;
insert into source_seq (id) select max(source_id)+1 from sources;
drop table if exists entry_types;
create table entry_types
(
```

Continued

Listing 13-1 *(Continued)*

```
    entry_type_id   tinyint not null auto_increment
    , entry_type    varchar(10) not null
, primary key (entry_type_id)
)
type=InnoDB
;
insert into entry_types (entry_type) values ('private');
insert into entry_types (entry_type) values ('public');

drop table if exists entry_type_seq;
create table entry_type_seq
(
  id tinyint not null auto_increment
, primary key (id)
)
type=InnoDB
;
insert into entry_type_seq (id) select max(entry_type_id)+1 from
entry_types;


drop table if exists staff;
create table staff
(
    staff_id        int not null auto_increment
    , username      varchar(20) not null
    , password      varchar(255) not null
    , staff_name    varchar(50) not null
    , active        tinyint default 1
, primary key (staff_id)
, unique (username)
)
type=InnoDB
;
insert into staff (username,password,staff_name) values
('fred',password('fred'),'Fred Flintstone')
, ('barney',password('barney'),'Barney Rubble')
;

drop table if exists staff_seq;
create table staff_seq
(
    id  int not null auto_increment
```

```
, primary key (id)
)
type=InnoDB
;
insert into staff_seq (id) select max(staff_id)+1 from staff;

drop table if exists customers;
create table customers
(
    customer_id     integer not null auto_increment
    , customer_code varchar(8)
    , firstname     varchar(40)
    , lastname      varchar(40)
    , address       varchar(40)
    , address2      varchar(40)
    , city          varchar(20)
    , state         char(2)
    , zip           char(5)
    , zip4          char(5)
    , email         varchar(255)
    , day_area      char(3)
    , day_prefix    char(3)
    , day_suffix    char(4)
    , day_ext       char(5)
    , day_start     char(8)
    , day_end       char(8)
    , eve_area      char(3)
    , eve_prefix    char(3)
    , eve_suffix    char(4)
    , eve_ext       char(5)
    , eve_start     char(8)
    , eve_end       char(8)
, primary key (customer_id)
)
type=InnoDB
;

drop table if exists customer_seq;
create table customer_seq
(
  id int not null auto_increment
, primary key (id)
)
```

Continued

Listing 13-1 *(Continued)*

```
type=InnoDB
;

drop table if exists problems;
create table problems
(
    problem_id       integer not null auto_increment
    , customer_id    integer not null
    , problem_code   char(8) not null
    , status_id      tinyint null
    , staff_id       integer null
    , summary        text
    , problem        text
    , entered_by     varchar(20) null
    , source_id      tinyint null
    , entry_dt       datetime
    , modify_dt      timestamp
    , last_public_entry_id  int null
    , last_entry_id int null
, primary key (problem_id)
, key (customer_id)
, foreign key (customer_id) references customers (customer_id) on
delete cascade
, key (status_id)
, foreign key (status_id) references status (status_id) on delete
set null
, key (source_id)
, foreign key (source_id) references sources (source_id) on delete
set null
, key (staff_id)
, foreign key (staff_id) references staff (staff_id) on delete set
null
, unique (problem_code)
)
type=InnoDB
;
drop table if exists problem_seq;
create table problem_seq
(
  id int not null auto_increment
, primary key (id)
)
type=InnoDB
```

```
;

drop table if exists history;
create table history
(
    entry_id        integer not null auto_increment
    , problem_id    integer not null
    , entry_type_id tinyint not null
    , entered_by    varchar(20) null
    , source_id     tinyint not null
    , entry_dt      timestamp
    , notes         text
, primary key (entry_id)
, key (problem_id), foreign key (problem_id) references problems
(problem_id) on delete cascade
, key (entry_type_id), foreign key (entry_type_id) references
entry_types (entry_type_id) on delete cascade
, key (source_id), foreign key (source_id) references sources
(source_id) on delete cascade
)
type=InnoDB
;
drop table if exists history_seq;
create table history_seq
(
  id int not null auto_increment
, primary key (id)
)
type=InnoDB
;
drop table if exists admin;
create table admin
(
    username    varchar(50) not null
    , password  varchar(255) not null
, primary key (username)
)
type=InnoDB
;
insert into admin values ('jay',password('rules'));

delete from mysql.db where Db = 'tracking';
```

Continued

Listing 13-1 *(Continued)*

```
grant delete, insert, select, update
    on tracking.*
    to nobody@localhost identified by 'ydobon'
;

flush privileges;
```

Code Overview

The only really new part of this example is that it uses the PEAR `Integrated Template` class. Templates are a common and useful way to separate an application's code from its design. Since these are frequently built by two different sets of people, working on different schedules, keeping these two parts of your application (not to mention the designers and the coders) at a distance from each other can make your life a lot easier. Plus, looking ahead, a site's design is something that is going to change much more frequently than its basic functionality, so maintenance becomes easier as well.

The idea behind a template is pretty easy to pick up. In one file you write all the HTML for a page (or part of a page – such as the navigational elements). Elements of the page that will be filled in with data from a database, or with values resulting from a calculation like "Total Amount Due," are represented by some kind of standardized placeholder, like so:

```
<tr>
<td><b>Total Amount Due:</b></td>
<td align="right"><b>{total_due}</b></td>
</tr>
```

We've picked the simplest templating system readily available, the `IntegratedTemplate` (or IT) class from PEAR. It looks just like the preceding example, shockingly enough, and also has some capacity for loops so you can repeat part of a template, like a row in a parts table, as many times as you have rows of data to fill it. There are lots of other, more advanced and complicated templating systems out there. Try changing this example around some until you get frustrated at not being able to do something – that's how you'll know what to look for.

You'll find `IntegratedTemplate` and its documentation here:

`http://pear.php.net/package-info.php?pacid=108.`

If IT isn't to your liking, you may want to investigate FastTemplate and Smarty, two other template engines.

Code Breakdown

This application makes more liberal use of includes than some of the previous ones you have seen. It contains a couple of very long forms that could really clutter up a page. They have been pushed off to templates.

Reusable functions from /book/tracking/ functions.php

The base function set, described in Chapter 9, will be used here once again. The first few of these functions are for convenience. The ones a little further down do some pretty heavy and cool work.

fetch_staff()

If you've looked at some of the other applications in this book, this type of function should be clear. Basically, this function takes a series of parameters that it uses to modify a generic `SELECT` query that's run against the staff table. If no parameters are sent to this function, the most basic `SELECT` is run:

```
SELECT * FROM staff;
```

If arguments exist, the code uses them to modify the `SELECT` statement. It employs a bit of intelligence here. If the arguments are numeric – the function uses `is_numeric` to figure this out – the code adjusts the `SELECT` statement to examine the `staff_id` field, like this:

```
SELECT * FROM staff; WHERE staff_id LIKE argument_value;
```

Alternatively, if the argument is a string (`is_string` comes into play for the job) the `SELECT` statement looks at the `username` field. For example:

```
SELECT * FROM staff; WHERE username LIKE argument_value;
```

Here's the full function.

```
function fetch_staff()
{
    $params = func_get_args();
    $wheres = array();
    $bind = array();
    foreach ($params as $arg)
    {
        if (is_string($arg))
        {
```

```
            $wheres[] = ' username like ? ';
            $bind[] = $arg;
        }
        elseif (is_numeric($arg))
        {
            $wheres[] = ' staff_id like ? ';
            $bind[] = $arg;
        }
        else
        {
            user_error(
                'Invalid argument to fetch_staff()
:'.var_export($arg,TRUE)
                , E_USER_NOTICE
            );
        }
    }
    $query = 'select * from staff ';
    if (count($wheres) > 0)
    {
        $query .= ' where '.implode(' or ', $wheres);
    }
    $result = db_connect()->getAll($query, $bind,
DB_FETCHMODE_ASSOC);
    if (is_array($result) && count($result) == 1)
    {
        $result = array_shift($result);
    }
    return $result;
}
```

fetch_customer()

This function works very much like `fetch_staff()`, except that there's no need to determine whether the argument is a string or a numeric value. Because we are building the query based on named parameters from the `$params` argument, we can look explicitly for the column values we need. So if we've been given a customer ID value, we use that. If not, we check for a customer code string, and if we have one, use that. If we don't have values for either of these columns, then we can't run the query, and we just error out of the function. DB lets us supply the column name we're using as a parameter by using the ! token character in its place in the query.

Here's the full function.

```
function fetch_customer(&$params)
{
    $query = 'select * from customers where ! = ?';
```

```
    if (!empty($params['customer_id']))
    {
        $bind = array('customer_id', (int)$params['customer_id']);
    }
    elseif (!empty($params['customer_code']))
    {
        $bind = array('customer_code', $params['customer_code']);
    }
    else
    {
        user_error(
            'Could not fetch customer - no ID or code specified'
            , E_USER_ERROR
        );
        return FALSE;
    }
    $dbh = db_connect();
    $record = $dbh->getRow($query, $bind, DB_FETCHMODE_ASSOC);
    if ($record === FALSE)
    {
        $private_error = 'fetch_customer: error in query: '
            . $dbh->last_query
        ;
        user_error(
            'Could not fetch customer from database'
            , E_USER_ERROR
        );
        return FALSE;
    }
    $params = array_merge($params, $record);
    return TRUE;
}
```

fetch_problem()

The difference between `fetch_problem()` and `fetch_customer()` is at the end of the function. When you get a problem from the database, you want more than the problem record itself. You want information about the customer who has the problem, and about the history of our work on the problem to date. So in addition to the usual query against the problems table, `fetch_problem()` also runs the `fetch_customer()` and `fetch_history()` functions. Here's the code:

```
function fetch_problem(&$params)
{
  $query = 'select * from problems where ! = ?';
  if (!empty($params['problem_id']))
```

```
    {
      $bind = array('problem_id', $params['problem_id']);
    }
    elseif (!empty($params['problem_code']))
    {
      $bind = array('problem_code', $params['problem_code']);
    }
    else
    {
      user_error(
        'Could not fetch problem: no ID or code specified'
        , E_USER_ERROR
      );
      return FALSE;
    }

    $dbh = db_connect();

    $record = $dbh->getRow($query, $bind, DB_FETCHMODE_ASSOC);
    if (!$record)
    {
      $private_error = 'fetch_problem: error with query: '
        . $dbh->last_query
      ;
      user_error(
        'Could not fetch problem from database'
        , E_USER_ERROR
      );
      return FALSE;
    }
    $params = array_merge($params, $record);
    if (empty($params['source']) && !empty($params['source_id']))
    {
      $params['source'] = source($params['source_id']);
    }

    if (!fetch_customer($params) or !fetch_history($params))
    {
      return FALSE;
    }

    return TRUE;
}
```

find_customer()

Remember that you would like to enable users to report their problems over the Web. In this application, we've decided that while a numeric primary key exists for each user, the application should be able to identify the user by either a phone number or an email address. So when a user enters information, you will need to check if someone with an identical email address or phone number has come along.

```
function find_customer($email=""
    ,$day_area='',$day_prefix='',$day_suffix=''
    ,$eve_area='',$eve_prefix='',$eve_suffix=''
)
{
    $wheres = array();
    $bind = array();
    if ($day_prefix != '')
    {
        // there must be a prefix for this to be a valid phone
number
        $wheres[] = '(day_area like ? and day_prefix like ? and
day_suffix like ?)';
        $bind[] = $day_area;
        $bind[] = $day_prefix;
        $bind[] = $day_suffix;
    }
    if ($eve_prefix != '')
    {
        // there must be a prefix for this to be a valid phone
number
        $wheres[] = '(eve_area like ? and eve_prefix like ? and
eve_suffix like ?)';
        $bind[] = $eve_area;
        $bind[] = $eve_prefix;
        $bind[] = $eve_suffix;
    }
    if ($email != '')
    {
        $wheres[] = '(email like ?)';
        $bind[] = $email;
    }
    if (count($wheres) == 0)
    {
        // nothing to look for
        user_error(
            'find_customer: no wheres supplied'
```

```
            , E_USER_NOTICE
        );
        return FALSE;
    }

    // run a query with the constructed qualification
    // and return the result.
    // separate each part of the qualification with OR -
    // any part constitutes a valid match.
    $query = 'select * from customers where '
        .  implode(' or ', $wheres)
        . ' order by customer_id '
    ;
    $results = db_connect()->getAll($query, $bind,
DB_FETCHMODE_ASSOC);
    return $results;
}
```

With this function you will know if the user has an existing record that can be used or that might need to be updated. Figure 13-6 shows the form for updating customer data.

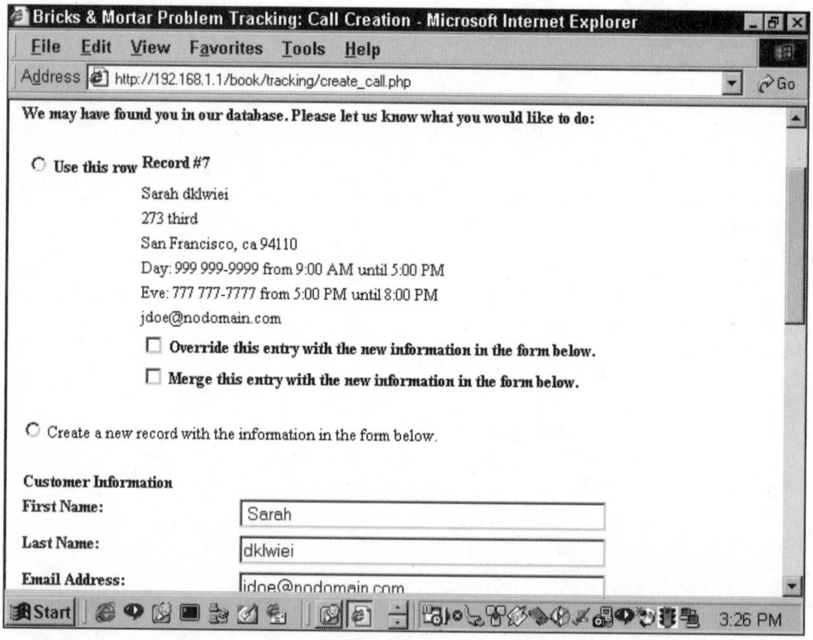

Figure 13-6: Form for updating customer information

If you are interested, you can set a cookie to make identifying the user a bit easier.

history_entry()

When a staff member enters an update on a problem, the step is stored in the history table. If the entry is public the user will be informed of the update by email; if not, no email will be sent.

```
function history_entry($problem_id=NULL
    , $entry_type_id=NULL
    , $entered_by=NULL
    , $source=NULL
    , $notes=NULL
)
{
    if (empty($problem_id))
    {
        user_error('Error: no problem ID for history entry',
E_USER_ERROR);
        return FALSE;
    }

    if (empty($entered_by)) { $entered_by = 'customer'; }

    $entry_type = entry_type($entry_type_id);
    $source_id = source_id($source);

    // create a record in the history table

    $dbh = db_connect();
    $entry_id = $dbh->nextId('history');
    $query = 'insert into history

(entry_id,problem_id,entry_type_id,entered_by,source_id,notes)
        values (?,?,?,?,?,?)
    ';
    $bind = array($entry_id,$problem_id,$entry_type_id,$entered_by
        ,$source_id,$notes
    );
    $result = $dbh->query($query,$bind);
    if (!$result)
```

```
    {
        $private_error = 'error: could not create history entry: '
            .'<li>query='.$query
            .'<li>result='.var_export($result,TRUE)
            .'<li>last_query='.$dbh->last_query
        ;
        user_error('Error: could not create history entry',
E_USER_ERROR);
        return FALSE;
    }

    // update the problem record
    $query = 'update problems set last_entry_id=? ';
    $bind = array($entry_id);
    if ($entry_type == 'public')
    {
        $query .= ', last_public_entry_id=? ';
        $bind[] = $entry_id;
    }
    $query .= ' where problem_id = ? ';
    $bind[] = $problem_id;
    $dbh->query($query,$bind);

    // get the email address of the customer who opened this call
    // if this was a public history entry, and if the email address
    // is not empty
    if ($entry_type == 'public')
    {
        $query = 'select c.email, p.problem_code from problems p,
customers c
            where p.problem_id = ? and p.customer_id = c.customer_id
                and trim(ifnull(c.email,"")) <> ""
        ';
        $email = NULL;
        list($email,$problem_code) = $dbh->getRow(
            $query
            , array($problem_id)
            , DB_FETCHMODE_ORDERED
        );
        if ($email)
        {
            // we have a valid email address - use it to
            // notify the customer that the call record
            // has been updated.
```

```
            notify_customer($problem_id,$email,$notes,$problem_code);
        }
    }
    return TRUE;
}
```

notify_customer()

This function constructs an email and sends it. The email informs the user that his or her problem is being tracked and provides a link to the page that gives the status of the problem in the system.

```
function notify_customer (
    $problem_id=NULL
    , $email=NULL
    , $notes=NULL
    , $problem_code=NULL
)
{
    // remove any HTML tags from $notes.
    $notes = cleanup_text($notes);

    $dbh = db_connect();

    if (!$problem_code)
    {
        $problem_code = $dbh->getOne(
            'select problem_code from problems where problem_id = ?'
            , array($problem_id)
        );
        if (!$problem_code)
        {
            $problem_code = create_problem_code();
            $dbh->query(
                'update problems set problem_code = ? where
problem_id = ?'
                , array($problem_code, $problem_id)
            );
        }
    }

    // build an absolute URL calling the problem_status.php page
    // to check on this problem
    $problem_url = regular_url(
        'problem.php?problem_code='.$problem_code
```

```
    );
    if (strpos($problem_url, '/staff') !== FALSE)
        $problem_url = str_replace('/staff', '', $problem_url);

    // set the body of the email
    $msgtext = <<<EOQ

Problem Update:

$notes

You can check the current status of this problem at

$problem_url

Thanks for your patience.

EOQ;

    // set the headers of the email
    // the Apache variable $_SERVER['SERVER_NAME'] is the name
    // of the server we're running on, minus any port number.

    $headers = 'From: webmaster@'.$_SERVER['SERVER_NAME']."\n"
        . 'Reply-To: webmaster@'.$_SERVER['SERVER_NAME']."\n"
        . 'X-Mailer: PHP/'.phpversion()
        . 'Bcc: webmaster@'.$_SERVER['SERVER_NAME']."\n"
    ;

    // send the email
    return mail($email, 'Problem Update', $msgtext, $headers);
}
```

PHP will have to be able to find sendmail or another SMTP-compliant mail server in order for this to work. Check your php.ini file if you're having problems.

status_change()

The status of a problem is going to be something like "open," "closed," or "pending." If it changes you are going to want to mark the exact change and record something like "Status changed to closed by John." The change should be recorded in the history table.

```
function status_change($problem_id=NULL
    , $entered_by='customer'
    , $new_status_id=NULL
    , $old_status_id=NULL
)
{
    $error = NULL;
    if (empty($problem_id))
    {
        $error = 'No problem ID supplied for status change';
    }
    elseif (empty($new_status_id))
    {
        $error = 'No new status ID supplied for status change';
    }
    elseif (!($new_status = status($new_status_id)))
    {
        $error = "New status ID $new_status_id is not valid.";
    }

    if ($error)
    {
        user_error($error, E_USER_WARNING);
        return FALSE;
    }

    // just return if no change - not an error condition,
    // just a no-op
    if ($old_status_id == $new_status_id)
    {
        return TRUE;
    }


    if (empty($entered_by)) { $entered_by = 'customer'; }

    // get the ID of the entry_type 'public', and construct
    // a string containing the new status value and either
    // the real name of the staff member who made the change,
    // or the value of $entered_by if no matching staff
    // member is found. for example, if the staff member Joe Blow
    // closes a call, the notes field will be set to
    // 'Status set to Closed by Joe Blow'. if a customer
    // re-opens a call, notes will be set to
```

```
    // 'Status set to Re-opened by customer'.

    $entry_type_id = entry_type_id('public');
    $notes = "Status set to $new_status by ";
    if ($entered_by != 'customer' && isset($GLOBALS['staff_name']))
    {
        $notes .= $_GLOBALS['staff_name'];
    }
    else
    {
        $notes .= $entered_by;
    }

    history_entry($problem_id, $entry_type_id, $entered_by,
'program', $notes);
}
```

create_problem_code()

This function creates a unique and highly random 8-character alphanumeric code.

```
function create_problem_code()
{
        return substr(md5(uniqid(rand())),0,8);
}
```

Scripts

Here are the pages that are actually called by URLs and `include` statements.

problem.php

This page does little but call either the `enter_problem()` or `update_problem()` function.

```
require_once('header.php');

$params = $_REQUEST;
$params['entered_by'] = 'customer';
$params['source'] = 'web';


if (empty($params['problem_code']))
{
    enter_problem($params);
}
```

```
else
{
    update_problem($params);
}
```

problem_entry_form.php

Mostly this form makes calls to the functions in your /book/functions/ folder. It prints the form shown in Figure 13-1 and determines the default information in the form. The call_entry.php page will include this page.

The interesting part of this script is its use of a `template` class to define the appearance of the generated HTML document. The variable `$tpl` is defined as a `template_object()`:

```
$tpl = template_object();
```

It is then loaded with an HTML template (problem_entry.html) that includes several named variables in its code.

These named variables come in handy when it's time to enter dynamic information into the HTML document. The general procedure for writing to a named block is this:

```
$tpl->setCurrentBlock(block_name');
$tpl->setVariable('template_variable_name',$local_variable_name);
$tpl->parseCurrentBlock();
```

This strategy enables you to enter programmatically determined values – typically from database lookups – into templates, and to have the templates apply standardized formatting. It insulates you from formatting issues, which can be no end of trouble. Here is the complete listing:

```
function problem_entry_form(&$params)
{
    global $default_page_title;


    $tpl = template_object();


    if ($tpl->loadTemplatefile('problem_entry.html') === FALSE)
    {
        user_error(
            'Could not load problem entry template'
            , E_USER_ERROR
        );
```

```
    }

    if (!empty($params['error_messages']))
    {
        foreach ((array)$params['error_messages'] as $error_message)
        {
            $tpl->setCurrentBlock('error_messages');
            $tpl->setVariable('error_message',$error_message);
            $tpl->parseCurrentBlock();
        }
    }

    if (!empty($params['dup_results']))
    {
        foreach ((array)$params['dup_results'] as $result)
        {
            $tpl->setCurrentBlock('dup_row');
            foreach ($result as $f => $v)
                $tpl->setVariable("dup_{$f}", $v);
            $tpl->parseCurrentblock();
        }
    }


    $tpl->setCurrentBlock('problem_entry_form');
    $tpl->setVariable($params);
    $tpl->setVariable('form_action', $_SERVER['PHP_SELF']);
    $tpl->parseCurrentBlock();

    // actually display something, finally...
    print start_page($default_page_title.': Enter New Report');
    $tpl->show();
    print end_page();
}
```

The form will be submitted to the page that called it. That page in turn ends up calling the `write_customer()` function, which is discussed next.

write_customer.php

This function is long, if not terribly complicated. We will mention interesting parts as they present themselves. It's easiest to figure out by actually looking at it the variety of actions this function can accomplish.

This page is largely a series of nested `if...else` statements. The simplest case is that in which all or part of the customer record—as identified by the `customer_id`—exists in the database already and when none of the information entered into the form conflicts with anything that's in the database. If that's so, we just pick up the customer information and move along.

A more complicated situation exists when more than one record matches the email and/or phone numbers entered into the form or when a single record matches but differs in other respects from what's in the database. The procedure here is to show all matching records to the customer and allow him or her to take any of several actions:

- Create a new record
- Choose one of the existing records to be used without modification
- Choose an existing record, merging it with the information in the form

Here is the complete listing of the function:

```
function write_customer(&$params)
{
  $dbh = db_connect();

  $output = TRUE;

  $action = 'insert';
  $duplicate = NULL;

  // set up default variables for all the fields in customers table
  // we end up with a key in params for every field in customers,
  // set to NULL if we have no value
  $customer_fields = $dbh->getCol('describe customers');
  foreach (array_diff($customer_fields, array_keys($params)) as $k)
    $params[$k] = NULL;

  // extract($params, EXTR_REFS);
  // workaround for "BOGUS" bug #24630 with extract() :
  // extracting with the EXTR_REFS flag will make any
  // variables used in *creating* the array into
  // references as well
  foreach (array_keys($params) as $k)
    $$k =& $params[$k];

  // the hours for day and evening phones are filled in by default.
  // if no phone number is given, set them to NULL

  if (empty($day_prefix)) { $day_start = NULL; $day_end = NULL; }
  if (empty($eve_prefix)) { $eve_start = NULL; $eve_end = NULL; }
```

```
    // the $action variable will be set to reflect what the script
    // should do with the customer data as it passes through a
    // myriad of tests.  by default, create a new customer record

    $errors = array();

    // if we've been through this once already, the user may
    // have passed on instructions
    $dup_action = NULL;
    if ($duplicate)
    {
      list($customer_id,$dup_action) = explode('-',$duplicate);
    }

    // use the validate_email() function (defined in
    // /book/functions/CheckEmail.php) to validate the format of the
    // email address. (note: this does *not* verify that the email
    // address is a real one, only that it looks like one.)

    if (!validate_email($email)
      && empty($day_prefix)
      && empty($eve_prefix)
    )
    {
      // we have to have either an email address or a phone number
      // to contact the user. if we don't, print out an error.
      $errors[] = <<<EOQ

Without either a valid email address or a phone number,
we can't contact you to resolve your problem.
Please enter at least one of these items
and submit your problem again. Thank you.

EOQ;
      $action = 'problems';
    }
    elseif ($customer_id)
    {
      // we have a database ID for a specific customer record
      $record = array('customer_id' => $customer_id);
      fetch_customer($record);

      if ($dup_action == 'merge')
      {
        // the user has checked a radio button indicating
```

```
    // that we should combine the information in the form
    // with the existing record in the customer table.

    // begin parsing customer record.
    foreach ($record as $field => $value)
    {
      if (is_string($value))
      {
        $value = trim($value);
      }
      if (is_string($$field))
      {
        $$field = trim($$field);
      }
      // for each column from the database record
      if ($value != $$field && empty($$field))
      {
        // the value from the form ($$field -
        // i.e. the variable with the same name
        // as the column) is blank, and the
        // current value of the column
        // in the database is not blank.
        // overwrite the form value with
        // the value from the database.
        $$field = $value;
      }
    }
    // end parsing customer record.

    // set $action to indicate that we should update
    // the customer record, using the information from
    // the form (which has been overwritten when called
    // for above).
    $action = 'update';
  }
  elseif ($dup_action == 'override')
  {
    // the user has checked a radio button indicating
    // that all the information in the current database
    // record should be overwritten by the values from
    // the form.

    // set $action to indicate that we should update
    // the customer record using the information from
```

```
        // the form.

        $customer_code = $record['customer_code'];
        $action = 'update';
      }
      else
      {
        // use the customer's record from the database
        extract($record);
        $action = 'none';
      }
    }
    elseif ($dup_action == 'add_as_new')
    {
      // the user has clicked on a radio field indicating that
      // a new customer record should be created.

      // set $action to indicate that we should create a new record.
      // with the information from the form.
      $action = 'insert';
    }
    else
    {
      // either we haven't checked for duplicate customer records yet,
      // or the user didn't tell us what to do about them.

      // use the find_customer() function (defined in functions.php)
      // to look for any existing customer records which might
      // match the customer described in the form.

      $result = find_customer($email
        , $day_area, $day_prefix, $day_suffix
        , $eve_area, $eve_prefix, $eve_suffix
      );
      if (count($result) == 0)
      {
        // either we don't have any contact information,
        // or no record was found matching this one.
        // set $action to indicate that we should go ahead
        // and create a new record.
        $action = 'insert';
      }
      else
      {
        $action = 'problems';
```

```
    if (count($result) == 1)
    {
      // we found exactly one record which might match
      // the form.
      // get that record from the database, trimming
      // strings and removing empty fields
      $row = array_filter($result[0], 'notempty');

      // do the same for current field values
      $current = array_filter($params,'notempty');

      // check for differences
      $diff = array_diff($row,$current);
      foreach (array_keys($diff) as $k)
      {
        if (empty($current[$k]))
        {
          unset($diff[$k]);
        }
      }
      if (!empty($diff))
      {
        // $errors[] = var_export($diff, TRUE);
        $customer_id = 0;
      }
      else
      {
        $action = 'none';
        extract($result[0]);
      }
    }
    if ($action == 'problems')
    {
      $params['dup_results'] = $result;
    }
  }
}

if ($action == 'problems' || count($errors) > 0)
{
  $params['error_messages'] = $errors;
  return FALSE;
}

if ($action == 'none')
```

```
{
  // no change to existing customer record
}
else
{
  // remove customer_id and customer_code from list of fields
  // at first
  $fields = array_diff(
    $customer_fields
    , array('customer_id', 'customer_code')
  );
  $bind = array_key_value($params,$fields,NULL,'list');
  $where = NULL;
  if ($action == 'insert')
  {
    // create a new customer record
    $customer_id = $dbh->nextId('customer');
    $bind[] = $customer_id;
    $fields[] = 'customer_id';
    // use the code for their first problem as a customer code
    if ($problem_code === NULL)
    {
      $problem_code = create_problem_code();
    }
    $customer_code = $problem_code;
    $bind[] = $customer_code;
    $fields[] = 'customer_code';
    $mode = DB_AUTOQUERY_INSERT;
  }
  elseif ($action == 'update')
  {
    // update an existing customer record
    $bind[] = $customer_id;
    $where = ' customer_id = ? ';
    $mode = DB_AUTOQUERY_UPDATE;
  }
  else
  {
    $private_error = "unknown value for action: $action";
    push_handler(E_ALL, H_DEBUG);
    $debug = E_ALL;
    user_error('Error creating problem record', E_USER_ERROR);
    return FALSE;
  }
  $stmt = $dbh->autoPrepare('customers', $fields, $mode, $where);
```

```
    $output = $dbh->execute($stmt, $bind);
    if (!$output)
    {
      $private_error = 'error updating customers: <pre>'
        .$dbh->last_query.'</pre>';
      user_error('Error updating customer record', E_USER_ERROR);
      return FALSE;
    }
    // $params = array_merge($params, compact($fields));
  }
  $params['action'] = $action;
  return $output;
}
```

staff/problems.php

This is where you expect the staff members to log in to the application. Note the use of the `staff_authenticate()` function, which calls the `authenticate()` function we've been using throughout the book. Before a staff member can log in, he or she must enter a valid password and username.

The page is going to show two lists of queries, a list of calls owned by the currently logged-in staff member, and a list of unowned calls, probably stuff that has been entered over the Web.

```
require_once(dirname(__FILE__).'/header.php');

$params = $_GET;
$last_list_value = NULL;

if (empty($params['customer_code']))
{
    // get a list of all open unowned problems (in the hopes
    // that the current user might grab one) and the current
    // user's open problems. include information from the
    // last entry in the history table for each problem.

    $params['where'] = ' status_id <> ? and ifnull(staff_id,?) = ?
';
    $params['bind'] = array(status_id('Closed'), $staff_id,
$staff_id);
    $params['order_by'] = ' staff_id, last_entry_dt asc ';
    $list_titles = array(
        '' => 'Unowned Calls'
        , $staff_id => 'Open Calls for '.$staff_name
    );
```

```
    $list_key = 'staff_id';

}
else
{
    fetch_customer($params);
    $list_titles = array(
        $params['customer_code'] =>
            'Calls for '.$params['firstname'].'
'.$params['lastname']
    );
    $list_key = 'customer_code';
    $last_list_value = $params[$list_key];

}

fetch_problems($params);

$tpl = template_object();

$tpl->loadTemplatefile('problem_list.html',TRUE,TRUE);

$neparams = array_filter($params, 'notempty');
$tpl->setVariable($neparams);

$first_list_value = $last_list_value;


foreach ($params['problems'] as $row)
{
    if ($row[$list_key] !== $last_list_value)
    {
        $tpl->setCurrentBlock('problems');
        $tpl->setVariable('list_title',
$list_titles[$last_list_value]);
        $tpl->parseCurrentBlock();
        $last_list_value = $row[$list_key];
    }
    if ($row['source_id'])
        $row['source'] = source($row['source_id']);
    else
        $row['source'] = 'No Source ID';
    if ($row['status_id'])
        $row['status'] = status($row['status_id']);
    else
```

```
        $row['status'] = 'No Status ID';
    $tpl->setCurrentBlock('problem');
    $tpl->setVariable($row);
    $tpl->parseCurrentBlock();
}
if (count($params['problems']) > 0 && $last_list_value !=
$first_list_value)
{
    $tpl->setCurrentBlock('problems');
    $tpl->setVariable('list_title', $list_titles[$last_list_value]);
    $tpl->parseCurrentBlock();
}
if (empty($params['customer_code']))
{
    $tpl->touchBlock('general_problem');
}
else
{
    $tpl->setCurrentBlock('customer_problem');
    $tpl->setVariable('customer_code', $params['customer_code']);
    $tpl->parseCurrentBlock();
}

print start_page();

$tpl->show();

print end_page();
```

Summary

The application presented in this chapter is very useful, as just about every information-services department will have some sort of system to track user complaints. As we stated at the beginning of this chapter, the problem-tracking system presented here is fairly generic. However, it can definitely be the basis for a more detailed application that you'd custom-design for use in the workplace.

Chapter 14

Shopping Cart

IN THIS CHAPTER

- Creating a secure site
- Working with PHP sessions
- Communicating with a credit-card-authorization service

IN THIS CHAPTER YOU are going to learn what you need to create a shopping-cart application using PHP and MySQL. But this application is different from the others in this book in that it's really impossible to talk about what you need for it without delving into some other topics. In addition to understanding the schema and the PHP code, you need to have a basic understanding of how to maintain state between pages. (If you don't know what that means, don't worry, we'll get to it momentarily.) Also, you need to know how to securely process credit-card transactions.

Don't read another sentence if you have not read through Chapter 12. You must understand how the catalog works before you can take this on. For reasons that shouldn't be too tough to understand, we built the shopping cart atop the catalog.

Determining the Scope and Goals of the Application

Anyone familiar with the Web knows what a shopping cart does. But it will be a bit easier to understand what the code for this application is doing if we explicitly state some of its purposes.

First, the application is going to have to display your wares; for this you reuse the code from Chapter 12. Further, users have to be able to choose items that they want to buy. Obvious, we know. Note what must happen after a user chooses an item: The exact item must be noted, and the user should have the opportunity to continue shopping. The server must remember what has been ordered. As the user continues to browse, the server must keep track of the user and allow him or her to check out with his or her requested items.

This functionality requires you to use some method for maintaining state – that is, the Web server needs to remember who the user is as he or she moves from page to page. Now, you might recall that in the introduction to this book we discussed the stateless nature of the Web and the HTTP protocol that the Web makes use of. After responding to an HTTP request, the server completely and totally forgets what it served to whom. The server takes care of requested information serially – one at a time, as requests come in. There is no persistence, no connection that lasts after a page has been served.

To give your site memory so that, in this case, the cart can remember who ordered what, some information that identifies the user must be sent with each page request. On the Web, you can store this information in exactly five ways:

- **You can set a large cookie (a nugget of information that's stored – possibly in a persistent file – on the client machine) containing all information about the state of the transaction and, in this case, the contents of the shopping cart.** Each time a request is made, the information stored in the cookie is sent to the server. Note that the browser stores the cookie information in a small text file (or in RAM) and sends the information to the server with each request.
- **You can set a small cookie that merely identifies the user to the server.** With the identifier, the server can find a database record that contains all further information about state.
- **You can make users use unique URLs (typically, they'll call server-side programs with unique, identifying, arguments).** These work like the previous "small cookie" strategy, but enable users to have cookies turned off.
- **You can send hidden data about the state to be kept on the user's screen and resent (posted) with the next request.** The session-identifying information can be stored in hidden form fields.
- **You can send hidden data to merely identify the user to be kept on the user's screen and resent (posted) with the next request.** Then the user-identifying data are used on the server to find a database record that contains all further information about state.

What do you need?

Since you are building this application atop the catalog, much of the code and information should be very familiar. The one notable thing that is going to be added to every page is a button that lets people go directly to the checkout. Figure 14-1 shows an example.

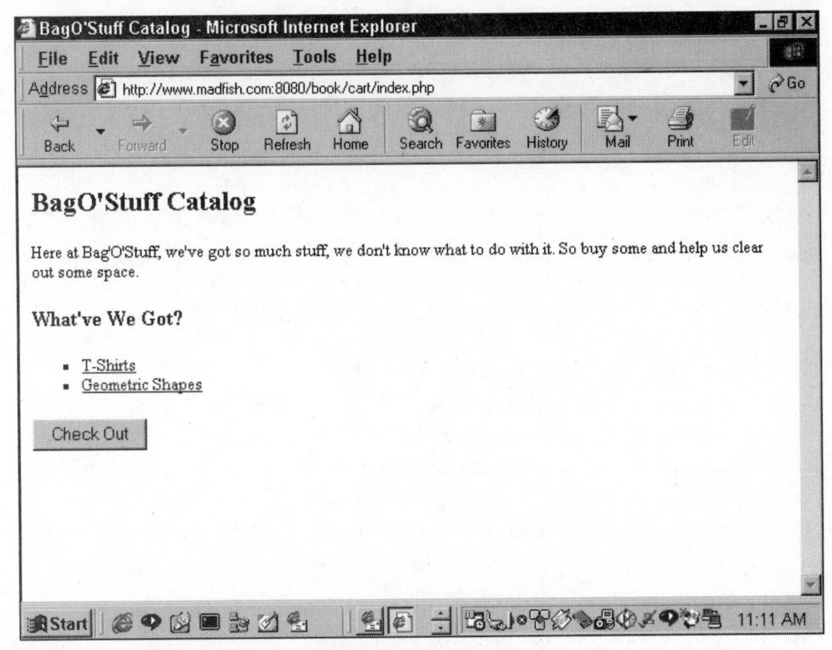

Figure 14-1: Category page with checkout button

What do you need to prevent?

You need to be careful about two things:

- Making sure you can track your users from page to page
- Keeping credit-card numbers and other personal information away from prying eyes

The Data

The database used here is added to the catalog database. Information about goods still comes from the tables reviewed there, while information on orders is stored in the tables shown here.

The data schema here, represented in Figure 14-2, should look familiar if you studied Chapter 1 and Chapter 12.

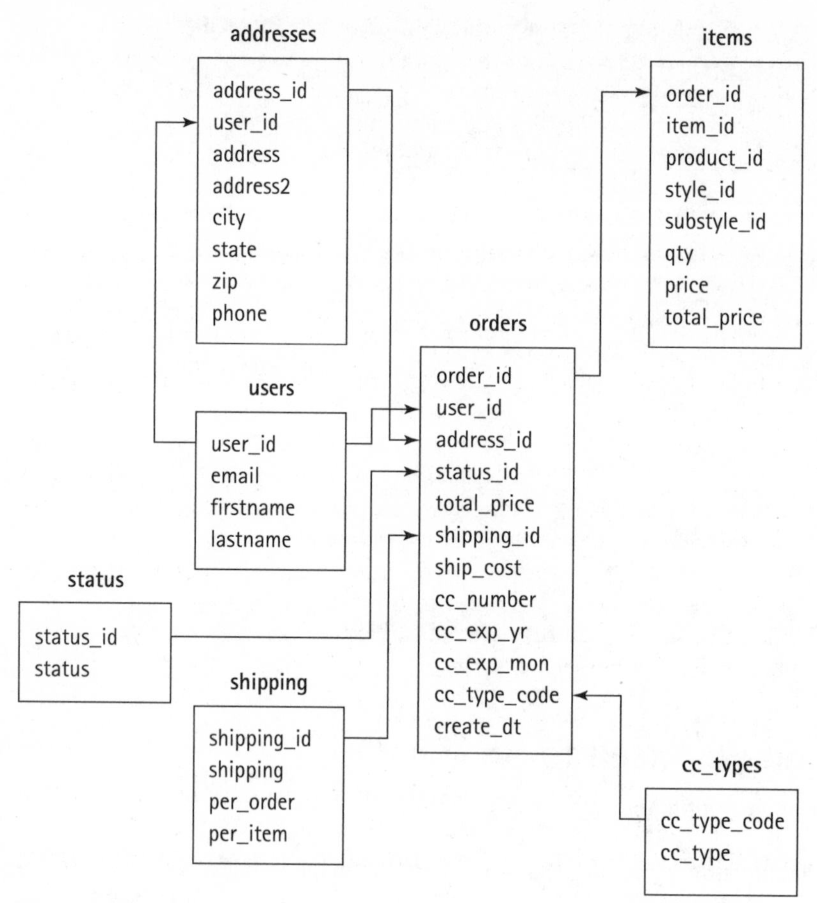

Figure 14-2: Cart schema

Configuration Overview

This application is specialized enough to require its own configuration. All the challenges discussed earlier (maintaining state, securely gathering credit-card information, and processing that information) not only require specialized code, they require some unique installation options.

Configuring for encryption and security

If you have a lot of experience with Apache and its related tools, this configuration might not be too big a deal; or if you are using an ISP and don't have the authority to install programs on a box, you won't need to worry about the specialized installation necessary to work with e-commerce.

But in any case, you should have an idea of the tools you need to get all of this working. First, we cover the basic theories behind encryption and Web security. We then cover some of the mandatory tools for your Apache installation. Finally, we cover some of the options PHP offers for maintaining state and processing credit-card transactions.

ENCRYPTION AND SECURITY THEORY

One of the best things about working around the Web is having first-hand knowledge of the work done by people smarter than yourself. Some of the most intense, complex, and difficult work being done is in the realm of security. This is algorithm-heavy stuff, and to really understand how the protocols work, you need to know quite a bit of math. Luckily, you don't need to have an advanced degree to understand the theories, and putting them into practice really isn't too bad.

PUBLIC-KEY/PRIVATE-KEY ENCRYPTION Machines on the Web make use of a *public-key/private-key* security scheme. Basically this means that computers that wish to communicate using encrypted data must have two keys to encrypt and decrypt data. First there is the *public key.* As the name suggests the public key is not hidden. It is available to all those you wish to communicate with.

However, the public key is good only for encrypting data. If you encrypt data with the public key and then try to decrypt it with the same key, it won't work, because of a very complicated piece of math called a *one-way hash*. The messages can be decrypted only by the private key. As the name implies, the private key is kept private. No one but you has access to it.

So, for example, suppose you want to send some credit-card information to a bank for processing. You have access to the bank's public key, with which you encrypt the information. But because of the complex algorithms involved, only the private key held by the bank can decrypt the data.

CERTIFICATES Even with the public-key/private-key safeguards, the banks have one major concern: that the messages they are getting are not from the sources they appear to be from. That is, if you are running `sofamegastore.com`, the bank needs to make sure that the request for credit-card authorization for that loveseat is actually from Sofa Megastore, not someone who is pretending to be Sofa Megastore. This confirmation requires a third party.

The encrypted messages that you send and receive have a signature of sorts, but that signature must be verified. For this reason, organizations that wish to communicate over the Web make use of organizations that distribute digital certificates that verify the sender of a message. Mechanisms for keeping certificates secure and making them useless if stolen are quite complicated. So it should make sense that you need to go to one of these organizations to get your public and private keys.

Probably the best-known organization involved in security certificates is VeriSign. You can find out about their offerings at this site: `http://www.verisign.com/products/site/ss/index.html`.

SECURE PROTOCOL HTTP by its very nature is open to eavesdropping. Packets that move across the Internet's routers are full of messages just waiting to be sniffed and read. Normally, the fact that you can easily read data sent via HTTP is a good thing. It makes the transfer and rendering of information quite simple. However, in cases where you need security, HTTP won't work well.

For example, if you are giving credit-card information to a site – for example, the commerce site you set up – you want to make sure that the information is unreadable. To ensure that, you need to make use of the Secure Sockets Layer, or SSL. SSL is an additional protocol by means of which the keys and certificates from your site are transferred to a browser or another server. Over SSL, your browser is able to verify the certificate from your site so that it knows you are who you say you are. Sites can also use it to verify each other's identity.

All the encryption in the world can't stop someone who has hacked into your box or who has legitimate access. Most credit-card theft is done by dishonest employees with too much access.

ENCRYPTION AND SECURITY TOOLS

Given what you have just read about encryption and security, it probably stands to reason that you are going to need some new tools. Here's a basic rundown.

First off, you are going to need to add SSL to Apache. As with everything else discussed in this book, adding SSL does not require you to pay for specialized software. All you need to do is install Apache with mod_ssl (which you can read more about at `http://www.modssl.org`). You'll want to have a look at the products of the Apache-SSL project as you configure your server for secure connectivity.

The process of installing SSL modules is documented by the project teams and is best found on the Web, so we won't cover it here. If you are having trouble getting mod_ssl, PHP, and MySQL to work for you, we recommend this site, which goes through the installation step by step: `http://www.devshed.com/Server_Side/PHP/SoothinglySeamless/page8.html`. Even though it deals with rsaref, which is no longer strictly required, the steps remain valid.

Configuring Apache for credit-card authorization

When Apache is configured with SSL your site is able to talk to browsers securely. If the URL starts with `https://` the browser knows to look on port 443 and to look for a certificate. However, the question of how your site talks with the entity that processes credit cards and either accepts or rejects the transaction still exists. Fortunately, PHP's integration of HTTP streams with its regular file-handling functions, like `fopen()` and `file_get_contents()`, has gotten even better. If PHP is built with SSL enabled, you can use these functions to exchange data with your credit-card processor via a secure connection. (Be aware, though, setting up the certificates for use in this way is more complicated than it is to go to an `https://` URL in your browser. The bank or service you choose will have more information on their requirements for you.)

Configuring for session handling

When we start breaking down the code, you can see the exact functions you need in order to work with sessions. But while talking about configuration options it's best to cover the different ways sessions can be implemented in PHP. However, first we present a little about what sessions in PHP actually do.

Suppose you want to track the activity of your users across a number of pages, as with this shopping cart. You need to remember who has put what in a cart. To do this you could pass some rather complex variables via a cookie that holds all the elements and their prices, but that approach is kind of messy and might expose more of the workings of your application than you are comfortable exposing. Moreover, the cookie specification (`http://www.netscape.com/newsref/std/cookie_spec.html`) allows only 20 cookies per domain and only 4 bytes per cookie.

A better idea is to give each person who visits your site a unique identifier, some value that identifies who that person is. Then, as the user adds items to the cart, information associated with the unique identifier can be stored on the server. If you were to code a function that stored the information by hand, you might create a unique string that would be put in a cookie; then, in some directory on the server, you could have a file that has the same name as the unique user ID. Within that file you could store all the variables associated with the user. For example, you might store an array of items that a specific user put in his or her cart.

In fact, this is a description of almost exactly what sessions do. When you indicate in your code (or by settings in your php.ini) that you'd like to start a session, PHP creates a unique identifier and an associated file, which is stored on the server (the location is set in the php.ini and, by default, is in the /tmp directory). Then, as a user moves from page to page, all the variable information that the user chooses can be stored in the file on the server, and all the script needs to keep track of is the unique identifier.

Many configuration options are possible when it comes to sessions, but probably the most important decision is whether the session ID is propagated in a URL or in a cookie. Most e-commerce sites make use of cookies. However, it is possible that some of your users will not be able to use your site properly if they have their browsers set to reject cookies. For this reason, in PHP it is very easy to include the session ID in the page request. You have two options.

- First, you can append the session identifier to the URL, as in this example: `http://www.fakeo.domain/?SID=ABCDEFG`. That corresponds to the HTTP `GET` operation.
- Alternately, you can include the session identifier in a hidden form field, which is submitted to the server when the form in which it is embedded is submitted. This corresponds to the HTTP `POST` operation.

However, this is NOT recommended. Though it's theoretically possible for a session to be "hijacked" in some way no matter how you set things up, putting the session cookie in as highly visible a place as the URL or the source of the form makes life easier for anyone trying to break in. It might be better in the long run to try to guide any recalcitrant users into allowing you to give them a cookie.

Code Overview

As you might have guessed by now, this example uses two function sets that are relatively unique:

- The functions that deal with sessions
- The functions associated with the cURL library

We cover both sets of functions in some detail in this section.

First, though, we need to make another note about the advantages of the object-oriented approach. When you read Chapter 12 (you did read Chapter 12, right?) you saw some of the principles of object-oriented programming in practice. Specifically, you might have noticed how inheritance is used. When a class inherits the properties and methods of a parent class, it has access to all of the methods and properties of the parent.

In this application you are extending the code you used in the catalog, so it makes sense that this application creates classes that extend the classes used in the catalog. Please be sure you are familiar with the catalog classes in Chapter 12 before proceeding.

Session functions

If you head over to the session page in the PHP manual (`http://www.php.net/manual/ref.session.php`), you will find at least 20 different functions. Depending on your needs, you may have to use a majority of these, but in many circumstances you can get away with using one: `session_start()`. The actual storing of variables in your session data, and removal of them, is just a matter of setting or unsetting a value in the $_SESSION superglobal array, once you've started your session.

session_start()

This function either starts a new session or resumes your current one, allowing you to maintain data across a number of request/response transactions. You'll call this every time you want to start session tracking. The most likely source of trouble you will have with this function is when you have stored an object in your session. The class definition must have already been loaded before the session is re-started. As of PHP 5, this will become less of a pain, however, since you can define an `__autoload()` function that will search your include path for any as-yet unloaded class files when the session begins.

session_destroy()

This function kills a session and all the variables associated with it. You might want to call this to enable a "fresh start" through an application, such as when a user completed a game or logged out from a special area.

session_set_save_handler()

This interesting function enables you to set your own methods for storing, retrieving, and writing your own session handlers:

```
void session_set_save_handler (string open, string close, string
read, string write, string destroy, string gc)
```

For a good deal of the time, the file-based session management in PHP is fine. However, in a couple of circumstances it might not suit you. If you happen to be working in a clustered environment (one in which several machines are serving the same site), writing to the local file system really won't work. Similarly, your SSL-enabled Apache installation may reside on a machine other than your main server.

In this case a better choice is to have all the machines connect to the same database and to have your database (MySQL, of course) store the session data. It was unnecessary for us to make use of this function when we created this application because we were working with only one physical server. However, if you need to store session data in a MySQL database, you can use the functions in Appendix H.

session_encode()

To write variables to a database you must put them in a format that makes sense to the database. That is what the `session_encode` function does. You can see examples of this in Appendix H.

```
$str = session_encode()
```

session_decode()

This function reverses the process of encoding, so that the variable is turned into a representation that PHP can work with. You can see examples of this in Appendix H.

Dealing with the credit-card processor

You are going to need to get some information directly from the entity processing the transaction. Most processing companies that we've seen work similarly. You send them a request with all the expected credit-card information – number, expiration date, address, and so forth – and they send you some codes in response.

Your PHP script needs to compare the codes it receives with the values you get from the processing agency.

For this application we use (well, pretend to use) Authorize.Net as the credit-card processor, which seems to work just fine.

Code Breakdown

As with the catalog, here you start by looking at the classes that come into play in this application. Again, the files accessed via the URLs are very high-level files; all the tough work is done in the class files.

As already mentioned, one of the goals of this application is to make use of the classes you created in the catalog. You want to write as little new code as possible, so the new classes here inherit the methods and properties in the classes you've already created.

One class from Chapter 12 doesn't quite do enough for inclusion in the cart. That is the `Base` class. In this chapter you're going to create another `Base` class with some extended functionality. Then all you have to do is make sure that the categories that extend `Base` call your new version. This is easily done with `require_once()` statements. In your classes.php file you include the `CartBase` class, and then, when a class that extends `CartBase` is included, the extending class sees the new class. When you look at the classes.php file, remember that the entire content of each of the included files is sucked into this file when the main file is parsed by PHP.

Classes

These classes have methods that look very much like the methods in the `Category`, `Product`, and other classes from Chapter 12. Those worked well because products have a natural hierarchy: Categories contain products, products contain styles, and styles contain substyles. For a shopping cart a hierarchy of user information exists: A user can have many addresses, many orders can go to an address, and many items can belong in a single order. These relationships are represented and managed in this application by the `Tree` class.

We start by looking at the `Request` class, another general purpose class similar to `Base` and `Tree`, that handles HTTP requests.

REQUEST CLASS

In the two example classes we provide for packaging up your user's credit card information all neatly for some card processing company, there's just one line that does quite a bit:

```
$results = Request::post($url, $args);
```

This sends an array of data and a URL off to the Request class, and receives the OK or not-OK from the card processor. Looks fairly simple on the outside, which is somewhat the point. But there's quite a bit going on inside.

This is especially true for POST requests (GET requests, being ultimately just long URLs, are easier to manage.) In previous versions, you had to explicitly open a socket to port 443 yourself, and do most of the work of reading data, checking for blocks, and so on. PHP 5 largely does that for you now. Instead, you need to set up what are called "stream context options." These are parameters to tell the PHP code handling the communication with the server what kind of content headers to send, where your SSL certificates are, among other things. Here's what that code looks like in the `Request` class:

```
$context = stream_context_create(
    array('http' => array(
        'method' => 'POST'
        , 'user_agent' => 'Mad/Fish 1.0'
    ))
);
stream_context_set_option(
    $context
    , 'http'
    , 'header'
    , "Content-type: {$content_type}\r\n"
     .'Content-length: '.strlen($request_content)."\r\n"
);
stream_context_set_option(
    $context
    , 'http'
    , 'content'
    , $request_content
);
```

We begin by creating a stream context of type 'http,' telling it that we will be doing a POST, and setting up a user agent. Then we spell out the content type and length – the type for a POST request is typically "application/x-www-form-encoded." Finally, we attach the actual content of the post – the URL-encoded version of the array we passed in as an argument to this function.

Then to do the POST and get a response, we have this tricky bit of coding:

```
$results= file_get_contents($url,false,$context);
```

Yes, that's it. Just like reading in a file, or downloading a web page from a URL. This will return the body of the response. To see the HTTP headers that came with it, you'll need to check the global variable `$http_response_header`.

TREE CLASS

We've set up this shopping-cart application to use a generalized tree structure to represent relationships among database records – individual records can have parents and children. Therefore, a `Tree` class exists for making queries against the database and interpreting the results in terms of tree structure.

Essentially, you pass to the `node()` method (shown following) the kind of object you want to organize in a hierarchy, which determines what table is queried, what the key field name is, and what class is created for each child record found.

```
function node($o=NULL)
{
    if ($o !== NULL)
    {
        if (is_object($o) && is_a($o, 'base'))
        {
            $class = get_class($o);
            if ($this->node !== NULL
                && $o !== $this->node
                && $class == $this->node_class
            )
            {
                $props = array_merge(
                    get_object_vars($this->node)
                    , get_object_vars($o)
                );
                foreach ($props as $k => $v)
                {
                    $o->$k = $v;
                }
            }
            $this->node = $o;
            $this->node_class = get_class($o);
            $this->idfield = $o->idfield;
            $this->table = $o->table;
        }
        else
```

```
            {
                return FALSE;
            }
        }
        elseif ($this->node === NULL)
        {
            return FALSE;
        }
        return $this->node;
    }
```

Once you have a tree in place in your database, you can use the `predict_children()` method to pull up all the descendants of a given ID value (or set of values) at one time, out to an arbitrary number of generations: the *depth*. The depth can be sent as a parameter, but it may be a better idea to let the method go to the default value set in the class constant `Depth` (referred to in code as `Tree::Depth`). You can set `Tree::Depth` to match the structure you've established for your data.

So what does a `predict_children()` query do? A query out to a depth of `3` looks like this:

```
select g0.product_id as g0_id
    , g1.product_id as g1_id
    , g2.product_id as g2_id
    , g3.product_id as g3_id
from products g0
    left join products g1 on g0.product_id = g1.parent_id
    left join products g2 on g1.product_id = g2.parent_id
    left join products g3 on g2.product_id = g3.parent_id
where g0.product_id in (1)
```

and the results look like this:

```
+-------+-------+-------+-------+
| g0_id | g1_id | g2_id | g3_id |
+-------+-------+-------+-------+
|     1 |     3 |     5 |     8 |
|     1 |     3 |     5 |     9 |
|     1 |     3 |     6 |  NULL |
|     1 |     3 |     7 |  NULL |
|     1 |     4 |    10 |  NULL |
|     1 |     4 |    11 |  NULL |
|     1 |     4 |    12 |  NULL |
|     1 |    22 |  NULL |  NULL |
+-------+-------+-------+-------+
```

In other words:

- Record 1 has three children: 3, 4, 22
- Record 3 has three children: 5, 6, 7
- Record 5 has two children: 8, 9
- Record 4 has three children: 10, 11, 12

The `predict_children()` method represents these data as a tree, creating a new object for each record. The actual data are stored in the `$all_data` property; the other properties are arrays of references into `$all_data`.

You know that the tree has been represented completely if the last column is `NULL` for all the records. If it's not, that can mean that more child records remain to be found, and the function can run again starting at that depth. In terms of the shopping cart application, this means we can extract the entire contents of our Tree objects.

ADDRESS CLASS

The `Address` class exists for the purpose of manipulating the Address table – a design characteristic of applications like this. The key function is `write_to_db()`, which verifies that a `user_id` value has been provided, and that either modifies an existing record or creates a new one corresponding to it.

```
class Address extends CartBase
{
    var $table = 'addresses';
    var $idfield = 'address_id';
    var $what = 'address';
    var $fields = array(

'address_id','user_id','address1','address2','city','state','zip','p
hone'
    );

    var $id = NULL;
    var $address_id = NULL;
    var $user_id = NULL;
    var $address1 = NULL;
    var $address2 = NULL;
    var $city = NULL;
    var $state = NULL;
    var $zip = NULL;
    var $phone = NULL;
```

```
    var $save_as_new = NULL;

    // Methods:

    function write_to_db()
    {
        if (empty($this->user_id))
        {
            $this->error = 'user_id required to save address';
            trigger_error($this->error, E_USER_WARNING);
            return FALSE;
        }
        if ($this->save_as_new)
        {
            // if the save_as_new property is set,
            // then create a new address record by setting
            // the id to NULL
            $this->address_id = NULL;
        }

        // update the addresses table
        $result = parent::write_to_db();
        return $result;
    }
}
```

ORDER CLASS

The `Order` class corresponds to the Order table and so features fields and methods that adjust and examine the contents of that table. It also contains the `charge_card()` function, which sends a transaction (over an SSL link, naturally) to an authorization center. Here is that code:

```
    function charge_card()
    {
        if (!$this->validate_card())
        {
            return FALSE;
        }

        $this->calculate_total();
        $total_charged = $this->total_price + $this->shipping_cost;

        // pass it off to one of the Charge subclasses
        return AuthorizeNet::sale($this);
        // return IONGATE::sale($this);
    }
```

Notice that near the end, the return value is forced TRUE. This is for testing purposes. In reality, your authorization house returns a value for auth_result that determines whether the function returns TRUE or FALSE.

Scripts

These are the pages called by URLs and the includes. You will probably notice that not much is involved here. Almost all the work is done in the classes. These scripts are concerned more with presentation of data and ways of manipulating them – as they should be, because such a design makes it more likely that you'll be able to reuse the classes somewhere else someday.

DISPLAY.PHP

This prints out either a list of categories or a specific product:

```
<?php
require_once('header.php');

$product_id = (int)array_key_value($_REQUEST,'product_id',0);
$submit = (string)array_key_value($_POST, 'submit');
$again = (string)array_key_value($_POST, 'again');

$p = new Product(array('product_id'=>$product_id));

if (empty($p->product_id))
{
    $p->description = "Here at Bag'O'Stuff, we've got so much stuff
we don't know what to do with it. So buy some and help us clear out
some space.";
    $p->product = "What've We Got?";
}
else
{
    $p->fetch_from_db();
}

// begin constructing the page title with a link to the main page
// of the catalog

// add a link back to the product level to the page title,
// followed by the name of this product, and print out the
// top of the page

$page_title = anchor_tag('index.php', "Bag'O'Stuff");
foreach ($p->parents() as $t)
{
```

```
    $page_title .= ' &gt; '.anchor_tag(
        'display.php?product_id='.$t->product_id
        , $t->product
    );
}
if ($p->product_id)
{
    $page_title .= ' &gt; '.anchor_tag(
        'display.php?product_id='.$p->product_id
        , $p->product
    );
}
else
{
    $page_title .= '<br><br>'.$p->product;
}
print start_page($page_title);

if ($submit == 'Add to Cart' || $again == 'please')
{
    include('cart.php');
}
else
{
    print print_product($p);
}
// print out the bottom of the page
print end_page();

?>
```

It doesn't get a whole lot more basic than this: If this page is to display a category (not a product), a category is loaded and then printed. The same happens for a product, if appropriate. If you remember the display.php page from Chapter 12, you might notice that the only real difference is that the objects instantiated here are created from the classes new to this application. That gives you access to the new print methods, which were designed to work with this application.

CART.PHP

Here's the page that creates your shopping cart:

```
<?php
$o = get_session_order();

$href = regular_url($_SERVER['PHP_SELF']);
```

```
// display the contents of the shopping cart
print start_form();
print hidden_field('again','please');
print '<h3>Shopping Cart</h3>';
print '<h5>(Change quantity to 0 to remove an item.)</h5>';
print start_table(array(
    'border'=>0
    , 'width'=>'80%'
    , 'cellpadding' => 5
));
print table_row(
    table_header_cell('Item')
    , table_header_cell(array('align'=>'right',
'value'=>'Quantity'))
    , table_header_cell(array('align'=>'right', 'value'=>'Price'))
    , table_header_cell(array('align'=>'right', 'value'=>'Total'))
);
print table_row('<hr>','<hr>','<hr>','<hr>');
$total_price = 0;
$total_quantity = 0;
foreach ($o->items() as $item)
{
    $tprice = $item->price * $item->quantity;
    $qfield = text_field(array(
        'name'=>"quantity[{$item->item_name}]"
        , 'value'=>$item->quantity
        , 'size'=>4
    ));
    print table_row(
        anchor_tag($href.'?product_id='.$item->product_id, $item-
>item_name)
        , table_cell(array('align'=>'right', 'value'=>$qfield))
        , table_cell(array('align'=>'right', 'value'=>money($item-
>price)))
        , table_cell(array('align'=>'right',
'value'=>money($tprice)))
    );

    // keep a running total of the quantity and price of items
    // in the cart.
    $total_price = $total_price + $tprice;
    $total_quantity = $total_quantity + $item->quantity;
}
$o->total_price = $total_price;
```

```
$o->total_quantity = $total_quantity;

// print out totals
print table_row('<hr>','<hr>','<hr>','<hr>');
print table_row(
    table_header_cell(array('align'=>'right', 'value'=>'Grand
Total'))
    , table_header_cell(array('align'=>'right',
'value'=>$total_quantity))
    , ' '
    , table_header_cell(array('align'=>'right',
'value'=>money($total_price)))
);

print table_row(
    table_cell(array(
        'colspan' => 4
        , 'value' => submit_field('Recalculate Order')
    ))
);

$url = 'display.php';
if (isset($p))
{
    $url .= '?product_id='.$p->product_id;
}
print table_row(
    table_cell(array(
        'align' => 'right'
        , 'colspan' => 4
        , 'value' => '<b>'
            . anchor_tag(regular_url($url), 'Continue Shopping')
            . '</b>'
    ))
);

print end_table();
print end_form();
save_session_order($o);
?>
```

CHECKOUT.PHP

Now, finally, it's time to check out. Note that this is really the only file that needs to be on the secure server. There's no need for the catalog portions or even the cart page to be on a secure server, because they don't contain information that needs to be protected. However, on this page you're going to be accepting credit-card information.

Extensive comments are contained within the script to help you get through the page's logic.

```
<?php
require_once('header.php');

// get the session variables for the shopping cart, the current
order,
// and the user's email address
$order = get_session_order();

// if a value for 'email' was posted to the script from a form, use
that
// in preference to the session variable
$_SESSION['email'] = array_key_value(
    $_POST
    , 'email'
    , array_key_value($_SESSION, 'email')
);
$order->email = $_SESSION['email'];

// set up variables defining the values of the buttons of the form
// (defining the values once helps avoid errors caused by spelling
problems.)
$order_button = 'ORDER NOW!';

// load data from form into order
$order->build($_POST);

$submit = array_key_value($_POST, 'submit');
if ($submit == $order_button)
{
    // the user hit the big ORDER button. validate their credit
    // card and charge it, using the ValidateCard() and ChargeCard()
    // functions of the Order class.

    if (!$order->charge_card())
    {
        print "could not charge card\n";
    }
    else
    {
```

```
        // the charge went through - write the order to the
        // database using the SaveOrder() method of the Order class.
        $order->write_to_db();

        // redirect the user to the receipt page for a receipt
        // they can print or save to a file, and exit the script.
        //  pass on the ID value of the new order record and
        // the session ID that was passed in to this script.

        $url = 'receipt.php?order_id='
            . $order->order_id
            . '&sessid='
            . session_id()
        ;
        // header('Location: $url');
        print paragraph(anchor_tag($url, $url));
        // exit;
    }
}

print start_page(
    anchor_tag('index.php', "Bag'O'Stuff")
    . '<br> <br>Check Out'
);

print paragraph(
    start_form()
    , submit_field(array('name'=>'reset_order','value'=>'Reset Order
Object'))
    , end_form()
);

// include the shopping cart form
print print_cart($order);

// begin the order form.
print start_form();

print hidden_field('sessid', session_id());


print subtitle('User Info');
// store the IDs of the user and address (if any)
print hidden_field('user_id', $order->user_id);
```

```
print hidden_field('address_id', $order->address_id);

start_table(array('_defaults'=>array('cellspacing'=>4)));

print start_table();

// display the user's email address, along with the button they
// can use to ask to check the database for address information.
print labeled_row(
    'Email:'
    , text_field(array(
            'name'=>'email'
            , 'value'=>$order->email
            , 'size'=>20
        ))
        . ' '
        . submit_field('Get My Info')
);

print labeled_row(
    'First Name:'
    , text_field(array(
        'name' => 'firstname'
        , 'value' => $order->firstname
        , 'size' => 42
        , 'maxlength' => 40
    ))
);
print labeled_row(
    'Last Name:'
    , text_field(array(
        'name' => 'lastname'
        , 'value' => $order->lastname
        , 'size' => 42
        , 'maxlength' => 40
    ))
);

print table_row(table_cell(array('colspan'=>2, 'value'=>' ')));

// these fields contain any address information that might have been
// directly entered by the user before the database was searched, or
// the information from an address from the database that has been
// selected by the user. in any case, *these* fields are what will
```

```
// be used in the order.

print labeled_row(
    'Address:'
    , text_field(array(
        'name' => 'address1'
        , 'value' => $order->address1.'-new'
        , 'size' => 42
        , 'maxlength' => 40
    ))
);
print labeled_row(
    ' '
    , text_field(array(
        'name' => 'address2'
        , 'value' => $order->address2
        , 'size' => 42
        , 'maxlength' => 40
    ))
);
print labeled_row(
    'City:'
    , text_field(array(
        'name' => 'city'
        , 'value' => $order->city
        , 'size' => 42
        , 'maxlength' => 40
    ))
);
print labeled_row(
    'State:'
    , select_field(array(
        'name' => 'state'
        , 'values' => states()
        , 'match' => $order->state
    ))
);
print labeled_row(
    'Zip:'
    , text_field(array(
        'name' => 'zip'
        , 'value' => $order->zip
        , 'size' => 12
        , 'maxlength' => 10
```

```
    ))
);
print labeled_row(
    'Phone:'
    , text_field(array(
        'name' => 'phone'
        , 'value' => $order->phone
        , 'size' => 22
        , 'maxlength' => 20
    ))
);

if ($order->address_id)
{
    // allow the user to create a new address
    print table_row(
        ' '
        , checkbox_field(array(
            'name' => 'save_as_new'
            , 'value' => 'yes'
            , 'label' => 'Save this as a new address'
        ))
    );
}

print end_table();

// display the available shipping methods
print subtitle('Shipping Info');

print start_table(array('cellspacing'=>4));

print table_row(
    table_header_cell('Shipping Method')
    , table_header_cell(array('value'=>'Per Order',
'align'=>'right'))
    , table_header_cell(array('value'=>'Per Item',
'align'=>'right'))
    , table_header_cell(array('value'=>'Total for Order',
'align'=>'right'))
);

// set up shipping methods

foreach ($order->shipping_methods() as $shipping_id => $r)
```

```
{
    // calculate the cost of using this method. we use a simplistic
    // system: a fixed cost per order, and a per item charge.
    $shiptotal = $r['per_order'] + ($order->total_quantity *
$r['per_item']);

    // display the shipping method with a radio field allowing the
    // user to choose it
    print table_row(
        radio_field(array(
            'name' => 'shipping_id'
            , 'value' => $shipping_id
            , 'label' => $r['shipping']
            , 'match' => $order->shipping_id
        ))
        , table_cell(array('value'=>money($r['per_order']),
'align'=>'right'))
        , table_cell(array('value'=>money($r['per_item']),
'align'=>'right'))
        , table_cell(array('value'=>money($shiptotal),
'align'=>'right'))
    );
}
print end_table();

// display payment information
print subtitle('Credit Card Info');

print start_table();

if ($order->error)
{
    // if the user tried to place an order and there was an error
    // when validating or charging the card, display it here.
    print table_row(
        table_cell(array(
            'style' => 'color:red'
            , 'value' => $order->error
            , 'colspan'=>2
        ))
    );
    $order->error = '';
}

// display a test card number in the form for this example by
default.
```

```
// it has a valid format, and since we're not really trying
// to charge any cards here, AuthorizeNet will accept it.
if (empty($order->cc_number))
{
    $order->cc_number = '4912-7398-07156';
}

// pick Visa as the default type, to match the default test card
number
if (empty($order->cc_type_code))
{
    $order->cc_type_code = 'vis';
}

// display the accepted credit card types as radio button fields
$cc_types = $order->dbh()->getAssoc('select cc_type_code, cc_type
from cc_types');

print labeled_row(
    'Credit Card:'
    , select_field(array(
        'name' => 'cc_type_code'
        , 'match' => $order->cc_type_code
        , 'values' => $cc_types
    ))
);

print labeled_row(
    'Number:'
    , text_field(array(
        'name'=>'cc_number'
        , 'value'=>$order->cc_number
        , 'size'=>22
    ))
);

// set the variables used to enter the credit card expiration date

// set the $months array to a list of possible months
$months = array(
    1 => 1
    , 2 => 2
    , 3 => 3
    , 4 => 4
    , 5 => 5
```

```
    , 6 => 6
    , 7 => 7
    , 8 => 8
    , 9 => 9
    , 10 => 10
    , 11 => 11
    , 12 => 12
);

// set the $years array to a list of plausible years
$y = date('Y');
$years = array(
    $y => $y++
    , $y => $y++
    , $y => $y++
    , $y => $y++
    , $y => $y++
    , $y => $y++
    , $y => $y++
    , $y => $y++
);

// use January of next year as a default expiration date
if (empty($order->cc_exp_mon))
{
    $order->cc_exp_mon = 1;
}
if (empty($order->cc_exp_yr))
{
    $order->cc_exp_yr = date('Y')+1;
}

print labeled_row(
    'Expires:'
    , select_field(array(
            'name' => 'cc_exp_mon'
            , 'values' => $months
            , 'match' => $order->cc_exp_mon
        ))
        . select_field(array(
            'name' => 'cc_exp_yr'
            , 'values' => $years
            , 'match' => $order->cc_exp_yr
        ))
);
```

```
print end_table();

// display the order button
print paragraph(
    submit_field($order_button)
    , submit_field('Test Submit')
);

print end_form();

print end_page();

$_SESSION['order'] = serialize($order);
?>
```

Summary

This chapter explained a lot of PHP concepts, using a shopping cart as a vehicle (no pun intended).

One of the most important concepts we discussed was persistence – the ability to store information related to a particular user (such as shopping-cart items) across multiple visits. PHP relies upon its connectivity to a database – a connection mediated by the PEAR classes, if you're smart – to store information.

Another key concept is state maintenance. Because HTTP is an inherently stateless protocol, you have to do a bit of work to correlate one HTTP request from someone with the next request from the same person, all the while distinguishing those requests from the hundreds of others that might be showing up at about the same time. PHP provides some useful state-management features. You saw, for example, that there's nothing to the process of registering a session identifier and examining it later to identify a particular use.

These capabilities are key in our shopping cart application. For one thing, we used persistence to store the contents of each shopping cart in a database, in such a way that they were kept separate from all others. Furthermore, we used session management to track users through our site – across many request/response transactions – as they browsed our wares and added and removed items from their carts.

Chapter 15

XML Parsing

IN THIS CHAPTER

- Learning how to work with XML documents
- Examining an XML document retrieved from a URL

WHAT HTML IS TO WEB PAGES, the eXtensible Markup Language, or XML, is to data. Whereas HTML is about presenting your information to the world – handling typefaces, sizes, colors, layout, and so on – XML concerns itself purely with structuring and identifying that information. Given the number of new and different Web platforms that seem to pop up each week – desktop computers, laptops, cell phones, televisions, wristwatches, car stereos – this separation of content from presentation is the great holy goal of Web programmers. Both languages are wildly successful because at heart they're both very simple, yet allow for a huge range of applications. They even look alike – which they should, considering they're both based on the Standard Generalized Markup Language (SGML).

In an XML document containing meteorological-observation data, for example, distinct tags can identify certain numbers as wind-velocity values and other numbers as wind-direction values. The question of how to represent these values visually – if they are to be displayed visually at all, rather than just read into a database or other processing environment – is a separate issue.

The other great thing about XML is that it's an excellent format for transmitting information not just data, but the kinds of queries and responses you might normally associate with a regular programming language (like PHP itself). This is because it's lightweight – it's just ASCII (or Unicode), after all – and transparent. You can look at an XML document for the first time and stand a good chance of understanding it right away. Yet it's also suitable for interpretation by machines, which are notoriously dim when it comes to understanding.

In this chapter we'll explore XML and the capabilities of PHP when it comes to processing it. We'll read a document in from a URL and reformat its contents for use in Netsloth, our content-management application.

The Web site Slashdot.org is used in this chapter merely for example purposes. Most sites like Slashdot.org have terms and conditions governing the use of the content they post, so be sure to pursue the proper permission before you publicly post any content taken from another Web site through your own Web application. For information about using headlines from Slashdot specifically, you should take a look at `http://slashdot.org/code.shtml`.

Scope and Goals of Application

Not long ago, we had this great application to show you here. It had XML parsers, and event handlers, and function callbacks, and all kinds of flashy bits. The idea was to grab the headlines from a Web site like Slashdot (`www.slashdot.org`), which makes their content available in about every format known to modern humanity. One of these formats is XML, and you can see it yourself at `http://slashdot.org/slashdot.xml`. We would read it, parse it, and spit it back out as HTML, to be included on our tiny yet distinctive example of a Web content site, Netsloth (which you might remember from Chapter 11).

But then the folks building PHP decided that they would change their underlying XML support, building it around the Gnome XML library libxml2, and introducing this new extension called Simplexml, and, this is how you would build our first example now. Completely.

```
<?php
// keep the errors off the page
ini_set('display_errors', 0);
$url = 'http://www.slashdot.org/slashdot.xml';
$cachefile = "/tmp/slashdot.xml.cache";

if (($xml = file_get_contents($url)))
{
    file_put_contents($cachefile, $xml);
}
else
{
    error_log('Unable to contact www.slashdot.org');
    if (($xml = file_get_contents($cachefile)) === FALSE)
    {
```

```
        error_log("Unable to open cache file: $cachefile");
        print <<<EOT
<p>
Unable to obtain Slashdot.org content.
Please try again later.
</p>
EOT;
        return;
    }
}
$stories = simplexml_load_string($xml);
print <<<EOT
<h3>Slashdot Stories:</h3>
<ul>
EOT;
foreach ($stories->story as $story)
{
    print <<<EOT
<li><a href="{$story->url}">{$story->title}</a>
EOT;
}
print <<<EOT
</ul>
EOT;
?>
```

This would make for a rather short chapter. You'll notice particularly that the "handle the XML" part of this code is just ten lines. So we've jazzed it up a bit.

We'll want to be able to include more information about each story, including the topic-representing images the site provides. At the same time, we want our own page at Netsloth to keep running if Slashdot gets slashdotted and goes off the air, while minimizing the amount that we add to their site's traffic. Both goals involve setting up local caches of content. Figure 15-1 shows you the new Netsloth home page.

The stories shown in Figure 15-1 are for example purposes only. None of the content in this chapter represents postings that ever actually appeared on Slashdot.org.

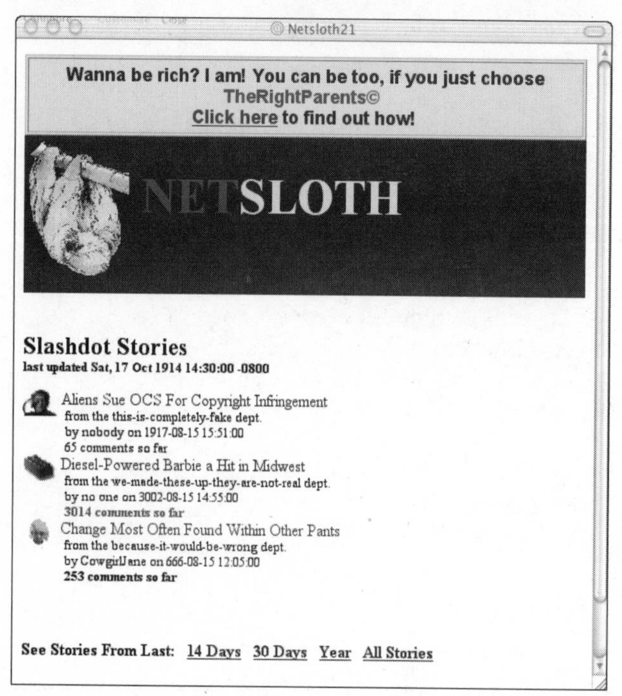

Figure 15-1: Netsloth21 home page with mock sample stories

Code Overview

The essential purpose of our application is to reach out across the Internet, grab an XML document, pick it apart, and reformat the chopped-up pieces into a form that's acceptable for use in our Netsloth content-management suite. To accomplish these goals, this software will need to be able to look at an XML document, distinguish the tags from the tagged text (also known as character data), and separate them if necessary. The piece of code that does this is generically called an *XML parser.* XML parsers can be designed in a couple of different ways.

An introduction to parsers

If you're going to work with XML, you need a parser. Parsers come in two different general varieties:

- **Tree-style parsers** (also called **Document Object Model (DOM) parsers**), which read through entire XML documents at once and convert the imported data into hierarchically organized objects representing whole documents at once. Microsoft's MSXML parser is of this kind.

- **Event-style parsers,** which read through XML documents just like tree-style parsers, but fire events as they go. These events correspond to different elements (such as opening tags, closing tags, and character data) encountered in the read-through. It's therefore possible to process different elements with code that listens for events of different kinds. The Simple API for XML (SAX) is an event-style parser implemented in a number of programming languages.

Both kinds of parsers do the job – it's possible to use either to examine an XML document programmatically. The difference between the two is performance. Because tree-style parsers have to read in a whole XML document and store it in memory as an object, they tend to be more resource-intensive than event-type parsers. Generally, tree-style parsers are a good idea if you're going to be examining the whole tree, or widely scattered parts of it – particularly more than once. Event-type parsers are better for quick, once-off examination of small parts of the tree.

Of course, you can just ignore the whole question of what style of parser suits you, and use Simplexml instead.

Using Simplexml

The Simplexml extension is, as of this writing, a work in progress. Still, it's hard to imagine that it could get much easier to use. It's a bit like one of those auto-focus, auto-everything-else cameras: you point it at some XML and, click, you've got an object:

```
$xml_object = simplexml_load_file("/path/to/my/file.xml");
$xml_object = simplexml_load_file("http://a.server/file.xml");
$xml_object = simplexml_load_string($some_xml_content);
```

Note especially the second example. Because PHP has general support for using URLs the same way you would use a path to a file on your server, you can go directly from an XML document from some far-off location to a useable object in your own code. Still, there are a few things to look out for. The nature of the properties of the `simplexml_element` object produced depends on the content of the XML. For example, we can make up a simplistic XML document and store it in a variable:

```
$doc = <<<EOT
<outer>
 <first>
 </first>
 <second>
  <name></name>
```

```
  </second>
  <third>
   <name>Joe</name>
  </third>
  <fourth>
   <name>Jill</name>
   <name>Bob</name>
  </fourth>
</outer>
EOT;
```

Then we can point Simplexml at it and print out the object we receive as a result:

```
$xml = simplexml_load_string($doc);
print_r($xml);
```

The results are as follows:

```
simplexml_element Object
(
    [first] => simplexml_element Object
        (
        )
    [second] => simplexml_element Object
        (
            [name] => simplexml_element Object
                (
                )
        )
    [third] => simplexml_element Object
        (
            [name] => Joe
        )
    [fourth] => simplexml_element Object
        (
            [name] => Array
                (
                    [0] => Jill
                    [1] => Bob
                )
        )
)
```

The first tag, <first>, had no content, so it becomes an empty simplexml_element object. The <second> tag did have some content, a <name> tag, but <name> itself was empty. We end up with an object having a single property, called name, whose value is another empty object. But now look at the <third> tag. This time <name> had a value, the string Joe. Now the name property, instead of pointing to another object, has a simple string value. And in the <fourth> tag, where the <name> tag was repeated, the result is an array of strings. This all makes good sense when you compare the output to the XML source.

But if you don't know what that source looked like, then discovering the nature of what you've received can be a little tricky. If you're going to be routinely parsing complicated documents that can have widely varying contents, then using something like the DOM XML Parser, which supports Xpath functions you can use to search through the XML in an easy yet powerful fashion, might be the way to go.

On the other hand, to use those routines, you have to learn new syntax rules, lots of new method calls, and so on. Whereas objects – we know from objects. Simplexml lets you focus more on the PHP side of the problem, and if that's where most of your real work lies, it can be a godsend.

Code Breakdown

Most of the work we'll be doing, as you saw in the smaller version earlier in the chapter, has to do with what happens at our end of the connection. We want to always be able to deliver some kind of content to our Netsloth front door, even if it isn't always current up to the instant the user sees the page. If we were delivering stock quotations, for instance, we'd have to worry much more about that subject. But for news headlines – particularly of the sort covered by a site like Slashdot, more valuable for their uniqueness than as the latest breaking stories – being roughly up-to-date is fine. Besides, they specifically request that you not hit their site more than once every 30 minutes, or else you might find yourself banned. One advantage we'll have is that we know what we'll be getting – the XML we'll receive from Slashdot is quite predictable. A typical Slashdot headline XML document is formatted like this (though, again, none of these stories are real):

```
<?xml version="1.0"?>
<backslash xmlns:backslash="http://slashdot.org/backslash.dtd">

    <story>
        <title>Aliens Sue OCS For Copyright Infringement</title>

<url>http://slashdot.org/article.pl?sid=03/08/15/1454224</url>
        <time>1917-08-15 15:51:00</time>
        <author>nobody</author>
```

```
        <department>this-is-completely-fake</department>
        <topic>107</topic>
        <comments>65</comments>
        <section>aliens</section>
        <image>topicms.gif</image>
    </story>

    <story>
        <title>Diesel-Powered Barbie a Hit in Midwest</title>

<url>http://slashdot.org/article.pl?sid=03/08/15/1451223</url>
        <time>3002-08-15 14:55:00</time>
        <author>no one</author>
        <department>we-made-these-up-they-are-not-real</department>
        <topic>126</topic>
        <comments>3014</comments>
        <section>basement</section>
        <image>topictoys.gif</image>
    </story>

    <story>
        <title>Change Most Often Found Within Other Pants</title>

<url>http://slashdot.org/article.pl?sid=03/08/14/2222214</url>
        <time>666-08-15 12:05:00</time>
        <author>CowgirlJane</author>
        <department>because-it-would-be-wrong</department>
        <topic>134</topic>
        <comments>253</comments>
        <section>science</section>
        <image>topicscience.gif</image>
    </story>

</backslash>
```

Note that each story element has associated title, URL, time, author, department, topic, comments, section, and image elements. Further note that the whole document is a backslash element—that is, it's bounded by `<backslash>` and `</backslash>` tags.

Laying the groundwork

All of the code is contained in a single file, slashdot.php, that lives in the /book/xml-rpc directory. But it gets displayed via an `include()` call from the front page of the enhanced version of Netsloth, which lives in /book/netsloth21. So the first order of business here, besides setting up the remote URL we're working with, is to figure out just where in the heck we are:

```
<?php
// example using new simplexml extension

// made possible by the nice folks at slashdot.org
$url = 'http://www.slashdot.org/slashdot.xml';

// let's get some stuff out of the way
$this_dir = dirname(__FILE__);
$root_dir = str_replace(
    $_SERVER['PHP_SELF']
    , ''
    , $_SERVER['PATH_TRANSLATED']
);
$src_dir = str_replace(
    $root_dir
    , ''
    , $this_dir
);
```

We are going to want to create URLs that point to content in the current directory – /book/xml-rpc – but that is not the "current directory" from the Web server's point of view, because we're being included from another script. That script name is in $_SERVER['PHP_SELF'], and the full file system path to that script is $_SERVER['PATH_TRANSLATED']. So we make the assumption that we share a common root directory with the script that called us, and do some string algebra to remove that common root from our current location – leaving us with, in theory, the correct Web server path to where we are.

Next, we check to see if it's time to get new stories from the Slashdot site. If that fails, because the network connection has trouble, or the remote site is down, or someone in Boise went nuts with a backhoe, we pick up the last copy we downloaded from a cache file. (If that fails, there's not much to do but apologize and give up.):

```
// a file to hold previously retrieved data
$cachefile = "{$this_dir}/slashdot.xml";

// We want nice clean error messages.
ini_set('display_errors', 0);

// first, we need to check whether we've hit their
// site within the last half-hour, BECAUSE:
//
```

```
//  "For those who don't know, you can get slashdot.rdf
//   or slashdot.xml to receive a list of headlines for
//   Slashdot. The document is fairly self explanatory,
//   and the rules are simple: Do whatever you want, but
//   don't access the file more than once every 30 minutes.
//   The server is plenty bogged down without adding a
//   hundred stock tickers refreshing themselves every
//   60 seconds. If your automated loading of slashdot
//   becomes too much of a burden on our servers, you
//   run the risk of having your IP banned, so play fair!"
//
//  -- http://slashdot.org/code.shtml
//

$xml = false;
if (    !file_exists($cachefile)     or !($last_time =
@filectime($cachefile))
)
{
    $last_time = 0;
}
else
{
    $xml = @file_get_contents($cachefile);
}

$this_time = time();
if ($last_time + 1800 < $this_time)
{
    // OK, try getting a new copy
    $newxml = @file_get_contents($url);
    if ($newxml === FALSE)
    {
        error_log("Unable to contact $url");
        if ($xml === FALSE)
        {
            error_log("Unable to open cache file: $cachefile");
            $msg = 'Unable to obtain Slashdot.org content.  Please
try again later.';
            error_log($msg);
            print "<h3>$msg</h3>\n";
            return;
        }
        $this_time = $last_time;
```

```
    }


}
```

Note that we use the built-in PHP function `filectime()` to get the date that the cache file was created. That lets us tell users how current the information they're looking at is.

If we are able to load the XML file from the URL, then we need to save it out as a new copy of the cache file, in preparation for times to come:

```
    else
    {
        $xml = $newxml;
        if (!@file_put_contents($cachefile, $xml))
        {
            // you might want to put an alert to the site webmaster
            // in here - if permission problems are preventing you
            // from caching the headlines, you'll hit the site too
            // often, and There Will Be Trouble. possibly including
            // flying monkeys.
            error_log("Problem caching Slashdot content to
$cachefile");
        }
    }
}
```

Then we run the XML that's now sitting in the variable `$xml` through Simplexml and create an object. We also check to see how many stories we're supposed to display. In the Netsloth21 home page, we set `$storycount` to the number we want to use. That variable will be visible here. In case we're being called by someone else, we also check to see if `$storycount` was passed as part of the URL, or from a form, by looking in the `$_REQUEST` superglobal. If no one has told us differently, we set the count to zero, meaning that we want to display every story we can get:

```
// load up the XML
$stories = simplexml_load_string($xml);

// and hey, presto
$last_updated = date('r', $last_time);
if (empty($storycount))
{
    if (empty($_REQUEST['storycount']))
        $storycount = 0; // all of 'em
```

```
    else
        $storycount = $_REQUEST['storycount'];
}
```

Now, to show off the goods. After opening an HTML table to contain the headlines, we create some variables pointing at the topic image directory on the Slashdot site and a local image directory on our own server. What we're going to do is copy the files from their site to ours. Since the images are based on general topics, the same ones are reused frequently. The first time we see each one, we make a local copy, and thereafter, that's what gets displayed on our pages. It's faster for us, and cheaper for them.

```
print <<<EOT
<p>
 <table cellspacing="0" cellpadding="0" border="0">
  <tr>
   <th colspan="4" align="left" style="font-size:large;">
    Slashdot Stories
   </th>
  </tr>
  <tr>
   <th colspan="4" align="left" style="font-size:smaller;">
    last updated {$last_updated}
    <br>
    <br>
   </th>
  </tr>

EOT;
// we are counting on this not changing..
$slashimage_dir = "http://images.slashdot.org/topics";
// they get enough traffic - let's store the Borg
// locally...
$ourimage_dir = "{$this_dir}/slashdot";
$i = 0;
foreach ($stories->story as $story)
{
    if (!file_exists("{$ourimage_dir}/{$story->image}"))
    {
        copy(
            "{$slashimage_dir}/{$story->image}"
            , "{$ourimage_dir}/{$story->image}"
        );
    }
```

Again, note how PHP's support for URLs-as-files makes this a snap. We just use the built-in `copy()` routine, which copies a file from one place to another, even though here, the file being copied is on some other server far off in the Net somewhere.

At this point, we're inside our main story loop, so we print out the headline, as well as the name of the person who posted it, the all-important department-of-strange-department-names line, and the number of comments about the story on the Slashdot site. In a bid to add a tiny bit of value to what is otherwise wholesale borrowing, we'll change the way we display the number of comments. You know a story is buzzing when the topic count goes through the roof, so the comments line will go from normal, to bold, to bright red for the big ones:

```
    // just to be fancy, let's be alarmed
    // by the number of comments
    $comment_style = '';
    $comment_count = (int)$story->comments;
    if ($comment_count > 200)
    {
        $comment_style .= 'font-weight:bold;';
        if ($comment_count > 500)
        {
            $comment_style .= 'color:red;';
        }
    }
    print <<<EOT
  <tr>
   <td align="center" valign="top" rowspan="2"><img height="25"
src="{$src_dir}/slashdot/{$story->image}"></td>
   <td align="left" valign="top" rowspan="2"> </td>
   <td align="left" valign="top" colspan="2"><a href="{$story->url}"
style="text-decoration:none;">{$story->title}</a></td>
  </tr>
  <tr>
   <td align="left" valign="top"> </td>
   <td style="font-size:smaller;" align="left" valign="top">
    from the {$story->department} dept.
    <br>
    by {$story->author} on {$story->time}
    <br>
    <span style="{$comment_style}">{$story->comments} comments so
far</span>
   </td>
  </tr>

EOT;
```

And that's it. Now we just check the story count and break out of the loop if we've reached our limit. Then we close the table, and we're done.

```
    ++$i;
    if ($storycount and $i >= $storycount)
        break;
}
print <<<EOT
 </table>
</p>

EOT;

?>
```

Summary

This chapter looked at the way in which PHP interacts with XML, which is an extraordinarily useful markup language for representing data in flat file form so that's it's more or less universally meaningful.

The new capabilities of PHP have made using an XML document feed – and there are lots of them out there – go from what was really something of a pain, to almost no trouble at all. Plus, obviously, headline feeds aren't the only kind of services available. The ease of using those services inside Web applications is going to make them a lot more popular.

If you're interested in getting deeper into XML and Web services, take a look in the /book/xml-rpc directory on the CD. We've put the code for an XML-RPC server and client there, along with some front-end pages you can use to see how they work. There, we use the new DOM extension of PHP 5, built around the libxml2 libraries, and Xpath, as well as the new object-oriented features and exception-handling capabilities, to make it almost as easy to call a function on someone else's server as it is on your own. For more information about XML-RPC, the best place to start is `http://www.xmlrpc.com`.

Next up: Simple Object Access Protocol (SOAP), a protocol for formatting messages with XML.

Chapter 16

SOAP

IN THIS CHAPTER

- Introducing Simple Object Access Protocol (SOAP)
- Introducing NuSOAP classes
- Examining application architecture built around public Web services and NuSOAP
- Looking at SOAP operations in PHP

WOULDN'T IT MAKE SENSE if software applications could talk to each other via something like email? You know, have one application send a message to another in order to invoke some function and have a message containing the result go back? Well, of course, it would, and a number of proprietary systems have served this purpose for a long time (IBM MQSeries is a long-standing example). Messaging systems enable applications – including those written in different languages, running on different processors, and created at different times – to work together to meet organizational-software-system requirements.

Messaging systems can be broken up, conceptually, into at least two parts: the transport protocol and the message format. Proprietary systems have traditionally used a closed protocol for at least one of those functions. Even relatively open standards, like remote procedure calls (RPCs) under Java, have relied on special facilities that can be perceived as security weaknesses by skeptical minds or under specific conditions.

This is the problem Simple Object Access Protocol (SOAP) is meant to solve. SOAP defines an XML document type for invoking objects' properties and functions. XML documents that conform to this specification are messages to be sent, like the body text of ordinary email messages between humans. SOAP messages, once written, can be sent via HTTP, or, indeed, by Simple Mail Transport Protocol (SMTP), the protocol normally used to send email. Hardly any routers or firewalls block the TCP ports required by those transport protocols, so moving SOAP messages around is a relatively straightforward process.

This chapter doesn't concern itself much with transport mechanisms. Instead, we're concerned here with the details of the SOAP message specification and the means by which you can make PHP comply with them.

Overview of SOAP

SOAP, at the end of the day, lives up to its first initial: It is indeed *simple*. SOAP messages are essentially text passages with some special tags applied, similar in some ways to HTML documents.

The SOAP specification is neither concerned with matters of transport (that's the role of the HTTP and SMTP specifications) nor with rules about what SOAP messages can carry (not much, anyway; that's up to the developers who build applications that employ SOAP). The SOAP definition has mainly to do with the structure of the documents that carry function calls to objects providing services and results back to the calling programs.

You can divide SOAP transactions into the request and the response. The client, via SOAP messages addressed to the server, says something like, "What's the CEO's inseam measurement?" This presumes, of course, that the server has a function that looks up or otherwise provides the boss's inseam length.

The server then executes the called function and returns some value or series of values. It might just return the integer 34, or return the integer 34 as well as the string `inches` so that the unit being used is clear.

Now it's time to have a look at the SOAP message itself. Though the SOAP specification includes information on a large number of special features (such as attachments), SOAP messages are essentially envelopes and their contents. The application we create in this chapter requires no SOAP features other than these critical ones.

You can view the full SOAP version 1.2 specifications on the Web at `http://www.w3.org/TR/soap12-part0`. (By the way, don't go to `http://www.soap.org` expecting to find information about the SOAP protocol. That site is run by the Society for Obstetric Anesthesia and Perinatology — "Celebrating Over 150 Years of Obstetric Anesthesia").

The SOAP envelope

The envelope surrounds the message *payload*, or body, and serves to define the XML namespaces used throughout the SOAP message.

Because it is an XML document, the SOAP text begins with a statement of its XML encoding and version:

```
<?xml version='1.0' encoding='UTF-8'?>
```

Then you have an opening `Envelope` tag, preceded by the `SOAP-ENV` namespace identifier. Indeed, the opening `Envelope` tag serves mainly to define three of the four namespaces used in the SOAP message. Here's the opening `Envelope` tag:

```
<SOAP-ENV:Envelope
   xmlns:SOAP-ENV="http://www.w3.org/2001/09/soap-encoding"
   xmlns:xsi="http://www.w3.org/2001/XMLSchema-instance"
   xmlns:xsd="http://www.w3.org/2001/XMLSchema">
```

Though the intricacies of XML namespaces are beyond the scope of this book, understand that the three namespaces defined in that passage of code serve the following roles:

- `SOAP-ENV` – Provides the definition of `Envelope` and `Body` elements in this SOAP message. The SOAP 1.2 specification is `http://www.w3.org/2001/09/soap-encoding`. That URL will render readably in Microsoft Internet Explorer; other browsers might require you to download the XML and look at it in a text viewer (such as vi, emacs, or Windows Notepad).
- `xsi` – The `xsi` schema defines aspects of function calls, such as values sent as arguments.
- `xsd` – The `xsd` schema deals with data types, such as integers, dates, strings, and Boolean values.

After the opening `Envelope` tag comes the whole of the `Body` element (to be discussed next). At the conclusion of the SOAP message, after the `Body` element, you find a closing `Envelope` tag, complete with its namespace identifier. It looks like this:

```
</SOAP-ENV:Envelope>
```

Now let's move on to the `Body` element.

The SOAP body

Inside the SOAP envelope is the SOAP body, the payload that's the whole point of having SOAP in the first place. A body begins with an opening `Body` tag, further distinguished by a `SOAP-ENV` namespace identifier:

```
<SOAP-ENV:Body>
```

Next comes the meat of the SOAP message – a call to a function, in this case. The name of the function you're calling is the name of the element that calls it. A namespace identifier – traditionally `ns1` – precedes the function name, like this:

```
<ns1:getInseam
xmlns:ns1="urn:referenceToWebService"
SOAP-ENV:encodingStyle="http://schemas.xmlsoap.org/soap/encoding/">
```

What's all that other stuff? Well, the namespace definition states where the function getInseam() can be found on the network. The SOAP-ENV:encodingStyle value further standardizes the way in which simple and complex data types are presented on each side of the SOAP transaction.

Next comes the question of whose inseam measurement you want to retrieve. This specifier should be presented to the function as an argument, which is to say that in a traditional (intra-program) call to the function the syntax looks something like this:

```
GetInseam("Joe Bloggs")
```

In SOAP you're obliged to do things a little differently. Remember that you are already inside a getInseam element, which means you have already made clear that getInseam is the function you're calling. You need to specify the argument now. Logically enough, you do that with an element whose name matches the argument name, as specified in the remote class:

```
<person xsi:type="xsd:string">Joe Bloggs</zipcode>
```

With that done, you close out the getInseam element and the Body element, as well:

```
</ns1:getInseam>
</SOAP-ENV:Body>
```

How does all this look in practice? The next section takes a look at a request/response pair in which a call to getInseam() is made and replied to.

A typical request/response pair

A SOAP transaction consists of a request and a response, similar in lots of ways to the request and response that are made when you order up a Web page with your browser. Remember, SOAP transmissions are nothing more than passages of text, marked up with XML in such a way that they serve special SOAP purposes.

THE REQUEST

Here's a complete request:

```
<?xml version='1.0' encoding='UTF-8'?>
<SOAP-ENV:Envelope
   xmlns:SOAP-ENV="http://schemas.xmlsoap.org/soap/envelope/"
   xmlns:xsi="http://www.w3.org/2001/XMLSchema-instance"
   xmlns:xsd="http://www.w3.org/2001/XMLSchema">
   <SOAP-ENV:Body>
      <ns1:getInseam
```

```
      xmlns:ns1="urn:referenceToWebService"
      SOAP-
ENV:encodingStyle="http://schemas.xmlsoap.org/soap/encoding/">
      <person xsi:type="xsd:string">Joe Bloggs</person>
      </ns1:getInseam>
   </SOAP-ENV:Body>
</SOAP-ENV:Envelope>
```

A request, at its simplest, is just a Body element inside an Envelope element. You can make things more complicated if you want – the specification allows for, among other things, a supplementary Header element that describes the relationship among several SOAP messages or that describes how the message should be routed.

THE RESPONSE

Responses, in terms of format, bear a close resemblance to requests. They have exactly the same envelope formats, and the body is different only in terms of the name given to the element being sent. Usually, that's the same as the element name specified in the request, with Response appended.

Here's a complete response to match your earlier request:

```
<?xml version='1.0' encoding='UTF-8'?>
<SOAP-ENV:Envelope
   xmlns:SOAP-ENV="http://schemas.xmlsoap.org/soap/envelope/"
   xmlns:xsi="http://www.w3.org/2001/XMLSchema-instance"
   xmlns:xsd="http://www.w3.org/2001/XMLSchema">
   <SOAP-ENV:Body>
      <ns1:getInseamResponse
      xmlns:ns1="urn:referenceToWebService"
      SOAP-
ENV:encodingStyle="http://schemas.xmlsoap.org/soap/encoding/">
         <return xsi:type="xsd:float">34.0</return>
      </ns1:getInseamResponse>
   </SOAP-ENV:Body>
</SOAP-ENV:Envelope>
```

Not too complicated, right? Joe Bloggs has an inseam measurement of 34. That's probably 34 inches. However, could Joe be a child with a 34-centimeter inseam? This response gives us no way to tell.

To encode complex data structures into SOAP messages (both requests and responses), you have to dig a bit deeper into the specification. The next section takes a look at how to encode an array into a SOAP message.

COMPLEX DATA TYPES

Complex data types are multipart data types. An *array* is an example of a complex data type in which the members are accessed by number. A *struct*, as those of you who code in C know, is an "associative array," in which the array elements are accessed by name rather than by number.

In the case of the inseam-returning Web service, it would be handy to know what unit applies to the floating-point number that comes back in response to a request. You can modify the contents of the `Body` element to hold this information in a struct.

The struct defined here contains two elements: the *value* (the floating-point value) and the *unit* (the string `inches`, `centimeters`, or whatever).

```
<return xmlns:ns1="urn:referenceToWebService"
xsi:type="ns1:inseamInfo">
<unit xsi:type="xsd:string">inch</unit>
<value xsi:type="xsd:double">34.0</value>
</return>
```

In this mode of using SOAP, the Web service referred to defines a struct called `inseamInfo`, which is comprised of a string called `unit` and a float called `value`. By stating in the opening `return` tag that the return value is of type `inseamInfo`, you make it legal to refer to these sub-elements.

There's a lot more to do with the SOAP specification, and not all of it obscure. Some of the more interesting and useful bits have to do with how errors and other exceptional conditions are noted via SOAP, while others have to do with how to describe other compound data types in SOAP messages. Such aspects of the specification are beyond the scope of this chapter, but are certainly worth studying.

There's lots of information on SOAP at the World Wide Web Consortium site, including an overview (`http://www.w3schools.com/soap/soap_intro.asp`) and a tutorial (`http://www.w3schools.com/soap/default.asp`).

Code Overview

Key to any successful career in software design is the ability to freely make use of the work of other people. The open-source movement is all about this practice, and, thankfully, a considerable amount of software is available for the taking. NuSphere Corporation – makers of PHPEd, a PHP development environment – have developed a set of classes called SOAPx4, which has since been modified and renamed NuSOAP. It's a remarkably capable SOAP suite, doing pretty much all the heavy lifting for you. If you're using a PHP development environment (such as NuSphere's PHPEd version 3 or later) you'll probably find it even easier to work with NuSOAP. You can add your own modules – such as new releases of PHP – to your environment after you set it up initially.

The best place to begin the process of getting NuSOAP is on the Web site of Dietrich Ayala (`http://dietrich.ganx4.com/nusoap/`). His site includes links to the latest version of NuSOAP, as well as links to documentation, mailing lists, and other resources for developers and architects.

The essence of NuSOAP

NuSOAP is a series of classes. You copy the downloaded files (most of them .php files) to your include directory and then make reference to them in your own PHP classes. The NuSOAP classes take care of such work as creating SOAP client and server objects and managing the transmission of SOAP messages among those objects. The NuSOAP classes even take care of something we discussed earlier in this chapter: the encoding of values into properly structured XML.

For the most part, you can think of the NuSOAP classes as black boxes. You just stick the PHP files in your include directory and then cease worrying about them. All you have to do is be aware, as you're writing PHP programs that you want to act as Web-service providers or consumers, that you have some new classes available to you.

Suppose you want to build a server. In other words, you want to make a PHP function available as a Web service. Once you've added the required include statement (as follows) you have a four-step process ahead of you.

```
require_once('nusoap.php');
```

1. Create a server object. All you need to do is set a variable equal to a `soap_server` object (`soap_server` being one of the classes made available by your inclusion of NuSOAP). It's easy:

   ```
   $server = new soap_server;
   ```

2. Register one of your local functions with that new `soap_server` object. Again, no problem. You simply invoke the `register()` function of the `soap_server` object, specifying one of your local functions as the sole argument. The complete syntax looks like this:

   ```
   $server->register('getInseam');
   ```

3. Define a function called `getInseam()`. This can contain whatever code you want. Presumably, in this case, it accesses a database to retrieve a named party's inseam measurement and then returns a value and unit. The skeleton of the function looks something like this:

   ```
   function getInseam($name) {
   // Function code...
   }
   ```

4. Tune the `soap_server` object in to the HTTP requests it's meant to monitor and enable it to respond to them. You do this with a standard piece of code that rarely varies across NuSOAP applications:

   ```
   $server->service($HTTP_RAW_POST_DATA);
   ```

Those are the key elements of a SOAP server as implemented under NuSOAP. What, then, about the client that speaks to this service? It's even simpler.

NuSOAP clients have to include the nusoap.php file as well. Once that's done, they need only to instantiate a `soapclient` object (the `soapclient` object, again, being part of the NuSOAP collection) with the URL of the service to be called as an argument. If you had a service called `getInseam()` on `http://www.wiley.com` (there isn't one, by the way), you could do this to create a SOAP client to call it:

```
$soapclient = new soapclient('http://www.wiley.com/getInseam.php');
```

Then you could send a call to the server via that client, like this:

```
write( $soapclient->call('getInseam',array('name'=>'Joe Bloggs')));
```

Pretty cool, eh? The arguments are sent as an array that enables you to match sent values to expected values as you like.

A simple NuSOAP service call

Now we take a quick look at a "Hello, user" program as written with the help of the NuSOAP classes. Really you see two programs here: a client and a server. The server exposes a simple routine that takes in a string (the user's name) and returns a string made up of the word `Hello` and the provided name followed by a period. In other words, if you send the service `Ralph` as an argument, the service says, `Hello, Ralph.`

First you need a server. The server has the same name as the service you want to expose, so in this case name it hello.php. Its full contents are as follows:

```
require_once('nusoap.php');

$server = new soap_server;

$server->register('hello');

function hello ($name){
        return "Hello $name.";
        }

$server->service($HTTP_RAW_POST_DATA);
```

Not complicated, really. It's just a matter of registering an otherwise ordinary function with a special server object and then setting that server to deal with HTTP activity.

Every server needs a client. The client file, in this case, can be called anything and can reside anywhere the server can be accessed via HTTP.

```
require_once('nusoap.php');

$soapclient = new soapclient('http://yourdomain.com/hello.php');

write($soapclient->call('hello',array('name'=>'Ralph')));
```

Pretty simple, really. You just bind your client to the service (this example assumes you know exactly where it is and what it's called) and call that client as you need values from it.

The glory of NuSOAP is its simplicity. There's more to it than we've just discussed – you will see some more complexity as the chapter continues – but there's no doubt that NuSOAP makes it unbelievably easy to incorporate SOAP client and server capability into PHP programs. It can be said that, other than for educational reasons, there's never a reason to write your own SOAP client and server classes anymore. You'd be reinventing an already highly refined wheel.

Determining the Goals of the Application

It's time to have a look at SOAP messaging under PHP, and at some of the ways you can communicate with publicly accessible Web services via SOAP. The rest of this chapter focuses on an application that requests information from different sources, parses it, and presents it to the user.

Our goal is to use the Web services made available by a couple of providers – the Barnes & Noble bookstore and the Babelfish translation service – to gather information. Specifically, we use the Barnes & Noble service to gather information about books that interest us, and the Babelfish service to translate a passage of text from English into a series of European languages.

The Barnes & Noble application takes an International Standard Book Number (ISBN) and returns the price of the book identified by that number at Barnes & Noble's Web site, `www.bn.com`. If you send it the value `0440234816`, which is the ISBN of Karen Marie Moning's novel *To Tame a Highland Warrior,* you can expect to see the following output from your local PHP program:

```
The price of book number 0440234816 is $6.99.
```

That price really is a bargain for "a medieval romance with paranormal overtones."

The Babelfish application (`http://babelfish.altavista.com`) enables you to translate a phrase from English to French, German, Italian, Spanish, or Portuguese. By default, the program is set up to send the value `From beneath you, it devours` to Babelfish. The application gives you the following translations, which are variously accurate. Generally, if you see the English word in the translation, it means Babelfish was stumped.

- French – *De sous vous, il devours.*
- German – *Von unter Ihnen es devours.*
- Italian – *Sotto da voi, esso devours.*
- Spanish – *Debajo de usted, él devours.*
- Portuguese – *Abaixo de você, ele devours.*

Clearly, Babelfish has problems with *devours.*

The interesting aspect of this is that everything is done with Web services. You send parameters (the ISBN in the former example, and the target language and original phrase in the latter), and the Web services (which aren't hosted locally, perhaps obviously) return the strings you need.

How does it work? The answer to this question requires a deeper exploration of our application's code, which follows in the next section.

Code Breakdown

To see what's going on in the two applications, you have to take a close look at the PHP code itself. Both the Babelfish application and the Barnes & Noble application are clients – they exist for the purpose of talking to servers that are implemented somewhere else.

In this case, both of them speak to servers on XMethods (`www.xmethods.com` or `www.xmethods.net`), a site that hosts a number of Web services for the purposes of testing and experimentation. You don't need to know how those remote services are implemented. They could be in Java, C, or PHP. It really makes no difference to you, because they're set up to work with SOAP requests from over the Internet.

The Barnes & Noble application

The Barnes & Noble client sends an ISBN value (which uniquely identifies a book in print) to a Web service, which returns the selling price of the corresponding book on the Barnes & Noble Web site, `www.bn.com`. It prints out a simple string, indicating either the price of the book, the fact that `www.bn.com` doesn't list the book, or the fact that there was an error in the execution of the Web service.

THE HEADER FILE

Many of the files in the Barnes & Noble and Babelfish applications call a header file initially. The header file, header.php, does two important things. First, it imports the critical nusoap.php file. It also specifies how the local applications deal with errors.

Here is header.php:

```
<?php

require_once(preg_replace('/soap.*/','book.php',realpath(__FILE__)))
;
function soap_errors()
{
    $oh = set_error_handler('error_handler');
    if (empty($oh))
    {
        set_handler(0, H_ERROR);
        set_handler(E_ALL, H_LOG);
    }
    else
    {
        restore_error_handler();
    }
}

soap_errors();

// include the class and function definitions for this application
require_once('lib/nusoap.php');
?>
```

THE CLIENT FILE

The client file actually handles the process of instantiating a SOAP client that connects to a publicly accessible Web service providing Barnes & Noble prices (really, it just tells NuSOAP to do the dirty work). Here it is:

```
<?php
// include the SOAP classes
require_once(dirname(__FILE__).'/header.php');
// define parameter array (ISBN number)
$param = array('isbn'=>'0385503954');
// define path to server application
$serverpath
='http://services.xmethods.net:80/soap/servlet/rpcrouter';
//define method namespace
$namespace="urn:xmethods-BNPriceCheck";
```

```
// create client object
$client = new soapclient($serverpath);
// make the call
$price = $client->call('getPrice',$param,$namespace);
// if a fault occurred, output error info
if (isset($fault)) {
        print "Error: ". $fault;
        }
else if ($price == -1) {
        print "The book is not in the database.";
} else {
        // otherwise output the result
        print "The price of book number ". $param['isbn'] ." is $".
$price;
        }
// kill object
unset($client);
?>
```

So, what's going on here? Some of it should look familiar. First of all, the program defines an array:

```
$param = array('isbn'=>'0385503954');
```

Then, it sets a variable (`$serverpath`) that contains, as a string, a URL:

```
$serverpath
='http://services.xmethods.net:80/soap/servlet/rpcrouter';
```

What's that URL? Well, if you call it up in an ordinary browser, you get an error. The error says, in effect, that you can't use a browser in this situation because this isn't a document at all – it's a remote procedure call (RPC) router. As such, you have to send it text (that is, SOAP XML) via the HTTP `POST` command. This makes sense, because you want to send something from your client to the remote Web service.

Then you specify, on that remote site, the namespace you're working with. This line of code serves that purpose:

```
$namespace="urn:xmethods-BNPriceCheck";
```

The purpose of the reference to that site is to examine the Web Services Description Language (WSDL) file that exists there. WSDL describes the Web services that exist at a particular site, and the particular methods they expose. You know that `BNPriceCheck` is a meaningful namespace on XMethods because you saw it advertised at `http://services.xmethods.net`. (It's also described programmatically at `http://www.xs.net/sd/2001/BNQuoteService.wsdl`.)

The next line should look familiar. It's the instantiation of a NuSOAP `soapclient` object that's bound to the XMethods RPC router:

```
$client = new soapclient($serverpath);
```

With all that done, you can make a call to the remote service, expecting a single value in return:

```
$price = $client->call('getPrice',$param,$namespace);
```

That line invokes the `call()` function of the local `soapclient` object (as contained in the `$client` handle). It sends along three arguments:

- `getPrice` – The name of the function you are calling
- `$param` – The struct you established earlier, containing the ISBN value
- `$namespace` – The namespace you got from the WSDL file, making it clear to the RPC router that you want to send your query to the Barnes & Noble service

After the request goes off – and remember, it's the job of NuSOAP to manage the mechanics of sending the request over HTTP (using `POST`) and dealing with the response when it comes – you have only to react to the string that you get back. It'll be one of three things: An indication that the service experienced an error, an indication that the ISBN you sent doesn't correspond to a book in the database, or a price value. Here's the code that figures out which:

```
if (isset($fault)) {
        print "Error: ". $fault;
        }
else if ($price == -1) {
        print "The book is not in the database.";
} else {
        print "The price of book number ". $param[isbn] ." is $".
$price;
```

From that code you see that you're expecting a floating-point value if the book is in the database, or `-1` if it's not. If a variable called `$fault` (defined in NuSOAP) exists, it means there was a problem in the service's execution and an error field in the `Header` element of the SOAP response was used (have a look at the SOAP specification for information on how `Header` elements indicate error conditions).

Be aware that floating-point values have some risk with respect to precision. If you work with lots of numbers, rounding errors can occur, and when the errors represent money, you can be in big trouble! Use the `math` functions to guarantee precision if you have to, but don't worry about it here — it's not a problem.

The Babelfish application

The Babelfish applications (there are three of them on the CD-ROM) are also SOAP clients, similarly concerned with talking to a Web service made available on the XMethods experimental site. The difference between these applications and the Barnes & Noble application, though, is that the Babelfish applications rely on the WSDL file exposed at XMethods (`www.xmethods.com` or `www.xmethods.net`) to learn about the Web service.

For discussion purposes, consider babel.php, the simplest of the Babelfish SOAP clients. The others vary mainly in that they do the same thing several times for different languages. Here is babel.php:

```
<?php
require_once(dirname(__FILE__).'/header.php');

$client = new soapclient(
    'http://www.xmethods.net/sd/2001/BabelFishService.wsdl'
    , 'wsdl'
);
$proxy = $client->getProxy();

$languages = array(
'English'    => 'en'
, 'French'    => 'fr'
, 'German'    => 'de'
, 'Italian'   => 'it'
, 'Spanish'   => 'es'
, 'Portugese' => 'pt'
);

$phrase = 'From beneath you, it devours.';

foreach ($languages as $language => $lc)
{
    if ($language == 'English')
        continue;
```

```
    $result = $proxy->BabelFish('en_'.$lc, $phrase);
    $result = $proxy->BabelFish($lc.'_en', $result);
    $result = $proxy->BabelFish('en_'.$lc, $result);
    $result = $proxy->BabelFish($lc.'_en', $result);
    print "English <-> $language : $result\n";
}
?>
```

The most readily obvious difference between this and the Barnes and Noble application is that the soapclient object (again, part of NuSOAP) uses a constructor that's different from the ones you saw earlier in this chapter. The soapclient constructor used here makes reference to a WSDL file:

```
$client = new soapclient(
    'http://www.xmethods.net/sd/2001/BabelFishService.wsdl'
    , 'wsdl'
);
```

What's that all about? Have a look at the WSDL file. It's an XML file itself, so you can call it up in your browser (or a text editor, if your browser won't show XML readably) if you like. The most interesting part of the file, for your purposes, is this passage:

```
<operation name="BabelFish">
<input message="tns:BabelFishRequest" />
<output message="tns:BabelFishResponse" />
</operation>
```

That means there's a function called BabelFish available to you. To call it you need to create what NuSOAP calls a proxy object, which you do by calling a function of the soapclient object:

```
$proxy = $client->getProxy();
```

With that done, your local PHP program sets a variable containing the phrase to be translated and an array containing abbreviations for the languages into which translation is to be made. Each individual call to the Babelfish service goes through the proxy object. The syntax for setting the variable looks like this:

```
$result = $proxy->BabelFish('en_'.$lc, $phrase);
```

The service is invoked, via the proxy object, with two arguments: the phrase to be translated and the from/to language pair that describes the desired translation procedure.

The seemingly redundant code in the `foreach` loop has a bit of fun with Babelfish, highlighting the fact that a translation from Language A to Language B and back again doesn't necessarily yield the original phrase! This results, among other things, from the gendered nature of many languages. Suppose you start with this phrase in English:

If I had a hammer

Babelfish translates it into Spanish like this:

Si tenía un martillo

If you ask Babelfish to translate that Spanish back into English, though, you get this:

If it had a hammer

This is because *tenía* can mean I had, you had, she had, he had, or it had (it's only in the subjunctive that Spanish is this vague). Only Babelfish's programmers know why the algorithm chooses *it* in this case.

Writing a SOAP server application

Sometimes, you just have to do things the hard way. Even though NuSOAP can make the job a lot easier, the file simple.php does the work of a SOAP server manually. It includes the code necessary to receive, parse, and evaluate SOAP requests, and to send out correct SOAP responses. Up until now, you've worked with clients; they requested data from publicly available Web services on the Internet.

Much of this file should look familiar to you. It receives a stream of raw text via an HTTP `POST` event and uses a combination of string manipulation and PHP's built-in XML parsing capability to extract an argument (either `CD` or `DVD`). The program kind of fakes a database lookup – you can put in actual code if you like – and formats the "results" of the "lookup" as a SOAP response.

That's the interesting part. The PHP program has to take on all the responsibility of properly formatting the SOAP response. Essentially, the whole SOAP response gets packed into a single variable, which is then returned:

```
$resp= <<<EOQ
<env:Envelope xmlns:env="http://schemas.xmlsoap.org/soap/envelope/"
xmlns:enc="http://schemas.xmlsoap.org/soap/encoding/"
env:encodingStyle="http://schemas.xmlsoap.org/soap/encoding/"
xmlns:xs="http://www.w3.org/1999/XMLSchema"
xmlns:xsi="http://www.w3.org/1999/XMLSchema-instance">
 <env:Header>
  <t:Transaction xmlns:t="urn:CDSpecial" env:mustUnderstand="0">
   5
  </t:Transaction>
 </env:Header>
```

```
 <env:Body>
  <a0:CDSpecial xmlns:a0="urn:CDSpecial">
   <CDSpecialResponse>
    <price xsi:type="xs:string">
     $price
    </price>
    <title xsi:type="xs:string">
     $title
    </title>
    <artist xsi:type="xs:string">
     $artist
    </artist>
   </CDSpecialResponse>
  </a0:CDSpecial>
 </env:Body>
</env:Envelope>
EOQ;
```

This passage should look very much like the standard SOAP response you saw in the theory sections earlier in this chapter. It's all here: the namespace declarations, the `Envelope`, `Header`, and `Body` elements, and the data-type designations describing the values that populate the `Body`.

Summary

This chapter covered a lot and in the process opened the door to a very exciting new capability of PHP. Web services, as made possible by SOAP messaging, enable you to extract information from the Internet without writing complicated text-parsing routines or having to hope that the HTML your programs parse remains formatted the same way forever. Web services are resources you can rely upon to give you correct answers in response to correctly formatted function calls.

SOAP isn't that hard to use, either, thanks in large part to the NuSOAP classes from NuSphere and Dietrich Ayala. NuSOAP handles the tedious work of managing HTTP requests and responses between clients and servers, and of formatting the XML in SOAP messages as required. It makes Web services under PHP simpler by a considerable margin.

Chapter 17

Project Management

IN THIS CHAPTER

- Introducing project management software
- Discussing the problems a project management application must solve
- Examining the database tables for a project management application

THE PROBLEM IS ALMOST NEVER the code. When you're developing a large application – or any project really – the hairiest difficulties have more to do with people working in teams than with any technical aspect of the job.

The program in this chapter aims to facilitate the process of collaboration between people working on a project. It will keep track of deadlines and keep notes on which person is responsible for which tasks in a project.

Determining the Goals of the Application

For the purposes of this application, project management has to do with the division of labor between two or more collaborators. We want them to be able to see who's responsible for what, to know when deadlines are (or were), and to view the contents of files. As an ancillary function, this application also requires authentication, so the software knows which user is which and can adjust its output accordingly.

Necessary pages

The catalog of pages our project management program requires closely resembles the list of requirements it must satisfy:

- The project management application must support user logins, and it must keep track of users as they use the application across many transactions. This makes session management a necessity. We use PHP's library of session-management functions and objects, just as we did in other applications in this book.

- Once users have logged in, they should be able to view the status of the projects they're involved in. They'll want to see which files they are responsible for (*own,* in the parlance), when they are or were due to be finished, what any revised expected completion dates are, and whether any problems have been noted with regard to individual files.
- Users should be able to share files that are relevant to a project.

The pages are straightforward – as you've guessed by now, we certainly didn't blow the budget on a designer. Figures 17-1 through 17-5 show you some of the main screens of the application.

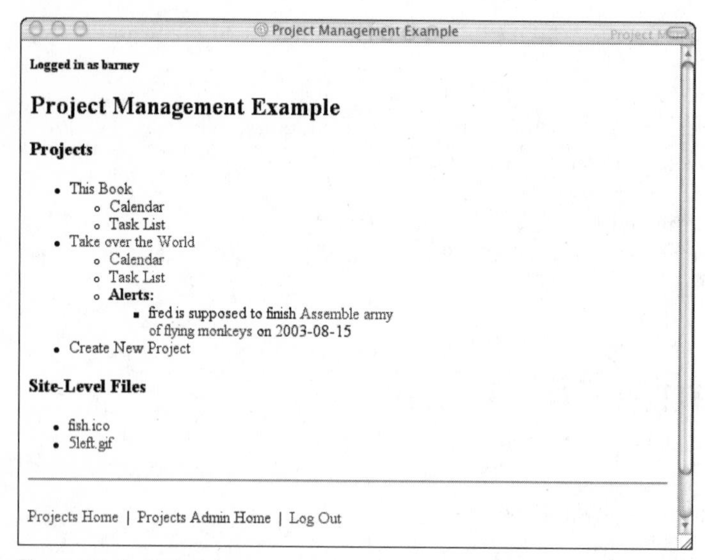

Figure 17-1: Project home page

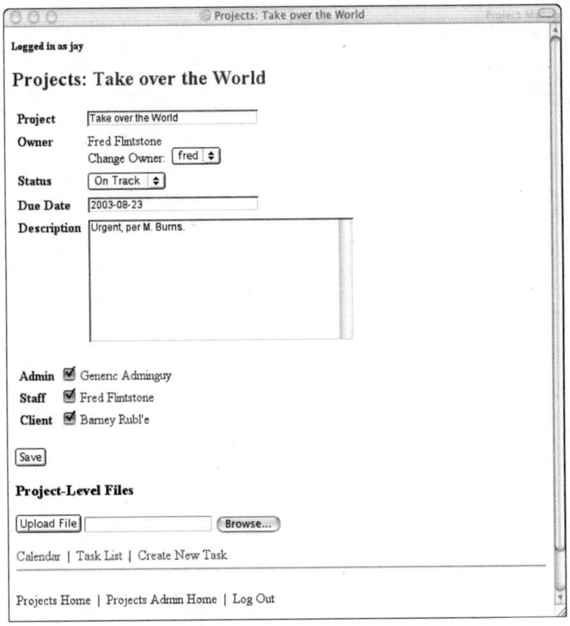

Projects: Take over the World

Logged in as jay

Projects: Take over the World

Project: Take over the World
Owner: Fred Flintstone
Change Owner: fred
Status: On Track
Due Date: 2003-08-23
Description: Urgent, per M. Burns.

Admin: Generic Adminguy
Staff: Fred Flintstone
Client: Barney Rubl'e

Save

Project-Level Files

Upload File Browse...

Calendar | Task List | Create New Task

Projects Home | Projects Admin Home | Log Out

Figure 17-2: Edit Project page

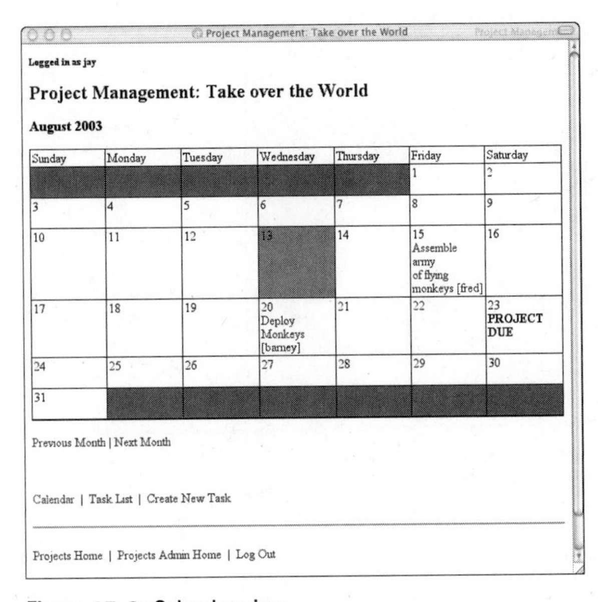

Figure 17-3: Calendar view

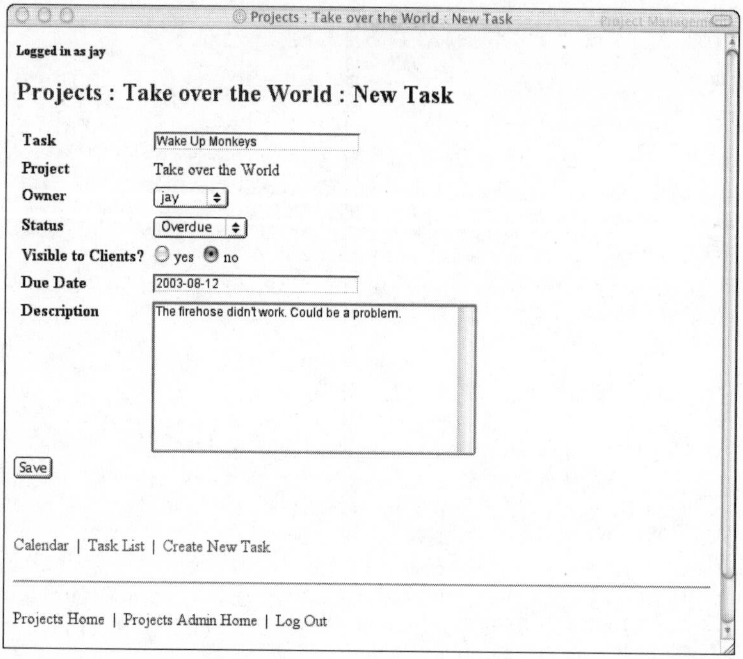

Projects : Take over the World : New Task

Logged in as jay

Projects : Take over the World : New Task

Task Wake Up Monkeys
Project Take over the World
Owner jay
Status Overdue
Visible to Clients? yes no
Due Date 2003-08-12
Description The firehose didn't work. Could be a problem.

Save

Calendar | Task List | Create New Task

Projects Home | Projects Admin Home | Log Out

Figure 17-4: Add New Task page

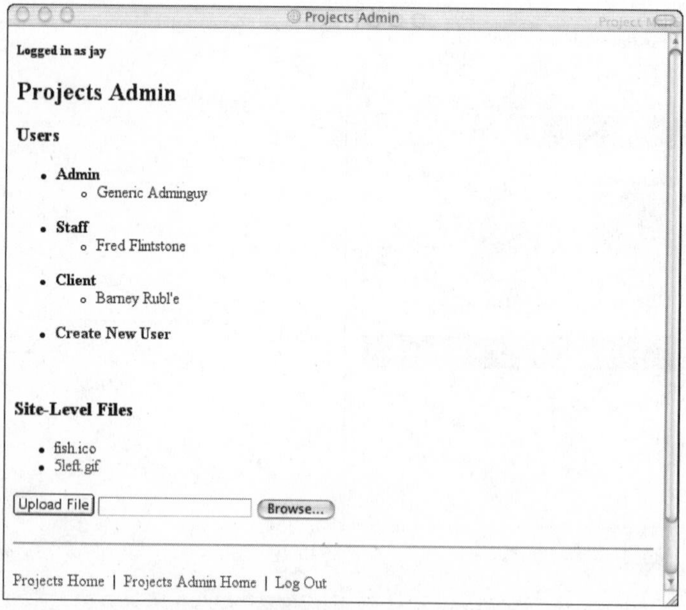

Projects Admin

Logged in as jay

Projects Admin

Users

- **Admin**
  - Generic Adminguy
- **Staff**
  - Fred Flintstone
- **Client**
  - Barney Rubl'e
- **Create New User**

Site-Level Files

- fish.ico
- 5left.gif

Upload File Browse...

Projects Home | Projects Admin Home | Log Out

Figure 17-5: Project Admin home page

Designing the Database

Key to this application is its database. Much of the work that the project-management application does is essentially note keeping about which files fit into which projects, where they are, who owns them, and what their status relative to established deadlines is. This information is the sort that databases like to contain for us.

The entirety of the project management information store is contained in a database called projects. The projects database contains a number of tables, each of which tracks various aspects of the project management mission. Figure 17-6 shows the complete schema:

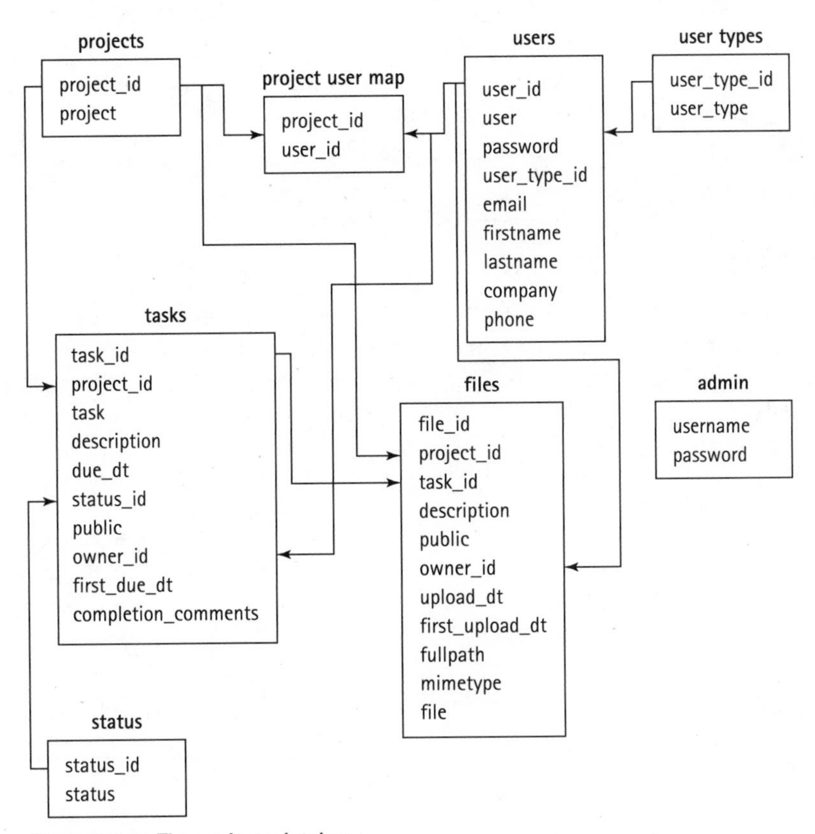

Figure 17-6: The projects database

User types

The values that can be assigned to users to dictate their privileges are contained in the `user_types` table. The table contains an incremented integer field called `user_type_id` that serves as the primary key, and a `user_type` field that contains English words that describe the type of user.

The SQL scripts that create the database and populate its tables initially put the values “staff,” “client,” and “admin” into the `user_type` fields of three records.

Application users

The `users` table defines the people who are allowed to use the database, as well as their usernames, passwords, and a bunch of personal contact information. The fields in this table are as follows:

- `user_id` – An auto-incrementing integer used as the primary key
- `user` – The username
- `password` – The password
- `user_type_id` – An integer that matches the primary key of one of the user type constants in the user_types table
- `email`, `firstname`, `lastname`, `company`, and `phone` – Strings representing personal details

Project and task status

The `status` table contains another set of values, describing whether a project or task is late, on schedule, on a delayed schedule, completed, or abandoned.

The descriptions of these values are “On Track,” “Slipped,” “Overdue,” “Done,” and “Cancelled.”

Projects

In this application, a project is defined as an entity in its own right. Though projects typically contain many files, it is the files that are mapped to projects, not the reverse. Projects are recorded in the `projects` table.

Project records contain seven columns:

- `project_id` – An auto-incrementing integer used as the primary key
- `project` – The project name
- `description` – A text description
- `due_dt` – The current due date of the project (possibly not the same as its original due date)
- `status_id` – The status of the project, defined by a reference to the status table
- `owner_id` – The manager of the project, defined by a reference to the users table
- `first_due_dt` – The original due date of the project; by comparing this field to `due_dt`, you can see whether or not the project has been delayed

Project-user mappings

The project_user_map table exists solely for the purpose of establishing a correlation between a project record, as identified by its project_id integer and stored in the project_id field, and a user, identified by its user_id integer and stored in the user_id field.

Tasks

Tasks are like files in that they are associated with project, and many of them can be associated with a single project. Tasks are recorded in a table called tasks, which contains 10 fields:

- task_id – An auto-incremented integer that serves as the table's primary key
- project_id – An integer that maps to a project_id value in the project table
- task – A varchar name for the job
- description – A text description of the task to be done
- due_dt – A date variable describing the originally scheduled completion date
- status_id – An integer that maps to the status_id field in the status table
- public – A Boolean value describing whether users other than the owner can see the task
- owner_id – An integer that maps to the user_id field of the users table to identify the task's owner
- first_due_dt – A date object denoting the current scheduled completion date for the task
- completion_comments – A text field for notes that are made upon completion

Files

Projects contain many files, and files map to projects. The project management application keeps track of projects' constituent files in a table called, logically enough, files. The files table contains 11 fields that describe the files:

- file_id – An auto-incrementing integer used as the primary key
- project_id – An integer that maps to a value in the project_id field in the projects table

- `task_id` – An integer that maps to the `task_id` field in the tasks table
- `description` – A text description of the file (not necessarily including its path)
- `public` – A Boolean value that describes whether users other than the owner can access the file
- `owner_id` – An integer that maps to the `user_id` field of the users table to identify the file's owner
- `upload_dt` – A date object describing when the file was last uploaded
- `first_upload_dt` – A date object describing when the file was first uploaded
- `fullpath` – The path and file name of the file in the file system, relative to the project root, recorded as text
- `mimetype` – A varchar description of the file's MIME characteristics
- `file` – The contents of the file itself

Code Overview

Aside from the database, the core of the project management application's functionality is in a series of PHP pages that closely parallel the application's essential functions (refer back to the requirements described earlier in this chapter in the "Necessary pages" section). The program also makes use of a series of classes that serve as software representations of logical entities, such as database connections. Further, it uses a library of PHP snippets to guarantee that HTML pages throughout the application have a consistent look, and that the pages' design can be updated easily.

Logging in and establishing a session

Users enter the application via the login page, login.php, which goes through the process of presenting the user with an HTML form that collects a username and password. The application validates these against the database before forwarding the user to index.php, the main interface page. The login page also serves the critical function of establishing a session with the user, enabling the application to distinguish him or her from other users across many request/response transactions.

Showing active projects

The main interface page, generated by index.php, provides the user with his or her main project management "dashboard." It shows the user, at a glance, what projects he or she owns, what the status of each is, and how each one is performing relative to its deadline. The user can see what tasks are associated with each project, and can establish a new project record in the database.

Creating a new project

If the user chooses to create a new project, he or she is prompted for all the details the database requires in its project record. The user gets an HTML form that asks for the project's title and description, its due date, its present status, and its owner (which may be someone other than the user who's adding the project).

Uploading a file

The application allows the user to associate files with projects. The application validates the path the user specifies and stores the file the user uploads – which the user does via a file upload interface of the sort that's standard to his or her operating system – in the files table of the database.

Viewing a file

When a version of a project file exists in the files table of the database, the application displays it to the user. The application lists the PHP code directly into the user's browser, where he or she can examine or save it.

Adding a user

Administrator-class users have the ability to add and edit users. They can determine usernames and passwords and adjust the personal information kept about each user.

Code Breakdown

How does the application do all this? The application is really quite modular and incorporates a lot of functions and other pieces you'll probably find useful in other kinds of applications. The details of the code are worth a look.

Session management

The first order of business on the login page is to figure out whether the user who has accessed the page is already in a PHP-managed session. If so, it may not be necessary for the user to log in manually at all. The application may be able to verify his or her credentials automatically and just present the requested page.

The code for doing this appears right at the top of the login page (and in several other locations throughout the application files, as well). It looks like this:

```
check_session();
if (!isset($_SESSION))
    global $_SESSION;
```

That code looks for a variable called $_SESSION. If the variable isn't around, it creates a new instance of it, effectively putting the user into a new session for tracking purposes.

The function check_session() is interesting. It's one of a library of functions written expressly for this book. It makes sure the user's environment (a browser, typically) is set to support persistent cookies, and if so, it starts a session:

```
function &check_session()
{
    if (!isset($_SESSION))
    {
        trace('_SESSION is not set');
        if (php_sapi_name() == 'cli')
        {
            global $_SESSION;
            $_SESSION = array();
            trace('can not use cookies, in CLI - set _SESSION to
array()');
        }
        else
        {
            trace('ok to use cookies, call session_start()');
            session_start();
        }
    }
    trace('results of check_session: _SESSION=', $_SESSION);
    return $_SESSION;
}
```

If the browser does not support cookies, or the user has them turned off, then the code reacts politely, and other operations continue without session tracking.

Authentication

Now you can have a look at the way the application handles user authentication. The file login.php handles the work of prompting the user for a username and password, using an HTML form. What's interesting is that this form makes use of the variables $_SERVER['PHP_AUTH_USER'] and $_SERVER['PHP_AUTH_PW'], which are PHP values that represent the username and password entered by the user.

Alternately, when the credentials are stored as part of a session, they can be referred to as `$_ SESSION ['PHP_AUTH_USER']` and `$_SESSION['PHP_AUTH_PW']`. This capability of PHP means that it's possible to refer to the entered values with a little more security than might otherwise exist during the authentication transaction.

The login.php file is called by the `session_auth()` function (a general-purpose authorization function found in /book/functions/basic), which makes use of the `validate_user()` function:

```
function validate_user()
{

    static $_defaults = array(
        'username' => NULL
        , 'password' => NULL
    );
    static $_simple = array('username','password');
    $args = func_get_args();
    $p = parse_arguments($args, $_simple, $_defaults);

    session_user()->user = $p['username'];
    session_user()->password = $p['password'];
    return (bool)session_user()->validate();
}
```

`validate_user()` calls in its last line a method of the User class object returned by `session_user()` called `validate()`. The `validate()` method is where the actual database query (the interrogation of the users table) takes place. Have a look:

```
    function validate()
    {

        $query = 'select u.* from users u
            left join user_types ut
                on u.user_type_id = ut.user_type_id
            where u.user = ? and u.password = ? '
        ;
        $bind = array($this->user, md5($this->password));
        if ($this->user_type())
        {
            $query .= ' and ut.user_type = ? ';
            $bind[] = $this->user_type();
        }
        $row = $this->dbh()-
>getRow($query,$bind,DB_FETCHMODE_ASSOC);
        if (count($row) > 0)
```

```
        {
            $this->build($row);
            return TRUE;
        }
        return FALSE;
    }
```

There's some code to deal with encryption in there (the password is passed as a hash), but essentially that function determines whether the user credentials the user has sent as a result of the login attempt match an entry in the users table. The `validate()` function returns a Boolean value, to which the lower functions react.

Viewing projects' status

The main part of the project management application's user interface is contained in the file index.php. That file concerns itself with displaying status information and other details, including deadline information, about the projects with which the user is associated. In doing that, the main interface page must do a lot of database queries and a fair bit of text-formatting work. Much of this work is delegated to other functions (many of them in other PHP files), which makes the application more modular and easier to maintain.

In index.php you see a strategy that's commonplace across all the display scripts in this application (and, indeed, in most HTML-generating PHP scripts everywhere). Early on, the script calls the `start_page()` function, like this:

```
print start_page('Project Management Example');
```

That function, defined in an imported file, does the work of generating opening HTML. The argument is inserted as the HTML `TITLE` element.

With that done, the application proceeds to determine if the user accessing the page is an administrator:

```
if (!session_user()->is_admin())
```

If so, then the status of all current projects is displayed; if the current user is not an administrator, then only the projects to which that user is assigned are displayed.

To query the database, the application makes use of a function called `dbh()`, which is contained in base.class.php (imported everywhere). The `dbh()` function establishes the link to the database and enables queries to be run against it:

```
function dbh()
{
    static $dbh = NULL;
    if ($dbh === NULL)
    {
```

```
            $dbh = db_connect($this->appname);
            if ($dbh === NULL)
            {
                user_error('Received NULL db connection',
E_USER_ERROR);
                return FALSE;
            }
            $dbh->setFetchMode(DB_FETCHMODE_ASSOC);
        }
        return $dbh;
```

With dbh() invoked, the index page can send a query to it:

```
$rows = session_user()->dbh()->getAll($query, $bind);
```

The index page gets a set of rows back. Those rows, looped through, form the bulk of what's on the index page. Here is the looping logic:

```
foreach ($rows as $row)
{
    extract($row, EXTR_OVERWRITE|EXTR_PREFIX_ALL, 'p');
    $tlinks = array();
    $tlinks[] = anchor_tag(
        'tasks/cal.php?project_id='.$p_project_id
        , 'Calendar'
    );
    $tlinks[] = anchor_tag(
        'tasks/list.php?project_id='.$p_project_id
        , 'Task List'
    );
    $query = 'select t.*, u.user as owner
        from tasks t left join users u on t.owner_id = u.user_id
        where t.project_id = ?
            and t.status_id <> ?
            and (t.due_dt >= curdate() - interval 3 day
                and t.due_dt <= curdate() + interval 3 day)
    ';
    $bind = array($p_project_id,$cancelled_id);
    $events = session_user()->dbh()->getAll($query,$bind);
    $elist = array();
    if (count($events) > 0)
    {
        $elinks = array();
        $today = strtotime(date('Y-m-d',strtotime('today')));
        foreach ($events as $e)
```

```
        {
            extract($e, EXTR_OVERWRITE|EXTR_PREFIX_ALL, 'e');
            session_user()->format_dt($e_due_dt);
            $e_task_tag = anchor_tag(
                'tasks/view_task.php?task_id='.$e_task_id
                , $e_task
            );
            $its_yours = FALSE;
            if ($e_owner_id == session_user()->user_id)
            {
                $e_owner = 'You';
                $its_yours = TRUE;
            }
            if ($e_status_id == $done_id)
            {
                $e_text = "$e_owner finished $e_task_tag on
$e_due_dt";
            }
            elseif ($e_status_id == $slipped_id)
            {
                $e_text = "$e_owner slipped $e_task_tag to
$e_due_dt";
            }
            else
            {
                $e_due_ts = strtotime($e_due_dt);
                $on_time = ($today <= $e_due_ts);
                if ($its_yours)
                {
                    $due_word = $on_time ? 'are' : 'were';
                }
                else
                {
                    $due_word = $on_time ? 'is' : 'was';
                }
                $e_text = "$e_owner $due_word supposed to finish
$e_task_tag on $e_due_dt";
            }
            $elinks[] = $e_text;
        }
        $tlinks[] = '<b>Alerts:</b>'.ul_list($elinks);
    }

    $links[] = anchor_tag(
            'project.php?project_id='.$p_project_id
```

```
            , $p_project
        )
        . ul_list($tlinks)
    ;
}
```

Some of the most interesting calls there are the ones to cal.php and list.php. These files contain functions that generate information about the due date and about the task list associated with the project at hand, respectively. They handle some of the bothersome aspects of PHP dates.

It's worth noting, as well, how the project management application deals with projects. Consider the following, for example:

```
    $links[] = anchor_tag(
            'project.php?project_id='.$p_project_id
            , $p_project
        )
        . ul_list($tlinks)
    ;
```

The call to project.php guarantees that the call to the database is made – the details of the project the user is interested in are retrieved and populated into a local object, which can then be manipulated. Here is that code:

```
$fetch_ok = TRUE;
if ($submit == 'Save')
{
    if (empty($p->owner_id))
    {
        print paragraph(array(
            'style' => 'color:red'
            , 'values' => 'Error: No owner is associated with this
project'
        ));
        $fetch_ok = FALSE;
    }
    else
    {
        $p->write_to_db();
    }
}
if ($fetch_ok)
{
    $p->fetch_from_db();
}
```

```
else
{
    $p->owner()->fetch_from_db();
    $p->status();
}
```

Uploading a file

The project management application provides its users with the ability to upload files to the files table of the database, which makes those files accessible to others with the proper access. It's interesting to see how the application goes about uploading a file from the user's local file system and encoding it into the database.

Upload duties are the domain of savefile.php, which capitalizes upon PHP's ability to work with a traditional computer file system and also its ability to interact with the contents of a relational database.

The code first sets out to determine whether the file already exists in the database. If it does not, the application proceeds to create a File object, complete with a file name, a MIME type, and the contents of the uploaded file itself:

```
$f = new File;
$f->build($_POST);
$uf = $_FILES['projectfile'];
$f->description = $uf['name'];
$f->mimetype = $uf['type'];

if (file_exists($uf['tmp_name']))        {
    $f->file = gzdeflate(
        file_get_contents($uf['tmp_name']), 9
    );
}
else
{
    error_log("could not find {$uf['tmp_name']}");
}

$f->write_to_db();
```

Where does the File object come from, anyway? It's defined in projects/classes/file.class.php and describes the mapping between its properties and the fields in the files database. Early in the File class definition, the fields are established in an array:

```
array('file_id','project_id','task_id','description','public','owner
_id','upload_dt','first_upload_dt','fullpath','mimetype','file');
```

Displaying the contents of a file

Our project management application needs to be able to display the files it's managing, which it does with the contents of displayfile.php, in which a named file is retrieved from the database:

```
$f = new File;
$f->build($_REQUEST);
$f->fetch_from_db();
if ($f->file)
{
    $f->display();
}
elseif ($f->fullpath)
{
    virtual($f->fullpath);
}
else
{
    print "<li>Duh, like what do I do now?\n";
}
unset($f);
```

That code segment, in turn, calls the `display()` function in the `File` class, defined in file.class.php. This function is a simple one:

```
function display()
{
    header('Content-type: '.$this->mimetype);
    echo gzinflate($this->file);
}
```

`display()` simply undoes the `gzdeflate()` function invoked at storage time and decompresses it after storage.

Summary

In this chapter we designed and built an application that manages projects, files, users, deadlines, and notes by storing everything in a database and presenting a coherent, useful user interface.

This exercise enabled you to explore the way PHP manages sessions persistently and to see how it goes about stuffing files from a file system into a database. You also got a further look at object orientation in PHP and ended up with both a library of reusable functions and a simple project management application.

Part V

Appendixes

APPENDIX A
What's on the CD-ROM

APPENDIX B
HTML Forms

APPENDIX C
Brief Guide to MySQL/PHP Installation and Configuration

APPENDIX D
MySQL Utilities

APPENDIX E
MySQL User Administration

APPENDIX F
PHP Function Reference

APPENDIX G
Regular Expressions Overview

APPENDIX H
Helpful User-Defined Functions

APPENDIX I
PHP and MySQL Resources

APPENDIX J
MySQL Function Reference

Appendix A

What's on the CD-ROM

THIS APPENDIX PROVIDES YOU with information on the contents of the CD that accompanies this book. For the latest and greatest information, please refer to the ReadMe file located at the root of the CD. Here is what you will find:

- System Requirements
- Using the CD
- What's on the CD
- Troubleshooting

System Requirements

Make sure that your computer meets the minimum system requirements listed in this section. If your computer doesn't match up to most of these requirements, you may have a problem using the contents of the CD.

For Windows 9x, Windows 2000, Windows NT4 (with SP 4 or later), Windows Me, or Windows XP:

- PC with a Pentium processor running at 120 MHz or faster
- At least 32MB of total RAM installed on your computer; for best performance, we recommend at least 64MB

For Linux/Unix:

- PC with a Pentium processor running at 90 MHz or faster
- At least 32MB of total RAM installed on your computer; for best performance, we recommend at least 64MB

For Macintosh:

- Mac OS computer running OS X or later
- At least 32MB of total RAM installed on your computer; for best performance, we recommend at least 64MB

Using the CD

The contents of this CD are set up as a folder structure. To access the files you want to work with, access the appropriate folder (apache, mysql, php, and so on). Note: To access the example applications from the book open the book folder and explore its contents.

What's on the CD

The following sections provide a summary of the software and other materials you'll find on the CD.

Example applications

To get the applications in Sections III and IV working you first need to install Apache, PHP, and MySQL. You can find these applications on this book's CD-ROM. You can follow the instructions in Appendix C to install these applications.

Once Apache, PHP, and MySQL are installed, you need to copy the PHP scripts that load the databases and run the applications. Copy the entire /book directory from the CD, with all of its subfolders, to somewhere under the htdocs/ directory of your Apache installation, so that you can browse to `http://myserver/book/` (or `http://myserver/monkeying/with/php5/book/`, and so on)

Check the README.TXT file in this directory for further instructions. Primarily, you will need to edit the book.ini file and set the values defined there to match your local configuration.

Applications

On the CD, in addition to the code for the examples detailed in this book (as well as some extra ones), you'll find the following:

- MySQL – Files for installing a recent version of MySQL 4.0. For more information, and a more recent version, check their Web site at `http://www.mysql.com`.
- Apache – Files for installing a recent version of the Apache Web server (go to `http://www.apache.org` for more information).
- PHP – Files for installing PHP 4 on your machine. Be sure to install Apache and MySQL first.

- **PHP 5 beta** – Files for installing the beta version of PHP 5 that was available at the time of publication. If you have access to the Web, check the PHP site at `http://www.php.net` for more recent developments. You can also find absolutely up-to-the-minute development versions at `http://snaps.php.net`.

- **Adobe Acrobat Reader** – Tool for reading files in the Portable Document Format (PDF).

- **Scripts** from Appendix H.

All files with .php extensions can simply be copied to the Web server directory and will execute when the page is accessed.

Files with .tar.gz extensions are intended for Unix systems and must be uncompressed before you will be able to use them. Use the following commands:

```
gunzip filename.tar.gz
tar xf filename.tar
```

All files with .zip extensions must be uncompressed using a Windows zip utility such as WinZip (available at `http://www.winzip.com`).

Once you've uncompressed the packages, see the README or INSTALL files for installation instructions.

For more information on installing and configuring MySQL, PHP, and Apache, see Appendix C.

Shareware programs are fully functional, trial versions of copyrighted programs. If you like particular programs, register with their authors for a nominal fee and receive licenses, enhanced versions, and technical support. *Freeware programs* are copyrighted games, applications, and utilities that are free for personal use. Unlike shareware, these programs do not require a fee or provide technical support. *GNU software* is governed by its own license, which is included inside the folder of the GNU product. See the GNU license for more details.

Trial, demo, or evaluation versions are usually limited either by time or functionality (such as being unable to save projects). Some trial versions are very sensitive to system date changes. If you alter your computer's date, the programs will "time out" and will no longer be functional.

eBook version of MySQL/PHP Database Applications, Second Edition

The complete text of this book is on the CD in Adobe's Portable Document Format (PDF). You can read and search through the file with the Adobe Acrobat Reader (also included on the CD).

Troubleshooting

If you have difficulty installing or using any of the materials on the companion CD, try the following solutions:

- **Turn off any antivirus software that you may have running** – Installers sometimes mimic virus activity and can make your computer incorrectly believe that it is being infected by a virus. (Be sure to turn the antivirus software back on later.)
- **Close all running programs** – The more programs you're running, the less memory is available to other programs. Installers also typically update files and programs; if you keep other programs running, installation may not work properly.
- **Reference the ReadMe** – Please refer to the ReadMe file located at the root of the CD-ROM for the latest product information at the time of publication.

If you still have trouble with the CD-ROM, please call the Wiley Product Technical Support phone number: (800) 762-2974. Outside the United States, call 1(317) 572-3994. You can also contact Wiley Product Technical Support at `www.wiley.com/techsupport`. Wiley Publishing will provide technical support only for installation and other general quality control items; for technical support on the applications themselves, consult the program's vendor or author.

To place additional orders or to request information about other Wiley products, please call (800) 225-5945.

Appendix B

HTML Forms

IF YOU WANT YOUR APPLICATIONS to take user data, you are going to need to provide a place for users to enter the data. That requires HTML forms (or, if you want to be fancy, PDF files or Macromedia Flash applications, but those are subjects unto themselves). HTML forms are easy enough to work with. Several commonly used input types are available, and in browsers that make use of HTML 4.0 and Cascading Style Sheets you can use certain techniques to make your forms a bit fancier. A full discussion of everything you can do with forms is beyond the scope of this book. If you need more information on forms and how they can work with CSS or JavaScript, or on some of the newer browser-specific form types, check out the documentation at `http://microsoft.com` or `http://mozilla.org`. There is also a great resource for questions about how different tags and attributes work in different browsers at the Index DOT Html site, `http://www.blooberry.com/indexdot/html/`. You'll find the official documentation at `http://www.w3c.org/MarkUp/`.

Form Basics

Each form is delimited by opening and closing `<form>` tags. The `<form>` tag takes the following attributes:

- `action` – This attribute specifies the URL of the page that a form will be sent to for processing. It can contain a relative URL (such as `myscript.php` or `../myfolder/myscript`) or a complete URL (such as `http://www.mydomain/myscript.php`).
- `method` – This attribute indicates the HTTP request type the browser will send to the server. It must be set to either `GET` or `POST`. If you set it to `GET`, the name/value pairs will appear in the browser's location bar (as in `http://mypage.com?name1=value1&name2=value2`). The advantage of using `GET` is that results can be bookmarked in the browser and that debugging is easier. The disadvantage is that the variables you send will be more transparent. If you set the `method` attribute to `POST` the name/value pairs will not be visible. The default value of this attribute is `GET`.
- `name` – This attribute is most useful for addressing portions of a form through JavaScript, though it can also be used for CGI applications. The form name is not sent to the server when the form is submitted.

- `enctype` – This attribute has a default value of `application-x-www-form-urlencoded`, and this is normally be fine. But if you are uploading files (using `<input type="file">`) you should use `multipart/form-data`.

A typical form shell will look something like this:

```
<form name="myform" action="processor.php" method="POST">
?
</form>
```

Input Types

Most of the work in your forms will be done by the input types. An input tag and the `type` attribute determine what kind of form element is rendered in your browser.

Every form field must have a `name` attribute. The name you give the form field is used by PHP to identify the value that was placed in it. See the code sample that follows shortly for a concrete example. (To be absolutely accurate, you don't need to supply `name` attributes to submit and reset buttons, but doing so makes it easier to retrieve values from form elements. Otherwise, you're stuck doing it via array position.)

As a quick example, the following would create a simple form with a single text box and a submit button. The text box has the default value of `"hello there"`, as shown in Figure B-1.

```
<form>
   <input type="text" size="50" maxlength="15"
    value="hello there"><br>
   <input type="submit" name="submit" value="OK?">
</form>
```

The input types are as follows. Note that different input types have different attributes associated with them. Each of them takes a `name` attribute.

- `text` – This type is shown in the preceding example. It can take these attributes:
  - `size` – Indicates the length of the box rendered in the Web browser.
  - `maxlength` – Limits the number of characters that can be inputted into the field. Keep in mind that older browsers will ignore `maxlength`; even in newer browsers you should not rely on this attribute to limit uploads.
  - `value` – The default value in the box. The user can override it by typing in different information.

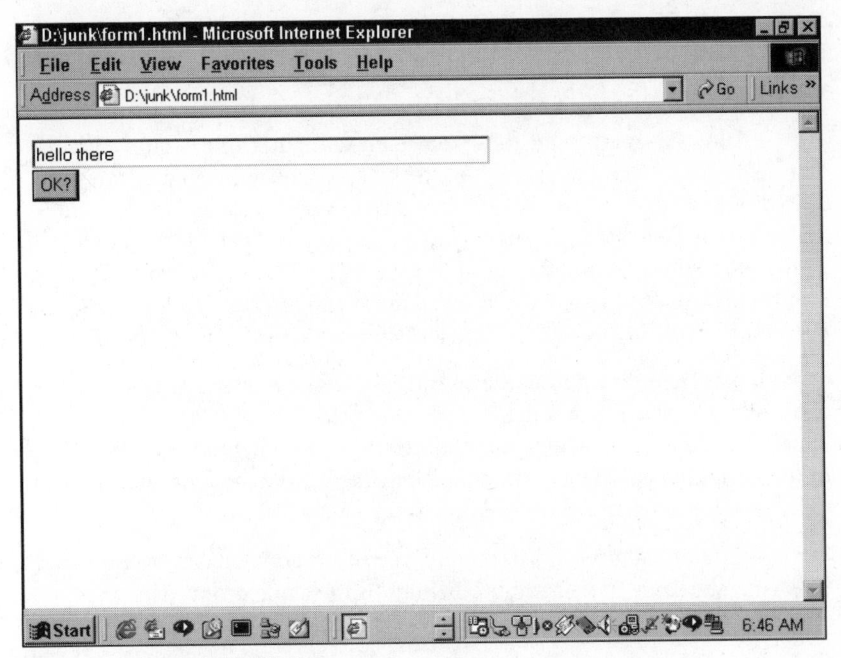

Figure B-1: A simple HTML form

- `password` – This type is identical to the text field, except that the text that is typed into the box is shown as asterisks.
- `hidden` – This type does not render on the screen. It is very useful for passing values between pages. The `name` and `value` attributes are all you need with `hidden` fields; consider using them if you're uncomfortable with cookies or sessions. Note that by simply viewing the source of your Web page, a savvy user will be able to see your `hidden` form elements. Do not put any sensitive data in `hidden` form fields.
- `submit` – Places a submit button on the page. The text in the `value` attribute will appear on the submit button. When the form is submitted, the `name` and `value` of the submit button are passed along like all other form elements. If you use name/value pairs for all of your submit buttons, you have the extra flexibility of having multiple submit buttons on a single form.
- `image` – Serves the same purpose as the submit button, but it enables you to specify an image to use instead of that ugly old submit button. Treat this form element as you would any `<img>` tag. Provide both `src` and `alt` attributes. If you're working with image maps, in which clicks on different regions of the same image have different functional significance, you can access the coordinates of a click through `name_x` and `name_y`.

- reset – This form field creates a button that, when pressed, returns the form to the state it was in when the page loaded. Any data that the user has entered into the form is cleared.
- file – Allows users to send files from their computer to a remote server. The field looks much like a text box that has a button labeled "Browse" placed next to it. When a user presses the Browse button, a file selection dialog box is displayed. The user can choose one file per file upload form field. A form can have multiple file upload fields. When using this input type, be sure to change the form enctype attribute to multipart/form-data. See Chapter 12 for a discussion of file uploads with PHP.
- checkbox – The name and value of the checkbox is passed only if the checkbox is checked when the form is submitted. If the word "checked" appears in the tag, the checkbox will be checked by default. Remember to use name=box_name[] to pass multiple checkboxes as an array. See Chapter 4 for a discussion of passing arrays with PHP.
- radio – Enable the user to select only one of several choices. Radio buttons with the same name attribute belong to the same group. The checked attribute signifies the default choice.

The following form makes use of all the form elements we just covered, except for the image type. Figure B-2 shows how it is rendered in the browser.

```
<h2>Please Enter Personal Information</h2>
<form>
   <input type="text" size="25" maxlength="15" name="name"
value="Name Here"><br>
   <input type="password" size="25" maxlength="15" name="password"
value=""><br>
   <input type="hidden" value="you can't see me">
   <input type="checkbox" name="telemmarket" value="yes" checked>If
checked, I have permission to clear out your bank account.
   <p>
   <b>What is your eye color?</b><br>
   <input type="radio" name="eye_color" value="blue"
checked>blue<br>
   <input type="radio" name="eye_color" value="green">green<br>
   <input type="radio" name="eye_color" value="brown">brown<br>
   <input type="radio" name="eye_color" value="red">red<br>
   <input type="submit" name="submit" value="submit">    
 
   <input type="Reset">
</form>
```

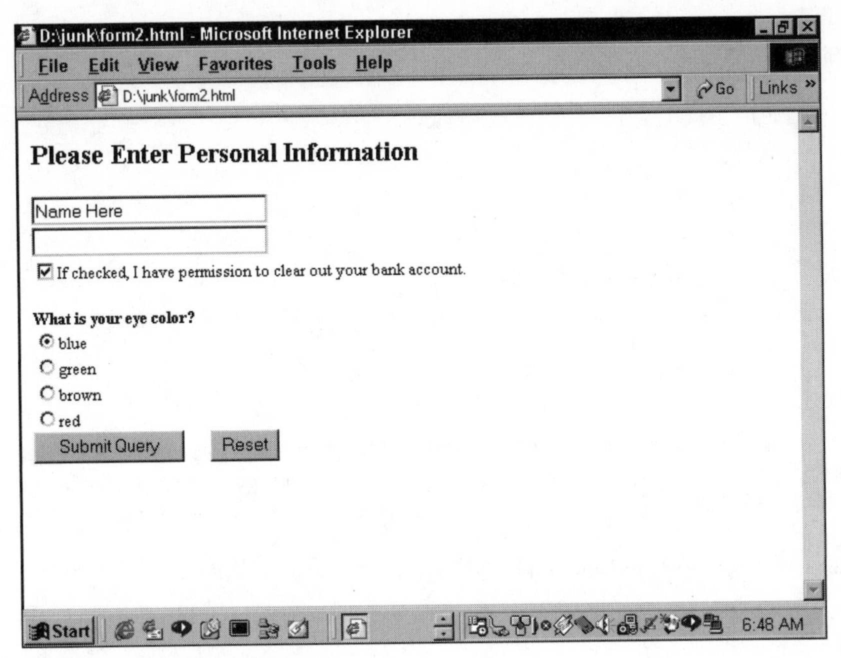

Figure B-2: More form elements

select, multiple select

The `select` form element creates drop-down boxes and (to use the Visual Basic term) list boxes. To create drop-down boxes you must use an opening `<select>` tag with a `name` attribute. Within the `select` element, `<option>` tags will indicate possible choices. Each of these can have a `value` attribute; without one, the value of the option is the text between the opening and closing `<option>` tags. If the word *selected* appears in the tag, that option is set as the default value of the `<select>` field (as with 'checked' for checkboxes and radio buttons).

The following HTML code creates a drop-down box with three elements:

```
<form name="tester" action="script.php" method="GET">
   <select name="dinner">
      <option value="1">chicken</option>
      <option value="2">fish</option>
      <option value="3">vegetarian</option>
   </select>
</form>
```

By adding the word `multiple` to the `select` element you enable the user to pick more than one of the choices. The `size` attribute determines how many of the options are visible at one time.

The following code creates a list box with three visible elements. Figure B-3 shows how this HTML code looks in the browser.

```
<form name="tester" action="script.php" method="GET">
   <select name="side_dishes" multiple size="3">
      <option value="1">potato</option>
      <option value="2">pasta</option>
      <option value="3">carrot</option>
      <option value="4">celery</option>
      <option value="5">mango</option>
   </select>
</form>
```

If you want that select list to support multiple selections (by holding down Ctrl), you have to put square brackets after the name value. In other words, the opening line of the preceding select box would be as follows:

```
<select name="side_dishes[]" multiple size="3">
```

textarea

The `textarea` element creates a large block for text entry. Add a `rows` and `columns` attribute to specify the size of the box. `textarea` is different from other form elements in that opening and closing tags surround the default text. For instance:

```
<textarea name="mytext" rows="5" columns="20">Here's the default text</textarea>
```

Keep in mind that if you have spaces or hard returns between your `<textarea>` tags, those characters will be carried to the form element.

Add the `wrap` attribute to change how text wraps when it reaches the end of a line in the box. If the value is `wrap="physical"`, carriage returns are added at the end of line; if the value is `wrap="virtual"`, the lines will appear to wrap but will be submitted as a single line. The latter is almost always the best choice for ease of processing on the server side—though `"virtual"` still preserves any manually inserted returns.

The attributes just listed came from the folks at Netscape, and you still might need to use them. The official W3C HTML 4.0 attribute values for `wrap` are `none`, `hard`, and `soft`, and these should work in the most of the recent browsers.

Figure B-3 adds the `select`, `multiple select` and `textarea` elements to a form with the following code:

```
<h2>Please Enter Personal Information</h2>
<form>
<fieldset id="fieldset1"
   style="postion:absolute;
   width:300;
   height:100;
   top:20;
   left:10;"
    >
<legend>Food Questions</legend>
<b>What did you eat for dinner?</b><br>
   <select name="dinner">
      <option value="1">chicken</option>
      <option value="2">fish</option>
      <option value="3">vegetarian</option>
   </select><br>
<b>Any Side dishes?</b><br>
   <select name="side_dishes[]" multiple size="3">
      <option value="1">potato</option>
      <option value="2">pasta</option>
      <option value="3">carrot</option>
      <option value="4">celery</option>
      <option value="5">mango</option>
   </select>
<br>
<b>How are you feeling about dinner?</b><br>
<textarea name="mytext" rows="5" columns="20">
Here's the default text</textarea>
</fieldset>
<p>
<button>
   <input type=img src="disk.gif" width="32" height="32" border="0"
alt="disk"><br>
   Pretty Little Button
</button>
</form>
```

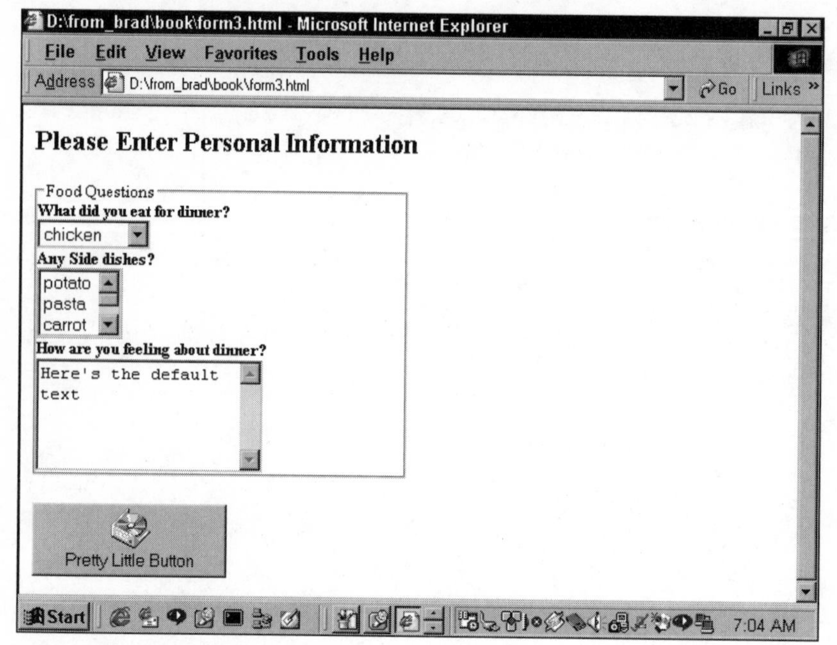

Figure B-3: Additional form elements

Other Attributes

With HTML 4.0 and the newest browsers some additional attributes have been introduced. Make sure to test these as part of your QA process, because they will not work on all browsers.

accesskey

An access key is the same as a hot key. If this attribute appears in a form element, the user can hit (on a PC) Alt and the designated key to be brought directly to that form element. The hot key is generally indicated by underlining of the hot letter.

```
<input type="text" name="mytext" accesskey="m"><u>M</u>y text box.
```

tabindex

Users can use the Tab key to move through form elements. The `tabindex` attribute specifies the order in which focus will move through form elements.

Other Elements

Internet Explorer 5 and Mozilla support a couple of new and seldom-used form elements that you might want to consider using.

button

The button is a fancier version of the submit button. It enables you to put both text and an image on the same button. There are opening and closing `<button>` tags, and everything inside of them appears on the button. Figure B-3 shows an example of the button.

fieldset and legend

These are nice for grouping elements in forms. All text and tags within the `<fieldset>` tags will be surrounded by a thin line. Text within the `<legend>` tags will serve as the caption for that grouping.

Figure B-3 shows all the form types.

At present, it is still not a great idea to use most of the HTML 4.0 form elements and attributes. Generally speaking, they add very little, and they may look very strange on many browsers.

Appendix C

Brief Guide to MySQL/PHP Installation and Configuration

WHEN INSTALLING MYSQL AND PHP, you are faced with all kinds of options. The variety of operating systems and installation options creates more permutations than could possibly be handled in this book. Luckily, installation procedures for all packages are documented well in each package's respective documentation.

In the first edition of this book, our installation instructions focused on compiling the individual packages from source files and then making changes to configuration files so that Apache, MySQL, and PHP would recognize each other. While there's still something to be said for compiling packages from source – you do get a finer level of control and may be able to invoke options not available with any other form of installation – it's likely that a simpler method of installation will work just fine for you. On just about any platform and operating system you can get the most recent version of all packages precompiled and packaged into an easy-to-install set of files. We make note of these installers in the following sections.

Windows Installation

At this point in computer history (in the opinion of these authors) far too many versions of Windows are in use. Windows 98, NT, 2000, and XP all have large user bases. Though each of these operating systems differs significantly from the others, the installation of the packages of concern to us is pretty similar on all Windows variants.

There are a few installers that make MySQL/PHP/Apache installation a truly painless process on Windows. We discuss two of these in the following sections.

phpdev

The phpdev bundles available at `http://www.firepages.com.au/` provide a very, very clean installation program. To install this package on a Windows machine, all you have to do is the following.

1. Go to the phpdev bundles area of the site.
2. Pick a version and download the installer file – in this case, the PHP5 beta bundle, dev5beta3.exe. This is an NSIS installer file.
3. Run the installer and choose the directory where you want your files to be installed – C:\phpdev5, for example.

And that's it. We're not including a phpdev package on the CD because it's likely that by the time you read this book a significant bug or security vulnerability will have be discovered in one of the included packages. So you're really better off getting the most current download available from the Web site.

You might also need to view any updated installation instruction files.

NuSphere

The NuSphere Corporation first got into the MySQL/PHP world by offering a transactional table for MySQL called Gemini. At the time of this writing, it's difficult to find any mention of Gemini on the NuSphere Web site. Instead, NuSphere seems to be concentrating its efforts on a PHP integrated development environment (IDE) called PHPed. (Incidentally, if you're on Windows or Linux, you might want to check this product out; it's pretty cool.)

At the time of this writing, NuSphere continues to make a very nice Web-based installer that installs PHP, MySQL, Apache, and mod_perl on Windows and Linux systems. All you really have to do is double-click the install file, and NuSphere did the rest.

It's entirely possible that NuSphere will no longer offer this installer by the time you read this book. Check its Web site (`http://www.nusphere.com/cgi-bin/nsp.cgi/custsrvc/utils/free_download.htm`) to see what's currently available.

Another installer, called Sokkit (formerly PHPtriad), used to be free for all but now is being re-written as part of a commercial effort.

Installing on Windows from assorted binaries

You can install all these packages separately and in the process let them know how to work together. We recommend getting the most recent binaries from the Web sites of the organizations that distribute the software. These packages are constantly updated, and there's no reason not to have access to the most recent features. (Of course, if you already installed these packages using phpdev or by means of some similar arrangement you should skip to the section on "PHP Configuration.")

Start by copying the MySQL binaries from the `http://mysql.com/downloads` site to your local drive. Do the same for Apache and PHP (the appropriate download sites here are `http://httpd.apache.org/download.cgi` and `http://www.php.net/download`). The names of the files will be something like the following (they may be slightly different, depending on the version you are using):

- mysql-4.0.14b-win.zip
- apache_1_3_22_win32_no_src.exe
- php-4.2.2-Win32.zip

Start by unzipping the MySQL file and PHP files with your favorite unzip tool. (If you don't have one, we recommend WinZip at `http://www.winzip.com/`.) Unzip them into a directory you find convenient. We prefer using a separate directory for each.

Start with MySQL.

1. In the directory in which you unzipped the file, you will have a file named setup.exe. Execute that file.
2. Choose a directory (for example, c:\mysql) in which you want to install it, and then in the next screen, select a Typical installation. (You might want to examine the custom options, but with the Windows installation very few real options exist.)

At this point your MySQL installation is complete. To test it, go to the DOS prompt and move to the directory you specified for your MySQL installation. Then move to the subcategory \bin. If you then type **mysqld**, the MySQL daemon should start. To test if your daemon is working, start up the MySQL command-line client by typing **mysql**.

Next, you should install Apache.

This installation requires little more than double-clicking the executable you copied from the `apache.org` site. The installation is pretty easy: all you really need to do is select a domain name (just use `localhost` if you're not actually putting it live on the Internet) and a directory in which you would like to install Apache. When the installation is completed an Apache HTTP Server group item is added to the Start menu. It's important to remember the directory in which you installed Apache. That is where you'll be putting all the PHP files that make up the applications. If you used the default settings, your default serving directory will be c:\Program Files\Apache Group\Apache\htdocs.

Don't start up Apache just yet. A little more configuration information follows.

Now on to PHP. You should have a folder into which you unzipped all the PHP files. (In the following instructions we are assuming the folder is c:\php.) Also, PHP 4 and later versions have a pretty good Apache module for Windows. In the previous version of this book we recommended using the CGI binary. The Apache module has a bit more in the way of functionality, so you should probably use that.

1. Copy php5ts.dll and php5apache.dll from c:\php into the c:\windows\system or c:\winnt\system32 directory, whichever is available on your version of Windows.

2. Next, copy the php.ini-dist file from the c:\php directory to c:\windows on Windows 95/98, or c:\winnt or winnt40 on NT/2000/XP. Rename the file php.ini. Now open the php.ini file and change the extension_dir entry so it matches the name of the folder where you placed the .dll files. For example:

   ```
   extension_dir = c:/windows/system32
   ```

3. Now you need to alter your Apache configuration file. The easiest way to do this is to go to the Start menu and select Apache HTTP Server → Configure Apache Server → Edit Configuration File.

4. Add the following three lines to the file. Note that the first line must match the name of the directory on your system:

   ```
   LoadModule php5_module c:/windows/system
   AddModule mod_php5.c
   AddType application/x-httpd-php .php
   ```

   The last line ensures that all files with .php extensions are processed as PHP applications. If you want other file extensions to by parsed by PHP, simply add another `AddType` line to the conf file, as follows:

   ```
   AddType application/x-httpd-php5 .phtml
   ```

You may have to make a couple of other alterations to your httpd.conf file, such as the following:

- If the server refuses to start, you may need to add something to the *ServerName* directive. If you are using TCP/IP in your local area network you may need to add the IP address of your machine, as follows:

  ```
  ServerName 192.168.1.2
  ```

  Or, if your machine is not networked, you may want to use the following *ServerName*:

  ```
  ServerName 127.0.0.1
  ```

- If you also have Microsoft Personal Web Server running on your machine you might want to change the port on which Apache runs. By default Web servers listen on port 80, but you can change that by altering the `port` line in httpd.conf to something else – perhaps `8080`.

And that should do it. Start Apache through the Start Menu. Add a file to your \htdocs folder that contains the `phpinfo()` function. When you call that function you should see that everything is working properly and that an entry for MySQL is there.

Note that you don't need to make any alterations to the php.ini file to make PHP work with MySQL. In fact, MySQL support is built into PHP for Windows.

If you uncomment the directive `extension=php_mysql.dll` you will have all kinds of problems getting a PHP page to load.

These are the basics you need to get going with PHP and MySQL on Windows. Note that you can also install PHP as an ISAPI filter for Internet Information Server (IIS) and PWS. The instructions for doing so are included in the readme.txt file included in the PHP Zip file.

As of this writing, running PHP as an IIS filter is tricky and unreliable and not recommended for a production environment. It's better to associate the .php extension with the PHP interpreter in the Internet Services Management console. It's much more reliable that way.

Installation on Unix/Mac OS X

On Unix, there are far more options that you might want to avail yourself of. You might want to install by compiling the source code yourself or (on Linux) by using .rpm files. This appendix covers only compiling from source. We strongly recommend that you do not use .rpm files. The convenience that .rpms sometimes offer does not extend to this type of configuration, largely because configuration can be tricky and manual work is the only way to get it right.

You can compile a variety of libraries and optional functions into PHP, and additional libraries and functions are being added all the time. In this quick guide, we cover only some highlights.

If you have other priorities, need .rpms, or want to include options not covered here, seek out the documentation in the online manuals. This really isn't a very difficult installation, and you should be able to customize as you see fit with minimal effort. First stop, MySQL.

MySQL installation

An option we have yet to discuss – and probably the best one for Unixes – is to get a set of binaries distributed by MySQL AB. If you go to `www.mysql.com/downloads` you can see binaries for about every major Unix distribution, including Solaris, Irix, HP-UX, FreeBSD, and Mac OS X. It would be impractical for us to include all these install files on the CD (and you're better off getting them from the site anyway), and the installation instructions can differ slightly from platform to platform. Installing from binaries, however, is exceedingly easy – and far quicker than compiling from source. If you download binaries for your platform you will see a set of instructions that comes with the package. You can have MySQL installed in under 10 minutes after running only a handful of commands.

Complete information on MySQL installation can be found in Chapter 2 of the MySQL online manual: `http://www.mysql.com/documentation/mysql/bychapter/manual_Installing.html`. Check it out if you are having problems.

If you decide that you do want to install from source, you need to get a compressed tarball of the source (a .tar.gz or .tgz file) from `http://www.mysql.com/downloads/`. Copy it to a directory you want to work in and then unpack it with a command like the following:

```
gunzip mysql-4.0.12.tar.gz
tar xf mysql-4.0.12.tar
```

This command creates a directory with the name of the MySQL distribution (for example, mysql-4.0.12). Use `cd` to move into the directory. Note that the exact version may be different, depending on when you download the software.

The first step is to run `configure`. You can set many options with `configure` flags; to get a complete list run `./configure --help`.

In the installations we've run, we have found it convenient to specify `--prefix`. If you do not specify a prefix, /usr/local is used, and this is almost always perfectly fine. Additionally, MySQL enables you to specify the location of any of the subdirectories (the data directory, the bin directory, and so on). Usually that will not be necessary. Normally you can run the following:

```
./configure --prefix=/path/to/installation
```

Now you have only two commands to execute:

```
make
make install
```

Note that you'll probably have to run the `make install` command as root. Either use `su` to switch to root, or, on platforms that support `sudo`, use that. The next thing you want to do is `cd` into the /bin directory and run the following command, which creates your default databases and permissions tables:

```
./mysql_install_db
```

You don't want to have to run the MySQL daemon as root. You're better off making a user and group specifically for running the daemon, mainly because your systems will be neater if you distribute responsibilities across users. Assign permissions to directories that allow the MySQL user to access everything he or she needs. In the following shell commands, we are creating a user and group named mysql and then assigning proper rights to that user; we're assuming an installation directory of /usr/local/mysql. These actions must also be performed as root.

```
shell> groupadd mysql
shell> useradd -g mysql mysql
shell> chown -R root /usr/local/mysql
shell> chown -R mysql /usr/local/mysql/var
shell> chgrp -R mysql /usr/local/mysql
```

At this point a directory listing of /usr/local/mysql should look about like this:

```
shell>  ls -Fla

drwxr-xr-x  13 root   mysql    442 Jun 26 13:31 ./
drwxr-xr-x   4 root   wheel    136 Jun 26 13:28 ../
drwxr-xr-x  40 root   mysql   1360 Jun 26 13:29 bin/
drwxr-xr-x   3 root   mysql    102 Jun 26 13:28 include/
drwxr-xr-x   3 root   mysql    102 Jun 26 13:28 info/
drwxr-xr-x   3 root   mysql    102 Jun 26 13:28 lib/
drwxr-xr-x   3 root   mysql    102 Jun 26 13:29 libexec/
drwxr-xr-x   3 root   mysql    102 Jun 26 13:29 man/
drwxr-xr-x   9 root   mysql    306 Jun 26 13:29 mysql-test/
drwxr-xr-x   3 root   mysql    102 Jun 26 13:29 share/
drwxr-xr-x  25 root   mysql    850 Jun 26 13:29 sql-bench/
drwx------  15 mysql  mysql    510 Aug 12 15:44 var/
```

You should now be able to start the mysql daemon using the `mysqld_safe` command from the /bin directory. With the permissions you've created you need to run the startup command as root while specifying that the daemon run as the user named mysql:

```
sudo /usr/local/mysql/bin/mysqld_safe --user=mysql &
```

By default MySQL uses port 3306 and keeps the all-important socket file at /tmp/myslq.sock. This is generally okay: PHP looks for the socket file in this location. However, if you have multiple installations of MySQL you need to change the port and socket location, which can be a pain. You need to play with your my.cnf file. See Chapter 4 of the MySQL manual for more information.

PHP/Apache

On Unix, PHP is loaded as an Apache module. Thus, the installation of the two must be done in concert. Once again you have many, many installation options. You can create PHP as an executable for use with CGI or command-line processing, as a shared Apache module (apxs), or for DSO. Here we cover only installation as an Apache module (except for OS X, which is discussed later in the appendix).

Start by unpacking both Apache and PHP.

```
gunzip apache 1.3.x.tar.gz
tar xf apache1.3.x.tar
gunzip php-4.2.tar.gz
tar xf php-4.2.tar.gz
```

Here *x* (in `apache_1.3.x.tar`) is the version number of Apache.

Use `cd` to move into the Apache directory and run `configure`, specifying the path to the directory in which you want to install Apache. You should be probably be running as the root account before you do this.

```
./configure --prefix=/path/to/apache
```

This prepares Apache to set up machine-specific information that PHP needs to compile. You come back later and finish up the Apache installation.

Then move to the directory holding PHP. Here you find a variety of flags you might or might not wish to specify. We suggest using the following:

```
./configure --with-mysql=/path/to/mysql --enable-trans-sid
```

Here, the two flags do the following:

- `--with-mysql` – Since the MySQL client libraries are no longer distributed as part of PHP, the MySQL extension is not enabled by default. You need to use this flag and, if you have installed MySQL somewhere other than the default location, specify the directory where it can be found.
- `--enable-trans-sid` – This option allows the session ID to be included automatically in URLs after a session is started. The Shopping Cart application in Chapter 14 makes use of this option.

Additionally, you might want to include one or more of the following flags:

- `--with-gd` – The GD functions enable you to create images on the fly, using nothing but code. A version of GD is bundled with PHP (at least, as of this writing).
- `--with-config-file-path=/path/to/file` – The php.ini file specifies many options for the PHP environment. PHP expects to find the file in /usr/local/lib/php.ini. If you wish to change the location, use this flag.

You can incorporate many other flags and libraries into PHP. Please see the online manual (`http://php.net/install.configure`) or run `--configure --help` for the latest and most complete list.

After running `configure`, run the following two commands, the latter as root:

```
make
make install
```

Now you need to go back to the Apache directory and rerun the `configure` command:

```
./configure --prefix=/path/to/apache --activate-module=
src/modules/php5/libphp5.a
```

Note that libphp5.a will not yet exist. It is created after the compiling is completed.

Now it's time to run the great twosome:

```
make
make install
```

Apache should now be installed in the directory you specified.

Now move back to the PHP directory and copy the file named php-ini.dist to /usr/local/lib/php.ini (or to the directory you specified in the `--config-file-path` flag).

The final step is to go into the /conf directory of your Apache installation and open the httpd.conf file. There you should uncomment the following line:

```
AddType application/x-httpd-php .php
```

Then move into the /bin directory and start Apache.

```
./apachectl start
```

Your installation should now be complete.

PHP looks for the socket to MySQL in /tmp/mysql.sock. If you have more than one MySQL installation and need PHP to connect to the socket in another location, you need to specify that in the `mysql_connect()` function, like this:

```
mysql_connect("localhost:/path/to/mysql.sock",
"username", "password");
```

In Mac OS X you probably want to use the version of Apache that ships with the OS. Therefore, you probably won't need to do any configuring or compiling of Apache. Simply start by configuring PHP the way you want it, using all the libraries and flags you need. Simply add the `--with-apxs` flag when compiling PHP, and PHP makes itself part of your Apache configuration.

Depending on the state of PHP 5 and OS X at the time you're installing, PHP may require some extra libraries, like libxml2. You should be able to get what you need from either Darwin Ports at `http://www.opendarwin.org/projects/darwinports/` or Fink at `http://fink.sourceforge.net/`.

You still need to make the changes listed earlier in this section to your httpd.conf file. In OS X, that file can be found in /etc/httpd.

PHP Configuration

The php.ini file is extremely large and has more options than we can cover here. A full list of options and potential settings can be found at `http://www.php.net/manual/configuration.php`. Here are a few highlights.

Globals

We've talked a lot in this book about the use of global variables. If possible you should have the `register_globals` line set to `Off`. This configuration requires you to use the `$_GET`, `$_POST`, `$_SERVER`, and other like-named arrays when using global variables, which keeps your applications more secure. But if you're working off legacy applications, it may be tough to make all the changes needed to have `register_globals` set to `Off`. If you are able to set `register_globals` to `Off`, you can prevent anyone from setting an internal PHP variable by referring to that variable in the URL or in a `POST`.

MySQL configuration entries

The following are some of the MySQL configuration entries:

```
mysql.allow_persistent  =
mysql.max_persistent    =
```

```
mysql.max_links    =
mysql.default_port  =
mysql.default_host  =
mysql.default_user  =
mysql.default_password  =
```

If you want to forbid persistent connections, change that setting to `Off`; if you want to limit the number of persistent links to MySQL, change the setting on `max_persistent` and `max_links` from `-1` to an appropriate number.

You can use the `default_user`, `default_host`, and `default_password` entries if you want to save yourself the trouble of entering these strings in your `mysql_connect()` command. Note that putting your MySQL password in the MySQL configuration file is a tremendous security risk.

You can make lots of other settings in your MySQL configuration file. The following sections explain some of the more useful ones.

MAGIC QUOTES

```
magic_quotes_gpc
magic_quotes_runtime
```

If `magic_quotes_gpc` is set to `On`, all single quotes (`'`), double quotes (`"`), backslashes (`\`), and `NULL`s are prepended with a backslash immediately upon being uploaded from a `form` element. This makes doing your inserts into MySQL a lot easier.

If `magic_quotes_runtime` is set to `On`, data retrieved from the file system or a database are automatically escaped with backslashes.

EXECUTION TIME

```
max_execution_time = 30
memory_limit = 8388608
```

These settings are intended to protect you in the event of an infinite loop or an endlessly recursive function. All scripts are automatically terminated if they reach either of these limits. If you want to use a script that you expect to take more than 30 seconds, you can set the maximum execution time within a script with the `set_time_limit ()` function. This function can contain a number of seconds; if you want to specify no limit, specify `set_time_limit(0)`.

AUTO PREPEND AND APPEND

```
auto_prepend_file       =
auto_append_file        =
```

With these settings you can specify files that are automatically included at the start and end of your PHP files. It might be useful for connection information or common headers.

INCLUDE PATH

```
include_path
```

This should contain a list of paths separated by colons (:). These paths are automatically searched for every `include()` and `require()`.

SESSION

You might want to change many session settings. Here are a few of them:

```
session.save_handler        = files
session.save_path           = /tmp
session.use_cookies         = 1
session.auto_start          = 0
```

Appendix F contains a set of functions for using MySQL for session handling. If you want to use it you must set `session.save.handler` to `user`.

`save_path` indicates where in the file system PHP saves session information.

If `use_cookies` is set to `0` you must use another means of storing cookies – either using `<?=SID ?>` or configuring PHP with the `--with-trans-sid` flag.

Finally, if `auto_start` is set to `1`, sessions are started automatically on every page, meaning you'll be able to track users through your pages by examining their session IDs.

Appendix D

MySQL Utilities

THIS APPENDIX PRESENTS a brief overview of some of the MySQL administrative utilities. These are the tools that you'll use to build and maintain your databases.

The best place to get the full details about the tools you have available to you is the Docs subdirectory of your local installation of MySQL. (Note: This is the install directory, not the data directory.) You can also check the online version of the MySQL documentation at `http://www.mysql.com/documentation/`.

Keep in mind that the online MySQL manual does not do a good job of indicating when features were added to a utility. This can be confusing as you may find yourself attempting to use a feature that is not available in your currently installed version. Don't be surprised if you can't find a utility – it may have been added in a later version.

mysql

This is the command-line interface to MySQL; it enables you to run any arbitrary SQL command, as well as the MySQL-specific commands like `describe table`. It's a tool you should get to know. You can use it to test out or debug queries for your code, create your database, create tables, add columns to existing tables – everything, really. It also has some batch-oriented options that make it handy to use in maintenance scripts, or as a quick no-frills reporting tool.

Syntax:

```
mysql [options] [databasename] [<inputfile] [>outputfile]
```

If you just type `mysql`, you'll start the tool up, but you won't be anywhere. When you try to do anything that involves interaction with a database, you'll get this error:

```
ERROR 1046: No Database Selected
```

To select one, type

```
use databasename;
```

use' is one of the mysql tool's built-in commands. Type help to see a list of them:

```
help     (\h)    Display this help.
?        (\?)    Synonym for `help'.
clear    (\c)    Clear command.
connect (\r)     Reconnect to the server. Optional arguments are db
                 and host.
edit     (\e)    Edit command with $EDITOR.
ego      (\G)    Send command to mysql server, display result
                 vertically.
go       (\g)    Send command to mysql server.
nopager (\n)     Disable pager, print to stdout.
notee    (\t)    Don't write into outfile.
pager    (\P)    Set PAGER [to_pager]. Print the query results via
                 PAGER.
print    (\p)    Print current command.
quit     (\q)    Quit mysql.
rehash   (\#)    Rebuild completion hash.
source   (\.)    Execute a SQL script file. Takes a file name as an
                 argument.
status   (\s)    Get status information from the server.
system   (\!)    Execute a system shell command (Linux only).
tee      (\T)    Set outfile [to_outfile]. Append everything into
                 given outfile.
use      (\u)    Use another database. Takes database name as
                 argument.
```

Once you're in a database you can run a SQL statement by typing it in, followed by a semicolon, \g, or \G, and hitting Return/Enter. When a query is terminated with a semicolon or \g the utility will return any result in tabular format; when a query is terminated with \G MySQL will give the listing in vertical format. The following listing demonstrates the difference:

```
mysql> show databases;
+----------+
| Database |
+----------+
| mysql    |
| test     |
+----------+
2 rows in set (0.01 sec)

mysql> show databases \G
*************************** 1. row ***************************
```

```
Database: mysql
*************************** 2. row ***************************
Database: test
2 rows in set (0.00 sec)
```

The vertical output can be helpful if you're feeding the output of your queries to another program, such as a Perl script, for processing, because this form is easier to parse. Alternatively, you can use the `-B` option to format things horizontally, but without the character-based line art.

Table D-1 lists some of the more useful command-line options.

TABLE D-1 COMMON `mysql` COMMAND-LINE CLIENT OPTIONS, PART I

Flag	Alternate Flag	Description
`-?`	`--help`	Displays help.
`-B`	`--batch`	Prints tab-delimited results, with each row on a new line.
`-D,`	`--database=..`	Specifies a database to use.
`-e`	`--execute=...`	Executes a command and quits.
`-E`	`--vertical`	Prints output vertically.
`-f`	`--force`	Gives the order to continue regardless of SQL errors.
`-h`	`--host=...`	Connects to a server.
`-H`	`--html`	Generates HTML output.
`-L`	`--skip-line-numbers`	Gives the order not to write line numbers for errors.
`-n`	`--unbuffered`	Flushes buffer after query.
`-p[password]`	`--password[=...]`	Specifies the password to use when connecting to the server.
`-P`	`--port=...`	Specifies the TCP/IP port to use for the connection.
`-q`	`--quick`	Gives the order not to cache the result, but to print it row by row.
`-r`	`--raw`	Writes column values without escape conversion.

Continued

TABLE D-1 COMMON mysql COMMAND-LINE CLIENT OPTIONS, PART I *(Continued)*

Flag	Alternate Flag	Description
--safe-mode		Sends this SQL statement to the MySQL server when the connection is opened: SET SQL_SAFE_UPDATES=1, SQL_SELECT_LIMIT=#select_limit#, SQL_MAX_JOIN_SIZE= #max_join_size#" #select_limit# and #max_join_size# are variables that you can specify on the mysql command line.
-t	--table	Specifies that the output is to be in table format.
-u	--user=#	Specifies the user to be used for login.
-w	--wait	Specifies the order to wait and retry instead of aborting if the connection is down.
-X	-XML	Formats output as XML.

The effect of the --safe-mode flag command is as follows:

- You are not allowed to do an UPDATE or DELETE if you don't have a key constraint in the WHERE portion. You can, however, force an UPDATE/DELETE by using LIMIT:

  ```
  UPDATE table_name SET not_key_column='some value' WHERE
  not_key_column='some value' LIMIT 1;
  ```

- All big results are automatically limited to #select_limit# rows.
- SELECTs that will probably need to examine more than #max_join_size row combinations will be aborted.

mysqladmin

You can use mysqladmin, a command-line tool, for performing all sorts of administrative tasks on a MySQL server – everything from simple tasks like creating new databases to getting detailed information on the status of your MySQL server.

mysqladmin takes a number of fairly generic flags that you can apply to any of the processes you'll see below. These flags, like -u, -p, and -h (which indicate username, password, and host, respectively), show up in about every MySQL client. You can get a listing of these flags by running mysqladmin --help.

Basic administrative commands

Many of the tasks that you can perform with the MySQL command-line client can also be performed with mysqladmin. The primary advantage of using mysqladmin for tasks like creating databases and setting passwords is that they can be entered from the shell or through a shell script without your having to worry about entering and exiting the command-line client. (Or, you can always use mysql with the -e option. That way, commands are standardized for you.)

From mysqladmin you can perform the following basic administrative functions: create a database, drop a database, and change a password. The following examples show how to perform each of these actions. (Note that for each of the examples, we're performing the actions as the MySQL root user.)

```
shell> mysqladmin -u root -p create store2
shell> mysqladmin -u root -p drop store2
```

The first command creates a database named store2 and the second one drops the same database. Note that the drop command will return a warning and ask you to confirm the drop action:

```
Dropping the database is potentially a very bad thing to do.
Any data stored in the database will be destroyed.

Do you really want to drop the 'store2' database [y/N]
```

This sort of response is fine, but it's something you want to avoid in an administrative shell script. You can ask mysqladmin to drop the database without confirmation by applying the -f or --force flag:

```
shell> mysqladmin -u root -p drop -f store2
```

You can also change passwords from mysqladmin. The following command changes the password for the MySQL root user from mypass to hispass.

```
shell> ./mysqladmin -u root -pmypass password hispass
```

Status-information commands

mysqladmin provides a means of determining the status and performance of your database server.

mysqladmin ping

For starters, you can check that a MySQL daemon is alive and running, using `mysqladmin ping`. If the command is successful it will return the message `mysqld is alive`. If it fails you will get an error message. Most often you will want to use `mysqladmin ping` when trying to establish that a connection is possible from a host other than localhost. In order to test the connection properly you'll need to supply a host name, username, and password. Within your MySQL installation you'll need to make sure that a user with that name from that host is allowed.

```
shell> mysqladmin -u jay -pmypass -h mysqlserver.myhost.com ping
mysqld is alive
```

If you simply want to find out whether the MySQL port is active, you can use a simple telnet client. If MySQL is running on the default port (3306) you can run telnet with the command:

```
telnet mysqlhost.myhost.com 3306
```

If the daemon is running you will get a response. You won't be able to connect through telnet, but you will get a response rather than a timeout.

mysqladmin version

You can get some interesting information about MySQL by running `mysqladmin version`:

```
shell> mysqladmin version
Server version          4.0.0-alpha
Protocol version        10
Connection              Localhost via UNIX socket
UNIX socket             /tmp/mysql.sock
Uptime:                 1 day 1 hour 15 min 10 sec

Threads: 73  Questions: 7168998  Slow queries: 119  Opens: 34482
Flush tables: 1  Open tables: 64 Queries per second avg: 29.983
```

The beginning of the listing shows very basic information. Below that, starting with `Threads`, you get some interesting information. Note that you can get just the information at the bottom of this listing (from `Threads` to `Queries per second avg`) plus some other goodies by running `mysqladmin status`.

mysqladmin status

This command can give you some very important information:

```
/mysqladmin status -u root -pmypass
Enter password:
Uptime: 239352  Threads: 68  Questions: 7175296  Slow queries: 119
Opens: 34509  Flush tables: 1  Open tables: 64 Queries per second
avg: 29.978
```

In this listing, you get the following information:

- **Uptime** – Number of seconds MySQL has been running
- **Threads** – Number of clients connected to MySQL
- **Questions** – Number of queries processed since the MySQL daemon was started
- **Slow queries** – Number of queries that have taken longer to process than the value of the variable `long_query_time`
- **Opens** – The number of table opens MySQL has performed
- **Flush tables** – Number of `flush`, `refresh`, and `reload` commands run
- **Open table** – Number of tables open when `mysqladmin status` was run
- **Queries per second avg** – A simple measurement of the queries run divided by the time the server has been running – not a measure of your server's performance

You can look at this information and start to make some decisions. If you have a lot of slow queries, it may be time to restart the server and log slow queries so you can see exactly what queries are problematic (see Chapter 4 of the MySQL manual concerning the slow query log). If you find that the number of active threads is often close to the maximum number allowed by the `max_connections` variable, you might want to increase the number of available threads. If the `Opens` item is very large (as it is in the previous listing), you should think about increasing the value of the `table_cache` variable.

Beyond these items, you can get far more information from your MySQL installation by running `mysqladmin extended-status`. This command returns a very long listing of system variables. You can get the definition for each of these items from the MySQL manual: `http://www.mysql.com/doc/S/H/SHOW_STATUS.html`.

mysqladmin processlist

Using `mysqladmin` you can also view all the server's active threads by running `mysqladmin processlist`. For example, the following listing contains five threads active in the MySQL server, including the thread that is running `mysqladmin`.

```
shell> ./mysqladmin -u root -pmypass processlist
+----+------+-----------+-------+---------+-------+-------+---------
---------+
| Id | User | Host      | db    | Command | Time  | State | Info
|
+----+------+-----------+-------+---------+-------+-------+---------
---------+
| 44 | jayg | localhost |       | Sleep   | 12359 |       |
|
| 50 | jayg | localhost | store | Sleep   | 12166 |       |
|
| 77 | phps | localhost | store | Sleep   | 22    |       |
|
| 81 | root | localhost | mysql | Sleep   | 2     |       |
|
| 82 | root | localhost |       | Query   | 0     |       | show
processlist |
+----+------+-----------+-------+---------+-------+-------+---------
---------+
```

You can get the same listing by logging in to the command-line client and running SHOW PROCESSLIST. (Note that you will need proper permissions to get a full listing of threads.) The Process_priv column of the user grant table stores these rights. If you don't have rights in this column, running mysqladmin processlist will show only the threads running with your username.

mysqladmin kill

Once you have a listing, you can end a process with mysqladmin. Try a command like this:

```
shell> mysqladmin -u root -pmypass kill 44
```

Flush commands

The flush commands reload or reset files, tables, or logs. You probably won't have to use these commands very often, but they are important.

mysqladmin flush-hosts

The first flush command is mysqladmin flush-hosts. MySQL maintains a cached table of all of the hosts connected to the MySQL server. If the connection from one of the hosts becomes problematic, MySQL will register the errors. Once the number of errors exceeds the value of the variable max_connect_errors, MySQL will cut off access for that host. At that point MySQL will produce the error Host hostname is blocked. Some sort of TCP/IP networking error normally causes these errors.

After the networking error is fixed, MySQL will continue to block the given host until the cached host tables are flushed. You can run this command from the MySQL command-line client with the command `FLUSH HOSTS`.

If you want to completely do away with blocking errors, you can set `max_connection_errors` to `99999999999`.

mysqladmin flush-logs

The `mysqladmin flush-logs` command closes and reopens all log files. Logging is a very important topic for database administrators, so if you're performing that function, see Chapter 4 of the MySQL manual regarding logging.

mysqladmin flush privileges

You can use `mysqladmin flush-privileges` to reload the grant tables you see in Appendix E. Normally you won't need to flush the grant tables. If you are using the `GRANT` statements, changes in permissions will be updated immediately. However, if you decide to change the GRANT tables with standard `UPDATE`, `INSERT`, and `DELETE` statements, you will need to flush the grant tables. You can also run this command from the command-line client with the command `FLUSH PRIVILEGES`.

mysqladmin flush-tables

The final flush command is `mysqladmin flush-tables`. This closes all open tables with the MySQL installation. MySQL is a multi-threaded environment and will open multiple copies of tables to serve different threads more efficiently. Running this command will close all tables associated with all threads. You can run this command from the command-line client with the command `FLUSH TABLES`.

mysqldump

On the accompanying CD is a file named /book/databases.sql. If you open that file in a text editor, you will see a series of SQL statements that includes both `CREATE` statements for tables and `INSERT` statements for table data. The commands look something like this:

```
# MySQL dump 8.14
#
# Host: localhost    Database: store
#-----------------------------------------------------
# Server version     4.01

#
```

```
# Table structure for table 'addresses'
#
create database store;
use store;

CREATE TABLE addresses (
  address_id int(11) NOT NULL auto_increment,
  user_id int(11) default NULL,
  place varchar(25) NOT NULL default '',
  addr_1 varchar(255) NOT NULL default '',
  addr_2 varchar(255) default NULL,
  city varchar(50) NOT NULL default '',
  state char(2) NOT NULL default '',
  ZIP varchar(5) NOT NULL default '',
  country varchar(5) default NULL,
  PRIMARY KEY  (address_id)
) TYPE=MyISAM;

#
# Dumping data for table 'addresses'
#

INSERT INTO addresses VALUES (5,3,'home','1845 Fair Oaks','Apt
6','San Francisco','CA','92147','USA');
INSERT INTO addresses VALUES (6,4,'home','30445 Haines St','Apt
8G','San Francisco','CA','92149','USA');
INSERT INTO addresses VALUES (7,5,'home','8 Oak
Rd',NULL,'Atlanta','GA','14119','USA');
```

It's a piece of cake to run all of these commands in a batch by directing this file into the command-line client.

```
shell> mysql -u root -pmypass < store.sql
```

The SQL statements in this file were created with the `mysqldump` utility. As you can see from the `.sql` file, this utility exports both table-structure information (`create table` statements) and table data (`insert` statements). By dumping the entirety of databases and tables into files you will create a backup of your data and make your data transportable.

The `mysqldump` utility is very flexible and can take a variety of flags that will return the exact MySQL data you need in a variety of formats. You can see the full set of `mysqldump` options by going to your mysql/bin directory and running `mysqldump --help`. In this appendix we address only some of `mysqldump`'s more commonly used options.

The basic format for a `mysqldump` command is as follows:

```
shell> mysqldump databasename
```

Or, optionally, you can add a table name after the database name to dump structure and data from a single table. And as you might expect, you need to have proper permissions to run `mysqldump`. Your `mysqldump` commands will look like one of the following; the first dumps a database named store, and the second dumps only the users table from that database. In the following statements, we've directed the output to files (store.sql and users.sql).

```
shell> mysqldump -u root -pmypass store > ~/store.sql
shell> mysqldump -u root -pmypass store users > ~/users.sql
```

If you want to dump more than one database you can include additional database names with the `--databases` flag; to dump all databases at once you can use the `--all-databases` flag.

```
shell> mysqldump -u root -pmypass --databases store otherdb > ~/dbs.sql
shell> mysqldump -u root -pmypass --all-databases > ~/alldbs.sql
```

On Unix systems you can use `mysqldump` with pipes to achieve some complex actions with a single command. The first command in the following code takes the output of `mysqldump`, compresses it using `gzip`, and then outputs the compressed data to a file. The second transfers data from one MySQL installation to another. It connects the output of `mysqldump` on one server to the command-line client on another host.

```
shell> mysqldump -u root -pmypass --all-databases | gzip > ~/dbs.sql
shell> mysqldump -u root -pmypass store | mysql -u jay -pmypass -h
mysqlhost.mydomain.com
```

(Note: Don't be misled by the appearance of the text here – that last command should be all one line.)

The MySQL manual recommends that when using `mysqldump` on DOS, you should indicate the location of any output file using the `--result-file` flag instead of the greater-than sign (>). So a sample command would look like this:

```
dos> mysqldump -u root -pmypass --result-file=c:\
store.sql store
```

You should be aware of some other important flags:

- **-c or --complete-insert:** mysqldump outputs each row as an SQL INSERT statement. But the INSERT statements do not use complete column listings; instead they list the values in the order in which the columns exist in the table. So in a table that has the following structure

  ```
  CREATE TABLE sample(
      id int not null primary key,
      fname char(15)
  )
  ```

  you have INSERT statements that look like this:

  ```
  INSERT INTO sample VALUES (1, 'Jay Greenspan');
  ```

  This is potentially problematic if you're transferring data to a table that may be slightly different or that is using a different SQL server. In these cases you want complete SQL statements like insert into sample (id, fname) values (1, 'Jay Greenspan'). The --complete-insert flag gives insert statements in this form.

- **-e or --extended-insert:** When you use this flag, each table's rows are inserted in a single statement, with row values surrounded by parentheses and separated by commas. Without this flag each row has its own INSERT statement. The first command in the following code is what an INSERT statement looks like when run with --extended-insert. The second and third are statements that insert the same information and are created by mysqldump if this flag is not used.

  ```
  INSERT INTO SAMPLE VALUES (1, 'jay'), (2, 'john');
  INSERT INTO SAMPLE VALUES (1, 'jay');
  INSERT INTO SAMPLE VALUES (1, 'john')
  ```

- **--delayed:** In MySQL you can indicate to the MySQL engine that an insert statement is of a relatively low priority by using the syntax insert delayed. When MySQL sees one of these statements it puts the statement in a queue rather than directly into the table if other insert or update statements are coming from other clients. This is especially helpful if other clients are inserting rows that must be available immediately. The delayed row will wait for other updates to finish before data are written to the actual table. Using insert delayed is a good idea when doing bulk inserts as might be the case with rows taken from mysqldump.

- **--add-drop-table:** MySQL's drop table command can return an error if a drop is attempted but the table does not exist. You can use the command drop table if exists to avoid potential errors with the DROP commands. This flag adds drop table if exists before every CREATE statement. If you use this flag with mysqldump you can be sure that any recovery done from this dump will create a clean set of tables and erase any data previously using those names in the tables.

- `-t` or `no-create-info`: Omits `create table` statements from the output.
- `-d` or `no-data`: Just dumps the `create table` statements with no row data.
- `--lock-tables`: Places a lock on all tables within a database before starting a dump.
- `--add-locks`: Adds a `lock tables` before and an `unlock tables` command after each set of inserts. This allows the `mysqldump` thread to move with the greatest speed because no other clients will be able to write to the tables at the same time.
- `--flush-logs` or `-f`: Flushes the log files before starting a dump operation.
- `-q` or `--quick`: By default `mysqldump` writes rows to memory before forcing the rows to standard output. This really isn't necessary. By using this flag you force `mysqldump` to deliver its contents directly to standard output, thereby saving some memory.
- `-w` or `--where`: Enables you to put a `where` condition on what is dumped. For example, from the store users table you can get a list of users with a `user_id` of greater than `5` with the following code. (Note that each `WHERE` condition must be put in quotes, and again, this is meant to be all on one line.)

  ```
  mysqldump -u root -pmypass --add-locks "-wuser_id>5" store
  users
  ```

If you're using `mysqldump` for backup, you'll probably want to use the `--opt` flag. This is the same as using `--quick`, `--add-drop-table`, `--add-locks`, `--extended-insert`, or `--lock-tables`. So for regular backups you should probably add something like the following command to your `cron` tab:

```
./mysqldump -u root -pmypass --opt --all-databases > /path/to/mybackup.sql
```

Other Utilities

Please check the /bin directory for other utilities that come with MySQL. If you are using 3.23 or 4.*x* you will want to look at `myisamchk` and `myisampack`. The first repairs corrupted tables and the second ensures that tables are set up as efficiently as possible. These utilities only work with the MyISAM tables. If you are using 3.22 or newer you will need to use of the `isamchk` utility, which operates on the ISAM tables used in this version of MySQL. And, of course, there's MySQL Control Center (MySQLCC) for those who prefer it.

Appendix E

MySQL User Administration

THIS APPENDIX TEACHES YOU to work with MySQL's permissions tables, which control permissions in MySQL.

Administration of any relational database management system (RDBMS) requires some work. Each system presents its own unique methods for administration, and you can expect difficulties when it comes to tasks like adding and deleting user accounts, backing up, and assuring security. Administering MySQL isn't especially difficult, but it can be a bit bewildering at first.

This book focuses on applications development, not server administration. Thus, extensive details on administration are beyond the scope of this book. If you are responsible for the backup and security of your server, you should delve deep into the MySQL online manual at `http://www.mysql.com/documentation/`.

For the purposes of this book, and we hope also for you, the application developer, it is enough to know a bit about user administration and the methods for assigning rights for users.

grant Tables

MySQL user rights are stored in a series of tables that are automatically created with the MySQL installation. These tables are kept in a database called mysql. If you start up the MySQL daemon (with `mysqld` or, better, `mysqld_safe`) and the MySQL monitor (with `mysql`), and run the query `show databases` just after installation, you see two databases, test and mysql.

Running the `show tables` query on the mysql database lists the tables that store user permissions.

```
mysql> use mysql

Database changed
mysql> show tables;
+-----------------+
| Tables in mysql |
+-----------------+
| columns_priv    |
| db              |
```

```
| func             |
| host             |
| tables_priv      |
| user             |
+------------------+
6 rows in set (0.00 sec)
```

Each of these tables corresponds to a level of access control. You can create any number of users, and users can be allowed access from any number of hosts. For each user/host combination you can grant access to an entire database, to specific tables within a database, or to a number of columns within a table. Additionally, these tables grant administrative privileges. Users can be given permission to add and drop databases or permission to grant other users permissions.

In practice you want to grant no more permissions than necessary. You want to protect your data from the overzealous and the incompetent. The best way to do that with MySQL is to use the proper grant table when assigning rights, keeping the following in mind:

- Rights are granted in a hierarchical way.
- Rights granted in the user table are universal. If a user is granted drop privileges in the user table, that user is able to drop any table in any database in that MySQL installation.
- The db table grants privileges on a database-specific basis. Using this table, you can grant rights for an entire database.
- For any one table or set of tables, make use of the tables_priv table.
- Finally, the columns_priv table enables you to grant rights on specific columns within a table. If you don't need to grant rights to an entire table, see that rights are assigned in the columns_priv table.

Recent releases of MySQL make use of a couple of very convenient commands that make creating users and assigning rights fairly easy. We'll discuss these commands after a brief look at the user, db, tables_priv, and columns_priv tables.

Remember, though, that managing user privileges manually is generally a bad idea. As in administering operating systems, it's better to define groups and manage rights through those groups. Even if you have a group of one, that's the better way to go. Why? Because there's less chance of someone being forgotten and retaining privileges he or she should not have.

The user table

Every user who needs to get at MySQL must be listed in the user table. Rights might be granted elsewhere, but without a listing here the user is refused a connection to the database server. Here is the listing of columns in the user table:

```
mysql> show columns from user;
 ----------------- ------------------- ------ ----- ------- -----
| Field            | Type               | Null | Key |Default|Extra|
 ----------------- ------------------- ------ ----- ------- -----
| Host             | varchar(60) binary |      | PRI |       |     |
| User             | varchar(16) binary |      | PRI |       |     |
| Password         | varchar(16) binary |      |     |       |     |
| Select_priv      | enum('N','Y')      |      |     | N     |     |
| Insert_priv      | enum('N','Y')      |      |     | N     |     |
| Update_priv      | enum('N','Y')      |      |     | N     |     |
| Delete_priv      | enum('N','Y')      |      |     | N     |     |
| Create_priv      | enum('N','Y')      |      |     | N     |     |
| Drop_priv        | enum('N','Y')      |      |     | N     |     |
| Reload_priv      | enum('N','Y')      |      |     | N     |     |
| Shutdown_priv    | enum('N','Y')      |      |     | N     |     |
| Process_priv     | enum('N','Y')      |      |     | N     |     |
| File_priv        | enum('N','Y')      |      |     | N     |     |
| Grant_priv       | enum('N','Y')      |      |     | N     |     |
| References_priv  | enum('N','Y')      |      |     | N     |     |
| Index_priv       | enum('N','Y')      |      |     | N     |     |
| Alter_priv       | enum('N','Y')      |      |     | N     |     |
| Show_db_priv     | enum('N','Y')      |      |     | N     |     |
| Super_priv       | enum('N','Y')      |      |     | N     |     |
| Create_tmp       | enum('N','Y')      |      |     | N     |     |
|   _table_priv    |                    |      |     |       |     |
| Lock_tables_priv| enum('N','Y')       |      |     | N     |     |
| Execute_priv     | enum('N','Y')      |      |     | N     |     |
| Repl_slave_priv  | enum('N','Y')      |      |     | N     |     |
| Repl_client_priv| enum('N','Y')       |      |     | N     |     |
| ssl_type         | enum('','ANY'      |      |     |       |     |
|                  |  ,'X509'           |      |     |       |     |
|                  |  ,'SPECIFIED')     |      |     |       |     |
| ssl_cipher       | blob               |      |     |       |     |
| x509_issuer      | blob               |      |     |       |     |
| x509_subject     | blob               |      |     |       |     |
| max_questions    | int(11) unsigned   |      |     | 0     |     |
| max_updates      | int(11) unsigned   |      |     | 0     |     |
| max_connections  | int(11) unsigned   |      |     | 0     |     |
 ----------------- ------------------- ------ ----- ------- -----
```

As you have seen, the PHP mysql_connect() function takes three arguments: username, host, and password. In the preceding listing you can see the corresponding field names. MySQL identifies a user by the combination of username and host. For instance, user jay can have a different set of rights for each host that he uses to connect to MySQL. If you or your PHP scripts are accessing MySQL from the local machine, you usually assign a host of localhost.

The other columns are intuitively named. As you can see, most of the columns allow only Y or N as column values. As we mentioned earlier, any of these rights that are set to Y are granted to every table of every database. Most of the columns' names correspond to SQL statements (such as delete, create, and so forth).

The user table also contains a set of columns that grant administrative rights. These columns are covered in detail in the "GRANT and REVOKE Syntax" section of the MySQL documentation. The following is a brief explanation of the meanings of some of these columns. If you are security-minded, grant these rights sparingly.

- File_priv — If granted, this privilege allows the database server to read and write files from the file system. You most often use it when loading a file into a database table.
- Grant_priv — A user with this right is able to assign his or her privileges to other users.
- Process_priv — This right gives a user the ability to view and kill all running processes and threads.
- Reload_priv — Most of the privileges granted by this column are not covered in the course of this book. This privilege is most often used with the mysqladmin utility to perform flush commands. See the MySQL online manual for more details.
- Shutdown_priv — Allows the user to shut down the database using mysqladmin shutdown.

The db table

For database-specific permissions, the db table is where you do most of your work. The following is a list of columns from the db table:

```
mysql> show columns from db;
 -------------------- --------------- ----- --- ------- -----
| Field              | Type            | Null |Key|Default|Extra|
 -------------------- --------------- ----- --- ------- -----
| Host               | char(60) binary |      |PRI|       |     |
| Db                 | char(64) binary |      |PRI|       |     |
| User               | char(16) binary |      |PRI|       |     |
| Select_priv        | enum('N','Y')   |      |   | N     |     |
| Insert_priv        | enum('N','Y')   |      |   | N     |     |
```

```
| Update_priv           | enum('N','Y')    |      |     | N       |       |
| Delete_priv           | enum('N','Y')    |      |     | N       |       |
| Create_priv           | enum('N','Y')    |      |     | N       |       |
| Drop_priv             | enum('N','Y')    |      |     | N       |       |
| Grant_priv            | enum('N','Y')    |      |     | N       |       |
| References_priv       | enum('N','Y')    |      |     | N       |       |
| Index_priv            | enum('N','Y')    |      |     | N       |       |
| Alter_priv            | enum('N','Y')    |      |     | N       |       |
| Create_tmp_table_priv| enum('N','Y')    |      |     | N       |       |
| Lock_tables_priv      | enum('N','Y')    |      |     | N       |       |
 --------------------- ----------------- ------ --- ------- -----
```

The db table works like the user table, except that permissions granted here work only for the database specified in the db column.

tables_priv and columns_priv

These two tables look pretty similar, and to save a bit of space, we show only the tables_priv table.

```
mysql> show columns from tables_priv;
 ------------- ---------------- ------ ----- --------- -------
| Field        | Type             | Null | Key | Default | Extra |
 ------------- ---------------- ------ ----- --------- -------
| Host         | char(60) binary |      | PRI |         |       |
| Db           | char(64) binary |      | PRI |         |       |
| User         | char(16) binary |      | PRI |         |       |
| Table_name   | char(60) binary |      | PRI |         |       |
| Grantor      | char(77)        |      | MUL |         |       |
| Timestamp    | timestamp(14)   | YES  |     | NULL    |       |
| Table_priv   | set('Select'    |      |     |         |       |
|              |  ,'Insert'      |      |     |         |       |
|              |  ,'Update'      |      |     |         |       |
|              |  ,'Delete'      |      |     |         |       |
|              |  ,'Create'      |      |     |         |       |
|              |  ,'Drop'        |      |     |         |       |
|              |  ,'Grant'       |      |     |         |       |
|              |  ,'References'  |      |     |         |       |
|              |  ,'Index'       |      |     |         |       |
|              |  ,'Alter')      |      |     |         |       |
| Column_priv  | set('Select'    |      |     |         |       |
|              |  ,'Insert'      |      |     |         |       |
|              |  ,'Update'      |      |     |         |       |
|              |  ,'References') |      |     |         |       |
 ------------- ---------------- ------ ----- --------- -------
```

For users who get access only to a table or set of tables within a database, the exact rights are stored in this table. Note the use of the `set` column type for table_priv and column_priv tables. All of the rights available to a specific user are crammed into these two cells.

At a couple of points in this book we advise against using the `set` column type. In fact, the db table is a good example of a place where using `set` makes sense. The column has few potential values, and the number of potential values is not likely to change.

grant and revoke Statements

Because the preceding tables are regular MySQL tables, you can alter them with the SQL statements you are already familiar with. But consider the nightmare that would be. If you wanted to grant a new user table-level access you would first need to insert a row into the user database with an SQL statement like the following:

```
INSERT INTO user
    (Host, User, Password, Select_priv, Insert_priv, Update_priv,
Delete_priv, Create_priv, Drop_priv, Reload_priv, Shutdown_priv,
Process_priv, File_priv, Grant_priv, References_priv, Index_priv,
Alter_priv)
VALUES
    ('localhost', 'juan', 'password', 'N', 'N', 'N', 'N', 'N', 'N',
'N', 'N', 'N', 'N', 'N', 'N', 'N', 'N')
```

Then you'd need to grant specific rights with another `insert` statement to another table.

If you are thinking you can script these functions with a Web front end, that is definitely a possibility. But you want to be very careful, because the script would have the equivalent of root access to the database, which could be very unsafe.

Happily, MySQL has some built-in statements that make user administration a whole lot easier. Knowing the `grant` and `revoke` statements saves you from having to send individual queries.

The grant statement

Before we get into specifics of this statement, take a look at the statement that grants all rights on the database named guestbook to user jim; jim's password is *pword*.

```
mysql> grant all on guestbook.* to jim@localhost identified by
"pword";
```

This command makes all the necessary changes to the user and db tables.

The first part of the grant statement can take the argument all (which must be followed by WITH GRANT if it's really to grant all privileges), or it can take any of the options listed in the user table. Most often you are granting rights to use SQL statements (select, create, alter, delete, drop, index, insert, and update).

The second portion of the grant statement (on guestbook in the example) identifies where privileges are to be applied: universally, to a single database, to tables, or to columns. Table E-1 shows how to indicate where privileges should be applied.

TABLE E-1 SETTING PERMISSIONS

Identifier	Meaning
grant all on *.*	Rights are universal; inserted into the user table
grant all on database.*	Rights apply to all tables in a single database
grant all on database.table_name	Rights apply to a single table
grant all(col1, col2) on database.table_name	Rights apply only to specific columns in a specific database and table

The third portion of the grant statement (to jim@localhost in the example) indicates the user to be given access. As we mentioned earlier, MySQL needs both a name and a host. In the grant statement these are separated by the @ symbol.

Finally, the identified by portion of the grant statement gives the user a password.

Here are a few more examples of grant statements:

```
grant select, update, insert  on guestbook2k.guestbook to
alvin@localhost identified by "pword";
```

The preceding statement allows alvin to view, update, and insert records into the table guestbook in database guestbook2k.

```
grant select, update (name, url)  on guestbook2k.guestbook to
chipmunk@localhost identified by "pword";
```

With the preceding statement the user can view and update only two columns (name and url). No deletes or inserts are allowed.

```
grant all on *.* to josh@localhost identified by "pword" WITH GRANT
OPTION;
```

The preceding statement gives this user all privileges, which means that josh@localhost is even allowed to grant privileges to other users.

The revoke statement

If you want to remove some of a user's privileges, you can use the revoke statement. To remove shutdown privileges from a user who had been granted all privileges, like josh in the preceding example, you can run the following:

```
revoke Shutdown on *.* from josh@localhost;
```

Notice that the word from is used in the revoke statement in place of to. Otherwise revoke works just like grant.

To remove a user entirely you must run a delete statement against the user table. Because the user is identified by a name and a host, the following should do it:

```
delete from user where user='username' and
host='hostname'
```

Viewing grants

You can use the SHOW GRANTS statement to see the exact grants available at a given time. All you need to know is the username and host.

```
mysql> show grants for jayg@localhost;

+-----------------------------------------------------------+
| Grants for jayg@localhost                                 |
+-----------------------------------------------------------+
| GRANT ALL PRIVILEGES ON my_test.* TO 'jayg'@'localhost'   |
+-----------------------------------------------------------+
1 row in set (0.00 sec)
```

Reloading grants

The grant tables are loaded into memory when the MySQL daemon is started. Changes made to the grant tables that do not make use of the `grant` command do not take effect until you tell MySQL to reload the grant tables. You can do this in the shell with the `mysqladmin` program:

```
shell> mysqladmin flush-privileges
```

or in the `mysql` client with the `flush privileges` command. Just run:

```
flush privileges
```

Appendix F

PHP Function Reference

PHP CONTAINS MORE FUNCTIONS than could possibly be listed in this book. The following tables present many of the most commonly used functions available as of PHP version 4. To keep up on exactly what's available in PHP, and to check out what new functions are available in PHP 5, make sure to check in with the online documentation: `http://www.php.net/docs.php`.

TABLE F-1 MYSQL FUNCTIONS

Function	Return Value	Action
`mysql_connect([string hostname [:port][:/path/to/socket]] [, string username] [, string password] [, bool new])`	resource	Opens a connection to a MySQL server
`mysql_pconnect([string hostname [:port][:/path/to/socket]] [, string username] [, string password])`	resource	Opens a persistent connection to a MySQL server
`mysql_close([int link_identifier])`	bool	Closes a MySQL connection
`mysql_select_db(string database_name [, int link_identifier])`	bool	Selects a MySQL database
`mysql_get_client_info(void)`	string	Returns a string that represents the client-library version
`mysql_get_host_info([int link_identifier])`	string	Returns a string describing the type of connection in use, including the server-host name

Continued

Table F-1 MYSQL FUNCTIONS *(Continued)*

Function	Return Value	Action
`mysql_get_proto_info([int link_identifier])`	int	Returns the protocol version used by the current connection
`mysql_get_server_info([int link_identifier])`	string	Returns a string that represents the server-version number
`mysql_create_db(string` *`database_name`* `[, int link_identifier])`	bool	Creates a MySQL database
`mysql_drop_db(string` *`database_name`* `[, int link_identifier])`	bool	Drops (deletes) a MySQL database
`mysql_query(string` *`query`* `[, int link_identifier] [, int` *`result_mode`*`])`	resource	Sends an SQL query to MySQL
`mysql_unbuffered_query(string` *`query`* `[, int link_identifier] [, int` *`result_mode`*`])`	resource	Sends an SQL query to MySQL, without fetching and buffering the result rows
`mysql_db_query(string` *`database_name`*`, string query [, int link_identifier])`	resource	Sends an SQL query to MySQL
`mysql_list_dbs([int link_identifier])`	resource	Lists the databases available on a MySQL server
`mysql_list_tables(string` *`database_name`* `[, int link_identifier])`	resource	Lists the tables in a MySQL database
`mysql_list_fields(string` *`database_name`*`, string` *`table_name`* `[, int link_identifier])`	resource	Lists the MySQL result fields
`mysql_error([int link_identifier])`	string	Returns the text of the error message from the previous MySQL operation

Function	Return Value	Action
`mysql_errno([int link_identifier])`	int	Returns the number of the error message from the previous MySQL operation
`mysql_affected_rows([int link_identifier])`	int	Gets the number of affected rows in the previous MySQL operation
`mysql_escape_string(string to_be_escaped)`	string	Escape string for a MySQL query
`mysql_insert_id([int link_identifier])`	int	Gets the ID generated from the previous `INSERT` operation
`mysql_result(int result, int row [, mixed field])`	mixed	Gets result data
`mysql_num_rows(int result)`	int	Gets the number of rows in a result
`mysql_num_fields(int result)`	int	Gets the number of fields in a result
`mysql_fetch_row(int result)`	array	Gets a result row as an enumerated array
`mysql_fetch_object(int result [, int result_type])`	object	Fetches a result row as an object
`mysql_fetch_array(int result [, int result_type])`	array	Fetches a result row as an array (associative, numeric, or both)
`mysql_fetch_assoc(int result)`	array	Fetches a result row as an associative array
`mysql_data_seek(int result, int row_number)`	bool	Moves the internal result pointer
`mysql_fetch_lengths(int result)`	array	Gets the maximum data size of each column in a result
`mysql_fetch_field(int result [, int field_offset])`	object	Gets the column information from a result and returns it as an object

Continued

Table F-1 MYSQL FUNCTIONS *(Continued)*

Function	Return Value	Action
mysql_field_seek(int *result*, int *field_offset*)	bool	Sets the result pointer to a specific field offset
mysql_*field_name*(int *result*, int *field_index*)	string	Gets the name of the specified field in a result
mysql_field_table(int *result*, int *field_offset*)	string	Gets the name of the table the specified field is in
mysql_field_len(int *result*, int *field_offset*)	int	Returns the length of the specified field
mysql_field_type(int *result*, int *field_offset*)	string	Gets the type of the specified field in a result
mysql_field_flags(int *result*, int *field_offset*)	string	Gets the flags associated with the specified field in a result
mysql_free_result(int *result*)	bool	Frees memory associated with the result

Table F-2 STRING-MANIPULATION FUNCTIONS

Function	Return Value	Action
bin2hex(string *data*)	string	Converts the binary representation of data to hex
strspn(string str, string *mask*)	int	Finds the length of the initial segment consisting entirely of characters found in mask
strcspn(string str, string *mask*)	int	Finds the length of the initial segment consisting entirely of characters not found in mask
nl_langinfo(int *item*)	string	Queries the language and locale information

Function	Return Value	Action
`strcoll(string` *str1*`, string` *str2*`)`	int	Compares two strings using the current locale
`chop(string` *str* `[, string` *character_mask*`])`	string	An alias for `rtrim`
`rtrim(string` *str* `[, string` *character_mask*`])`	string	Removes trailing white space
`trim(string` *str* `[, string` *character_mask*`])`	string	Strips white space from the beginning and end of a string
`ltrim(string` *str* `[, string` *character_mask*`])`	string	Strips white space from the beginning of a string
`wordwrap(string` *str* `[, int` *width* `[, string` *break* `[, int` *cut*`]]])`	string	Wraps a string to a given number of characters using a string break character.
`explode(string` *separator*`, string` *str* `[, int` *limit*`])`	array	Splits a string-on-the string *separator* and returns an array of components
`join(array` *src*`, string` *glue*`)`	string	An alias for `implode`
`implode(array` *src*`, string` *glue*`)`	string	Joins array elements by placing the glue string between items and returns one string
`strtok([string str,] string` *token*`)`	string	Tokenizes a string
`strtoupper(string` *str*`)`	string	Makes a string upper case
`strtolower(string` *str*`)`	string	Makes a string lower case
`basename(string` *path* `[, string` *suffix*`])`	string	Returns the file-name component of the path
`dirname(string` *path*`)`	string	Returns the directory-name component of the path

Continued

Table F-2 STRING-MANIPULATION FUNCTIONS *(Continued)*

Function	Return Value	Action
`pathinfo(string path)`	array	Returns information about a certain string
`stristr(string haystack, string needle)`	string	Finds the first occurrence of a string within another (case-insensitive)
`strstr(string haystack, string needle)`	string	Finds the first occurrence of a string within another
`strchr(string haystack, string needle)`	string	An alias for `strstr`
`strpos(string haystack, string needle [, int offset])`	int	Finds the position of the first occurrence of a string within another
`strrpos(string haystack, string needle)`	int	Finds the position of the last occurrence of a character in a string within another
`strrchr(string haystack, string needle)`	string	Finds the last occurrence of a character in a string within another
`chunk_split(string str [, int chunklen [, string ending]])`	string	Returns a split line
`substr(string str, int start [, int length])`	string	Returns part of a string
`substr_replace(string str, string repl, int start [, int length])`	string	Replaces part of a string with another string
`quotemeta(string str)`	string	Quotes meta-characters
`ord(string character)`	int	Returns the ASCII value of a character
`chr(int ascii)`	string	Converts ASCII code to a character
`ucfirst(string str)`	string	Makes a string's first character upper case

Function	Return Value	Action
`ucwords(string str)`	string	Renders the first character of every word in a string in upper case
`strtr(string str, string from, string to)`	string	Translates characters in `str` using given translation tables
`strrev(string str)`	string	Reverses a string
`similar_text(string str1, string str2 [, float percent])`	int	Calculates the similarity between two strings
`addcslashes(string str, string charlist)`	string	Escapes all characters mentioned in `charlist` with backslashes. Creates octal representations if asked to backslash characters with eighth-bit set or with ASCII<32 (except `\n`, `\r`, `\t`, and so on)
`addslashes(string str)`	string	Escapes single quotes, double quotes, and backslash characters in a string with backslashes
`stripcslashes(string str)`	string	Strips backslashes from a string (uses C-style conventions)
`stripslashes(string str)`	string	Strips backslashes from a string
`str_replace(mixed search, mixed replace, mixed subject [, bool boyer])`	mixed	Replaces all occurrences of `search` in `haystack` with `replace`
`hebrev(string str [, int max_chars_per_line])`	string	Converts logical Hebrew text to visual text
`hebrevc(string str [, int max_chars_per_line])`	string	Converts logical Hebrew text to visual text with newline conversion

Continued

Table F-2 STRING-MANIPULATION FUNCTIONS *(Continued)*

Function	Return Value	Action
`nl2br(string str)`	string	Converts newlines to HTML line breaks
`strip_tags(string str [, string allowable_tags])`	string	Strips HTML and PHP tags from a string
`setlocale(mixed category, string locale)`	string	Sets locale information
`parse_str(string encoded_string [, array result])`	void	Parses `GET`/`POST`/`COOKIE` data and sets global variables
`str_repeat(string input, int mult)`	string	Returns the input string repeated `mult` times
`count_chars(string input [, int mode])`	mixed	Returns information about what characters are used in input
`strnatcmp(string s1, string s2)`	int	Returns the result of a string comparison using a "natural" algorithm
`localeconv(void)`	array	Returns numeric formatting information based on the current locale
`strnatcasecmp(string s1, string s2)`	int	Returns the result of a case-insensitive string comparison using a "natural" algorithm
`substr_count(string haystack, string needle)`	int	Returns the number of times a substring occurs in the string
`str_pad(string input, int pad_length [, string pad_string [, int pad_type]])`	string	Returns the input string, padded on the left or right to a specified length with `pad_string`
`sscanf(string str, string format [, string ...])`	mixed	Implements an ANSI C-compatible `sscanf`
`str_rot13(string str)`	string	Performs the rot13 transform on a string

Table F-3 ARRAY FUNCTIONS

Function	Return Value	Action
`krsort(array array_arg [, int sort_flags])`	bool	Sorts an array by key value in reverse order
`ksort(array array_arg [, int sort_flags])`	bool	Sorts an array by key
`count(mixed var [, int mode])`	int	Counts the number of elements in a variable (usually an array)
`natsort(array array_arg)`	void	Sorts an array using natural sort
`natcasesort(array array_arg)`	void	Sorts an array using case-insensitive natural sort
`asort(array array_arg [, int sort_flags])`	bool	Sorts an array and maintains index association
`arsort(array array_arg [, int sort_flags])`	bool	Sorts an array in reverse order and maintains index association
`sort(array array_arg [, int sort_flags])`	bool	Sorts an array
`rsort(array array_arg [, int sort_flags])`	bool	Sorts an array in reverse order
`usort(array array_arg, string cmp_function)`	bool	Sorts an array by values using a user-defined comparison function
`uasort(array array_arg, string cmp_function)`	bool	Sorts an array with a user-defined comparison function and maintains index association
`uksort(array array_arg, string cmp_function)`	bool	Sorts an array by keys using a user-defined comparison function

Continued

TABLE F-3 ARRAY FUNCTIONS *(Continued)*

Function	Return Value	Action
`end(array array_arg)`	mixed	Advances the array argument's internal pointer to the last element and returns it
`prev(array array_arg)`	mixed	Moves the array argument's internal pointer to the previous element and returns it
`next(array array_arg)`	mixed	Moves the array argument's internal pointer to the next element and returns it
`reset(array array_arg)`	mixed	Sets the array argument's internal pointer to the first element and returns it
`current(array array_arg)`	mixed	Returns the element currently pointed to by the internal array pointer
`key(array array_arg)`	mixed	Returns the key of the element currently pointed to by the internal array pointer
`min(mixed arg1 [, mixed arg2 [, mixed ...]])`	mixed	Returns the lowest value in an array or a series of arguments
`max(mixed arg1 [, mixed arg2 [, mixed ...]])`	mixed	Returns the highest value in an array or a series of arguments
`array_walk(array input, string funcname [, mixed userdata])`	bool	Applies a user function to every member of an array
`in_array(mixed needle, array haystack [, bool strict])`	bool	Checks if the given value exists in the array

Function	Return Value	Action
`array_search(mixed needle, array haystack [, bool strict])`	mixed	Searches the array for a given value and returns the corresponding key if successful
`extract(array var_array [, int extract_type [, string prefix]])`	int	Imports variables into the symbol table from an array
`compact(mixed var_names [, mixed ...])`	array	Creates a hash containing variables and their values
`array_fill(int start_key, int num, mixed val)`	array	Creates an array containing `num` elements, starting with index `start_key`, each initialized to `val`
`range(mixed low, mixed high)`	array	Creates an array containing the range of integers or characters from low to high (inclusive)
`shuffle(array array_arg)`	bool	Randomly shuffles the contents of an array
`array_push(array stack, mixed var [, mixed ...])`	int	Pushes elements onto the end of the array
`array_pop(array stack)`	mixed	Pops an element off the end of the array
`array_shift(array stack)`	mixed	Pops an element off the beginning of the array
`array_unshift(array stack, mixed var [, mixed ...])`	int	Pushes elements onto the beginning of the array
`array_splice(array input, int offset [, int length [, array replacement]])`	array	Removes the elements designated by `offset` and `length` and replaces them with the supplied array
`array_slice(array input, int offset [, int length])`	array	Returns the elements specified by `offset` and `length`

Continued

TABLE F-3 ARRAY FUNCTIONS *(Continued)*

Function	Return Value	Action
`array_merge(array arr1, array arr2 [, array ...])`	array	Merges the elements from passed arrays into one array
`array_merge_recursive(array arr1, array arr2 [, array ...])`	array	Recursively merges elements from passed arrays into one array
`array_keys(array input [, mixed search_value])`	array	Returns just the keys from the input array, optionally only for the specified `search_value`
`array_values(array input)`	array	Returns just the values from the input array
`array_count_values(array input)`	array	Returns an array using the values of the *input* array as keys and their frequency in *input* as values
`array_reverse(array input [, bool preserve keys])`	array	Returns *input* as a new array with the order of the entries reversed
`array_pad(array input, int pad_size, mixed pad_value)`	array	Returns a copy of the *input* array padded with `pad_value` to size `pad_size`
`array_flip(array input)`	array	Returns an array with the key <-> value flipped
`array_change_key_case(array input [, int case=CASE_LOWER])`	array	Returns an array with all string keys rendered in lower case (or upper cased)
`array_unique(array input)`	array	Removes duplicate values from the array

Function	Return Value	Action
`array_intersect(array arr1, array arr2 [, array ...])`	array	Returns the entries of `arr1` that have values that are present in all the other arguments
`array_diff(array arr1, array arr2 [, array ...])`	array	Returns the entries of `arr1` that have values that are not present in any of the other arguments
`array_multisort(array` *`ar1`* `[, SORT_ASC|SORT_DESC [, SORT_REGULAR|SORT_NUMERIC|SORT_STRING]] [, array ar2 [, SORT_ASC|SORT_DESC [, SORT_REGULAR|SORT_NUMERIC|SORT_STRING]], ...])`	bool	Sorts multiple arrays at once, much as the `ORDER BY` clause does in SQL
`array_rand(array input [, int` *`num_req`*`])`	mixed	Returns the key/keys for random entry/entries in the array
`array_sum(array input)`	mixed	Returns the sum of the array entries
`array_reduce(array input, mixed callback [, int` *`initial`*`])`	mixed	Iteratively reduces the array to a single value via the callback
`array_filter(array input [, mixed callback])`	array	Filters elements from the array via the callback
`array_map(mixed callback, array` *`input1`* `[, array` *`input2`* `,...])`	array	Applies the callback to the elements in given arrays
`array_key_exists(mixed` *`key`*`, array` *`search`*`)`	bool	Checks if the given key or index exists in the array
`array_chunk(array input, int` *`size`* `[, bool` *`preserve_keys`*`])`	array	Splits the array into chunks

TABLE F-4 DATE/TIME FUNCTIONS

Function	Return Value	Action
`time(void)`	int	Returns the current Unix timestamp
`Mktime(int hour, int min, int sec, int mon, int day, int year)`	int	Gets the Unix timestamp for a date
`gmmktime(int hour, int min, int sec, int mon, int day, int year)`	int	Gets the Unix timestamp for a GMT date
`date(string format [, int timestamp])`	string	Formats a local time/date
`gmdate(string format [, int timestamp])`	string	Formats a GMT/UTC date/time
`localtime([int timestamp [, bool associative_array]])`	array	Returns the results of the C-system call `localtime` as an associative array if the *associative_array* argument is set to 1; otherwise it is a regular array
`getdate([int timestamp])`	array	Gets date/time information
`checkdate(int month, int day, int year)`	bool	Returns `true` if the given values represent a valid date in the Gregorian calendar
`strftime(string format [, int timestamp])`	string	Formats a local time/date according to locale settings
`gmstrftime(string format [, int timestamp])`	string	Formats a GMT/UCT time/date according to locale settings
`strtotime(string time, int now)`	int	Converts a string representation of the date and time to a timestamp

TABLE F-5 DIRECTORY FUNCTIONS

Function	Return Value	Action
opendir(string *path*)	mixed	Opens a directory and returns a dir_handle
dir(string *directory*)	class	Returns a directory pseudo-class, with properties *handle* and *path*, and methods read(), rewind() and close()
closedir([resource *dir_handle*])	void	Closes the directory connection identified by the dir_handle
chroot(string *directory*)	bool	Changes the root directory
chdir(string *directory*)	bool	Changes the current directory
getcwd(void)	mixed	Gets the current directory
rewinddir([resource *dir_handle*])	void	Rewinds dir_handle back to the start
readdir([resource *dir_handle*])	string	Reads the directory entry from dir_handle

TABLE F-6 DNS-RELATED FUNCTIONS

Function	Return Value	Action
gethostbyaddr(string *ip_address*)	string	Gets the Internet host name corresponding to a given IP address
gethostbyname(string *hostname*)	string	Gets the IP address corresponding to a given Internet host name

Continued

Table F-6 DNS-RELATED FUNCTIONS *(Continued)*

Function	Return Value	Action
gethostbynamel(string *hostname*)	array	Returns a list of IP addresses that a given host name resolves to
checkdnsrr(string *host* [, string *type*])	int	Checks DNS records corresponding to a given Internet host name or IP address
getmxrr(string *hostname*, array *mxhosts* [, array *weight*])	int	Gets MX records corresponding to a given Internet host name

Table F-7 EXECUTION FUNCTIONS

Function	Return Value	Action
exec(string *command* [, array *output* [, int *return_value*]])	string	Executes an external program
system(string *command* [, int *return_value*])	int	Executes an external program and displays output
passthru(string *command* [, int *return_value*])	void	Executes an external program and displays raw output
escapeshellcmd(string *command*)	string	Escapes shell meta-characters
escapeshellarg(string *arg*)	string	Quotes and escapes an argument for use in a shell command that has been opened via popen()

Table F-8 FUNCTIONS FOR WORKING WITH FILES

Function	Return Value	Action
`flock(resource fp, int operation [, int wouldblock])`	bool	Portable file locking
`get_meta_tags(string filename [, bool use_include_path])`	array	Extracts all metatag content attributes from a file and returns an array
`file(string filename [, bool use_include_path])`	array	Reads the entire file into an array
`tempnam(string dir, string prefix)`	string	Creates a unique file name in a directory
`tmpfile(void)`	resource	Creates a temporary file that will be deleted automatically after use
`fopen(string filename, string mode [, bool use_include_path])`	resource	Opens a file or a URL and returns a file pointer
`fclose(resource fp)`	bool	Closes an open file pointer
`popen(string command, string mode)`	resource	Executes a command and opens either a read or a write pipe to it
`pclose(resource fp)`	int	Closes a file pointer opened by `popen()`
`feof(resource fp)`	bool	Tests for end-of-file on a file pointer
`socket_set_blocking(resource socket, int mode)`	bool	Sets blocking/non-blocking mode on a socket
`set_socket_blocking(resource socket, int mode)`	bool	Sets blocking/non-blocking mode on a socket
`socket_set_timeout(int socket_descriptor, int seconds, int microseconds)`	bool	Sets timeout on socket read to *seconds* plus *microseconds*
`socket_get_status(resource socket_descriptor)`	array	Returns an array describing socket status

Continued

Table F-8 FUNCTIONS FOR WORKING WITH FILES *(Continued)*

Function	Return Value	Action
`fgets(resource fp[, int length])`	string	Gets a line from the file pointer
`fgetc(resource fp)`	string	Gets a character from the file pointer
`fgetss(resource fp, int length [, string allowable_tags])`	string	Gets a line from the file pointer and strips HTML tags
`fscanf(string str, string format [, string ...])`	mixed	Implements a mostly-ANSI-compatible `fscanf()`
`fwrite(resource fp, string str [, int length])`	int	Binary-safe file write
`fflush(resource fp)`	bool	Flushes output
`set_file_buffer(resource fp, int buffer)`	int	Sets file write buffer
`rewind(resource fp)`	bool	Rewinds the position of a file pointer
`ftell(resource fp)`	int	Gets the file pointer's read/write position
`fseek(resource fp, int offset [, int whence])`	int	Seeks on a file pointer
`mkdir(string pathname [, int mode])`	bool	Creates a directory
`rmdir(string dirname)`	bool	Removes a directory
`readfile(string filename [, int use_include_path])`	int	Outputs a file or a URL
`umask([int mask])`	int	Returns or changes the `umask`
`fpassthru(resource fp)`	int	Outputs all remaining data from a file pointer

Function	Return Value	Action
`rename(string` *old_name*, `string` *new_name*`)`	bool	Renames a file
`unlink(string` *filename*`)`	bool	Deletes a file
`ftruncate(resource` *fp*, `int` *size*`)`	int	Truncates file to length *size*
`fstat(resource` *fp*`)`	int	`Stat()` on a file handle
`copy(string` *source_file*, `string` *destination_file*`)`	bool	Copies a file
`fread(resource` *fp*, `int length)`	string	Binary-safe file read
`fgetcsv(resource` *fp*, `int length [, string` *delimiter*`])`	array	Gets a line from the file pointer and parses it for CSV fields
`realpath(string` *path*`)`	string	Returns the resolved path

TABLE F-9 FILE STATUS FUNCTIONS

Function	Return Value	Action
`disk_total_space(string` *path*`)`	float	Gets total disk space for the file system that *path* is on
`disk_free_space(string` *path*`)`	float	Gets free disk space for the file system that *path* is on
`chgrp(string filename, mixed group)`	bool	Changes the file group
`chown (string filename, mixed user)`	bool	Changes the file owner
`chmod(string filename, int mode)`	bool	Changes the file mode
`touch(string filename [, int time [, int atime]])`	bool	Sets the modification time for the file
`clearstatcache(void)`	void	Clears the file's stat cache

Continued

TABLE F-9 FILE STATUS FUNCTIONS *(Continued)*

Function	Return Value	Action
`fileperms(string filename)`	int	Gets file permissions
`fileinode(string filename)`	int	Gets the file `inode`
`filesize(string filename)`	int	Gets the file size
`fileowner(string filename)`	int	Gets the file owner
`filegroup(string filename)`	int	Gets the file group
`fileatime(string filename)`	int	Gets the last access time for the file
`filemtime(string filename)`	int	Gets the last modification time for the file
`filectime(string filename)`	int	Gets the `inode`-modification time for the file
`filetype(string filename)`	string	Gets the file type
`is_writable(string filename)`	int	Returns `true` if the file can be written
`is_readable(string filename)`	int	Returns `true` if the file can be read
`is_executable(string filename)`	int	Returns `true` if the file is executable
`is_file(string filename)`	int	Returns `true` if the file is a regular file
`is_dir(string filename)`	int	Returns `true` if the file is a directory
`is_link(string filename)`	int	Returns `true` if the file is a symbolic link
`file_exists(string filename)`	bool	Returns `true` if the file name exists
`lstat(string filename)`	array	Gives information about a file or symbolic link
`stat(string filename)`	array	Gives information about a file

TABLE F-10 FSOCK FUNCTIONS

Function	Return Value	Action
fsockopen(string hostname, int *port* [, int *errno* [, string *errstr* [, float *timeout*]]])	int	Opens an Internet or Unix domain-socket connection
pfsockopen(string hostname, int *port* [, int *errno* [, string *errstr* [, float *timeout*]]])	int	Opens a persistent Internet or Unix domain-socket connection

TABLE F-11 HTTP HEADER FUNCTIONS

Function	Return Value	Action
header(string *header* [, bool *replace*])	void	Sends a raw HTTP header
setcookie(string *name* [, string *value* [, int *expires* [, string *path* [, string *domain* [, bool *secure*]]]]])	bool	Sends a cookie
headers_sent(void)	int	Returns true if headers have already been sent, false otherwise

TABLE F-12 HTML-RELATED FUNCTIONS

Function	Return Value	Action
htmlspecialchars(string *string* [, int *quote_style*][, string *charset*])	string	Converts special characters into HTML entities
htmlentities(string *string* [, int *quote_style*][, string *charset*])	string	Converts all applicable characters into HTML entities

Continued

Table F-12 HTML-RELATED FUNCTIONS *(Continued)*

Function	Return Value	Action
get_html_translation_table([int *table* [, int *quote_style*]])	array	Returns the internal translation table used by htmlspecialchars and htmlentities

Table F-13 PHP-INFORMATION FUNCTIONS

Function	Return Value	Action
phpinfo([int *what*])	void	Outputs a page of useful information about PHP and the current request
phpversion([string *extension*])	string	Returns the current PHP version
phpcredits([int *flag*])	void	Prints the list of people who've contributed to the PHP project
php_sapi_name(void)	string	Returns the current SAPI module name
php_uname(void)	string	Returns information about the system PHP was built on

Table F-14 MATH FUNCTIONS

Function	Return Value	Action
abs(int *number*)	int	Returns the absolute value of the number
ceil(float *number*)	float	Returns the next highest integer value from the number

Function	Return Value	Action
`floor(float number)`	float	Returns the next lowest integer value from the number
`round(float number [, int precision])`	float	Returns the number rounded to the specified precision
`sin(float number)`	float	Returns the sine of the number in radians
`cos(float number)`	float	Returns the cosine of the number in radians
`tan(float number)`	float	Returns the tangent of the number in radians
`asin(float number)`	float	Returns the arc sine of the number in radians
`acos(float number)`	float	Return the arc cosine of the number in radians
`atan(float number)`	float	Returns the arc tangent of the number in radians
`atan2(float y, float x)`	float	Returns the arc tangent of *y*/*x*, with the resulting quadrant determined by the sines of *y* and *x*
`sinh(float number)`	float	Returns the hyperbolic sine of the number, defined as (exp(*number*) – exp(–*number*))/2
`cosh(float number)`	float	Returns the hyperbolic cosine of the number, defined as (exp(*number*) + exp(–*number*))/2
`tanh(float number)`	float	Returns the hyperbolic tangent of the number, defined as sinh(*number*)/cosh(*number*)

Continued

TABLE F-14 MATH FUNCTIONS *(Continued)*

Function	Return Value	Action
`asinh(float number)`	float	Returns the inverse hyperbolic sine of the number, that is, the value whose hyperbolic sine is *number*
`acosh(float number)`	float	Returns the inverse hyperbolic cosine of the number, that is, the value whose hyperbolic cosine is *number*
`atanh(float number)`	float	Returns the inverse hyperbolic tangent of the number, that is, the value whose hyperbolic tangent is *number*
`pi(void)`	float	Returns an approximation of pi
`is_finite(float val)`	bool	Returns whether argument is finite
`is_infinite(float val)`	bool	Returns whether argument is infinite
`is_nan(float val)`	bool	Returns whether argument is not a number
`pow(number base, number exponent)`	number	Returns *base* raised to the power of *exponent*; returns the integer result when possible
`exp(float number)`	float	Returns *e* raised to the power of *number*
`expm1(float number)`	float	Returns *exp(number)* – 1, computed in a way that is accurate even when the value of *number* is close to 0

Function	Return Value	Action
`log1p(float number)`	float	Returns log(1 + *number*), computed in a way that is accurate even when the value of number is close to 0
`log(float number)`	float	Returns the natural logarithm of the number
`log10(float number)`	float	Returns the base-10 logarithm of the number
`sqrt(float number)`	float	Returns the square root of the number
`deg2rad(float number)`	float	Converts the number in degrees to the radian equivalent
`rad2deg(float number)`	float	Converts the radian number to the equivalent number in degrees
`bindec(string binary_number)`	int	Returns the decimal equivalent of the binary number
`hexdec(string hexadecimal_number)`	int	Returns the decimal equivalent of the hexadecimal number
`octdec(string octal_number)`	int	Returns the decimal equivalent of an octal string
`decbin(int decimal_number)`	string	Returns a string containing a binary representation of the number
`decoct(int decimal_number)`	string	Returns a string containing an octal representation of the given number
`dechex(int decimal_number)`	string	Returns a string containing a hexadecimal representation of the given number

Continued

Table F-14 MATH FUNCTIONS *(Continued)*

Function	Return Value	Action
`base_convert(string number, int frombase, int tobase)`	string	Converts a number in a string from any base smaller than or equal to 36 to any base smaller than or equal to 36
`_format(float number [, int num_decimal_places [, string dec_seperator, string thousands_separator]])`	string	Formats a number with grouped thousands
`fmod(float x, float y)`	float	Returns the remainder of dividing *x* by *y* as a float

Table F-15 RANDOM-NUMBER FUNCTIONS

Function	Return Value	Action
`srand([int seed])`	void	Seeds the random-number generator
`mt_srand([int seed])`	void	Seeds the Mersenne Twister random-number generator
`rand([int min, int max])`	int	Returns a random number
`mt_rand([int min, int max])`	int	Returns a random number from the Mersenne Twister
`getrandmax(void)`	int	Returns the maximum value a random number can have
`mt_getrandmax(void)`	int	Returns the maximum value a random number from the Mersenne Twister can have

TABLE F-16 REGULAR EXPRESSION FUNCTIONS

Function	Return Value	Action
ereg(string *pattern*, string *string* [, array *registers*])	int	Regular expression match
eregi(string *pattern*, string *string* [, array *registers*])	int	Case-insensitive regular expression match
ereg_replace(string *pattern*, string *replacement*, string *string*)	string	Replaces a regular expression
eregi_replace(string *pattern*, string *replacement*, string *string*)	string	Case-insensitive replace regular expression
split(string *pattern*, string *string* [, int *limit*])	array	Splits the string into an array by regular expression
spliti(string *pattern*, string *string* [, int *limit*])	array	Splits the string into an array by regular expression (case-insensitive)
sql_regcase(string *string*)	string	Makes a regular expression for case-insensitive match

TABLE F-17 PERL-COMPATIBLE REGULAR EXPRESSION FUNCTIONS

Function	Return Value	Action
preg_match(string *pattern*, string *subject* [, array *subpatterns*])	int	Performs a Perl-style regular-expression match
preg_match_all(string *pattern*, string *subject*, array *subpatterns* [, int *order*])	int	Performs a Perl-style global-regular-expression match
preg_replace(mixed *regex*, mixed *replace*, mixed *subject* [, int *limit*])	string	Performs a Perl-style regular-expression replacement

Continued

TABLE F-17 PERL-COMPATIBLE REGULAR EXPRESSION FUNCTIONS *(Continued)*

Function	Return Value	Action
`preg_replace_(mixed` *regex*`, mixed callback, mixed` *subject* `[, int` *limit*`])`	string	Performs a Perl-style regular-expression replacement using replacement callback
`preg_split(string` *pattern*`, string` *subject* `[, int` *limit* `[, int` *flags*`]])`	array	Splits the string into an array using a Perl-style regular expression as a delimiter
`preg_quote(string str, string` *delim_char*`)`	string	Quotes regular-expression characters plus an optional character
`preg_grep(string` *regex*`, array input)`	array	Searches the array and returns entries that match *regex*

TABLE F-18 VARIABLE-TYPING FUNCTIONS

Function	Return Value	Action
`gettype(mixed` *var*`)`	string	Returns the type of the variable
`settype(mixed` *var*`, string` *type*`)`	bool	Sets the type of the variable
`intval(mixed` *var* `[, int` *base*`])`	int	Gets the integer value of a variable using the optional base for the conversion
`floatval(mixed` *var*`)`	float	Gets the float value of a variable
`strval(mixed` *var*`)`	string	Gets the string value of a variable
`is_null(mixed` *var*`)`	bool	Returns `true` if the variable is `NULL`

Function	Return Value	Action
`is_resource(mixed var)`	bool	Returns `true` if the variable is a resource
`is_bool(mixed var)`	bool	Returns `true` if the variable is a Boolean
`is_long(mixed var)`	bool	Returns `true` if the variable is a long (integer)
`is_float(mixed var)`	bool	Returns `true` if the variable is a floating point value
`is_string(mixed var)`	bool	Returns `true` if the variable is a string
`is_array(mixed var)`	bool	Returns `true` if the variable is an array
`is_object(mixed var)`	bool	Returns `true` if the variable is an object
`is_numeric(mixed value)`	bool	Returns `true` if the value is a number or a numeric string
`is_scalar(mixed value)`	bool	Returns `true` if the value is a scalar
`is_callable(mixed var [, bool syntax_only [, string callable_name]])`	bool	Returns `true` if *var* is callable

Table F-19 SESSION FUNCTIONS

Function	Return Value	Action
`session_set_cookie_params(int lifetime [, string path [, string domain [, bool secure]]])`	void	Sets the session-cookie parameters
`session_get_cookie_params(void)`	array	Returns the session-cookie parameters

Continued

Table F-19 SESSION FUNCTIONS *(Continued)*

Function	Return Value	Action
session_name([string *newname*])	string	Returns the current session name; if *newname* is given, the session name is replaced with *newname*
session_module_name([string *newname*])	string	Returns the current module name used for accessing session data; if *newname* is given, the module name is replaced with *newname*
session_set_save_handler(string *open*, string *close*, string *read*, string *write*, string *destroy*, string *gc*)	void	Sets the user-level functions
session_save_path([string *newname*])	string	Returns the current save path passed to *module_name*; if *newname* is given, the save path is replaced with *newname*
session_id([string *newid*])	string	Returns the current session ID; if *newid* is given, the session ID is replaced with *newid*
session_cache_limiter([string *new_cache_limiter*])	string	Returns the current cache limiter; if *new_cache_limiter* is given, the current cache limiter is replaced with *new_cache_limiter*
session_cache_expire([int *new_cache_expire*])	int	Returns the current *cache_expire*; if *new_cache_expire* is given, the current *cache_expire* is replaced with *new_cache_expire*

Function	Return Value	Action
`session_register(mixed *var_names* [, mixed ...])`	bool	Adds *var_name(s)* to the list of variables that are frozen at the session's end
`session_unregister(string *varname*)`	bool	Removes *varname* from the list of variables that are frozen at the session's end
`session_is_registered(string *varname*)`	bool	Checks if a variable is registered in the session
`session_encode(void)`	string	Serializes the current setup and returns the serialized representation
`session_decode(string *data*)`	bool	Deserializes data and reinitializes the variables
`session_start(void)`	bool	Begins session – reinitializes frozen variables, registers browsers, and so on
`session_destroy(void)`	bool	Destroys the current session and all data associated with it
`session_unset(void)`	void	Unsets all registered variables
`session_write_close(void)`	void	Writes session data and ends the session

TABLE F-20 XPAT XML FUNCTIONS

Function	Return Value	Action
`xml_parser_create([string *encoding*])`	int	Creates an XML parser
`xml_parser_create_ns([string *encoding* [, string *sep*]])`	int	Creates an XML parser

Continued

TABLE F-20 XPAT XML FUNCTIONS *(Continued)*

Function	Return Value	Action
xml_set_object(int *pind*, object *&obj*)	int	Sets up an object that should be used for callbacks
xml_set_element_handler(int *pind*, string *shdl*, string *ehdl*)	int	Sets up start and end element handlers
xml_set_character_data_handler (int *pind*, string *hdl*)	int	Sets up a character-data handler
xml_set_processing_instruction_ handler(int *pind*, string *hdl*)	int	Sets up a processing-instruction (PI) handler
xml_set_default_handler(int *pind*, string *hdl*)	int	Sets up a default handler
xml_set_unparsed_entity_decl_ handler(int *pind*, string *hdl*)	int	Sets up an unparsed-entity-declaration handler
xml_set_notation_decl_handler (int *pind*, string *hdl*)	int	Sets up a notation-declaration handler
xml_set_external_entity_ref_ handler(int *pind*, string *hdl*)	int	Sets up an external entity-reference handler
xml_set_start_namespace_decl_ handler(int *pind*, string *hdl*)	int	Sets up a character-data handler
xml_set_end_namespace_decl_ handler(int *pind*, string *hdl*)	int	Sets up a character-data handler
xml_parse(int *pind*, string *data* [, int *isFinal*])	int	Starts parsing an XML document
xml_parse_into_struct(int *pind*, string *data*, array *&struct*, array *&index*)	int	Parsing a XML document
xml_get_error_code(int *pind*)	int	Gets XML parser-error code
xml_error_string(int *code*)	string	Gets XML parser-error string
xml_get_current_line_number (int *pind*)	int	Gets the current line number for an XML parser
xml_get_current_column_number (int *pind*)	int	Gets the current column number for an XML parser

Function	Return Value	Action
`xml_get_current_byte_index (int pind)`	int	Gets the current byte index for an XML parser
`xml_parser_free(int pind)`	int	Frees an XML parser
`xml_parser_set_option(int pind, int option, mixed value)`	int	Sets options in an XML parser
`xml_parser_get_option(int pind, int option)`	int	Gets options from an XML parser
`utf8_encode(string data)`	string	Encodes an ISO-8859-1 string to UTF-8
`utf8_decode(string data)`	string	Converts a UTF-8–encoded string to ISO-8859-1

TABLE F-21 WDDX FUNCTIONS

Function	Return Value	Action
`wddx_serialize_value(mixed var [, string comment])`	string	Creates a new packet and serializes the given value
`wddx_serialize_vars(mixed var_name [, mixed ...])`	string	Creates a new packet and serializes given variables into a structure
`wddx_packet_start ([string comment])`	int	Starts a WDDX packet with an optional comment and returns the packet ID
`wddx_packet_end(int packet_id)`	string	Ends the specified WDDX packet and returns the string containing the packet
`wddx_add_vars(int packet_id, mixed var_names [, mixed ...])`	int	Serializes given variables and adds them to the packet given by `packet_id`
`wddx_deserialize(string packet)`	mixed	Deserializes the given packet and returns a PHP value

TABLE F-22 BC MATH FUNCTIONS

Function	Return Value	Action
bcadd(string *left_operand*, string *right_operand* [, int *scale*])	string	Returns the sum of two arbitrary-precision numbers
bcsub(string *left_operand*, string *right_operand* [, int *scale*])	string	Returns the difference between two arbitrary-precision numbers
bcmul(string *left_operand*, string *right_operand* [, int *scale*])	string	Returns the product of two arbitrary-precision numbers (multiplication)
bcdiv(string *left_operand*, string *right_operand* [, int *scale*])	string	Returns the quotient of two arbitrary-precision numbers (division)
bcmod(string *left_operand*, string *right_operand*)	string	Returns the modulus of the two arbitrary-precision operands
bcpow(string *x*, string *y* [, int *scale*])	string	Returns the value of an arbitrary-precision number raised to the power of another
bcsqrt(string *operand* [, int *scale*])	string	Returns the square root of an arbitrary-precision number
bccomp(string *left_operand*, string *right_operand* [, int *scale*])	string	Compares two arbitrary-precision numbers
bcscale(int *scale*)	string	Sets the default scale parameter for all BC math functions

TABLE F-23 CURL FUNCTIONS

Function	Return Value	Action
`curl_version(void)`	string	Returns the CURL version string
`curl_init([string url])`	int	Initializes a CURL session
`curl_setopt(int ch, string option, mixed value)`	bool	Sets an option for a CURL transfer
`curl_exec(int ch)`	bool	Performs a CURL session
`curl_getinfo(int ch, int opt)`	string	Gets information regarding a specific transfer
`curl_error(int ch)`	string	Returns a string containing the last error for the current session
`curl_errno(int ch)`	int	Returns an integer containing the last error number for the current session
`curl_close(int ch)`	void	Closes a CURL session

TABLE F-24 FTP FUNCTIONS

Function	Return Value	Action
`ftp_connect(string host [, int port [, int timeout)]])`	resource	Opens an FTP stream
`ftp_login(resource stream, string username, string password)`	bool	Logs in to the FTP server
`ftp_pwd(resource stream)`	string	Returns the present working directory
`ftp_cdup(resource stream)`	bool	Changes to the parent directory

Continued

Table F-24 FTP FUNCTIONS *(Continued)*

Function	Return Value	Action
`ftp_chdir(resource stream, string directory)`	bool	Changes directories
`ftp_exec(resource stream, string command)`	bool	Requests execution of a program on the FTP server
`ftp_mkdir(resource stream, string directory)`	string	Creates a directory and returns the absolute path for the new directory, or `false` on error
`ftp_rmdir(resource stream, string directory)`	bool	Removes a directory
`ftp_nlist(resource stream, string directory)`	array	Returns an array of file names in the given directory
`ftp_rawlist(resource stream, string directory)`	array	Returns a detailed listing of a directory as an array of output lines
`ftp_systype(resource stream)`	string	Returns the system-type identifier
`ftp_fget(resource stream, resource fp, string remote_file, int mode)`	bool	Retrieves a file from the FTP server and writes it to an open file
`ftp_pasv(resource stream, bool pasv)`	bool	Turns passive mode on or off
`ftp_get(resource stream, string local_file, string remote_file, int mode)`	bool	Retrieves a file from the FTP server and writes it to a local file
`ftp_fput(resource stream, string remote_file, resource fp, int mode)`	bool	Stores a file from an open file to the FTP server
`ftp_put(resource stream, string remote_file, string local_file, int mode)`	bool	Stores a file on the FTP server

Function	Return Value	Action
ftp_size(resource *stream*, string filename)	int	Returns the size of the file, or -1 on error
ftp_mdtm(resource *stream*, string filename)	int	Returns the last modification time for the file, or -1 on error
ftp_rename(resource *stream*, string *src*, string *dest*)	bool	Renames the given file to a new path
ftp_delete(resource *stream*, string *file*)	bool	Deletes a file
ftp_site(resource *stream*, string *cmd*)	bool	Sends a SITE command to the server
ftp_close(resource *stream*)	void	Closes the FTP stream
ftp_set_option(resource *stream*, int *option*, mixed *value*)	bool	Sets an FTP option
ftp_get_option(resource *stream*, int *option*)	mixed	Gets an FTP option

TABLE F-25 CYBERCASH FUNCTIONS

Function	Return Value	Action
cybercash_encr(string *wmk*, string *sk*, string *data*)	array	CyberCash encrypt
cybercash_decr(string *wmp*, string *sk*, string *data*)	array	CyberCash decrypt
cybercash_base64_encode(string *data*)	string	base64 encode data for CyberCash
cybercash_base64_decode(string *data*)	string	base64 decode data for CyberCash

Table F-26 GD FUNCTIONS

Function	Return Value	Action
imageloadfont(string filename)	int	Loads a new font
imagesetstyle(resource *im*, array *styles*)	void	Sets the line-drawing styles for use with imageline() and IMG_COLOR_STYLED
imagecreatetruecolor(int *x_size*, int *y_size*)	int	Creates a new true-color image
imagetruecolortopalette(resource *im*, bool *ditherFlag*, int *colorsWanted*)	void	Converts a true-color image to a palette-based image with a number of colors, optionally using dithering
imagesetthickness(resource *im*, int *thickness*)	void	Sets line thickness for drawing lines, ellipses, rectangles, polygons, and so on
imageellipse(resource *im*, int *cx*, int *cy*, int *w*, int *h*, int *color*)	void	Draws an ellipse
imagefilledellipse(resource *im*, int *cx*, int *cy*, int *w*, int *h*, int *color*)	void	Draws a filled ellipse
imagefilledarc(int *im*, int *cx*, int *cy*, int *w*, int *h*, int *s*, int *e*, int *col*, int *style*)	int	Draws a filled partial ellipse
imagealphablending(resource *im*, bool *on*)	void	Turns alpha-blending mode on or off for the given image
imagecolorresolvealpha(resource *im*, int *red*, int *green*, int *blue*, int *alpha*)	int	Resolves/allocates a color with an alpha level. Works for true-color and palette-based images
imagecolorclosestalpha(resource *im*, int *red*, int *green*, int *blue*, int *alpha*)	int	Finds the closest matching color with alpha transparency

Function	Return Value	Action
imagecolorexactalpha(resource *im*, int *red*, int *green*, int *blue*, int *alpha*)	int	Finds an exact match for the color with transparency
imagecopyresampled(int *dst_im*, int *src_im*, int *dst_x*, int *dst_y*, int *src_x*, int *src_y*, int *dst_w*, int *dst_h*, int *src_w*, int *src_h*)	int	Copies and resizes part of an image using resampling to help ensure clarity
imagesettile(resource *image*, resource *tile*)	int	Sets the tile image to `$tile` when filling `$image` with the `IMG_COLOR_TILED` color
imagesetbrush(resource *image*, resource *brush*)	int	Sets the brush image to `$brush` when filling `$image` with the `IMG_COLOR_BRUSHED` color
imagecreate(int *x_size*, int *y_size*)	int	Creates a new image
imagetypes(void)	int	Returns the types of images supported in a bitfield – 1 = GIF, 2 = JPEG, 4 = PNG, 8 = WBMP, 16 = XPM
imagecreatefromstring(string *image*)	int	Creates a new image from the image stream in the string
imagecreatefromgif(string filename)	int	Creates a new image from a GIF file or URL
imagecreatefromjpeg(string filename)	int	Creates a new image from a JPEG file or URL
imagecreatefrompng(string filename)	int	Creates a new image from a PNG file or URL
imagecreatefromxbm(string filename)	int	Creates a new image from an XBM file or URL

Continued

TABLE F-26 GD FUNCTIONS *(Continued)*

Function	Return Value	Action
`imagecreatefromxpm(string filename)`	int	Creates a new image from an XPM file or URL
`imagecreatefromwbmp(string filename)`	int	Creates a new image from a WBMP file or URL
`imagecreatefromgd(string filename)`	int	Creates a new image from a GD file or URL
`imagecreatefromgd2(string filename)`	int	Creates a new image from a GD2 file or URL
`imagecreatefromgd2part(string filename, int srcX, int srcY, int width, int height)`	int	Creates a new image from a given part of a GD2 file or URL
`imagegif(int im [, string filename])`	int	Outputs a GIF image to a browser or file
`imagepng(int im [, string filename])`	int	Outputs a PNG image to a browser or file
`imagejpeg(int im [, string filename [, int quality]])`	int	Outputs a JPEG image to a browser or file
`imagewbmp(int im [, string filename, [, int foreground]])`	int	Outputs a WBMP image to a browser or file
`imagegd(int im [, string filename])`	int	Outputs a GD image to a browser or file
`imagegd2(int im [, string filename])`	int	Outputs a GD2 image to a browser or file
`imagedestroy(int im)`	int	Destroys an image
`imagecolorallocate(int im, int red, int green, int blue)`	int	Allocates a color for an image
`imagepalettecopy(int dst, int src)`	int	Copies the palette from the `src` image onto the `dst` image
`imagecolorat(int im, int x, int y)`	int	Gets the index of the color of a pixel

Function	Return Value	Action
imagecolorclosest(int *im*, int *red*, int *green*, int *blue*)	int	Gets the index of the closest color to the specified color
imagecolorclosesthwb(int *im*, int *red*, int *green*, int *blue*)	int	Gets the index of the color that has the hue, white, and blackness nearest to those of the given color
imagecolordeallocate(int *im*, int *index*)	int	De-allocates a color for an image
imagecolorresolve(int *im*, int *red*, int *green*, int *blue*)	int	Gets the index of the specified color or its closest possible alternative
imagecolorexact(int *im*, int *red*, int *green*, int *blue*)	int	Gets the index of the specified color
imagecolorset(int *im*, int *col*, int *red*, int *green*, int *blue*)	int	Sets the color for the specified palette index
imagecolorsforindex(int *im*, int *col*)	array	Gets the colors for an index
imagegammacorrect(int *im*, float *inputgamma*, float *outputgamma*)	int	Applies gamma correction to a GD image
imagesetpixel(int *im*, int *x*, int *y*, int *col*)	int	Sets a single pixel
imageline(int *im*, int *x1*, int *y1*, int *x2*, int *y2*, int *col*)	int	Draws a line
imagedashedline(int *im*, int *x1*, int *y1*, int *x2*, int *y2*, int *col*)	int	Draws a dashed line
imagerectangle(int *im*, int *x1*, int *y1*, int *x2*, int *y2*, int *col*)	int	Draws a rectangle
imagefilledrectangle(int *im*, int *x1*, int *y1*, int *x2*, int *y2*, int *col*)	int	Draws a filled rectangle

Continued

Table F-26 GD FUNCTIONS *(Continued)*

Function	Return Value	Action
imagearc(int *im*, int *cx*, int *cy*, int *w*, int *h*, int *s*, int *e*, int *col*)	int	Draws a partial ellipse
imagefilltoborder(int *im*, int *x*, int *y*, int *border*, int *col*)	int	Flood fills the image to the specific color
imagefill(int *im*, int *x*, int *y*, int *col*)	int	Flood fills the image
imagecolorstotal(int *im*)	int	Finds out the number of colors in an image's palette
imagecolortransparent(int *im* [, int *col*])	int	Defines a color as transparent
imageinterlace(int *im* [, int *interlace*])	int	Enables or disables interlace
imagepolygon(int *im*, array *point*, int *num_points*, int *col*)	int	Draws a polygon
imagefilledpolygon(int *im*, array *point*, int *num_points*, int *col*)	int	Draws a filled polygon
imagefontwidth(int *font*)	int	Gets the font width
imagefontheight(int *font*)	int	Gets the font height
imagechar(int *im*, int *font*, int *x*, int *y*, string *c*, int *col*)	int	Draws a character
imagecharup(int *im*, int *font*, int *x*, int *y*, string *c*, int *col*)	int	Draws a character rotated 90 degrees counter-clockwise
imagestring(int *im*, int *font*, int *x*, int *y*, string str, int *col*)	int	Draws a string horizontally
imagestringup(int *im*, int *font*, int *x*, int *y*, string str, int *col*)	int	Draws a string vertically (rotated 90 degrees counter-clockwise)

Function	Return Value	Action
imagecopy(int *dst_im*, int *src_im*, int *dst_x*, int *dst_y*, int *src_x*, int *src_y*, int *src_w*, int *src_h*)	int	Copies part of an image
imagecopymerge(int *src_im*, int *dst_im*, int *dst_x*, int *dst_y*, int *src_x*, int *src_y*, int *src_w*, int *src_h*, int *pct*	int	Merges one part of an image with another
imagecopymergegray(int *src_im*, int *dst_im*, int *dst_x*, int *dst_y*, int *src_x*, int *src_y*, int *src_w*, int *src_h*, int *pct*)	int	Merges one part of an image with another, converting the pixels of the destination image to grayscale before copying from the source image
imagecopyresized(int *dst_im*, int *src_im*, int *dst_x*, int *dst_y*, int *src_x*, int *src_y*, int *dst_w*, int *dst_h*, int *src_w*, int *src_h*)	int	Copies and resizes part of an image
imagesx(int *im*)	int	Gets the image width
imagesy(int *im*)	int	Gets the image height
imageftbbox(int *size*, int *angle*, string *font_file*, string *text*[, array *extrainfo*])	array	Gives the bounding box of a text using fonts via FreeType2
imagefttext(int *im*, int *size*, int *angle*, int *x*, int *y*, int *col*, string *font_file*, string *text*, [array *extrainfo*])	array	Writes text to the image using fonts via FreeType2
imagettfbbox(int *size*, int *angle*, string *font_file*, string *text*)	array	Gives the bounding box of a text using TrueType fonts
imagettftext(int *im*, int *size*, int *angle*, int *x*, int *y*, int *col*, string *font_file*, string *text*)	array	Writes text to the image using a TrueType font

Continued

TABLE F-26 GD FUNCTIONS *(Continued)*

Function	Return Value	Action
`imagepsloadfont(string pathname)`	int	Loads a new font from the specified file
`imagepscopyfont(int font_index)`	int	Makes a copy of a font for purposes such as extending or re-encoding
`imagepsfreefont(int font_index)`	bool	Frees memory used by a font
`imagepsencodefont(int font_index, string filename)`	bool	Changes a font's character-encoding vector
`imagepsextendfont(int font_index, float extend)`	bool	Extends or condenses (if `extend` is greater than `1`) a font
`imagepsslantfont(int font_index, float slant)`	bool	Slants a font
`imagepstext(int image, string text, int font, int size, int xcoord, int ycoord [, int space, int tightness, float angle, int antialias])`	array	Rasterizes a string over an image
`imagepsbbox(string text, int font, int size [, int space, int tightness, int angle])`	array	Returns the bounding box needed by a string if rasterized
`image2wbmp(int im [, string filename [, int threshold]])`	int	Outputs a WBMP image to a browser or file
`jpeg2wbmp (string f_org, string f_dest, int d_height, int d_width, int threshold)`	void	Converts a JPEG image to a WBMP image
`png2wbmp (string f_org, string f_dest, int d_height, int d_width, int threshold)`	void	Converts a PNG image to a WBMP image

Table F-27 PAYFLOW PRO FUNCTIONS

Function	Return Value	Action
`pfpro_version()`	string	Returns the version of the Payflow Pro library
`pfpro_init()`	void	Initializes the Payflow Pro library
`pfpro_cleanup()`	void	Shuts down the Payflow Pro library
`pfpro_process_raw(string` *`parmlist`* `[, string` *`hostaddress`* `[, int` *`port`*`, [, int` *`timeout`* `[, string` *`proxyAddress`* `[, int` *`proxyPort`* `[, string` *`proxyLogon`* `[, string` *`proxyPassword`*`]]]]]]])`	string	Raw Payflow Pro transaction processing
`pfpro_process(array` *`parmlist`* `[, string` *`hostaddress`* `[, int` *`port`*`, [, int` *`timeout`* `[, string` *`proxyAddress`* `[, int` *`proxyPort`* `[, string` *`proxyLogon`* `[, string` *`proxyPassword`*`]]]]]]])`	array	Payflow Pro transaction processing using arrays

Table F-28 PDF FUNCTIONS

Function	Return Value	Action
`pdf_set_info(int` *`pdfdoc`*`, string` *`fieldname`*`, string` *`value`*`)`	bool	Fills an `info` field of the document
`pdf_set_info_creator(int` *`pdfdoc`*`, string` *`creator`*`)`	bool	Fills the `creator` field of the document
`pdf_set_info_title(int` *`pdfdoc`*`, string` *`title`*`)`	bool	Fills the `title` field of the document
`pdf_set_info_subject(int pdfdoc, string` *`subject`*`)`	bool	Fills the `subject` field of the document

Continued

TABLE F-28 PDF FUNCTIONS *(Continued)*

Function	Return Value	Action
pdf_set_info_author(int pdfdoc, string *author*)	bool	Fills the author field of the document
pdf_set_info_keywords(int pdfdoc, string *keywords*)	bool	Fills the keywords field of the document
pdf_close(int pdfdoc)	void	Closes the PDF document
pdf_begin_page(int pdfdoc, float *width*, float *height*)	void	Starts a page
pdf_end_page(int pdfdoc)	void	Ends a page
pdf_show(int pdfdoc, string *text*)	void	Outputs text at the current position
pdf_show_xy(int pdfdoc, string *text*, float x_koor, float y_koor)	void	Outputs text at a position
pdf_show_boxed(int pdfdoc, string *text*, float x_koor, float y_koor, float *width*, float *height*, string *mode* [, string *feature*])	int	Outputs text formatted in a box
pdf_set_font(int pdfdoc, string *font*, float *size*, string *encoding* [, int *embed*])	void	Selects the current font face, size, and encoding
pdf_set_value(int pdfdoc, string *key*, float *value*)	void	Sets an arbitrary value
pdf_get_value(int pdfdoc, string *key*, float *modifier*)	float	Gets an arbitrary value
pdf_get_font(int pdfdoc)	int	Gets the current font
pdf_get_fontname(int pdfdoc)	string	Gets the current font name
pdf_get_fontsize(int pdfdoc)	float	Gets the current font size
pdf_set_leading(int pdfdoc, float *distance*)	void	Sets the distance between text lines
pdf_set_text_rendering(int pdfdoc, int *mode*)	void	Determines how text is rendered

Function	Return Value	Action
pdf_set_horiz_scaling(int pdfdoc, float *scale*)	void	Sets the horizontal scaling of text
pdf_set_text_rise(int pdfdoc, float *value*)	void	Sets the text rise
pdf_set_char_spacing(int pdfdoc, float *space*)	void	Sets the character spacing
pdf_set_word_spacing(int pdfdoc, float *space*)	void	Sets the spacing between words
pdf_set_text_pos(int pdfdoc, float *x*, float *y*)	void	Sets the position of text for the next pdf_show call
pdf_continue_text(int pdfdoc, string text)	void	Outputs text in the next line
pdf_stringwidth(int pdfdoc, string *text* [, int *font*, float *size*])	float	Returns the width of the text in the current font
pdf_save(int pdfdoc)	void	Saves the current environment
pdf_restore(int pdfdoc)	void	Restores the formerly saved environment
pdf_translate(int pdfdoc, float *x*, float *y*)	void	Sets the origin of the coordinate system
pdf_scale(int pdfdoc, float *x_scale*, float *y_scale*)	void	Sets the scaling
pdf_rotate(int pdfdoc, float *angle*)	void	Sets the rotation
pdf_skew(int pdfdoc, float *xangle*, float *yangle*)	void	Skews the coordinate system
pdf_setflat(int pdfdoc, float *value*)	void	Sets the flatness
pdf_setlinejoin(int pdfdoc, int *value*)	void	Sets the linejoin parameter
pdf_setlinecap(int pdfdoc, int *value*)	void	Sets the linecap parameter

Continued

TABLE F-28 PDF FUNCTIONS *(Continued)*

Function	Return Value	Action
pdf_setmiterlimit(int pdfdoc, float *value*)	void	Sets the miter limit
pdf_setlinewidth(int pdfdoc, float *width*)	void	Sets the line width
pdf_setdash(int pdfdoc, float *black*, float *white*)	void	Sets the dash pattern
pdf_moveto(int pdfdoc, float *x*, float *y*)	void	Sets the current point
pdf_curveto(int pdfdoc, float *x1*, float *y1*, float *x2*, float *y2*, float *x3*, float *y3*)	void	Draws a curve
pdf_lineto(int pdfdoc, float *x*, float *y*)	void	Draws a line
pdf_circle(int pdfdoc, float *x*, float *y*, float *radius*)	void	Draws a circle
pdf_arc(int pdfdoc, float *x*, float *y*, float *radius*, float start, float *end*)	void	Draws an arc
pdf_rect(int pdfdoc, float *x*, float *y*, float *width*, float *height*)	void	Draws a rectangle
pdf_closepath(int pdfdoc)	void	Closes a path
pdf_closepath_stroke(int pdfdoc)	void	Closes a path and draws a line along the path
pdf_stroke(int pdfdoc)	void	Draws a line along a path
pdf_fill(int pdfdoc)	void	Fills the current path
pdf_fill_stroke(int pdfdoc)	void	Fills and strokes the current path
pdf_closepath_fill_stroke(int pdfdoc)	void	Closes, fills, and strokes the current path
pdf_endpath(int pdfdoc)	void	Ends the current path

Function	Return Value	Action
pdf_clip(int pdfdoc)	void	Clips to the current path
pdf_set_parameter(int pdfdoc, string *key*, string *value*)	void	Sets arbitrary parameters
pdf_get_parameter(int pdfdoc, string *key*, mixed *modifier*)	string	Gets arbitrary parameters
pdf_setgray_fill(int pdfdoc, float *value*)	void	Sets the filling color to gray value
pdf_setgray_stroke(int pdfdoc, float *value*)	void	Sets the drawing color to gray value
pdf_setgray(int pdfdoc, float *value*)	void	Sets the drawing and filling color to gray value
pdf_setrgbcolor_fill(int pdfdoc, float *red*, float *green*, float *blue*)	void	Sets the filling color to the RGB color value
pdf_setrgbcolor_stroke(int pdfdoc, float *red*, float *green*, float *blue*)	void	Sets the drawing color to the RGB color value
pdf_setrgbcolor(int pdfdoc, float *red*, float *green*, float *blue*	void	Sets the drawing and filling color to the RGB color value
pdf_add_bookmark(int pdfdoc, string *text* [, int *parent*, int *open*])	int	Adds a bookmark for the current page
pdf_set_transition(int pdfdoc, int *transition*)	void	Sets a transition between pages
pdf_set_duration(int pdfdoc, float *duration*)	void	Sets a duration between pages
pdf_open_gif(int *pdf*, string *giffile*)	int	Opens a GIF file and returns an image for placement in a PDF object
pdf_open_jpeg(int *pdf*, string *jpegfile*)	int	Opens a JPEG file and returns an image for placement in a PDF document

Continued

Table F-28 PDF FUNCTIONS *(Continued)*

Function	Return Value	Action
pdf_open_png(int *pdf*, string *pngfile*)	int	Opens a PNG file and returns an image for placement in a PDF document
pdf_open_tiff(int *pdf*, string *tifffile*)	int	Opens a TIFF file and returns an image for placement in a PDF document
pdf_open_image_file(int *pdf*, string *type*, string *file*, string *stringparam*, int *intparam*)	int	Opens an image file of the given type and returns an image for placement in a PDF document
pdf_open_memory_image(int *pdf*, int *image*)	int	Takes an GD image and returns an image for placement in a PDF document
pdf_close_image(int *pdf*, int *pdfimage*)	void	Closes the PDF image
pdf_place_image(int *pdf*, int *pdfimage*, float *x*, float *y*, float *scale*)	void	Places an image in the PDF document
pdf_get_image_width(int *pdf*, int *pdfimage*)	int	Returns the width of an image
pdf_get_image_height(int *pdf*, int *pdfimage*)	int	Returns the height of an image
pdf_add_weblink(int pdfdoc, float *llx*, float *lly*, float *urx*, float *ury*, string *url*)	void	Adds a link to a Web resource
pdf_add_pdflink(int pdfdoc, float *llx*, float *lly*, float *urx*, float *ury*, string filename, int *page*, string *dest*)	void	Adds a link to a PDF document
pdf_set_border_style(int pdfdoc, string *style*, float *width*)	void	Sets the style of the box surrounding all kinds of annotations and links

Function	Return Value	Action
`pdf_set_border_color(int pdfdoc, float` *red*`, float` *green*`, float` *blue*`)`	void	Sets the color of the box surrounding all kinds of annotations and links
`pdf_set_border_dash(int pdfdoc, float` *black*`, float` *white*`)`	void	Sets the border-dash style of all kinds of annotations and links
`pdf_new()`	int	Creates a new PDF object
`pdf_get_majorversion()`	int	Returns the major version number of the PDFlib
`pdf_get_minorversion()`	int	Returns the minor version number of the PDFlib
`pdf_delete(int pdfdoc)`	bool	Deletes the PDF object
`pdf_open_file(int pdfdoc [, char filename])`	int	Opens a new PDF document; if the file name is `NULL`, the document is created in memory
`pdf_get_buffer(int pdfdoc)`	int	Fetches the full buffer containing the generated PDF data
`pdf_findfont(int pdfdoc, string` *fontname*`, string` *encoding* `[, int` *embed*`])`	int	Prepares the font *fontname* for later use with `pdf_setfont()`
`pdf_setfont(int pdfdoc, int` *font*`, float` *fontsize*`)`	void	Sets the current font in the given fontsize
`pdf_setpolydash(int pdfdoc, float` *darray*`)`	void	Sets complicated dash pattern
`pdf_concat(int` *pdf*`, float` *a*`, float` *b*`, float` *c*`, float` *d*`, float` *e*`, float` *f*`)`	void	Concatenates a matrix to the current transformation matrix for text and graphics
`pdf_open_ccitt(int` *pdf*`, string filename, int` *width*`, int` *height*`, int` *bitreverse*`, int` *k*`, int` *blackls1*`)`	int	Opens an image file with raw CCITT G3- or G4-compressed bitmap data

Continued

TABLE F-28 PDF FUNCTIONS *(Continued)*

Function	Return Value	Action
pdf_open_image(int *pdf*, string *type*, string *source*, string *data*, long length, int *width*, int *height*, int *components*, int *bpc*, string *params*)	int	Opens an image of the given type and returns an image for placement in a PDF document
pdf_attach_file(int *pdf*, float *lly*, float *lly*, float *urx*, float *ury*, string filename, string *description*, string *author*, string *mimetype*, string *icon*)	void	Adds a file-attachment annotation at the rectangle specified by the given lower left-hand and upper right-hand corners
pdf_add_note(int pdfdoc, float *llx*, float *lly*, float *urx*, float *ury*, string *contents*, string *title*, string *icon*, int *open*)	void	Sets the annotation
pdf_add_locallink(int pdfdoc, float *llx*, float *lly*, float *urx*, float *ury*, int *page*, string *dest*)	void	Adds a link annotation to a target within the current PDF file
pdf_add_launchlink(int pdfdoc, float *llx*, float *lly*, float *urx*, float *ury*, string filename)	void	Adds a launch annotation to a target of arbitrary file type
pdf_place_pdi_page(int *pdf*, int *page*, float *x*, float *y*, float *sx*, float *sy*)	void	Places a PDF page with the lower left-hand corner at (*x*, *y*) and scales it
pdf_setmatrix(int *pdf*, float *a*, float *b*, float *c*, float *d*, float *e*, float *f*)	void	Explicitly sets the current transformation matrix

Appendix G

Regular Expressions Overview

REGULAR EXPRESSIONS PROVIDE a means for pattern matching in strings. Patterns may be as simple as a literal string (like `my dog spot`) or a literal string with a wildcard character (like `Mr. .* Baggins`), or they can grow to be very complex. How complex? Check out the following example, which is intended to perform email validation. If you're new to regular expressions this may look nasty, but to tell the truth it's not nearly nasty enough. In fact, to properly validate an email takes about 200 lines of regular expressions.

```
^[_\.0-9a-z-]+@([0-9a-z][0-9a-z-]+\.)+[a-z]{2,3}$
```

When you're working with PHP and MySQL, three variants of regular expressions exist that you might need to use: the regular PHP regular-expression functions, the Perl-Compatible Regular Expression (PCRE) functions, and MySQL regular-expression functions. The PHP `ereg()`, `eregi()`, `ereg_replace()`, `eregi_replace()`, `split()`, and `spliti()` functions use these patterns.

The PCREs are quite different from the standard `ereg()` functions in places, and they offer some functionality that can't be replicated with the `ereg()` functions. After you have a good feel for regular expressions, you should probably head over to `http://www.perldoc.com/perl5.6/pod/perlre.html` to view some of the differences for yourself. The major PCRE functions are `preg_match()`, `preg_match_all()`, and `preg_replace()`.

Finally, another slight variant of the regular expressions used in MySQL exists. It is described in the Appendix G of the MySQL manual (`http://www.mysql.com/doc/en/Regexp.html`).

Literal Patterns

The simplest possible pattern match is to a series of known characters. For instance, to match `jay` within a string, you can do the following:

```
$str = "this is a string with my name: jay";
if ( ereg("jay", $str))
{
```

```
    echo "pattern found";
}
else
{
    echo "string not found";
}
```

This tests `true` and prints `pattern found`. However, with a simple string like this, you don't need a regular expression. One of PHP's string functions works and is a good deal faster. For example, in the preceding example, `strstr($str, "jay")` works equally well and is faster.

Characters

In regular expressions you can make use of the following characters.

- `\n` – Newline
- `\t` – Tab
- `\r` – Return
- `\f` – Form feed
- `^` (Shift+6) – Start of string (also known as *caret*)
- `$` – End of string
- `.` (dot) – Matches any non-newline character

So if you need to match the word `jay` at the beginning of a string, you can do this:

```
ereg("^jay", $str)
```

And if you want to make sure nothing exists before or after `jay` in the string, you can do the following:

```
ereg("^jay$", $str)
```

In the preceding listing, notice the meaning of the dot (`.`). It stands for any non-newline character. If you want to print whatever four characters follow `jay` in a string, you can do the following:

```
ereg("jay(....)", $str, $arr);
echo $arr[1];
```

Note that the parentheses here represent a substring. When `ereg()` is processed and a match is found, the array in the third argument contains the entire matched string (including substrings) in `$arr[0]`, and each additional substring indicated by parentheses in the regular expression is assigned to an additional array element. In the preceding example, therefore, the four characters following `jay` are in `$arr[1]`.

Character Classes

Often you need to see if a string contains a group of characters. For instance, you might need to make sure that a single character or given set of characters is alphanumeric or consists of a digit or digits. For this you can make use of character classes, either the built-in ones or the ones you make yourself. The built-in character classes are surrounded by two sets of brackets and colons, as seen in the following section. Character classes of your own making are surrounded by a single set of brackets.

Built-in character classes

- `[[:alpha:]]` – Any letter, upper or lower case
- `[[:digit:]]` – Digits (0–9)
- `[[:space:]]` – Matches any whitespace character, including spaces, tabs, newlines, returns, and form feeds
- `[[:upper:]]` – Matches only uppercase letters
- `[[:lower:]]` – Matches only lowercase letters
- `[[:punct:]]` – Matches any punctuation mark
- `[[:xdigit:]]` – Matches possible hexadecimal characters (0–9, A–F)

For example, suppose you want to make sure a letter contains punctuation after the salutation “Dear Sir or Madam”:

```
ereg("Madam[[:punct:]]", $str);
```

Note that if you use the caret symbol (^) within a character class it has the effect of saying “not.” So, `ereg("Madam[^[:punct:]]", $str)` matches only if “Madam” is *not* followed by a punctuation mark.

The caret symbol can get confusing because it has two distinct meanings. At the beginning of a regular expression it indicates the start of a string, and so the following regular expression matches only a string in which a digit is the first character:

```
^[[:digit]]
```

But if the caret is not in the first position in the regular expression, it means "not." The following regular expression matches a string that does not contain any digits:

```
[^[:digit:]]
```

And to put it all together, the following matches a string that starts with a digit but has a second character that is not a digit:

```
^[[:digit:]][^[:digit:]]
```

Self-made character classes

You can use brackets to construct your own character classes, either by using ranges of characters or by mixing characters of your choosing. Here are some typical ranges:

- `a-z` – Any lowercase letter
- `A-Z` – Any uppercase letter
- `0-9` – Any digit

Note that though these are the ranges you see most frequently, you can specify a range of `a-m` or `0-4` if you wish.

Be aware that the ASCII sequence of characters does not always follow human logic. Therefore, the expression `[A-z]` does indeed define a range of ASCII characters that includes all the upper-and lowercase letters, but also a lot of other, non-alphabetic characters. Better to define the upper- and lowercase ranges separately, or use the predefined character classes.

These ranges must be put within brackets to become character classes. So

```
[a-zA-Z]
```

is identical to `[[:alpha:]]`.

Self-made classes don't have to contain a range; they can contain any characters you want. For example:

```
[dog0-9]
```

This class matches the letters *d*, *o*, or *g*, or any digit.

```
$str="drat";
if(ereg("^[dog0-9]", $str))
{
    echo "true";
}
else
{
    echo "false";
}
```

This code prints `true`, because the first character in `$str` is in the class we have defined. If we replaced the `d` in `drat` with a `b`, this code prints `false`.

If you need to include a hyphen within a class, the hyphen must be the final character before the closing bracket of the class. For example, `[a-zA-Z-]`.

Multiple Occurrences

The real fun in regular expressions comes when you deal with multiple occurrences, which is when the syntax starts getting a little thick. We'll start by looking at three commonly used special characters.

- `*` (asterisk) – Zero or more of the previous character
- `+` – One or more of the previous character
- `?` – Zero or one of the previous character

Note that if you want to match any of these characters literally you need to escape them with a backslash. So, for example, if you want to match the querystring of a URL `http://www.mysqlphpapps.com/index.php?foo=mystring`, you can do the following:

```
\?.*$
```

The first two characters (\?) match the question mark character (?). Note that the query matches the literal question mark because the question mark is escaped with a backslash. If the question mark were not escaped, its meaning would be as given in the previous listing.

Then, the dot matches any non-newline character. The asterisk matches zero or more of the previous character. So the combination (.*) matches any number of characters until a new line. The .* combination is a common one. The dollar sign is the end-of-string character. So .*$ matches every non-newline character to the end of the string.

You probably want to use a regular expression like the previous one if you need to make use of the querystring in some other context.

The following is code that retrieves a string from a URL and then picks out the relevant portion with a regular expression. It then pops that matched portion into an array and echoes it to output:

```
$str="http://domain.com/index.php?foo=mystring&bar=otherstring";
//see the use of the parenthesized substring
//this will assign the matched portion to $array[1]
if (ereg("\?(.*)$", $str, $array) )
{
    echo "The querystring is ", $array[1];

}
```

Now that you have the querystring in the variable `$array[1]`, you can do further processing on it.

Before you incorporate this code into your script, note that you don't have to. You can use the PHP variables `$_SERVER['QUERY_STRING']` or the `$_GET` array.

Because the plus sign means one or more of the previous character, the following code matches a single digit or multiple digits:

```
[0-9]+
```

Consider the following statement:

```
if (ereg("jay[0-9]+", $str) )
```

`jay1` tests `true`, but `jayg` tests `false`. `jay2283092002909303` tests `true` because it's still `jay` followed by one or more numbers. Even `jay8393029jay` tests `true`.

If you need to get more specific about the number of characters you need to match, you can make use of curly braces.

- `{3}` – If a single digit is surrounded by brackets, it indicates that you want to match exactly that number of the previous character. `j{3}` matches only `jjj`.

- `{3,5}` – If two digits are surrounded by brackets, it indicates an upper and lower limit to the matches of the previous character. `j{3,5}` matches `jjj`, `jjjj`, and `jjjjj` only.
- `{3, }` – If an integer followed by a comma and no second integer are surrounded by brackets, it matches as many times or more of the previous character. So `j{3, }` matches `jjj`, `jjjj`, `jjjjjj`, and so on.

Specifying "Or"

If you want to specify one combination of characters or another, you need to make use of the pipe character (|). Most often the pipe is used with parentheses, which group portions of strings. If you want to match either `jay` or `brad` within a string, you can use the following:

```
(jay|brad)
```

Or you might want to check that URLs have a suffix you were familiar with:

```
(com|org|edu)
```

Example Regular Expressions

This has been a pretty quick review of regular expressions. If you're interested, entire books have been written on the subject. To get more comfortable with regular expressions, you can take a look at the following practical example.

Suppose you want to write a regular expression that matches the contents of an `href` attribute of an anchor tag. An anchor looks something like this:

```
<a href="../my_link.php">this is my link text</a>
```

At first, you might be tempted to look at this link and think all you need to do is match everything between the `href="` and the closing quotation mark. Something like this:

```
if (eregi('<a href="(.*)"', $anchor, $array))
{
    echo $array[1];
}
```

However, you really can't be sure that the `href` immediately follows the `<a`; another attribute or perhaps a JavaScript event might precede the `href`. So you need to account for that possibility in your regular expression.

```
if (eregi('<a.*href="(.*)"', $anchor, $array))
{
    echo $array[1];
}
```

Be aware that because of the greedy nature of POSIX regular expressions (such as those in MySQL) regular expression could grab several anchors. You might want to alter your code to check for that possibility, and break it up if that's what happens.

You've seen anchor tags with a space before the equals sign and anchor tags with a space after the equals sign, so you need to account for both possibilities:

```
if (eregi('<a.*href[[:space:]]?=[[:space:]]?"(.*)"',
$anchor, $array))
{
    echo $array[1];
}
```

Because the question-mark character means "zero or one of the previous character," the pairing `[[:space:]]?` means that one whitespace character can exist, or none. If you want to allow for more than one whitespace character, you can use `[[:space:]]*`.

Finally, you need to deal with the actual contents of the `href` attribute. So far you've accounted only for cases in which the link destination is delimited by double quotes. But at the very least you should account for delimiters of either double quotes or single quotes. To do that you need to put double quotes and single quotes within a character class. Because you've surrounded the entire regular expression with single quotes, you need to escape single quotes within the regular expression with backslashes. The class will be `["\']`.

```
if (eregi('<a.*href[[:space:]]?=[[:space:]]?["\'](.*)["\']',
        $anchor, $array))
{
    echo $array[1];
}
```

To be even more complete, the regular expression should account for cases in which no quotation mark at all is used to delimit the value of the `href`. For example, browsers are just fine with a tag like this: `<a href=mylink.php>`. In a case like this it might be a good idea to add a question mark character after the `["\']` class that marks the beginning of the `href`, and to include `[:space:]` and the greater-than sign (>) to mark the end of the `href`. All you need to do is add them to the last character class:

```
if (
```

```
eregi(
  '<a.*href[[:space:]]?=[[:space:]]?["\']?(.*)["\'>[:space:]]'
  , $anchor
  , $array
 )
)
{
    echo $array[1];
}
```

However, this arrangement presents some problems that you may not have anticipated. Imagine that the preceding code is attempting to match this string: `<a href = ../my_link.php>this is my link text</a>`. When you add the greater-than sign to the character class, the regular expression does not match the first greater-than sign in the string – it matches the final greater-than sign. This situation is known as *greedy matching,* and you can't get around it using `ereg()` or `ereg_replace()`.

If you need to match the first occasion of a character in a string you need to make use of the PCRE functions. With PCRE, the combination `.*?` matches all characters until the first occasion of the character you indicate. The following series matches everything until the first double quote, single quote, or greater-than sign:

```
.*?["\'>]
```

With `preg_match()` the final function looks like this:

```
if
(preg_match('/<a.*?href[[:space:]]?=[[:space:]]?["\']?(.*?)["\'>]/i'
,
        $anchor, $array))
{
    echo $array[1];
}
```

Appendix H

Helpful User-Defined Functions

THIS APPENDIX CONTAINS a series of PHP functions and classes that you might find useful in creating your scripts. It starts with a run-through of the base functions kept in the /book/functions folder.

Base Functions Set Used in This Book

We discuss these in detail in Chapter 8, but we include them here for quick reference.

From functions/basic/

These functions deal with authentication and text manipulation.

authenticate()

This function gets a username and password, either from the browser by sending a 401 header or from a regular Web page, and verifies the results against a database table named admin.

```
void authenticate([string realm [, string message]])
```

cleanup_text()

This function removes HTML and PHP tags using the `strip_tags()` function and replaces <, >, &, and " characters with their HTML entities. If the second argument is not empty `strip_tags` will not be run, and only the HTML-entity replacement will occur. The third argument can specify tags that should not be removed.

```
string cleanup_text ([string value [, string preserve [, string
allowed_tags]]])
```

make_page_title()

This function cleans up a string to make it suitable for use as the value of an HTML `<TITLE>` tag, removing any HTML tags and replacing all HTML entities with their literal-character equivalents by using `get_html_translation_table (HTML_ENTITIES)`.

```
string make_page_title ([string title])
```

money()

This function formats the sole argument as a standard U.S. dollar value, rounding any decimal value to two decimal places for cents and prepending a dollar sign to the returned string. Commas serve as thousands separators. However, remember that you can run into rounding errors with numbers of type float. This is only an issue in complex applications, though.

```
string money ([mixed value])
```

states()

This function returns an associative array, the key being the two-letter abbreviation of the states, the value being the state name.

```
array states(void)
```

From functions/database/

These are common functions that help you work with MySQL databases.

db_connect()

This function creates a database connection using the `PEAR DB` class. It accepts a variable list of parameters. The most common one used in the examples in this book is `application`, which is used as an index into values retrieved from an .ini file (typically stored outside the document root of the Web server).

```
void db_connect ()
```

db_fetch_record()

This function selects values from the MySQL table specified by the first argument. If the optional second and third arguments are not empty, the select gets the row from that table in which the column named in the second argument has the value given by the third argument. The second and third arguments can also be arrays, in which case the query builds its `where` clause using the values of the second array of arguments as the table-column names and the corresponding values of the third array of a arguments as the required values for those table columns.

```
db_fetch_record(string table [,string key [,string value]])
```

db_values_array()

This function builds an associative array out of the values in the MySQL table specified in the first argument. The data from the column named in the second argument are set to the keys of the array. If the third argument is not empty, the data from the column it names are the values of the array; otherwise, the values are equal to the keys. If the third argument is not empty, the data are ordered by the column that is named; otherwise, they are ordered by the key column. The optional fourth argument specifies any additional qualification for the query against the database table; if it is empty, all rows in the table are retrieved.

If either the first or second argument is empty, no query is run and an empty array is returned. The function presumes that whoever calls it knows what he or she is doing – that the table exists, that all the column names are correct, and so on.

```
array db_values_array ([string table name [, string value field [,
string label field [, string sort field [, string where clause]]]]])
```

From functions/html/

These functions create common HTML elements, including anchors and unordered lists.

font_tag()

This function creates an HTML font tag. Default size is `2`; default font face is `sans-serif`. Any additional attributes in the third argument are added to the tag. It is expecting an associative array, the key of which is the name of the attribute; the value of the array element is the attribute value.

```
string font_tag ([int size [, string typeface [, array attributes]]])
```

anchor_tag()

This function creates an HTML anchor tag. The first argument is the `href` value; the second the string to be surrounded by the anchor. It is expecting an associative array, the key of which is the name of the attribute; the value of the `array` element is the attribute value.

```
string anchor_tag ([string href [, string text [, array attributes]]])
```

image_tag()

This function returns an HTML image tag (`<img>`). The first argument gives the URL of the image to be displayed. Additional attributes can be supplied as an array in the third argument.

```
string image_tag ([string src [,array attributes]])
```

subtitle()

This function returns an HTML <h3> tag. It is used for the titles of secondary areas within pages in our examples. The reason to display these via a function rather than just literal <h3> tags is that this will enable you to change the format of these subtitles in one place, instead of in each script.

```
string subtitle(string string)
```

paragraph()

This function returns a string inside HTML paragraph (<p>) tags. Attributes for the <p> tag can be supplied in the first argument. Any additional arguments are included inside the opening and closing <p> tags, separated by newlines.

```
string paragraph([array attributes [, mixed ...]])
```

ul_list()

This function returns an HTML unordered (bulleted) list (<ul> tags). If the argument is an array, each value from the array is included as a list item (<li>) in the list. Otherwise, the argument is simply included inside the <ul> tags as is.

```
string ul_list(mixed values)
```

The following functions create opening and closing <table> tags, as well as <tr> and <td> tags.

start_table()

This function returns an opening HTML table tag inside a pair of paragraph (<p>...</p>) tags. Attributes for the table can be supplied as an array.

```
string start_table([array attributes])
```

end_table()

This function returns a closing table tag.

```
string end_table(void)
```

table_row()

This function returns a pair of HTML table row (<tr>) tags enclosing a variable number of table cell (<td>) tags. If any of the arguments to the function is an array, it is uses as attributes for the <tr> tag. All other arguments are used as values for the cells of the row. If an argument begins with a <td> tag, the argument is added to the row as is; otherwise, it is passed to the `table_cell()` function and the resulting string is added to the row.

```
string table_row ([array attributes], [indefinite number of string
arguments])
```

table_cell()

This function returns an HTML table cell (`<td>`) tag. The first argument is used as the value of the tag. Attributes for the `<td>` tag are supplied as an array in the second argument. By default the table cell is aligned left horizontally and to the top vertically.

```
string table_cell ([string value [, array attributes]])
```

From functions/forms/

These functions create all common form elements, as well as the opening and closing `<form>` tags.

start_form()

This function returns an HTML `<form>` tag. If the first argument is empty, the value of the global Apache variable `SCRIPT_NAME` is used for the `action` attribute of the `<form>` tag. Other attributes for the form can be specified in the optional second argument; the default method of the form is `post`. The behavior of this function on servers other than Apache has not been tested. It's likely that it will work, because `SCRIPT_NAME` is part of the CGI 1.1 specification.

```
string start_form ([string action, [array attributes]])
```

end_form()

This function returns a closing form tag.

```
string end_form(void)
```

text_field()

Returns an HTML `<input type=text>` form element. Default size is `10`.

```
string text_field ([string name [, string value [, int size [, int
maximum length]]]])
```

textarea_field()

This function returns an HTML `textarea` field. The default size is 50 columns and 10 rows, and the default wrap mode is `soft`, which means no hard newline characters are inserted after line breaks in what the user types into the field. The alternative wrap mode is `hard`', which means that hard newlines are inserted.

```
string textarea_field([string name [, string value [, int cols [,
int rows [, string wrap mode]]]]])
```

password_field()

This function returns an HTML password field. This is like a text field, but the value of the field is obscured (only stars or bullets are visible for each character). The default size of the field is `10`. A starting value and maximum data length may be supplied.

```
string password_field ([string name [, string value [, int size [,
int maximum length]]]])
```

hidden_field()

This function returns an HTML hidden-form element. A name and value may be supplied.

```
string hidden_field ([string name [, string value]])
```

file_field()

This function returns a text field from an HTML form.

```
string file_field([string name])
```

This function returns an HTML file field. These are used to specify files on the user's local hard drive, typically for uploading as part of the form.

See `http://www.zend.com/manual/features.file-upload.php` for more information about how PHP interacts with the local file system.

submit_field()

This function returns an HTML submit field. The value of the field is the string displayed by the button displayed by the user's browser. The default value is `Submit`.

```
string submit_field ([string name [, string value]])
```

image_field()

This function returns an HTML image field. An image field works like a submit field, except that the image specified by the URL given in the second argument is displayed instead of a button.

```
string image_field ([string name [, string src [, string value]]])
```

reset_field()

This function returns an HTML reset field.

```
string reset_field ([string name, [string value]])
```

checkbox_field()

This function returns an HTML checkbox field. The optional third argument is included immediately after the checkbox field, and the pair are included between a `<nobr>` tag and `</nobr>` tag – meaning that they are displayed together on the same line. If the value of the second or third argument matches that of the fourth argument, the checkbox is checked (that is, flipped on).

```
string checkbox_field ([string name [, string value [, string label
[, string match]]]])
```

radio_field()

This function returns an HTML radio button field. The optional third argument is included immediately after the radio button, and the pair are included between a `<nobr>` tag and `</nobr>` tag – meaning that they are displayed together on the same line. If the value of the second or third argument matches that of the fourth argument, the radio button is checked (that is, flipped on).

```
string radio_field ([string name [, string value [, string label [,
string match]]]])
```

select_field()

This function returns an HTML select field (popup field). If the optional second argument is an array, each key in the array is set to the value of an option of the select field, and the corresponding value from the array is the displayed string for that option. If the key or the value from the array matches the optional third argument, that option is designated as the default value of the select field.

```
string select_field ([string name [, array items [, string default
value]]])
```

Additional Functions Not Used in This Book

Here are a couple of functions that may make dealing with common queries a bit easier.

insert_row()

This is a generic function to run SQL `insert` statements.

```
function insert_row($table="", $atts="")
{
    if(empty($table) || !is_array($atts))
    {
        return False;
    }
    else
    {
        while (list ($col, $val) = each ($atts))
        {
            //if null go to the next array item
            if ($val=="")
            {
                continue;
            }
            $col_str .= $col . ",";
            if (is_int($val) || is_double($val))
            {
                $val_str .= $val . ",";
            }
            else
            {
                $val_str .= "'$val',";
            }
        }
        $query = "insert into $table
            ($col_str)
                values($val_str)";
        //trim trailing comma from both strings
        $query = str_replace(",)", ")", $query);
    }
    safe_query($query);

    return mysql_affected_rows();
}
```

This function takes two attributes: the first is the table name, and the second should be an associative array, with the key being the column name and the value being the value to be inserted. Single quotes that should surround a string are included if the variable is not an integer or a double. The function returns `false` if the query fails to perform an action. It does not work in all circumstances, because it doesn't check for the column type from the database. But it can be nice for creating pages quickly.

Empty values in the array are not added to the query. For columns left out of the query, MySQL inserts either null values or empty strings, depending on whether or not the column allows nulls.

Note that you can create the associative array from a set of variables using the `compact()` function. For example, the following creates an associative array named `$array` and then inserts a row into a table named mytable. (It's assumed that you have already connected to the database.)

```
$category="";
$category_id=6;
$category_name="my category";
$array=compact("category", "category_id", "category_name");
if (!insert_row("mytable", $array))
{
    echo "insert failed";
}
```

update_row()

This function will run SQL `update` statements.

```
function update_row($table="", $atts="", $where="")
{
    if(empty($table) || !is_array($atts))
    {
        return FALSE;
    }
    else
    {
        while(list ($col, $val) = each ($atts))
        {
            if ($val=="")
            {
                continue;
            }
            if(is_int($val) || is_double($val))
            {
                $str .= "$col=$val,";
```

```
            }
            elseif($val=="NULL" || $val=="null")
            {
                $str .= "$col=NULL,";
            }
            else
            {
                $str .= "$col='$val',";
            }
        }
    }
    $str = substr($str, 0, -1);
    $query = "update $table set $str";
    if (!empty($where))
    {
        $query .= " where $where";
    }
    mysql_query($query) or
        die (mysql_error());
    return mysql_affected_rows();
}
```

This function takes three arguments: `$table`, a string, `$atts`, an associative array containing keys of column names and values to be inserted, and `$where`, which is the condition – for example `column_id = 1`.

Again, this function is not robust enough to work in all circumstances.

delete_row()

This function takes two arguments: `$table`, the table name, and `$where`, the value in the `where` clause. It returns `false` on failure or `0` if nothing was deleted.

```
function delete_row($table="", $where="")
{
        if (empty($table) || empty($where))
        {
                return FALSE;
        }
        $query = "delete from $table where $where";
        mysql_query($query) or die (mysql_error());
        return mysql_affected_rows();
}
```

select_to_table()

This function takes a query and lays it out in a simple HTML table. It assumes that a database connection has already been made.

```
function select_to_table($query)
{
    $result=mysql_query($query);
    $number_cols = mysql_num_fields($result);
    echo "<b>query: $query</b>";
    //layout table header
    echo "<table border = 1>\n";
    echo "<tr align=center>\n";
    for ($i=0; $i<$number_cols; $i++)
    {
           echo "<th>" . mysql_field_name($result, $i). "</th>\n";
    }
    echo "</tr>\n";//end table header
    //layout table body
    while ($row = mysql_fetch_row($result))
    {
           echo "<tr align=left>\n";
        for ($i=0; $i<$number_cols; $i++)
        {
        echo "<td>";
              if (!isset($row[$i])) //test for null value
                {
                echo "NULL";
             }
              else
                 {
                echo $row[$i];
             }
                echo "</td>\n";
        } echo "</tr>\n";
    }
    echo "</table>";
}
```

enum_to_array()

This function returns the values defined in an enum field into an array.

```
function enum_to_array($table="", $col = "")
{

    if (empty($table) || empty($col))
    { return False; }
    else
    {
        $query = "describe $table $col";
        $result = mysql_query($query);
        list( , $col) = mysql_fetch_array($result);
        echo $col;
        if (substr($col, 0, 4) != "enum")
        {
            return false;
        }
        $col = str_replace ("'","" ,
                    substr($col, 5, -1)
        );
        $col = explode(",", $col);
    }
    return $col;
}
```

You can use the `enum` field type in MySQL to limit possible values in a column, which might be helpful for restricting column values to `Y` or `N`, for example. But to get at these values in PHP you need to run one of the MySQL queries that retrieves column information. In the preceding example we use the `describe` query, and we assume that the column of interest is included in the query.

The query returns six columns. In order, they are as follows: `Field`, `Type`, `Null`, `Key`, `Default`, and `Extra`. The second, `Type`, contains the column type – something like `enum('yes','no')`. In the preceding function, this value is assigned to `$col`. That string can then be stripped of the extraneous parentheses and the letters `enum`. The remainder is exploded into an array.

You can then use the array however you wish, perhaps in a drop-down box.

Session handling with MySQL

If you wish to use these functions, set your `session.save_handler` to `user` in your php.ini. This set of functions is intended to work with a table that looks something like this:

```
create table sessions (
    session_id char(32) not null primary key,
    sess_data text,
    last_update timestamp
```

```
);


function mysql_session_open()
{
        mysql_pconnect("localhost", "root", "")
            or die (mysql_error());
        $db_sess = mysql_select_db("test")
            or die (mysql_error());
}


//this function receives the session_id as the only argument
function mysql_session_read($id)
{
        $data = "";
         $query = "select sess_data from sessions
               where session_id = '$id'";
        $result= mysql_query($query) or die (mysql_error());
        if ($row = mysql_fetch_row($result) )
        {
               $data=session_decode($row[0]);
        }
        return $data;
}

//this takes the sessionid and the session data
//as arguments
function mysql_session_write($id, $data)
{
    $data = session_encode($data);
    $query = "replace into sessions (session_id, sess_data)
        values ('$id', '$data')";
    mysql_query($query) or
        die(mysql_error ());
    return true;
}


function mysql_session_close()
{
        return true;
}

//takes only the session id for an argument
```

```
function mysql_session_destroy($id)
{
        $query = "delete from sessions where session_id = '$id'";
        mysql_query($query) or
            die (mysql_error());
            return true;
}

//this function receives the maximum lifetime setting
//from php.ini. It is by default set to 1440 seconds.
//the session.gc_probability setting in the php.ini determines
//what percentage of the time this function will run.
function mysql_session_gc($time)
{
        $query = "delete from sessions where
                  last_update < ( subdate(now(),
                   INTERVAL $time SECOND) )";
        mysql_query($query) or
               die (mysql_error() )_;
}
session_set_save_handler(
        "mysql_session_open",
        "mysql_session_close",
        "mysql_session_read",
        "mysql_session_write",
        "mysql_session_destroy",
        "mysql_session_gc"
);
```

Email Validation

A lot of simple regular expressions can be used to ensure that a string more or less resembles the format of a proper email address, but if you want something that is a bit more thorough, try this function. It is not entirely RFC-compliant, but it is pretty close. It is included in the /book/functions folder.

```
#CheckEmail
#
#mailbox      =  addr-spec                    ; simple address
#             /  phrase route-addr            ; name & addr-spec
#
#route-addr   =  "<" [route] addr-spec ">"
#
#route        =  1#("@" domain) ":"           ; path-relative
```

```
#
#addr-spec    =  local-part "@" domain        ; global address
#
#local-part   =  word *("." word)             ; uninterpreted
#                                             ; case-preserved
#
#domain       =  sub-domain *("." sub-domain)
#
#sub-domain   =  domain-ref / domain-literal
#
#domain-ref   =  atom                         ; symbolic reference
#
#atom         =  1*<any CHAR except specials, SPACE and CTLs>
#
#specials     =  "(" / ")" / "<" / ">" / "@"  ; Must be in quoted-
#              /  "," / ";" / ":" / "\" / <">  ;  string, to use
#              /  "." / "[" / "]"              ;  within a word.
#
#                                             ; (  Octal, Decimal.)
#CHAR         =  <any ASCII character>        ; (  0-177,  0.-127.)
#ALPHA        =  <any ASCII alphabetic character>
#                                             ; (101-132, 65.- 90.)
#                                             ; (141-172, 97.-122.)
#DIGIT        =  <any ASCII decimal digit>    ; ( 60- 71, 48.- 57.)
#CTL          =  <any ASCII control           ; (  0- 37,  0.- 31.)
#                 character and DEL>          ; (    177,     127.)
#CR           =  <ASCII CR, carriage return>  ; (     15,      13.)
#LF           =  <ASCII LF, linefeed>         ; (     12,      10.)
#SPACE        =  <ASCII SP, space>            ; (     40,      32.)
#HTAB         =  <ASCII HT, horizontal-tab>   ; (     11,       9.)
#<">          =  <ASCII quote mark>           ; (     42,      34.)
#CRLF         =  CR LF
#
#LWSP-char    =  SPACE / HTAB                 ; semantics = SPACE
#
#linear-white-space =  1*([CRLF] LWSP-char)  ; semantics = SPACE
#                                             ; CRLF => folding
#
#delimiters   =  specials / linear-white-space / comment
#
#text         =  <any CHAR, including bare    ; => atoms, specials,
#                 CR & bare LF, but NOT       ;  comments and
#                 including CRLF>             ;  quoted-strings are
#                                             ;  NOT recognized.
#
```

```
#quoted-string = <"> *(qtext/quoted-pair) <">; Regular qtext or
#                                              ;   quoted chars.
#
#qtext        =  <any CHAR excepting <">,     ; => may be folded
#                 "\" & CR, and including
#                 linear-white-space>
#
#domain-literal =  "[" *(dtext / quoted-pair) "]"
#
#
#
#
#dtext        =  <any CHAR excluding "[",     ; => may be folded
#                 "]", "\" & CR, & including
#                 linear-white-space>
#
#comment      =  "(" *(ctext / quoted-pair / comment) ")"
#
#ctext        =  <any CHAR excluding "(",     ; => may be folded
#                 ")", "\" & CR, & including
#                 linear-white-space>
#
#quoted-pair  =  "\" CHAR                     ; may quote any char
#
#phrase       =  1*word                       ; Sequence of words
#
#word         =  atom / quoted-string
#

#mailbox      =  addr-spec                    ; simple address
#             /  phrase route-addr            ; name & addr-spec
#route-addr   =  "<" [route] addr-spec ">"
#route        =  1#("@" domain) ":"           ; path-relative
#addr-spec    =  local-part "@" domain        ; global address

#validate_email("insight\@bedrijfsnet.nl");

function print_validate_email ($eaddr="")
{
    $result = validate_email($eaddr) ? "is valid" : "is not valid";
    print "<h4>email address (".htmlspecialchars($eaddr).")
$result</h4>\n";
}

function validate_email ($eaddr="")
```

```
{

    if (empty($eaddr))
    {
#print "[$eaddr] is not valid\n";
        return false;
    }
    $laddr = "";
    $laddr = $eaddr;

# if the addr-spec is in a route-addr, strip away the phrase and <>s

    $laddr = preg_replace('/^.*</','', $laddr);
    $laddr = preg_replace('/>.*$/','',$laddr);
    if (preg_match('/^\@.*:/',$laddr))    #path-relative domain
    {
        list($domain,$addr_spec) = preg_split('/:/',$laddr);
        $domain = preg_replace('/^\@/','',$domain);
        if (!is_domain($domain)) { return false; }
        $laddr = $addr_spec;
    }
    return(is_addr_spec($laddr));
}

function is_addr_spec ( $eaddr = "" )
{
    list($local_part,$domain) = preg_split('/\@/',$eaddr);
    if (!is_local_part($local_part) || !is_domain($domain))
    {
#print "[$eaddr] is not valid\n";
        return false;
    }
    else
    {
#print "[$eaddr] is valid\n";
        return true;
    }
}

#local-part  =  word *("." word)             ; uninterpreted
function is_local_part ( $local_part = "" )
{
    if (empty($local_part)) { return false; }

    $bit_array = preg_split('/\./',$local_part);
```

```
    while (list(,$bit) = each($bit_array))
    {
        if (!is_word($bit)) { return false; }
    }
    return true;
}

#word          =  atom / quoted-string
#quoted-string = <"> *(qtext/quoted-pair) <">; Regular qtext or
#                                              ;   quoted chars.
#qtext         =  <any CHAR excepting <">,     ; => may be folded
#                  "\" & CR, and including
#                  linear-white-space>
#quoted-pair =  "\" CHAR                        ; may quote any char
function is_word ( $word = "")
{

    if (preg_match('/^".*"$/i',$word))
    {
        return(is_quoted_string($word));
    }
    return(is_atom($word));
}

function is_quoted_string ( $word = "")
{
    $word = preg_replace('/^"/','',$word);    # remove leading quote
    $word = preg_replace('/"$/','',$word);    # remove trailing
quote
    $word = preg_replace('/\\+/','',$word);    # remove any quoted-
pairs
    if (preg_match('/\"\\\r/',$word))    # if ", \ or CR, it's bad
qtext
    {
        return false;
    }
    return true;
}


#atom          =  1*<any CHAR except specials, SPACE and CTLs>
#specials      =  "(" / ")" / "<" / ">" / "@"  ; Must be in quoted-
#              /  "," / ";" / ":" / "\" / <">  ;  string, to use
#              /  "." / "[" / "]"              ;  within a word.
#SPACE         =  <ASCII SP, space>            ; (     40,      32.)
```

```
#CTL         =  <any ASCII control            ; (  0- 37,  0.- 31.)
#                character and DEL>           ; (    177,     127.)
function is_atom ( $atom = "")
{

    if (
    (preg_match('/[\(\)\<\>\@\,\;\:\\\"\.\[\]]/',$atom))    #
specials
        || (preg_match('/\040/',$atom))            # SPACE
        || (preg_match('/[\x00-\x1F]/',$atom))        # CTLs
    )
    {
        return false;
    }
    return true;
}

#domain      =  sub-domain *("." sub-domain)
#sub-domain  =  domain-ref / domain-literal
#domain-ref  =  atom                           ; symbolic reference
function is_domain ( $domain = "")
{

    if (empty($domain)) { return false; }

# this is not strictly required, but is 99% likely sign of a bad
domain
    if (!preg_match('/\./',$domain)) { return false; }

    $dbit_array = preg_split('/./',$domain);
    while (list(,$dbit) = each($dbit_array))
    {
        if (!is_sub_domain($dbit)) { return false; }
    }
    return true;
}
function is_sub_domain ( $subd = "")
{
    if (preg_match('/^\[.*\]$/',$subd))    #domain-literal
    {
        return(is_domain_literal($subd));
    }
    return(is_atom($subd));
}
#domain-literal =  "[" *(dtext / quoted-pair) "]"
```

```
#dtext        =  <any CHAR excluding "[",     ; => may be folded
#                 "]", "\" & CR, & including
#                 linear-white-space>
#quoted-pair =  "\" CHAR                       ; may quote any char
function is_domain_literal ( $dom = "")
{
    $dom = preg_replace('/\\+/','',$dom);          # remove quoted
pairs
    if (preg_match('/[\[\]\\\r]/',$dom))     # bad dtext characters
    {
        return false;
    }
    return true;
}

?>
```

You would probably want to put all of these functions in one file and then include it when needed. It returns 1 (for true) or nothing (for false). You'd probably want to use it like so:

```
if ( !validate_email("myaddress@mydomain.com") )
{
    echo "this is not a valid email";
}
```

sitemap.php

We wrote the following code to help us take a look at all the documents installed on the Web server. It prints every document and provides a link to these documents.

```
<?php include('book.php'); ?>
<b><a href=".">back to directory</a></b>
<h2>Site Map</h2>
<?php
function printdir($dir='.',$path=NULL, $print_ok=FALSE)
{
    if ($path === NULL)
        $path = $dir;
    $pursue = TRUE;
    $old_print_ok = $print_ok;
    if ($print_ok)
    {
        // np
```

```
    }
    elseif (strpos($path, BOOK_ROOT) === FALSE)
    {
        if (strpos($path, DSN_ROOT) === FALSE)
        {
            if (strpos(BOOK_ROOT, $path) === FALSE
                && strpos(DSN_ROOT, $path) === FALSE
            )
            {
                $pursue = FALSE;
            }
        }
        else
        {
            $print_ok = TRUE;
        }
    }
    else
    {
        $print_ok = TRUE;
    }
    $printdir = $dir;
    if ($print_ok && !$old_print_ok)
        $printdir = $path;
    $url = NULL;
    if (strpos($path, DOC_ROOT) !== FALSE)
    {
        $url = str_replace(DOC_ROOT, '', $path);
        $printdir = "<a href=\"$url\">$printdir</a>";
    }
    if ($dh = opendir($path))
    {
        if ($print_ok)
            print "<li>$printdir/\n<ul>\n";
        while (($file = readdir($dh)) !== FALSE)
        {
            if ($file == '.' or $file == '..' or $file == 'CVS' or
substr($file,-4) == '.swp')
                continue;

            $wholefile = "{$path}/{$file}";
            if ($url)
                if (substr($file,-4) == '.php')
                    $printfile = '<a href="'
                        . BOOK_URL_ROOT
```

```
                            . '/source'
                            . str_replace(BOOK_URL_ROOT, '/book/',
"{$url}/{$file}")
                            . '">'
                            . $file
                            . '</a>'
                        ;
                else
                    $printfile = "<a
href=\"{$url}/{$file}\">$file</a>";
            else
                $printfile = $file;

            if (is_link($wholefile))
            {
                if ($print_ok)
                    print "<li>@{$printfile}\n";
            }
            elseif (is_dir($wholefile))
            {
                if ($pursue)
                    printdir($file, $wholefile, $print_ok);
            }
            elseif ($print_ok)
            {
                print "<li>$printfile\n";
            }
        }
        closedir($dh);
        if ($print_ok)
            print "</ul>\n";
    }
    else
    {
        print "<li>could not open '$dir'\n";
    }
}
printdir('/usr/local/book/apache');
?>
```

Appendix 1

PHP and MySQL Resources

THIS APPENDIX PRESENTS SOME resources that should be extremely useful in increasing your knowledge of both PHP and MySQL.

PHP Resources

Here are some sites that are great for all things PHP.

php.net

This site, along with its many international mirrors, should be your home away from home. From the home page, you can search the manual or one of the many mailing lists. Among the many helpful resources are the following:

- **PHP Annotated Manual** (`http://www.php.net/manual/`) – The online manual is really terrific; it includes user comments, some of which clarify the use of some of the trickier functions in PHP.
- **Downloads** (`http://www.php.net/downloads.php`) – Here you can find not only the various distributions, but also an HTML manual that you can download and put on your local machine.
- **Daily snapshots** (`http://snaps.php.net`) – PHP is an active open-source project, and features and bug fixes are constantly added to the code base. Before official releases are made, you can get the most up-to-date code here: Source code is updated daily. Note that this service is best for the true hacker with a box devoted to development; if you have room for only one installation, get the most recent stable source code. A link to the most recent stable source is always available from `http://www.php.net/`.
- **Bug database** (`http://bugs.php.net`) – Wondering if there is a problem with a function? Head over to this site to search through the bug reports, or to add one yourself – but be very sure that you've found a bug before submitting a report.
- **FAQ** (`http://www.php.net/FAQ.php`) – Before you post to any mailing list or start writing an application, read the FAQ.

PHP mailing lists

One of the great things about the Web, and about open-source projects in particular, is the quality of the advice available on the mailing lists. Many lists, covering many specific topics, are available. The ones discussed in this section are all part of `php.net` and use the `lists.php.net` mail domain. You can subscribe to any of these lists on `http://www.php.net/mailing-lists.php`, and they are all archived at `http://marc.theaimsgroup.com/`. The core developers monitor the list and respond to questions and complaints.

If you want to keep up with the goings-on of any of the lists but would rather not stuff up your inbox, you can also get to these mailing lists via a newsgroup reader. Just connect to `news.php.net`.

- **PHP general** – This is the generic support area. Over the course of a typical day over 100 emails are posted to this list. It is amazingly helpful, even if you don't have an interest in posting questions or supplying answers. Your comrades have some interesting techniques and knowledge, which they share daily.

Please practice good etiquette when posting to the mailing lists. First check one of the searchable archives to make sure your question is something resembling unique. And please, read the FAQ.

- **Database list** – This one is a natural for most everyone reading this book because it has to do with how PHP interacts with databases. This is key to almost all Web applications.
- **Installation list** – If you are having problems getting PHP installed on your box, this is the place to go.

zend.com

At the core of the PHP is the Zend engine, which was built by Zeev Suraski and Andi Gutmans. Their work became the foundation for a company that is offering products that make PHP even more powerful. Zend products include a cache, which can really increase speed, an optimizer, which can help make badly written code run faster, a compiler, which makes PHP unreadable (which is great if you're planning on distributing code that you would rather not be open source), and an integrated development environment (IDE). And who wouldn't want that?

The `zend.com` site includes some valuable resources:

- **Code Gallery** (`http://zend.com/codex.php`) – This is one of the better code galleries out there. Browse it and see if it contains functions that will make your life easier.
- **Applications** (`http://zend.com/apps.php`) – What? What you have here isn't enough?
- **Tutorials** (`http://zend.com/zend/tut/`) – Zend provides a growing number of very informative tutorials that cover a variety of topics.
- **Weekly Summary** (`http://zend.com/zend/week/`) – Avi Lewin writes a weekly article that summarizes the major issues the core developers discussed over the past week. It's interesting stuff, and can give you a heads-up about what will be happening in PHP's future.

phpbuilder.com

PHPBuilder was once the best source for PHP articles. Tim Perdue, who used to run PHPBuilder, built a great base of articles that cover topics including databases, Cascading Style Sheets, and other topics of interest to developers who work in the Web environment. PHPBuilder also has discussion boards, job boards, and a code library. It is really worth checking with frequently, although the quality has dropped off over the past year or so.

phpMyAdmin on Sourceforge

Earlier in the book we recommended the phpMyAdmin, a PHP tool for Web-based administration of MySQL. Tobias Ratschiller and Till Gerken provide several other useful tools. It's all on SourceForge at `http://sourceforge.net/projects/phpmyadmin/`.

PEAR

PEAR stands for the PHP Extension and Application Repository, and we've mentioned it many times already in this book. It is a set of code being written by some very skilled programmers whose goal is a common set of well-written extensions the rest of us can incorporate into our own PHP applications. The extensions include a templating engine, a database-abstraction layer, and much much more. Stig Bakken, one of the core developers, is heading up the project.

You can most easily obtain a current copy of PEAR through the PHP CVS repository (cvs.php.net).

PHPclasses

A Portuguese programmer named Manuel Lemos is among the most prolific PHP coders on the planet, and he shares his code at http://www.phpclasses.org. In fact, PHPclasses is now a code repository for anyone who has classes to share with the PHP world. The following are of particular note:

- **Manuel's Form Processing Class** – This class provides a uniform method for creating and validating forms. It accounts for about every type of validation imaginable.
- **Metabase** – This is a very complete database-abstraction layer.
- **Mail Class** – This class makes sending e-mail with attachments quite a bit easier.

Midgard

The Midgard project team is building a content-management system with PHP and MySQL. If you need content management, http://www.midgard-project.com is definitely worth a look. Or you can just work on the application we created in Chapter 11.

Phorum

Phorum (www.phorum.org) has an excellent discussion server written in PHP and MySQL. You might want to compare it to the threaded discussion application in Chapter 10.

weberdev.com

Of the many Web-development sites that have PHP articles, tutorials, and code, weberdev.com (http://weberdev.com/) is among the most extensive.

Webmonkey

Both Brad and Jay have worked at Webmonkey. Jay is a former producer of the site, and Brad has written several articles. Check out its PHP-related material at http://hotwired.lycos.com/webmonkey/programming/php/.

MySQL Resources

There's no shortage of resources here either. We've mentioned mainly Web-based resources in this appendix; however, we must mention one hard-copy MySQL resource. Jay Greenspan, the co-author of this book, also wrote *MySQL Weekend Crash Course* (Wiley 2002).

mysql.com

Predictably, this is probably the best place to find answers to any questions you might have about MySQL. Some specific portions of the site are worth particular note:

- **Downloads** (`http://www.mysql.com/downloads/`) – This is the place to find the latest version of MySQL in all the popular formats, including rpms, source code, and Windows binaries.
- **Contributions** (`http://www.mysql.com/downloads/contrib.html`) – A lot of developers have put together tools that you might be able to use when working with MySQL. Of these, the GUI clients are particularly interesting.
- **Documentation** (`http://www.mysql.com/documentation/`) – The online manual for MySQL is pretty good and available in several languages. It covers many topics that this book did not. For example, the manual's language reference should be bookmarked on your browser.

Both PHP and MySQL have downloadable HTML manuals. We keep them on our local machine so we don't have to connect to the Web every time we have a question.

Mailing lists

The MySQL mailing list is monitored by many of the core developers. If you have a question about the product and post it on the mailing list, someone who is working on the product itself will surely see it. In addition, they're really a very nice bunch of guys. Information about subscribing to any of the mailing lists can be found here: `http://www.mysql.com/documentation/lists.html`. A searchable archive of the mailing lists can be found here: `http://lists.mysql.com`.

General Client-Side Resources

Here are a few of the sites we find ourselves returning to frequently.

HTML 4.0 character entity references

About the most comprehensive list we know of can be found here: `http://www.hclrss.demon.co.uk/demos/ent4_frame.html`.

Netscape's tag reference

If you are still dealing with the mess that is Netscape 4, this tag reference should be of some assistance:

`http://devedge.netscape.com/library/manuals/1998/htmlguide/`

Apache References

Apache will likely be your Web server, and when you are new to it, it can be tricky. Apache.org (`www.apache.org`) is the home site for the Apache Software Foundation, which is now working on many interesting projects. In particular, some very cool things are happening in the XML space. Apache can be opaque when you first come to it, but when you grow accustomed to using its documentation, you will see that it really isn't very difficult to work with.

Appendix J

MySQL Function Reference

MYSQL HAS MANY FUNCTIONS, and only some of these were used in the course of this book. You should, however, have a good idea of what other MySQL functions are available, as you might find they come in handy at times. To see the complete MySQL function reference check out MySQL AB's documentation at `http://www.mysql.com/documentation/mysql/bychapter/manual_Reference.html`.

String Comparison Functions

This set of functions should not be confused with PHP's string handling functions. Normally, if any expression in a string comparison is case-sensitive, the comparison is performed in a case-sensitive way.

LIKE

This function conducts a pattern match using basic SQL wildcard characters:

```
expr LIKE pattern
RETURNS: int
```

With `like` you can use the following two wildcard characters in the pattern: `%`, which matches any number of characters, even zero characters, and `_`, which matches exactly one character. To test for literal instances of a wildcard character, precede the character with the escape character, usually a backslash (`\`).

In MySQL you can specify a different escape character, but this is rarely useful. This function returns `1` (`true`) if the pattern is found or `0` (`false`) if not:

```
mysql> select 'jay greenspan' like 'jay%';
+-----------------------------+
| 'jay greenspan' like 'jay%' |
+-----------------------------+
|                           1 |
+-----------------------------+
1 row in set (0.00 sec)
```

NOT LIKE

A `NOT LIKE` pattern match uses the same syntax and escaping as `like`.

```
expr NOT LIKE pattern
RETURNS: int
```

As you could probably have predicted, `NOT LIKE` returns `true` if the pattern and the expression do not match:

```
mysql> select 'jay greenspan' NOT LIKE 'jay%';
+---------------------------------+
| 'jay greenspan' NOT LIKE 'jay%' |
+---------------------------------+
|                               1 |
+---------------------------------+
```

REGEXP

This function performs a pattern match of a string expression (`expr`) against a regular expression (`pat`). See Appendix G for a discussion of regular expressions. But be aware that MySQL does not support regular expressions to the extent you find in PHP.

```
expr REGEXP pat
RETURNS: int
```

`REGEXP` returns `1` (`true`) if the pattern is found or `0` (`false`) if not:

```
mysql> select name from guestbook WHERE name regexp '^j.*g';
+---------------+
| name          |
+---------------+
| Jay Greenspan |
| Jay Green     |
+---------------+
2 rows in set (0.00 sec)
```

NOT REGEXP

This function works identically to `REGEXP`, except that patterns that fail to match the expression test `true` and those that do match test `false`.

STRCMP

This function compares two strings, like the PHP function of the same name:

```
STRCMP(expr1,expr2) (used in examples)
RETURNS: int
```

STRCMP returns 0 if the strings are the same, -1 if the first argument is smaller than the second, and 1 if the second argument is smaller than the first:

```
mysql> select strcmp('foo', 'bar');
+----------------------+
| strcmp('foo', 'bar') |
+----------------------+
|                    1 |
+----------------------+
1 row in set (0.11 sec)

mysql> select strcmp('bar', 'bar');
+----------------------+
| strcmp('bar', 'bar') |
+----------------------+
|                    0 |
+----------------------+
1 row in set (0.00 sec)

mysql> select strcmp('bar', 'foo');
+----------------------+
| strcmp('bar', 'foo') |
+----------------------+
|                   -1 |
+----------------------+
1 row in set (0.00 sec)
```

MATCH...AGAINST

Starting in MySQL version 3.23, MySQL incorporates full-text searching. Using full-text searching you test the relevance of given rows against a string pattern. We didn't use full-text searching in the applications in this book, but if you're interested in this feature we recommend reading Section 6.8 of the MySQL manual, available at http://www.mysql.com/doc/F/u/Fulltext_Search.html.

Cast Operators

You will encounter only one cast operator in MySQL.

BINARY

```
BINARY
RETURNS: string
```

The BINARY operator casts the string following it to a binary string. Using it is an easy way to force a column comparison to be case-sensitive even if the column isn't defined as BINARY or BLOB.

```
mysql> select binary('Foo') = 'foo', binary('Foo') = 'Foo';
+-----------------------+-----------------------+
| binary('Foo') = 'foo' | binary('Foo') = 'Foo' |
+-----------------------+-----------------------+
|                     0 |                     1 |
+-----------------------+-----------------------+
1 row in set (0.06 sec)
```

Control Flow Functions

Two functions allow for varying results depending on conditions.

IFNULL

```
IFNULL(expr1,expr2) (used in examples)
RETURNS: type of expr1 or expr2
```

If expr1 is not NULL, IFNULL() returns expr1; otherwise, it returns expr2. IFNULL() returns either a numeric or a string value depending on the context in which it is used.

```
mysql> select ifnull(1/0, 'exp 1 is null');
+------------------------------+
| ifnull(1/0, 'exp 1 is null') |
+------------------------------+
|                exp 1 is null |
+------------------------------+
1 row in set (0.00 sec)

mysql> select ifnull(1/1, 'exp 1 is not null');
+----------------------------------+
```

```
| ifnull(1/1, 'exp 1 is not null') |
+----------------------------------+
|                             1.00 |
+----------------------------------+
1 row in set (0.00 sec)
```

IF

Lots of times, you need to do something only if one or more conditions are true. `IF` serves that purpose in MySQL queries.

```
IF(expr1,expr2,expr3) (used in examples)
```

If `expr1` is `true` (`expr1 <> 0` and `expr1 <> NULL`), `IF()` returns `expr2`; otherwise it returns `expr3`. `IF()` returns a numeric or string value depending on the context in which it is used. `expr1` is evaluated as an integer value, which means that if you are testing floating-point or string values you should do so using a comparison operation.

```
mysql> select if(name like 'jay%', 'Yes', 'No') as 'Jay Names'
    -> from guestbook;
+-----------+
| Jay Names |
+-----------+
| Yes       |
| Yes       |
| No        |
| Yes       |
| No        |
| No        |
| No        |
+-----------+
10 rows in set (0.00 sec)
```

NULLIF

```
NULLIF(expr1,expr2)
```

The `NULLIF` function compares the two expressions. If they are equal the function returns a `NULL` value. If they are not equal it returns the value of `expr1`.

```
mysql> select NULLIF('jay', 'jay');
+----------------------+
| NULLIF('jay', 'jay') |
+----------------------+
| NULL                 |
```

```
+----------------------+
1 row in set (0.00 sec)

mysql> select NULLIF('jay', 'jack');
+----------------------+
| NULLIF('jay', 'jack') |
+----------------------+
| jay                  |
+----------------------+
1 row in set (0.00 sec)
```

Mathematical Functions

You can see the most current list of MySQL's math functions at `http://www.mysql.com/doc/M/a/Mathematical_functions.html`. All mathematical functions return `NULL` in case of an error.

ABS

This function returns the absolute value of *X*:

```
ABS(X)
RETURNS: type of X

mysql> select abs(22), abs(-22);
+---------+----------+
| abs(22) | abs(-22) |
+---------+----------+
|      22 |       22 |
+---------+----------+
```

SIGN

This function returns the sign of the argument as `-1`, `0`, or `1`, depending on whether `X` is negative, `0`, or positive:

```
SIGN(X)RETURNS: intmysql> select sign(10), sign(-10), sign(0);
+----------+-----------+---------+
| sign(10) | sign(-10) | sign(0) |
+----------+-----------+---------+
|        1 |        -1 |       0 |
+----------+-----------+---------+
1 row in set (0.00 sec)
```

MOD

Modulo is like the % operator in C. It returns the remainder of *N* divided by *M*:

```
MOD(N,M) or N % M
RETURNS: int

mysql> select mod(10,3), mod(10,4);
+-----------+-----------+
| mod(10,3) | mod(10,4) |
+-----------+-----------+
|         1 |         2 |
+-----------+-----------+
1 row in set (0.05 sec)
```

FLOOR

This function returns the largest integer value not greater than X:

```
FLOOR(X)
RETURNS: int

mysql> select floor(8.5);
+------------+
| floor(8.5) |
+------------+
|          8 |
+------------+
1 row in set (0.00 sec)
```

CEILING

This function returns the smallest integer value not less than X:

```
CEILING(X)
RETURNS: int

mysql> select ceiling(8.5);
+--------------+
| ceiling(8.5) |
+--------------+
|            9 |
+--------------+
1 row in set (0.00 sec)
```

ROUND

This function returns the argument *X*, rounded to an integer, rounded to the specified number of decimal places (or zero places by default):

```
Round ROUND(X [,D])
RETURNS: int or float
```

ROUND returns the argument *X* rounded to a number with *D* decimals. If *D* is 0, or does not exist, the result will have no decimal point or fractional part.

```
mysql> select round(8.53), round(8.47), round(8.534,2);
+-------------+-------------+----------------+
| round(8.53) | round(8.47) | round(8.534,2) |
+-------------+-------------+----------------+
|           9 |           8 |           8.53 |
+-------------+-------------+----------------+
1 row in set (0.33 sec)
```

TRUNCATE

TRUNCATE returns the number *X* truncated to *D* decimals. If D is 0, the result will have no decimal point or fractional part.

```
TRUNCATE(X,D)
RETURNS: decimal
```

```
mysql> select truncate(8.53,0), truncate(8.43,0), truncate(8.534,2);
+------------------+------------------+-------------------+
| truncate(8.53,0) | truncate(8.43,0) | truncate(8.534,2) |
+------------------+------------------+-------------------+
|                8 |                8 |              8.53 |
+------------------+------------------+-------------------+
1 row in set (0.05 sec)
```

EXP

This function returns the value of e (the base of natural logarithms) raised to the power of *X*:

```
EXP(X)
RETURNS: float
```

LOG

This function returns the natural logarithm of *X*. If you want the log of a number *X* to some arbitrary base *B*, use the formula `LOG(X)/LOG(B)`.

```
LOG(X)
RETURNS: float
```

LOG10

`LOG10` returns the base-10 logarithm of *X*:

```
LOG10(X)
RETURNS: float
```

POW

This function returns the value of *X* raised to the power of *Y*:

```
POW(X,Y)
RETURNS: float
```

SQRT

This function returns the non-negative square root of *X*:

```
SQRT(X)
RETURNS: float
```

PI

This function returns an approximation of pi:

```
PI()
RETURNS: float
```

By default, only five decimal places of precision are returned. Additional precision can be gained by adding the result of `PI()` to `0`, formatted as a floating point number with many decimal places:

```
SELECT PI() + 0.0000000000
```

COS

COS returns the cosine of *X*, where *X* is given in radians:

```
COS(X)
RETURNS: float
```

SIN

SIN returns the sine of *X*, where *X* is given in radians:

```
SIN(X)
RETURNS: float
```

TAN

This function returns the tangent of *X*, where *X* is given in radians:

```
TAN(X)
RETURNS: float
```

ACOS

This function returns the arc cosine of *X* – that is, the value whose cosine is X. It returns NULL if *X* is not in the range -1 to 1.

```
ACOS(X)
float
```

ASIN

This returns the arc sine of *X* – that is, the value whose sine is *X*. It returns NULL if *X* is not in the range -1 to 1.

```
ASIN(X)
RETURNS: float
```

ATAN

ATAN returns the arc tangent of *X* – that is, the value whose tangent is *X*:

```
ATAN(X)
RETURNS: float
```

ATAN2

ATAN2 returns the arc tangent of the two arguments *X* and *Y*. The process is similar to that of calculating the arc tangent of *Y*/*X*, except that the sines of both arguments are used to determine the quadrant of the result.

```
ATAN2(X,Y)
RETURNS: float
```

COT

This function returns the cotangent of *X*:

```
COT(X)
RETURNS: float
```

RAND

This function returns a random floating-point value in the range 0 to 1.0.

```
RAND()
```

or

```
RAND(N)
RETURNS: float
```

If an integer argument *N* is specified, it is used as the seed value. You can't use a column with RAND() values in an order by clause because in that case order by would evaluate the column multiple times. In MySQL 3.23 and later you can, however, do the following: `select * from table_name order by RAND()`. This is useful for getting a random sample. Note that a RAND() in a WHERE clause will be reevaluated every time the WHERE is executed.

LEAST

With two or more arguments, this function returns the smallest (minimum-valued) argument:

```
LEAST(X,Y,...)
RETURNS: type of X
```

Some unusual stuff goes on with LEAST, most of it having to do with casting arguments into alternate forms before comparison. Here are some examples of the behavior of this function:

- LEAST(22, 2.2) returns 2.2.
- LEAST(now(), 'a') returns the current date/time as a string.
- LEAST(now(), 50000000000000) returns the current date as a number.
- LEAST('a', 10) returns 0.
- LEAST('a', '10') returns 10.
- LEAST(2.2, '22') returns 2.2.

```
mysql> select least(2,7,9,1);
+----------------+
| least(2,7,9,1) |
+----------------+
|              1 |
+----------------+
1 row in set (0.00 sec)
```

GREATEST

GREATEST returns the largest (maximum-valued) argument. In MySQL versions prior to 3.22.5, you can use MAX() instead of GREATEST. Type conversion and casting works in the same way it does with LEAST, discussed previously.

```
GREATEST(X,Y,...)
RETURNS: type of X
```

```
mysql> select greatest(2,7,9,1);
+-------------------+
| greatest(2,7,9,1) |
+-------------------+
|                 9 |
+-------------------+
1 row in set (0.00 sec)
```

DEGREES

This function returns the argument *X*, converted from radians to degrees:

```
DEGREES(X)
RETURNS: float
```

RADIANS

This function returns the argument *X*, converted from degrees to radians:

```
RADIANS(X)
RETURNS: float
```

String Functions

MySQL's string functions return `NULL` if the length of the result would be greater than the `max_allowed_packet` server parameter. You can set this parameter by starting MySQL with a command like this:

```
safe_mysqld -O max_allowed_packet=16M
```

For functions that operate on string positions, the first position is numbered `1`.

ASCII

This function returns the ASCII-code value of the leftmost character in the string `str`. It returns `0` if `str` is the empty string and `NULL` if `str` is `NULL`.

```
ASCII(str)
RETURNS: int

mysql> select ascii('\n');
+-------------+
| ascii('\n') |
+-------------+
|          10 |
+-------------+
1 row in set (0.00 sec)
```

ORD

If the leftmost character in the string `str` is a multi-byte character, this function returns the code of the multi-byte character by returning the ASCII-code value of the character in the following format: `((`*`first byte ASCII code`*`)*256+(`*`second byte ASCII code`*`))[*256+`*`third byte ASCII code`*`...]`. If the leftmost character is not a multi-byte character, `ORD` returns the same value as the similar `ASCII()` function.

```
ORD(str)
RETURNS: int
```

CONV

This function converts numbers between different number bases:

```
CONV(N,from_base,to_base)
RETURNS: string
```

It returns a string representation of the number *N*, converted from base `from_base` to base `to_base`. It returns `NULL` if any argument is `NULL`. The argument *N* is interpreted as an integer, but may be specified as an integer or as a string. The minimum base is 2, and the maximum base is 36. If `to_base` is a negative number, *N* is regarded as a signed number; otherwise `N` is treated as unsigned. `CONV` works with 64-bit precision.

```
mysql> select conv(3,10,2);
+--------------+
| conv(3,10,2) |
+--------------+
| 11           |
+--------------+
```

BIN

This function returns the value of *N* as a binary (base-2) number. `BIN` treats *N* as a 64-bit signed integer value. Any decimal remainder is discarded. Negative numbers consist of 64 bits. Positive numbers have leading zeroes discarded. It returns `NULL` if `N` is `NULL`.

```
BIN(N)
RETURNS: string
```

```
mysql> select bin(3);
+--------+
| bin(3) |
+--------+
| 11     |
+--------+
```

OCT

This function returns a string representation of the octal value of *N*, where *N* is a long (`BIGINT`) number. It is equivalent to `CONV(N,10,8)`. It returns `NULL` if *N* is `NULL`.

```
OCT(N)
RETURNS: string
```

HEX

This function returns a string representation of the hexadecimal value of N, where N is a long (BIGINT) number. This is equivalent to CONV(N,10,16). It returns NULL if *N* is NULL.

```
HEX(N)
RETURNS: string
```

```
mysql> select hex(1000);
+-----------+
| hex(1000) |
+-----------+
| 3E8       |
+-----------+
1 row in set (0.00 sec)
```

CHAR

This function interprets the arguments as integers and returns a string consisting of the ASCII-code values of those integers. NULL values are skipped.

```
CHAR(N,...)
RETURNS: string
```

```
mysql> select char(74,65,89);
+----------------+
| char(74,65,89) |
+----------------+
| JAY            |
+----------------+
1 row in set (0.00 sec)
```

CONCAT

This function returns the string that results from the concatenation of the arguments. It returns NULL if any argument is NULL. CONCAT may have more than two arguments. A numeric argument is converted to the equivalent string form.

```
CONCAT(str1,str2,...) (used in examples)
RETURNS: string
```

This function is used in the following example to prepend a wildcard character onto the column in the WHERE clause of a query:

```
select 1 from blocked_domains
    WHERE '$REMOTE_HOST' like concat('%',domain)
    and release_dt is null
```

LENGTH

This function returns the length of the string str. If a numeric value is used as the argument, it's converted to a string first. Note that for CHAR_LENGTH() multi-byte characters are counted only once.

```
LENGTH(mixed)
```

or

```
CHAR_LENGTH(mixed)

RETURNS: int
mysql> select length('mysql functions');
+--------------------------+
| length('mysql functions') |
+--------------------------+
|                       15 |
+--------------------------+
1 row in set (0.00 sec)
```

LOCATE

This function returns the position of the first occurrence of substring substr in string str. Returns 0 if substr is not in str.

```
LOCATE(substr,str [,pos])
```

or

```
POSITION(substr IN str)
RETURNS: int
```

The optional third argument enables you to specify an offset at which to start the search:

```
mysql> select locate('s', 'mysql functions') as example1,
    -> locate('s', 'mysql functions',4) as example2;
+----------+----------+
```

```
| example1 | example2 |
+----------+----------+
|        3 |       15 |
+----------+----------+
1 row in set (0.00 sec)
```

INSTR

This function returns the position of the first occurrence of substring `substr` in string `str`. It is the same as `LOCATE()`, except that the arguments are swapped and no argument that indicates position is allowed.

```
INSTR(str,substr)
RETURNS: int
```

LPAD

This function returns the string `str`, left-padded with the string `padstr` until `str` is `len` characters long.

```
LPAD(str,len,padstr)
RETURNS: string

mysql> select lpad('foo', 15, 'k');
+----------------------+
| lpad('foo', 15, 'k') |
+----------------------+
| kkkkkkkkkkkkfoo      |
+----------------------+
1 row in set (0.00 sec)
```

RPAD

This function returns the string `str`, right-padded with the string `padstr` until `str` is `len` characters long.

```
RPAD(str,len,padstr)
RETURNS: string
```

LEFT

This function returns the leftmost `len` characters from the string `str`:

```
LEFT(str,len)
RETURNS: string
```

```
mysql> select left('mysql functions', 10);
+----------------------------+
| left('mysql functions', 10) |
+----------------------------+
| mysql func                 |
+----------------------------+
1 row in set (0.02 sec)
```

RIGHT

This function returns the rightmost `len` characters from the string `str`:

```
RIGHT(str,len)
RETURNS: string
```

SUBSTRING

This function returns a substring `len` characters long from string `str`, starting at position `pos` and continuing for `len` number of characters. The variant form that uses `FROM` is ANSI SQL92 syntax.

```
SUBSTRING(str,pos[,len])
```

or

```
SUBSTRING(str FROM pos FOR len)
```

or

```
MID(str,pos,len) (used in examples)
RETURNS: string
```

```
mysql> select mid('mysqlfunctions',6,8);
+--------------------------+
| mid('mysqlfunctions',6,8) |
+--------------------------+
| function                 |
+--------------------------+
1 row in set (0.00 sec)
```

SUBSTRING_INDEX

This function returns the substring from string `str` after `count` occurrences of the delimiter `delim`. If `count` is positive, everything to the left of the final delimiter (counting from the left) is returned; if `count` is negative, everything to the right of the final delimiter (counting from the right) is returned. If count is 0, nothing is returned.

```
SUBSTRING_INDEX(str,delim,count) (used in examples)
RETURNS: string

mysql> select substring_index('mysqlfunctionsmysql', 'fu', 1);
+----------------------------------------------+
| substring_index('mysqlfunctions', 'fu', 1) |
+----------------------------------------------+
| mysql                                        |
+----------------------------------------------+
1 row in set (0.00 sec)

mysql> select substring_index('mysqlfunctionsmysql', 'fu', -1);
+-----------------------------------------------+
| substring_index('mysqlfunctionsmysql', 'fu', -1) |
+-----------------------------------------------+
| nctionsmysql                                  |
+-----------------------------------------------+
1 row in set (0.00 sec)
```

LTRIM

This function returns the string str with leading spaces (and only spaces – no other whitespace characters) removed:

```
LTRIM(str)
RETURNS: string
```

RTRIM

This function returns the string str with trailing-space characters removed:

```
RTRIM(str)
RETURNS: string
```

TRIM

This function returns the string str with all remstr prefixes and/or suffixes removed. If none of the specifiers BOTH, LEADING, and TRAILING is given, BOTH is assumed. If remstr is not specified, spaces are removed.

```
TRIM([[BOTH | LEADING | TRAILING] [remstr] FROM] str) (used in
examples)
RETURNS: string
```

```
mysql> select trim(both '\n' from '\n mystring');
+----------------------------------+
| trim(both '\n' from '\n mystring') |
+----------------------------------+
|  mystring                          |
+----------------------------------+
1 row in set (0.00 sec)
```

Note that remstr will exactly match only the exact sequence of characters. So putting \t\n\ in the remstr argument in the preceding example removes only occurrences where tabs and newlines appear consecutively.

REPLACE

This function returns the string str with all occurrences of the string from_str replaced by the string to_str:

```
REPLACE(str,from_str,to_str)
RETURNS: string
```

SOUNDEX

This function returns a soundex string from str:

```
SOUNDEX(str)
RETURNS: string
```

Two strings that sound "about the same" in English should have identical soundex strings. A "standard" soundex string is four characters long, but the SOUNDEX() function returns a string of arbitrary length. You can use SUBSTRING() on the result to get a "standard" soundex string. All non-alphanumeric characters are ignored in the given string. All international alpha characters outside the A–Z range are treated as vowels.

```
mysql> select soundex('functions'), soundex('junctions'),
soundex('fiction');
+----------------------+----------------------+--------------------+
| soundex('functions') | soundex('junctions') | soundex('fiction') |
+----------------------+----------------------+--------------------+
| F52352               | J52352               | F235               |
+----------------------+----------------------+--------------------+
1 row in set (0.00 sec)
```

SPACE

This function returns a string consisting of `N` space characters:

```
SPACE(N)
RETURNS: string
```

REPEAT

This function returns a string consisting of the string `str` repeated `count` times. If `count` is less than or equal to `0`, it returns an empty string. It returns `NULL` if `str` or `count` are `NULL`.

```
REPEAT(str,count)
RETURNS: string
```

```
mysql> select repeat('foo', 10);
+-------------------------------+
| repeat('foo', 10)             |
+-------------------------------+
| foofoofoofoofoofoofoofoofoofoo |
+-------------------------------+
```

REVERSE

This function returns the string `str` with the order of the characters reversed:

```
REVERSE(str)
RETURNS: string
```

INSERT

This function returns the string `str`, with the substring `len` characters long beginning at position `pos` replaced by the string `newstr`:

```
INSERT(str,pos,len,newstr)
RETURNS: string
```

```
mysql> select insert('mysqlfunctions', 6,2,'FU');
+-----------------------------------+
| insert('mysqlfunctions', 6,2,'FU') |
+-----------------------------------+
| mysqlFUnctions                    |
+-----------------------------------+
1 row in set (0.44 sec)
```

ELT

This function returns str1 if *N* equals 1, str2 if *N* equals 2, and so on. It returns NULL if *N* is less than 1 or greater than the number of arguments. ELT() is the complement of FIELD().

```
ELT(N,str1,str2,str3,...)
RETURNS: string
```

```
mysql> select elt(2, 'foo', 'bar', 'foobar');
+--------------------------------+
| elt(2, 'foo', 'bar', 'foobar') |
+--------------------------------+
| bar                            |
+--------------------------------+
1 row in set (0.00 sec)
```

FIELD

This function returns the index of str in the str1, str2, str3, ... list. It returns 0 if str is not found. FIELD() is the complement of ELT().

```
FIELD(str,str1,str2,str3,...)
RETURNS: int
```

```
mysql> select field('foobar', 'foo', 'bar', 'foobar');
+-----------------------------------------+
| field('foobar', 'foo', 'bar', 'foobar') |
+-----------------------------------------+
|                                       3 |
+-----------------------------------------+
1 row in set (0.01 sec)
```

LCASE

This function returns the string str with all characters changed to lower case according to the current character-set mapping (the default is ISO-8859-1 Latin1):

```
LCASE(str) or LOWER(str) (used in examples)
RETURNS: string
```

UCASE

This function returns the string `str` with all characters changed to upper case according to the current character-set mapping (the default is ISO-8859-1 Latin1):

```
UCASE(str) or UPPER(str)
RETURNS: string
```

Date and Time Functions

MySQL offers many functions for calculating dates. Of all the MySQL functions available, these are the ones you will probably use most frequently.

The `DATE_FORMAT` function enables you to format dates to take the form of MySQL timestamps. In addition, several functions will enable you to get specific date information from a column with ease. For example, to find the day of the week of all the entries in a timestamp column, you could use the following code:

```
mysql> select dayname(created) from guestbook;
+------------------+
| dayname(created) |
+------------------+
| Sunday           |
| Sunday           |
| Wednesday        |
| Sunday           |
| Sunday           |
| Wednesday        |
| Wednesday        |
| Wednesday        |
+------------------+
```

DAYOFWEEK

This function returns the weekday index for `date` (`1` for Sunday, `2` for Monday, and so on up to `7` for Saturday). These index values correspond to the ODBC standard. If an invalid date is supplied to the date functions, they return `null`.

```
DAYOFWEEK(date) (used in examples)
RETURNS: int
mysql> select dayofweek('2001-01-01');
+-------------------------+
| dayofweek('2001-01-01') |
```

```
+-------------------------+
|                       2 |
+-------------------------+
1 row in set (0.33 sec)
```

WEEKDAY

This function returns the weekday index for `date` (`0` for Monday, `1` for Tuesday, and so on up to `6` for Sunday):

```
WEEKDAY(date) (used in examples)
RETURNS: int
```

DAYOFMONTH

This function returns the day of the month for `date`, in the range of `1` to `31`:

```
DAYOFMONTH(date)
RETURNS: int
```

DAYOFYEAR

This function returns the day of the year for `date`, in the range of `1` to `366`:

```
DAYOFYEAR(date)
RETURNS: int

mysql> select dayofmonth('02-01-2000');
+-------------------------+
| dayofmonth('02-01-2000') |
+-------------------------+
|                      20 |
+-------------------------+
1 row in set (0.00 sec)
```

MONTH

This function returns the month for `date`, in the range of `1` to `12`:

```
MONTH(date)
RETURNS: int
```

DAYNAME

This function returns the full name of the weekday for date:

```
DAYNAME(date)
RETURNS: string
```

```
mysql> select dayname('10/01/2000');
+-----------------------+
| dayname('10/01/2000') |
+-----------------------+
| Wednesday             |
+-----------------------+
1 row in set (0.00 sec)
```

MONTHNAME

This function returns the full English-language name of the month for date:

```
MONTHNAME(date)
RETURNS: string
```

QUARTER

This function returns the quarter of the year for date, in the range of 1 to 4:

```
QUARTER(date)
RETURNS: int
```

To find all the people who signed your guestbook in the second quarter of the year, you could use the following command:

```
select name from guestbook WHERE quarter(created) = 2;
```

WEEK

With a single argument, this function returns the week for date, in the range of 0 to 53:

```
WEEK(date [, first])
RETURNS: int
```

The optional second argument enables you to specify whether the week starts on Sunday or Monday. The week starts on Sunday if the second argument is 0 and on Monday if the second argument is 1.

YEAR

This function returns the year for `date`, in the range of `1000` to `9999`:

```
YEAR(date) (used in examples)
RETURNS: int
```

YEARWEEK

This function returns the year and week for a date, in the format *YYYYWW*. The second argument works exactly like the second argument in `WEEK()`.

```
YEARWEEK(date [,first])
RETURNS: int
```

HOUR

This function returns the hour for `time`, in the range of `0` to `23`:

```
HOUR(time)
RETURNS: int
```

MINUTE

This function returns the minute for `time`, in the range of `0` to `59`:

```
MINUTE(time)
RETURNS: int
```

SECOND

This function returns the second for `time`, in the range of 0 to 59:

```
SECOND(time)
RETURNS: int
```

PERIOD_ADD

This function adds *N* months to period *P* (in the format *YYMM* or *YYYYMM*) and returns a value in the format *YYYYMM*:

```
PERIOD_ADD(P,N)
RETURNS: int
```

Note that the period argument *P* is *not* a date value.

```
mysql> select period_add(200006,7);
+------------------------+
| period_add(200006,7) |
+------------------------+
|                 200101 |
+------------------------+
1 row in set (0.00 sec)
```

PERIOD_DIFF

This function returns the number of months between periods *P1* and *P2*. *P1* and *P2* should be in the format *YYMM* or *YYYYMM*.

```
PERIOD_DIFF(P1,P2)
RETURNS: int
```

Note that the period arguments *P1* and *P2* are *not* date values.

```
mysql> select period_diff(200106,200001);
+--------------------------------+
| period_diff(200106,200001) |
+--------------------------------+
|                             17 |
+--------------------------------+
1 row in set (0.00 sec)
```

DATE_ADD

These functions perform date arithmetic.

```
DATE_ADD(date,INTERVAL expr type)
```

or

```
DATE_SUB(date,INTERVAL expr type)
```

or

```
ADDDATE(date,INTERVAL expr type)
```

or

```
SUBDATE(date,INTERVAL) (used in examples)
RETURNS: date
```

ADDDATE() and SUBDATE() are identical to DATE_ADD() and DATE_SUB(), respectively. In all versions of MySQL since version 3.23 you can use + and - symbols, respectively, instead of DATE_ADD() and DATE_SUB(). (See the following example.) date is a DATETIME or DATE value specifying the starting date. expr is an expression specifying the interval value to be added or subtracted from the starting date. expr is a string; it may start with a - for negative intervals. type is a keyword indicating how the expression should be interpreted.

Table J-1 shows how the type and expr arguments are related.

TABLE J-1 DATE_ADD() OPERATORS

Type	Meaning	Expected expr Format Value
SECOND	Seconds	*SS*
MINUTE	Minutes	*MM*
MINUTE_SECOND	Minutes and seconds	*MM:SS*
HOUR	Hours	*HH*
HOUR_SECOND	Hours, minutes, seconds	*HH:MM:SS*
HOUR_MINUTE	Hours and minutes	*HH:MM*
DAY	Days	*DAYS*
DAY_SECOND	Days, hours, minutes, seconds	*DAYS HH:MM:SS*
DAY_MINUTE	Days, hours, minutes	*DAYS HH:MM*
DAY_HOUR	Days and hours	*DAYS HH*
MONTH	Months	*MONTHS*
YEAR	Years	*YEARS*
YEAR_MONTH	Years and months	*YEARS-MONTHS*

MySQL allows any punctuation delimiter in the expr format. The ones shown in the table are the suggested delimiters. If the date argument is a DATE value and your calculations involve only YEAR, MONTH, and DAY parts (that is, no time parts), the result is a DATE value. Otherwise, the result is a DATETIME value.

```
mysql> select '2001-01-01 13:00:00' + interval 10 m
+-------------------------------------------+
| '2001-01-01 13:00:00' + interval 10 minute |
+-------------------------------------------+
| 2001-01-01 13:10:00                        |
+-------------------------------------------+
1 row in set (0.39 sec)

mysql> select '2000-01-01 00:00:00' - interval 1 second;
+-------------------------------------------+
| '2000-01-01 00:00:00' - interval 1 second |
+-------------------------------------------+
| 1999-12-31 23:59:59                        |
+-------------------------------------------+
1 row in set (0.00 sec)

mysql> select date_add('2000-01-01 00:00:00', interval '1:1:1'
hour_second);
+---------------------------------------------------------------+
| date_add('2000-01-01 00:00:00', interval '1:1:1' hour_second) |
+---------------------------------------------------------------+
| 2000-01-01 01:01:01                                            |
+---------------------------------------------------------------+
1 row in set (0.00 sec)

mysql> select date_sub('2000-01-01 00:00:00', interval '1' month);
+---------------------------------------------------+
| date_sub('2000-01-01 00:00:00', interval '1' month) |
+---------------------------------------------------+
| 1999-12-01 00:00:00                                |
+---------------------------------------------------+
1 row in set (0.00 sec)
```

If you specify an interval value that is too short (one that does not include all the interval parts that would be expected from the `type` keyword), MySQL assumes you have left out the leftmost parts of the interval value. For example, if you specify a `type` of `DAY_SECOND`, the value of `expr` is expected to have days, hours, minutes, and seconds parts. If you specify a value like `1:10`, MySQL assumes that the days and hours parts are missing and that the value represents minutes and seconds.

TO_DAYS

Given a date date, this function returns a daynumber (the number of days since year 0):

```
TO_DAYS(date) (used in examples)
RETURNS: int
```

```
mysql> select to_days('2003-01-01');
+-----------------------+
| to_days('2003-01-01') |
+-----------------------+
|                731581 |
+-----------------------+
```

TO_DAYS() is not intended for use with values that precede the advent of the Gregorian calendar (1582). Note that it is not the same as the PHP mktime() function, which gets the date relative to January 1, 1970. See the entry for the MySQL UNIX_TIMESTAMP function, later in this appendix, if you need that information.

FROM_DAYS

Given a daynumber *N*, this function returns a DATE calculated from year 0:

```
FROM_DAYS(N) (used in examples)
RETURNS: date
```

```
mysql> select from_days('731581');
+---------------------+
| from_days('731581') |
+---------------------+
| 2003-01-01          |
+---------------------+
```

FROM_DAYS() is not intended for use with values that precede the advent of the Gregorian calendar (1582).

DATE_FORMAT

This function formats the date value according to the format string:

```
DATE_FORMAT(date,format) (used in examples)
RETURNS: string
```

The specifiers in Table J-2 can be used in the format string.

TABLE J-2 DATE_FORMAT SPECIFIERS

Specifier	Meaning
%M	Month name (January through December)
%W	Weekday name (Sunday through Saturday)
%D	Day of the month with English ordinal suffix (1st, 2nd, 3rd, and so on)
%Y	Year, numeric, four digits
%y	Year, numeric, two digits
%a	Abbreviated weekday name (Sun...Sat)
%d	Day of the month, two numeric digits (01...31)
%e	Day of the month, numeric (1...31)
%m	Month, two numeric digits (01...12)
%c	Month, numeric (1...12)
%b	Abbreviated month name (Jan...Dec)
%j	Day of year (001...366)
%H	Hour (00...23)
%k	Hour (0...23)
%h	Hour (01...12)
%I	Hour (01...12)
%i	Minutes, numeric (00...59)
%r	Time, 12-hour (*hh*:*mm*:*ss* [AP]M)
%T	Time, 24-hour (*hh*:*mm*:*ss*)
%S	Seconds (00...59)
%s	Seconds (00...59)
%p	AM or PM
%w	Day of the week (0=Sunday...6=Saturday)
%U	Week (0...53), where Sunday is the first day of the week

Continued

TABLE J-2 DATE_FORMAT SPECIFIERS *(Continued)*

Specifier	Meaning
%u	Week (0...53), where Monday is the first day of the week
%V	Week (1...53), where Sunday is the first day of the week; used with %X
%v	Week (1...53), where Monday is the first day of the week; used with %x
%X	Year for the week, where Sunday is the first day of the week; numeric, four digits, used with %V
%x	Year for the week, where Monday is the first day of the week; numeric, four digits, used with %v
%%	A literal %

All other characters are just copied to the result without interpretation:

```
mysql> select date_format('2001-01-01', '%W %M %d, %Y');
+-----------------------------------------+
| date_format('2001-01-01', '%W %M %d, %Y') |
+-----------------------------------------+
| Monday January 01, 2001                 |
+-----------------------------------------+
1 row in set (0.00 sec)

mysql> select date_format('2001-01-01 15:30:20',
    ->'%W %M %d, %Y %I:%i:%S %p');
+----------------------------------------------------------+
| date_format('2001-01-01 15:30:20', '%W %M %d, %Y %I:%i:%S %p') |
+----------------------------------------------------------+
| Monday January 01, 2001 03:30:20 PM                      |
+----------------------------------------------------------+
1 row in set (0.00 sec)
```

For MySQL 3.23 and later versions, the % character is required before format-specifier characters. In earlier versions of MySQL, % was optional.

TIME_FORMAT

This function is used like the DATE_FORMAT() function just discussed, but the format string can contain only those format specifiers that handle hours, minutes, and seconds. If specifiers other than those for hours, minutes, and seconds are included, the function will return a `NULL` value.

```
TIME_FORMAT(time,format) (used in examples)
RETURNS: string
```

CURDATE

This function returns today's date as a value in *YYYY-MM-DD* or *YYYYMMDD* format, depending on whether the function is used in a string or a numeric context:

```
CURDATE() or CURRENT_DATE (used in examples)
RETURNS: mixed
```

CURTIME

This function returns the current time as a value in *HH:MM:SS* or *HHMMSS* format, depending on whether the function is used in a string or a numeric context:

```
CURTIME() or CURRENT_TIME
RETURNS: mixed
```

NOW

This function returns the current date and time as a value in *YYYY-MM-DD HH:MM:SS* or *YYYYMMDDHHMMSS* format, depending on whether the function is used in a string or a numeric context:

```
NOW()
```

or

```
SYSDATE()
```

or

```
CURRENT_TIMESTAMP (used in examples)
RETURNS: string
```

UNIX_TIMESTAMP

If this function is called with no argument, it returns a Unix timestamp (seconds since 1970-01-01 00:00:00 GMT). If `UNIX_TIMESTAMP()` is called with a `date` argument, it returns the value of the argument as seconds since 1970-01-01 00:00:00 GMT. `date` may be a `DATE` string, a `DATETIME` string, a `TIMESTAMP`, or a number in the format *YYMMDD* or *YYYYMMDD* in local time.

```
UNIX_TIMESTAMP([date])
RETURNS: int
```

FROM_UNIXTIME

This function returns a representation of the `unix_timestamp` argument as a value in "*YYYY-MM-DD HH:MM:SS*" or "*YYYYMMDDHHMMSS*" format, depending on whether the function is used in a string or numeric context:

```
FROM_UNIXTIME(unix_timestamp) (used in examples)
RETURNS: string
```

SEC_TO_TIME

This function returns the `seconds` argument, converted to hours, minutes, and seconds, as a value in *HH:MM:SS* or *HHMMSS* format, depending on whether the function is used in a string or numeric context:

```
SEC_TO_TIME(seconds)
RETURNS: string
```

TIME_TO_SEC

This function returns the `time` argument, converted to seconds:

```
TIME_TO_SEC(time) (used in examples)
RETURNS: int
```

The date portion of a supplied date/time value is discarded.

Miscellaneous Functions

Here are a few other functions that don't fall under any of the previous categories.

DATABASE

This function returns the current database name. If no current database exists, `DATABASE()` returns the empty string.

```
DATABASE()
RETURNS: string
```

USER

This function returns the current MySQL username. In MySQL 3.22.11 or later, it includes the client host name as well.

```
USER()
```

or

```
SYSTEM_USER()
```

or

```
SESSION_USER() (used in examples)
RETURNS: string
```

VERSION

This function returns a string indicating the MySQL server version:

```
VERSION()
RETURNS: string
```

PASSWORD

This function calculates a password string from the plain-text password `str`:

```
PASSWORD(str) (used in examples)
RETURNS: string
```

This is the function that encrypts MySQL passwords for storage in the `Password` column of the user table. `PASSWORD()` encryption is one-way. `PASSWORD()` does not perform password encryption in the same way in which Unix passwords are encrypted. You should not assume that if your Unix password and your MySQL password are the same, `PASSWORD()` will result in the same encrypted value that is stored in the Unix password file. See `ENCRYPT()`.

ENCRYPT

This function encrypts `str` using the Unix `crypt()` system call:

```
ENCRYPT(str[,salt])
RETURNS: string
```

The salt argument should be a string with two characters. (As of MySQL 3.22.16, salt may be longer than two characters.) If crypt() is not available on your system, ENCRYPT() always returns NULL. ENCRYPT() ignores all but the first eight characters of str on most systems.

ENCODE

This function encrypts str using pass_str as the password:

```
ENCODE(str,pass_str)
RETURNS: binary string
```

To decrypt the result, use DECODE(). The result is a binary string. If you want to save it in a column, use a BLOB column type.

DECODE

This function decrypts the encrypted string crypt_str using pass_str as the password. crypt_str should be a string returned from ENCODE().

```
DECODE(crypt_str,pass_str)
RETURNS: string
```

MD5

This function calculates an MD5 checksum for the string. The value is returned as a 32-character alphanumeric string. This is the same as the md5() function used by PHP.

```
MD5(string)
RETURNS: string
```

LAST_INSERT_ID

This function returns the last automatically generated value that was inserted into an AUTO_INCREMENT column:

```
LAST_INSERT_ID()
RETURNS: int
```

GET_LOCK

This function tries to obtain a lock with a name given by the string str, with a timeout of timeout seconds. It returns 1 if the lock was obtained successfully, 0 if the attempt timed out, and NULL if an error occurred (such as running out of memory or the thread being killed with mysqladmin kill). A lock is released, RELEASE_LOCK() is executed, a new GET_LOCK() is executed, or the thread terminates.

```
GET_LOCK(str,timeout)
RETURNS: int
```

RELEASE_LOCK

This function releases the lock named by the string str that was obtained with GET_LOCK(). It returns 1 if the lock was released, 0 if the lock wasn't locked by this thread (in which case the lock is not released), and NULL if the named lock didn't exist.

```
RELEASE_LOCK(str)
RETURNS: int
```

Functions for Use with GROUP BY Clauses

Most of the functions used with the GROUP BY clause were covered in Chapter 3. There are three additional functions that we did not cover there.

STD/STDDEV

This function returns the standard deviation of expr. It is an extension of ANSI SQL. The STDDEV() form of this function is provided for Oracle compatibility.

```
STD(expr)
```

or

```
STDDEV(expr)
RETURNS: float
```

BIT_OR

This function returns the bitwise OR of all bits in expr. The calculation is performed with 64-bit (BIGINT) precision.

```
BIT_OR(expr)
RETURNS: int
```

BIT_AND

This function returns the bitwise AND of all bits in expr. The calculation is performed with 64-bit (BIGINT) precision.

```
BIT_AND(expr)
RETURNS: int
```

Index

Symbols

A

continued

B

continued

continued

G

H

continued

M

N

O

P

Q

R

continued

S

continued

T

V

W

X

Y

Z

Wiley Publishing, Inc. End-User License Agreement

5. Limited Warranty.
   (a) WPI warrants that the Software and Software Media are free from defects in materials and workmanship under normal use for a period of sixty (60) days from the date of purchase of this Book. If WPI receives notification within the warranty period of defects in materials or workmanship, WPI will replace the defective Software Media.
   (b) WPI AND THE AUTHOR(S) OF THE BOOK DISCLAIM ALL OTHER WARRANTIES, EXPRESS OR IMPLIED, INCLUDING WITHOUT LIMITATION IMPLIED WARRANTIES OF MERCHANTABILITY AND FITNESS FOR A PARTICULAR PURPOSE, WITH RESPECT TO THE SOFTWARE, THE PROGRAMS, THE SOURCE CODE CONTAINED THEREIN, AND/OR THE TECHNIQUES DESCRIBED IN THIS BOOK. WPI DOES NOT WARRANT THAT THE FUNCTIONS CONTAINED IN THE SOFTWARE WILL MEET YOUR REQUIREMENTS OR THAT THE OPERATION OF THE SOFTWARE WILL BE ERROR FREE.
   (c) This limited warranty gives you specific legal rights, and you may have other rights that vary from jurisdiction to jurisdiction.
6. Remedies.
   (a) WPI's entire liability and your exclusive remedy for defects in materials and workmanship shall be limited to replacement of the Software Media, which may be returned to WPI with a copy of your receipt at the following address: Software Media Fulfillment Department, Attn.: MySQL/PHP Database Applications, Second Edition, Wiley Publishing, Inc., 10475 Crosspoint Blvd., Indianapolis, IN 46256, or call 1-800-762-2974. Please allow four to six weeks for delivery. This Limited Warranty is void if failure of the Software Media has resulted from accident, abuse, or misapplication. Any replacement Software Media will be warranted for the remainder of the original warranty period or thirty (30) days, whichever is longer.
   (b) In no event shall WPI or the author be liable for any damages whatsoever (including without limitation damages for loss of business profits, business interruption, loss of business information, or any other pecuniary loss) arising from the use of or inability to use the Book or the Software, even if WPI has been advised of the possibility of such damages.
   (c) Because some jurisdictions do not allow the exclusion or limitation of liability for consequential or incidental damages, the above limitation or exclusion may not apply to you.
7. U.S. Government Restricted Rights. Use, duplication, or disclosure of the Software for or on behalf of the United States of America, its agencies and/or instrumentalities "U.S. Government" is subject to restrictions as stated in paragraph (c)(1)(ii) of the Rights in Technical Data and Computer Software clause of DFARS 252.227-7013, or subparagraphs (c) (1) and (2) of the Commercial Computer Software - Restricted Rights clause at FAR 52.227-19, and in similar clauses in the NASA FAR supplement, as applicable.
8. General. This Agreement constitutes the entire understanding of the parties and revokes and supersedes all prior agreements, oral or written, between them and may not be modified or amended except in a writing signed by both parties hereto that specifically refers to this Agreement. This Agreement shall take precedence over any other documents that may be in conflict herewith. If any one or more provisions contained in this Agreement are held by any court or tribunal to be invalid, illegal, or otherwise unenforceable, each and every other provision shall remain in full force and effect.

GNU GENERAL PUBLIC LICENSE

Preamble

The licenses for most software are designed to take away your freedom to share and change it. By contrast, the GNU General Public License is intended to guarantee your freedom to share and change free software—to make sure the software is free for all its users. This General Public License applies to most of the Free Software Foundation's software and to any other program whose authors commit to using it. (Some other Free Software Foundation software is covered by the GNU Library General Public License instead.) You can apply it to your programs, too.

When we speak of free software, we are referring to freedom, not price. Our General Public Licenses are designed to make sure that you have the freedom to distribute copies of free software (and charge for this service if you wish), that you receive source code or can get it if you want it, that you can change the software or use pieces of it in new free programs; and that you know you can do these things.

To protect your rights, we need to make restrictions that forbid anyone to deny you these rights or to ask you to surrender the rights. These restrictions translate to certain responsibilities for you if you distribute copies of the software, or if you modify it.

For example, if you distribute copies of such a program, whether gratis or for a fee, you must give the recipients all the rights that you have. You must make sure that they, too, receive or can get the source code. And you must show them these terms so they know their rights.

We protect your rights with two steps: (1) copyright the software, and (2) offer you this license which gives you legal permission to copy, distribute and/or modify the software.

Also, for each author's protection and ours, we want to make certain that everyone understands that there is no warranty for this free software. If the software is modified by someone else and passed on, we want its recipients to know that what they have is not the original, so that any problems introduced by others will not reflect on the original authors' reputations.

Finally, any free program is threatened constantly by software patents. We wish to avoid the danger that redistributors of a free program will individually obtain patent licenses, in effect making the program proprietary. To prevent this, we have made it clear that any patent must be licensed for everyone's free use or not licensed at all.

The precise terms and conditions for copying, distribution and modification follow.

TERMS AND CONDITIONS FOR COPYING, DISTRIBUTION AND MODIFICATION

0. This License applies to any program or other work which contains a notice placed by the copyright holder saying it may be distributed under the terms of this General Public License. The "Program", below, refers to any such program or work, and a "work based on the Program" means either the Program or any derivative work under copyright law: that is to say, a work containing the Program or a portion of it, either verbatim or with modifications and/or translated into another language. (Hereinafter, translation is included without limitation in the term "modification".) Each licensee is addressed as "you".

   Activities other than copying, distribution and modification are not covered by this License; they are outside its scope. The act of running the Program is not restricted, and the output from the Program is covered only if its contents constitute a work based on the Program (independent of having been made by running the Program). Whether that is true depends on what the Program does.

1. You may copy and distribute verbatim copies of the Program's source code as you receive it, in any medium, provided that you conspicuously and appropriately publish on each copy an appropriate copyright notice and disclaimer of warranty; keep intact all the notices that refer to this License and to the absence of any warranty; and give any other recipients of the Program a copy of this License along with the Program.

   You may charge a fee for the physical act of transferring a copy, and you may at your option offer warranty protection in exchange for a fee.

2. You may modify your copy or copies of the Program or any portion of it, thus forming a work based on the Program, and copy and distribute such modifications or work under the terms of Section 1 above, provided that you also meet all of these conditions:

   (a) You must cause the modified files to carry prominent notices stating that you changed the files and the date of any change.

   (b) You must cause any work that you distribute or publish, that in whole or in part contains or is derived from the Program or any part thereof, to be licensed as a whole at no charge to all third parties under the terms of this License.

   (c) If the modified program normally reads commands interactively when run, you must cause it, when started running for such interactive use in the most ordinary way, to print or display an announcement including an appropriate copyright notice and a notice that there is no warranty (or else, saying that you provide a warranty) and that users may redistribute the program under these conditions, and telling the user how to view a copy of this License. (Exception: if the Program itself is interactive but does not normally print such an announcement, your work based on the Program is not required to print an announcement.)

   These requirements apply to the modified work as a whole. If identifiable sections of that work are not derived from the Program, and can be reasonably considered independent and separate works in themselves, then this License, and its terms, do not apply to those sections when you distribute them as separate works. But when you distribute the same sections as part of a whole which is a work based on the Program, the distribution of the whole must be on the terms of this License, whose permissions for other licensees extend to the entire whole, and thus to each and every part regardless of who wrote it.

Thus, it is not the intent of this section to claim rights or contest your rights to work written entirely by you; rather, the intent is to exercise the right to control the distribution of derivative or collective works based on the Program.

In addition, mere aggregation of another work not based on the Program with the Program (or with a work based on the Program) on a volume of a storage or distribution medium does not bring the other work under the scope of this License.

3. You may copy and distribute the Program (or a work based on it, under Section 2) in object code or executable form under the terms of Sections 1 and 2 above provided that you also do one of the following:

   (a) Accompany it with the complete corresponding machine-readable source code, which must be distributed under the terms of Sections 1 and 2 above on a medium customarily used for software interchange; or,

   (b) Accompany it with a written offer, valid for at least three years, to give any third party, for a charge no more than your cost of physically performing source distribution, a complete machine-readable copy of the corresponding source code, to be distributed under the terms of Sections 1 and 2 above on a medium customarily used for software interchange; or,

   (c) Accompany it with the information you received as to the offer to distribute corresponding source code. (This alternative is allowed only for noncommercial distribution and only if you received the program in object code or executable form with such an offer, in accord with Subsection b above.)

   The source code for a work means the preferred form of the work for making modifications to it. For an executable work, complete source code means all the source code for all modules it contains, plus any associated interface definition files, plus the scripts used to control compilation and installation of the executable. However, as a special exception, the source code distributed need not include anything that is normally distributed (in either source or binary form) with the major components (compiler, kernel, and so on) of the operating system on which the executable runs, unless that component itself accompanies the executable.

   If distribution of executable or object code is made by offering access to copy from a designated place, then offering equivalent access to copy the source code from the same place counts as distribution of the source code, even though third parties are not compelled to copy the source along with the object code.

4. You may not copy, modify, sublicense, or distribute the Program except as expressly provided under this License. Any attempt otherwise to copy, modify, sublicense or distribute the Program is void, and will automatically terminate your rights under this License. However, parties who have received copies, or rights, from you under this License will not have their licenses terminated so long as such parties remain in full compliance.

5. You are not required to accept this License, since you have not signed it. However, nothing else grants you permission to modify or distribute the Program or its derivative works. These actions are prohibited by law if you do not accept this License. Therefore, by modifying or distributing the Program (or any work based on the Program), you indicate your acceptance of this License to do so, and all its terms and conditions for copying, distributing or modifying the Program or works based on it.

6. Each time you redistribute the Program (or any work based on the Program), the recipient automatically receives a license from the original licensor to copy, distribute or modify the Program subject to these terms and conditions. You may not impose any further restrictions on the recipients' exercise of the rights granted herein. You are not responsible for enforcing compliance by third parties to this License.
7. If, as a consequence of a court judgment or allegation of patent infringement or for any other reason (not limited to patent issues), conditions are imposed on you (whether by court order, agreement or otherwise) that contradict the conditions of this License, they do not excuse you from the conditions of this License. If you cannot distribute so as to satisfy simultaneously your obligations under this License and any other pertinent obligations, then as a consequence you may not distribute the Program at all. For example, if a patent license would not permit royalty-free redistribution of the Program by all those who receive copies directly or indirectly through you, then the only way you could satisfy both it and this License would be to refrain entirely from distribution of the Program.

   If any portion of this section is held invalid or unenforceable under any particular circumstance, the balance of the section is intended to apply and the section as a whole is intended to apply in other circumstances.

   It is not the purpose of this section to induce you to infringe any patents or other property right claims or to contest validity of any such claims; this section has the sole purpose of protecting the integrity of the free software distribution system, which is implemented by public license practices. Many people have made generous contributions to the wide range of software distributed through that system in reliance on consistent application of that system; it is up to the author/donor to decide if he or she is willing to distribute software through any other system and a licensee cannot impose that choice.

   This section is intended to make thoroughly clear what is believed to be a consequence of the rest of this License.
8. If the distribution and/or use of the Program is restricted in certain countries either by patents or by copyrighted interfaces, the original copyright holder who places the Program under this License may add an explicit geographical distribution limitation excluding those countries, so that distribution is permitted only in or among countries not thus excluded. In such case, this License incorporates the limitation as if written in the body of this License.
9. The Free Software Foundation may publish revised and/or new versions of the General Public License from time to time. Such new versions will be similar in spirit to the present version, but may differ in detail to address new problems or concerns.

   Each version is given a distinguishing version number. If the Program specifies a version number of this License which applies to it and "any later version", you have the option of following the terms and conditions either of that version or of any later version published by the Free Software Foundation. If the Program does not specify a version number of this License, you may choose any version ever published by the Free Software Foundation.
10. If you wish to incorporate parts of the Program into other free programs whose distribution conditions are different, write to the author to ask for permission. For software which is copyrighted by the Free Software Foundation, write to the Free